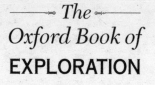

The
Oxford Book of
EXPLORATION

Robin Hanbury-Tenison, Gold Medallist of the Royal Geographical Society, has been on over twenty expeditions, including the first land crossing of South America at its widest point. He led the Royal Geographical Society's longest expedition to date, taking 140 scientists to study the rain forests of Sarawak, Borneo. He is one of the founders, now President, of Survival International, which campaigns for the rights of threatened tribal peoples. His passionate concern for them, and his recognition that most of what we call exploration is merely following in the footsteps of those who went before but left no written record, shine through the extracts he has chosen for this book.

His many books include *Mulu: The Rainforest*, *White Horses over France*, *A Ride Along the Great Wall*, *A Question of Survival for the Indians of Brazil*, and his autobiography, *Worlds Apart*. When not on his travels, he runs a hill farm on Bodmin Moor in Cornwall.

The
Oxford Book of
EXPLORATION

Selected by

ROBIN HANBURY-TENISON

Oxford   New York

OXFORD UNIVERSITY PRESS

1994

Oxford University Press, Walton Street, Oxford OX2 6DP

Oxford New York
Athens Auckland Bangkok Bombay
Calcutta Cape Town Dar es Salaam Delhi
Florence Hong Kong Istanbul Karachi
Kuala Lumpur Madras Madrid Melbourne
Mexico City Nairobi Paris Singapore
Taipei Tokyo Toronto
and associated companies in
Berlin Ibadan

Oxford is a trade mark of Oxford University Press

Introduction and selection © Robin Hanbury-Tenison 1993

Further copyright information can be found on page 523

First published by Oxford University Press 1993
First issued as an Oxford University Press paperback 1994

British Library Cataloguing in Publication Data
Data available

Library of Congress Cataloging in Publication Data
The Oxford book of exploration / selected by Robin Hanbury-Tenison.
p. cm.
Includes bibliographical references and index.
1. Discoveries in geography. I. Hanbury-Tenison, Robin.
G80.094 1993 910'.9—dc20 93–10770
ISBN 0-19-282396-5

1 3 5 7 9 10 8 6 4 2

Printed in Great Britain by
Biddles Ltd
Guildford and King's Lynn

THIS BOOK IS DEDICATED TO THE
ROYAL GEOGRAPHICAL SOCIETY
AND ITS STAFF, PAST, PRESENT
AND FUTURE.

'Exploring is delightful to look forward to and back upon, but it is not comfortable at the time, unless it be of such an easy nature as not to deserve the name.'

Samuel Butler, *Erewhon*

ACKNOWLEDGEMENTS

IT is thanks to the initiative of the Royal Geographical Society that most of the greatest expeditions of the last 163 years have taken place. Many of the explorers whose writings appear in this anthology were inspired and financed by the Society, and I have used the Award of a Gold Medal as one of the most valid touchstones for inclusion.

Over the years I have, myself, received much encouragement and kindness from successive members of staff. Sir Laurence Kirwan, the Director and Secretary from 1945 to 1975, challenged my youthful enthusiasm in such a way as to make me determined not to let him down. John Hemming, my oldest friend, has been a worthy successor. Nigel Winser, the Deputy Director, and Shane Winser, Information Officer, have helped me unstintingly as always. Jayne Dunlop, the Librarian, Janet Turner and Timothy Collinson, her assistants, put up with my constant presence during the year in which I blighted their lives with requests for books I could not find on my own. I am very grateful for their patience.

I was also helped immensely by many modern explorers and academics who responded to my request for suggestions about suitable passages to include. Although lack of space has prevented using much fascinating material, I would like to thank all who took the trouble to write to me. They include Michael Asher, John Bartholomew, Phil Barton, Sir George Bishop, John Blashford-Snell, Chris Bonington, Denis Brunsden, Pat Cannings, Roger Chapman, Brian Cheeseman, Miles Clark, R. H. Cockburn, A. W. Cockerill, Bill Colegrave, Nick Crane, Andrew Croft, David Curtis, Christina Dodwell, Lady Elton, Sir Robert Fellowes, Nik Fleming, Sir Vivian Fuchs, Nigel Gifford, Laurence Gordon-Clark, Andrew Goudie, Jack Hanbury-Tenison, Richard Hanbury-Tenison, Wally Herbert, Robin Hodgkin, Lord Hunt, Patrick Hutton, Tristan Jones, Sylvia Kantaris, Monica Kristensen, John Maggs, Ella Maillart, David Mason, Viscount Norwich, Martin Pailthorpe, Rob Palmer, Ghillean Prance, John Ridgeway, Jane Robinson, William Ruxton, Lord Shackleton, Clio Smeeton, Anthony Sturt, Marjorie Sweeting, Wilfred Thesiger, Sarah Tolley, Lord Walsingham, Germaine Warkentin, Helen Webb.

Quite exceptional help was given by Dorothy Middleton and John

Bockstoce, while Anna Rawlinson and Jamie Williams did some useful research for me. I hope those whose names I have accidentally omitted will forgive me. Whether or not I took their advice only they will be able to deduce from the text.

CONTENTS

Introduction x

I. ASIA 1

II. AFRICA 125

III. NORTH AMERICA 219

IV. CENTRAL AND SOUTH AMERICA 319

V. THE PACIFIC, AUSTRALIA, AND NEW ZEALAND 377

VI. THE ARCTIC 467

VII. THE ANTARCTIC 487

Bibliography 521

Source acknowledgements 523

Index 525

INTRODUCTION

TIME and again the European explorer, as he 'discovers' some new land, makes a passing reference to his native guide. If I had been allowed just one illustration in this anthology, it would have been a cartoon seen many years ago in the *Geographical Magazine*. Two pith-helmeted explorers stand at the foot of a huge waterfall, their baggage-bearers snaking out behind them. Pointing across the river to a group of natives beside some thatched huts, one explorer says to the other, 'You don't suppose they might have discovered it already, do you?'

Explorers are quite different from travellers. They are driven by a desire to discover which transcends the urge to conquer, the pursuit of trade, the curiosity of the scientist, the zeal of the missionary, or the simple search for adventure which first sent them abroad. Their achievements and, indeed, their failures have a lasting significance which may affect the destiny of mankind. As a result they tend to take themselves rather seriously. And yet, by the time explorers had begun to write down their adventures, almost every habitable corner of this planet had long been discovered, investigated, and, where possible, settled. The real explorers were those who for tens of thousands of years before history began searched the world for uninhabited land.

The explorers in this anthology were, therefore, seldom the first human beings to experience what they describe: only the first to write it down. What is significant about their writings is that they were the first from a particular culture to see new lands and describe them. This gives their observations an edge which later descriptions, however good they may be as travel writing, can never equal. Occasionally it has been possible to include examples of how the native inhabitants saw the new arrivals, but the vast majority of extracts are by Europeans, and the majority of them British. I am very aware how ethnocentric my selection has turned out to be. As one whose main life's work has been the promotion of the rights and recognition of indigenous peoples, I have let their voice be heard as well. It is there, hidden in the text, but—fortunately for those of us whose first language is English—much of the best writing by explorers that has survived is in English or has been translated. It was through the writings of explorers that the world outside was revealed. The more lurid and colourful their descriptions, the more popular were their books. During the high days of Victorian travel, when the Empire was spreading its red blush across the globe, travel and exploration books were regular bestsellers. They informed and they revealed, but they also titillated with glimpses of societies free of the puritanical strait-laces under which the readers, particularly female ones, laboured.

The extracts I have selected are intended to reveal something about the explorer. Some are moments of despair, others of euphoria; some are failures, such as last entries before death; others are successes, the moment of achievement after a long and painful search. Some are long; some are short. I have concentrated on some of the places which have captured the imagination of their time, such as the search for the source of the Nile, or the desire to enter Lhasa. Certain themes seem to have consistently excited explorers, too: first contacts with new peoples, first sightings of new lands, always with a background of suffering and danger. Only a flavour of what lies behind can be tasted in these pages. Fortunately, there is a multitude of excellent general books on exploration to which the reader wishing to know more about the subject may refer, and some of the best are listed in the Bibliography. Many of these, such as the Royal Geographical Society's *History of Exploration*, contain maps which show where the explorers went and relate this to the discoveries of others.

There are men and women in their prime today whose names history will rank alongside the greats. But reputations take time to mature, and so I have included only three living explorers: Edmund Hillary who, with Sherpa Norgay Tenzing, was the first to reach the highest place on earth; Wally Herbert, because he may well have been the first person to reach the North Pole on foot; and Wilfred Thesiger, who once turned up on an expedition of mine deep in the heart of Borneo, having blithely ignored the bureaucracy which surrounded those wishing to reach our base camp. He said he thought it was time he experienced a rain forest, but that on the whole he preferred an environment where water was better appreciated. In spite of a bad knee, he set off to climb our highest mountain. When I wrote to him about this anthology, he suggested the two short pieces I have included. They come from his great book *Arabian Sands*, and encapsulate beautifully his feelings about exploration. Whether one agrees with his sentiments or not, they should also make anyone who has not already done so want to read the whole book. And that must be the prime purpose of an anthology: to inspire the reader to go to the original source and decide which bits he or she would have selected; to expand on the brief glimpse here into the mind of the explorer. This is what I have tried to do, rather than to instruct or to be definitive. If anyone is tempted to read more of the original than there is room for here, then I will have achieved my purpose.

R.H.-T.

Cabilla Manor, Cornwall
February 1993

Note: Spelling and punctuation have been modernized as far as was necessary to render the narratives accessible to the modern reader. The date following the title of each extract indicates the year (as far as can be ascertained) of the event described.

I

——✦❧✦——

ASIA

——✦❧✦——

Fa Hsien (319–414) 3

Hsuan Tsang (596–664) 5

Giovanni de Piano Carpini (1182–1252) 7

William of Rubruck (c.1212–1295) 9

Marco Polo (c.1254–1324) 12

Ibn Battúta (1304–1377) 17

Cheng Ho (1371–1435) 21

Vasco da Gama (c.1460–1524) 23

Sir Hugh Willoughby (c.1500–1554) 25

Anthony Jenkinson (d. 1611) 26

Timofeyevich Yermak (d. 1584) 27

Willem Barents (d. 1579) 29

Johann Grueber (1623–1680) 31

Ippolito Desideri (1684–1733) 33

Vitus Bering (1681–1741) 34

Thomas Manning (1772–1840) 38

William Moorcroft (1765–1825) 41

Sir Joseph Dalton Hooker (1817–1911) 44

Sir Spencer St John (1825–1910) 52

William Gifford Palgrave (1826–1888) 55

Nain Singh (fl. 1865–1877) 59

Alfred Russell Wallace (1823–1913) 60

Nikolai Mikhailovich Przhevalsky (1839–1888) 62

Charles Montagu Doughty (1843–1926) 66

Adolf Erik Nordenskjöld (1832–1901) 70

Ney Elias (1844–1897) 75

Sir Francis Younghusband (1863–1942) 78

Sven Hedin (1865–1952) 82

Sir (Mark) Aurel Stein (1862–1943) 93

Boris Andreyevich Vilkitskiy (1885–1961) 98

Roald Amundsen (1872–1928) 100

Alexandra David-Neel (1868–1969) 103

Frank Kingdon-Ward (1885–1958) 105

Bertram Thomas (1892–1950) 111

Eric Shipton (1907–1977) 113

Wilfred Thesiger (b. 1910) 118

Sir Edmund Hillary (b. 1919) 120

FA HSIEN

(319–414)

Chinese Buddhist monk who made the first recorded journey overland from China to India in 399, returning by sea and taking fifteen years.

Travels of Fah-Hian and Sung-Yun, ed. S. Beal (London, 1869).

1. CROSSING THE GOBI (399)

There are fortifications here extending about 80 *li* (i.e. about 16 miles) east and west, and half that distance north and south. They all stopped here a month and some odd days, after which Fa Hsien and his four companions made arrangements to set out in advance of the others, and so they were again separated. The military governor of Dunhuang, Li Ho, provided them with all necessaries for crossing the Desert. In this desert there are a great many evil demons; there are also sirocco winds, which kill all who encounter them. There are no birds or beasts to be seen; but so far as the eye can reach, the route is marked out by the bleached bones of men who have perished in the attempt to cross the desert. After travelling thus for seventeen days, a distance of about 1508 *li*, they arrived at the kingdom of Shen-Shen.

2. OVER THE PAMIRS

From this country, proceeding westward towards North India, after a journey of one month, we succeeded in passing the Tsung Ling Mountains. These mountains are covered with snow both in winter and summer. They shelter venomous dragons also, which, if once provoked, spit out their poison. Scarcely one person out of ten thousand survives after encountering the various difficulties which oppose their advance—the wind, and the rain, and the snow, and the driving sand and gravel. The men of these districts are also known as men of the Snowy Mountains. On passing this mountain chain we arrive in North India. . . .

Keeping along the incline of the Tsung Ling Mountains, in a south-westerly direction, they travelled onwards for fifteen days. The road is difficult and fatiguing. Steep crags and precipices constantly intercept the way. These mountains are like walls of rock, standing up 10,000 ft. in height. On looking over the edge the sight becomes confused, and then, on advancing, the foot loses its hold and you are lost. At the base there is a stream called the Sin-to (Indus). Men of old days have cut away the cliff so as to make a passage, and have carved out against the rock steps for descent, amounting altogether to 700 in number. Having passed these, there is, suspended across the river, a bridge of ropes, by which travellers pass over it. From one side of the river to the other is eighty paces. . . .

In the second month of winter, Fa Hsien and his two companions, going to the south, crossed the Little Snowy Mountains. The snow continually accumulates on these mountains, both in winter and summer. The exceeding cold which came on suddenly in crossing the northern slope of the mountain, which lies in the shade, caused the men generally to remain perfectly silent through fear. The pilgrim Hwui Ying was unable, after repeated efforts, to proceed any further. His mouth was covered with a white foam; at last he addressed Fa Hsien and said, 'It is impossible for me to recover; whilst there is time do you press forward, lest we all perish', and upon this he presently died. Fa Hsien embraced him and piteously invoked him by his familiar name, but it was all ineffectual to restore life. Submitting therefore to his destiny, he once more gathered up his strength and pressed forward.

3. DESCRIPTION OF INDIA

To the south of this, the country is called Madya Desa (the middle country). The climate of this region is exceedingly equable: there is neither frost nor snow. The inhabitants are prosperous and happy. There are no boards of population and revenue. Those only who farm the royal demesnes, pay a portion of the produce as rent. Nor are they bound to remain in possession longer than they like. The king in the administration of justice inflicts no corporal punishment, but each culprit is fined in money according to the gravity of his offence; and even in cases where the culprit has been guilty of repeated attempts to excite rebellion, they restrict themselves to cutting off his right hand. The chief officers of the king have all allotted revenues. The people of this country kill no living creature, nor do they drink intoxicating liquors. And, with the exception of the Chandalas, they eat neither garlic or onions. The word 'chandala' signifies a wicked man, who lives apart from others. If such a man enters a town or a market-place, he strikes a piece of wood, in order to keep himself separate; people, hearing this sound, know what it means and avoid touching him or brushing against him. In this country they do not keep swine or fowls, they do not deal in living animals, nor are there shambles or wine shops round their markets. They use shells for money in their traffic.

4. PERSUADED TO WRITE AN ACCOUNT

After Fa Hsien left Tchang'an, he was five years in reaching mid-India. He resided there six years, and was three years more before he arrived at Tsing Chow. He had passed through thirty different countries. In all the countries of India, after passing the Sandy Desert (of Gobi), the dignified carriage of the priesthood and the surprising influence of religion (amongst the people) cannot be adequately described. But, because our learned doctors had not heard of these things, he was induced, regardless of all personal considerations, to cross the seas, and to encounter every conceivable danger in returning home. Having been preserved therefore by divine power (by the influences of the Three Honourable Ones), and brought through all dangers safely, he was further induced to commit to writing these records of his travels, desiring that the virtuous of all ages may be informed of them together, as well as himself. . . .

. . . when they pressed him to write a full record of all that happened to him from first to last, then he said, 'If I were to recall all which has occurred to me, then persons of unstable minds would be excited to strive how they might enter on similar dangers and encounter corresponding risks, reckless of their personal safety. For they would argue in this way, "Here is a man who has escaped all and come back safe and sound"; and so these foolish persons would set about jeopardizing their lives in lands impossible to explore, and to pass through which, not one in ten thousand could hope for.' On hearing these remarks, they all said, with a sigh of assent, 'This man, in order to preserve the knowledge of old things and new, has himself penetrated to the eastern source of the great doctrine, and is yet alive.'

✻

HSUAN TSANG

(596–664)

Chinese explorer. He spent sixteen years between 629 and 645 visiting Central Asia and India before returning overland with over 700 religious

*manuscripts. At the emperor's command, he spent the rest of his life trans-
lating them and compiling his memoirs, a work many times longer than the
Bible.*

Buddhist Records of the Western World, trans. S. Beale (London, 1890).

1. DANGERS OF TRAVEL IN THE MOUNTAINS (629)

Going 300 *li* or so to the north-west of this country, crossing a stony desert,
we come to Ling Shan (ice-mountain). This is, in fact, the northern plateau
of the Tsung Ling range, and from this point the waters mostly have an
eastern flow. Both hills and valleys are filled with snow-piles, and it freezes
both in spring and summer; if it should thaw for a time, the ice soon forms
again. The roads are steep and dangerous, the cold wind is extremely
biting, and frequently fierce dragons impede and molest travellers with
their inflictions. Those who travel this road should not wear red garments
nor carry loud-sounding calabashes. The least forgetfulness of these precautions entails certain misfortune. A violent wind suddenly rises with
storms of flying sand and gravel; those who encounter them, sinking through
exhaustion, are almost sure to die.

Going 400 *li* or so, we come to the great Tsing lake. This lake is about
1,000 *li* in circuit, extended from east to west, and narrow from north to
south. On all sides it is enclosed by mountains, and various streams empty
themselves into it and are lost. The colour of the water is a blueish-black,
its taste is bitter and salt. The waves of this lake roll along tumultuously
as they expend themselves on the shores. Dragons and fishes inhabit it
together. At certain portentous occasions scaly monsters rise to the surface, at which travellers passing by offer up prayers for good fortune.
Although the water animals are numerous, no one dares to catch them by
fishing.

2. ARRIVAL IN THE HINDU KUSH

The country of U-chang-na is about 5,000 *li* in circuit; the mountains and
valleys are continously connected, and the valleys and marshes alternate
with a succession of high plateaux. Though various kinds of grain are sown,
yet the crops are not rich. The grape is abundant, the sugar cane scarce.
The earth produces gold and iron, and is favourable to the cultivation of
the scented shrub called Yo-kin (turmeric). The forests are thick and shady,
the fruits and flowers abundant. The cold and heat are agreeably tempered, the wind and rain come in their season. The people are soft and

effeminate, and in disposition are somewhat sly and crafty. They love learning yet have no application. They practise the art of using charms. Their clothing is white cotton, and they wear little else.

✼

GIOVANNI DE PIANO CARPINI

(1182–1252)

Italian Franciscan monk. A contemporary and friend of St Francis, he was sent by Pope Innocent IV as ambassador to the Mongol Khans.

A *General History & Collection of Voyages & Travels,* ed. Robert Kerr (Edinburgh, 1811–24).

1. INTRODUCTORY EPISTLE (1245–1247)

To all the faithful in Christ, to whom this writing may come, I, friar John de Piano Carpini, of the order of minorites, legate and messenger from the Apostolic see to the Tartars and other nations of the east, wish the Grace of God in this life, and glory in the next, and perpetual triumph over all the enemies of the Lord. Having learnt the will of our lord the Pope, and the venerable Cardinals, and received the commands of the holy see, that we should go to the Tartars and other nations of the east, we determined to go in the first place to the Tartars; because we dreaded that the most imminent and nearest danger to the Church of God arose from them . . . Hence, what we now write is for your advantage, that you may be on your guard, and more secure; being what we saw with our own eyes, while we sojourned with and among these people, during more than a year and four months, or which we have learnt from Christian captives residing among them, and whom we believe to be worthy of credit.

2. THE APPEARANCE OF THE TARTARS

The appearance of the Mongols or Tartars is quite different from all other nations, being much wider between the eyes and cheeks, and their cheeks are very prominent, with small flat noses, and small eyes, having the upper lids opened up to the eyebrows, and their crowns are shaven like priests

7

on each side, leaving some long hair in the middle, the remainder being allowed to grow long like women, which they twist into two tails or locks, and bind behind their ears. The garments of the men and women are alike, using neither cloaks, hats, nor caps, but they wear strange tunics made of buckram, purple, or baldequin. Their gowns are made of skins, dressed in the hair, and open behind. They never wash their clothes, neither do they allow others to wash, especially in time of thunder, till that be over. Their houses are round, and artificially made like tents, of rods and twigs interwoven, having a round hole in the middle of the roof for the admission of light and the passage of smoke, the whole being covered with felt, of which likewise the doors are made. Some of these are easily taken to pieces or put together, and are carried on sumpter-cattle; while others are not capable of being taken to pieces, and are carried on carts. Wherever they go, whether to war, or only travelling to fresh pastures, these are carried with them. They have vast numbers of camels, oxen, sheep, and goats, and such prodigious multitudes of horses and mares, as are not to be found in all the rest of the world; but they have no swine. Their emperor, dukes, and other nobles are extremely rich in gold and silver, silks, and gems. They eat of every thing that is eatable, and we have even seen them eat vermin.

3. RECEPTION AT COURT

On our arrival at the court of Cuyne, he ordered us to be provided with a tent, and all necessary expenses, after the Tartar customs, and his people treated us with more attention and respect than they showed to any other messengers. We were not admitted into his presence, as he had not been formally elected and invested in the empire; but the translation of the Pope's letters, and of our speech, had been transmitted to him by Baatu. After remaining in this place for five or six days, we were sent to his mother, who kept a solemn court. In this place we beheld an immense tent, so vast, in our opinion, that it could have contained two thousand men; around which there was an enclosure of planks, painted with various figures. All the Tartar dukes were assembled in this neighbourhood, with their attendants, and amused themselves in riding about the hills and valleys. The first day these were all clothed in white robes. The second day, on which Cuyne came to the great tent, they were dressed in scarlet. The third day they were dressed in blue, and on the fourth in rich robes of Baldakin.[1] In the wall of boards, encircling the great tent, there were two gates, through one of which the emperor alone was allowed to enter;

---

[1] This term probably signifies the manufacture of Baldach or Bagdat, and may refer to silken stuffs damasked, or woven with gold flowers.

and though it stood continually open, there were no guards, as no one
dared to enter or come out by that way. All who were admitted entered
by the other gate, at which there were guards, armed with bows, arrows,
and swords. If any one presumed to approach the tent beyond the assigned
limits, he was severely beaten if caught; or if he attempted to run away, he
was shot at with arrows. Many of the people whom we saw here had upon
their saddles, bridles, and other trappings of their horses, to the value of
twenty marks in pure gold, according to our estimation.

The dukes assembled in the great tent, and consulted together, as we
thought, about the election of the emperor. The rest of the people were
collected all round the wooden walls, and at a considerable distance; and
in this manner they continued till almost noon. Then they began to drink
mare's milk, or cosmos, and continued to drink amazing quantities till
evening. We were invited among them, and they treated us with ale, as we
did not drink cosmos. They intended this as a great honour, but they made
us drink so much, in comparison with our ordinary diet, as we were not
able to endure; but on making them understand that it was hurtful to us,
they desisted from insisting on our compliance.

✳

WILLIAM OF RUBRUCK

(*c.*1212–1295)

*Flemish Franciscan monk. He was sent by Louis IX of France to the Tartar
Khan Mangu.*

The Journey of William of Rubruck to the Eastern Parts of the World, 1253–1255,
ed. W. W. Rockhill (Cambridge, 1900).

1. THE PEOPLE OF TEBET (1253)

Beyond these are the Tebet, a people in the habit of eating their dead
parents, so that for piety's sake they should not give their parents any other
sepulchre than their bowels. They have given this practice up, however, as
they were held an abomination among all nations. They still, however,
make handsome cups out of the heads of their parents, so that when
drinking out of them they may have them in mind in the midst of their

merry-making. This was told me by one who had seen it. These people have much gold in their country, so that when one lacks gold he digs till he finds it, and he only takes so much as he requires and puts the rest back in the ground; for if he put it in a treasury or a coffer, he believes that God would take away from him that which is in the ground.

2. AT THE COURT OF THE GREAT KHAN

When we had sung this hymn, they searched our legs and breasts and arms to see if we had knives upon us. They had the interpreter examined, and made him leave his belt and knife in the custody of a door-keeper. Then we entered, and there was a bench in the entry with *cosmos* [mare's milk], and near by it they made the interpreter stand. They made us, however, sit down on a bench near the ladies. The house was all covered inside with cloth of gold, and there was a fire of briars and wormwood roots—which grow here to great size—and of cattle dung, in a grate in the centre of the dwelling. He [Mangu] was seated on a couch, and was dressed in a skin spotted and glossy, like a seal's skin. He is a little man, of medium height, aged forty-five years, and a young wife sat beside him; and a very ugly, full-grown girl called Cirina, with other children sat on a couch after them. This dwelling had belonged to a certain Christian lady, whom he had much loved, and of whom he had had this girl. Afterwards he had taken this young wife, but the girl was the mistress of all this *ordu*, which had been her mother's.

He had us asked what we wanted to drink, wine or *terracina*, which is rice wine (*cervisia*), or *caracosmos*, which is clarified mare's milk, or *bal*, which is honey mead. For in winter they make use of these four kinds of drinks. I replied: 'My lord, we are not men who seek to satisfy our fancies about drinks; whatever pleases you will suit us.' So he had us given of the rice drink, which was clear and flavoured like white wine, and of which I tasted a little out of respect for him, but for our misfortune our interpreter was standing by the butlers, who gave him so much to drink, that he was drunk in a short time. After this the khan had brought some falcons and other birds, which he took on his hand and looked at, and after a long while he bade us speak. Then we had to bend our knees. He had his interpreter, a certain Nestorian, who I did not know was a Christian, and we had our interpreter, such as he was, and already drunk. Then I said: 'In the first place we render thanks and praise to God, who has brought us from so far to see Mangu Khan, to whom God has given so much power on earth. And we pray Christ, by whose will we all live and die, to grant him a happy and long life.' For it is their desire, that one shall pray for their lives. . . . 'We have neither gold, nor silver nor precious stones to present to you, but only ourselves to offer to you to serve God, and to pray to God for you. At all events give us leave to remain here till this cold has passed away, for my companion is so feeble that he cannot with safety to his life stand any more the fatigue of travelling on horse-back.'

My companion had told me of his infirm condition, and had adjured me to ask for permission to stay, for we supposed that we would have to go back to Baatu, unless by special grace he gave us permission to stay. Then he began his reply: 'As the sun sends its rays everywhere, likewise my sway and that of Baatu reach everywhere, so we do not want your gold or silver.' So far I understood my interpreter, but after that I could not understand the whole of any one sentence: it was by this that I found out he was drunk, and Mangu himself appeared to me tipsy. . . .

Mangu had at Karakoram a great palace, situated next to the city walls, enclosed within a high wall like those which enclose monks' priories among us. Here is a great palace, where he has his drinkings twice a year: once about Easter, when he passes there, and once in summer, when he goes back (westward). And the latter is the greater (feast), for then come to his court all the nobles, even though distant two months journey; and then he makes them largesse of robes and presents, and shows his great glory. There are there many buildings as long as barns, in which are stored his provisions and his treasures. In the entry of this great palace, it being unseemly to bring in there skins of milk and other drinks, master William the Parisian had made for him a great silver tree, and at its roots are four lions of silver, each with a conduit through it, and all belching forth white milk of mares. And four conduits are led inside the tree to its tops, which are bent downward, and on each of these is also a gilded serpent, whose tail twines round the tree. And from one of these pipes flows wine, from another *caracosmos*, or clarified mare's milk, from another *bal*, a drink made with honey, and from another rice mead, which is called *terracina*; and for each liquor there is a special silver bowl at the foot of the tree to receive it. Between these four conduits in the top, he made an angel holding a trumpet, and underneath the tree he made a vault in which a man can be hid. And pipes go up through the heart of the tree to the angel. In the first place he made bellows, but they did not give enough wind. Outside the palace is a cellar in which the liquors are stored, and there are servants all ready to pour them out when they hear the angel trumpeting. And there are branches of silver on the tree, and leaves and fruit. When then drink is wanted, the head butler cries to the angel to blow his trumpet. Then he who is concealed in the vault, hearing this, blows with all his might in the pipe leading to the angel, and the angel places the trumpet to his mouth,

11

and blows the trumpet right loudly. Then the servants who are in the cellar, hearing this, pour the different liquors into the proper conduits, and the conduits lead them down into the bowls prepared for that, and then the butlers draw it and carry it to the palace to the men and women. . . .

When I came before the Khan, I had to bend the knees, and so did the Tuin beside me, with his interpreter. Then the Khan said to me: 'Tell me the truth, whether you said the other day, when I sent my secretaries to you, that I was a Tuin.' I replied: 'My lord, I did not say that; I will tell you what I said, if it pleases you.' Then I repeated to him what I had said, and he replied: 'I thought full well that you did not say it, for you should not have said it; but your interpreter translated badly.' And he held out toward me the staff on which he leaned, saying: 'Fear not.' And I, smiling, said in an undertone: 'If I had been afraid, I should not have come here.' He asked the interpreter what I had said, and he repeated it to him. After that he began confiding to me his creed.

✵

MARCO POLO

(*c*.1254–1324)

Venetian trader and traveller. Accompanying his father and uncle, who had been there already, he travelled to China overland from 1271 to 1275. They stayed there for sixteen years, during which the young Marco Polo became a favourite of Kublai Khan. They returned to Venice in 1295. Subsequently imprisoned by the Genoese, he dictated his story to one Rustichello, a writer of romances.

The Book of Marco Polo the Venetian, ed. H. Yule (London, 1903).

1. THE PROVINCE OF BADASHAN (1271–1275)

There is also in the same country another mountain, in which azure is found; it is the finest in the world, and is got in a vein like silver. There are also other mountains which contain a great amount of silver ore, so that the country is a very rich one; but it is also (it must be said) a very cold one. It produces numbers of excellent horses, remarkable for their speed. They are not shod at all, although constantly used in mountainous country, and on very bad roads. . . .

The mountains of this country also supply Saker falcons of excellent flight, and plenty of Lanners likewise. Beasts and birds for the chase there are in great abundance. Good wheat is grown, and also barley without husk. They have no olive oil, but make oil from sesame, and also from walnuts. In the mountains there are vast numbers of sheep—400, 500, or 600 in a single flock, and all of them wild; and though many of them are taken, they never seem to get aught the scarcer.

Those mountains are so lofty that it is a hard day's work, from morning till evening, to get to the top of them. On getting up, you find an extensive plain, with great abundance of grass and trees, and copious springs of pure water running down through rocks and ravines. In those brooks are found trout and many other fish of dainty kinds; and the air in those regions is so pure, and residence there so healthful, that when the men who dwell below in the towns, and in the valleys and plains, find themselves attacked by any kind of fever or other ailment that may hap, they lose no time in going to the hills; and after abiding there two or three days, they quite recover their health through the excellence of that air. And Messer Marco said he had proved this by experience: for when in those parts he had been ill for about a year, but as as soon as he was advised to visit that mountain, he did so and got well at once.

In this kingdom there are many narrow and perilous passes, so difficult to force that the people have no fear of invasion. Their towns and villages also are on lofty hills, and in very strong positions. They are excellent archers, and much given to the chase; indeed, most of them are dependent for clothing on the skins of beasts, for stuffs are very dear among them. The great ladies, however, are arrayed in stuffs, and I will tell you the style of their dress! They all wear drawers made of cotton cloth, and into the making of these some will put 60, 80, or even 100 ells of stuff. This they do to make themselves look large in the hips, for the men of those parts think that to be a great beauty in a woman. . . .

There are numbers of wild beasts of all sorts in this region. And when you leave this little country, and ride three days north-east, always among mountains, you get to such a height that it is said to be the highest place in the world! And when you have got to this height you find . . . a fine river running through a plain clothed with the finest pasture in the world: a lean beast there will fatten to your heart's content in ten days. There are great numbers of all kinds of wild beasts; among others, wild sheep of great size, whose horns are good six palms in length. From these horns the shepherds make great bowls to eat from, and they use the horns also to enclose folds for their cattle at night. . . .

The plain is called Pamier, and you ride across it for twelve days together, finding nothing but a desert without habitations or any green thing, so that travellers are obliged to carry with them whatever they have need of. The region is so lofty and cold that you do not even see any birds flying. And I must note also that, because of this great cold, fire does not burn so brightly, nor give out so much heat as usual, nor does it cook food so effectually.

2. POSSIBLE DESCRIPTION OF ASBESTOS

Chingintalas is also a province at the verge of the desert, and lying between north-west and north. It has an extent of sixteen days' journey, and belongs to the Great Khan, and contains numerous towns and villages. There are three different races of people in it—Idolaters, Saracens, and some Nestorian Christians. At the northern extremity of this province there is a mountain in which are excellent veins of steel and ondanique. And you must know that in the same mountain there is a vein of the substance from which Salamander is made. For the real truth is that the Salamander is no beast, as they allege in our part of the world, but is a substance found in the earth; and I will tell you about it.

Everybody must be aware that it can be no animal's nature to live in fire, seeing that every animal is composed of all the four elements. Now I, Marco Polo, had a Turkish acquaintance of the name of Zurficar, and he was a very clever fellow. And this Turk related to Messer Marco Polo how he had lived three years in that region on behalf of the Great Khan, in order to procure those Salamanders for him. He said that the way they got them was by digging in that mountain until they found a certain vein. The substance of this vein was then taken and crushed, and when so treated it divides, as it were, into fibres of wool, which they set forth to dry. When dry, these fibres were pounded in a great copper mortar, and then washed, so as to remove all the earth and to leave only the fibres like fibres of wool. These were then spun, and made into napkins. When first made these napkins are not very white, but by putting them into the fire for a while they come out as white as snow. And so again whenever they become dirty they are bleached by being put in the fire.

Now this, and nought else, is the truth about the Salamander, and the people of the country all say the same. Any other account of the matter is fabulous nonsense. And I may add that they have at Rome a napkin of this stuff, which the Grand Khan sent to the Pope to make a wrapper for the Holy Sudarium of Jesus Christ.

3. PAPER MONEY (1275–1295)

The Emperor's mint, then, is in this same city of Cambaluc [Peking], and the way it is wrought is such that you might say he hath the secret of alchemy in perfection, and you would be right! For he makes his money after this fashion.

He makes them take of the bark of a certain tree, in fact of the mulberry tree, the leaves of which are the food of the silkworms—these trees being so numerous that whole districts are full of them. What they take is a certain fine white bast or skin which lies between the wood of the tree and the thick outer bark, and this they make into something resembling sheets of paper, but black. When these sheets have been prepared they are cut up into pieces of different sizes. The smallest of these sizes is worth a half tornesel; the next, a little larger, one tornesel; one, a little larger still, is worth half a silver groat of Venice; another a whole groat; others yet two groats, five groats, and ten groats. There is also a kind worth one bezant of gold, and others of three bezants, and so up to ten. All these pieces of paper are issued with as much solemnity and authority as if they were of pure gold or silver; and on every piece a variety of officials, whose duty it is, have to write their names, and to put their seals. And when all is prepared duly, the chief officer deputed by the Khan smears the seal entrusted to him with vermilion, and impresses it on the paper, so that the form of the seal remains stamped upon it in red; the money is then authentic. Anyone forging it would be punished with death. And the Khan causes every year to be made such a vast quantity of this money, which costs him nothing, that it must equal in amount all the treasure in the world.

With these pieces of paper, made as I have described, he causes all payments on his own account to be made; and he makes them to pass current universally over all his kingdoms and provinces and territories, and wherever his power and sovereignty extends. And nobody, however important he may think himself, dares to refuse them on pain of death. And, indeed, everybody takes them readily, for wherever a person may go throughout the Great Khan's dominions he shall find these pieces of paper current, and shall be able to transact all sales and purchases of goods by means of them just as well as if they were coins of pure gold. And all the while they are so light that ten bezants' worth does not weigh one golden bezant.

Furthermore, all merchants arriving from India or other countries, and bringing with them gold or silver or gems and pearls, are prohibited from selling to any one but the Emperor. He has twelve experts chosen for this business, men of shrewdness and experience in such affairs; these appraise the articles, and the Emperor then pays a liberal price for them in those pieces of paper. The merchants accept his price readily, for in the first place they would not get so good a one from anybody else, and secondly they are paid without any delay. And with this paper money they can buy what they like anywhere over the Empire, whilst it is also vastly lighter to carry about on their journeys. And it is a truth that the merchants will several times in the year bring wares to the amount of 400,000 bezants, and the Grand Sire pays for all in that paper. So he buys such a quantity of those precious things every year that his treasure is endless, whilst all the time the money he pays away costs him nothing at all. Moreover, several times in the year proclamation is made through the city that any one who may have gold or silver or gems or pearls, by taking them to the mint shall get a handsome price for them. And the owners are glad to do this, because they would find no other purchaser give so large a price. Thus the quantity they bring in is marvellous, though those who do not choose to do so may let it alone. Still, in this way, nearly all the valuables in the country come into the Khan's possession.

When any of those pieces of paper are spoilt—not that they are so very flimsy—the owner carries them to the mint, and by paying 3 per cent on the value he gets new pieces in exchange. And if any baron, or any one else, hath need of gold or silver or gems or pearls, in order to make plate, or girdles or the like, he goes to the Mint and buys as much as he list, paying in this paper-money.

4. COAL

It is a fact that all over the country of Cathay there is a kind of black stone existing in beds in the mountains, which they dig out and burn like firewood. If you supply the fire with them at night, and see that they are well kindled, you will find them still alight in the morning; and they make such capital fuel that no other is used throughout the country. It is true that they have plenty of wood also, but they do not burn it, because those stones burn better and cost less.

Moreover, with that vast number of people, and the number of hot baths that they maintain—for every one has such a bath at least three times a week, and in winter if possible every day, whilst every nobleman and man of wealth has a private bath for his own use—the wood would not suffice for the purpose.

IBN BATTÚTA
(MOHAMMED IBN ABDULLAH IBN BATUTA)
(1304–1377)

A Moroccan Muslim often called the greatest traveller of all time. His first journey started in 1325 as a pilgrimage to Mecca but eventually took him half-way round the world to China before his triumphant return home in 1349.

Travels in Asia and Africa 1325–1354, trans. and selected by H. A. R. Gibb (London, 1929).

DESCRIPTION OF CHINA (1345)

The land of China is of vast extent, and abounding in produce, fruits, grain, gold, and silver. In this respect there is no country in the world that can rival it. It is traversed by the river called the 'Water of Life', which rises in some mountains, called the 'Mountain of Apes', near the city of Khan-Baliq [Peking] and flows through the centre of China for the space of six months' journey, until finally it reaches Sin as-Sin [Canton]. It is bordered by villages, fields, fruit gardens, and bazaars, just like the Egyptian Nile, only that the country through which runs this river is even more richly cultivated and populous, and there are many waterwheels on it. In the land of China there is abundant sugar cane, equal, nay superior, in quality to that of Egypt, as well as grapes and plums. I used to think that the Othmani plums of Damascus had no equal, until I saw the plums in China. It has wonderful melons too, like those of Khwarizm and Isfahan. All the fruits which we have in our country are to be found there, either much the same or of better quality. Wheat is very abundant in China— indeed, better wheat I have never seen—and the same may be said of their lentils and chick-peas.

The Chinese pottery [porcelain] is manufactured only in the towns of Zaytun and Sin-kalan. It is made of the soil of some mountains in that district, which takes fire like charcoal, as we shall relate subsequently. They mix this with some stones which they have, burn the whole for three days, then pour water over it. This gives a kind of clay which they cause to ferment. The best quality of porcelain is made from clay that has fermented for a complete month, but no more, the poorer quality from clay that has fermented for ten days. The price of this porcelain there is the

17

same as, or even less than, that of ordinary pottery in our country. It is exported to India and other countries, even reaching as far as our own lands in the West, and it is the finest of all makes of pottery.

The hens and cocks in China are very big indeed, bigger than geese in our country, and hen's eggs there are bigger than our goose eggs. On the other hand their geese are not all large. We bought a hen once and set about cooking it, but it was too big for one pot, so we put it in two. Cocks over there are about the size of ostriches; often a cock will shed its feathers and nothing but a great red body remains. The first time I saw a Chinese cock was in the city of Kawlam. I took it for an ostrich and was amazed at it, but its owner told me that in China there were some even bigger than that, and when I got to China I saw for myself the truth of what he had told me about them.

The Chinese themselves are infidels, who worship idols and burn their dead like the Hindus. The king of China is a Tartar, one of the descendants of Ghenkis Khan. In every Chinese city there is a quarter for Muslims in which they live by themselves, and in which they have mosques both for the Friday services and for other religious purposes. The Muslims are honoured and respected. The Chinese infidels eat the flesh of swine and dogs, and sell it in their markets. They are wealthy folk and well-to-do, but they make no display either in their food or their clothes. You will see one of their principal merchants, a man so rich that his wealth cannot be counted, wearing a coarse cotton tunic. But there is one thing that the Chinese take a pride in, that is, gold and silver plate. Every one of them carries a stick, on which they lean in walking, and which they call 'the third leg'. Silk is very plentiful among them, because the silk-worm attaches itself to fruits and feeds on them without requiring much care. For that reason it is so common to be worn by even the very poorest there. Were it not for the merchants it would have no value at all, for a single piece of cotton cloth is sold in their country for the price of many pieces of silk. It is customary amongst them for a merchant to cast what gold and silver he has into ingots, each weighing a hundredweight or more or less, and to put those ingots above the door of his house.

The Chinese use neither gold dinars nor silver dirhams in their commerce. All the gold and silver that comes into their country is cast by them into ingots, as we have described. Their buying and selling is carried on exclusively by means of pieces of paper, each of the size of the palm of the hand, and stamped with the sultan's seal. Twenty-five of these pieces of paper are called a *balisht*, which takes the place of the dinar with us. When these notes become torn by handling, one takes them to an office corresponding to our mint, and receives their equivalent in new notes on delivering up the old ones. This transaction is made without charge and involves no expense, for those who have the duty of making the notes receive regular salaries from the sultan. Indeed, the direction of that office is given to one of their principal amirs. If anyone goes to the bazaar with a silver dirham or a dinar, intending to buy something, no one will accept it from him or pay any attention to him until he changes if for *balisht*, and with that he may buy what he will.

All the inhabitants of China and of Cathay use in place of charcoal a kind of lumpy earth found in their country. It resembles our fuller's earth, and its colour too is the colour of fuller's earth. Elephants are used to carry loads of it. They break it up into pieces about the size of pieces of charcoal with us, and set it on fire and it burns like charcoal, only giving out more heat than a charcoal fire. When it is reduced to cinders, they knead it with water, dry it, and use it again for cooking, and so on, over and over again, until it is entirely consumed. It is from this clay that they make the Chinese porcelain ware, after adding to it some other stones, as we have related.

The Chinese are of all peoples the most skilful in the arts and possessed of the greatest mastery of them. This characteristic is well known, and has frequently been described at length in the works of various writers. In regard to portraiture there is none, whether Greek or any other, who can match them in precision, for in this art they show a marvellous talent. I myself saw an extraordinary example of this gift of theirs. I never returned to any of their cities after I had visited it a first time without finding my portrait and the portraits of my companions drawn on the walls and on sheets of paper exhibited in the bazaars. When I visited the sultan's city I passed with my companions through the painters' bazaar on my way to the sultan's palace. We were dressed after the Iraqi fashion. On returning from the palace in the evening, I passed through the same bazaar, and saw my portrait and those of my companions drawn on a sheet of paper which they had affixed to the wall. Each of us set to examining the other's portrait and found that the likeness was perfect in every respect. I was told that the sultan had ordered them to do this, and that they had come to the palace while we were there and had been observing us and drawing our portraits without our noticing it. This is a custom of theirs, I mean making portraits of all who pass through their country. In fact they have brought this to such perfection that if a stranger commits any offence that obliges him to flee from China, they send his portrait far and wide. A search is then made for him and wherever the person bearing a resemblance to that portrait is found, he is arrested.

When a Mohammedan merchant enters any town in China, he is given the choice between staying with some specified merchant among the Muslims domiciled there, or going to a hostelry. If he chooses to stay with the merchant, his money is taken into custody and put under the charge of the resident merchant. The latter then pays from it all his expenses with honesty and charity. When the visitor wishes to depart, his money is examined, and if any of it is found to be missing, the resident merchant who was put in charge of it is obliged to make good the deficit. If the visitor chooses to go to the hostelry, his property is deposited under the charge of the keeper of the hostelry. The keeper buys for him whatever he desires and presents him with an account. If he desires to take a concubine, the keeper purchases a slave-girl for him and lodges him in an apartment opening out of the hostelry, and purveys for them both. Slave-girls fetch a low price; yet all the Chinese sell their sons and daughters, and consider it no disgrace. They are not compelled, however, to travel with those who buy them, nor on the other hand, are they hindered from going if they choose to do so. In the same way, if a stranger desires to marry, marry he may; but as for spending his money in debauchery, no, that he may not do. They say, 'We will not have it noised about amongst Muslims that their people waste their substance in our country, because it is a land of riotous living and women of surpassing beauty.'

China is the safest and best regulated of countries for a traveller. A man may go by himself a nine months' journey, carrying with him large sums of money, without any fear on that account. The system by which they ensure his safety is as follows. At every post-station in their country they have a hostelry controlled by an officer, who is stationed there with a company of horsemen and foot-soldiers. After sunset, or later in the evening, the officer visits the hostelry with his clerk, registers the names of all travellers staying there for the night, seals up the list, and locks them into the hostelry. After sunrise he returns with his clerk, calls each person by name, and writes a detailed description of them on the list. He then sends a man with them to conduct them to the next post-station and bring back a clearance certificate from the controller there to the effect that all these persons have arrived at that station. If the guide does not produce this document, he is held responsible for them. This is the practice at every station in their country from Sin as-Sin to Khan-Baliq. In these hostelries there is everything that the traveller requires in the way of provisions, especially fowls and geese. Sheep, on the other hand, are scarce with them.

20

CHENG HO

(1371–1435)

Chinese mariner, the Grand Eunuch. Although most emperors forbade travel outside China, he was sent by the emperor Ch'eng Tsu on six rare voyages of exploration, reaching as far west as Arabia and the coast of Africa. His chronicler was Ma Huan.

The Overall Survey of the Ocean's Shores (1433), trans. J. V. G. Mills (Cambridge, 1970).

1. MA HUAN'S FOREWORD (1416)

I once looked at a book called *A Record of the Islands and their Barbarians*, which recorded variations of season and of climate, and differences in topography and in peoples. I was surprised and said, 'How can there be such dissimilarities in the world?'

In the eleventh year of the Yung-lo period, the cyclic year *kuei-ssu*, the Grand Exemplar the Cultured Emperor issued an imperial order that the principal envoy, the grand eunuch Cheng Ho, should take general command of the treasure-ships and go to the various foreign countries in the Western Ocean to read out the imperial commands and to bestow rewards.

I too was sent in a subordinate capacity as a translator of foreign documents. I followed the mission wherever it went, over vast expanses of huge waves for I do not know how many millions of *li*; I passed through the various countries, with their different seasons, climates, topography, and peoples; and I saw these countries with my own eyes and I walked through them in person. After that I knew that the statements in *A Record of the Islands and their Barbarians* were no fabrications, and that even greater wonders existed.

So I collected notes about the appearance of the people in each country, and about the variations of the local customs, also about the differences in the natural products, and about the boundary-limits. I arranged my notes in order so as to make a book, which I have entitled *The Overall Survey of the Ocean's Shores*. It enables an interested reader at a brief glance to learn all the important facts about the various foreign countries; and in particular he will see how the civilizing influence of the Emperor has spread to an extent which could not be matched during former dynasties.

But I am ashamed of my own foolishness, for I am a mere simpleton, who was privileged to accompany the imperial envoy, and with him made this 'Overall Survey'. It was in truth a wonderful opportunity such as occurs only once in a thousand years. As regards this volume, in formulating my ideas and expressing myself in words I am incapable of literary elegances, but I write of these matters with an honest pen and nothing more. I hope that the reader will not ridicule my book because of the superficiality of its style.

This note will serve as a foreword.

The lucky day of the yellow cup moon, in the fourteenth year (the cyclic year *ping-shen*) of the Yung-lo period of the Great Ming dynasty.

Written by Ma Huan, the mountain-woodcutter of Kuei chi.

2. A CHINESE VIEW OF MECCA (1432)

This country is the country of Mecca. Setting sail from the country of Calicut, you proceed towards the south-west—the point *shen* on the compass; the ship travels for three moons, and then reaches the jetty of this country. The foreign name for it is Jidda, and there is a great chief who controls it. From Jidda you go west, and after travelling for one day you reach the city where the king resides; it is named the capital city of Mecca.

They profess the Muslim religion. A holy man first expounded and spread the doctrine of his teaching in this country, and right down to the present day the people of the country all observe the regulations of the doctrine in their actions, not daring to commit the slightest transgression.

The people of this country are stalwart and fine-looking, and their limbs and faces are of a very dark purple colour. The menfolk bind up their heads; they wear long garments; and on their feet they put leather shoes. The women all wear a covering over their heads, and you cannot see their faces. They speak the A-la-pi [Arabic] language. The law of the country prohibits wine-drinking. The customs of the people are pacific and admirable. There are no poverty-stricken families. They all observe the precepts of their religion, and law-breakers are few. It is in truth a most happy country. As to the marriage and funeral rites: they all conduct themselves in accordance with the regulations of their religion.

If you travel on from here for a journey of more than half a day, you reach the Heavenly Hall mosque; the foreign name for this Hall is K'ai-a-pai [?Ka'ba]. All round it on the outside is a wall; this wall has 466 openings; on both sides of the openings are pillars all made of white jade-stone; of these pillars there are altogether 467—along the front 99, along

22

the back 101, along the left-hand side 132, and along the right-hand side 135.

The Hall is built with layers of five-coloured stones; in shape it is square and flat-topped. Inside there are pillars formed of five great beams of sinking incense wood, and a shelf made of yellow gold. Throughout the interior of the Hall, the walls are all formed of clay mixed with rosewater and ambergris, exhaling a perpetual fragrance. Over the Hall is a covering of black hemp-silk. They keep two black lions to guard the door.

Every year on the tenth day of the twelfth moon all the foreign Muslims—in extreme cases making a long journey of one or two years—come to worship inside the Hall. Everyone cuts off a piece of the hemp-silk covering as a memento before he goes away. When it has been completely cut away, the king covers over the Hall again with another covering woven in advance; this happens again and again, year after year, without intermission.

❄

VASCO DA GAMA

(c.1460–1524)

Portuguese navigator. Following a route pioneered by Bartolomeo Dias around the Cape of Good Hope in 1488, he took on provisions on the East African coast and sailed to India in 1498.

The Three Voyages of Vasco da Gama and His Viceroyalty (London, 1869).

DEPARTURE FROM AFRICA AND ARRIVAL AT CALICUT (1498)

This same day, in the evening, the pilots went on board the ships, one with Paulo da Gama, and the other with Vasco da Gama, and with him the Mozambique pilot, and they gave them cabins in which to stow their property. Then the King sent boats to the ships laden with biscuit, which he had ordered to be made in the Moorish fashion, which is like mouthfuls of bread, and much rice, and butter, cocoa-nuts, sheep salted whole like salt meat, and others alive, many fowls and vegetables, separately for each ship, and in great abundance, and much sugar in powder in sacks. And as they were equipped with everything and ready to set sail next day, which was the day of the Transfiguration of our Lord (6 August), they took leave

23

of the King, who could not endure it, and embarked in his boat and went with them, saying very affectionate things, with which he bade farewell to each of them at the side of the ships; and he remained looking at them for a space as they hoisted in the boats; and bidding each other farewell the trumpets sounded, and all the crews gave a shout of 'Lord God have mercy, farewell!', after which night fell. The next day they arose with the ships dressed out with flags, and as it was a fine day they loosed the sails, sounding the trumpets with much joy, all upon their knees, giving great praise to the Lord for so much favour as He had shown to them in their affairs. Sailing with a fair wind in twenty days they got sight of land, which the pilots foretold before that they saw it, this was a great mountain which is on the coast of India, in the Kingdom of Cananor, which the people of the country in their language call the mountain Delielly, and they call it of the rat, and they call it Mount Dely, because in this mountain there were so many rats that they never could make a village there. As it was the custom to give the fees of good news to the pilots when they see the land, they gave to each of the pilots a robe of red cloth, and ten testoons; and they went on approaching the land until they saw the beach, and they ran along it and passed within sight of a large town of thatched houses inside a bay, which the pilots said was named Cananor, where many skiffs were going about fishing; and several came near to see the ships and were much surprised, and went ashore to relate that these ships had so much rigging and so many sails and white men . . .

The ships continued running along the coast close to land for the coast was clear, without banks against which to take precautions; and the pilots gave orders to cast anchor in a place which made a sort of bay, because there commenced the city of Calicut. This town is named Capocate, and on anchoring there a multitude of people flocked to the beach, all dark and naked, only covered with cloths half-way down the thigh, with which they concealed their nakedness. All were much amazed at seeing what they had never before seen. When news was taken to the King he also came to look at the ships, for all the wonder was at seeing so many ropes and so many sails, and because the ships arrived when the sun was almost set; and at night they lowered out the boats, and Vasco da Gama went at once for his brother and Nicolas Coelho, and they remained together conversing upon the method of dealing with this King, since here was the principal end which they had come to seek; it seemed to him that it would be best to comport himself as an ambassador, and to make him his present, always saying that they had been separated from another fleet which they came to seek for there, and that the captain-major had come and brought him letters from the King.

SIR HUGH WILLOUGHBY

(*c*.1500–1554)

British military officer and explorer. He sailed in 1553 with three ships to seek the North-East Passage. One ship, commanded by Richard Chancellor, reached the White Sea, and he travelled overland to Moscow before returning to England. The other two wintered on the coast of Lapland and all aboard died.

'Voyage, wherein he unfortunately perished at Arzina Reca in Lappland', in *Principal Navigations by Richard Hakluyt*, vol. i (London, 1599).

WILLOUGHBY'S INSTRUCTIONS FROM SEBASTIAN CABOT, GOVERNOR OF THE COMPANY OF MERCHANT VENTURERS (1554)

Item, if people shall appear gathering of stones, gold, metal, or other like, on the sand, your pinnaces may draw nigh, marking what things they gather, using or playing upon the drum, or such other instruments, as may allure them to harkening, to fantasy, or desire to see, and hear your instruments and voices, but keep you out of danger, and show to them no point or sign of rigour and hostility . . .

Item, there are people that can swim in the sea, havens, and rivers, naked, having bows and shafts, coveting to draw nigh your ships, which if they shall find not well watched, or warded, they will assault, desirous of the bodies of men, which they covet for meat: if you resist them, they dive, and so will flee, and therefore diligent watch is to be kept both day & night, in some Islands.

Item, if occasion shall serve, that you may give advertisements of your proceedings in such things as may correspond to the expectation of the company, and likelihood of success in the voyage, passing such dangers of the seas, perils of ice, intolerable colds, and other impediments, which by sundry authors & writers, have ministered matter of suspicion in some heads, that this voyage could not succeed for the extremity of the North Pole, lack of passage, and such like, which have caused wavering minds, and doubtful heads, not only to withdraw themselves from the adventure of this voyage, but also dissuaded others from the same, the certainty wherof, when you shall have tried by experience (most certain Master of all worldly knowledge), then for declaration of the truth, which you shall have experted [i.e. experienced], you may by common assent of counsel send either by land, or otherwise, such two or one person, to bring the same by credit, as you shall think may pass in safety.

✲

ANTHONY JENKINSON

(d. 1611)

English merchant. He has been described as the first great English explorer. Following Chancellor's route to Moscow, he continued south to the Caspian, which he sailed across, and eventually reached Bukhara.

Early Voyages and Travels to Russia and Persia, ed. E. Delmar Morgan (London, 1886).

1. FIRST ENGLISH DESCRIPTION OF THE TARTARS (1557)

The Nagayans when they flourished, lived in this manner: they were divided into divers companies called Hordes, and every Horde had a ruler, whom they obeyed as their king, and was called a Murse. Town or house they had none, but lived in the open fields, every Murse or King having his Hordes or people about him, with their wives, children, and cattle, who, having consumed the pasture in one place, removed unto another: and when they remove they have houses like tents set upon wagons or carts, which are drawn from place to place with camels, and therein their wives, children, and all their riches, which is very little, is carried about, and every man hath at the least four or five wives besides concubines. Use of money they have none, but do barter their cattle for apparel and other necessaries. They delight in no art nor science, except the wars, wherein they are expert, but for the most part they be pasturing people, and have great store of cattle, which is all their riches. They eat much flesh, and especially the horse, and they drink mare's milk, wherewith they be oftentimes drunk: they are seditious and inclined to theft and murder. Corn they sow not, neither do eat any bread, mocking the Christians for the same, and disabling our strengths, saying we live by eating the top of a weede, and drink a drink made of the same, allowing their great devouring of flesh, and drinking of milk, to be the increase of their strength.

2. ARRIVAL IN BUKHARA

So upon the 23rd day of December we arrived at the city of Boghar [Bukhara] in the land of Bactria. This Boghar is situated in the lowest part of all the land, walled about with a high wall of earth, with divers gates into the same: it is divided into 3 partitions, whereof two parts are the king's, and the 3rd part is for merchants and markets, and every science hath their dwelling and market by themselves. The city is very great, and the houses for the most part of earth, but there are also many houses, temples, and monuments of stone sumptuously builded, and gilt, and specially bathstones so artificially built that the like thereof is not in the world . . . There is a little river running through the midst of the said city, but the water thereof is most unwholesome, for it breedeth sometimes in men that drink thereof, and especially in them that be not there born, a worm of an ell long, which lieth commonly in the leg betwixt the flesh and the skin, and is plucked out about the ankle with great art and cunning, the surgeons being much practised therein, and if she break in plucking out, the part dieth, and every day she cometh out about an inch, which is rolled up, and so worketh till she be all out. And yet it is there forbidden to drink any other thing than water, and mares' milk, and whosoever is found to break that law is whipped and beaten most cruelly through the open markets, and there are officers appointed for the same who have authority to go into any man's house, to search if he have either aquavita, wine, or brage, and finding the same, do break the vessels, spoil the drink, and punish the masters of the house most cruelly, yea, and many times, if they perceive but by the breath of a man that he hath drunk, without further examination he shall not escape their hands.

✳

TIMOFEYEVICH YERMAK
(d. 1584)

Russian Cossack. Leading a force of 800 men, he overthrew the Tartar khanate of Kuchum and so destroyed the last of the Golden Horde. This opened up Siberia for Russian conquest, an area comparable to that unveiled by Columbus.

Yermak's Campaign in Siberia, ed. T. Armstrong (London, 1975).

THE DEFEAT OF KUCHUM (1581)

All the cossacks decided on a final blow, and this was the fourth battle with Kuchum's men. Kuchum was standing on the hill with his son Mametkul by the barrage when the cossacks, by God's will, issued forth from the town saying of one accord: 'God is with us! Understand this, ye peoples, and submit, for God is with us!' And all together they joined battle, and the fighting was terrible on the 23rd day of October, hand to hand, foe cutting down foe. Kuchum was shooting from the hill while the cossacks raked them with their fire so that they died of wounds or were killed. The unbelievers, driven by Kuchum, suffered great losses at the hands of the cossacks; they lamented, fought unwillingly, and died.

Kuchum's men had no guns, only bows and arrows, spears and swords. The Chuvash had two cannon which the cossacks silenced, so they hurled these down the hill into the Irtysh. Kuchum, as he stood on the Chuvash hill, saw the carnage wrought among his men and lamented with all the unbelievers, and ordered his chanters and mullahs to shout their prayers to their idols because their gods were asleep. Helpless and dishonoured, hard pressed by God's might, he meditated flight. They fought on ceaselessly for three days without respite.

On the 24th day of October, the Ostyak princelings of the lower reaches were the first to disobey Kuchum's orders, and fled on horseback to their homeland without return, to live there like animals in wild forests, keeping out of sight of the Russian people. And to this day it is their custom to flee and disappear when our people come.

On the 25th day of October, Kuchum, as he lay on his couch at night, weary and sorrowful, had a vision sent by God: the skies suddenly opened at the four corners of the universe and there issued forth to destroy him shining warriors armed, winged, and terrible, who on reaching his residence surrounded the whole of his army, saying: 'Unclean son of the dark demon Bakhmet, leave this land, for the land and its fulness is the Lord's and all the Christians living in it are blessed; fly to your habitations near the abyss of the thrice-accursed demon Bakhmet.' Kuchum rose trembling in his whole body and said: 'Let us flee from here, from this terrible place, so as not to perish.' And God's angel drove them along, for the way for them was dark and slippery.

On the same date, in the evening, the Voguls also secretly abandoned Kuchum's defences, fleeing to their homes beyond the impassable swamps and lakes of Yaskalba so as not to be tracked down by Yermak and die a cruel death. They took refuge with their families in inaccessible places to remain undiscovered, and to this day a man on skis can see, in the over-grown swamps and lakes, earth-walls in front and behind.

Kuchum, after seeing in the night vision the final loss of his kingdom and wholesale devastation, fled from his city Kashlyk, which is called Sibir, on the 26th day of October. He secretly rose and said to all his people: 'Let us flee immediately so as not to die a cruel death at the hands of the cossacks.' And without looking back all fled from the city to the steppe, to the Kazakh horde, to their former habitations, leaving empty the towns of Chuvash and Kashlyk, Suzgun, Bishik, Abalak, and others, driven by God's invisible power. . . .

The rumour about Yermak and the cossacks sped over the entire land of Sibir, and the fear of God seized all the infidels living in that country. And on the fourth day after the taking of Sibir Boyar, prince of Demyan, came to Yermak with many gifts, bringing all needful provisions and de-livering tribute. Yermak received them with honour and dismissed them. There also began to come to him Tatars living in the neighbourhood with their wives and children and kinsfolk, bringing tribute. And Yermak ordered them to go on living in their homes as before, as they had done under Kuchum.

✾

WILLEM BARENTS

(d. 1579)

Dutch Arctic explorer. He searched for the North-East Passage on three expeditions, on the last of which he died after wintering near Novaya Zemlya.

G. de Veer, *The Second Voyage of William Barents into the North Seas, 1595,* in John Harris, *A Complete Collection of Voyages and Travels* (London, 1705).

A LANDING IN SAMOYED COUNTRY AND AN ENCOUNTER WITH A BEAR (1595)

On the last of August, William Barents, our Captain, sailed to the south side of Weygates, and going on shore, our men, being nine in number, went about a mile into the land, not thinking to find any men there (because they had been on shore in the Weygates at other times, and saw none), and being misty weather, they perceived about twenty men, who were very near them before they knew it. Our interpreter went alone towards them to speak with them, which they, perceiving, sent one towards us who, coming almost to our men, took an arrow out of his quiver, offering to shoot at him; wherewith our interpreter called unto him in the Russian tongue, 'Shoot not, we are friends'; which the other, hearing, cast his bow and arrows to the ground, and said, 'You are welcome', and saluting each other, by bending their heads towards the ground after the Russian manner, our interpreter questioned him about the situation and stretching of the sea eastward of the strait of Weygates. He answered that, when we should pass a point of land about five days' sailing from thence (pointing with his hand towards the north-east), then we should come to a great sea (pointing towards the south-east), saying that he knew it very well, because one had been there who was sent thither by their king with certain soldiers, whereof he had been captain.

They are for the most part low of stature, with broad, flat faces, small eyes, short legs, their knees standing outwards, and are very nimble. They are apparelled in deer-skins from head to foot, and wear long hair, which they pleat and fold, letting it hang down their backs. Their sleds stood always ready with one or two deer in them, which will carry a man or two swifter than our horses.

One of our men shot a musket toward the sea, wherewith they were in so great fear that they ran and leapt like madmen. We told them by our interpreter that we used our pieces instead of bows; and to convince them, one of our men took a flat stone and set it upon a hill a good distance from him, and with a bullet struck the stone asunder, whereat they wondered exceedingly.

After they were gone from us, one of them came riding to the shore, to fetch a rough-hewn image which our men had taken off the shore and put into their boat; as soon as he saw it in the boat, he made us a sign that we had not done well in taking it away; whereupon we gave it him again. Not far from thence we found hundreds of such carved images, having a little hill instead of a nose, and two cuts in places of eyes, and under the nose a cut in place of a mouth. Before the images we found great store of ashes and bones of deer, whereby we supposed that they there offered unto them.

On the second of September we set sail, but by reason of the ice, the mist, and the shifting of the wind, we could hold no course. On the fourth we sailed between the firm land and the States Island.

On the sixth some of our men went ashore on the firm land, to seek for stones which looked like diamonds, and two of our men lying together in one place, a great, lean, white bear came stealing out, and caught one of them fast by the neck, who, not perceiving what it was, cried out and said, 'Who is it that pulls me so by the neck?', wherewith the other, lifting up his head to see who it was, cried out, and said, 'Oh mate, it is a bear', and therewith presently rose up and ran away.

The bear at the first, falling upon the man, bit his head asunder, and sucked out his blood, wherewith the rest of the men that were on the land, being about twenty, ran presently thither, either to save the man, or else to drive the bear from the dead body, and having charged their pieces and bent their pikes, set upon her, who was still devouring the man; but she, perceiving them to come towards her, fiercely ran at them, and, getting another of them out from the company, tore him in pieces, wherewith all the rest ran away.

✻

JOHANN GRUEBER

(1623–1680)

Jesuit priest. He and another Jesuit, Albert d'Orville, set out from China and became, in 1661, probably the first Europeans to enter Lhasa. D'Orville died in India on their way back to Rome, which Grueber reached in 1664.

Account of Travels of Johann Grueber, Jesuit, in A New General Collection of Voyages and Travels, published by Thomas Astley (London, 1745–7).

1. DESCRIPTION OF THE GREAT WALL (1661)

The Missionary set out for China, as we conjecture, in the year 1656. According to the first letter, he went from Venice to Smyrna by sea; from thence to Ormuz by land in five months; from Ormuz by sea in seven months to Macao. There landing, he passed through China partly by water, partly by land, to Peking in three months. He stayed in China three years: in one of which, 1660, he says the fifty-six Jesuits who were then in that empire baptized more than 50,000 men.

In his return he took a road never perhaps attempted by any European before. Grueber left Peking in June 1661, in company with Albert d'Orville, of the same society. In thirty days he came to Singan-fu, and in thirty more to Sining-fu, crossing the Huang-ho, or Yellow River, twice in the way.

Sining is a great and populous city, built at the vast Wall of China, through the gate of which the merchants from India enter Katay or China. Here they stay till they have licence from the Emperor to proceed forward. The Wall at this place is so broad that six horsemen may run abreast on it without embarrassing each other. Here the citizens of Sining take the air (which is very healthful, coming from the desert), and recreate themselves with the prospect as well as other diversions. There are stairs to the top of the Wall, and many travel on it from the gate at Sining to the next at Suchow, which is eighteen days' journey. This they do by the Governor's licence, out of curiosity, having a delightful prospect all the way from the Wall, as from a high tower, of the innumerable habitations on one side, and the various kinds of wild beast which range the desert on the other side. Besides wild bulls, here are tigers, lions, elephants, rhinoceroses, and monoceroses, which are a kind of horned ass. Thus the merchants view the beasts free from danger.

2. TIBET AND NEPAL

From Sining they, in three months, entered the kingdom of Lhasa, which the Tatars call Barantola. The King is styled Deva, or Teva, descended from an ancient race of the Tangut Tatars, and resides at Butala [Potala], a castle built on a high mountain, after the European fashion, where he has a numerous court. The great priest of this country is called Lama Konju, and is adored as a god. He resides at Barantola, and is the Pope of the Chinese and Tatars, called by them God the Father, whose religion in all essential points tallies with the Romish, although, says the author, no Christian ever was in the country before.

Here they stayed a month, and might have converted many of the natives, but for that devilish God the Father (as the author calls him), who puts to death such as refuse to adore him. However, they were kindly treated by the people and King, who was the brother of that God the Father....

From Lhasa, or Barantola, they came in four days to the foot of the mountain Langur, which being exceedingly high, travellers can hardly breathe at top, the air is so very thin; neither is it to be crossed in summer without great danger from the exhalations of certain poisonous herbs. Besides, as no waggons or beasts can pass it for the rocks and precipices, they must proceed on foot almost a month till they come to Kuthi, one of the two chief cities of the kingdom of Nepal. This mountainous tract is plentifully furnished with springs both hot and cold, which issue from all parts of the mountain, affording store of fish and pasture.

✷

IPPOLITO DESIDERI

(1684–1733)

Italian Jesuit. Regarded as the first of the great Tibetan explorers, he crossed from Kashmir to Lhasa in 1715 and then stayed for five years.

Letter from Father Ippolito Desideri to Father Ildebrando Grassi, Lhasa, 10 April 1716, in *A New General Collection of Voyages and Travels*, published by Thomas Astley (London, 1745–7).

DIFFICULTIES OF TRAVEL IN THE MOUNTAINS (1715)

Great Tibet begins at the summit of an enormous, snow-clad mountain called Kantel. One side of the mountain belongs to Kashmir, and the other to Tibet. We had left Kashmir on 17 May 1715, and on the 30th, the festival of Our Lord's Ascension, we crossed the mountain and entered Tibet. Much snow had fallen on the path, which winds between mountains as far as Leh, or Ladak, the fortress where the King resides, which are the very picture of desolation, horror, and death itself. They are piled one atop of another. And so close as scarcely to leave room for the torrents which course impetuously from their heights, and dash with such deafening noise against the rocks as to appal the stoutest traveller. Above and at their foot the mountains are equally impassable; you are therefore forced to make your way about half-way down the slope, and the path, as a rule, is so narrow as barely to leave room for you to set down your feet; this obliges you to pick your way with extreme care. A false step, and you are precipitated down the abyss with the loss of your life, or at the least with broken limbs, as befell some of our fellow-travellers. Were there bushes you might cling by them, but these mountains are so barren that neither plants nor even a blade of grass grows thereon. Would you wish to cross from one mountain to another, you must pass over the foaming torrents between, and there is no bridge, save some narrow, unsteady planks, or some ropes stretched across and interwoven with green branches. Often you are obliged to take off your shoes in order to get a better foothold. I assure you that

I shudder now at the bare remembrance of these dreadful episodes in our journey. . . .

One's eyes are terribly tired with the reflection of the sun's rays from the snow, which dazzles and nearly blinds them. I was obliged to bandage mine, and admit only just enough light to see my way. Then, every other day or so, we encountered customs officers, who, not content with demanding the usual dues, exacted all they pleased by any right they fancied.

✻

VITUS BERING

(1681–1741)

Danish navigator in the service of Russia. He was sent by Peter the Great, in whose navy he served, to establish whether the Asian and American continents were linked. He passed through the Bering Strait in 1728 and was then sent back to check what land lay to the east. The Great Northern Expedition took ten years to prepare (1733–43), and Bering was sixty when he finally reached Alaska. He died of scurvy on one of the Aleutian islands. The brilliant scientist who accompanied him and wrote the following was Georg Wilhelm Steller (1709–46).

Journal of a Voyage with Bering, 1741–1742, by Georg Wilhelm Steller, ed. O. W. Frost (Stanford, Calif., 1988).

ALASKA (1741)

We saw land as early as 15 July, but because I was the first to announce it and because forsooth it was not so distinct that a picture could be made of it, the announcement, as usual, was regarded as one of my peculiarities; yet on the following day, in very clear weather, it came into view in the same place. The land was here very much elevated; the mountains, observed extending inland, were so lofty that we could see them quite plainly at sea at a distance of sixteen Dutch miles. I cannot recall having seen higher mountains anywhere in Siberia and Kamchatka. The coast was everywhere much indented and therefore provided with numerous bays and inlets close to the mainland.

Once having determined to tell the truth and be impartial in all things. I must not fail to mention one circumstance which perhaps may not escape the notice of the high authorities but may receive an interpretation different from the actual facts.—It can easily be imagined how happy everyone was when land was finally sighted; nobody failed to congratulate the Captain Commander, whom the glory for the discovery mostly concerned. He, however, received it all not only very indifferently and without particular pleasure, but in the presence of all he even shrugged his shoulders while looking at the land. Had the Commander survived and had he intended to take any action against his officers because of their misdoings, they would have been ready to point to his conduct then as evidence of his evil-minded disposition. But the good Captain Commander was much superior to his officers in looking into the future, and in the cabin he expressed himself to me and Mr Plenisner as follows: 'We think now we have accomplished everything, and many go about greatly inflated, but they do not consider where we have reached land, how far we are from home, and what may yet happen; who knows but that perhaps trade winds may arise, which may prevent us from returning? We do not know this country; nor are we provided with supplies for a wintering. . . .

When I was once more on the top of the mountain, and turned my eyes towards the mainland to take a good look at least at that country on which I was not vouchsafed to employ my endeavours more fruitfully, I noticed smoke some versts away ascending from a charming hill covered with spruce forest, so that I could now entertain the certain hope of meeting with people and learning from them the data I needed for a complete report. For that reason I returned in great haste and went back, loaded with my collections, to the place where I had landed. Through the men who were just ready to hurry back to the ship in the boat I informed the Captain Commander, and asked him for the small yawl and a few men for a couple of hours. Dead tired, I made in the mean time descriptions on the beach of the rarer plants which I was afraid might wither, and was delighted to be able to test out the excellent water for tea.

In an hour or so I received the patriotic and courteous reply that I should betake myself on board quickly or they would leave me ashore without waiting for me. I reflected that God gives to each one the place and the opportunity to do that which he is ordered to do, so as to enable one to present one's services favourably to the highest authorities and after long waiting and untold expenses to the Empress [i.e. Government] work out one's destinies. However, as matters now stand, it is probable that at our departure we all saw Russia for the last time, since under the present circumstances it is impossible to expect the divine help on the return voyage, if wind and weather were to become as hostile toward us as we have been to the general object of the expedition and thereby to our own good fortune. However, since there was now no time left for moralizing, only enough to scrape together as much as possible before our fleeing the country, and as evening was already nearing, I sent my cossack out to shoot some rare birds that I had noticed, while I once more started off to the westward, returning at sunset with various observations and collections. Here I was given once more the strict command that, unless I came on board this time, no more notice would be taken of me. I consequently betook myself with what I had collected to the ship and there, to my great astonishment, was treated to chocolate. . . .

I had been on the ship scarcely an hour when Khitrov with his party of about fifteen men also returned in the great boat and made the following report. He had discovered among the islands lying close to the mainland a harbour where one could anchor without any danger. Although he had seen no human beings on land, he had nevertheless come across a small dwelling built of wood, the walls of which were so smooth that it seemed as if they had been planed and in fact as if it had been done with cutting tools. Out of this building he brought with him various tangible tokens, for instance, a wooden vessel, such as is made in Russia of linden bark and used as a box; a stone which perhaps, for lack of something better, served as a whet-stone, on which were seen streaks of copper, as if the savages, like the ancient Siberian tribes, possessed cutting tools of copper; further, a hollow ball of hard-burned clay, about two inches in diameter, containing a pebble, which I regarded as a toy for small children; and finally a paddle and the tail of a blackish grey fox.

These, then, are all our achievements and observations, and these not even from the mainland, on which none of us set foot, but only from an island which seemed to be three miles long and a half-mile wide and the nearest to the mainland (which here forms a large bay studded with many islands) and separated from it by a channel less than half a mile wide. The only reason why we did not attempt to land on the mainland is a sluggish obstinacy and a dull fear of being attacked by a handful of unarmed and still more timid savages, from whom there was no reason to expect either friendship or hostility, and a cowardly homesickness which they probably thought might be excused, especially if those high in authority would pay no more attention to the testimony of the malcontents than did the commanding officers themselves. The time here spent in investigation bears an arithmetical ratio to the time used in fitting out: ten years the preparations for this great undertaking lasted, and ten hours were devoted to the work itself. Of the mainland we have a sketch on paper; of the country itself an imperfect idea, based upon what could be discovered on the island and upon conjectures.

What can be said from comparison and observations at a distance may be summed up about as follows. The American continent (on this side), as far as the climate is concerned, is notably better than that of the extreme north-eastern part of Asia. For, although the land, wherever it faces the sea, whether we looked at it from near or far, consists of amazingly high mountains, most of which had the peaks covered with perpetual snow, yet these mountains, in comparison with those of Asia, are of a much better nature and character.

2. BLUE FOXES

Of four-footed land animals there occur on Bering Island only the stone or Arctic foxes (*Lagopus*), which doubtless have been brought there on drift ice and which, fed on what was cast up by the sea, have increased indescribably. I had opportunity during our unfortunate sojourn on this island to become acquainted only too closely with the nature of this animal, which far surpasses the common fox in impudence, cunning, and roguishness. . . . They crowded into our dwellings by day and by night and stole everything that they could carry away, including articles that were of no use to them, like knives, sticks, bags, shoes, socks, caps, and so forth. They knew in such an unbelievably cunning way how to roll off a weight of several poods from our provision casks and to steal the meat from thence that at first we could hardly ascribe it to them. While skinning sea animals it often happened that we stabbed two or three foxes with our knives, because they wanted to tear the meat from our hands. However well we might bury something and weight it down with stones, they not only found it but, like human beings, pushed the stones away with their shoulders and, lying under them, helped each other do this with all their might. If we cached something up in the air on a post, they undermined the post so that it had to fall down, or one of them climbed up it like a monkey or a cat and threw down the object with incredible skill and cunning. They observed all that we did and accompanied us on whatever project we undertook. . . .

Where we sat down by the wayside they waited for us and played innumerable tricks in our sight, became constantly more impudent, and when we sat still came so near that they began to gnaw the straps on our new-fashioned, self-made shoes, and even the shoes themselves. If we lay down as if sleeping they sniffed at our nostrils to see whether we were dead or alive; if one held one's breath they even nipped our noses and were about to bite. When we first arrived they bit off the noses, fingers, and toes of our dead while their graves were being dug; they also attacked the weak

37

and ill to such extent that one could hardly hold them off. One night when a sailor on his knees wanted to urinate out of the door of the hut, a fox snapped at the exposed part and, in spite of his cries, did not soon want to let go.

❋

THOMAS MANNING

(1772–1840)

English scholar and eccentric. Having learned Chinese, he attempted to reach China overland from India, but got no further than Lhasa, which he was the first Englishman to enter.

Narrative of the Journey of Thomas Manning to Lhasa, ed. C. R. Markham (London, 1878).

1. ARRIVAL AT LHASA (1811)

We had not gone many miles before we were met by a respectable person on horseback, who dismounted and saluted me; then, mounting again, rode on with our guide. Upon inquiry, I found this was a person sent out by the Grand Lama or his people, or by the Tibet magistrate of Lhasa, to welcome and honour me, and conduct me to the metropolis. We hurried into the town where we were to change horses, but our haste was fruitless. There we were obliged to wait until our baggage came up long, long after us, and until it was adjusted upon fresh cattle. If we now had galloped all the way to Lhasa the sun would have been in the south before we could have been in the august presence of the Tagin. This was exceeding discomfort to my Munshi, but great comfort to me. I much disliked the idea of hurrying to Lhasa, and without any kind of refreshment going before the mandarins, sweltering and heated, my boots hurting me every step I set; and I could not comprehend what crime it was for travellers like us, who could not command prompt attendance, arriving an hour sooner or an hour later.

As there was no use in hurrying now, we proceeded calmly on. As soon as we were clear of the town, the palace of the Grand Lama presented itself to our view. It seemed close at hand, but taking an eye observation upon the change of certain angles as I advanced 80 or 100 paces, I sagaciously informed my Munshi that it was still four of five miles off. As we approached, I perceived that under the palace on one side lay a considerable extent of marshy land. This brought to my mind the Pope, Rome, and what I had read of the Pontine Marshes. We passed under a large gateway whose gilded ornaments at top were so ill-fixed that some leaned one way and some another, and reduced the whole to the rock appearance of castles and turrets in pastry-work. The road here, as it winds past the palace, is royally broad; it is level and free from stones, and combined with the view of the lofty towering palace, which forms a majestic mountain of building, has a magnificent effect. The road about the palace swarmed with monks; its nooks and angles with beggars lounging and basking in the sun. This again reminded me of what I have heard of Rome. My eye was almost perpetually fixed on the palace, and roving over its parts, the disposition of which being irregular, eluded my attempts at analysis. As a whole, it seemed perfect enough; but I could not comprehend its plan in detail. Fifteen or twenty minutes now brought us to the entrance of the town of Lhasa.

If the palace had exceeded my expectations, the town as far fell short of them. There is nothing striking, nothing pleasing in its appearance. The habitations are begrimed with smut and dirt. The avenues are full of dogs, some growling and gnawing bits of hide which lie about in profusion, and emit a charnel-house smell; others limping and looking livid; others ulcerated; others starved and dying, and pecked at by the ravens; some dead and preyed upon. In short, everything seems mean and gloomy, and excites the idea of something unreal. Even the mirth and laughter of the inhabitants I thought dreamy and ghostly. The dreaminess no doubt was in my mind, but I never could get rid of the idea; it strengthened upon me afterwards. A few turns through the town brought us into a narrow bylane, and to the gate of a courtyard, where we dismounted, and, passing through that yard, entered another smaller one surrounded by apartments. We mounted a ladder, and were shown into the room provided for us.

2. AUDIENCE WITH THE DALAI LAMA

At length we arrived at the large platform roof, off which is built the house, or hall of reception. There we rested awhile, arranged the presents, and conferred with the Lama's Chinese interpreter. This interpreter was not an absolute stranger to us; he had been to visit us at our lodging. He was a Chinaman by the father's side and a Tibetan by the mother's. He had resided many years at Peking and in Chinese Tatary. He spoke many languages, but having never learned to read or write in any one, was utterly unlearned. He was a strange, melancholy man, severe in his manner, and extraordinarily sparing in his words, except when he made a narration or continued speech, and then he was equally profuse. Whether it was avarice or poverty I do not know, but notwithstanding he had a good place, he seemed straitened in his circumstances. They say he lavished his money on women; for though he had the title of Lama and wore the lama dress, he was not bound to celibacy. He had a wife and son.

The Ti-mu-fu [head magistrate] was in the hall with the Grand Lama. I was not informed of this until I entered, which occasioned me some confusion. I did not know how much ceremony to go through with one before I began with the other. I made the due obeisance, touching the ground three times with my head to the Grand Lama, and once to the Ti-mu-fu. I presented my gifts, delivering the coin with a handsome silk scarf with my own hands into the hands of the Grand Lama and the Ti-mu-fu. While I was ketesing, the awkward servants contrived to let fall and break the bottle of lavender water intended for the Ti-mu-fu. Of course, I seemed not to observe it, though the odoriferous stream flowed close to me, and I could not help seeing it with the corner of my eye as I bowed down my head. Having delivered the scarf to the Grand Lama, I took off my hat, and humbly gave him my cleanshaved head to lay his hands upon. The ceremony of presentation being over, Munshi and I sat down on two cushions not far from the Lama's throne, and had *suchi* brought us. It was most excellent, and I meant to have mended my draught and emptied the cup, but it was whipped away suddenly, before I was aware of it. The Lama's beautiful and interesting face and manner engrossed almost all my attention. He was at that time about seven years old: had the simple and unaffected manners of a well-educated princely child. His face was, I thought, poetically and affectingly beautiful. He was of a gay and cheerful disposition; his beautiful mouth perpetually unbending into a graceful smile, which illuminated his whole countenance. Sometimes, particularly when he had looked at me, his smile almost approached to a gentle laugh. No doubt my grim beard and spectacles somewhat excited his risibility, though I have afterwards, at the New Year's festival, seen him smile and unbend freely, while sitting myself unobserved in a corner, and watching his reception of various persons, and the notice he took of the strange variety of surrounding objects.

WILLIAM MOORCROFT

(1765–1825)

British vet with the East India Company. A compulsive Himalayan explorer, he pioneered much unknown country. His last and longest journey ended in Bukhara, where he probably died. He was the first European to arrive from India and only the second Englishman since Anthony Jenkinson 250 years before. Some of his diaries were found many years later.

Travels in the Himalayan Provinces of Hindustan and the Punjab . . . , prepared by H. H. Wilson (London, 1841).

1. CROSSING THE OXUS (1825)

The Oxus, at the ferry of Khwaja Salah, appeared to be about as broad as the Thames opposite the Temple gardens . . . This river begins to rise in April, and remains full till July, when it again falls. When at its height it inundates the plain on either side, but especially on the right bank. The extent of its inundation is marked by a belt of sedge and weeds, and then by a thick jungle of dwarf trees and brushwood. Of the former the principal is called Patta, and is of great service to the people, as the boats are constructed of its timber. The Oxus is said to be navigable from Syah to Urganj . . . No use of it, however, is made for commerce, and the only boats upon it are ferryboats. These are made of the entire trunks of the Patta tree, used as planks simply squared and fastened together by clamps of iron. The oars are two crooked pieces of timber, not in the least trimmed, whilst a third serves the purpose of a rudder: these are sufficient in calm weather, and when the current is moderate. At other periods a different mode of crossing is had recourse to.

We arrived at the river on the morning of the 11th, but the wind was too violent to permit our making the passage. After several boats had crossed the wind increased, on which the boatmen adopted the novel plan of employing horses to tow the boats over the river. Two horses were fastened, one behind the other, to each boat, on the side next the current; two locks of the mane were tied together to form a noose, through which a halter was passed and fastened to a stout bight in the bow; a bridle was put into the horse's mouth, and that of the leader was secured to a stout staff held by a man opposite his head: the bridle of the rear horse was held by a man in the boat, the object being not only to guide the horses, but to keep their heads above water. A second man, attached to each horse,

41

prevented him from being carried under the boat, either with his leg over the side or with a pole. The horses were taken indiscriminately from our train, and although at first somewhat frightened, yet soon overcame their fear, and worked with good will, carrying the boats across in about ten or fifteen minutes. We encamped on the right bank close to the water.

On the following day we passed through an owal, or station of Khirgahs and Kappahs, or circular huts of mats and reeds, with a conical top. Horses stood saddled at the doors of the tents, and mares and foals, and many camels, were grazing in the adjoining jungle. The cows were stabled in holes made in the ground, roofed with branches of trees and grass, and covered with sand and bushes. The dogs were of middle size, of a foxy colour, but strong and courageous. There were also many good-looking greyhounds. The people were Kazaks. We met here some Turkman women, some riding on camels, some on horseback behind men; they had turbans on their heads, with a yellow silk veil, which some of them dropped over their faces, whilst others indulged their curiosity freely. The faces we saw were broad and plump, of the true Uzbek character.

2. Audience with an Uzbek Prince and Arrival in Bukhara

It had been intimated to us that on the third day after our arrival we were expected to wait upon the Prince, Tora Bahadar, who was the governor of Karshi, a lad of about sixteen, the son of the king by a bondmaid, and, accordingly, on the 19th, at an early hour, we were summoned to an audience, and desired to bring our soldiers with their arms. As we passed along the streets we found them knee-deep in mud, under which the surface, which it concealed, was broken into ruts and holes which rendered it dangerous to proceed. I had seen bad roads in other countries, and particularly the cross roads of some parts of Normandy in a wet winter, but they were absolutely good in comparison with the streets of the second city of the kingdom of Bokhara. We managed, however, to make way without any serious mishap, until we were desired to stop in an open area, fronted by three large brick and mortar colleges of two storeys, of which the iron latticed windows gave them the aspect of prisons rather than of seminaries of learning. We halted here for about a quarter of an hour, during which several Uzbeks, whose clothing bespoke them of a respectable class of the community, passed us, as if on their way to the court. From hence we proceeded to a gate-house, where we were desired to dismount. Within the gateway was a raised apartment on either hand, open to the front, in which a number of persons were seated. On entering an interior road, walled on each side, with a seat of earth the whole length, we saw other persons, of whom the principal was a fair, stout, short, good-humoured looking personage, in a dress of China gold-flowered brocade; this was the master of the ceremonies. He was attended by his deputy, who was dressed in a coat of purple broadcloth, and held a painted and gilded stick. After instructing us in the manner of paying our respects, which consists in crossing the arms upon the breast, and bowing the head, these officers conducted us to a large court, opposite to the gateway of which was a line of men with white wands. When arrived at the middle of the area, the sides of which were lined by well-dressed persons, we saw the Prince sitting on the floor, in the opening of a small door opposite. After making our obeisance, we were desired to sit, or rather kneel, and then, in imitation of the master of the ceremonies, raised our hands, open, with the palms inwards, to a level with our faces, whilst our prompter recited the usual prayer. At the conclusion we stroked our beards, rose, sat down again, repeated our salutation, and once more stood up, when we were told we might depart.

The Prince was a ruddy, well-looking youth, whose face was in a con-stant smile whilst we were in his presence, which scarcely exceeded three minutes. The master of the ceremonies attended us to the court-door, when his deputy conducted us to seats in the passage, and we stopped about ten minutes longer, during which many of those who had had an audience came forth. It was then signified that the ceremonial was over, and that we might depart on the morrow. The manner in which we had been received was, according to Uzbek etiquette, highly respectful, and augured well for our reception at Bukhara. The conduct of the people was also very civil, and although their curiosity was somewhat troublesome, it was never rude. They pressed upon us in great numbers both in the streets and at our tents, but when they crowded too much about us the Yasawal rushed amongst them, and with a long and thick stick distributed blows at random, which speedily cleared the ground. The more respectable who were allowed to approach repeatedly said that we were objects of great interest to them, as they had never seen any of our countrymen. The questions they asked us were very much alike, and were not very sapient. It was a remark which frequently occurred to us, on our journey in Turkistan, that a singularly uniform mediocrity of intellect prevailed amongst even the best informed of the Uzbek population. It was rare indeed to find an individual shrewd or sagacious beyond his fellows.

We left Karshi on 21 February, and resumed our journey to Bukhara. The country we traversed resembled that we had passed between Karshi and the Oxus: after quitting the confines of the strip of cultivated ground

43

on which that city stands, we again came to a sandy and sterile tract, less undulating than the nearer the river, but equally unproductive. It was with no slender satisfaction that on the morning of 25 February 1825, we found ourselves at the end of our protracted pilgrimage, at the gates of that city which had for five years been the object of our wanderings, privations, and perils.

✧

SIR JOSEPH DALTON HOOKER

(1817–1911)

English botanist to whom Darwin first confided his theory of natural selection. He explored the northern frontiers of India between 1847 and 1851 while searching for new species.

Himalayan Journals (London, 1905).

1. BOTANIZING IN WILD COUNTRY (1848)

The path lay north-west up the valley, which became thickly wooded with silver fir and juniper; we gradually ascended, crossing many streams from lateral gulleys, and huge masses of boulders. Evergreen rhododendrons soon replaced the firs, growing in inconceivable profusion, especially on the slopes facing the south-east, and with no other shrubs or tree vegetation, but scattered bushes of rose, *Spiraea*, dwarf juniper, stunted birch, willow, honeysuckle, berberry, and a mountain ash (*Pyrus*). What surprised me more than the prevalence of rhododendron bushes was the number of species of this genus, easily recognized by the shape of their capsules, the form and woolly covering of the leaves; none were in flower, but I reaped a rich harvest of seed. At 12,000 feet the valley was wild, open, and broad, with sloping mountains clothed for 1,000 feet with dark-green rhododendron bushes; the river ran rapidly, and was broken into falls here and there. Huge angular and detached masses of rock were scattered about, and to the right and left snowy peaks towered over the surrounding mountains, while amongst the latter narrow gulleys led up to blue patches of glacial ice, with trickling streams and shoots of stones. Dwarf rhododendrons with strongly scented leaves (*R. anthopogon* and

44

setosum), and abundance of a little *Andromeda*, exactly like ling, with woody stems and tufted branches, gave a heathery appearance to the hillsides. The prevalence of lichens, common to this country and to Scotland (especially *L. geographicus*), which coloured the rocks, added an additional feature to the resemblance to Scotch Highland scenery. Along the narrow path I found the two commonest of all British weeds, a grass (*Poa annua*), and the shepherd's purse! They had evidently been imported by man and yaks, and as they do not occur in India, I could not but regard these little wanderers from the north with the deepest interest.

Such incidents as these give rise to trains of reflection in the mind of the naturalist traveller; and the farther he may be from home and friends, the more wild and desolate the country he is exploring, the greater the difficulties and dangers under which he encounters these subjects of his earliest studies in science; so much keener is the delight with which he recognizes them, and the more lasting is the impression which they leave. At this moment these common weeds more vividly recall to me that wild scene than does all my journal, and remind me how I went on my way, taxing my memory for all it ever knew of the geographical distribution of the shepherd's purse, and musing on the probability of the plant having found its way thither over all Central Asia, and the ages that may have been occupied in its march.

2. Riding on an Elephant (1849)

A good many plants grow along the streams, the sandy beds of which are everywhere covered with the marks of tigers' feet. The only safe way of botanizing is by pushing through the jungle on elephants; an uncomfortable method, from the quantity of ants and insects which drop from the foliage above, and from the risk of disturbing pendulous bees' and ants' nests. . . .

The latter part of the journey I performed on elephants during the heat of the day, and a more uncomfortable mode of conveyance surely never was adopted; the camel's pace is more fatiguing, but that of the elephant is extremely trying after a few miles, and is so injurious to the human frame that the Mahouts (drivers) never reach an advanced age, and often succumb young to spine diseases, brought on by the incessant motion of the vertebral column. The broiling heat of the elephant's black back, and the odour of its oily driver, are disagreeable accompaniments, as are its habits of snorting water from its trunk over its parched skin, and the consequences of the great bulk of green food which it consumes.

3. ILLEGAL ENTRY INTO TIBET

On the 16th [October] we were up early. I felt very anxious about the prospect of our getting round by Donkia pass and Cholamoo, which would enable me to complete the few remaining miles of my long survey of the Teesta river, and which promised immense results in the views I should obtain of the country, and of the geology and botany of these lofty snowless regions. Campbell, though extremely solicitous to obtain permission from the Tibetan guard (who were waiting for us on the frontier), was nevertheless bound by his own official position to yield at once to their wishes, should they refuse us a passage.

The sun rose on our camp at 7.30 a.m., when the north wind fell; and within an hour afterwards the temperature had risen to 45°. Having had our sticks[1] warmed and handed to us, we started on ponies, accompanied by the Lama only, to hold a parley with the Tibetans; ordering the rest of the party to follow at their leisure. We had not proceeded far when we were joined by two Tibetan sepoys, who, on our reaching the pass, bellowed lustily for their companions; when Campbell and the Lama drew up at the chait of Kongra Lama, and announced his wish to confer with their commandant.

My anxiety was now wound up to a pitch; I saw men with matchlocks emerging from amongst the rocks under Chomiomo, and despairing of permission being obtained, I goaded my pony with heels and stick, and dashed on up the Lachen valley, resolved to make the best of a splendid day, and not turn back till I had followed the river to the Cholamoo lakes. The sepoys followed me a few paces, but running being difficult at 16,000 feet, they soon gave up the chase. . . .

A few miles further, on rounding a spur of Kanchenjunga, I arrived in sight of Cholamoo lakes, with the Donkia mountain rearing its stupendous precipices of rock and ice on the east. My pony was knocked up, and I felt very giddy from the exertion and elevation; I had broken his bridle, and so led him on by my plaid for the last few miles to the banks of the lake; and there, with the pleasant sound of the waters rippling at my feet, I yielded for a few moments to those emotions of gratified ambition which, being unalloyed by selfish considerations for the future, become springs of happiness during the remainder of one's life.

The landscape about Cholamoo lake was simple in its elements, stern

---

[1] It was an invariable custom of our Lepcha and Tibetan attendants to warm the handles of our sticks in cold weather, before starting on our daily marches. This is one of many little instances I could adduce of their thoughtfulness and attention to the smallest comforts of the stranger and wanderer in their lands.

and solemn; and though my solitary situation rendered it doubly impressive to me, I doubt whether the world contains any scene with more sublime associations than this calm sheet of water, 17,000 feet above the sea, with the shadows of mountains 22,000 to 24,000 feet high, sleeping on its bosom.

There was much short grass about the lake, on which large antelopes, 'Chiru' (*Antilope Hodgsoni*), and deer, 'Goa' (*Procapra picticaudata*), were feeding. There were also many slate-coloured hares with white rumps (*Lepus oiostolus*), with marmots and tailless rats. The abundance of animal life was wonderful, compared with the want of it on the south side of the Donkia pass, not five miles distant in a straight line! It is partly due to the profusion of carbonate of soda, of which all ruminants are fond, and partly to the dryness of the climate, which is favourable to all burrowing quadrupeds. A flock of common English teal were swimming in the lake, the temperature of which was 55°.

I had come about fifteen miles from the pass, and arrived at 1 p.m., remaining half an hour. I could not form an idea as to whether Campbell had followed or not, and began to speculate on the probability of passing the night in the open air, by the warm side of my steed. Though the sun shone brightly, the wind was bitterly cold, and I arrived at the stone dykes of Yeumtso at 3 p.m., quite exhausted with fatigue and headache. I there found, to my great relief, the Tchebu Lama and Lachen Phipun: they were in some alarm at my absence, for they thought I was not aware of the extreme severity of the temperature on the north side of the snows, or of the risk of losing my way; they told me that after a long discourse with the Dingpun (or commander) of the Tibetan sepoys, the latter had allowed all the party to pass; that the sepoys had brought on the coolies, who were close behind, but that they themselves had seen nothing of Campbell; of whom the Lama then went in search.

The sun set behind Chomiomo at 5 p.m., and the wind at once dropped; so local are these violent atmospheric currents, which are caused by the heating of the upper extremities of these lofty valleys, and consequent rarefaction of the air. Intense terrestrial radiation immediately follows the withdrawal of the sun's rays, and the temperature sinks rapidly.

Soon after sunset the Lama returned, bringing Campbell, who, having mistaken some glacier-fed lakes at the back of Kanchenjunga for those of Cholamoo, was looking for me. He too had speculated on having to pass the night under a rock, with one plaid for himself and servant; in which case I am sure they would both have been frozen to death, having no pony to lie down beside. He told me that, after I had quitted Kongra Lama, leaving him with the Tchebu Lama and Phipun, the Dingpun and twenty men came up, and very civilly but formally forbade their crossing the frontier; but that, upon explaining his motives, and representing that it would save him ten days' journey, the Dingpun had relented, and promised to conduct the whole party to the Donkia pass.

We pitched our little tent in the corner of the cattle-pen, and our coolies soon afterwards came up; mine were in capital health, though suffering from headaches, but Campbell's were in a distressing state of illness and fatigue, with swollen faces and rapid pulses, and some were insensible from symptoms like pressure on the brain; these were chiefly Ghurkas (Nepalese). The Tibetan Dingpun and his guard arrived last of all: he was a droll little object, short, fat, deeply marked with smallpox, swarthy, and greasy; he was robed in a green woollen mantle, and was perched on the back of a yak, which also carried his bedding, and cooking utensils, the latter rattling about its flanks, horns, neck, and every point of support: two other yaks bore the tents of the party. His followers were tall, savage-looking fellows, with broad swarthy faces, and their hair in short pigtails. They wore the long-sleeved cloak, short trousers, and boots, all of thick woollen, and felt caps on their heads. Each was armed with a long matchlock slung over his back, with a moveable rest having two prongs like a fork, and a hinge, so as to fold up along the barrel, when the prongs project behind the shoulders like antelope horns, giving the uncouth warrior a droll appearance. A dozen cartridges, each in an iron case, were slung round the waist, and they also wore the long knife, flint, steel, and iron tobacco-pipe, pouch, and purse, suspended to a leathern girdle.

The night was fine, but intensely cold, and the vault of heaven was very dark, and blazing with stars; the air was electrical, and flash lightning illumined the sky . . .

This being the migrating season, swallows flitted through the air; finches, larches, and sparrows were hopping over the sterile soil, seeking food, though it was difficult to say what. The geese, which had roosted by the river, cackled; the wild ducks quacked and plumed themselves; ouzels and waders screamed or chirped: and all rejoiced as they prepared themselves for the last flight of the year, to the valleys of the southern Himalaya, to the Teesta, and other rivers of the Terai and plains of India.

4. Seizure and Torture of Dr Campbell

We went into the hut, and were resting ourselves on a log at one end of it, when, the evening being very cold, the people crowded in; on which Campbell went out, saying that we had better leave the hut to them, and that he would see the tents pitched. He had scarcely left, when I heard

48

him calling loudly to me, 'Hooker! Hooker! the savages are murdering me!'
I rushed to the door, and caught sight of him striking out with his fists, and
struggling violently; being tall and powerful, he had already prostrated a
few, but a host of men bore him down, and appeared to be trampling on
him; at the same moment I was myself seized by eight men, who forced
me back into the hut, and down on the log, where they held me in a sitting
posture, pressing me against the wall; here I spent a few moments of
agony, as I heard my friend's stifled cries grow fainter and fainter. I struggled but little, and that only at first, for at least five-and-twenty men crowded
round and laid their hands upon me, rendering any effort to move useless;
they were, however, neither angry nor violent, and signed to me to keep
quiet. I retained my presence of mind, and felt comfort in remembering
that I saw no knives used by the party who fell on Campbell, and that if
their intentions had been murderous, an arrow would have been the more
sure and less troublesome weapon. It was evident that the whole animus
was directed against Campbell, and that though at first alarmed on my own
account, all the inferences which, with the rapidity of lightning my mind
involuntarily drew, were favourable.

After a few minutes, three persons came into the hut, and seated themselves opposite to me. I only recognized two of them; namely, the Singtam
Soubah, pale, trembling like a leaf, and with great drops of sweat trickling
from his greasy brow; and the Tchebu Lama, stolid, but evidently under
restraint, and frightened. The former ordered the men to leave hold of me,
and to stand guard on either side, and, in a violently agitated manner, he
endeavoured to explain that Campbell was a prisoner by the orders of the
Rajah, who was dissatisfied with his conduct as a government officer during the past twelve years; and that he was to be taken to the Durbar and
confined till the supreme government at Calcutta should confirm such
articles as he should be compelled to subscribe to; he also wanted to know
from me how Campbell would be likely to behave. I refused to answer any
questions till I should be informed why I was myself made prisoner, on
which he went away, leaving me still guarded. My own Sirdar then explained
that Campbell had been knocked down, tied hand and foot, and taken
to his tent, and that all his coolies were also bound, our captors claiming
them as Sikkimites, and subjects of the Rajah.

Shortly afterwards the three returned, the Soubah looking more spectral
than ever, and still more violently agitated, and I thought I perceived that
whatever were his plans he had failed in them. He asked me what view
the Governor-General would take of this proceeding, and receiving no
answer, he went off with the Tchebu Lama, and left me with the third
individual. The latter looked steadily at me for some time, and then asked

if I did not know him. I said I did not, when he gave his name as Dingpun Tinli, and I recognized in him one of the men whom the Dewan had sent to conduct us to the top of Mainom the previous year. This opened my eyes a good deal, for he was known to be a right-hand man of the Dewan's, and had within a few months been convicted of kidnapping two Brahmin girls from Nepal, and had vowed vengeance against Campbell for the duty he performed in bringing him to punishment.

I was soon asked to go to my tent, which I found pitched close by; they refused me permission to see my fellow-prisoner, or to be near him, but allowed me to hang up my instruments, and arrange my collections. My guards were frequently changed during the night, Lepchas often taking a turn; they repeatedly assured me that there was no complaint or ill-feeling against me, that the better classes in Sikkim would be greatly ashamed of the whole affair, that Tchebu Lama was equally a prisoner, and that the grievances against Campbell were of a political nature, but what they were they did not know.

The night was very cold, and two inches of snow fell. I took as many of my party as I could into my tent, they having no shelter fit for such an elevation at this season. Through the connivance of some of the people, I managed to correspond with Campbell, who afterwards gave me the following account of the treatment he had received. He stated that on leaving the hut he had been met by Meepo, who told him the Soubah had ordered his being turned out. A crowd of sepoys then fell on him and brought him to the ground, knocked him on the head, trampled on him, and pressed his neck down to his chest as he lay, as if endeavouring to break it. His feet were tied, and his arms pinioned behind, the wrist of the right hand being bound to the left arm above the elbow; the cords were then doubled, and he was violently shaken. The Singtam Soubah directed all this, which was performed chiefly by the Dingpun Tinli and Jongpun Sangabadoo. After this the Soubah came to me, as I have related; and returning, had Campbell brought bound before him, and asked him, through Tchebu Lama, if he would write from dictation. The Soubah was violent, excited, and nervous; Tchebu Lama scared. Campbell answered, that if they continued torturing him (which was done by twisting the cords round his wrist with a bamboo-wrench), he might say or do anything, but that his government would not confirm any acts thus extorted. The Soubah became still more violent, shook his bow in Campbell's face, and drawing his hand significantly across his throat, repeated his questions, adding others . . .

Early next morning . . . I was obliged to call upon the Soubah and Dingpun to explain their conduct of the previous day, which they declared arose from no ill-feeling, but simply from their fear of my interfering in

Campbell's behalf; they could not see what reason I had to complain, so long as I was neither hurt nor bound. I tried in vain to explain to them that they could not so play fast and loose with a British subject, and insisted that, if they really considered me free, they should place me with Campbell, under whose protection I considered myself, he being still the Governor-General's agent.

Much discussion followed this ... My course was, however clear as to the propriety of keeping as close to Campbell as I was allowed, so they reluctantly agreed to take me with him to the Durbar. . . .

We were summoned by the Dingpun to march at 10 a.m.: I demanded an interview with Campbell first, which was refused; but I felt myself pretty safe, and insisting upon it, he was brought to me. He was sadly bruised about the head, arms, and wrists, walked very lame, and had a black eye to boot, but he was looking stout and confident. . . .

During the march down to Laghep, Campbell was treated by the Dingpun's men with great rudeness. I kept as near as I was allowed, quietly gathering rhododendron seeds by the way. At the camping-ground we were again separated, at which I remonstrated with the Dingpun, also complaining of his people's insolent behaviour towards their prisoner, which he promised should be discontinued.

The next day we reached Rungpo, where we halted for further instructions: our tents were placed apart, but we managed to correspond by stealth. On the 10th of November we were conducted to Tumloong. A pony was brought for me, but I refused it, on seeing that Campbell was treated with great indignity, and obliged to follow at the tail of the mule ridden by the Dingpun, who thus marched him in triumph up to the village.

I was taken to a house at Phadong, and my fellow traveller was confined in another at some distance to the eastward, a stone's throw below the Rajah's; and thrust into a little cage-like room. . . .

The hut being small, and intolerably dirty, I pitched my tent close by, and lived in it for seven days: I was not guarded, but so closely watched, that I could not go out for the most trifling purpose, except under surveillance. They were evidently afraid of my escaping; I was however treated with civility, but forbidden to communicate either with Campbell or with Darjeeling. . . . [*Hooker was subsequently permitted to join Campbell, and eventually they were both released.*]

I found my friend in good health and spirits, strictly guarded in a small thatched hut, of bamboo wattle and clay: the situation was pretty, and commanded a view of the Ryott valley and the snowy mountains; there were some picturesque chaits hard by, and a blacksmith's forge. Our walks were confined to a few steps in front of the hut, and included a puddle and a spring of water. We had one black room with a small window, and a fire in the middle on a stone; we slept in the narrow apartment behind it, which was the cage in which Campbell had been at first confined, and which exactly admitted us both, lying on the floor. Two or three sepoys' occupied an adjoining room, and had a peep-hole through the partition-wall.

✻

SIR SPENCER ST JOHN

(1825–1910)

British civil servant. He spent thirteen years in Borneo and was trusted by all. He spent as much time as possible travelling in the interior.

Life in the Forests of the Far East (London, 1862).

ASCENT OF MT. KINABALU (1858)

To ascend Kina Balu had been an ambition of mine, even before I ever saw Borneo. To have been the first to do it would have increased the excitement and the pleasure. However, this satisfaction was not for me. Mr Low, colonial treasurer of Labuan, had long meditated the same scheme, and in 1851 made the attempt. It was thought at the time but little likely to succeed, as the people and the country were entirely unknown; but by determined perseverance Mr Low reached what may fairly be entitled the summit, though he did not attempt to climb any of the rugged peaks, rising a few hundred feet higher than the spot where he left a bottle with an inscription in it. . . .

In 1858, Mr Low and I determined to make another attempt; and early in April I went over from Brunei to Labuan to join him. We waited till the 15th for a vessel, which we expected would bring us a supply of shoes, but as it did not arrive we started. This was the cause of most of our mishaps, as a traveller can make no greater mistake than being careless of his feet, particularly in Borneo, where all long journeys must be performed on foot. . . .

Our path lay along the side of the hill in which the village stands, we followed it about four miles in an easterly direction, and then descended to a torrent, one of the feeders of the Tampasuk, where we determined to spend the night, as Mr Low's feet were becoming very swollen and painful, and it was as well to collect the party. We had passed through considerable fields of sweet potatoes, kiladi, and tobacco, where the path was crossed occasionally by cool rills from the mountains. We enjoyed the cold water very much, and had a delightful bath. The torrent comes tumbling down, and forms many fine cascades. Mr Low botanized a little, notwithstanding his feet were suppurating. The hut in which we spent the night was very pretty-looking, flat-roofed, built entirely of bamboos. . . .

Next morning, Mr Low found it impossible to walk, and I was therefore obliged to start without him. We showed our perfect confidence in the villagers of Kiau by dividing our party, leaving only four men with Mr Low to take care of the arms; we carried with us up the mountain nothing but our swords and one revolver. They must have thought us a most extraordinary people; but we knew that their demonstrations of hostility were really harmless, and more aimed against each other than against us. Probably, had we appeared afraid, it might have been a different matter. . . .

I observed a fine yellow, sweet-scented rhododendron on a decayed tree, and requested my men on their return to take it to Mr Low; continuing the ascent, after an hour's tough walking, reached the top of the ridge. There it was better for a short time; but the forest, heavily hung with moss, is exposed to the full force of the south-west monsoon, and the trees are bent across the path, leaving occasionally only sufficient space to crawl through. We soon came upon the magnificent pitcher-plant, the *Nepenthes Lowii*, that Mr Low was anxious to get. We could find no young plants, but took cuttings, which the natives said would grow.

We stopped to breakfast at a little swampy spot, where the trees are becoming very stunted, though in positions protected from the winds they grow to a great height. Continuing our course, we came upon a jungle that appeared to be composed almost entirely of rhododendrons, some with beautiful pink, crimson, and yellow flowers. I sat near one for about half an hour apparently in intense admiration but, in fact, very tired and breathless, and anxious about my followers, only one of whom had kept up with me.

Finding it useless to wait longer, as the mist was beginning to roll down from the summit, and the white plain of clouds below appeared rising, I pushed on to the cave, which we intended to occupy. It was a huge granite boulder, resting on the hill side, that sheltered us but imperfectly from the cold wind. . . .

During the night, the thermometer at the entrance of the cave fell to 36°5′; and on my going out to have a look at the night-scene, all the bushes and trees appeared fringed with hoar frost.

After breakfasting at the cave, we started for the summit. Our course lay at first through a thick, low jungle, full of rhododendrons; it then changed into a stunted brushwood, that almost hid the rarely used path; gradually the shrubs gave way to rocks, and then we commenced our ascent over the naked granite. . . . The rocks were often at an angle of nearly forty degrees, so that I was forced to ascend them, at first, with woollen socks, and when they were worn through, with bare feet. It was a sad alternative, as the rough stone wore away the skin and left a bleeding and tender surface. After hard work, we reached the spot where Mr Low had left a bottle, and found it intact—the writing in it was not read, as I returned it unopened to its resting-place. Low's Gully is one of the most singular spots in the summit. We ascend an abrupt ravine, with towering perpendicular rocks on either side, till a rough natural wall bars the way. Climbing on this, you look over a deep chasm, surrounded on three sides by precipices, so deep that the eye could not reach the bottom; but the twitter of innumerable swallows could be distinctly heard, as they flew in flocks below. . . .

I was now anxious to reach one of those peaks which are visible from the sea; so we descended Low's Gully, through a thicket of rhododendrons bearing a beautiful blood-coloured flower, and made our way to the westward. It was rough walking at first, while we continued to skirt the rocky ridge that rose to our right; but gradually leaving this, we advanced up an incline composed entirely of immense slabs of granite, and reaching the top, found a noble terrace, half a mile in length, whose sides sloped at an angle of thirty degrees on either side. The ends were the southern peak and a huge cyclopean wall.

I followed the guides to the former and, after a slippery ascent, reached the summit. I have mentioned that this peak has a rounded aspect when viewed form the eastward; but from the northward it appears to rise sharply to a point; and when with great circumspection I crawled up, I found myself on a granite point, not three feet in width, with but a water-worn way a few inches broad to rest on, and prevent my slipping over the sloping edges.

During the climbing today, I suffered slightly from shortness of breath, and felt some disinclination to bodily exertion; but as soon as I sat down on this lofty point, it left me, and a feeling came on as if the air rendered me buoyant and made me long to float away.

William Gifford Palgrave

(1826–1888)

British Jesuit explorer. Working as a spy for Napoleon III, he made the first west–east crossing of Arabia in 1862.

A Year's Journey through Central and Eastern Arabia (1862–1863) (London, 1883).

1. Camels and Wells (1862)

I have, while in England, heard and read more than once of the 'docile camel'. If 'docile' means stupid, well and good; in such a case the camel is the very model of docility. But if the epithet is intended to designate an animal that takes an interest in its rider so far as a beast can, that in some way understands his intentions or shares them in a subordinate fashion, that obeys from a sort of submissive or half fellow-feeling with his master, like the horse and elephant, then I say that the camel is by no means docile, very much the contrary; he takes no heed of his rider, pays no attention whether he be on his back or not, walks straight on when once set a-going, merely because he is too stupid to turn aside; and then, should some tempting thorn or green branch allure him out of the path, continues to walk on in this new direction simply because he is too dull to turn back into the right road. His only care is to cross as much pasture as he conveniently can while pacing mechanically onwards; and for effecting this his long, flexible neck sets him at great advantage, and a hard blow or a downright kick alone has any influence on him whether to direct or impel. He will never attempt to throw you off his back, such a trick being far beyond his limited comprehension; but if you fall off, he will never dream of stopping for you, and walks on just the same, grazing while he goes, without knowing or caring an atom what has become of you. If turned loose, it is a thousand to one that he will never find his way back to his accustomed home or pasture, and the first comer who picks him up will have no particular shyness to get over; Jack or Tom are all the same to him, and the loss of his old master and of his own kith and kin gives him no regret and occasions no endeavour to find them again. One only symptom will he give that he is aware of his rider, and that is when the latter is about to mount him, for on such an occasion, instead of addressing him in the style of Balaam's more intelligent beast, 'Am not I thy camel upon which thou hast ridden ever since I was thine, unto this day?', he will bend back his long, snaky neck towards his master, open his enormous jaws to bite if he dared, and roar out a tremendous sort of groan, as if to complain of some entirely new and unparalleled injustice about to be done him. In a word, he is from first to last an undomesticated and savage animal, rendered serviceable by stupidity alone, without much skill on his master's part or any co-operation on his own, save that of an extreme passiveness. Neither attachment nor even habit impress him; never tame, though not wide awake enough to be exactly wild. . . .

The breeze is fresh, and will continue so till noon. Before us are high palm-trees and dark shadows; the ground is velvet green with the autumn crop of maize and vetches, and intersected by a labyrinth of water-courses, some dry, others flowing; for the wells are at work.

These wells are much the same throughout Arabia; their only diversity is in size and depth, but their hydraulic machinery is everywhere alike. Over the well's mouth is fixed a cross-beam, supported high in air on pillars of wood or stone on either side, and in this beam are from three to six small wheels, over which pass the ropes of as many large leathern buckets, each containing nearly twice the ordinary English measure. These are let down into the depth, and then drawn up again by camels or asses, who pace slowly backwards and forwards on an inclined plane leading from the edge of the well itself to a pit prolonged for some distance. When the buckets rise to the verge they tilt over, and pour out their contents by a broad channel into a reservoir hard by, from which part the water-courses that irrigate the garden. The supply thus obtained is necessarily discontinuous, and much inferior to what a little more skill in mechanism affords in Egypt and Syria; while the awkward shaping and, not infrequently, the ragged condition of the buckets themselves causes half the liquid to fall back into the well before it reaches the brim. The creaking, singing noise of the wheels, the rush of water as the buckets attain their turning-point, the unceasing splash of their overflow dripping back into the source, all are a message of life and moisture very welcome in this dry and stilly region, and may be heard far off amid the sand-hills, a first intimation to the sun-scorched traveller of his approach to a cooler resting-place.

2. Dangerous Encounter at the Court of Riyadh

The royal messenger and myself then left the house, and proceeded in silence and darkness through the winding streets to the palace of 'Abd-Allah. Arrived there, a short parley ensued between my conductor and the guards, who then resumed their post, while the former passed on to give the prince notice, leaving me to cool myself for a minute or two in the night air of the courtyard. A negro then came out, and beckoned me to enter.

The room was dark, there was no other light than that afforded by the flickering gleams of the firewood burning on the hearth. At the further end sat 'Abd-Allah, silent and gloomy . . .

When I entered, all remained without movement or return of greeting. I saluted 'Abd-Allah, who replied in an undertone and gave me a signal to sit down at a little distance from him but on the same side of the divan. My readers may suppose that I was not at the moment ambitious of too intimate a vicinity.

After an interval of silence, 'Abd-Allah turned half round towards me, and with his blackest look and a deep voice said, 'I now know perfectly well what you are; you are no doctors, you are Christians, spies, and revolutionists ("mufsideen") come hither to ruin our religion and state in behalf of those who sent you. The penalty for such as you is death, that you know, and I am determined to inflict it without delay.'

'Threatened folks live long,' thought I, and had no difficulty in showing the calm which I really felt. So looking him coolly in the face, I replied, 'Istaghfir Allah', literally, 'Ask pardon of God'. This is the phrase commonly addressed to one who has said something extremely out of place.

The answer was unexpected; he started, and said, 'Why so?'

'Because', I rejoined, 'you have just now uttered a sheer absurdity. "Christians", be it so; but "spies", "revolutionists"—as if we were not known by everybody in your town for quiet doctors, neither more nor less! And then to talk about putting me to death! You cannot, and you dare not.'

'But I can and dare,' answered 'Abd-Allah, 'and who shall prevent me? you shall soon learn that to your cost.'

'Neither can nor dare,' repeated I. 'We are here your father's guests and yours for a month and more, known as such, received as such. What have we done to justify a breach of the laws of hospitality in Nejed? It is impossible for you to do what you say,' continued I, thinking the while that it was a great deal too possible after all; 'the obloquy of the deed would be too much for you.'

He remained a moment thoughtful, then said, 'As if any one need know who did it. I have the means, and can dispose of you without talk or rumour. Those who are at my bidding can take a suitable time and place for that, without my name being ever mentioned in the affair.'

The advantage was now evidently on my side; I followed it up, and said with a quiet laugh, 'Neither is that within your power. Am I not known to your father, to all in his palace? to your own brother Sa'ood among the rest? Is not the fact of this my actual visit to you known without your gates? Or is there no one here', added I, with a glance at Maḥboob, 'who can report elsewhere what you have just now said? Better for you to leave off this nonsense; do you take me for a child of four days old?'

He muttered a repetition of his threat. 'Bear witness, all here present,' said I, raising my voice so as to be heard from one end of the room to the other, 'that if any mishap befalls my companion or myself from Riyadh to the shores of the Persian Gulf, it is all 'Abd-Allah's doing. And the consequences shall be on his head, worse consequences than he expects or dreams.'

The prince made no reply. All were silent; Maḥboob kept his eyes steadily fixed on the fireplace; 'Abd-el-Laṭeef looked much and said nothing.

'Bring coffee,' called out 'Abd-Allah to the servants. Before a minute had elapsed, a black slave approached with one and only one coffee-cup in his hand. At a second sign from his master he came before me and presented it.

Of course the worst might be conjectured of so unusual and solitary a draught. But I thought it highly improbable that matters should have been so accurately prepared; besides, his main cause of anger was precisely the refusal of poisons, a fact which implied that he had none by him ready for use. So I said, 'Bismillah', took the cup, looked very hard at 'Abd-Allah, drank it off, and then said to the slave, 'Pour me out a second.' This he did; I swallowed it, and said, 'Now you may take the cup away.'

The desired effect was fully attained. 'Abd-Allah's face announced defeat, while the rest of the assembly whispered together. . . .

I purposely kept my seat, to show the unconcern of innocence, till Maḥboob made me a sign that I might safely retire. On this I took leave of 'Abd-Allah and quitted the palace unaccompanied. It was now near midnight, not a light to be seen in the houses, not a sound to be heard in the streets; the sky too was dark and overcast . . . for the first time, a feeling of lonely dread came over me, and I confess that more than once I turned my head to look and see if no one was following with 'evil', as Arabs say, in his hand. But there was none, and I reached the quiet alley and low door where a gleam through the chinks announced the anxious watch of my companions, who now opened the entrance, overjoyed at seeing me back sound and safe from so critical a parley.

NAIN SINGH

(*fl.* 1865–1877)

No. 1 Pundit. The Pundits were native surveyors recruited originally by T. G. Montgomerie of the Survey of India. Between 1865 and 1875 they marched thousands of miles through the Himalayas, always in great danger, mapping vast areas forbidden to Europeans. Nain Singh was the first and perhaps the greatest. On his first journey he obtained the first accurate bearings for the location of Lhasa.

Proceedings of the Royal Geographical Society, 1876–1877 (London, 1877).

PRESENTATION OF THE PATRON'S MEDAL OF THE ROYAL GEOGRAPHICAL SOCIETY TO NAIN SINGH IN HIS ABSENCE BY THE PRESIDENT, SIR RUTHERFORD ALCOCK (1877)

Colonel H. Yule, CB, then came forward to receive the Medal on behalf of the Pundit Nain Singh. The President addressed him as follows:

'Colonel Yule—Since Nain Singh's absence from this country precludes my having the pleasure of handing to him in person, this, the Victoria or Patron's Medal, which has been awarded to him for his great journeys and surveys in Tibet and along the Upper Brahmaputra, during which he determined the positions of Lhasa, and added largely to our positive knowledge of the map of Asia, I beg to place it in your charge for transmission to the Pundit.

'I will myself address a letter to the Viceroy in India calling his attention to this award of one of the two medals of the year, the highest honour this Society can confer on any geographer, however distinguished by his services to geographical science or discovery, and with a request that His Excellency will take such steps as he may deem best for its presentation to Nain Singh.

'But, in the mean time, I would beg you, who were the first to propose that this medal should be so conferred, and took such generous and earnest interest in the recognition by the Society of Nain Singh's high claims to that distinction, to convey to him from me, as the President of the Royal Geographical Society, the satisfaction the Council have felt in thus publicly marking their high appreciation of the noble qualities of loyalty, courage, and endurance, by the display of which in no ordinary degree he achieved success, and was enabled to add so largely to our knowledge of that portion

of Asia which no European could explore. I would ask you also to add that
the Council have not failed to see that he has not worked as a mere
topographical automaton; and were perfectly aware that, notwithstanding
he was a native of Asia and familiar with Tibetan dialects, his journeys
were not accomplished without great peril to life. I would finally wish you
to convey to Nain Singh, who in the performance of these distinguished
services has suffered seriously in health by the extreme hardships attending his journeys, that I trust this public recognition of his merits as a
geographer from the Royal Geographical Society, which in its awards knows
no distinction of nationality, race, or creed, will be a source of satisfaction
to him in his retirement, of which nothing can ever deprive him, to the
end of a life he has devoted so faithfully to the public service and the
advancement of geographical knowledge.'

✳

ALFRED RUSSELL WALLACE

(1823–1913)

*English naturalist. After spending five years travelling in Amazonia he
spent a further eight in the Far East, during which time he formulated a
theory of natural selection similar to Darwin's.*

*The Malay Archipeligo: The Land of the Orang-Utan and the Bird of Paradise.
A Narrative of Travel with Studies of Man and Nature* (London, 1872).

1. THE PLEASURE OF COLLECTING (1869)

I have rarely enjoyed myself more than during my residence here. As I sat
taking my coffee at six in the morning, rare birds would often be seen on
some tree close by, when I would hastily sally out in my slippers, and
perhaps secure a prize I had been seeking after for weeks. The great
hornbills of Celebes (*Buceros cassidix*) would often come with loud-
flapping wings, and perch upon a lofty tree just in front of me; and the
black baboon-monkeys, *Cynopithecus nigrescens*, often stared down in
astonishment at such an intrusion into their domains; while at night herds
of wild pigs roamed about the house, devouring refuse, and obliging us to
put away everything eatable or breakable from our little cooking-house. A
few minutes' search on the fallen trees around my house at sunrise and

sunset would often produce me more beetles than I would meet with in a day's collecting, and odd moments could be made valuable which when living in villages or at a distance from the forest are inevitably wasted. Where the sugar-palms were dripping with sap, flies congregated in immense numbers, and it was by spending half an hour at these when I had the time to spare that I obtained the finest and most remarkable collection of this group of insects that I have ever made.

Then what delightful hours I passed wandering up and down the dry river-courses, full of water-holes and rocks and fallen trees, and overshadowed by magnificent vegetation! I soon got to know every hole and rock and stump, and came up to each with cautious step and bated breath to see what treasures it would produce. At one place I would find a little crowd of the rare butterfly *Tachyris zarinda*, which would rise up at my approach, and display their vivid orange and cinnabar-red wings, while among them would flutter a few of the fine blue-banded *Papilios*. Where leafy branches hung over the gully, I might expect to find a grand *Ornithoptera* at rest and an easy prey. At certain rotten trunks I was sure to get the curious little tiger beetle, *Therates flavilabris*. In the denser thickets I would capture the small metallic blue butterflies (*Amblypodia*) sitting on the leaves, as well as some rare and beautiful leaf-beetles of the families *Hispidae* and *Chrysomelidae*.

2. The Failure of Our Civilization

During the last century, and especially in the last thirty years, our intellectual and material advancement has been too quickly achieved for us to reap the full benefit of it. Our mastery over the forces of nature has led to a rapid growth of population, and a vast accumulation of wealth; but these have brought with them such an amount of poverty and crime, and have fostered the growth of so much sordid feeling and so many fierce passions, that it may well be questioned, whether the mental and moral status of our population has not on the average been lowered, and whether the evil has not overbalanced the good. Compared with our wondrous progress in physical science and its practical applications, our system of government, of administering justice, of national education, and our whole social and moral organization, remains in a state of barbarism. And if we continue to devote our chief energies to the utilizing of our knowledge of the laws of nature with the view of still further extending our commerce and our wealth, the evils which necessarily accompany these when too eagerly pursued, may increase to such gigantic dimensions as to be beyond our power to alleviate.

We should now clearly recognize the fact, that the wealth and knowledge and culture of *the few* do not constitute civilization, and do not of themselves advance us towards the 'perfect social state'. Our vast manufacturing system, our gigantic commerce, our crowded towns and cities, support and continually renew a mass of human misery and crime *absolutely* greater than has ever existed before. They create and maintain in lifelong labour an ever-increasing army, whose lot is the more hard to bear by contrast with the pleasures, the comforts, and the luxury which they see everywhere around them, but which they can never hope to enjoy; and who, in this respect, are worse off than the savage in the midst of his tribe.

✻

Nikolai Mikhailovich Przhevalsky

(1839–1888)

Russian soldier and explorer. He led five expeditions to Central and Eastern Asia, collecting botanical and zoological specimens. He discovered, for Western science, the horse which was named after him.

Mongolia, the Tangut Country and the Solitudes of Northern Tibet: Being a Narrative of Three Years' Travel in Eastern High Asia, trans. E. D. Morgan (London, 1876).

1. Wild Horses

Wild horses, called by the Mongols *dzerlik-adu*, are rare in Western Tsaidam, but more numerous near Lob-nor. They are generally in large herds, very shy, and when frightened continue their flight for days, not returning to the same place for a year or two. Their colour is uniformly bay, with black tails and long manes hanging down to the ground. They are never hunted owing to the difficulties of the chase.

2. A Narrow Escape (1873)

In such arid mountains as these one would have supposed that we should not have incurred the slightest risk from water; but fate willed that we should experience every misfortune which can possibly overtake the traveller in these countries, for without giving us the slightest warning, a deluge, such as we never remember to have seen, swept suddenly down upon us.

It was on the morning of the 13th July; the summits of the mountains were enveloped in mist, a sure indication of rain. Towards midday, however, it became perfectly clear and gave every promise of a fine day, when, three hours later, all of a sudden, clouds began to settle on the mountains, and the rain poured down in buckets. Our tent was soon soaked through, and we dug small trenches to drain off the water which made its way into the interior. This continued for an hour without showing any signs of abatement, although the sky did not look threatening. The rainfall was so great that it was more than could be absorbed by the soil or retained on the steep slopes of the mountains; the consequence was that streams formed in every cleft and gorge, even falling from the precipitous cliffs, and uniting in the principal ravine, where our tent happened to be pitched, descended in an impetuous torrent with terrific roar and speed. Dull echoes high up in the mountains warned us of its approach, and in a few minutes the deep bed of our ravine was inundated with a turbid, coffee-coloured stream, carrying with it rocks and heaps of smaller fragments, while it dashed with such violence against the sides that the very ground trembled as though with the shock of an earthquake.... the rain continued with undiminished violence, and the torrent kept ever swelling. The deep bed of the ravine was soon choked with stones, mud, and fallen timber, which forced the water out of its channel on to higher ground. Barely twenty feet from our tent rushed the torrent, destroying everything in its course. Another minute, another foot of water, and our collections, the fruit of our expedition, were irrevocably gone! The flood had been so sudden that we had not a chance of rescuing them; all we could have done would have been to save our own lives by climbing on the nearest rocks. The disaster was so unexpected, the ruin so imminent, that a feeling of apathy took possession of me, and although face to face with so terrible a misfortune I could not realize it.

Fortune, however, again befriended us. Before our tent was a small projecting ledge of rock upon which the waves threw up stones which soon formed a breakwater, and this saved us. Towards evening the rain slackened, the torrent quickly subsided, and the following morning beheld only a small stream flowing where the day before the waters of a mighty river had swept along. A bright sun lit up the scene of yesterday's destruction, and displayed so complete a change in the appearance of the valley that we could not recognize it for the same.

On returning to Din-yuan-ing we equipped our caravan, bartered away our bad camels, bought new ones, and on the morning of the 26th July started on our journey. . . .

Another long series of hardships now awaited us. We suffered most from the July heat, which at midday rose to 113°F. in the shade, and at night was never less than 73°. No sooner did the sun appear above the horizon than it scorched us mercilessly. In the daytime the heat enveloped us on all sides, above from the sun, below from the burning ground; the wind, instead of cooling the atmosphere, stirred the lower strata and made it even more intolerable. On these days the cloudless sky was of a dirty hue, the soil heated to 145°F., and even higher where the sands were entirely bare, whilst at a depth of two feet from the surface it was 79°.

Our tent was no protection, for it was hotter within than without, although the sides were raised. We tried pouring water on it, and on the ground inside, but this was useless, in half an hour everything was as dry as before, and we knew not whither to turn for relief. . . .

To avoid the heat as much as possible we rose before daybreak; tea-drinking and loading the camels, however, took up so much time that we never got away before four or even five o'clock in the morning. We might have lightened the fatigue considerably by night-marching, but in that case we should have had to forego the survey which formed so important a part of our labours. . . .

The commencement of our journey was unpropitious, for on the sixth day after we left Din-yuan-ing, we lost our faithful friend 'Faust', and we ourselves nearly perished in the sands.

It was on the 31st July; we had left Djarataidabas and had taken the direction of the Khan-ula mountains; our guide having informed us that a march of eighteen miles lay before us that day, but that we should pass two wells about five miles apart.

Having accomplished that distance, we arrived at the first, and after watering our animals, proceeded, in the full expectation of finding the second, where we intended to halt; for though it was only seven in the morning, the heat was overpowering. So confident were we that the Cossacks proposed to throw away the supply of water that we had taken in the casks, in order not to burden our camels needlessly, but fortunately I forbade their doing this. After nearly seven miles more, no well was to be seen, and the guide announced that we had gone out of our road. So he proceeded to the top of a hillock in the immediate neighbourhood to obtain a view over the surrounding country, and soon afterwards beckoned to us to follow. On rejoining him, he assured us that although we had missed the second well, a third, where he purposed passing the night, was scarcely four miles further. We took the direction indicated. In the meanwhile it was near midday and the heat intolerable. A strong wind stirred the hot lower atmosphere, enveloping us in sand and saline dust. Our animals suffered frightfully; especially the dogs, obliged to walk over the burning sand. We stopped several times to give them drink, and to moisten their heads as well as our own. But the supply of water now failed! Less than a gallon remained, and this we reserved for the last extremity. 'How much further is it?' was the question we constantly put to our guide, who invariably answered that it was near, that we should see it from the next sand hill or the one after; and so we passed on upwards of seven miles without having seen a sign of the promised well. In the meanwhile the unfortunate 'Faust' lay down and moaned, giving us to understand that he was quite unable to walk. I then told my companion and guide to ride on, charging the latter to take 'Faust' on his camel as he was completely exhausted. After they had ridden a mile in advance of the caravan the guide pointed out the spot where he said the well should be, apparently about three miles off. Poor 'Faust's' doom was sealed; he was seized with fits, and Mr Pyltseff, finding it was impossible to hurry on, and too far to ride back to the caravan for a glass of water, waited till we came up, laying 'Faust' under a clump of *saxaul* and covering him with saddle-felt. The poor dog became less conscious every minute, gasped two or three times, and expired. Placing his body on one of the packs, we moved on again, sorely doubting whether there were really any well in the place pointed out to us by the guide; for he had already deceived us more than once. Our situation at this moment was desperate. Only a few glasses of water were left, of which we took into our mouths just enough to moisten our parched tongues; our bodies seemed on fire, our heads swam, and we were close upon fainting.

In this last extremity I desired a Cossack to take a small vessel and to ride as hard as he could to the well, accompanied by the guide, ordering him to fire at the latter if he attempted to run away. They were soon hidden in a cloud of dust which filled the air, and we toiled onwards in their tracks in the most anxious suspense. At length, after half an hour, the Cossack appeared. What news does he bring? and spurring our jaded horses, which could hardly move their legs to meet him, we learned, with the joy of a man who has been snatched from the jaws of death, that the well had been found! After a draught of fresh water from the vesselful that he brought, and having wet our heads, we rode in the direction pointed out, and soon reached the well of Boro-Sondji. It was now two o'clock in the afternoon; we had, therefore, been exposed for nine consecutive hours to frightful heat, and had ridden upwards of twenty miles.

After unloading the camels, I sent a Cossack back with the Mongol for the pack which had been left on the road, by the side of which our other

(Mongol) dog, who had been with us nearly two years, was laid. The poor brute had lain down underneath the pack but was still alive, and after getting a draught of water he was able to follow the men back to camp. Notwithstanding the complete prostration of our physical and moral energies, we felt the loss of 'Faust' so keenly that we could eat nothing, and slept but little all night. The following morning we dug a small grave and buried in it the remains of our faithful friend.

3. Bad Water

On crossing the frontier of the Khalka country we entered the principality of Tushetu-khan, and hastened by forced marches to Urga, which was now the goal we were so desirous of reaching. Nearly three years of wanderings, attended by every kind of privation and hardship, had so worn us out physically and morally that we felt most anxious for a speedy termination of our journey; besides which we were now travelling through the wildest part of the Gobi, where want of water, heat, storms of wind, in short every adverse condition, combined against us, and day by day undermined what little of our strength remained.

I need only describe the water we had to drink, after crossing the Hurku hills, to give some idea of our discomforts. Shortly before we passed through this country a heavy fall of rain had choked up most of the wells and had formed temporary lakes, by the side of which Mongols were as usual encamped: some of these lakes were but a hundred yards across and two or three feet deep, yet a dozen or more yurtas would often be seen pitched by them, and their brackish water was rendered muddy and filthy in the extreme by the large herds daily driven to drink in it, the heat of the sun raising its temperature to 77°. The first sight of this water was enough to disgust anyone; but we, like the Mongols, were obliged to use it, taking care to boil it first and to add brick-tea.

✻

Charles Montagu Doughty

(1843–1926)

English scholar and poet. He spent two years, starting in 1876, exploring Arabia alone, during which he was subjected to extremes of discomfort. His subsequent book, Travels in Arabia Deserta, *is deliberately written in archaic prose.*

Travels in Arabia Deserta (Cambridge, 1888).

1. FROM THE INTRODUCTION BY T. E. LAWRENCE

The realism of the book is complete. Doughty tries to tell the full and exact truth of all that he saw. If there is a bias it will be against the Arabs, for he liked them so much; he was so impressed by the strange attraction, isolation, and independence of this people that he took pleasure in bringing out their virtues by a careful expression of their faults. 'If one live any time with the Arab he will have all his life after a feeling of the desert.' He had experienced it himself, the test of nomadism, that most deeply biting of all social disciplines, and for our sakes he strained all the more to paint it in its true colours, as a life too hard, too empty, too denying for all but the strongest and most determined men. Nothing is more powerful and real than this record of all his daily accidents and obstacles, and the feelings that came to him on the way. His picture of the Semites, sitting to the eyes in a cloaca, but with their brows touching Heaven, sums up in full measure their strength and weakness, and the strange contradictions of their thought which quicken our curiosity at our first meeting with them.

To try and solve their riddle many of us have gone far into their society, and seen the clear hardness of their belief, a limitation almost mathematical, which repels us by its unsympathetic form. Semites have no half-tones in their register of vision. They are a people of primary colours, especially of black and white, who see the world always in line. They are a certain people, despising doubt, our modern crown of thorns. They do not understand our metaphysical difficulties, our self-questionings. They know only truth and untruth, belief and unbelief, without our hesitating retinue of finer shades.

2. CAMELS AND EVENING (1876)

The camels now jezzin, 'not drinking', we wandered without care of great watering places. The people drank of any small waters of the suffa, or ground rock. There are in all this desert mountain soil pit-like places of rock choked with old blown sand. In these sandpools, a water of the winter rains is long time preserved, but commonly thick and ill-smelling in the wet sand, and putrefying with rotten fibres of plants and urea of the nomads' cattle, which have been watered here from the beginning. Of such, the nomads (they prefer the thick desert water to pure water) now boiled their daily coffee, which is not then ill-tasting. The worst is that blackish water drawn from pits long forsaken, until they have been voided once.

Sooner than drink their water I suffered thirst, and very oft passed the nights half sleepless. . . .

Pleasant, as the fiery heat of the desert daylight is done, is our homely evening fire. The sun gone down upon a highland steppe of Arabia, whose common altitude is above three thousand feet, the thin dry air is presently refreshed, the sand is cold (yet at three fingers' depths is left a sunny warmth of the past day's heat until the new sunrise). After a half hour it is the blue night, the clear hoary starlight in which there shines the girdle of the milky way with a marvellous clarity.

As the sun is setting, the nomad housewife brings in a truss of sticks and dry bushes which she had pulled or hoed in the wilderness. She casts down this provision by our hearth side for the sweet-smelling evening fire. But to Hirfa, his sheikhly young wife, Zeyd had given a little Beduin maid to help her. The housewife has upon her woman's side of the tent a hearth apart, which is the cooking fire. Commonly Hirfa baked then, under the ashes, a bread-cake for the stranger. Zeyd eats not yet, but only near midnight.

At this first evening hour, the Beduin are all in their households to sup of such wretchedness as they may have. There is no more wandering through the wide encampment, and the coming in then of any persons, not strangers, were an unseemly 'ignorance'.

The foster-camels lie couched before the booth of hair, and these Beduins let them lie still an hour before the milking. The great feeble brutes have wandered all day upon the droughty face of the wilderness; they may hardly crop their fill, in those many hours, of so slender pastures. The mare stands tethered before the booth at the woman's side, where there is not much passage.

When the Arabs have eaten their morsel and drunken buttermilk of the flock, the few men of our encampment begin to assemble about the sheikh's hearth, where is some expectation of coffee. Glad at the fall of the empty daylight, the householders sit again to make talk, or silent and listless with the drooping gravity of brute animals. Old men, always weary, and the herdmen which were all day abroad in the sun, are lying now upon an elbow (this is the right nomad posture, and which Zeyd would have me learn and use) about the common fire. But the reposing of the common sort at home is to lie heels out backward about the hearth, as the spokes of a wheel, and flat upon their bellies (which they even think appeases the gnawing of hunger); and a little raising themselves, they discourse staying upon their breasts and two elbows. Thus the men of this lean nation will later sleep, spreading only their tattered cloaks under them, upon the wild soil, a posture even reproved by themselves.

They asking me of our custom, I said, 'You are ground-sitters, but we sit high upon stools like the Turk.' The legs of chair-sitters to hang all day they thought an insufferable fatigue. The Arabs asked me often if we sat gathered in this kindly sort about our evening fires. And if neighbours went about to neighbour houses, seeking company of friends and coffee-drinking. . . .

3. SUFFERING

They halted bye and bye, and Eyad dismounted. Merjan, who was still sitting upon the dromedary's back, struck fire with flint: I thought it might be for their pipes, since they had bought a little sweet tobacco with my money at Hayil. But Eyad kindled the cord of his musket!

I said, 'What is this?'

They answered, 'A hare!'

'Where is your hare? I say, show me this hare!' Eyad had yet to put priming to the eye of his piece: they stumbled in their words, and remained confused. I said to them, 'Do I seem to you like this hare? By the life of Him who created us, in what instant you show me a gun's mouth, I will lay dead your hares' carcasses upon this earth. Put out that match!' He did so.

The cool of the evening approached; we marched on slowly in silence, and doubtless they rolled it in their hollow hearts what might signify that vehement word of the Nasrany [foreigner or Christian]. 'Look,' I said to them, '*rizelleyn*, you two vile dastards. I tell you plainly, that in that moment you drive me to an extremity ye are but dead dogs; I will take this carrion camel!'

My adventure in such too unhappy case had been nearly desperate; nigher than the Syrian borders I saw no certain relief. Syria was a great mark to shoot at, and terribly far off—and yet upon a good dromedary, fresh watered (for extremities make men bold, and the often escaping from dangers) I would not despair to come forth; and one watering in the midway, if I might once find water, would save both dromedary and rider.— Or should I ride towards Teyma, two hundred miles from hence? But seeing the great landmarks from this direction, how might I know them again?—And if I found any nomads westward, yet they would be Bishr, these men's tribesmen.—Should I ride eastward in unknown habitations?— Or hold over the fearful Nefud sand billows to seek the Sherarat tribe? Wherever I rode I was likely to faint before I came to any human relief; and might not strange nomads sooner kill the stranger, seeing one arrive thus, than receive me? My eyes were dim with the suffered ophthalmia, and not knowing where to look for them, how in the vastness of the desert landscape should I descry any nomads? If I came by the mercy of God to any wells, I might drink drop by drop by some artifice, but not water the camel.

Taking up stones I chafed my blood-stained hands, hoping to wash them when we should come to the nomads. But this was the time of the spring pasture, when the great cattle are dry, and ofttimes the nomads have no water by them because there is buttermilk to drink.

Eyad thought the game turned against him! When we came to a habitation, I might complain of them and he would have a scorn. 'Watch,' said he, 'and when any camel stales, run thou and rinse the hands; for truly seeing blood on thy hands, there will none of the nomads eat with thee.'

Thus it continued for several days, finding some rest and sustenance only at night, with nomads in their tents, or herdsmen in the open.

The gravel stones were sharp; the soil in the sun soon glowed as a hearth under my bare feet. The naked pistol (hidden under my tunic) hung heavily upon my panting chest. The air was breathless, and we had nothing to drink. It was hard for me to follow on foot, notwithstanding the weak pace of their camel. A little spurn of a rider's heel and she would trot out of my sight. Hard is this human patience! Showing myself armed, I might compel them to deliver the dromedary. But who would not afterward be afraid to become my rafik? If I provoked them, they (supposing me unarmed) might come upon me with their weapons; and must I then take their poor lives! But was that just? In this faintness of body and spirit I could not tell. I thought that a man should forsake life rather than justice.

✳

ADOLF ERIK NORDENSKJÖLD

(1832–1901)

Swedish explorer and scientist. After many Arctic expeditions he became the first man to take a ship through the North-East Passage. Leaving Tromsö in Norway in July 1878, he missed reaching the Pacific that year by one day and so was frozen in until the following summer.

1. *The Arctic Voyages of Adolf Erik Nordenskiold*, by Alexander Leslie (London, 1879); 2. *The Voyage of the Vega round Asia and Europe*, trans. A. Leslie (London, 1881).

70

1. ADDRESS TO THE SWEDISH GOVERNMENT

The ocean lying north of the Siberian coast from the mouth of the Yenissey to Tschaun Bay has never been ploughed by the keel of any proper sea-going vessel, still less has been traversed by any steamer specially equipped for navigation among ice.

The small vessels with which it has been attempted to navigate this part of the ocean never ventured very far from the coast.

An open sea with a fresh breeze was as destructive for them, indeed more destructive, than a sea covered with drift-ice.

They almost always sought some convenient winter harbour just at the season of the year when the sea is freest of ice, namely late summer or autumn.

Although the sea from Cape Chelyuskin to Bering's Straits has been repeatedly traversed, none has yet succeeded in traversing the whole extent at once.

The covering of ice formed during winter along the coast, but probably not in the open sea, is every summer broken up, giving origin to extensive fields of drift-ice, which are driven, now by a northerly wind towards the coast, now by a southerly wind out to sea, yet not so far but that it comes back to the coast after some days of northerly wind, whence it appears probable that the Siberian Sea is, so to speak, shut off from the Polar Sea proper by a series of islands, of which for the present we know only Wrangel's Land and the islands which form New Siberia.

I consider it probable that a well-equipped steamer would be able, without meeting with too many obstacles from ice, to force a passage this way during autumn in a few days, and thus that it would be possible not only to solve a geographical problem of several centuries' standing but also, with all the means now at the disposal of the man of science in carrying on researches in geography, hydrography, geology, and natural history, to survey a hitherto almost unknown sea of enormous extent.

I am also fully convinced that it is not only possible to sail along the north coast of Asia, provided circumstances are not too unfavourable, but that such an enterprise will be of incalculable practical importance, by no means directly as opening up a new commercial route, but indirectly by the impression which would thereby be communicated of the practical utility of a communication between the ports of north Scandinavia and the Obi and Yenisey on the one hand and between the Pacific Ocean and the Lena on the other.

Should the expedition, contrary to expectation, not succeed in carrying out the programme which has been arranged in its entirety, it ought not to be looked upon as having failed. In such a case the expedition will remain for a considerable time at places on the north coast of Siberia, suitable for scientific research. Every mile beyond the mouth of the Yenisey is a step forward to a complete knowledge of our globe, an object which some time or other must be attained, and towards which it is an affair of honour for every civilized nation to contribute in its proportion. ...

2. Caught by the Ice (1878)

On 22 [September] I made, along with Captain Palander, an excursion in the steam launch to take soundings farther to the east. We soon succeeded in discovering a channel of sufficient depth and not too much blocked with ice, and on the 23rd the *Vega* was able to resume her voyage among very closely packed drift-ice, often so near the land that she had only a fourth of a metre of water under her keel. We went forward, however, if slowly.

The land here formed a grassy plain, still clear of snow, rising inland to gently sloping hills or earthy heights. The beach was strewn with a not inconsiderable quantity of driftwood, and here and there were seen the remains of old dwelling-places. On the evening of 23 September we lay to at a ground-ice in a pretty large opening of the ice-field. This opening closed in the course of the night, so that on the 24th and 25th we could make only very little progress, but on the 26th we continued our course, at first with difficulty, but afterwards in pretty open water to the headland which on the maps is called Cape Onman. The natives too, who came on board here, gave the place that name. The ice we met with on that day was heavier than before, and bluish-white, not dirty. It was accordingly formed further out at sea.

On the 27th we continued our course in somewhat open water to Kolyutschin Bay. No large river debouches in the bottom of this great fjord, the only one on the north coast of Asia which, by its long narrow form, the configuration of the neighbouring shores, and its division into two at the bottom, reminds us of the Spitzbergen fjords which have been excavated by glaciers. The mouth of the bay was filled with very closely packed drift-ice that had gathered round the island situated there, which was inhabited by a large number of Chukchi families. In order to avoid this ice, the *Vega* made a considerable detour up the fjord. The weather was calm and fine, but new ice was formed everywhere among the old drift-ice where it was closely packed. Small seals swarmed by hundreds among the ice, following the wake of the vessel with curiosity. Birds, on the contrary, were seen in limited numbers. Most of them had evidently already migrated to more southerly seas. At 4.45 p.m. the vessel was anchored to an ice-floe near the eastern shore of the fjord. It could be seen from this point that the ice at the headland, which bounded the mouth of the fjord to the east, lay so near land that there was a risk that the open water next the shore would not be deep enough for the *Vega*.

Lieutenant Hovgaard was therefore sent with the steam launch to take soundings. He returned with the report that the water off the headland was sufficiently deep. At the same time, accompanied by several of the naturalists, I made an excursion on land. In the course of this excursion the hunter Johnsen was sent to the top of the range of heights which occupied the interior of the promontory, in order to get a view of the state of the ice farther to the east. Johnsen too returned with the very comforting news that a very broad, open channel extended beyond the headland along the coast to the south-east. I was wandering about, along with my comrades, on the slopes near the beach in order, so far as the falling darkness permitted, to examine its natural conditions, when Johnsen came down; he informed us that from the top of the height one could hear bustle and noise and see fires at an encampment on the other side of the headland. He supposed that the natives were celebrating some festival. I had a strong inclination to go thither in order, as I thought, 'to take farewell of the Chukchis', for I was quite certain that on some of the following days we should sail into the Pacific. But it was already late in the evening and dark, and we were not yet sufficiently acquainted with the disposition of the Chukchis to go by night, without any serious occasion, in small numbers and provided only with the weapons of the chase, to an encampment with which we were not acquainted. It was not until afterwards that we learned that such a visit was not attended with any danger. Instead of going to the encampment, as the vessel in any case could not weigh anchor this evening, we remained some hours longer on the beach and lighted there an immense log fire of drift-wood, round which we were soon all collected, chatting merrily about the remaining part of the voyage in seas where not cold but heat would trouble us, and where our progress at least would not be obstructed by ice, continual fog, and unknown shallows. None of us then had any idea that, instead of the heat of the tropics, we would for the next ten months be experiencing a winter at the pole of cold, frozen in on an unprotected road, under almost continual snow-storms, and with a temperature which often sank below the freezing-point of mercury.

The evening was glorious, the sky clear, and the air so calm that the flames and smoke of the log fire rose high against the sky. The dark surface of the water, covered as it was with a thin film of ice, reflected its light as a fire-way straight as a line, bounded far away at the horizon by a belt of ice, whose inequalities appeared in the darkness as the summits of a distant high mountain chain. The temperature in the quite draught-free air was felt to be mild, and the thermometer showed only 2° under the freezing-point. This slight degree of cold was, however, sufficient to cover the sea in the course of the night with a sheet of newly-frozen ice, which, as the following days' experience showed, at the opener places could indeed only delay, not obstruct the advance of the *Vega*, but which, however, bound together the fields of drift-ice collected off the coast so firmly that a vessel, even with the help of steam, could with difficulty force her way through.

When on the following day, 28 September, we had sailed past the headland which bounds Kolyutschin Bay on the east, the channel next the coast, clear of drift-ice, but covered with newly formed ice, became suddenly shallow. The depth was too small for the *Vega*, for which we had now to seek a course among the blocks of ground-ice and fields of drift-ice in the offing. The night's frost had bound these so firmly together that the attempt failed. We were thus compelled to lie to at a ground-ice so much the more certain of getting off with the first shift of the wind, and of being able to traverse the few miles that separated us from the open water at Bering's Straits, as whalers on several occasions had not left this region until the middle of October.

When we were frozen in, there was ice-free water some minutes further east. A single hour's steaming of the *Vega* at full speed had probably been sufficient to traverse this distance, and a day earlier the drift-ice at this point would not have formed any serious obstacle to the advance of the vessel.

This misfortune of being frozen in so near the goal is the one mishap during all my Arctic journeys that I have had most difficulty in reconciling myself to, but I console myself with the brilliant result, almost unexampled in the history of Arctic exploration, that has been already won, with our excellent winter harbour, and with prospect of being able to continue our voyage next summer. A winter's meteorological and magnetical observations at this place, and the geological, botanical, and zoological researches which our being frozen in will give us an opportunity of prosecuting, are, besides, of sufficient interest to repay all the difficulties and troubles which a wintering involves. . . .

NEY ELIAS

(1844–1897)

British civil servant and explorer. In 1872, accompanied only by one Chinese attendant, he left Peking, crossed western Mongolia 2,500 miles to the Russian frontier, then travelled another 2,300 miles to the then railhead at Nijni Novgorod. One of the very greatest of Asian explorers, he never wrote a book of reminiscences: his domineering mother forbade the writing of a memoir of his life. He is therefore less well known than he deserves to be. In the library of the Royal Geographical Society is a slim, leather-bound collection of the obituaries written after his sudden death at the age of fifty-three. The one from The Times *was written by his friend and admirer Francis Younghusband, who stated in a letter to Ney's sister Jessie: 'I have always thought him the best traveller there has ever been in Central Asia . . .' Pressed between the pages is a bunch of wild flowers.*

Royal Geographical Society archives.

1. OBITUARY IN *THE TIMES* (2 JUNE 1897)

Mr Ney Elias, late Consul-General at Meshed, died in London on Monday from blood poisoning after only a short illness, but after being in indifferent health for some time. Though almost the least known he was one of the most courageous, the most clear-sighted, and most observant of all recent-day explorers in Asia. He was exceptionally modest, and as his most important journey was made, and his most valuable reports were written, when employed in confidential service under the Government of India, it has come about that a man who, a quarter of a century ago, earned the gold medal of the Royal Geographical Society for a solitary journey made from Peking to St Petersburg, in the depth of winter and in the midst of a fanatical Chinese rebellion, and who since then has almost continuously been employed on daring journeys and delicate political missions in south-western China, in Burma, in Chinese Turkestan, the Pamirs, Afghan Turkestan, Chitral, Siam, and Persia, is scarcely known to any Englishmen beyond a few officials of the Government of India and readers of the Geographical Society's *Journal*.

Ney Elias, at an early age, found his way to China, where he was employed for a time in a business office, and, in 1871, conceived the daring project of returning to Europe overland across the entire continent of Asia.

He set out with a single Chinese servant, he crossed the terrible desert of Gobi by a route never before explored, he unconcernedly travelled amid the opposing factions of the great Mahomedan rebellion of those times, and he traversed the breadth of Siberia to Russia. The report of this journey is contained in no pretentious book of travels, and received none of the advertisement which other far less intrepid or important journeys have obtained. It was merely recorded in the sober pages of the *Journal* of the Geographical Society. But the record of this, as of all the other journeys made by Ney Elias, was so transparently truthful and interesting in detail as to gain the unstinted admiration of such men as the late Sir Henry Yule and Sir Henry Rawlinson, who were then the highest authorities upon Asiatic geography. After his return from this great journey Mr Elias formed the conception of penetrating to the mysterious city of Lhassa, in Tibet, but being detained through political difficulties he accepted service under the Government of India, and was sent, first, to Yunan, and afterwards to Ladak. From this latter place he was sent on a political mission to Chinese Turkestan, with the object of establishing relations between the Government of India and the Government of the Great Province of China which bounds our Indian Empire on the north. In 1885 he again visited the same countries, and made one of his greatest and most valuable journeys, traversing the entire length of the Pamirs, visiting the interesting little States that lie on either side of the Oxus, travelling through Badakhshan and Afghan Turkestan to the neighbourhood of Herat, and returning to India by way of Chitral and Gilgit. In 1889–90 Mr Elias demarcated the frontier between Siam and the Shan States of Burma, and in 1891 he was appointed Consul-General at Meshed, in Persia, from which post he only recently retired.

Mr Elias had for years past suffered from bad health contracted under the hardships of travel in every contrast of climate—in Siberian cold and Indian heat, in the moist malarial atmosphere of Burma and Siam, and then in the parched climates of Central Asia. All his latter journeys were made, at the call of duty, when he was suffering acutely from depressing illnesses. He was remarkable alike for his unswerving courage and determination in pursuing his object and for his modesty in recording the results of his labour when the object was attained. He was as restive and sensitive of constraint from his superiors as he was devoted to the interests of those serving under him; and only those few who have followed close upon his footsteps in China and Central Asia and those who have had opportunities of noting his work can truly appreciate the sterling value of the services he has rendered his country. For those services the single reward he received was the Companionship of the Order of the Indian

Empire, conferred at the conclusion of his great journey across the Pamirs and Afghanistan. But the reason why he received no further distinction afterwards will be understood when it is related that, on finding it was impossibled to return the decoration which had already been given him, he requested that at any rate no other honour should ever be bestowed upon him. He loved his work for the work's sake, and he was almost morbidly sensitive of anything which might be construed into popularity-hunting or cheap advertisement.

2. OBITUARY IN *THE SCOTSMAN*

Much regret has been caused both in Anglo-Indian and geographical circles by the unexpected news of the death of Mr Ney Elias, the Central Asian traveller. Mr Elias was naturally of a disposition so modest, shy, and retiring that his achievements, remarkable as they were, never obtained for him a tithe of the popular applause and recognition accorded to men who had done nothing that could be put in comparison with his work. I have heard distinguished Anglo-Indians say that Mr Ney Elias knew more of the geography of Central Asia than any other man, and that he had himself done more, certainly than any other Englishman, probably than any other European, with the possible exception of the famous Russian explorer Przhevalsky, to extend our knowledge of the heart of Asia. He was the first to make the great overland journey between Pekin and India across the Gobi desert, and his explorations of the Himalayas and the Pamirs are almost too numerous to make an enumeration of them possible. I remember in this connection hearing a story that illustrates both Ney Elias's retiring disposition and his work as an explorer. At a dinner at Simla, given to a traveller who had recently arrived in India from Russian Turkestan, the guest of the evening was loudly proclaiming the magnitude of his achievement in having crossed a certain pass. Mr Elias, who was present, made no remark until one of the hosts, a little irritated at the self-satisfaction displayed by the guest of the evening, turned to him and asked, 'You've crossed this pass more than once, haven't you, Elias?' The simple reply, 'Yes, eighteen times', had an instantaneous effect—intensified when further questions elicited the fact that some of these crossings had been made in winter. Almost the last piece of work on which Mr Elias was engaged was the preparation of a statement of what remained to be done in the exploration of Asia, which he had drawn up at the request of Sir Clements Markham, President of the Royal Geographical Society.

SIR FRANCIS YOUNGHUSBAND

(1863–1942)

Indian Army officer and explorer. In 1887 he travelled from Peking to India via the Gobi and Kashgar. In 1904 he was to lead the British military expedition to Lhasa.

The Heart of a Continent (London, 1937; first published 1896).

1. CROSSING AN UNEXPLORED PASS (1887)

It was altogether a bad day's march for both men and ponies, but at last, toward evening, we found the valley opening to a wide plain, with plenty of scrub on it, and here we encamped. Before us rose a great wall of snowy mountains, with not the very smallest sign of a pass, though the guide said we should have to cross them on the following day. I felt some misgivings on looking at this barrier which now stopped our way, for the guide frankly confessed that he had forgotten the way across, and of course there was no sign of a path to guide us. He said, however, that possibly, as we got nearer, he might remember which turning we should have to take, and with that amount of consolation we had to settle down for the night.

We now had our first taste of real cold. We were about fifteen thousand feet above the sea-level, and as soon as the sun set one could almost *see* the cold stealing over the mountains—a cold grey creeps over them, the running streams become coated with ice, and as soon as we had had our dinner—we always dined together, to save trouble and time in cooking—and darkness had fairly fallen, we took up our beddings from the places where we had ostentatiously laid them out to mislead any prowling Kanjutis, and hurried off to deposit them behind any rock which would shelter us from the icy wind which blew down from the mountains. It is a curious fact, but when real difficulties seem to be closing around, one's spirits rise. As long as you have health—that is the main point to look after, but it is easily attained in mountain travel—and provided that you take plenty of food, difficulties seem only to make you more and more cheery. Instead of depressing you, they only serve to brace up all your faculties to their highest pitch; and though, as I lay down that night, I felt that for the next two or three weeks we should have harder and harder work before us, I recollect that evening as one of those in all my life in which I have felt in the keenest spirits.

78

At the first dawn of day on the following morning we were astir. The small stream was frozen solid, and the air bitingly cold; so we hurried about loading up, had a good breakfast, and, as the sun rose, started off straight at the mountain wall—a regular battlement of rocky peaks covered with snow, where it was possible, but for the most part too steep for snow to lie. After travelling for three or four miles, a valley suddenly opened up to the left. The guide immediately remembered it, and said that up it was an easy pass which would completely outflank the mountain barrier. The going was good. I left the ponies, and in my eagerness hurried on rapidly in front of them, straining to see the top of the pass, and the 'other side'—that will-o'-the-wisp which ever attracts explorers and never satisfies them, for there is ever another side beyond. The height was beginning to tell, and the pass seemed to recede the nearer I approached it. One rise after another I surmounted, thinking it would prove the summit, but there was always another beyond. The valley was wide and open, and the going perfectly easy, leading sometimes over round boulders, but more often loose soil. At length I reached a small lake, about a quarter of a mile in length, and a small rise above it at the farther end was the summit of the pass. I rushed up it, and there before me lay the 'other side', and surely no view which man has ever seen can excel that. To describe the scene in words would be impossible. . . .

Before me rose tier after tier of stately mountains, among the highest in the world—peaks of untainted snow, whose summits reached to heights of twenty-five thousand, twenty-six thousand, and, in one supreme case, twenty-eight thousand feet above sea-level. There was this wonderful array of mountain majesty set out before me across a deep, rock-bound valley, and away in the distance, filling up the head of this, could be seen a vast glacier, the outpourings of the mountain masses which give it birth. It was a scene which, as I viewed it, and realized that this seemingly impregnable array must be pierced and overcome, seemed to put the iron into my soul and stiffen all my energies for the task before me.

2. THE VIRTUE OF HOLDING ONE'S TONGUE

Everything here was on a gigantic scale, and what seemed to be not more than an hour's walk from the camp was in fact a six hours' climb. It was nearly midday when we reached the top of the pass . . . There was nothing but a sheer precipice, and those first few moments on the summit of the Mustagh Pass were full of intense anxiety to me. If we could but get over, the crowning success of my expedition would be gained. But the thing seemed to me simply an impossibility. I had had no experience of Alpine climbing, and I had no ice-axes or other mountaineering appliances with me. I had not even any proper boots. All I had for foot-gear were some native boots of soft leather, without nails and without heels—mere leather stockings, in fact—which gave no sort of grip upon an icy surface. How, then, I should ever be able to get down the icy slopes and rocky precipices I now saw before me I could not think; and if it had rested with me alone, the probability is we never should have got over the pass at all.

What, however, saved our party was my holding my tongue. I kept quite silent as I looked over the pass, and waited to hear what the men had to say about it. They meanwhile were looking at me, and, imagining that an Englishman never went back from an enterprise he had once started on, took it as a matter of course that, as I gave no order to go back, I meant to go on. So they set about their preparations for the descent. We had brought an ordinary pickaxe with us, and Wali went on ahead with this, while the rest of us followed one by one behind him, each hanging on to a rope tied round Wali's waist to support him in case he slipped while hewing steps across the ice-slope. This slope was of hard ice, very steep, and, thirty yards or so below the line we took, ended in an ice-fall, which again terminated far beneath in the head of a glacier at the foot of the pass. Wali with his pickaxe hewed a way step by step across the ice-slope, so as to reach the rocky cliff by which we should have to descend on to the glacier below. We slowly edged across the slope after him, but it was hard to keep cool and steady. From where we stood we could see nothing over the end of the slope but the glacier many hundreds of feet below us.

Some of the men were so little nervous that they kicked the fragments of ice hewed out by Wali down the slope, and laughed as they saw them hop down it and with one last bound disappear altogether. But an almost sickening feeling came on me as I watched this, for we were standing on a slope as steep as the roof of a house. We had no ice-axes with which to anchor ourselves or give us support; and though I tied handkerchiefs, and the men bits of leather and cloth, round the insteps of our smooth native boots, to give us a little grip on the slippery ice, I could not help feeling that if any one of us had lost his foothold, the rest of us would never have been able to hold him up with the rope, and that in all likelihood the whole party would have been carried away and plunged into the abyss below. Outwardly I kept as cool and cheerful as I could, but inwardly I shuddered at each fresh step I took. The sun was now pouring down on to the ice, and just melted the surface of the steps after they were hewn, so that by the time those of us who were a few paces behind Wali reached a step, the ice was just covered over with water, and this made it still more slippery for our soft leather boots, which had now become almost slimy on the surface. It was under these circumstances that my Ladaki servant, Drogpa, gave in. He was shaking all over in an exaggerated shiver, and so unsteady, I thought he would slip at any moment, and perhaps carry us all with him. We were but at the beginning of our trials. We had not even begun the actual descent yet, but were merely crossing to a point from which we should make it. It was dangerous to have such a man with us, so I told him he might return to the ponies and go round with them. . . .

We reached the bottom of the cliff without accident, and then found ourselves at the head of a long ice-slope extending down to the glacier below. Protruding through the ice were three pieces of rock, which would serve us as successive halting-places, and we determined upon taking a line which led by them. We had brought with us every scrap of rope that could be spared from the ponies' gear, and we tied these and all the men's turbans and waist-clothes together into one long rope, by which we let a man down the ice-slope on to the first projecting rock. As he went down he cut steps, and when he had reached the rock we tied the upper end of the rope firmly on to a rock above, and then one by one we came down the slope, hanging on to the rope and making use of the steps which had been cut. This was, therefore, a comparatively easy part of the descent; but one man was as nearly as possible lost. He slipped, fell over on his back, and came sliding down the slope at a frightful pace. Luckily, however, he still managed to keep hold of the rope with one hand, and so kept himself from dashing over the ice-fall at the side of the slope; but when he reached the rock his hand was almost bared of skin, and he was shivering with fright. Wali, however, gave him a sound rating for being so careless, and on the next stage made him do all the hardest part of the work. . . .

At last, just as the sun set, we reached the glacier at the foot of the pass. We were in safety once more. The tension was over, and the last and greatest obstacle in my journey had been surmounted. Those moments when I stood at the foot of the pass are long to be remembered by me— moments of intense relief, and of deep gratitude for the success that had been granted. Such feelings as mine were now cannot be described in words, but they are known to everyone who has had his heart set on one great object and has accomplished it. I took one last look at the pass, never before or since seen by a European, and then we started away down the glacier to find some bare spot on which to lay our rugs and rest.

SVEN HEDIN

(1865–1952)

Swedish explorer. He made many tough and dramatic expeditions through-out Central Asia.

My Life as an Explorer (London, 1926).

1. DYING OF THIRST IN THE GOBI (1895)

That night I wrote what I supposed were to be my last lines in my diary: 'Halted on a high dune, where the camels dropped. We examined the east through the field-glasses; mountains of sand in all directions, not a straw, no life. All, men as well as camels, are extremely weak. God help us!' May Day, a spring-time feast of joy and light at home in Sweden, was for us the heaviest day on our *via dolorosa* through the desert.

The night had been quiet, clear and cold; but the sun was hardly above the horizon when it grew warm. The men squeezed the last drops of the rancid oil out of a goatskin and gave them to the camels. The day before I had not had a single drop of water, and the day before that, only two cups. I was suffering from thirst; and when by chance I found the bottle in which we kept the Chinese spirits for the Primus stove, I could not resist the temptation to drink some of it. It was a foolish thing to do; but nevertheless I drank half the bottle. Yoldash heard the gurgling sound and came toward me, wagging his tail. I let him have a sniff. He snorted and went away sadly. I threw the bottle away and the rest of the liquid flowed out into the sand.

That treacherous drink finished me. I tried to rise but my legs would not support me. The caravan broke camp but I remained behind. Islam Bai led, compass in hand, going due east. The sun was already burning hot. My men probably thought I would die where I lay. They went on slowly, like snails. The sound of the bells grew fainter and finally died away altogether. On every dune-crest the caravan reappeared like a dark spot, smaller and smaller; in every hollow between the dunes it remained concealed for a while. Finally I saw it no more. But the deep trail, with its dark shadows from the sun, which was still low, reminded me of the danger of my situation. I had not strength enough to follow the others. They had left me. The horrible desert extended in all directions. The sun was burning and blinding; there was not a breath of air.

Then a terrible thought struck me. What if this was the quiet preceding a storm? At any moment, then, I might see the black streak across the horizon in the east, which heralded the approach of a sand-storm. The trail of the caravan would then be obliterated in a few moments, and I would never find my men and camels again, those wrecks of the ships of the desert. I exerted all my will-power, got up, reeled, fell, crawled for a while along the trail, got up again, dragged myself along, and crawled. One hour passed, and then another. From the ridge of a dune I saw the caravan. It was standing still. The bells had ceased tinkling. By superhuman efforts I managed to reach it.

Islam stood on a ridge, scanning the eastern horizon and shading his eyes with his hand. Again he asked permission to hurry eastward with the jugs. But seeing my condition he quickly abandoned the idea. Mohammed Shah was lying on his face, sobbingly invoking Allah. Kasim sat in the shadow of a camel, his face covered with his hands. He told me that Mohammed Shah had been raving about water all the way. Yolchi lay on the sand as if he were dead.

Islam suggested that we continue and look for a spot of hard clay ground, where we might dig for water. All the camels were lying down. I climbed on the white one. Like the others, he refused to get up. Our plight was desperate. Here we were to die. Mohammed Shah lay babbling, toying with the sand and raving about water. I realized that we had reached the last act of our desert-drama. But I was not yet ready to give in altogether.

The sun was now glowing like an oven. 'When the sun has gone down', I said to Islam, 'we will break camp and march all night. Up with the tent!' The camels were freed from their burdens and lay in the blazing sun all day. Islam and Kasim pitched the tent. I crawled in, undressed completely, and lay down on a blanket, my head pillowed on a sack. Islam, Kasim, Yoldash and the sheep went into the shade, while Mohammed Shah and Yolchi stayed where they had fallen. The hens were the only ones to keep up their spirits. This death-camp was the unhappiest I lived through in all my wanderings in Asia.

It was only half-past nine in the morning, and we had hardly traversed three miles. I was absolutely done up and unable to move a finger. I thought I was dying. I imagined myself already lying in a mortuary chapel. The church bells had stopped tolling for the funeral. My whole life flew past me like a dream. There were not many hours left me on the threshold of eternity. But most of all, I was tormented by the thought of the anxiety and uncertainty which I would cause my parents and brother and sisters. When I should be reported missing, Consul Petrovsky would make investigations. He would learn that I had left Merket on April 10. All traces after that, however, would then have been swept away; for several storms would have passed over the desert since then. They would wait and wait at home. One year would pass after another. But no news would come, and finally they would cease hoping.

About noon the slack flaps of the tent began to bulge, and a faint southerly breeze moved over the desert. It blew stronger, and after a couple of hours it was so fresh that I rolled myself up in my blanket.

And now a miracle happened! My debility vanished and my strength returned! If ever I longed for the sunset it was now. I did not want to die: I *would not* die in this miserable, sandy desert! I could run, walk, crawl on my hands and feet. My men might not survive, but I had to find water! The sun lay like a red-hot cannon ball on a dune in the west. I was in the best of condition. I dressed and ordered Islam and Kasim to prepare for departure. The sunset glow spread its purple light over the dunes. Mohammed Shah and Yolchi were in the same position as in the morning. The former had already begun his death-struggle; and he never regained consciousness. But the latter woke to life in the cool of the evening. With his hands clenched he crawled up to me and cried pitifully: 'Water! Give us water, sir! Only a drop of water!' Then he crawled away.

'Is there no liquid here, whatever?' I said.

'Why, the rooster!' So they cut off the rooster's head and drank his blood. But that was only a drop in the bucket. Their eyes fell on the sheep, which had followed us as faithfully as a dog without complaining. Everyone hesitated. It would be murder to kill the sheep to prolong our lives for only one day. But Islam led it away, turned its head toward Mecca and slashed its carotids. The blood, reddish-brown and ill-smelling, flowed slowly and thickly. It coagulated immediately into a cake, which the men gulped down. I tried it, too; but it was nauseous, and the mucous membrane of my throat was so dry that it stuck there, and I had to get rid of it quickly.

Mad with thirst, Islam and Yolchi collected camel's urine in a receptacle, mixed it with sugar and vinegar, held their noses, and drank. Kasim and I declined to join in this drinking-bout. The two who had drunk this poison were totally incapacitated. They were overcome with violent cramps and vomiting, and lay writhing and groaning on the sand.

Islam recovered slightly. Before darkness fell we went over our baggage. I laid everything that was irreplaceable in one pile: notebooks, itineraries, maps, instruments, pencils and paper, arms and ammunition, the Chinese silver (about £260), lanterns, candles, a pail, a shovel, provisions for three days, some tobacco and a few other things. A pocket Bible was the only book included. Among the things abandoned were the cameras and about a thousand plates, of which about one hundred had already been exposed, the medicine chest, saddles, clothes, presents intended for the natives, and much besides. I removed a suit of clean clothing from the pile of discarded things and changed everything from head to foot; for if I was to die and be buried by the sand-storms in the eternal desert, I would at least be robed in a clean, new shroud.

The things we had decided to take along were packed in soft saddle-bags, and these were fastened to the camels. All the pack-saddles were discarded, as they would only have added unnecessary weight.

Yolchi had crawled into the tent to lie down on my blanket. He looked repulsive, soiled as he was with blood from the lungs of the sheep. I tried to brace him up and advised him to follow our track during the night. He did not answer. Mohammed Shah was already delirious. In his delirium he muttered the name of Allah. I tried to make his head comfortable, passed my hand over his burning forehead, begged him to crawl along our trail as far as he could, and told him that we would return to rescue him as soon as we found water.

The two men eventually died in the death-camp, or near it. They were never heard of; and when, after a year had elapsed, they were still missing, I gave a sum of money to their respective widows and children.

All five camels were induced to get up, and they were tied to one another in single file. Islam led and Kasim brought up the rear. We did not take the two dying men along, because the camels were too weak to carry them; and, indeed, in their deplorable condition, they could not have kept their seats between the humps. We also cherished the hope that we would find water, in which case we were going to fill the two goatskins that we still carried, and hurry back to save the unfortunate ones.

The hens, having satisfied their keen hunger with the dead sheep's blood, had gone to rest. A silence more profound than that of the grave prevailed around the tent. As twilight was about to merge into darkness, the bronze bells sounded for the last time. We headed eastward as usual, avoiding the highest ridges. After a few minutes' walk I turned about, and gave a fare-well glance at the death-camp. The tent stood out distinctly in the vanishing daylight that still lingered in the west. It was a relief to get away from this ghastly place. It was soon swallowed up by the night. . . .

Thus we walked on through the night and the sand. After two hours of it, we were so exhausted from fatigue and from lack of sleep, that we flung ourselves headlong on the sand, and dozed off. I was wearing thin, white, cotton clothes, and was soon awakened by the cold night-air. Then we walked again, till the limit of our endurance was reached. We slept once more on a dune. My stiff-topped boots, reaching to my knees, made progress difficult. I was on the point of throwing them away several times; but fortunately I did not do so.

After another halt we walked on for five hours more, that is, from four to nine in the morning. This was on May 2. Then one hour's rest again, and one and a half hour's slow march. The sun was blazing. All became black before our eyes as we sank down on the sand. Kasim dug out, from a northerly slope, sand which was still cold from the night. I stripped and laid myself down in it, while Kasim shovelled sand over me up to my neck. He did the same for himself. Our heads were quite close to each other, and we shaded ourselves from the sun by hanging our clothes on the spade, which we had stuck in the ground.

All day long we lay like this, speaking not a word, and not getting a wink of sleep. The turquoise-blue sky arched over us, and the yellow sea of the desert extended around us, stretching to the horizon.

When the ball of the sun again rested on the ridge of a dune in the west, we got up, shook off the sand, dressed, and dragged ourselves slowly with innumerable interruptions, towards the east, until one o'clock in the morning.

The sand-bath, although cooling and pleasant during the heat of the day, was also weakening. Our strength was ebbing. We could not cover as much ground as the night before. Thirst did not torment us, as it had done during the first days; for the mouth-cavity had become as dry as the outside skin, and the craving was dulled. An increasing feebleness set in instead. The functioning of all the glands was reduced. Our blood got thicker, and flowed through the capillaries with increasing sluggishness. Sooner or later this process of drying-up would reach its climax in death.

From one o'clock until half-past four in the morning, on May 3, we lay inanimate; and not even the cold night-air could rouse us to go on. But at dawn we dragged ourselves forward again. We would take a couple of steps intermittently. We managed to get down the sandy slopes fairly well; but climbing the waves of sand was heavy work.

At sunrise, Kasim caught me by the shoulder, stared, and pointed east, without saying a word.

'What is it?' I whispered.

'A tamarisk,' he gasped.

A sign of vegetation at last! God be praised! Our hopes, which had been close to extinction, flamed up once more. We walked, dragged ourselves, and staggered for three hours, before we reached that first bush—an olive branch intimating that the sea of the desert had a shore. We thanked God for this blessed gift, as we chewed the bitter green needles of the tamarisk. Like a water-lily the bush stood on its wave of sand, basking in the sun. But how far below was the water that nourished its roots?

About ten o'clock, we found another tamarisk; and we saw several more in the east. But our strength was gone. We undressed, buried ourselves in the sand, and hung our clothes on the branches of the tamarisk to make shade.

We lay in silence for nine hours. The hot desert-air dried our faces into parchment. At seven o'clock, we dressed and continued onward. We went more slowly than ever. After three hours' walk in the dark, Kasim stopped short, and whispered: 'Poplars!'

Between two dunes there appeared three poplars, standing close together. We sank down at their base, exhausted with fatigue. Their roots, too, must derive nourishment from below. We took hold of the spade, intending to dig a well; but the spade slipped from our hands. We had no strength left. We lay down and scratched the ground with our nails, but gave up the attempt as useless.

Instead, we tore off the fresh leaves and rubbed them into our skins. Then we collected dry, fallen twigs, and made a fire on the nearest crest as a signal to Islam, should he prove to be still alive, which I very much doubted. The fire might also, perhaps, attract the attention of a shepherd in the woods along the Khotan-daria. But even if a shepherd should see this fire in an area of deathly silence, he was more likely to become frightened and believe it was the desert-spirit who haunted the place and practised witchcraft. For fully two hours we kept the fire going, regarding it as a companion, a friend, and a chance of rescue. Nowadays, those who are shipwrecked at sea have other means of sending out their SOS in moments of extreme danger. We had only this fire; and our eyes were glued to its flames.

The night was coming to an end; and the sun, our worst enemy, would soon rise again above the dunes on the eastern horizon, to torment us anew. At four on the morning of May 4 we started off, stumbling along for five hours. Then our strength gave out. Our hope was again on the decline. In the east there were no more poplars, no more tamarisks, to stimulate our dying vitality with their verdure. Only mounds of sand, as far as the eye could reach.

We collapsed on the slope of a dune. Kasim's ability to dig out cold sand for me was gone. I had to help myself as best I could. For fully ten hours we lay silent in the sand. It was strange that we were still alive. Would we have strength enough to drag ourselves through one more night—our last one?

I rose at twilight and urged Kasim to come. Hardly audible was his gasp: 'I can't go on.' And so I left the last remnant of the caravan behind and continued on alone. I dragged myself along, and fell. I crawled up slopes, and staggered down the other side. I lay quiet for long periods, listening.

Not a sound! The stars shone like electric torches. I wondered whether I was still on earth, or whether this was the valley of the shadow of death. I lit my last cigarette. Kasim had always received the butts; but now I was alone, and so I smoked this one to the end. It afforded me a little relief and distraction.

Six hours had passed since the beginning of my solitary journey, when, totally overcome with feebleness, I sank down by a new tamarisk, and went off into the doze which I feared, for death might come while I was asleep. As a matter of fact, I hardly slept at all. All the time, in the grave-like silence, I heard the beating of my heart and the ticking of the chronometers. And after a couple of hours I heard the swish of steps in the sand, and saw a phantom stagger and struggle to my side.

'Is that you, Kasim?' I whispered.

'Yes, sir.'

'Come! We have not far to go!'

Heartened by our reunion, we struggled on. We slid down the dunes; we struggled upwards. We would lie motionless where we fell, in our battle against the insidious desire for sleep. We slackened our pace, and grew more and more indolent. We were like sleep-walkers; but still we fought for our lives.

Suddenly Kasim grabbed my arm and pointed downwards at the sand. There were distinct tracks of human beings!

In a twinkling we were wide awake. It was plain that the river *must* be near! It was possible that some shepherds had noticed our fire and had come to investigate. Or maybe a sheep, astray in the desert, had been searched for by these men who had so recently passed over the sand.

Kasim bent down, examined the prints, and gasped:

'It is our own trail!'

In our listless, somnolent state, we had described a circle without knowing it. That was enough for a while; we could not endure any more. We collapsed on the trail and fell asleep. It was half-past two in the morning.

When the new day dawned, on May 5, we rose heavily, and with difficulty. Kasim looked terrible. His tongue was white and swollen, his lips blue, his cheeks were hollow, and his eyes had a dying glassy lustre. He was tortured by a kind of death-hiccup, which shook his whole frame. When the body is so completely dried up that the joints almost creak, every movement is an effort.

It grew lighter. The sun rose. From the top of a dune, where nothing obstructed the view towards the east, we noticed that the horizon, which for two weeks had revealed a row of yellow saw-teeth, now disclosed an absolutely even, dark-green line. We stopped short, as though petrified,

88

and exclaimed simultaneously: 'The forest!' And I added: 'The Khotan-daria! Water!'

Again we collected what little strength we had left and struggled along eastward. The dunes grew lower, we passed a depression in the ground at the bottom of which we tried to dig; but we were still too weak. We went on. The dark-green line grew, the dunes diminished, stopped altogether, and were replaced by level soft ground. We were but a few hundred yards from the forest. At half-past five we reached the first poplars, and wearied, sank down in their shade. We enjoyed the fragrance of the forest. We saw flowers growing between the trees, and heard the birds sing and the flies and gadflies hum. At seven o'clock we continued. The forest grew thinner. We came upon a path, showing traces of men, sheep, and horses, and we thought it might lead to the river. After following it for two hours, we collapsed in the shade of a poplar grove.

We were too weak to move. Kasim lay on his back. He looked as if he were going to die. The river *must* be quite near. But we were as if nailed down. A tropical heat surrounded us. Would the day never come to an end? Every hour that passed brought us closer to certain death. We would have to drag ourselves on to the river before it got too late! But the sun did not go down. We breathed heavily and with effort. The will to live was about to desert us.

At seven p.m. I was able to get up. . . . Again I urged Kasim to accom-pany me to the river to drink. He signalled with his hand that he could not rise, and he whispered that he would soon die under the poplars.

Alone I pulled myself along through the forest. Thickets of thorny bushes, and dry fallen branches obstructed my way. I tore my thin clothes and scratched my hands; but gradually I worked my way through. I rested frequently, crawled part of the way on all-fours, and noticed with anxiety how the darkness grew denser in the woods. Finally the new night came— the last one. I could not have survived another day.

The forest ended abruptly, as though burnt by a fire. I found myself on the edge of a six-foot-high terrace, which descended almost perpendicu-larly to an absolutely even plain, devoid of vegetation. The ground was packed hard. A withered leafless twig was sticking out of it. I saw that it was a piece of drift-wood, and that I was in the river-bed of the Khotan-daria. And it was dry, as dry as the sandy desert behind me! Was I to die of thirst in the very bed of the river, after having fought my way so suc-cessfully to its bank? No! I was not going to lie down and die without first crossing the Khotan-daria and assuring myself that the whole bed was dry, and that all hope was irretrievably gone. . . .

Like the beds of all desert-rivers in Central Asia, that of the

Khotan-daria is very wide, flat, and shallow. A light haze floated over the desolate landscape. I had gone about one mile when the outlines of the forest on the eastern shore appeared below the moon. Dense thickets of bushes and reeds grew on the terraced shore. A fallen poplar stretched its dark trunk down towards the river-bed. It looked like the body of a crocodile. The bed still remained as dry as before. It was not far to the shore where I must lie down and die. My life hung on a hair.

Suddenly I started, and stopped short. A water-bird, a wild duck or goose, rose on whirring wings, and I heard a splash. The next moment, I stood on the edge of a pool, seventy feet long and fifteen feet wide! The water looked as black as ink in the moonlight. The overturned poplar-trunk was reflected in its depths.

In the silent night I thanked God for my miraculous deliverance. Had I continued eastward I should have been lost. In fact, if I had touched shore only a hundred yards north or south of the pool, I would have believed the entire river-bed to be dry. I knew that the freshets from melting snow-fields and glaciers in northern Tibet flowed down through the Khotan-daria bed only in the beginning of June, to dry up in the late summer and autumn, leaving the bed dry during the winter and spring. I had also heard that in certain places, separated sometimes by a day's journey or more, the river forms eddies, which scoop the bed into greater depths, and that the water may remain the year round in these hollows near the terraced shore. And now I had come upon one of these extremely rare bodies of water!

I sat down calmly on the bank and felt my pulse. It was so weak that it was hardly noticeable—only forty-nine beats. Then I drank, and drank again. I drank without restraint. The water was cold, clear as crystal, and as sweet as the best spring-water. And then I drank again. My dried-up body absorbed the moisture like a sponge. All my joints softened, all my movements became easier. My skin, hard as parchment before, now became softened. My forehead grew moist. The pulse increased in strength; and after a few minutes it was fifty-six. The blood flowed more freely in my veins. I had a feeling of well-being and comfort. I drank again, and sat caressing the water in this blessed pool. Later on, I christened this pool Khoda-verdi-kol, or 'the Pool of God's Gift'. . . .

My thoughts now flew to Kasim, who lay faint from thirst on the edge of the wood on the western shore. Of the stately caravan of three weeks ago, I, a European, was the only one that had held out till the moment of rescue. If I did not waste my minutes, perhaps Kasim, too, might be saved. But in what was I to carry the water? Why, in my waterproof boots! There was, in fact, no other receptacle. I filled them to the top, suspended them at either end of the spade-handle, and carefully recrossed the river-bed. Though the moon was low, my old track was plainly visible. I reached the forest. The moon went down, and dense darkness descended among the trees. I lost my trail, and went astray among thorny bushes and thickets, which would not give under my stockinged feet. From time to time, I called 'Kasim!' at the top of my voice. But the sound died away among the tree-trunks; and I got no answer but the 'clevitt' of a frightened night-owl.

If I lost my way, perhaps I would never again find the trail and then Kasim would be lost. I stopped at an impenetrable thicket of dry branches and brush, set fire to the whole thing, and enjoyed seeing the flames lick and scorch the nearest poplars. Kasim could not be far away; he was certain both to hear and to see the fire. But he did not come. I had no choice but to await the dawn. At the foot of a poplar, out of reach of the fire, I lay down and slept for some hours. The fire protected me against any prowling wild beasts.

When dawn came the night-fire was still glowing, and a black column of smoke was rising above the forest. It was easy now to find my trail and the place where Kasim lay. He was still in the same position as the night before. Upon seeing me, he whispered: 'I am dying!' 'Will you have some water?' I asked, letting him hear the splashing sound. He sat up, dazed and staring. I handed him one of the boots. He lifted it to his lips and emptied it to the last drop. After a short pause he emptied the other one, too.

2. COMPARES HIS MOTIVES WITH THOSE OF AUREL STEIN

It would not surprise me if some of my readers were to raise the question: 'What was the good of your exposing your own life, as well as those of your men and camels, and your whole outfit to the tremendous risks of those long journeys across sandy deserts devoid of water?'

To this I should like to reply that, though the best existing maps of the interior of Asia indicated sandy deserts in the section of eastern Turkestan in question, no European had ever traversed them; and thus an investigation into the nature of this part of the earth's crust remained an unfinished task for geographical research. Nor was it beyond question that traces of ancient civilization might be discovered in the regions which had been completely buried in the drift sand. We have also seen, in a previous chapter, that those hopes of mine were finally crowned with success through my discovery of two ancient cities.

I have also mentioned my hope that these ruined cities would some time be made the subject of expert archaeological excavation and examination. In this, too, I was not disappointed, although my hopes were not realized until twelve years afterwards. It was my friend, Sir M. Aurel Stein, the famous English archaeologist, a Hungarian by birth, who, supported by the Indian Government, took upon himself this difficult but grateful task. And my old cities could hardly have fallen into better hands than his. For his achievements there, as well as in other parts of Asia, the Retzius Gold Medal of the Swedish Geographical Society was later awarded to him, on my recommendation.

Once, at the beginning of February, 1908, he boldly ventured to follow the same route along the Keriya-daria and through the desert which I have described . . . He was guided by my maps. But he made the journey in the opposite direction, from north to south. He describes it thus:

Now I knew well by experience the difficulty of steering a correct course by the compass alone in a real sea of sand devoid of all directing features. Nor could I overlook the fact that, however justified my reliance in Hedin's careful mapping was, differences in longitude deduced from mere route-traverses were bound to be considerable on such ground, and in our case all depended on the assumed longitude being right. If we failed to strike the river-end in the confused delta of dry beds which the river has formed since early periods in its death-struggles with the sands, our position was certain to be dangerous. There would be nothing to indicate whether the actual bed, in which we might hope to find at least subsoil-water by digging wells, lay to the east or west. If we continued our course to the south, there would be great risk of our water-supply getting completely exhausted, and of animals—if not of men, too—succumbing through thirst long before the line of wells and oases at the foot of the Kun-lun could be reached.

Thus his own life, as well as those of his men and his caravan animals, depended on my map. Had this been unreliable, and he been led to steer to the right or the left of the point where I had found the river-end in the sand desert, he would have been lost beyond rescue. I had, therefore, a great responsibility; and even to this day I am happy in the confidence he reposed in my map. One cannot stake more on a single card than one's own and other people's lives. He had one advantage over me, in that he knew from my account that the dunes *could* be traversed with camels and donkeys. I was in the dark about that when I ventured into the desert from the point where the river ended. . . .

The same geographical problem which had tempted me to undertake the disastrous journey in the Takla-makan Desert also prompted Stein, eighteen years later, to take the same route. . . . He chose the same starting-point as I did—the southern end of the long lake I had discovered. When, after sixteen miles, I found that the range did not continue through the desert, I changed my course to one straight east and crossed the entire desert. When Stein, after twenty-five miles, found the enterprise a too risky one, he abandoned it and returned to the lake. He says about this:

Next morning, I ascended the highest dune near our camp and, carefully scanning the horizon, saw nothing but the same expanse of formidable sand-ridges, like huge waves of an angry ocean suddenly arrested in movement. There was a strange allurement in this vista, suggesting Nature in the contortions of death. But hard as it seemed to resist the siren voices of the desert which called me onwards, I felt forced to turn northward. . . . It was as well that I took that hard decision in time; for, by the third day after, there sprung up a violent *buran* (storm). . . .

He still had eighty-five miles to go, from his turning-point, to the little mountain of Masar-tagh, on the western shore of the Khotan-daria. It was no doubt fortunate for him and his companions that he turned in time. In a similar situation I should never have made such a decision. I should have continued through the desert. It might have been the death of me and my men. I might have lost everything, as in 1895. But the adventure, the conquest of an unknown country, the struggle against the impossible, all have a fascination which draws me with irresistible force.

✵

SIR (MARK) AUREL STEIN

(1862–1943)

Hungarian-British archaeologist. He discovered the Cave of the Thousand Buddhas in the Takla Makan. This was perhaps the greatest find of early Buddhist manuscripts (many of them being the very ones Hsuan Tsang (q.v.) brought from India in the seventh century), and Stein has been criticized for removing them to the British Museum. However, many of those left behind have since been stolen or destroyed.

Ruins of Desert Cathay (London, 1912).

THE DISCOVERY (1907)

I left the Ssu-yeh behind to make the most of the favourable impression produced, and to urge an early loan of the promised manuscript specimens. But the priest had again become nervous and postponed their delivery in a vague way 'until later'. There was nothing for me but to wait.

All doubt, however, disappeared in the end. Late at night Chiang groped his way to my tent in silent elation with a bundle of Chinese rolls which Wang Tao-shih had just brought him in secret, carefully hidden under his flowing black robe, as the first of the promised 'specimens'. The rolls looked unmistakably old as regards writing and paper, and probably contained Buddhist canonical texts; but Chiang needed time to make sure of their character. Next morning he turned up by daybreak and, with a face expressing both triumph and amazement, reported that these fine rolls of paper contained Chinese versions of certain 'Sutras' from the Buddhist canon which the colophons declared to have been brought from India and translated by Hsuan-tsang himself. The strange chance which thus caused us to be met at the very outset by the name of my Chinese patron saint, and by what undoubtedly were early copies of his labours as a sacred translator, struck both of us as a most auspicious omen. Was it not 'T'ang-seng' himself, so Chiang declared, who at the opportune moment had revealed the hiding-place of that manuscript hoard to an ignorant priest in order to prepare for me, his admirer and disciple from distant India, a fitting antiquarian reward on the westernmost confines of China proper?

Of Hsuan-tsang's authorship, Wang Tao-shih in his ignorance could not possibly have had any inkling when he picked up that packet of 'specimens'. Chiang-ssu-yeh realized at once that this discovery was bound to impress the credulous priest as a special interposition on my behalf of the great traveller of sacred memory. So he hastened away to carry the news to the Tao-shih, and, backed up by this visible evidence of support from the latter's own cherished saint, to renew his pleading for free access to the hidden manuscript store. The effect was most striking. Before long Chiang returned to report that the portent could be trusted to work its spell. Some hours later he found the wall blocking the entrance to the recess of the temple removed, and on its door being opened by the priest, caught a glimpse of a room crammed full to the roof with manuscript bundles. I had purposely kept away from the Tao-shih's temple all the forenoon, but on getting this news I could no longer restrain my impatience to see the great hoard myself. The day was cloudless and hot, and the 'soldiers' who had followed me about during the morning with my cameras were now taking their siesta in sound sleep soothed by a good smoke of opium. So accompanied only by Chiang I went to the temple.

I found the priest there evidently still combating his scruples and nervous apprehensions. But under the influence of that quasi-divine hint he now summoned up courage to open before me the rough door closing the narrow entrance which led from the side of the broad front passage into the rock-carved recess, on a level of about four feet above the floor of the former. The sight of the small room disclosed was one to make my eyes open wide. Heaped up in layers, but without any order, there appeared in the dim light of the priest's little lamp a solid mass of manuscript bundles rising to a height of nearly ten feet, and filling, as subsequent measurement showed, close on 500 cubic feet. The area left clear within the room was just sufficient for two people to stand in. It was manifest that in this 'black hole' no examination of the manuscripts would be possible, and also that the digging out of all its contents would cost a good deal of physical labour.

A suggestion to clear out all the bundles into the large cella [main area] of the cave-temple, where they might have been examined at ease, would have been premature; so much oppressed at the time was Wang Tao-shih by fears of losing his position—and patrons—by the rumours which any casual observers might spread against him in the oasis. So for the present I had to rest content with his offer to take out a bundle or two at a time, and to let us look rapidly through their contents in a less cramped part of the precincts. . . .

It was clear to me from the first that the deposit of the manuscripts must have taken place some time after the middle of the ninth century. But until we could find dated records among the manuscripts themselves there was no other indication of the lower date limit than the style of the frescoes which covered the passage walls. . . . On various grounds it seemed improbable that they could be later than the period of the Sung dynasty, which immediately preceded the great Mongol conquest of the thirteenth century.

So there was evidence from the first to encourage my hopes that a search through this big hoard would reveal manuscripts of importance and interest. But the very hugeness of the deposit was bound to give rise to misgivings. Should we have time to eat our way through this mountain of ancient paper with any thoroughness? Would not the timorous priest, swayed by his worldly fears and possible spiritual scruples, be moved to close down his shell before I had been able to extract any of the pearls? There were reasons urging us to work with all possible energy and speed, and others rendering it advisable to display studied insouciance and calm assurance. Somehow we managed to meet the conflicting requirements of the situation. But, I confess, the strain and anxieties of the busy days which followed were great.

The first bundles which emerged from that 'black hole' consisted of thick rolls of paper about one foot high, evidently containing portions of canonical Buddhist texts in Chinese translations. All were in excellent preservation and yet showed in paper, arrangement, and other details, unmistakable signs of great age. . . . Mixed up with the Chinese bundles there came to light Tibetan texts also written in roll form, though with clearly marked sections, as convenience of reading required in the case of a writing running in horizontal lines, not in vertical columns like Chinese. I could not doubt that they contained portions of the great canonical collections now known as the Tanjur and Kanjur. . . .

All the manuscripts seemed to be preserved exactly in the same condition they were in when deposited. Some of the bundles were carelessly fastened with only rough cords and without an outer cloth wrapper; but even this had failed to injure the paper. Nowhere could I trace the slightest effect of moisture. And, in fact, what better place for preserving such relics could be imagined than a chamber carved in the live rock of these terribly barren hills, and hermetically shut off from what moisture, if any, the atmosphere of this desert valley ever contained? Not in the driest soil could relics of a ruined site have so completely escaped injury as they had here, in a carefully selected rock chamber where, hidden behind a brick wall and protected by accumulated drift sand, these masses of manuscripts had lain undisturbed for centuries.

How grateful I felt for the special protection thus afforded when, on opening a large packet wrapped in a sheet of stout coloured canvas, I found it full of paintings on fine gauze-like silk and on linen, ex-votos in all kinds of silk and brocade, with a mass of miscellaneous fragments of painted papers and cloth materials. Most of the paintings first found were narrow pieces from two to three feet in length, and proved by their floating streamers and the triangular tops provided with strings for fastening to have served as temple banners. These mountings made them look much more imposing when hung up. Many of them were in excellent condition, and all exactly as they had been deposited, after longer or shorter use. . . . The silk used for these pictures was almost invariably a transparent gauze of remarkable fineness. As these banners floated in the air they would allow a good deal of light to pass through—an important point, since in order to be properly seen these paintings would have to be hung up across or near the porches through which alone the cellas of the temple caves would receive their lighting. . . .

Whatever the technical advantages in the use of such a delicate material might have been, the attendant risks were evident when I came upon convolutes of silk paintings much larger in size, showing, as subsequently ascertained, dimensions up to six feet or more. Closely and often carelessly folded up at the time of their deposition, and much creased in consequence as they were, any attempt to open them out would have implied obvious risk of damage to the thin material which centuries of compression in the driest air had rendered terribly brittle. But by lifting a fold here and there I could see that the scenes represented were almost as elaborate as the fresco panels on the walls of the old grottoes. Greatly tempted as I was to search for votive inscriptions likely to contain dates, I had to leave the opening till later from fear of possible damage.

Nor was there time for any closer study, such as I should have loved to give there and then to these delicate, graceful paintings. My main care was how many of them I might hope to rescue from their dismal imprisonment and the risks attending their present guardian's careless handling. To my surprise and relief he evidently attached little value to these beautiful relics of pictorial art in the T'ang times. So I made bold to put aside rapidly 'for further inspection' the best of the pictures on silk, linen, or paper I could lay my hands on, more than a dozen from the first bundle alone. I longed to carry away all its contents; for even among the fragments there were beautiful pieces, and every bit of silk would have its antiquarian and artistic value. But it would not have been wise to display too much *empressement*. So I restrained myself as well as I could, and put the rest away, with the firm resolve to return to the charge as soon as the ground was prepared for more extensive acquisitions.

To remains of this kind the priest seemed indifferent. The secret hope of diverting by their sacrifice my attention from the precious rolls of Chinese canonical texts or 'Ching' made him now more assiduously grope for and hand out bundles of what he evidently classed under the head of miscellaneous rubbish. . . .

Flushed as I was with delight at these unhoped-for discoveries, I could not lose sight of the chief practical task, all-important for the time being. It was to keep our priest in a pliable mood, and to prevent his mind being overcome by the trepidations with which the chance of any intrusion and of consequent hostile rumours among his patrons would fill him. With the help of Chiang-ssu-yeh's genial persuasion, and what reassuring display I could make of my devotion to Buddhist lore in general and the memory of my patron saint in particular, we succeeded better than I had ventured to hope. I could see our honest Tao-shih's timorous look changing gradually to one of contentment at our appreciation of all this, to him valueless, lore. Though he visibly grew tired climbing over manuscript heaps and dragging out heavy bundles, it seemed as if he were becoming resigned to his fate, at least for a time.

When the growing darkness in the cave compelled us to stop further efforts for the day, a big bundle of properly packed manuscripts and painted fabrics lay on one side of our 'reading room' awaiting removal for what our diplomatic convention styled 'closer examination'. The great question was whether Wang Tao-shih would be willing to brave the risks of this removal, and subsequently to fall in with the true interpretation of our proceeding. It would not have done to breathe to him unholy words of sale and purchase; it was equally clear that any removal would have to be effected in strictest secrecy. So when we stepped outside the temple there was nothing in our hands or about our persons to arouse the slightest suspicion. . . .

It was late at night when I heard cautious footsteps. It was Chiang who had come to make sure that nobody was stirring about my tent. A little later he returned with a big bundle over his shoulders. It contained everything I had picked out during the day's work. The Tao-shih had summoned up courage to fall in with my wishes, on the solemn condition that nobody besides us three was to get the slightest inkling of what was being transacted, and that as long as I kept on Chinese soil the origin of these 'finds' was not to be revealed to any living being. He himself was afraid of being seen at night outside his temple precincts. So the Ssu-yeh, zealous and energetic as always, took it upon himself to be the sole carrier. For seven nights more he thus came to my tent, when everybody had gone to sleep, with the same precautions, his slight figure panting under loads which grew each time heavier, and ultimately required carriage by instalments. For hands accustomed only to wield pen and paper it was a trying task, and never shall I forget the good-natured ease and cheerful devotion with which it was performed by that most willing of helpmates. . . .

But my time for feeling true relief came when all the twenty-four cases, heavy with manuscript treasures rescued from that strange place of hiding, and the five more filled with paintings and other art relics from the same cave, had been deposited safely in the British Museum.

✿

ADMIRAL BORIS ANDREYEVICH VILKITSKIY

(1885–1961)

Russian admiral. While his father was hydrographer of the Imperial Russian Navy (1901–13) he was put in command of an expedition which made the last major discoveries, off Siberia, of land within the Arctic Circle. During 1914–15 he made the first east–west traverse of the North-East Passage. After the Revolution he emigrated to the West.

L. M. Starokadomskiy, *Charting the Russian Northern Sea Route*, trans. and ed. W. Barr (Montreal, 1976).

1. DEPARTURE (1914)

Taymyr lay at the mouth of the Anadyr until 12 August, waiting for a reply from the Chief Hydrographic Directorate to the telegram we had sent. Finally a reply was received. We were ordered to continue our mission. Farewell telegrams arrived simultaneously from the Naval Minister and from the head of the Chief Hydrographic Directorate.

Some of the officers and men received this order with sore hearts; their dreams of heroic war feats were postponed, or even became totally unattainable. But many members of the expedition were delighted at the possibility of continuing the through passage, fraught with difficulties as it was, and of finally reaching the goal we had been set. They consoled themselves with the fact that the war would not end quickly, and that in any case they too would be able to take part in war activities. The future would show that they were not mistaken: on our arrival in Arkangel many members of the expedition took part in war operations with the ships of the Russian Fleet, or fought in military units ashore. . . .

Somebody among the officers presented a request to the leader of the expedition that we should call at Nome once more, in order to get the latest news on the course of the hostilities; we were, of course, faced with the prospect of being away from land for a long time. However, the majority of the members of the expedition considered that it was better to head out into the Arctic Ocean not knowing what was happening, rather than possibly to receive bad news. Strange as it may seem, this second point of view prevailed. We sailed out into the ocean, and thus found out nothing further about the war.

2. ARRIVAL IN ARKANGEL (1915)

The through passage was completed. For the first time in history sea-going ships had traversed the Northern Sea Route from Bering Strait to the White Sea. The expedition had closed the circle around Europe and Asia, which we had begun surveying in 1909. Here is how the local newspaper, *Severnoe Utro*, described the welcome:

It is a dull, northern day. Since morning it has been drizzling rain, but even by 10 o'clock the wharf near Sobornoy quay had begun to fill up with people. The Arkangel anchorage, despite the fact that it is autumn, somehow looks festive: the

mass of sailing ships and steamers have been dressed overall with flags since
morning. . . . *Taymyr* is the first to come alongside the quay, followed by *Vaygach*
and *Eclipse*. A hymn rings out, played by an orchestra, and incessant cheers roll
along the ranks of people. . . .

Slowly, without any haste, *Eclipse* comes alongside *Taymyr*. Her old
captain, the famous Otto Sverdrup, in a green hat and yellow jacket, stands
calmly on deck. It is as if the old sea-dog is totally uninterested in all this
worldly excitement. The crew go about their duties confidently, without
hurrying. This picture somehow conveys something of the northern sailor's
spirit quite clearly. With joyfully ringing barks the polar dogs come pouring on deck; like their masters, they have not seen a noisy city for one-and-
a-half years. Among these four-footed friends is one who has almost travelled
right round the world, having been with Amundsen at the South Pole.

✻

ROALD AMUNDSEN

(1872–1928)

*Norwegian explorer. The first man to the South Pole was also the second to
navigate the North-East Passage from west to east, setting out in July 1918.*

My Life as an Explorer (London, 1927).

1. ENCOUNTER WITH A POLAR BEAR (1918)

We made the lee of the islets and tied up to the land ice two hundred
yards from the beach. We named this rather uncertain haven Maud Harbour, and in spite of its unfavourable first aspect, it sheltered us safely for
a year. . . .

The searching Arctic winds are the greatest handicap to comfort in winter
quarters, so our next enterprise was to shovel snow against the sides of the
Maud until we had piled up a snowbank all around her nearly to the deck
level and sloping steeply downward to the level of the ice. For convenience
we made a gangplank at an easier grade, in such a manner as to make a
runway leading from the ice up to the deck of the *Maud* at the point nearest
to the door to the cabin. One side of this runway was provided with a rope
hand rail to which, in slippery weather, one could cling to keep from falling.

One of the dogs was a female who was expecting shortly to have a litter. She was very fond of me, and every morning when I came out of the cabin she would come running to me to be petted. I would pick her up in my arms and carry her down the runway to the ice so that she could accompany me on the morning walk which I took to keep in good condition. One morning, when I had got her in my arms and was just about to start down the runway, Jacob, the watchdog of the *Maud*, came running toward me and bumped against me so that my feet went out from under me and I plunged headlong down the steep slope at the side of the runway, landing on my right shoulder with the weight of my whole body on top of it. For a few moments I saw stars. When I came to, I managed to sit up on the ice, but found that my shoulder was giving me excruciating pain. I had no doubt it was a bad fracture, as X-rays three years later proved was the case. I succeeded in climbing aboard again and into my cabin. Here Wisting, who had studied first aid at a hospital in Oslo, did his best to get the fracture set. The pain was so intense and the swelling so bad that neither he nor I could tell at the time whether he had succeeded. I was so entirely knocked out by the shock that I kept my bed for eight days. Then I got Wisting to put my arm in a sling and started going about again. But my bad luck was not yet through with me.

On 8 November I came up on deck so early in the morning that it was still almost as dark as night. A fog added to the gloom. Jacob, the watchdog, came running to me, and after leaping about me in demonstrative fashion for some moments, dashed down the runway and disappeared off on the ice. I did not venture to follow him for fear of another fall, so made my way down the gangway and proceeded alongside the ship, watching carefully to avoid the ice and snow pieces that littered this passage. I had stood below the bow for only a moment when I heard a faint sound so odd that I pricked up my ears to listen better. It seemed like the first faint soughing of the wind in the rigging when a breeze springs up. In a moment it grew louder and was clearly the sound of heavy breathing. Straining my eyes in the direction from which it came, I finally discerned Jacob headed for the ship at the best pace he could muster, and the next instant I saw behind him the huge form of a Polar bear in hot pursuit. It was the breathing of this bear approaching rapidly that I had heard.

Instantly I realized the situation. This was a mother bear with her cub. Jacob had found them and teased the cub. The mother's fury had quickly decided Jacob that he had urgent business on board the ship. The situation had its humorous side, but I did not pause to enjoy that, because I saw it also had its dangers for me. When the bear saw me she sat down and gazed at me. I certainly did the same at her. However, I think our feelings were different. We were both at about the same distance from the gangway. What should I do? I was alone—no assistance—only one arm—the left. Well, I had not much choice. I started to run as quickly as possible for the gangplank, but the bear did the same thing. Now started a race between a healthy, furious bear and an invalid. Not much chance for the latter. As soon as I reached the gangway and turned to run on board, the bear stretched me to the ground with a well-aimed blow on my back. I fell on my broken arm—face down—and expected to be finished right away. But no—my lucky star had not stopped shining yet. Jacob, who had been on board all this time, took suddenly into his head to return—probably to play with the cub. In doing so, he had to pass where mother bear was busy with me. When she saw Jacob passing, she jumped high in the air and left me for Jacob. It did not take me long to get up and disappear into safety. It was one of the narrowest escapes of my life.

2. ESKIMOS JOIN THE CREW

As the winter wore on, the men in this settlement became greatly attached to us and we to them. When the spring thaw should come, our first concern would be, of course, to get the *Maud* back to Seattle for repairs. Pondering upon the necessity of working the ship through the ice under sail, I decided that it would be wise to add to our crew. I therefore asked five of the men if they would be willing to accompany us when we made our start. Their reply touched me to the heart. 'Anywhere you go, we will go with you; anything you ask us to do, we will do—except, if you asked us to commit suicide, we would ask you to repeat your question.' I joyfully took them at their word, and they remained with us for a year as most useful men and loyal helpers.

No task was too heavy or hours too long for them. They were calm and cheerful in every situation. But when we reached Seattle, the noise of the city nearly drove two of them insane, and they could not rest until they were free to return on a northbound steamer which would set them down on the Siberian mainland, whence they could make their way overland to their home.

Alexandra David-Neel

(1868–1969)

*French scholar and explorer. A student of Oriental Buddhism, she made
five expeditions into Tibet and became a lama in her own right. She was
the first European woman to enter Lhasa (in 1924).*

My Journey to Lhasa (London, 1927).

Entering the Forbidden City (1924)

At last, after four months of tramping, filled with adventures and observations of which I have been able to relate but a very small part, I left
Dechen one morning at dawn, and set out upon the last stage to Lhasa.
The weather was clear, dry, and cold, the sky luminous. In the rosy light
of the rising sun, we sighted the Potala, the huge palace of the lamaist
ruler, still far away, yet already majestic and impressive.

'This time we have won,' I said to my young friend.

He silenced me.

'Hush! Do not speak too soon! Do not rejoice yet. We have still to cross
the river Kyi. Who knows if there is not a post of watchmen there?' . . .

Arrived at the river, which in the winter is but a narrow stream, we
embarked on a rustic ferry adorned with the head of an animal, which the
artist probably intended to be a horse. A mixed crowd of men and beasts
was packed on the boat. A few minutes later we landed on the opposite
bank. Neither the busy ferrymen nor any of the passengers had given us
so much as a glance. Hundreds of ragged pilgrims cross the Kyi chu each
year, and nothing distinguished us from our fellow *arjopas*.

We were now in Lhasa territory, but still far from the city itself. Yongden
once more repressed my desire to rejoice, even in a whisper. What could
he still fear? Had we not reached our goal? And now, nature itself gave us
a token of her maternal complicity. . . . No sooner had we landed than the
air, till then so calm, became agitated. All of a sudden a furious storm
arose, lifting clouds of dust high into the sky. I have seen the simoon in
the Sahara, but was it worse than this? No doubt it was. Yet, that terrible,
dry lashing rain of dust gave me the impression of being once more in the
great desert. Indistinct forms passed us, men bent in two, hiding their
faces in the laps of their dresses, or whatever piece of cloth they might
happen to have with them.

Who could see us coming? Who could know us? An immense yellow curtain of whirling sand was spread before the Potala, blinding its guests, hiding from them Lhasa, the roads leading to it, and those who walked upon them. I interpreted it as a symbol promising me complete security, and the future justified my interpretation. For two months I was to wander freely in the lamaist Rome, with none to suspect that, for the first time in history, a foreign woman was beholding the Forbidden City. . . .

At that time of the year, a large number of people from all the provinces of Tibet congregate in the capital to enjoy the various festivals and merry-makings, which take place there. The inns are full. All those who can vacate a room or any shelter rent them. Travellers sleep in the stables and camp in the courtyards. I could have gone from door to door for hours, in quest of a lodging, without any other result than showing myself to a number of householders of both sexes and being compelled to answer a lot of questions. Fortunately, I was spared the trouble and danger of this. The storm abated as suddenly as it had arisen. Newcomers, unacquainted with the city, we stood a little at a loss amid the crowd without knowing where to go. Unexpected help came again to me in the shape of a young woman.

'You want a room, Mother?' she said. 'You come from very far. You must be exceedingly tired. Follow me. I know a place where you will be all right.'

I only smiled at her, uttering thanks. I felt rather astonished. Obliging people are many in Tibet, and the kindness of the unknown woman was not altogether extraordinary, but how did she know that 'I had come from very far'? This puzzled me a little, but no doubt she had gained that idea from the sight of my pilgrim staff, and I was lean enough, after so many fasts and so much fatigue, to inspire compassion.

Our guide was not communicative. We followed her like sheep, a little bewildered by the noise and the traffic after months spent in the solitudes, and perhaps still more bewildered by our good luck. She led us outside the town to a place from which one enjoyed an extended view of most beautiful scenery, including the Potala. This detail struck me particularly; for all along the road I had wanted to get a lodging from which I could see it.

I was granted the use of a narrow cell, in a ramshackle cottage occupied by beggarly people. This was indeed the best hostelry one could have wished for the security of my incognito. The idea of looking there for a foreign lady traveller would not have occurred to anybody; and the poor beggars who frequented the place never suspected my identity. The woman went away smiling after a brief farewell. All had happened so quickly that it seemed a dream. We never saw our guide again.

In our hovel that evening, lying on the ground amongst our miserable luggage, I said to my faithful companion: 'Do you allow me now to say that we have won the game?'

'Yes,' he said, and he shouted in a suppressed, yet most triumphant tone: '*Lha gyalo. De tamche pam!* We are at Lhasa!'

I was in Lhasa. No doubt I could be proud of my victory, but the struggle, with cunning and trickery as weapons, was not yet over. I was in Lhasa, and now the problem was to stay there. Although I had endeavoured to reach the Tibetan capital rather because I had been challenged than out of any real desire to visit it, now that I stood on the forbidden ground at the cost of so much hardship and danger, I meant to enjoy myself in all possible ways. I should really have felt ashamed of myself had I been caught, locked up somewhere, and taken back to the border, having only had a superficial and brief glance at the exterior of the palaces and temples. This should not be! No! I would climb to the top of the Potala itself; I would visit the most famous shrines, the large historical monasteries in the vicinity of Lhasa, and I would witness the religious ceremonies, the races, and the pageants of the New Year festival. All sights, all things which are Lhasa's own beauty and peculiarity, would have to be seen by the lone woman explorer who had had the nerve to come to them from afar, the first of her sex. It was my well-won reward after the trials on the road and the vexations by which for several years various officials had endeavoured to prevent my wanderings in Tibet. This time I intended that nobody should deprive me of it.

✿

FRANK KINGDON-WARD

(1885–1958)

British botanist. One of the great plant collectors, he made important discoveries, such as establishing the source of the Irrawaddy, while botanizing.

Explorers All, ed. Sir P. Sykes (London, 1939).

A JOURNEY THROUGH THE TSANGPO GORGE (1926)

The name of Tibet is instinct with the spirit of the land, a spirit aloof and mysterious, brooding over the vast, white roof-top of the world in an icy silence broken by the blare of trumpets or the heavy throbbing of drums from some dim temple, or the crash of mighty waters as the lost rivers break their way through the greatest mountain range in the world to the unseen sea.

There are two Tibets. There is the Chang Tang, the plateau country, including the lake region and the upper courses of the great rivers, and there is the little-known, or unknown, gorge country, seamed by the middle courses of these rivers, where they change direction to the south and force the barrier-ranges on their way to India and China. . . . Tibet possesses the largest unexplored areas in the world and one of the richest mountain floras; and it was to collect and bring to England specimens and seeds of Tibetan plants, as well as to add to geographers' knowledge of the country, that I set out from Bengal, accompanied by Lord Cawdor, on a journey to the Gorge of the Tsangpo itself.

We expected to be lost to civilization for a year, and in addition to our tents, equipment, scientific instruments, and personal belongings, we had to take with us all our money in silver rupees. We travelled via Sikkim, and in Gangtok received our passports for Tibet, which had been specially obtained for us direct from Lhasa. For two days we rode our ponies through the wonderland of the Sikkim forest, and then crossed the Nathu La (14,500 feet) and entered Tibet. Leaving Yatung, we began the sharp ascent to the Tibetan plateau. The valley of the Ammo Chu was as pleasant as England in May. Steep grass-slopes glowed honey-yellow in the mild sunshine, or glimmered with the lilac shadow of *Primula denticulata*. Barberry bushes shone red as Chinese lacquer against the turquoise sky, and silver tails of willows glistened on the half-fledged twigs. But when we entered the rhododendron-juniper forest bleak winter shut us in like night, nor did we see again the face of spring till we reached the Tsangpo a month later. . . .

In the Tsangpo valley the villagers plant crab, walnut and peach trees, and the terraces were covered with a thick scrub of rose, potentilla and cotoneaster. These were occasional birch trees.

We usually marched from ten to four, with a midday luncheon halt. As we had to cut our baggage to a minimum, we lived on the country as much as possible, buying eggs and chickens, yak milk, yak or goat meat, and *tsamba*—roast barley flour. We carried a small supply of tinned foods, and such provisions as cocoa, chocolate, coffee, and Quaker Oats. Birthdays, special achievements, or chance meetings were celebrated by breaking into our small store of luxuries.

We crossed the Lung La, lifted heavenward between two snow peaks, and, in driving snow and gathering darkness . . . we came to the monastery of Chokorchye. Sitting by a huge charcoal fire and drinking buttered tea, one degree less hot than the charcoal, we forgot the storm. Next day we pushed on to Tsegyu, and by night reached Gyatsa Dzong. . . . Beyond this the river looked to be twisted sharply, but it did not change its character. It still wound slowly along—like our transport! We had a dozen girls carrying the overflow of bundles which were not strapped on our oxen or little stubborn ponies. Round Gyantse the ladies stretch their hair over frames of wood and wire, projecting some eight inches at the sides and decorated with coloured beads. Our female porters were small and very strong in build, and, to enhance their attractions (we thought unsuccessfully), they covered their faces with black varnish—in contrast to the shades affected by Western womanhood.

We came to the village of Trungsasho, birthplace of the then Dalai Lama, and here we met his sister, taking her ponies to water. She still lived her old life as a peasant, unaltered by the knowledge that her brother was ruler of all Tibet and venerated by millions of believers in other lands. . . .

Transport troubles increased. According to the custom of the country, we had to change transport at each village; and when the villages lie close together, you are lucky if you change only four times in the day. Ponies were badly broken and often bolted, strewing the track with the wreckage of packing-cases and boxes which contained our worldly all. However, we were near Tsela Dzong, where we planned to make our first halt. Firewood and pine torches were plentiful—and local provisions also. We saw peas and beans occasionally—a great luxury—and we could always procure small and strong-flavoured onions. The main fruit crops are walnuts and peaches. The peaches are sun-dried on the roofs of the houses—and that, as Cawdor said, is 'a sound investment, for, sucked conscientiously, a sun-dried peach lasts a long time'. . . .

Soon after our arrival at Tsela, we called on the *Dzongpon*, but found his manager, with whom we exchanged presents and arranged for the delivery of our mails. His Tibetan mastiffs almost broke their chains in a dutiful attempt to accomplish our deaths. Luckily the chains stood the strain. Besides these mastiffs they breed a Tibetan poodle, which is something like a Pekingese, but longer in the leg and shorter-coated. He is black, and may have a small, white patch on the chest. There are pariahs here, as everywhere in Asia, and—a feature often found in hill countries—many of them are wall-eyed.

Tibetans are not, by English standards, 'kind to animals', in the sense that they do not make a cult of them; but they are not unkind. Simply they live hard lives themselves, and expect their animals to follow their example and take stoically what comes next. We saw here nothing of the 'Oriental

107

cruelty' of which one hears so much in the West. We did see one criminal, a thief who was condemned to wear leg-irons for life, and passed on from *dzong* to *dzong* as a Horrible Warning. He was clanking cheerfully about his work when we saw him.

We now decided to leave Tsela Dzong, and make our permanent base at Tumbatse, in the upper valley of the Rong Chu. We went down the Tsangpo in skin boats to Luding, and then up the Temo Valley till we saw above us Temo Gompa, raised heavenward on a hill between two racing streams. So in the golden evening we rode through the narrow street, past silent, quiet-moving Lamas, and were made welcome at the guest house.

The *Depa* of Temo was a young man, 'easy to look at' as the Americans say, with native courtesy and a cosmopolitan urbanity. He had visited India, and said that he had learned of many of the material benefits of Western civilization. He had certainly learned of one, for he had brought back an awe-inspiring collection of firearms. He dressed in Chinese style: jacket of imperial yellow silk, black plush boots, and a hat with a scarlet mandarin tassel.

We constituted Temo our rationing base for the season. After leaving Tsetang we made the horrible discovery that we had forgotten the curry powder—a serious matter in a country where cooking does not rank as one of the arts, and raw materials are sometimes questionable. However, we summoned up our courage, and sampled the *masala* which they make in Kongbo of dried fruits and chips of bark and wood and seeds, pounded in a mortar with a stone. We found it excellent.

In early June we left Temo Gompa and crossed the Temo La. We were now on the range which runs northward to the Nambu La, and divides the Gyamda River to the west from the Rong Chu. I climbed the peak opposite Tumbatse, 16,008 feet. The night was bitter and the dawn mist-blinded, but in the last precious hour of evening I saw one of those sights which never quite leave one throughout life—the setting sun firing the great snowbergs of the Salween Divide.

Beyond the Temo La we reached the rhododendron moorland, which was later awash with the sea-foam flowers of an aromatic-leafed 'Anthopogon' and the pinks and purples of other dwarf alpine rhododendrons. By mid-June three alpine poppies flowered. One was the lovely azure *Meconopsis simplicifolia*—the true colour, as originally shown in the *Botanical Magazine*. Later a dingy violet form, said to be perennial, reached England. Not till Major F. R. Bailey sent home in 1913 seed of a rich blue form, collected in the Eastern Himalaya, did we recover the true *M. simplicifolia*, under the name of Bailey's variety. Ours from the Temo La was a fragrant form; but this must not be confused with *Meconopsis Baileyi*, which I brought back and which has done very well in English parks and gardens.

Other lovely poppies from this region were *M. impedita*, with small gold and violet silken flowers, twenty or more to a cluster, and a beautiful yellow-flowered species covered with silky, honey-coloured hairs. This aspiring plant grew only between 15,000 and 17,000 feet. I collected a very fine barberry with jet black stems and coral fruits. In the autumn its flame-red and old gold foliage is very beautiful. . . .

In June the open boggy places are flushed with the rose of *Primula tibetica*; in September its small capsules fill with gold-dust seed. Edging a stream I found a lovely 'Sibirica' iris, violet coloured, with a cobweb of gold spun over the falls. We returned to Tumbatse at the beginning of July, and there I collected . . . another plant which has taken kindly to English gardens (especially when wet and shady)—the giant cowslip, *Primula Florindae*. When conditions suit it this plant sends up flower-stalks four feet high, bearing a hundred flowers in a cluster. . . .

Rope bridges supply one of the more doubtful joys of a traveller's life in the gorge country. They are of various types. A common one hereabouts consists of two cables of twisted bamboo, some five inches thick. These are tied to trees above the river on either bank, and on them rides a yoke-shaped wooden carrier with a two-foot span, notched on each side to hold the safety-rope in place. The ordinary mortal attaches himself to this carrier, with his arms free for hauling, and courageously but ungracefully pulls himself across. Superior persons (we, thank heaven, were superior persons) are literally tied hand and foot to two carriers, and pulled across by slow jerks which shake every tooth in the head and rack every nerve in the body. . . .

There was trouble at Drukla, which had formerly been an important monastery housing eight hundred monks. Wars with the Pobas and the Chinese had wasted the neighbourhood, and the strength of Drukla dwindled to one hundred and thirty. Now the enemy within the gates—the very old enemy of man—had been active; sixty monks had been discovered in the error of their ways, and the Commissioner had ordered immediate expulsion. This would leave the monastery a mere shell. We felt sympathy for the *Labrang Lama*, but, on looking at the sixty delinquents, we also felt sympathy for the world without, upon which they were suddenly to be released in force.

At Napo Dzong we were guests in the house of a magnate of the first water. The windows of the room where we supped were fitted with glass, protected without by wire netting and embellished within by curtains. The paved yard was bright with flowers like an English cottage garden—stocks, asters, hollyhocks. The *Dzongpon* had visited Calcutta and returned with a tin of Sutton's seeds, which provided all this display. The apartments allotted to us were furnished in the Chinese style, with chairs, tables, and a carved and curtained bedstead fit for an Empress. There was also a painted prayer-drum in a pagoda. . . .

We sent home seeds of 250 species, many travelling in thermos flasks for protection against the violent changes of temperature through which they had to pass.

At Pe we saw three Lopas, the Tibetan name for the most savage of the Assam jungle tribes. These dwarfs had small animal eyes, bulging fore-heads, and projecting muzzles which called to mind the Neanderthal man. They are evidently the people we call Abors. They were unfriendly, spoke no Tibetan, and wore next to no clothes; but they carried 80-lb loads over tracks that would kill a white man, and crossed the Doshong La almost naked in deep snow, and in the teeth of the awful interstellar wind which eternally scours the Tibetan uplands.

The *Depa* at Pe gave an entertainment for us, and by the smoky light of burning pine-chips we watched a Tibetan dance, stamped out to the accompaniment of a weird and wonderful song, without tune or rhythm. After this a *Monba*, a tall, good-looking fellow, sang one of the slow, sad songs of his own jungle. Even the Pobas gave a 'turn', though they were very drunk by that time. . . .

Some time after this we saw the sun glitter on the snow peaks of the Trans-Himalayan range, the first of the three great barriers which still separated us from India. We pressed on now, making short marches and short halts. At Tating we had the exciting experience of losing the trail (and ourselves) for two hours, on a 15,000-foot plateau, during a winter's night. And at Dengshu I myself was ill and passed into a strange stupor, in which my mind was active, but my body nearly unconscious. I was glad that it lasted only for a day.

When we reached Tsona we were worn out, bloodshot, and frost-bitten—and here we met further transport difficulty. However, on 9 January transport of a sort was found for us, and we reached the Po La, in Monyul, and stood at last upon the third barrier. Behind us the plateau lay, dead and shrouded. No sound of bird or beast, no crack of twig or stir of leaf, could be heard, only the eternal fierce call of the wind in that unearthly empti-ness. Below us, dark and full of promise, the forest began—the forest full of life and loveliness, through which our road lay to the flowery plains of Hindustan.

BERTRAM THOMAS

(1892–1950)

English explorer. He made the first crossing of the Empty Quarter, the Rub'al-Khali, in 1930–1, much to the annoyance of Harry St John Philby, who had for some time been planning to be the first to do so. Philby later made a much more arduous crossing.

Arabia Felix (London, 1938).

1. CAMEL AND OTHER TRACKS IN THE DESERT (1931)

As we went we crossed many recent camel tracks which showed Farajja to be a popular water-hole. The grouped tracks of four camels walking in line arrested my companion's attention, and he turned to me and asked me in play which camel I saw in the sands to be best. I pointed—pardonably, I persuaded myself—to the wrong one. 'There,' he said, 'do you see that cuffing up of the toes? It is a good sign: but not that skidding' (pointing to mine) 'between the footmarks.' 'That', he said of the third, 'is an animal that has recently been in the steppe. Do you see the rugged impressions of her feet? Camels that have long been in the sands leave smooth impressions, and that' (pointing to the fourth) 'is her baby. Your camel is big with young—see the deep impressions of her small hind feet.' And thus and thus. It was not the least important part of Hamad's lore—a lore shared by nearly every dweller of the sands in varying degree—to read the condition of the strange camel, as yet unseen, from her marks, and hence to know whether to flee or to pursue.

Tracking in Arabia is an exact science, beside which the finger-print methods of the West are limited in scope, for the sands are a perfect medium. . . .

And now, six months later, in the centre of Rub'al Khali I was enjoying serener moments studying the tracks of the smaller animals. To a Badu, their simple story is immediately intelligible. For a European they have another appeal, the charm of graceful line or subtle invention; the sweep of drooping *gasis* in the wind makes a tiny picture of the prayer-ring the Badu sweeps with his cane towards the setting sun; the straight stride of birds' claws spaced one immediately before the other, a contrast with the earthy meanderings of some small quadruped; the neat little rosette pattern of a rat leads to a thicket, where you will find its tiny hole, a heap of newly turned red sand at the entrance; the crooked but beautiful intricacies of a lizard like a miniature arabesque lead to a sprig of herbage where it has played maypole and rolled over in joyous repletion; that futuristic riot marks the fallen twigs bowled over and over by the whims of the wind.

2. The End of the Journey

The famous water-hole of Banaiyan lay but a day's march ahead. An hour and a half after leaving our overnight's *hadh* pastures, we breasted the red sand-hills of Khiyut al Buraidan that marked the northern border of Sanam. The wind had dropped and the pure smooth surface of the rosy sand-hills —here called Hamarur—was in refreshing contrast to the white smoking plains of the recent marches. Patches of vivid green *haram* lined the gravelly troughs in the sand-hills and our hungry camels occasionally snatched at a tuft as we passed, though without encouragement, for *haram* is a saline feed which does no good to the animal not used to it. 'Now the Manasir', said a Badu with a sweep of his arm to the eastwards, 'have little else and their camels are reared on it and grow humps like this'—here he caught the elbow of one arm held out before him, the forearm bent upwards on the palm of the other hand—a favourite gesture to indicate a large hump and therefore a thriving animal.

Rare ridges of red sand in the plain, long and low, and patches of *gadha* growing out of elephant-mask accretions of sand about their roots, formed an area called Qadha Za'aza and brought us to more rolling red hills. In the midst of these we halted over the water-hole of Banaiyan. The caravan had dragged out, as all tired caravans do. Ramadan was telling on the men, the saline pastures on the camels, and the long marches and cold north wind on both. Hamad and I were the first arrivals.

'Drink, Sahib,' he said, 'the water of Banaiyan is good.'

Hamad, even had it not been the fast month, would himself have forborne. It was their code after a thirsty day's march that when we arrived at a water-hole no drop of water should pass the lips of the advance party until those in the rear had come up, nor would any man eat a crust with me on the march unless his companions were there to share it. If this precarious condition of life produces savagery between enemies, it breeds none the less a fine humanity among friends.

Banaiyan was a real well, stone-lined and therefore unlike the mere pits in the sand that are the water-holes of the south. As my party straggled in there was a visible change in their mood. Cheerfulness prevailed with the merry shouts and noise of spilling water that they love to make, while their

112

great thirsty brutes, with long necks stretched down to the scooped-out water trough, gurgled their fill.

The want of pastures forbade a halt in these barren, rolling hills, and the first animals to be watered were already on the march before the last had come up. I delayed to accompany the rear party. Soon we had to halt for the sunset prayer, and after that we found growing difficulty in following the tracks of our advance guard; the failing light soon made it impossible. So with Polaris before our left shoulder—as the Badu has it, with his hand over his corresponding collar-bone so that you shall not err—we made our way through the night. An hour had passed when there was a shout from a man behind me. Turning, I saw the glimmer of a camp fire away to the eastwards. We turned and made camp at seven o'clock. I was thoroughly exhausted after ten and a half hours in the saddle, but comfort came from the realization that the great central wastes of Rub'al Khali lay behind me, the sea was but eighty miles to the northward, success was in sight.

✿

ERIC SHIPTON

(1907–1977)

English mountaineer. He climbed all over the Himalayas in the 1930s, including achieving 26 peaks over 6,000 m. in 1935 alone. With Bill Tilman he trekked great distances into unknown valleys in search of new peaks.

Nanda Devi (London, 1936).

INTO THE NANDA DEVI SANCTUARY (1934)

In the evening we wandered down to the lower end of the valley, and looked straight down a 5,000 foot precipice into what must be one of the most fantastic gorges in the world. It has never yet been penetrated by any human being, and is believed by the locals to be the abode of demons— a superstition we were quite ready to share. . . .

We could identify the furthest points reached by the Graham and Longstaff parties, just beyond the junction of the Rhamani Valley with the Rishi Nala, and it was about there that we proposed to put our base camp. Beyond was the untrodden section of the gorge, the key to the sanctuary of the Nanda Devi Basin. The view we got of it from here proved of the greatest value to us later.

Clouds soon began to form on the peaks around, but Nanda Devi remained clear. . . . Now we obtained an uninterrupted view of the great southern ridge of the mountain. It was by this ridge that we entertained some slight hope of finding a practicable route to the summit, although we were not sufficiently equipped to make the attempt that year. But as we looked at the mighty upward sweep of the ridge all hope died, for the thing appeared utterly unclimbable, as indeed I still think it is. . . .

We went on for a bit until we arrived at the edge of a deep gulley which descended steeply to the Rishi. While Tilman and I examined the possibility of getting on to a higher line of traverse, Kusang and Angtharkay went down the gulley to see if the shore of the river would help us. By now the sky had become very dark and a fierce gusty wind was blowing up the valley. It was evident that we were in for a fairly considerable storm. The Dotials huddled together, their teeth chattering.

When the two Sherpas returned with the news that they had only been able to get a hundred yards or so along the shore, we nevertheless gave the word for a general descent to the river, for it was obvious that, apart from everything else, the storm would prevent any intricate climbing on the precipitous ground in front of us. On reaching the river we set to work cutting down trees for the construction of a bridge, while the Dotials made fires on the shore and squatted round them. The actual bridging was not a difficult task with so many hands to assist, as the river was now quite low. By 5.30 p.m. we were safely across.

With a good deal of persuasion we induced the Dotials to come on a little further, telling them that if they did reach the Rhamani junction that night, we would discharge them on the following morning. We told them too that it would take another two hours (though we had not ourselves the haziest notion of how long we should need). A strip of pine forest lay along the southern shore at this point, and as this was free from undergrowth and offered such excellent going, we had actually reached our goal by 6.15. A few minutes later the storm broke, and in a whirl of falling snow we pitched the tents and struggled with a reluctant fire, while the Dotials made themselves snug in a little cave beyond. We did not bother much about food that evening, as darkness had fallen before we had stowed our kit away, and the whirling snow made mock of our efforts to get a fire going.

When preparations for the night were complete, Passang and I retired to the shelter of a small overhanging rock, while the others took to the tents. Until late into the night the two of us sat huddled over a fire which, after many unsuccessful attempts, we had managed to light in our shelter. . . .

The snow stopped falling in the early hours of the morning and the dawn broke on a cloudless sky. The Dotials paid us an early visit, and we gave them their well-earned pay. They said they did not like leaving us up here alone, but after a touching farewell ceremony, they took their departure. And sorry I was to see them go. They had served us well and faithfully, carrying huge loads over country where a slip would have had serious consequences. Nor should I easily forget their pleasant humour and their courtesy. The morning was spent in moving our stuff over to the overhang which had been occupied by the Dotials, sorting things out, taking stock of food, and many other little jobs. We found that we had thirty-five days' food left . . . .

Whatever may have been my enthusiasm or impatience to be up and doing on the night before, the hour for getting up always finds me with no other ambition in the world than to be permitted to lie where I am and sleep, sleep, sleep. Not so Tilman. I have never met anyone with such a complete disregard for the sublime comforts of the early morning bed. However monstrously early we might decide, the night before, to get up, he was about at least half an hour before the time. He was generally very good about it, and used to sit placidly smoking his pipe over the fire, with no more than a few mild suggestions that it might be a good idea to think about starting. . . .

It was useless trying to hurry along the traverse. Each section had to be tackled with the utmost caution. It was slow work, but very far from tedious, as the job required all our attention. As we gradually became used to the gigantic depth of the ravine above which we were making our way, the early feeling of nervousness changed to one of exhilaration, a glorious feeling almost of being part of this giant creation of Nature. Towards the end of the traverse, the links became very fragile. One spot in particular caused us such trouble that it produced a fairly forceful protest from Angtharkay, and caused Kusang to pause momentarily in his monotonous flow of song. But above and below us the cliffs were smooth and sheer, and the passage could not be avoided. This section came to be known as the 'Mauvais Pas', and was certainly the most hair-raising bit of the traverse. The last bit went comparatively easily, and by the middle of the afternoon we reached the river at the point where we had made our first crossing three days before. After stowing the loads under a rock, we hurriedly retreated along the traverse, and reached our camp before dark. . . .

On the opposite side of the river there was a wider strip of shore, on which grew a small clump of stunted birches. There was also a fair-sized

115

cave. It was obviously the ideal base from which to tackle the final section of the upper gorge, and the sooner we got there and made ourselves snug, the better, so as soon as the snowstorm had abated we collected all the loads at the water's edge, and prepared for the crossing. There were ten loads to be carried across. The river appeared to be slightly swollen but, as the snow had been melting as it fell, this was only to be expected. We did not anticipate that the difficulties would be much greater than they had been before.

Fastening an end of the rope to my waist and shouldering a load, I paddled up the edge of the stream, probing with my ice-axe and searching for the best place to begin the crossing. Then I started to wade slowly out into the raging waters. I soon realized that, although the river appeared only slightly higher than it had been before, it confronted us with an obstacle twice as formidable. The force of the current was terrific. As I moved a foot forward, it would be whirled sideways, and it was only by shuffling along that I could make any headway. My legs were slashed by stones swept down by the force of the river, but soon the numbing cold robbed my lower limbs of all sensation. The whirling motion of the water made me giddy, and I was hard put to it to keep my balance. In midstream the water was nearly up to my waist; had it been an inch higher it must have carried me away, but by a desperate effort I kept my feet. I tried to turn round, but found that the current was impossible to face or turn my back upon, so I had to go on, and at length emerged with bleeding legs upon the opposite beach.

Tilman was a short way behind me. Being shorter, he was having an even tougher struggle. Passang and Angtharkay were already well in the water, holding on to each other, and on to the rope which was now stretched across the river. My wits must have been numbed by the cold, for I missed the brief opportunity I had of preventing them from coming any further. Too late I realized what they were in for. Passang was carrying a load of satu, Angtharkay had a load of clothes and bedding, which came down to his buttocks. He was very slight of build and easily the shortest of the five of us. When he got out towards the middle of the stream, the water was well above his waist, and it was obvious that he was prevented from being swept away only by hanging on to the rope and Passang's firm hand, which clutched him by the arm. Soon, however, his load became waterlogged, and started to drag him down. How he managed to keep his feet will always remain a mystery to me for, in spite of the help afforded him by the rope, his difficulties must have been vastly greater than my own, and I knew that I had had just as much as I could cope with. But then these Sherpas have standards of their own. As they were approaching the northern bank, however, Angtharkay actually did lose his balance and, as he went in up to his neck, I thought he was lost. But he retained his hold on the rope, and Passang, clutching frantically at his arm, dragged him ashore. They were both rather badly shaken, but immediately set about the task of pitching camp and lighting a fire. . . .

We now commanded both sides of the river, and it was decided that Tilman and Angtharkay should explore the possibilities of the southern side, while Passang and I tried to get through on the northern side. . . . But after some desperate rock-climbing, we were forced to admit defeat, and returned to camp, satisfied that at least there was no route along the northern side of the gorge.

It was a cold grey afternoon, and towards evening rain began to fall gently. The gorge wore a grim and desolate aspect, which increased my dejection as I sat in the cave, waiting for the others to return and wondering what our next move would be. If we were forced to retreat from here, we would have to abandon our attempt to penetrate into the Nanda Devi Basin, as there was no other line of possibility. As the evening wore on, we began to scan the crags of the opposite side anxiously for any sign of the others. Their delay in returning gave me some hope that they might after all have found a way; but towards dark I began to fear that an accident had occurred, for they must have realized our failure, and desperation is apt to make people run unjustifiable risks. Then all at once we spotted them, descending through the mist at a seemingly reckless speed. As they approached the river I went over to the bridge to await them. Angtharkay was in front and, as he came nearer, I could see that he was in a state of great excitement; as he balanced his way precariously over the water, above the roar of the torrent I caught the words: 'Bahut achcha, sahib, bahut achcha.'

When Tilman arrived, I heard from him the glad news that they had found, 1,500 feet above the river, a break in that last formidable buttress, guarding the mystic shrine of the 'Blessed Goddess'. From where they had stood, they could see that the way was clear into the Nanda Devi Basin. The last frail link in that extraordinary chain of rock-faults, which had made it possible to make our way along the grim precipices of the gorge, had been discovered; and this meant at least a certain measure of success to our undertaking.

As I lay in the mouth of the cave after our evening meal, watching the spectral shadows hover in the ghostly clefts of the opposite wall of the gorge, and listening to the mighty boom of the torrent echoing to a great height above our heads, my feeling of despondency was changed to one of deep content.

117

Towards sunset the rain cleared off and, as we sat round our juniper fire, we witnessed a heavenly unveiling of the great peaks of the basin. First appeared the majestic head of Nanda Devi herself, frowning down upon us from an incredible height, utterly detached from the earth. One by one the white giants of the unnamed ranges to the north followed suit; until at last it seemed as if the entire mountain realm stood before us bathed in the splendour of the dying sun, paying homage to the majesty of their peerless queen.

We were now actually in the inner sanctuary of the Nanda Devi Basin, and at each step I experienced that subtle thrill which anyone of imagination must feel when treading hitherto unexplored country. Each corner held some thrilling secret to be revealed for the trouble of looking. My most blissful dream as a child was to be in some such valley, free to wander where I liked, and discover for myself some hitherto unrevealed glory of Nature. Now the reality was no less wonderful than that half-forgotten dream; and of how many childish fancies can that be said, in this age of disillusionment?

✤

WILFRED THESIGER

(b. 1910)

English explorer. He twice crossed the Empty Quarter, the Rub'al-Khali, between 1946 and 1949. His sensitive writing and remarkable photographs record a life of almost constant travel. The extracts which follow were his own choice.

Arabian Sands (London, 1959).

1. FEELINGS AFTER CROSSING THE EMPTY QUARTER (1946)

In the evening, now that we needed no longer measure out each cup of water, bin Kabina made extra coffee, while Musallim increased our rations of flour by a mugful. This was wild extravagance, but we felt that the occasion called for celebration. Even so, the loaves he handed us were woefully inadequate to stay our hunger, now that our thirst was gone.

The moon was high above us when I lay down to sleep. The others still talked round the fire, but I closed my mind to the meaning of their words, content to hear only the murmur of their voices, to watch their outlines sharp against the sky, happily conscious that they were there and beyond them the camels to which we owed our lives.

For years the Empty Quarter had represented to me the final, unattainable challenge which the desert offered. Suddenly it had come within my reach. I remembered my excitement when Lean had casually offered me the chance to go there, the immediate determination to cross it, and then the doubts and fears, the frustrations, and the moments of despair. Now I had crossed it. To others my journey would have little importance. It would produce nothing except a rather inaccurate map which no one was ever likely to use. It was a personal experience, and the reward had been a drink of clean, nearly tasteless water. I was content with that.

Looking back on the journey I realized that there had been no high moment of achievement such as a mountaineer must feel when he stands upon his chosen summit. Over the past days new strains and anxieties had built up as others eased, for, after all, this crossing of the Empty Quarter was set in the framework of a longer journey, and already my mind was busy with the new problems which our return journey presented.

2. THOUGHTS ON EXPLORATION

I was sailing on this dhow because I wanted to have some experience of the Arab as a sailor. Once they had been a great sea-going race, sailing their dhows round the coasts of India to the East Indies and perhaps even farther. The Trucial Coast which we had just left had been known and dreaded as the Pirate Coast; in the early nineteenth century Juasimi pirates had fought our frigates on level terms on these very waters. But there was a deeper reason that had prompted me to make this journey. I had done it to escape a little longer from the machines which dominated our world. The experience would last longer than the few days I spent on the journey. All my life I had hated machines. I could remember how bitterly at school I had resented reading the news that someone had flown across the Atlantic or travelled through the Sahara in a car. I had realized even then that the speed and ease of mechanical transport must rob the world of all diversity.

For me, exploration was a personal venture. I did not go to the Arabian desert to collect plants nor to make a map; such things were incidental. At heart I knew that to write or even to talk of my travels was to tarnish the achievement. I went there to find peace in the hardship of desert travel and the company of desert peoples. I set myself a goal on these journeys, and, although the goal itself was unimportant, its attainment had to be worth every effort and sacrifice. Scott had gone to the South Pole in order to stand for a few minutes on one particular and almost inaccessible spot on the earth's surface. He and his companions died on their way back, but even as they were dying he never doubted that the journey had been worthwhile. Everyone knew that there was nothing to be found on the top of Everest, but even in this materialistic age few people asked, 'What point is there in climbing Everest? What good will it do anyone when they get there?' They recognized that even today there are experiences that do not need to be justified in terms of material profit.

No, it is not the goal but the way there that matters, and the harder the way the more worthwhile the journey. Who, after all, would dispute that it is more satisfying to climb to the top of a mountain than to go there in a funicular railway? Perhaps this was one reason why I resented modern inventions; they made the road too easy. I felt instinctively that it was better to fail on Everest without oxygen than to attain the summit with its use. If climbers used oxygen, why should they not have their supplies dropped to them from aeroplanes, or landed by helicopter? Yet to refuse mechanical aids as unsporting reduced exploration to the level of a sport, like big-game shooting in Kenya when the hunter is allowed to drive up to within sight of the animal but must get out of the car to shoot it. I would not myself have wished to cross the Empty Quarter in a car. Luckily this was impossible when I did my journeys, for to have done the journey on a camel when I could have done it in a car would have turned the venture into a stunt.

✴

SIR EDMUND HILLARY

(b. 1919)

New Zealand mountaineer. He is best known for his first ascent of Everest with Norgay Tenzing, just in time for the news to arrive before the coronation of Queen Elizabeth II.

High Adventure (London, 1955).

ARRIVAL AT THE SUMMIT (1953)

I lay on the little rock ledge panting furiously. Gradually it dawned on me that I was up the step, and I felt a glow of pride and determination that completely subdued my temporary feelings of weakness. For the first time on the whole expedition I really knew I was going to get to the top. 'It will have to be pretty tough to stop us now' was my thought. But I couldn't entirely ignore the feeling of astonishment and wonder that I'd been able to get up such a difficulty at 29,000 feet even with oxygen.

When I was breathing more evenly I stood up and, leaning over the edge, waved to Tenzing to come up. He moved into the crack and I gathered in the rope and took some of his weight. Then he, in turn, commenced to struggle and jam and force his way up until I was able to pull him to safety—gasping for breath. We rested for a moment. Above us the ridge continued on as before—enormous overhanging cornices on the right and steep snow slopes on the left running down to the rock bluffs. But the angle of the snow slopes was easing off. I went on chipping a line of steps, but thought it safe enough for us to move together in order to save time. The ridge rose up in a great series of snakelike undulations which bore away to the right, each one concealing the next. I had no idea where the top was. I'd cut a line of steps around the side of one undulation and another would come into view. We were getting desperately tired now and Tenzing was going very slowly. I'd been cutting steps for almost two hours, and my back and arms were starting to tire. I tried cramponing along the slope without cutting steps, but my feet slipped uncomfortably down the slope. I went on cutting. We seemed to have been going for a very long time and my confidence was fast evaporating. Bump followed bump with maddening regularity. A patch of shingle barred our way, and I climbed dully up it and started cutting steps around another bump. And then I realised that this was the last bump, for ahead of me the ridge dropped steeply away in a great corniced curve, and out in the distance I could see the pastel shades and fleecy clouds of the highlands of Tibet.

To my right a slender snow ridge climbed up to a snowy dome about forty feet above our heads. But all the way along the ridge the thought had haunted me that the summit might be the crest of a cornice. It was too late to take risks now. I asked Tenzing to belay me strongly, and I started cutting a cautious line of steps up the ridge. Peering from side to side and thrusting with my ice-axe, I tried to discover a possible cornice, but everything seemed solid and firm. I waved Tenzing up to me. A few more whacks of the ice-axe, a few very weary steps, and we were on the summit of Everest.

It was 11.30 a.m. My first sensation was one of relief—relief that the long grind was over; that the summit had been reached before our oxygen supplies had dropped to a critical level; and relief that in the end the mountain had been kind to us in having a pleasantly rounded cone for its summit instead of a fearsome and unapproachable cornice. But mixed with the relief was a vague sense of astonishment that I should have been the lucky one to attain the ambition of so many brave and determined climbers. It seemed difficult at first to grasp that we'd got there. I was too tired and too conscious of the long way down to safety really to feel any great elation. But as the fact of our success thrust itself more clearly into my mind, I felt a quiet glow of satisfaction spread through my body—a satisfaction less vociferous but more powerful than I had ever felt on a mountain top before. I turned and looked at Tenzing. Even beneath his oxygen mask and the icicles hanging from his hair, I could see his infectious grin of sheer delight. I held out my hand, and in silence we shook in good Anglo-Saxon fashion. But this was not enough for Tenzing, and impulsively he threw his arm around my shoulders and we thumped each other on the back in mutual congratulations.

But we had no time to waste! First I must take some photographs and then we'd hurry down. I turned off my oxygen and took the set off my back. I remembered all the warnings I'd had of the possible fatal consequences of this, but for some reason felt quite confident that nothing serious would result. I took my camera out of the pocket of my windproof and clumsily opened it with my thickly gloved hands. I clipped on the lens-hood and ultra-violet filter and then shuffled down the ridge a little so that I could get the summit into my viewfinder. Tenzing had been waiting patiently, but now, at my request, he unfurled the flags wrapped around his ice-axe and, standing on the summit, held them above his head. Clad in all his bulky equipment and with the flags flapping furiously in the wind, he made a dramatic picture, and the thought drifted through my mind that this photograph should be a good one if it came out at all. I didn't worry about getting Tenzing to take a photograph of me—as far as I knew, he had never taken a photograph before and the summit of Everest was hardly the place to show him how.

I climbed up to the top again and started taking a photographic record in every direction. The weather was still extraordinarily fine. High above us were long streaks of cirrus wind cloud and down below fluffy cumulus hid the valley floors from view. But wherever we looked, icy peaks and sombre gorges lay beneath us like a relief map. Perhaps the view was most spectacular to the east, for here the giants Makalu and Kanchenjunga dominated the horizon and gave some idea of the vast scale of the Himalayas.

Makalu in particular, with its soaring rock ridges, was a remarkable sight; it was only a few miles away from us. From our exalted viewpoint I could see all the northern slopes of the mountain and was immediately struck by the possibility of a feasible route to its summit. With a growing feeling of excitement, I took another photograph to study at leisure on returning to civilization. The view to the north was a complete contrast—hundreds of miles of the arid high Tibetan plateau, softened now by a veil of fleecy clouds into a scene of delicate beauty. To the west the Himalayas stretched hundreds of miles in a tangled mass of peaks, glaciers, and valleys.

But one scene was of particular interest. Almost under our feet, it seemed, was the famous North Col and the East Rongbuk glacier, where so many epic feats of courage and endurance were performed by the earlier British Everest Expeditions. Part of the ridge up which they had established their high camps was visible, but the last thousand feet, which had proved such a formidable barrier, was concealed from our view as its rock slopes dropped away with frightening abruptness from the summit snow pyramid. It was a sobering thought to remember how often these men had reached 28,000 feet without the benefits of our modern equipment and reasonably efficient oxygen sets. Inevitably my thoughts turned to Mallory and Irvine, who had lost their lives on the mountain thirty years before. With little hope I looked around for some sign that they had reached the summit, but could see nothing.

Meanwhile Tenzing had also been busy. On the summit he'd scratched out a little hole in the snow, and in this he placed some small offerings of food—some biscuits, a piece of chocolate, and a few sweets—a small gift to the Gods of Chomolungma which all devout Buddhists (as Tenzing is) believe to inhabit the summit of this mountain. Besides the food, I placed the little cross that John Hunt had given me on the South Col. Strange companions, no doubt, but symbolical at least of the spiritual strength and peace that all peoples have gained from the mountains. We made seats for ourselves in the snow, and sitting there in reasonable comfort we ate with relish a bar of mintcake. My camera was still hanging open on my chest so I decided to put it safely away. But my fingers seemed to have grown doubly clumsy. With slow and fumbling movements, I closed the camera and did up the leather case. I suddenly realised that I was being affected by the lack of oxygen—it was nearly ten minutes now since I'd taken my set off. I quickly checked the gauges on our bottles—1,450-lb pressure; roughly 350 litres of oxygen; nearly two hours' endurance at three litres a minute. It wasn't much, but it would have to do. I hastily put my set on and turned on the oxygen. I felt better immediately. Tenzing had removed the flags from his ice-axe and, as there was nothing to tie them to, he thrust them down into the snow. They obviously wouldn't stay there for long. We slowly got to our feet again. We were tired all right, and all my tension and worry about reaching the summit had gone, leaving a slight feeling of anticlimax. But the smallness of our supply of oxygen filled me with a sense of urgency. We must get back to the South Summit as quickly as possible.

I took up my ice-axe, glanced at Tenzing to see if he were ready, and then looked at my watch—it was 11.45, and we'd only been on top fifteen minutes. I had one job left to do. Walking easily down the steps I'd made in the ridge I descended forty feet from the summit to the first visible rocks, and taking a handful of small stones thrust them into my pocket—it seemed a bit silly at the time, but I knew they'd be rather nice to have when we got down.

II

AFRICA

IBN BATTÚTA (1304–1377)   127
LEO AFRICANUS (*c.*1485–*c.*1554)   131
JAMES BRUCE (1730–1794)   134
MUNGO PARK (1771–1806)   138
HUGH CLAPPERTON (1788–1827)   140
RENÉ CAILLIÉ (1799–1838)   143
RICHARD LEMON LANDER (1804–1834)   150
JOHANN LUDWIG KRAPF (1810–1881)   154
SIR FRANCIS GALTON (1822–1911)   155
HEINRICH BARTH (1821–1865)   156
DR WILLIAM BALFOUR BAIKIE (1825–1864)   161
SIR RICHARD BURTON (1821–1890)   164
JOHN HANNING SPEKE (1827–1864)   170
DR DAVID LIVINGSTONE (1813–1873)   175
SIR HENRY MORTON STANLEY (1841–1904)   182
SIR SAMUEL WHITE BAKER (1821–1893)   189
FLORENCE VON SASS BAKER (*c.*1841–1918)   195
REVD CHARLES NEW (1840–1875)   200
GEORG AUGUST SCHWEINFURTH (1836–1925)   202
JOSEPH THOMSON (1858–1895)   203
COUNT SAMUEL TELEKI (1845–1916)   208
MARY KINGSLEY (1862–1900)   210

IBN BATTÚTA

(MOHAMMED IBN ABDULLAH IBN BATUTA)

(1304–1377)

The greatest of all Muslim travellers. After his travels in Asia (page 17), he set out once more in 1352, crossing the Sahara to reach the Niger river, which he believed to be the Nile.

Travels of Ibn Battúta (London, 1983).

1. CROCODILE (1353)

I saw a crocodile in this part of the Nile, close to the bank; it looked just like a small boat. One day I went down to the river to satisfy a need, and lo, one of the blacks came and stood between me and the river. I was amazed at such lack of manners and decency on his part, and spoke of it to someone or other. He answered, 'His purpose in doing that was solely to protect you from the crocodile, by placing himself between you and it.'

2. IN THE KINGDOM OF THE BLACKS

I was at Mali during the two festivals of the sacrifice and the fast-breaking. On these days the sultan takes his seat on the *pempi* [throne] after the mid-afternoon prayer. The armour-bearers bring in magnificent arms—quivers of gold and silver, swords ornamented with gold and with golden scabbards, gold and silver lances, and crystal maces. At his head stand four amirs driving off the flies, having in their hands silver ornaments resembling saddle-stirrups. The commanders, qadi, and preacher sit in their usual places. The interpreter Dugha comes with his four wives and his slave-girls, who are about a hundred in number. They are wearing beautiful robes, and on their heads they have gold and silver fillets, with gold and silver balls attached. A chair is placed for Dugha to sit on. He plays on an instrument made of reeds, with some small calabashes at its lower end, and chants a poem in praise of the sultan, recalling his battles and deeds of valour. The women and girls sing along with him and play with bows. Accompanying them are about thirty youths, wearing red woollen tunics

127

and white skull-caps; each of them has his drum slung from his shoulder and beats it. Afterwards come his boy pupils who play and turn wheels in the air, like the natives of Sind. They show a marvellous nimbleness and agility in these exercises and play most cleverly with swords. Dugha also makes a fine play with the sword. Thereupon the sultan orders a gift to be presented to Dugha and he is given a purse containing two hundred *mithqals* of gold dust, and is informed of the contents of the purse before all the people. The commanders rise and twang their bows in thanks to the sultan. The next day each one of them gives Dugha a gift, every man according to his rank. Every Friday after the '*asr* prayer, Dugha carries out a similar ceremony to this that we have described.

On feast-days, after Dugha has finished his display, the poets come in. Each of them is inside a figure resembling a thrush, made of feathers, and provided with a wooden head with a red beak, to look like a thrush's head. They stand in front of the sultan in this ridiculous make-up and recite their poems. I was told that their poetry is a kind of sermonizing in which they say to the sultan: 'This *pempi* which you occupy was that whereon sat this king and that king, and such and such were this one's noble actions and such and such the other's. So do you too do good deeds whose memory will outlive you.' After that, the chief of the poets mounts the steps of the *pempi* and lays his head on the sultan's lap, then climbs to the top of the *pempi* and lays his head first on the sultan's right shoulder and then on his left, speaking all the while in their tongue, and finally he comes down again. I was told that this practice is a very old custom amongst them, prior to the introduction of Islam, and that they have kept it up.

The negroes disliked Mansa Suleiman because of his avarice. His predecessor was Mansa Magha, and before him reigned Mansa Musa, a generous and virtuous prince, who loved the whites and made gifts to them. . . .

The negroes possess some admirable qualities. They are seldom unjust, and have a greater abhorrence of injustice than any other people. Their sultan shows no mercy to anyone who is guilty of the least act of it. There is complete security in their country. Neither traveller nor inhabitant in it has anything to fear from robbers or men of violence. They do not confiscate the property of any white man who dies in their country, even if it be uncounted wealth. On the contrary, they give it into the charge of some trustworthy person among the whites, until the rightful heir takes possession of it. They are careful to observe the hours of prayer, . . . and in bringing up their children to them. On Fridays, if a man does not go early to the mosque, he cannot find a corner to pray in, on account of the crowd. It is a custom of theirs to send each man his boy with his prayer-mat; the boy spreads it out for his master in a place befitting him until he comes to the mosque. Their prayer-mats are made of the leaves of a tree resembling a date-palm, but without fruit.

Another of their good qualities is their habit of wearing clean white garments on Fridays. Even if a man has nothing but an old worn shirt, he washes it and cleans it, and wears it to the Friday service. Yet another is their zeal for learning the Koran by heart. They put their children in chains if they show any backwardness in memorizing it, and they are not set free until they have it by heart. I visited the qadi in his house on the day of the festival. His children were chained up, so I said to him, 'Will you not let them loose?' He replied, 'I shall not do so until they learn the Koran by heart.' Among their bad qualities are the following. The women servants, slave-girls, and young girls go about in front of everyone naked, without a stitch of clothing on them. Women go into the sultan's presence naked and without coverings, and his daughters also go about naked. Then there is their custom of putting dust and ashes on their heads, as a mark of respect, and the grotesque ceremonies we have described when the poets recite their verses. Another reprehensible practice among many of them is the eating of carrion, dogs, and asses.

The date of my arrival at Mali was [28 June 1352] and of my departure from it [27 February 1353]. I was accompanied by a merchant called Abu Bakr ibn Ya'qub. We took the Mima road. I had a camel which I was riding, because horses are expensive, and cost a hundred *mithqals* each. We came to a wide channel which flows out of the Nile and can only be crossed in boats. The place is infested with mosquitoes, and no one can pass that way except by night. We reached the channel three or four hours after nightfall on a moonlit night. On reaching it I saw sixteen beasts with enormous bodies, and marvelled at them, taking them to be elephants, of which there are many in that country. Afterwards I saw that they had gone into the river, so I said to Abu Bakr, 'What kind of animals are these?' He replied, 'They are hippopotami which have come out to pasture ashore.' They are bulkier than horses, have manes and tails, and their heads are like horses' heads, but their feet like elephants' feet. I saw these hippopotami again when we sailed down the Nile from Timbuktu to Gao. They were swimming in the water, and lifting their heads and blowing. The men in the boat were afraid of them and kept close to the bank in case the hippopotami should sink them.

They have a cunning method of catching these hippopotami. They use spears with a hole bored in them, through which strong cords are passed. The spear is thrown at one of the animals, and if it strikes its leg or neck it goes right through it. Then they pull on the rope until the beast is brought to the bank, kill it and eat its flesh. Along the bank there are quantities of hippopotamus bones.

We halted near this channel at a large village, which had as governor a negro, a pilgrim, and man of fine character, named Farba Magha. He was one of the negroes who made the pilgrimage in the company of Sultan Mansa Musa. Farba Magha told me that when Mansa Musa came to this channel, he had with him a qadi, a white man. This qadi attempted to make away with four thousand *mithqals* and the sultan, on learning of it, was enraged at him and exiled him to the country of the heathen cannibals. He lived among them for four years, at the end of which the sultan sent him back to his own country. The reason why the heathens did not eat him was that he was white, for they say that the white is indigestible because he is not 'ripe', whereas the black man is 'ripe' in their opinion.

Sultan Mansa Suleiman was visited by a party of these negro cannibals, including one of their amirs. They have a custom of wearing in their ears large pendants, each pendant having an opening of half a span. They wrap themselves in silk mantles, and in their country there is a gold mine. The sultan received them with honour, and gave them as his hospitality-gift a servant, a negress. They killed and ate her, and having smeared their faces and hands with her blood came to the sultan to thank him. I was informed that this is their regular custom whenever they visit his court. Someone told me about them that they say that the choicest parts of women's flesh are the palm of the hand and the breast. . . .

From Timbuktu I sailed down the Nile on a small boat, hollowed out of a single piece of wood. We used to go ashore every night at the villages and buy whatever we needed in the way of meat and butter in exchange for salt, spices, and glass beads. I then came to a place the name of which I have forgotten, where there was an excellent governor, a pilgrim, called Farba Suleiman. He is famous for his courage and strength, and none ventures to pluck his bow. I have not seen anyone among the blacks taller or bulkier than him. At this town I was in need of some millet, so I visited him (it was on the Prophet's birthday) and saluted him. He took me by the hand, and led me into his audience hall. We were served with a drink of theirs called *daqnu*, which is water containing some pounded millet mixed with a little honey or milk. They drink this in place of water, because if they drink plain water it upsets them. If they have no millet they mix the water with honey or milk. Afterwards a green melon was brought in and we ate some of it.

A young boy, not yet full-grown, came in, and Farba Suleiman, calling him, said to me, 'Here is your hospitality-gift; keep an eye on him in case he escapes.' So I took the boy and prepared to withdraw, but he said, 'Wait till the food comes.' A slave-girl of his joined us; she was an Arab girl, of Damascus, and she spoke to me in Arabic. While this was going on we heard cries in his house, so he sent the girl to find out what had happened. She returned to him and told him that a daughter of his had just died. He said, 'I do not like crying, come, we shall walk to the river', meaning the Nile, on which he has some houses. A horse was brought, and he told me to ride, but I said, 'I shall not ride if you are walking', so we walked together. We came to his houses by the Nile, where food was served, and after we had eaten I took leave of him and withdrew. I met no one among the blacks more generous or upright than him. The boy whom he gave me is still with me.

✻

LEO AFRICANUS
(AL-HASSAN IBN MUHAMMED AL-WAZZANI, SHORTENED TO AL-FASI, THE MAN OF THE FEZ)
(c.1485–c.1554)

One of the most colourful medieval travellers in Africa. He crossed the Sahara twice to Timbuktu and claimed to have visited fifteen Sudanese kingdoms. Captured by pirates, he was converted to Christianity by Pope Leo X, who encouraged him to write accounts of his travels. In these he reinforced for 200 years myths about the source of the Congo, and that the Niger flowed west from Lake Chad past Timbuktu to the Atlantic coast.

Leo Africanus: *The History and Description of Africa*, trans. J. Pory, ed. R. Brown (London, 1896).

1. THE CONGO (1540)

The principal river of all Congo called Zaire, taketh his chief original out of the second lake of Nilus, lying under the Equinoctial line: and albeit this is one of the mightiest rivers of all Africa, being eight and twenty miles broad at the mouth, yet was it utterly unknown to ancient writers. Amongst other rivers it receiveth Vumba and Barbela, which sprung out of the first great lake. In this country are sundry other rivers also, which fetch their original out of the lake of Aquelunda: the principal whereof are Coanza, which divideth the kingdom of Congo from that of Angola, and the river Lelunda, which breedeth crocodiles and water-horses which the Greeks call hippopotami, of which creatures the isle of horses in the mouth of the river Zaire taketh denomination. The Hippopotamus or water-horse is somewhat tawny, of the colour of a lion; in the night he comes on land to feed upon the grass, and keepeth in the water all the day time. The Africans tame and manage some of these horses, and they prove exceeding swift; but a man must beware how he passes over deep rivers with them, for they will suddenly dive under water. Also in these rivers of Ethiopia are bred a kind of oxen, which live every night upon the land. Here likewise breedeth another strange creature, called in the Congonian language Ambize Angulo, that is to say, a hog-fish, being so exceeding fat, and of such greatness, that some of them weigh above five hundred pound. This abundance of waters, together with the heat of the climate, which proceedeth from the nearness of the sun, causeth the country to be most fruitful of plants, herbs, fruits, and corn; and much more fertile would it be, if nature were helped forward by the industry of the inhabitants. Here also, besides goats, sheep, deer, Gugelle, conies, hares, civet-cats, and ostriches, are great swarms of tigers, which are very hurtful both to man and beast. The Zebra or Zabra of this country being about the bigness of a mule, is a beast of incomparable swiftness, streaked about the body, legs, ears, and other parts, with black, white, and brown circles of three fingers broad; which do make a pleasant show. Buffles, wild asses, called by the Greeks Onagri, and Dantes (of whose hard skins they make all their targets) range in herds up and down the woods. Also here are infinite store of elephants of such monstrous bigness, that by the report of sundry credible persons, some of their teeth do weigh two hundred pounds, at sixteen ounces the pound: upon the plains this beast is swifter than any horse, by reason of his long steps; only he cannot turn with such celerity. Trees he overturneth with the strength of his back, or breaketh them between his teeth; or standeth upright upon his hinder feet, to browse upon the leaves and tender sprigs. The she elephants bear their brood in their wombs two years before they bring forth young ones: neither are they great with young, but only from seven years to seven years. This creature is said to live 150 years; he is of a gentle disposition; and relying upon his great strength, he hurteth none but such as do him injury; only he will in a sporting manner gently heave up with his snout such persons as he meeteth. He loveth the water beyond measure and will stand up to the mid-body therein, bathing the ridge of his back and other parts with his long promuscis or trunk. His skin is four fingers thick; and it is reported that an elephant of this country, being stricken with a little gun called Petrera, was not wounded therewith, but so sore bruised inwardly, that within three days after he died. Here are likewise reported to be mighty adders or snakes of five and twenty spans long, and five spans broad, which will swallow up a whole stag, or any other creature of that bigness. Neither are they here destitute of Indie-cockes and hens, partridges, pheasants, and innumerable birds of prey, both of the land and of the sea; whereof some dive under the water, which the Portugals call Pelicans.

2. SALT FROM TEGAZA

In this region is great store of salt digged, being whiter than any marble. This salt is taken out of certain caves or pits, at the entrance whereof stand their cottages that work in the salt-mines. And these workmen are all strangers, who sell the salt which they dig, unto certain merchants that carry the same upon camels to the kingdom of Timbuktu, where there would otherwise be extreme scarcity of salt. Neither have the said diggers of salt any victuals but such as the merchants bring unto them: for they are distant from all inhabited places, almost twenty days' journey, insomuch that oftentimes they perish for lack of food, whenas the merchants come not in due time unto them. Moreover the south-east wind doth so often blind them, that they cannot live here without great peril. I myself contin-ued three days amongst them, all which time I was constrained to drink salt-water drawn out of certain wells not far from the salt-pits.

3. THE NIGER

This kingdom called by the merchants of our nation Gheneoa, by the natural inhabitants thereof Genni, and by the Portugals and other people of Europe Guinea standeth in the midst between Gualata on the north, Timbuktu on the east, and the kingdom of Mali on the south. In length it containeth almost five hundred miles, and extendeth two hundred and fifty miles along the river of Niger, and bordereth upon the Ocean sea in the same place, where Niger falleth into the said sea. This place exceedingly aboundeth with barley, rice, cattle, fishes, and cotton: and their cotton they sell unto the merchants of Barbary, for cloth of Europe, for brazen vessels, for armour, and other such commodities. Their coin is of gold without any stamp or inscription at all: they have certain iron-money also, which they use about matters of small value, some pieces whereof weigh a pound, some half a pound, and some one-quarter of a pound. In all this kingdom there is no fruit to be found but only dates, which are brought hither either out of Gualata or Numidia. Here is neither town nor castle, but a certain great village only, wherein the prince of Guinea, together with his priests, doctors, merchants, and all the principal men of the region inhabit. The walls of their houses are built of chalk, and the roofs are covered with straw: the inhabitants are clad in black or blue cotton, wherewith they cover their heads also: but the priests and doctors of their law go apparelled in white cotton. This region during the three months of July, August, and September, is yearly environed with the overflowings of Niger in manner of an lsland; all which time the merchants of Timbuktu convey their merchandise hither in certain Canoas or narrow boats made of one tree, which they row all the day long, but at night they bind them to the shore, and lodge themselves upon the land.

❊

JAMES BRUCE
(LAIRD OF KINNAIRD)
(1730–1794)

Scottish explorer. The first modern traveller in Africa, he reached the headwaters of the Blue Nile, which he mistakenly believed to be the main source of the Nile. He was ridiculed on his return but his eventual book, written twenty years after the event, fascinated and titillated Victorian society. He died falling down his own stairs.

Travels to Discover the Source of the Nile (Edinburgh, 1790).

1. I CALL IT HOT

I call it *hot*, when a man sweats at rest, and excessively on moderate motion. I call it *very hot*, when a man, with thin or little clothing, sweats much, though at rest. I call it *excessive hot*, when a man in his shirt, at rest, sweats excessively, when all motion is painful, and the knees feel feeble, as if after a fever. I call it *extreme hot*, when the strength fails, a disposition to faint comes on, a straitness is found round the temples, as if a small cord were drawn round the head, the voice impaired, the skin dry, and the head seems more than ordinary large and light. This, I apprehend, denotes death at hand.

2. 'DISCOVERY' OF THE SOURCE OF THE NILE (1770)

Half undressed as I was by loss of my sash, and throwing my shoes off, I ran down the hill, towards the little island of green sods, which was about two hundred yards distant; the whole side of the hill was thick grown over with flowers, the large bulbous roots of which appearing above the surface of the ground, and their skins coming off on treading upon them, occasioned me two very severe falls before I reached the brink of the marsh; I after this came to the island of green turf, which was in form of an altar, apparently the work of art, and I stood in rapture over the principal fountain which rises in the middle of it.

It is easier to guess than to describe the situation of my mind at that moment—standing in that spot which had baffled the genius, industry, and inquiry, of both ancients and moderns, for the course of near three thousand years. Kings had attempted this discovery at the head of armies, and each expedition was distinguished from the last, only by the difference of the numbers which had perished, and agreed alone in the disappointment which had uniformly, and without exception, followed them all. Fame, riches, and honour, had been held out for a series of ages to every individual of those myriads these princes commanded, without having produced one man capable of gratifying the curiosity of his sovereign, or wiping off this stain upon the enterprise and abilities of mankind, or adding this desideratum for the encouragement of geography. Though a mere private Briton, I triumphed here, in my own mind, over kings and their armies; and every comparison was leading nearer and nearer to presumption, when the place itself where I stood, the object of my vain-glory, suggested what depressed my short-lived triumph. I was but a few minutes arrived at the sources of the Nile, through numberless dangers and sufferings, the least of which would have overwhelmed me, but for the continual goodness and protection of Providence; I was, however, but then half through my journey, and all those dangers which I had already passed, awaited me again on my return. I found a despondency gaining ground fast upon me, and blasting the crown of laurels I had too rashly woven for myself. I resolved, therefore, to divert, till I could, on more solid reflection, overcome its progress.

3. THE KING'S LADIES

About four o'clock that same afternoon I was again sent for to the palace, when the king told me that several of his wives were ill, and desired that I would give them my advice, which I promised to do without difficulty, as all acquaintance with the fair sex had hitherto been much to my advantage. I must confess, however, that calling these the fair sex is not preserving a precision in terms. I was admitted into a large square apartment, very ill-lighted, in which were about fifty women, all perfectly black, without any covering but a very narrow piece of cotton rag about their waists. While I was musing whether or not these all might be queens, or whether there was any queen among them, one of them took me by the hand and led me rudely enough into another apartment. This was much better lighted than the first. Upon a large bench, or sofa, covered with blue Surat cloth, sat three persons cloathed from the neck to the feet with blue cotton shirts.

One of these, who, I found, was the favourite, was about six feet high, and corpulent beyond all proportion. She seemed to me, next to the elephant and rhinoceros, the largest living creature I had met with. Her features were perfectly like those of a Negro; a ring of gold passed through her under lip, and weighed it down, till, like a flap, it covered her chin, and left her teeth bare, which were very small and fine. The inside of her lip she had made black with antimony. Her ears reached down to her shoulders, and had the appearance of wings; she had in each of them a large ring of gold, somewhat smaller than a man's little finger, and about five inches diameter. The weight of these had drawn down the hole where her ear was pierced so much, that three fingers might easily pass above the ring. She had a gold necklace, like what we used to call *esclavage*, of several rows, one below another, to which were hung rows of sequins pierced. She had on her ankles two manacles of gold, larger than any I had ever seen upon the feet of felons, with which I could not conceive it was possible for her to walk, but afterwards I found they were hollow. The others were dressed pretty much in the same manner; only there was one that had chains, which came from her ears to the outside of each nostril, where they were fastened. There was also a ring put through the gristle of her nose, and which hung down to the opening of her mouth. I think she must have breathed with great difficulty. It had altogether something of the appearance of a horse's bridle. Upon my coming near them, the eldest put her hand to her mouth, and kissed it, saying, at the same time, in very vulgar Arabic, 'Kifhalek howaja?' (how do you do, merchant)—I never in my life was more pleased with distant salutations than at this time. I answered, 'Peace be among you! I am a physician, and not a merchant.'

I shall not entertain the reader with the multitude of their complaints; being a lady's physician, discretion and silence are my first duties. It is sufficient to say, that there was not one part of their whole bodies, inside and outside, in which some of them had not ailments. The three queens insisted upon being blooded, which desire I complied with, as it was an operation that required short attendance; but, upon producing the lancets, their hearts failed them. They then all cried out for the Tabange, which, in Arabic, means a pistol; but what they meant by this word was, the cupping instrument, which goes off with a spring like the snap of a pistol. I had two of these with me, but not at that time in my pocket. I sent my servant home, however, to bring one, and, that same evening, performed the operation upon the three queens with great success. The room was overflowed with an effusion of royal blood, and the whole ended with their insisting upon my giving them the instrument itself, which I was obliged to do, after cupping two of their slaves before them, who had no complaints, merely to show them how the operation was to be performed.

Another night I was obliged to attend them, and gave the queens, and two or three of the great ladies, vomits. I will spare my reader the recital of so nauseous a scene. The ipecacuanha had great effect, and warm water was drunk very copiously. The patients were numerous, and the floor of the room received all the evacuations. It was most prodigiously hot, and the horrid, black figures, moaning and groaning with sickness all around me, gave me, I think, some slight idea of the punishment in the world below. My mortifications, however, did not stop here. I observed that, on coming into their presence, the queens were all covered with cotton shirts; but no sooner did their complaints make part of our conversation, than, to my utmost surprise, each of them, in her turn, stript herself entirely naked, laying her cotton shirt loosely on her lap, as she sat cross-legged like a tailor. The custom of going naked in these warm counties abolishes all delicacy concerning it. I could not but observe that the breasts of each of them reached the length of their knees.

This exceeding confidence on their part, they thought, merited some consideration on mine; and it was not without great astonishment that I heard the queen desire to see me in the like dishabille in which she had spontaneously put herself. The whole court of female attendants flocked to the spectacle. Refusal, or resistance, were in vain. I was surrounded with fifty or sixty women, all equal in stature and strength to myself. The whole of my clothing was, like theirs, a long loose shirt of blue Surat cotton cloth, reaching from the neck down to the feet. The only terms I could possibly, and that with great difficulty, make for myself were, that they should be contented to strip me no farther than the shoulders and breast. Upon seeing the whiteness of my skin, they gave all a loud cry in token of dislike, and shuddered, seeming to consider it rather the effects of disease than natural. I think in my life I never felt so disagreeably. I have been in more than one battle, but surely I would joyfully have taken my chance again in any of them to have been freed from that examination. I could not help likewise reflecting, that, if the king had come in during this exhibition, the consequence would either have been impaling, or stripping off that skin whose colour they were so curious about; though I can solemnly declare there was not an idea in my breast, since ever I had the honour of seeing these royal beauties, that could have given his majesty of Sennaar the smallest reason for jealousy; and I believe the same may be said of the sentiments of the ladies in what regarded me. Ours was a mutual passion, but dangerous to no one concerned. I returned home with very different sensations from those I had felt after an interview with the beautiful Aiscach of Teawa. Indeed, it was impossible to be more chagrined at, or more disgusted with, my present situation than I was, and the more so, that my delivery from it appeared to be very distant, and the circumstances were more and more unfavourable every day.

✵

Mungo Park

(1771–1806)

Scottish explorer. Commissioned in 1775 by the African Association in London to trace the Niger, he proved that it flowed east. returning in 1805, he was drowned after being ambushed at Bussa.

Travels in the Interior Districts of Africa (London, 1799).

1. Arrival at the Niger (1796)

Just before it was dark, we took up our lodging for the night at a small village, where I procured some victuals for myself, and some corn for my horse, at the moderate price of a button; and was told that I should see the Niger (which the Negroes call Joliba, or *the great water*) early the next day. The lions are here very numerous: the gates are shut a little after sunset, and nobody allowed to go out. The thoughts of seeing the Niger in the morning, and the troublesome buzzing of musketoes, prevented me from shutting my eyes during the night; and I had saddled my horse, and was in readiness before daylight; but, on account of the wild beasts, we were obliged to wait until the people were stirring, and the gates opened. This happened to be a market-day at Sego, and the roads were everywhere filled with people, carrying different articles to sell. We passed four large villages, and at eight o'clock saw the smoke over Sego.

As we approached the town, I was fortunate enough to overtake the fugitive Kaartans, to whose kindness I had been so much indebted in my journey through Bambarra. They readily agreed to introduce me to the king; and we rode together through some marshy ground, where, as I was anxiously looking around for the river, one of them called out, *geo affilli* (see the water); and looking forwards, I saw with infinite pleasure the great object of my mission; the long sought for, majestic Niger, glittering to the morning sun, as broad as the Thames at Westminster, and flowing slowly *to the eastward*.

2. ROBBED ON THE WAY BACK

I heard somebody holloa; and looking behind, saw those I had taken for elephant-hunters, running after me, and calling out to me to turn back. I stopped until they were all come up; when they informed me that the King of the Foulahs had sent them on purpose to bring me, my horse, and everything that belonged to me, to Fooladoo; and that therefore I must turn back, and go along with them. Without hesitating a moment, I turned round and followed them, and we travelled together near a quarter of a mile, without exchanging a word; when coming to a dark place in the wood, one of them said, in the Mandingo language, 'this place will do'; and immediately snatched my hat from my head. Though I was by no means free of apprehension, yet I resolved to show as few signs of fear as possible, and therefore told them, that unless my hat was returned to me, I should proceed no further. But before I had time to receive an answer, another drew his knife, and seizing upon a metal button which remained upon my waistcoat, cut it off, and put it into his pocket. Their intentions were now obvious; and I thought that the easier they were permitted to rob me of everything, the less I had to fear. I therefore allowed them to search my pockets without resistance, and examine every part of my apparel, which they did with the most scrupulous exactness. But observing that I had one waistcoat under another, they insisted that I should cast them both off; and at last, to make sure work, they stripped me quite naked. Even my half boots (though the sole of one of them was tied on to my foot with a broken bridle-rein) were minutely inspected. Whilst they were examining the plunder, I begged them, with great earnestness, to return my pocket compass; but when I pointed it out to them, as it was lying on the ground, one of the banditti, thinking I was about to take it up, cocked his musket and swore that he would lay me dead upon the spot, if I presumed to put my hand upon it. After this, some of them went away with my horse, and the remainder stood considering whether they should leave me quite naked, or allow me something to shelter me from the sun. Humanity at last prevailed: they returned me the worst of the two shirts, and a pair of trousers; and, as they went away, one of them threw back my hat, in the crown of which I kept my memorandums; and this was probably the reason they did not wish to keep it. After they were gone, I sat for some time, looking around me with amazement and terror. Whichever way I turned, nothing appeared but danger and difficulty. I saw myself in the midst of a vast wilderness, in the depth of the rainy season; naked and alone; surrounded by savage animals, and men still more savage. I was five hundred miles from the nearest European settlement. All these circumstances crowded at once on my recollection; and I confess that my spirits began to fail me.

✿

HUGH CLAPPERTON

(1788–1827)

Scottish explorer. He crossed the Sahara in 1823–4 from Tripoli with Walter Oudney and Major Dixon Denham, discovering Lake Chad and reaching the kingdoms of Bornu and Fulani. Returning in 1825 with Richard Lander as his servant, he died in Sokoto.

D. Denham, H. Clapperton, and W. Oudney, *Narrative of Travels in Northern and Central Africa in 1822–24* (London, 1826).

1. ENTRY INTO KANO (1824)

Jan. 20. By El Wordee's advice, I prepared myself this morning for entering Kano, which was now at hand. Arrayed in naval uniform, I made myself as smart as circumstances would permit. For three miles to the north of Duakee, the country was open and well cultivated. It then became thickly covered with underwood, until we ascended a rising ground, whence we had a view of two little mounts within the walls of Kano. The soil here is a tough clay mixed with gravel, the stones of which appear to be clay ironstone. The country was now clear of wood, except here and there a few large shady trees, resorted to as usual by the women of the country selling refreshments. The villages were numerous, and the road was thronged with people of all descriptions.

At eleven o'clock we entered Kano, the great emporium of the kingdom of Haussa; but I had no sooner passed the gates, than I felt grievously disappointed; for from the flourishing description of it given by the Arabs, I expected to see a city of surprising grandeur: I found, on the contrary, the houses nearly a quarter of a mile from the walls, and in many parts scattered into detached groups, between large stagnant pools of water. I might have spared all the pains I had taken with my toilet; for not an individual turned his head round to gaze at me, but all, intent on their own business, allowed me to pass by without notice or remark.

I went with El Wordee directly to the house of Hadje Hat Salah, to whom I had a letter of recommendation from the sheikh of Bornou. We found Hat Salah sitting under a rude porch in front of his house amid a party of Arabs, Tuaregs, and people of the town. When El Wordee presented me, and told him of the sheikh's letter of recommendation, he bade me welcome, and desired me to sit down by his side. After exchanging many compliments, I inquired for the house he had hired for me, as El Wordee had sent a messenger on horseback the day before, to inform him of my approach, and to request him to have a house ready for my reception. Hat Salah now sent one of his slaves to conduct us to the house.

We had to retrace our steps more than half a mile through the market-place, which is bordered to the east and west by an extensive swamp covered with reeds and water, and frequented by wild ducks, cranes, and a filthy kind of vulture. The last is extremely useful, and by picking up offal serves as a sort of town scavenger. The house provided for me was situated at the south end of the morass, the pestilential exhalations of which, and of the pools of standing water, were increased by the sewers of the houses all opening into the street. I was fatigued and sick, and lay down on a mat that the owner of the house spread for me.

2. HAUSSA BOXERS

Having heard a great deal of the boxers of Haussa, I was anxious to witness their performance. Accordingly I sent one of my servants last night to offer 2,000 whydah for a pugilistic exhibition in the morning. As the death of one of the combatants is almost certain before a battle is over, I expressly prohibited all fighting in earnest; for it would have been disgraceful, both to myself and my country, to hire men to kill one another for the gratification of idle curiosity. About half an hour after the massi dubu were gone, the boxers arrived, attended by two drums, and the whole body of butchers, who here compose 'the fancy'. A ring was soon formed, by the master of the ceremonies throwing dust on the spectators to make them stand back. The drummers entered the ring, and began to drum lustily. One of the boxers followed, quite naked, except a skin round the middle. He placed himself in an attitude as if to oppose an antagonist, and wrought his muscles into action, seemingly to find out that every sinew was in full force for the approaching combat; then coming from time to time to the side of the ring, and presenting his right arm to the bystanders, he said, 'I am a hyena'; 'I am a lion'; 'I am able to kill all that oppose me'. The spectators, to whom he presented himself, laid their hands on his shoulder, repeating, 'The blessing of God be upon thee'; 'Thou art a hyena'; 'Thou art a lion'. He then abandoned the ring to another, who showed off in the same manner. The right hand and arm of the pugilists were now bound with narrow country cloth, beginning with a fold round the middle finger, when, the hand being first clinched with the thumb between the fore and mid fingers, the cloth was passed in many turns round the fist, the wrist, and the fore arm. After about twenty had separately gone through their attitudes of defiance, and appeals to the bystanders, they were next brought forward by pairs. If they happened to be friends, they laid their left breasts together twice, and exclaimed, 'We are lions'; 'We are friends'. One then left the ring, and another was brought forward. If the two did not recognize one another as friends, the set-to immediately commenced. On taking their stations, the two pugilists first stood at some distance, parrying with the left hand open, and, whenever opportunity offered, striking with the right. They generally aimed at the pit of the stomach, and under the ribs. Whenever they closed, one seized the other's head under his arm, and beat it with his fist, at the same time striking with his knee between his antagonist's thighs. In this position, with the head in chancery, they are said sometimes to attempt to gouge or scoop out one of the eyes. When they break loose, they never fail to give a swinging blow with the heel under the ribs, or sometimes under the left ear. It is these blows which are so often fatal. The combatants were repeatedly separated by my orders, as they were beginning to lose their temper. When this spectacle was heard of, girls left their pitchers at the wells, the market people threw down their baskets, and all ran to see the fight. The whole square before my house was crowded to excess. After six pairs had gone through several rounds, I ordered them, to their great satisfaction, the promised reward, and the multitude quietly dispersed.

RENÉ CAILLIÉ

(1799–1838)

French explorer. The first European to reach Timbuktu and survive. He arrived from the Atlantic coast in 1828 and returned with a camel caravan across the Sahara, to receive a prize of 10,000 francs from the Société Géographique of Paris.

Travels through Central Africa to Timbuktoo, and across the great desert, to Morocco, performed in the years 1824–28 (London, 1830).

1. ARRIVAL IN TIMBUKTU (1828)

On the 20th of April, at half past three, I set out for Timbuktu, escorted by Sidi-Abdallah Chebir's slaves. Our road lay northward. The slaves who had been on board our canoe also accompanied us, so that we formed a numerous caravan. The youngest slaves were mounted upon asses, as the road is very sandy and wearisome. Near Cabra we passed two lakes, the banks of which were overgrown with mimosas from five to six feet high. A little further the eye was refreshed by some signs of vegetation. The country presented the same scenery until we had proceeded half-way on our journey, and then it began to be more naked, and the sand becoming exceedingly loose, rendered travelling very difficult. On the road we were followed by a Tuareg, mounted on a superb horse. This marauder, who appeared to be about fifty years of age, showed a disposition to appropriate to himself a young negro slave. Sidi-Abdallah Chebir's men represented to him that the slave belonged to their master, and that if, on arriving at the city, he would pay him a visit, he would doubtless receive a present. This appeared to satisfy him, and he ceased to molest us. He eyed me narrowly, and several times enquired who I was, and whence I came. They told him I was poor, and he relinquished the hope of getting anything from me.

At length, we arrived safely at Timbuktu, just as the sun was touching the horizon. I now saw this capital of the Soudan, to reach which had so long been the object of my wishes. On entering this mysterious city, which is an object of curiosity and research to the civilized nations of Europe, I experienced an indescribable satisfaction. I never before felt a similar emotion and my transport was extreme. I was obliged, however, to restrain my feelings, and to God alone did I confide my joy. With what gratitude did I return thanks to Heaven, for the happy result which attended my

143

enterprise! How many grateful thanksgivings did I pour forth for the protection which God had vouchsafed to me, amidst obstacles and dangers
which appeared insurmountable. This duty being ended, I looked around
and found that the sight before me, did not answer my expectations. I had
formed a totally different idea of the grandeur and wealth of Timbuktu.
The city presented, at first view, nothing but a mass of ill-looking houses,
built of earth. Nothing was to be seen in all directions but immense plains
of quicksand of a yellowish white colour. The sky was a pale red as far as
the horizon: all nature wore a dreary aspect, and the most profound silence
prevailed; not even the warbling of a bird was to be heard. Still, though I
cannot account for the impression, there was something imposing in the
aspect of a great city, raised in the midst of sands, and the difficulties
surmounted by its founders cannot fail to excite admiration. I am inclined
to think that formerly the river flowed close to Timbuktu; though at present
it is eight miles to the north of that city, and five miles from Cabra, in the
same direction.

I took up my abode with Sidi-Abdallahi, who received me in the most
friendly manner. He had already been indirectly acquainted with the al-
leged circumstances, which, as I pretended, had occasioned my journey
across the Soudan. He invited me to sup with him; and an excellent couscous
of millet and mutton was served up. Six of us partook of the dish, and we
ate with our fingers; but in as cleanly a way as was possible under such
circumstances. Sidi-Abdallahi, according to the custom of his countrymen, did not say a word to me. He was a mild, quiet, reserved man. His
age might be about forty or forty-five. He was five feet high, stout and
pitted with the smallpox. His countenance was pleasing, his manners grave,
and rather dignified. He had no fault but his religious fanaticism.

After bidding my host good-night, I went to repose upon a mat which
was spread upon the ground in my new lodging. At Timbuktu the nights
are as hot as the days, and I could get no rest in the chamber which had
been prepared for me. I removed to the court adjoining the house, but still
found it impossible to sleep. The heat was oppressive; not a breath of air
freshened the atmosphere. In the whole course of my travels I never found
myself more uncomfortable.

On the morning of 21 April, I went to pay my respects to my host, who
received me with affability; afterwards I took a turn round the city. I found
it neither so large nor so populous as I had expected. Its commerce is not
so considerable as fame has reported. There was not as at Jenne, a concourse
of strangers from all parts of the Soudan. I saw in the streets of Timbuktu
only the camels, which had arrived from Cabra laden with the merchandise
of the flotilla, a few groups of the inhabitants sitting on mats, conversing

together, and Moors lying asleep in the shade before their doors. In a word, everything had a dull appearance.

I was surprised at the inactivity, I may even say, indolence, displayed in the city. Some colat-nut vendors were crying their goods in the streets, as at Jenne.

About four in the afternoon, when the heat had diminished, I saw several negro traders, all well clothed and mounted on good horses richly harnessed, go out to ride. Prudence forbids them to venture far from the city, for fear of the Tuaregs, who would make them pay dearly for their excursions.

In consequence of the oppressive heat the market is not held until three in the afternoon. There were few strangers to be seen except the Moors of the neighbouring tribe of Zawat, who often come hither; but in comparison with Jenne, the market is a desert.

At Timbuktu, it is very unusual to see any other merchandise except what is brought by the vessels and a few articles from Europe, such as glass wares, amber, coral, sulphur, paper, etc.

I saw three shops kept in small rooms, well stored with stuffs of European manufacture. The merchants put out at their doors cakes of salt for sale, but they never exhibit them in the market. Such as do business at the market have stalls made of stakes covered with mats, to protect them against the heat of the sun. My host Sidi-Abdallahi was obliging enough to show me over one of his magazines in which he stowed his European merchandise. I observed there many double-barrel guns, with the mark of Saint-Étienne, and other manufactories. In general French muskets are much prized, and sell at a higher rate than those of other nations. I also saw some beautiful elephants' teeth. My host told me that he procured some from Jenne, but the larger ones had been bought at Timbuktu; they are brought hither by the Tuaregs or Soorgoos, the Kissoors, and the Dirimans, who inhabit the banks of the river. They do not hunt the elephant with firearms, but catch it in snares. I regret having never seen one of these animals caught. . . .

The city of Timbuktu is principally inhabited by negroes of the Kissoor nation. Many Moors also reside there. They are engaged in trade, and, like Europeans, who repair to the colonies in the hope of making their fortunes, they usually return to their own country to enjoy the fruits of their industry. They have considerable influence over the native inhabitants of Timbuktu, whose king or governor is a negro. This prince, who is named Osman, is much respected by his subjects. He is very simple in his manners: his dress is like that of the Moors of Morocco; and his house is no better furnished than those of the Moorish merchants. He is himself a merchant, and his sons trade with Jenne. He inherited a considerable fortune from his ancestors, and is very rich. He has four wives, besides an infinite number of slaves, and is a zealous Mahometan.

The sovereignty is hereditary, descending to the eldest son. The king does not levy any tribute on his subjects or on foreign merchants, but he receives presents. There is no regular government. The king is like a father ruling his children. He is mild and just, and has nothing to fear from his subjects. The whole community, indeed, exhibits the amiable and simple manners of the patriarchs. In case of war, all are ready to serve; but the mild and inoffensive manners of these people afford little ground for quarrels, and when they arise the natives of Timbuktu repair to their chief, who assembles a council of the elders, all of whom are blacks. Though the Moors are not permitted to take part in these councils, yet my host Sidi-Abdallahi, the friend of Osman, was sometimes allowed to be present at them. The Moors acknowledge a superior among themselves; but they are, nevertheless, amenable to the authorities of the country. I requested my host to present me to the king, which, with his usual good nature, he consented to do.

The prince received me in the midst of is court. He was seated on a beautiful mat with a rich cushion. We seated ourselves for a few moments at a little distance from him. Sidi-Abdallahi, after briefly relating my adventures, told him that I wished to pay my respects to him. I could not understand their conversation, for they spoke in the language of the Kissoors. The king afterwards addressed me in Arabic, asking some questions about the Christians, and the manner in which they had treated me. After a short time we took our leave: I wished to have seen the interior of the house, but my curiosity could not be gratified. The king appeared to be of an exceedingly amiable disposition; his age might be about fifty-five, and his hair was white and curly. He was of the middling height, and his colour was jet black. He had an aquiline nose, thin lips, a grey beard, and large eyes, and his whole countenance was pleasing; his dress, like those of the Moors, was composed of stuff of European manufacture. On his head was a red cap, bound round with a large piece of muslin in the form of a turban. His shoes were of morocco, shaped like our morning slippers, and made in the country. He often visited the mosque.

There are, as I have already mentioned, many Moors in Timbuktu, and they occupy the finest houses in the city. They very soon become rich in trade, and they receive consignments of merchandise from Adrar, Tafilet, Tawat, Ardamas, Tripoli, Tunis, and Algiers. They receive from Europe tobacco and other articles, which they send by canoes to Jenne and elsewhere. Timbuktu may be regarded as the principal entrepôt of this part of Africa. All the salt obtained from the mines of Toudeyni is brought hither on camels. The Moors of Morocco and other countries who travel to the Soudan, remain six or eight months at Timbuktu to sell their goods, and get their camels re-laden.

The cakes of salt are tied together with cords, made of a sort of grass which grows in the neighbourhood of Tandaye. This grass is dry when gathered; but it is afterwards moistened, and then buried under ground to keep it from the sun and the east wind, which would dry it too rapidly. When sufficiently impregnated with moisture, it is taken out of the earth and platted into cord, which the Moors use for various purposes. The camels frequently throw their loads off their backs, and when the cakes of salt arrive in the town they are frequently broken. This would spoil their sale, if the merchants did not take the precaution of making the slaves join them together again. When the pieces are fastened together, the cakes are packed up again with a stronger kind of cord made of bull's hide. The cakes are ornamented with little designs, such as stripes, lozenges, etc., traced in black. The slaves are very fond of executing these ornaments, an employment which enables them to collect a little supply of salt for their own use. In general, the slaves are better treated at Timbuktu than in other countries. They are well clothed and fed, and seldom beaten. They are required to observe religious duties, which they do very punctually; but they are nevertheless regarded as merchandise, and are exported to Tripoli, Morocco, and other parts of the coast, where they are not so happy as at Timbuktu. They always leave that place with regret, though they are ignorant of the fate that awaits them elsewhere.

At the time of my departure, I saw several slaves affectionately bidding each other adieu. The conformity of their melancholy condition excites among them a feeling of sympathy and mutual interest. At parting, they recommended good behaviour to each other; but the Moors frequently hurry their departure, and interrupt these affecting scenes, which are so well calculated to excite commiseration for their fate.

When I was at the mosque, a middle-aged Moor stepped up to me gravely, and without saying a word slipped a handful of cowries into the pocket of my coussabe. He withdrew immediately, without affording me time to thank him. I was much surprised at this delicate way of giving alms.

The city of Timbuktu forms a sort of triangle, measuring about three miles in circuit. The houses are large, but not high, consisting entirely of a ground-floor. In some, a sort of little closet is constructed above the entrance. They are built of bricks of a round form, rolled in the hands, and baked in the sun. The walls, except as far as regards their height, resemble those of Jenne.

The streets of Timbuktu are clean, and sufficiently wide to permit three horsemen to pass abreast. Both within and without the town there are many straw huts of a circular form, like those of the pastoral Foulahs. They serve as dwellings for the poor, and for the slaves who sell merchandise for their masters.

Timbuktu contains seven mosques, two of which are large; each is surmounted by a brick tower.

This mysterious city, which has been an object of curiosity for so many ages, and of whose population, civilization, and trade with the Soudan, such exaggerated notions have prevailed, is situated in an immense plain of white sand, having no vegetation but stunted trees and shrubs, such as the *mimosa ferruginea*, which grows no higher than three or four feet. The city is not closed by any barrier, and may be entered on any side. Within the town are seen some of the *balanitis egyptiaca*, and in the centre is a palm tree.

Timbuktu may contain at most about ten or twelve thousand inhabitants; all are engaged in trade. The population is at times augmented by the Arabs, who come with the caravans, and remain awhile in the city. In the plain several species of grass and thistles afford food for the camels. Firewood is very scarce, being all brought from the neighbourhood of Cabra. It is an article of trade, and the women sell it in the market-place. It is only burnt by the rich; the poor use camel-dung for fuel. Water is also sold in the market-place; the women give a measure containing about half a pint for a cowrie.

2. Wives and Slaves

The inhabitants of Timbuktu are exceedingly neat in their dress and in the interior of their dwellings. Their domestic articles consist of calabashes and wooden platters. They are unacquainted with the use of knives and forks, and they believe that, like them, all people in the world eat with their fingers. Their furniture merely consists of mats for sitting on; and their beds are made by fixing four stakes in the ground at one end of the room, and stretching over them some mats or a cow-hide. The rich have cotton mattresses, and coverlets, which the neighbouring Moors manufacture from camel's hair and sheep's wool. I saw a woman of Cabra employed in spinning these coverlets.

The natives of Timbuktu, as I before observed, have several wives, and to these many add their slaves. The Moors, indeed, cohabit only with their slaves, and these females are employed in vending merchandise in the streets, such as colats, allspice, etc. Some also have a little stall in the market-place, while the favourite stays at home, superintending those whose

148

business it is to cook for the household: the favourite herself prepares the husband's meals. These women are very neatly dressed: their costume consists of a coussabe, like that worn by the men, except that it has not large sleeves. Their shoes are of morocco. The fashion of the head-dress sometimes varies; it principally consists of a *fatara* of fine muslin, or some other cotton stuff of European manufacture. Their hair is beautifully plaited. The principal tress, which is about an inch thick, comes from the back to the front of the head, and is terminated by a piece of cornelian of a round form and concave in the centre; they put a little cushion under the tress to support it, and add to that ornament several other trinkets, made of imitation of amber or coral, and bits of cornelian cut like that just mentioned. They also anoint the head and the whole body with butter, but less profusely than the Bambaras and the Mandingoes. The great heat, which is augmented by the scorching east wind, renders this custom necessary. The women of the richer class have always a great number of glass beads about their necks and in their ears. Like the women of Jenne, they wear nose-rings; and the female who is not rich enough to procure a ring, substitutes a bit of red silk for it; they wear silver bracelets, and ankle-rings of plated steel, the latter of which are made in the country; instead of being round, like the bracelets, are flat, and about four inches broad. Some pretty designs are engraved on them.

The female slaves of rich masters have gold ornaments about their necks; instead of wearing ear-rings as in the environs of the Senegal, they have little plates in the form of a necklace. A few days after my arrival at Timbuktu I fell in with a negro, who was parading about the streets two women, whom I recollected to have been fellow-passengers with me on board the canoe. These women were not young, but their master, to give them the appearance of an age better suited to the market, had dressed them well. They wore fine white pagnes, large gold ear-rings, and each had two or three necklaces of the same metal. When I passed them, they looked at me, and smiled. They did not appear in the least mortified at being exhibited in the streets for sale, but manifested an indifference which I could easily enough account for, by the state of degradation to which they had been reduced and their total ignorance of the natural rights of mankind. They thought that things should be so, and that they had come into this world to be bought and sold.

RICHARD LEMON LANDER

(1804–1834)

Cornish explorer. He travelled with Clapperton until his death in 1827. Sent back by the British government in 1830 with his brother John (1807–39), he finally solved the problem of the Niger's route. Returning together to Africa a third time, they were attacked on the island of Fernando Po and Richard was killed.

1, 2: *The Journal of Richard Lander from Kano to the Sea-coast* (London, 1829); 3: R. and J. Lander, *Journal of an Expedition to Explore the Course and Termination of the Niger* (London, 1932).

1. BURIAL OF CLAPPERTON (1827)

The violence of my grief having subsided, Pasko and Mudey, whom my exclamations had brought into the apartment, fetched me water, with which I washed the corpse, and with their assistance, carried it outside the hut, laid it on a clean mat, and wrapped it in a sheet and blanket. After leaving it in this state nearly two hours, I put a large neat mat over the whole, and sent a messenger to make Bello acquainted with the mournful event, as well as to obtain his permission to have the body buried after the manner of my own country; and also to learn in what particular place the Sultan would wish to have it interred. The man soon returned with a favourable answer to the former part of my request, and about twelve o'clock on the morning of the same day, a person came into the hut, accompanied by four slaves, to dig the grave; and wished me to follow him with the corpse. Accordingly, saddling my camel, the body was placed on the animal's back, and throwing a British flag over it, I requested the men to proceed. Having passed through the dismal streets of Soccatoo, we travelled almost unobservedly, at a solemn pace, and halted near Jungavie, a small village, built on a rising ground about five miles south-east of the city. The body was then taken from the camel's back, and placed in a shed, whilst the slaves were employed in digging the grave. Their task being speedily accomplished, the corpse was borne to the brink of the pit, and I planted the flag close to it; then, uncovering my head, and opening a prayer-book, amidst showers of tears, I read the impressive funeral service of the Church of England over the remains of my valued master—the English flag waving slowly and mournfully over them at the same moment. Not a single soul

150

listened to this peculiarly distressing ceremony; for the slaves were quarreling with each other the whole of the time it lasted.

2. ORDEAL BY POISON

In the private fetish-hut of the King Adolee, at Badagry, the skull of that monarch's father is preserved in a clay vessel, placed in the earth. Human blood, as well as the blood of birds and beasts, is occasionally sprinkled on it; and when the king goes to war, that same skull is invariably carried with him, with which he frequently converses, and gently rebukes it, if his success does not happen to answer his expectations. 'If this custom be neglected', said Adolee, 'the virtues and martial energy of my deceased father would cease to influence my actions, and defeat and disgrace would attend all my warlike undertakings.' The people of Badagry regard this skull with the same veneration as the Turks do the sacred banner of their Prophet; and believe that should it be missed through any casualty, or captured by the enemy, the destiny of their prince would be sealed for ever, and the pillars of their monarchy crumble into dust, so that they would no longer be a people!

There is another fetish-hut at Badagry, the interior of which is positively ornamented with rows of human skulls, and other emblems of mortality, whitened by time, and having a most terrific appearance. In this Pagan sanctuary all suspected persons go through the ordeal of bitter (poisonous) water, in order to ascertain their guilt or innocence; and death, which in almost all cases ensues shortly after the prisoner receives the fatal draught into his stomach, is considered by the people as a sure criterion of the former; whilst, if the culprit has the good fortune to escape with life, which rarely happens, he is pronounced free of the allegations brought against him, and immediately acquitted.

At a short distance from this gloomy hut stands a fetish-tree, on the branches of which the headless bodies of human beings, slaughtered under them, are invariably suspended.

I did not think, as I strolled one day to the spot, and scrutinized the exterior of the fetish-hut, that I myself was so shortly to enter its doors, and be tried with bitter water by its inexorable priests, in order to prove whether I was a good or bad man, a friend or foe to their nation!

But the calumnies of the Portuguese had recently begun to display their effects very strikingly; Adolee had latterly behaved in a cold and distant manner to me; and his chiefs studiously shunned my presence whenever they observed me approaching them.

One morning, as I was taking my solitary breakfast of palm oil and

Indian corn, I was startled by a message from the king, commanding me to repair at noon-tide to the fetish-hut, and be examined by the priests, who would be there assembled, to answer certain charges that would be brought against me. I was well aware in what manner my trial was to be conducted; and I could not forbear exclaiming to myself, as I mused on the dreadful fate which I imagined awaited me: 'Well then, here will be an end to my wanderings and my life; yet, having escaped so many dangers, and encountered such grievous afflictions, it is hard, after all, to cast off the fardel of existence thus prematurely; it is hard, when almost within hearing of my countrymen, that my life should be destroyed; that my skull should be preserved as a trophy by heartless savages, and my body be devoured by ravens and other birds of prey.' As I was making this saddening, and perhaps unmanly soliloquy, tears rushed involuntarily into my eyes, but, hastily wiping them off, I employed the little time allotted me in making my peace with Heaven, so that when the fellows came to conduct me to the fetish-hut, I was calm and collected, and prepared to undergo the severest punishment which the power of man could inflict upon me.

The news of the white man's arrest, and approaching trial, spread like wild-fire through the town, and the inhabitants, assembling from all parts, armed with axes, spears, clubs, and bows and arrows, followed the procession to the dismal spot. On entering the hut, I beheld a number of priests and elders of the people, seated in a circle, who desired me to stand in the midst of them. When I had complied with their request, one of the priests arose, and presenting me with a bowl, containing about a quart of a clear liquid, scarcely distinguishable from water, cried out in a loud voice, and with much emphasis, 'You are accused, white man, of designs against our king and his government, and are therefore desired to drink the contents of this vessel, which, if the reports to your prejudice be true, will surely destroy you; whereas, if they be without foundation, you need not fear, Christian; the fetish will do you no injury, for our gods will do that which is right.'

I took the bowl in my trembling hand, and gazed for a moment on the sable countenances of my judges; but not a single look of compassion shone upon any of them; a dead silence prevailed in the gloomy sanctuary of skulls; every eye was intently fixed upon me; and seeing no possibility of escape, or of evading the piercing glance of the priests and elders, I offered up, internally, a short prayer to the Throne of Mercy—to the God of Christians—and hastily swallowed the fetish, dashing the poison-chalice to the ground. A low murmur ran through the assembly; they all thought I should instantly have expired, or at least have discovered symptoms of severe agony, but detecting no such tokens, they arose simultaneously, and made way for me to leave the hut. On getting into the open air, I found my poor slaves in tears; they had come, they said, to catch a last glimpse of their master; but when they saw me alive and at liberty, they leaped and danced for joy, and prepared a path for me through the dense mass of armed people. These set up an astounding shout at my unexpected appearance, and seemed greatly pleased (if I might be allowed to judge) that I had not fallen a victim to the influence of their fearful fetish. On arriving at my dwelling, I took instant and powerful means to eject the venomous potion from my stomach, and happily succeeded in the attempt.

I was told that the liquid I had swallowed was a decoction of the bark of a tree abounding in the neighbourhood, and that I was the only individual who, for a long season, had escaped its poisonous qualities. It had a disagreeably bitter taste, but I experienced no other ill effects from it than a slight dizziness, which wore off completely a few hours after the conclusion of the trial.

The dreadful charm having been thus providentially broken, all the cold reserve and stiffness of Adolee and his chiefs suddenly disappeared; and they visited me voluntarily a few days afterwards with presents of provisions, & c. observing frequently that the Portuguese were wicked men, but that I was a good man, under the special protection of the white man's God, who would suffer no evil to come near me.

3. ARRIVAL AT BADAGRY (1830)

March 22nd. Cheered by six hearty huzzas, good-naturedly given us by the crew of the Clinker, at the desire of her gallant commander, we sailed towards the beach in one of the brig's boats in the earlier part of the afternoon, and having been taken into a canoe that was waiting at the edge of the breakers to receive us, we were plied over a tremendous surf, and flung with violence on the burning sands.

Wet and uncomfortable as this accident had rendered us, we had no change of linen at hand, and we walked to a small creek about the distance of a quarter of a mile from the sea-shore, where we were taken into a native canoe, and conveyed safely through an extremely narrow channel, overhung with luxuriant vegetation, into the Badagry river, which is a branch of the Lagos. It is a beautiful body of water, resembling a lake in miniature: its surface is smooth and transparent as glass, and its picturesque banks are shaded by trees of a lively verdure. We were soon landed on the opposite side, when our road lay over a magnificent plain, on which deer, antelopes, and buffaloes are often observed to feed. Numbers of men, women, and children followed us to the town of Badagry, and they made the most terrific noises at our heels, but whether these were symptoms of satisfaction or displeasure, admiration or ridicule, we could not at first understand. We were soon, however, satisfied that the latter feeling was predominant; and indeed our clothing was exceedingly grotesque, consisting of a straw hat larger than an umbrella, a scarlet Mohammedan tobe or tunic and belt, with boots and full Turkish trousers. So unusual a dress might well cause the people to laugh heartily; they were all evidently highly amused, but the more modest of the females, unwilling to give us any uneasiness, turned aside to conceal the titter from which they were utterly unable to refrain.

✻

JOHANN LUDWIG KRAPF

(1810–1881)

German missionary with the English Church Missionary Society. He travelled with Johann Rebmann (1820–1876), who contributed to the subsequent publication. They were the first explorers of East Africa to see and describe snow-capped mountains, descriptions greeted at first with disbelief in Europe.

Travels, Researches and Missionary Labours by the Rev. Dr. J. L. Krapf (London, 1860).

1. AMONG THE WANYIKA TRIBES (1844)

After a three hours' walk we reached the village of Endila, which consists of only some eight or ten huts. The elders were sitting under a tree, and I felt rather strange on beholding these naked savages who said scarcely anything when I appeared, and did not even stand up, but looked sadly and gloomily on the ground, often gazing at me as if I were a higher being. The chief went at last into his hut and fetched a bowl of milk, mixed with blood as I afterwards found; for they believe that thus taken, blood helps to nourish their natural strength. . . . Their legs and arms, necks and hair, were covered with white and blue beads, which in combination with their nudity gave them a striking and singular appearance; for many of the men were perfectly naked, whilst others wore a mere rag in imitation of the fig-leaf of sculptors, and even the women had a very scant covering below the waist, being otherwise completely naked from head to foot. Behind, a kind of leather caudal appendage was worn, fastened round the loins with a thong. No wonder then that people say 'there are people with tails in the interior of Africa!'

2. FIRST SIGHTING OF SNOW ON KILIMANJARO
(REBMANN'S JOURNAL, 1848)

May 11. In the midst of a great wilderness, full of wild beasts, such as rhinoceroses, buffaloes, and elephants, we slept beneath thorn-bushes, quietly and securely under God's gracious protection! This morning we discerned the mountains of Jagga more distinctly than ever; and about ten o'clock, I fancied I saw the summit of one of them covered with a dazzlingly white cloud. My guide called the white which I saw, merely *Beredi*, cold; it was perfectly clear to me, however, that it could be nothing else but snow. . . .

Rungua, king of Majame, the father of Mamkinga, once sent a large expedition to investigate the nature of snow. He hoped it might prove to be silver, or something of the kind; but only one of the party survived, and with frozen hands and feet announced to the king the melancholy fate of his companions, who had been destroyed not only by the cold, but by fear and terror; for in their ignorance they ascribed the effects of the cold to evil spirits, and fled away, only to meet with destruction in severer frost and cold. My guide told me that he had seen the poor man, whose frost-bitten hands and feet were bent inwards by the cold, and that he had heard from his own lips the story of his adventures.

❄

SIR FRANCIS GALTON

(1822–1911)

English scientist. He received the Royal Geographical Society's Gold Medal for his travels in Africa. His Art of Travel *became the standard explorers' handbook.*

The Art of Travel (London, 1860).

1. REPUTED DANGERS OF TRAVEL

A young man of good constitution, who is bound on an enterprise sanctioned by experienced travellers, does not run very great risks. Let those who doubt, refer to the history of the various expeditions encouraged by the Royal Geographical Society, and they will see how few deaths have occurred; and of those deaths how small a proportion among young travellers. Savages rarely murder newcomers; they fear their guns, and have a superstitious awe of the white man's power: they require time to discover that he is not very different to themselves, and easily to be made away with. Ordinary fevers are seldom fatal to the sound and elastic constitution of youth, which usually has power to resist the adverse influences of two or three years of wild life.

2. MANAGEMENT OF SAVAGES

A frank, joking, but determined manner, joined with an air of showing more confidence in the good faith of the natives than you really feel, is the best. It is observed that a sea-captain generally succeeds in making an excellent impression on savages: they thoroughly appreciate common sense, truth, and uprightness; and are not half such fools as strangers usually account them. If a savage does mischief, look on him as you would on a kicking mule, or a wild animal, whose nature is to be unruly and vicious, and keep your temper quite unruffled. Evade the mischief, if you can: if you cannot, endure it; and do not trouble yourself overmuch about your dignity, or about retaliating on the man, except it be on the grounds of expediency. There are even times when any assumption of dignity becomes ludicrous, and the traveller must, as Mungo Park had once to do, 'lay it down as a rule to make himself as useless and as insignificant as possible, as the only means of recovering his liberty'.

✻

HEINRICH BARTH

(1821–1865)

German scholar and explorer. He joined the British Government's Central African Expedition in 1850 under the leadership of James Richardson

(1806–51) and with another German, the geologist Alfred Overweg (1822–52). They crossed the Sahara from Tripoli to Lake Chad, where both his companions died. Barth continued to carry out meticulous research and travel vast distances, reaching Timbuktu before returning to Europe in 1855.

Travels and Discoveries in North and Central Africa, 1849–55 (London, 1858).

1. IN TIMBUKTU (1853)

The style of the buildings was various. I could see clay houses of different characters, some low and unseemly, others rising with a second storey in front to greater elevation, and making even an attempt at architectural ornament, the whole being interrupted by a few round huts of matting. The sight of this spectacle afforded me sufficient matter of interest, although, the streets being very narrow, only little was to be seen of the intercourse carried on in them, with the exception of the small market in the northern quarter, which was exposed to view on account of its situation on the slope of the sand-hills, which, in course of time, have accumulated round the mosque.

But while the terrace of my house served to make me well acquainted with the character of the town, it had also the disadvantage of exposing me fully to the gaze of the passers-by, so that I could only slowly, and with many interruptions, succeed in making a sketch of the scene thus offered to my view, and which is represented in the frontispiece. At the same time I became aware of the great inaccuracy which characterizes the view of the town as given by M. Caillié; still, on the whole, the character of the single dwellings was well represented by that traveller, the only error being that in his representation the whole town seems to consist of scattered and quite isolated houses, while in reality the streets are entirely shut in, as the dwellings form continuous and uninterrupted rows. But it must be taken into account that Timbuktu, at the time of Caillié's visit, was not so well off as it is at present, having been overrun by the Fulbe the preceding year, and he had no opportunity of making a drawing on the spot.

Although I was greatly delighted at the pleasant place of retreat for refreshing my spirits and invigorating my body by a little exercise which the terrace afforded me, I was disgusted by the custom which prevails in the houses like that in which I was lodged, of using the terrace as a sort of closet; and I had great difficulty in preventing my guide, Ammer el Walati, who still stayed with me and made the terrace his usual residence, from indulging in this filthy practice.

Being anxious to impart to my friends in Europe the news of my safe arrival in this far-famed town, I was busily employed in writing letters, which gave fresh impulse to my energy. My tormentor Sidi Alawate himself seemed anxious to rouse my spirits, which he could not but be conscious of having contributed a great deal to depress, by sending me word that he himself would undertake to accompany me on my home journey, as he intended making the pilgrimage to Mecca; but, having once had full opportunity of judging of the character of this man, I placed but little confidence in his words.

... suddenly, on the morning of the 10th, while I was suffering from another attack of fever, I was excited by the report being circulated that the party opposed to my residence in the town was arming in order to attack me in my house. Now I must confess that, notwithstanding the profession of sincere friendship made to me by Sidi Alawate, I am inclined to believe that he himself was not free from treachery, and, perhaps, was in some respect implicated in this manoeuvre, as he evidently supposed that, on the first rumour of such an attack being intended, I should abandon my house, or at least my property, when he might hope to get possession underhand of at least a good portion of the latter before the arrival of his brother, whom he knew to be a straightforward man, and who would not connive at such intrigues. With this view, I have no doubt, he sent a female servant to my house, advising me to deposit all my goods in safety with the Taleb el Wafi, as the danger which threatened me was very great; but this errand had no other effect than to rouse my spirits. I armed immediately, and ordered my servants to do the same, and my supposed protector was not a little astonished when he himself came shortly afterward with the Walati (who, no doubt, was at the bottom of the whole affair) and found me ready to defend myself and my property, and to repulse any attack that might be made upon my residence, from whatever quarter it might proceed. He asked me whether I meant to fight the whole population of the town, uttering the words 'guwet e' Rum', 'strength of the Christians'; and protested that I was quite safe under his protection, and had nothing to fear, and certainly, for the moment, my energetic conduct had dispersed the clouds that might have been impending over my head.

But notwithstanding his repeated protestations of sincere friendship, and although he confirmed with his own mouth what I had already heard from other people, that he himself was to accompany me on my return journey as far as Bornu, he did not discontinue for a moment his importunity in begging for more presents day by day.

One day he called on me in company with his principal pupils, and earnestly recommended me to change my religion, and from an unbeliever to become a true believer. Feeling myself strong enough in arguments to defend my own religious principles, I challenged him to demonstrate to me the superiority of his creed, telling him that in that case I should not fail to adopt it, but not till then. Upon this he and his pupils began with alacrity a spirited discussion, in the firm hope that they would soon be able to overcome my arguments; but after a little while they found them rather too strong, and were obliged to give in without making any further progress at the time in their endeavours to persuade me to turn Mohammedan. This incident improved my situation in an extraordinary degree, by basing my safety on the sincere esteem which several of the most intelligent of the inhabitants contracted for me.

2. DAILY FOOD

The course of my material existence went on very uniformly, with only slight variations. My daily food, when I was in the town, consisted of some milk and bread in the morning, a little couscous, which the sheikh used to send, about two in the afternoon, and a dish of negro millet, containing a little meat, or seasoned with the sauce of the kobewa, or *Cucurbita Melopepo*, after sunset. The meat of Timbuktu, at least during the cold season, agreed with me infinitely better than that of any other part of Negroland; but this was not the case with the *Melopepo*, although it is an excellent and palatable vegetable. In the beginning of my stay I had consumed a great many young pigeons, which form a favourite dainty in this city. They are sold at the almost incredibly cheap rate of ten shells each, or at the rate of three hundred for a dollar; but the poor little things were used for culinary purposes so soon after breaking the shell as to be almost tasteless. A very rare dainty was formed by an ostrich egg, which was one day brought to me. This article is more easily to be obtained in the desert than in the towns, and such strong food, moreover, is not well adapted to the stomach of a resident. The sheikh used also to send me a dish late at night, sometimes long after midnight; but, on account of the late hour, I never touched it, and left it to my servants.

3. A FEAST

It was highly interesting for me to be thus brought into close contact with these people, who owe allegiance to the chief that had murdered Major Laing; and, well aware that I could not fail to entertain a strong prejudice against them, they all thronged round me on my arrival, and hastened to assure me of their friendly disposition. They were armed with double-barrelled guns, a weapon which, owing to the trade with the French, is now common through the whole of this part of the desert, the long single-barrelled gun, the only favourite weapon with the Arabs to the north, being here regarded with contempt as befitting only the slave. In general, the people were of middle stature, although some of them were fine tall men and of a warlike and energetic appearance, having their shirts, mostly of a light blue colour, tied up over their shoulder and girt round the waist with a belt, the powder-horn hanging over the shoulder, quite in the same style as is the custom of their brethren nearer the shores of the Atlantic. Their head was uncovered, with the exception of their own rich black hair, or guffa, which, I am sorry to add, was full of vermin.

The same evening, although it was late, my host, who was certainly not wanting in hospitality, slaughtered five oxen, and in consequence we partook of supper about an hour after midnight. But that was not at all unusual here; and nothing during my stay in Timbuktu was more annoying to me, and more injurious to my health, than this unnatural mode of living, which surpasses in absurdity the late hours of London and Paris.

Early the next morning two more head of cattle were slaughtered, and enormous quantities of rice and meat were cooked for the great numbers of guests, who had flocked here together from the town and from all parts of the neighbouring district. . . . The way in which the guests dealt with the enormous dishes, some of which were from four to five feet in diameter, and could only be carried by six persons, bore testimony to the voracity of their appetites; one of these immense dishes was upset, and the whole of the contents spilt in the sand.

But the people were not long left to enjoy their festivity, for just while they were glutting themselves a troop of Kel-hekikan, the tribe who waged the bloody feud with the Gwanin, passed by, throwing the whole encampment into the utmost confusion. When at length it had again settled down, the festivities proceeded, and Mohammed el 'Aish, with some of his countrymen from Tawat, rode a race up the slope of the downs toward the tents, firing their guns at the same time; but altogether the exhibition was rather shabby, and some of the men were very poor riders, having probably never been on horseback before, as they were natives of the desert where the camel prevails. The inhabitants of Timbuktu, who possess horses, are continually pestered with the request to lend them to strangers; and, with regard to these animals, a sort of communism prevails in the town; but they are of a very poor description, only the sheikh himself possessing some good horses, brought from the Gibleh, or western quarter of the desert.

Dr William Balfour Baikie

(1825–1864)

Scottish naval surgeon and naturalist. He explored the Niger and the Benue. He pioneered the effective use of quinine, and settled on the Benue to run a government trading station and breed several children.

Narrative of an Exploring Voyage up the Rivers Kwora and Binue in 1854 (London, 1856).

The Great Dulti Chase (1854)

About half-past ten we entered a creek on the north side, running nearly parallel with the river, and shortly afterwards sighted a village, at which we soon arrived. To our astonishment the first thing which brought us up was our running the bow of the gig against a hut, and on looking around we found the whole place to be flooded. We advanced right into the middle of the village, and found no resting-place; right and left, before and behind, all was water. People came out of the huts to gaze at the apparition, and standing at the doors of their abodes were, without the smallest exaggeration, immersed nearly to their knees, and one child I particularly observed up to its waist. How the interiors of the huts of these amphibious creatures were constructed I cannot conjecture, but we saw dwellings from which, if inhabited, the natives must have dived like beavers to get outside. We pulled in speechless amazement through this city of waters, wondering greatly that human beings could exist under such conditions. We had heard of wild tribes living in caverns and among rocks, we had read of races in Hindustan roosting in trees, of whole families in China spending their lives on rafts and in boats in their rivers and their canals; we knew, too, of Tuariks and Shanbah roaming over vast sandy deserts, and of Eskimo burrowing in snow retreats, but never had we witnessed or even dreamt of such a spectacle as that of creatures endowed like ourselves, living by choice like a colony of beavers, or after the fashion of the hippopotami and crocodiles of the neighbouring swamps.

A little distance from us we espied a large tree, round the foot of which was a patch of dry land, towards which we pulled, but grounding before reaching quite to it, Mr May and I waded to it, instruments in hand, to take observations. We were barely allowed to conclude, when nearly the entire population of the place, half-wading, half-swimming across a small creek, came upon us, and stared at us in wild astonishment. A hurried set of sights being taken, we carried our things back into the boat, and as we wished to get another set about three-quarters of an hour after noon, we tried to amuse ourselves and to spend the intervening time as we best could. We were now able to look a little more attentively at our new friends, who in large numbers crowded round, and who, male and female, were nearly all equally destitute of a vestige of clothing. One young man understood a few words of Hausa, and by this means we learnt that this was the Dulti of which we had heard at Djin, and that the inhabitants were of the same stock as at the other villages; but they were by far more rude, more savage, and more naked than any of the other Baibai whom we had encountered. A canoe came near us, lying in the bottom of which was a curious large fish, of which I had just time to make a rough eye-sketch, when I had to retreat to the boat, and Mr May, who had been exploring in another direction, also returned. The behaviour of these wild people now attracted our notice; the men began to draw closer around us, to exhibit their arms, and to send away the women and children. Their attentions became momentarily more and more familiar, and they plainly evidenced a desire to seize and plunder our boat. A sour-looking old gentleman, who was squatting on the branch of a tree, was mentioned as their king; but if so, he made no endeavours to restrain the cupidity of his *sans-culottes*. Part of a red shirt belonging to one of our crewmen was seen peeping out from below a bag, and some advanced to lay hold of it, when suddenly my little dog, who had been lying quietly in the stern sheets, raised her head to see what was causing such a commotion. Her sudden appearance startled the Dulti warriors, who had never seen such an animal before, so they drew back to take counsel together, making signs to me to know if she could bite, to which I replied in the affirmative. Matters were beginning to look serious; our crew, as usual, were timid, and Mr May and I had only ourselves to depend upon in the midst of three or four hundred armed savages, who were now preparing to make a rush at us. There was no help for it; we had to abandon all hopes of our remaining observations, and of so fixing an exact geographical position. As at Djin, I seized a few trinkets, and handing them hastily to those nearest to us, we shoved off while the people were examining these wondrous treasures.

Still anxious, if possible, to get some further observations not far removed from the spot where the former ones were taken, we pulled about among trees and bushes, but without any success, At length we shoved in among some long grass, hoping to find dry land, but after having proceeded until completely stopped by the thickness of the growth, we still found upwards of a fathom of water. At this moment Mr May's ear caught a voice not far behind us; so we shoved quietly back, and found a couple of canoes trying to cut off our retreat. Seeing this we paddled vigorously back, there not being room for using our oars, and the canoes did not venture to molest us. We were quickly padding across the flooded plain, when suddenly a train of canoes in eager pursuit issued out upon us. There were ten canoes, each containing seven or eight men, and they were sufficiently close to us to allow us to see their stores of arms. Our crewboys worked most energetically, and we went ahead at such a rate that our pursuers had complete occupation found them in paddling, and could not use their weapons. At this moment we were about a couple of hundred yards from the river, towards which we made as straight a course as possible. Not knowing how matters might terminate, we thought it advisable to prepare for defence, so I took our revolver to load it, but now, when it was needed, the ramrod was stiff and quite immoveable. Mr May got a little pocket-pistol ready, and we had if required a cutlass, and a ship's musket, which the crewmen, by this time in a desperate fright, wished to see prepared, as they kept calling out to us, 'Load de big gun, load de big gun'. Could an unconcerned spectator have witnessed the scene, he would have been struck with the amount of the ludicrous it contained. There were our crewboys, all as pale as black men could be, the perspiration starting from every pore, exerting to the utmost their powerful muscles, while Mr May and I were trying to look as unconcerned as possible, and, to lessen the indignity of our retreat, were smiling and bowing to the Dulti people, and beckoning to them to follow us. Their light canoes were very narrow, and the people were obliged to stand upright. The blades of their paddles, instead of being of the usual lozenge shape, were oblong and rectangular, and all curved in the direction of the propelling stroke. It was almost a regatta, our gig taking and keeping the lead. Ahead we saw an opening in the bush, by which we hoped to make our final retreat, but we were prepared, should the boat take the ground, to jump out at once and shove her into deep water. Fortune favoured us, we reached the doubtful spot, and with a single stroke of our paddles shot into the open river. Here we knew we were comparatively safe, as if the natives tried to molest us in the clear water, all we had to do was to give their canoes the stem and so upset them; our only fear had been that of being surrounded by them while entangled among the bushes. Our pursuers apparently guessed that we had now got the advantage, as they declined following us into the river, but turning paddled back to their watery abodes, and so ended the great Dulti chase.

SIR RICHARD BURTON

(1821–1890)

*British explorer. After visiting Mecca and Medina in disguise, he set out,
in 1854, on an expedition to Harar, the forbidden city deep in Somali
territory. Back on the coast he and his companions, Speke and Lt. Stroyan,
were attacked by Somalis. In 1857 he and Speke went in search of the
source of the Nile, a journey which culminated in their famous row.*

1–3: *First Footsteps in East Africa* (London, 1856); 4: *The Lake Regions of Central
Africa* (London, 1860).

1. ILL ON THE WAY TO HARAR (1855)

On the morning after my arrival at Sagharrah I felt too ill to rise, and was
treated with unaffected kindness by all the establishment. The Gerad sent
to Harar for millet beer, Ao Samattar went to the gardens in search of Kat
[a stimulating vegetable drug], the sons Yusuf Dera and a dwarf insisted
upon firing me with such ardour that no refusal could avail: and Khayrah
the wife, with her daughters, two tall, dark, smiling, and well-favoured girls
of thirteen and fifteen, sacrificed a sheep as my Fida, or Expiatory offering.
Even the Galla Christians, who flocked to see the stranger, wept for the
evil fate which had brought him so far from his fatherland, to die under
a tree. Nothing, indeed, would have been easier than such operation: all
required was the turning face to the wall, for four or five days. But to
expire of an ignoble colic!—the thing was not to be thought of, and a firm
resolution to live on sometimes, methinks, effects its object.

On the 1st January, 1855, feeling stronger, I clothed myself in my Arab
best, and asked a palaver with the Gerad. We retired to a safe place behind
the village, where I read with pomposity the Hajj Sharmarkay's letter. The
chief appeared much pleased by our having preferred his country to that
of the Eesa: he at once opened the subject of the new fort, and informed
me that I was the builder, as his eldest daughter had just dreamed that
the stranger would settle in the land. Having discussed the project to the
Gerad's satisfaction, we brought out the guns and shot a few birds for the
benefit of the vulgar. Whilst engaged in this occupation appeared a party
of five strangers, and three mules with ornamented Morocco saddles, bridles,
bells, and brass neck ornaments, after the fashion of Harar. Two of these
men, Haji Umar and Nur Ambar, were citizens: the others, Ali Hasan,

Husayn Araleh, and Haji Mohammed, were Somal of the Habr Awal tribe, high in the Amir's confidence. They had been sent to settle with Adan the weighty matter of Blood-money. After sitting with us almost half-an-hour, during which they exchanged grave salutations with my attendants, inspected our asses with portentous countenances, and asked me a few questions concerning my business in those parts, they went privily to the Gerad, told him that the Arab was not one who bought and sold, that he had no design but to spy out the wealth of the land, and that the whole party should be sent prisoners in their hands to Harar. The chief curtly replied that we were his friends, and bade them 'throw far those words'. Disappointed in their designs, they started late in the afternoon, driving off their 200 cows, and falsely promising to present our salams to the Amir.

2. ISABEL BURTON'S DESCRIPTION OF THE ATTACK

But he would not 'let well alone'; he wanted to make a new expedition, Nilewards via Harar, on a large and imposing scale, and he went and came back from Aden with forty-two armed men, established an agency, and a camp in a place where he could have the protection of an English gunboat which brought them; but unfortunately the Government drew off the gunboat, and 300 of the natives swarmed round them in the night, and tried to throw the tents down, and trap them like mice. They fought desperately, but Speke received eleven wounds, poor Stroyan was killed, Herne was untouched, and Richard Burton, sabreing his way through the crowd, heard a friendly voice behind him, hesitated for a moment, and received a javelin through both cheeks, carrying away four teeth, and transfixing the palate. He could not draw it out on account of its barb and had to wander up and down on the coast for hours from night to daylight. They all managed to escape to the water's edge, where they hailed a native craft, which was just sailing out, and to whose master and crew Richard fortunately had shown great hospitality. They picked them up and managed to extract the javelin and bind up his jaws till they reached Aden. They were so badly wounded that they had to return to England, and as soon as he recovered, he proceeded to the Crimea.

3. BURTON'S OWN DESCRIPTION

Between 2 and 3 a.m. of 19 April I was suddenly aroused by the Balyuz, who cried aloud that the enemy was upon us. Hearing a rush of men like a stormy wind, I sprang up, called for my sabre, and sent Lt. Herne to ascertain the force of the foray. Armed with a 'Colt', he went to the rear and left of the camp, the direction of danger, collected some of the guard—others having already disappeared—and fired two shots into the assailants. Then finding himself alone, he turned hastily towards the tent; in so doing he was tripped up by the ropes, and as he arose, a Somali appeared in the act of striking at him with a club. Lt. Herne fired, floored the man, and rejoining me, declared that the enemy was in great force and the guard nowhere. Meanwhile, I had aroused Lts. Stroyan and Speke, who were sleeping in the extreme right and left tents. The former, it is presumed, arose to defend himself, but, as the sequel shows, we never saw him alive. Lt. Speke, awakened by the report of fire-arms, but supposing it the normal false alarm—a warning to plunderers—he remained where he was: presently hearing clubs rattling upon his tent, and feet shuffling around, he ran to my Rowtie [tent], which we prepared to defend as long as possible.

The enemy swarmed like hornets with shouts and screams intending to terrify, and proving that overwhelming odds were against us: it was by no means easy to avoid in the shades of night the jobbing of javelins, and the long heavy daggers thrown at our legs from under and through the opening of the tent. We three remained together: Lt. Herne knelt by my right, on my left was Lt. Speke guarding the entrance, I stood in the centre, having nothing but a sabre. The revolvers were used by my companions with deadly effect: unfortunately there was but one pair. When the fire was exhausted, Lt. Herne went to search for his powder-horn, and that failing, to find some spears usually tied to the tent-pole. Whilst thus engaged, he saw a man breaking into the rear of our Rowtie, and came back to inform me of the circumstance.

At this time, about five minutes after the beginning of the affray, the tent had been almost beaten down, an Arab custom with which we were all familiar, and had we been entangled in its folds we should have been speared with unpleasant facility. I gave the word for escape, and sallied out, closely followed by Lt. Herne, with Lt. Speke in the rear. The prospect was not agreeable. About twenty men were kneeling and crouching at the tent entrance, whilst many dusk figures stood further off, or ran about shouting the war-cry, or with shouts and blows drove away our camels. Among the enemy were many of our friends and attendants: the coast being open to them, they naturally ran away, firing a few useless shots and receiving a modicum of flesh wounds.

After breaking through the mob at the tent entrance, imagining that I saw the form of Lt. Stroyan lying upon the sand, I cut my way towards it amongst a dozen Somal, whose war-clubs worked without mercy, whilst the Balyuz, who was violently pushing me out of the fray, rendered the strokes of my sabre uncertain. This individual was cool and collected:

166

though incapacitated by a sore right-thumb from using the spear, he did not shun danger, and passed unhurt through the midst of the enemy: his efforts, however, only illustrated the venerable adage, 'defend me from my friends'. I turned to cut him down: he cried out in alarm; the well-known voice caused an instant's hesitation: at that moment a spearman stepped forward, left his javelin in my mouth, and retired before he could be punished. Escaping as by a miracle, I sought some support: many of our Somal and servants lurking in the darkness offered to advance, but 'tailed off' to a man as we approached the foe. Presently the Balyuz reappeared, and led me towards the place where he believed my three comrades had taken refuge. I followed him, sending the only man that showed presence of mind, one Golab of the Yusuf tribe, to bring back the Aynterad craft from the Spit into the centre of the harbour.[1]

Again losing the Balyuz in the darkness, I spent the interval before dawn wandering in search of my comrades, and lying down when overpowered with faintness and pain: as the day broke, with my remaining strength I reached the head of the creek, was carried into the vessel, and persuaded the crew to arm themselves and visit the scene of our disasters.

Meanwhile, Lt. Herne, who had closely followed me, fell back, using the butt-end of his discharged six-shooter upon the hard heads around him: in so doing he came upon a dozen men, who though they loudly vociferated, 'Kill the Franks who are killing the Somal!' allowed him to pass uninjured.

He then sought his comrades in the empty huts of the town, and at early dawn was joined by the Balyuz, who was similarly employed. When day broke he sent a Negro to stop the native craft, which was apparently sailing out of the harbour, and in due time came on board. With the exception of sundry stiff blows with the war-club, Lt. Herne had the fortune to escape unhurt.

On the other hand, Lt. Speke's escape was in every way wonderful. Sallying from the tent he levelled his 'Dean and Adams' close to his assailant's breast. The pistol refused to revolve. A sharp blow of a war-club upon the chest felled our comrade, who was in the rear and unseen. When he fell, two or three men sprang upon him, pinioned his hands behind, felt him for concealed weapons—an operation to which he submitted in some alarm—and led him towards the rear, as he supposed to be slaughtered. There, Lt. Speke, who could scarcely breathe from the pain of the blow, asked a captor to tie his hands before, instead of behind, and begged a

---

[1] At this season native craft quitting Berberah make for the Spit late in the evening, cast anchor there, and set sail with the land breeze before dawn. Our lives hung upon a thread. Had the vessel departed, as she intended, the night before the attack, nothing could have saved us from destruction.

drop of water to relieve his excruciating thirst. The savage defended him against a number of the Somal who came up threatening and brandishing their spears, he brought a cloth for the wounded man to lie upon, and lost no time in procuring a draught of water.

Lt. Speke remained upon the ground till dawn. During the interval he witnessed the war-dance of the savages—a scene striking in the extreme. The tallest and largest warriors marched in a ring round the tents and booty, singing, with the deepest and most solemn tones, the song of thanksgiving. At a little distance the grey uncertain light disclosed four or five men, lying desperately hurt, whilst their kinsmen kneaded their limbs, poured water upon their wounds, and placed lumps of dates in their stiffening hands.[2] As day broke, the division of plunder caused angry passions to rise. The dead and dying were abandoned. One party made a rush upon the cattle, and with shouts and yells drove them off towards the wild, some loaded themselves with goods, others fought over pieces of cloth, which they tore with hand and dagger, whilst the disappointed, vociferating with rage, struck at one another and brandished their spears. More than once during these scenes, a panic seized them; they moved off in a body to some distance; and there is little doubt that had our guard struck one blow, we might still have won the day.

Lt. Speke's captor went to seek his own portion of the spoil, when a Somali came up and asked in Hindustani, what business the Frank had in their country, and added that he would kill him if a Christian, but spare the life of a brother Moslem. The wounded man replied that he was going to Zanzibar, that he was still a Nazarene, and therefore that the work had better be done at once—the savage laughed and passed on. He was succeeded by a second, who, equally compassionate, whirled a sword round his head, twice pretended to strike, but returned to the plunder without doing damage. Presently came another manner of assailant. Lt. Speke, who had extricated his hands, caught the spear levelled at his breast, but received at the same moment a blow from a club which, paralysing his arm, caused him to lose his hold. In defending his heart from a succession of thrusts, he received severe wounds on the back of his hand, his right shoulder, and his left thigh. Pausing a little, the wretch crossed to the other side, and suddenly passed his spear clean through the right leg of the wounded man: the latter, 'smelling death', then leapt up, and taking advantage of his assailant's terror, rushed headlong towards the sea. Looking behind, he avoided the javelin hurled at his back, and had the good fortune to run, without further accident, the gauntlet of a score of missiles.

[2] The Somal place dates in the hands of the fallen to ascertain the extent of injury: he who cannot eat that delicacy is justly decided to be *in articulo*.

When pursuit was discontinued, he sat down faint from loss of blood upon a sandhill. Recovering strength by a few minutes' rest, he staggered on to the town, where some old women directed him to us. Then, pursuing his way, he fell in with the party sent to seek him, and by their aid reached the craft, having walked and run at least three miles, after receiving eleven wounds, two of which had pierced his thighs. A touching lesson how difficult it is to kill a man in sound health![3]

4. BURTON ON SPEKE'S ILLNESS (1858)

At Hanga my companion was taken seriously ill. He had been chilled on the line of march by the cruel easterly wind, and at the end of the second march from Kazeh he appeared trembling as if with ague. Immediately after arrival at the foul village of Hanga—where we lodged in a kind of cow-house, full of vermin, and exposed directly to the fury of the cold gales—he complained, in addition to a deaf ear, an inflamed eye, and a swollen face, of a mysterious pain which often shifted its seat, and which he knew not whether to attribute to liver or to spleen. It began with a burning sensation, as by a branding-iron, above the right breast, and then extended to the heart with sharp twinges. After ranging around the spleen, it attacked the upper part of the right lung, and finally it settled in the region of the liver. On 10 October, suddenly waking about dawn from a horrible dream, in which a close pack of tigers, leopards, and other beasts, harnessed with a network of iron hooks, were dragging him like the rush of a whirlwind over the ground, he found himself sitting up on the side of his bedding, forcibly clasping both sides with his hands. Half stupefied by pain, he called Bombay, who, having formerly suffered from the *kichyoma-chyoma*—the 'little irons'—raised his master's right arm, placed him in a sitting position, as lying down was impossible, and directed him to hold the left ear behind the head, thus relieving the excruciating and torturing twinges by lifting the lung from the liver. The next spasm was less severe, but the sufferer's mind had begun to wander, and he again clasped his sides, a proceeding with which Bombay interfered.

Early on the next morning, my companion, supported by Bombay and Gaetano, staggered toward the tent. Nearing the doorway, he sent in his Goanese to place a chair for sitting, as usual during the toils of the day, outside. The support of an arm being thus removed, ensued a second and violent spasm of cramps and twinges, all the muscles being painfully

[3] In less than a month after receiving such injuries, Lieut. Speke was on his way to England: he has never felt the least inconvenience from the wounds, which closed up like cuts in Indian-rubber.

contracted. After resting for a few moments, he called his men to assist him into the house. But neglecting to have a chair previously placed for him, he underwent a third fit of the same epileptic description, which more closely resembled those of hydrophobia than aught I had ever witnessed. He was once more haunted by a crowd of hideous devils, giants, and lion-headed demons, who were wrenching, with superhuman force, and stripping the sinews and tendons of his legs down to the ankles. At length, sitting, or rather lying upon the chair, with limbs racked by cramps, features drawn and ghastly, frame fixed and rigid, eyes glazed and glassy, he began to utter a barking noise, and a peculiar chopping motion of the mouth and tongue, with lips protruding—the effect of difficulty of breathing—which so altered his appearance that he was hardly recognizable, and completed the terror of the beholders. When this, the third and the severest spasm, had passed away, he called for pen and paper, and fearing that increased weakness of mind and body might presently prevent any exertion, he wrote an incoherent letter of farewell to his family. That, however, was the crisis. He was afterward able to take the proper precautions, never moving without assistance, and always ordering a resting-place to be prepared for him. He spent a better night, with the inconvenience, however, of sitting up, pillow-propped, and some weeks elapsed before he could lie upon his sides. Presently the pains were mitigated, though they did not entirely cease: this he expressed by saying that 'the knives were sheathed'. Such, gentle reader, in East Africa, is the *kichyoma-chyoma*.

❖

JOHN HANNING SPEKE

(1827–1864)

British army officer and explorer. He named Lake Victoria, the source of the Nile, in 1858 while travelling with but separated from Richard Burton. Returning with James Grant between 1860 and 1863, he spent some time in Buganda. He died in a shooting accident just before a meeting of the British Association for the Advancement of Science in Bath, at which he and Burton were due to confront each other.

1: *Blackwood's Magazine*, 1859; 2, 3: *Journal of the Discovery of the Source of the Nile* (Edinburgh and London, 1863).

1. A BEETLE IN THE EAR (1858)

At night a violent storm of rain and wind beat on my tent with such fury that its nether parts were torn away from the pegs, and the tent itself was only kept upright by sheer force. On the wind's abating, a candle was lighted to rearrange the kit, and in a moment, as though by magic, the whole interior became covered with a host of small black beetles, evidently attracted by the glimmer of the candle. They were so annoyingly determined in their choice of place for peregrinating, that it seemed hopeless my trying to brush them off the clothes or bedding; for as one was knocked aside another came on, and then another, till at last, worn out, I extinguished the candle, and with difficulty—trying to overcome the tickling annoyance occasioned by these intruders crawling up my sleeves and into my hair, or down my back and legs—fell off to sleep. Repose that night was not destined to be my lot. One of these horrid little insects awoke me in his struggles to penetrate my ear, but just too late: for, in my endeavour to extract him, I aided his immersion. He went his course, struggling up the narrow channel, until he got arrested by want of passage-room. This impediment evidently enraged him, for he began with exceeding vigour, like a rabbit at a hole, to dig violently away at my tympanum. The queer sensation this amusing *measure* excited in me is past description. I felt inclined to act as our donkeys once did when beset by a swarm of bees, who buzzed about their ears and stung their heads and eyes until they were so irritated and confused that they galloped about in the most distracted order, trying to knock them off by treading on their heads, or by rushing under bushes, into houses, or through any jungle they could find. Indeed, I do not know which was worst off. The bees killed some of them, and this beetle nearly did for me. What to do I knew not. Neither tobacco, oil, nor salt could be found: I therefore tried melted butter; that failing, I applied the point of a penknife to his back, which did more harm than good; for though a few thrusts kept him quiet, the point also wounded my ear so badly that inflammation set in, severe suppuration took place, and all the facial glands extending from that point down to the point of the shoulder became contorted and drawn aside, and a string of buboes decorated the whole length of that region. It was the most painful thing I ever remember to have endured; but, more annoying still, I could not open my mouth for several days, and had to feed on broth alone. For many months the tumour made me almost deaf, and ate a hole between that orifice and the nose, so that when I blew it, my ear whistled so audibly that those who heard it laughed. Six or seven months after this accident happened, bits of the beetle, a leg, a wing, or parts of its body, came away in the wax.

2. A MATTER OF DIGNITY AT THE COURT OF THE KABAKA
(1862)

I was requested to sit on the ground outside in the sun with my servants. Now, I had made up my mind never to sit upon the ground as the natives and Arabs are obliged to do, nor to make my obeisance in any other manner than is customary in England, though the Arabs had told me that from fear they had always complied with the manners of the court. I felt that if I did not stand up for my social position at once, I should be treated with contempt during the remainder of my visit, and thus lose the vantage-ground I had assumed of appearing rather as a prince than a trader, for the purpose of better gaining the confidence of the king. To avert over-hastiness, however—for my servants began to be alarmed as I demurred against doing as I was bid—I allowed five minutes to the court to give me a proper reception, saying, if it were not conceded I would then walk away.

Nothing, however, was done. My own men, knowing me, feared for me, as they did not know what a 'savage' king would do in case I carried out my threat; whilst the Waganda, lost in amazement at what seemed little less than blasphemy, stood still as posts. The affair ended by my walking straight away home, giving Bombay orders to leave the present on the ground, and to follow me.

Although the king is said to be unapproachable, excepting when he chooses to attend court—a ceremony which rarely happens—intelligence of my hot wrath and hasty departure reached him in an instant. He first, it seems, thought of leaving his toilet-room to follow me, but, finding I was walking fast and had gone far, changed his mind, and sent Wakungu running after me. Poor creatures! they caught me up, fell upon their knees, and implored I would return at once, for the king had not tasted food, and would not until he saw me. I felt grieved at their touching appeals; but, as I did not understand all they said, I simply replied by patting my heart and shaking my head, walking if anything all the faster.

On my arrival at my hut, Bombay and others came in, wet through with perspiration, saying the king had heard of all my grievances. Suwarora's hongo [tribute] was turned out of court, and, if I desired it, I might bring my own chair with me, for he was very anxious to show me great respect—although such a seat was exclusively the attribute of the king, no one else in Uganda daring to sit on an artificial seat.

My point was gained, so I cooled myself with coffee and a pipe, and returned rejoicing in my victory, especially over Suwarora. . . .

At noon Mtesa sent his pages to invite me to his palace. I went, with my guard of honour and my stool, but found I had to sit waiting in an ante-hut three hours with his commander-in-chief and other high officers before he was ready to see me. During this time Wasoga minstrels, playing on tambira, and accompanied by boys playing on a harmonicon, kept us amused; and a small page, with a large bundle of grass, came to me and said, 'The king hopes you won't be offended if required to sit on it before him; for no person in Uganda, however high in office, is ever allowed to sit upon anything raised above the ground, nor can anybody but himself sit upon such grass as this; it is all that his throne is made of. The first day he only allowed you to sit on your stool to appease your wrath.'

On consenting to do in 'Rome as the Romans do', when my position was so handsomely acknowledged, I was called in, and found the court sitting much as it was on the first day's interview, only that the number of squatting Wakungu was much diminished; and the king, instead of wearing his ten brass and copper rings, had my gold one on his third finger. This day, however, was cut out for business, as, in addition to the assemblage of officers, there were women, cows, goats, fowls, confiscations, baskets of fish, baskets of small antelopes, porcupines, and curious rats caught by his gamekeepers, bundles of mbugu, etc., made by his linen-drapers, coloured earths and sticks by his magician, all ready for presentation; but, as rain fell, the court broke up, and I had nothing for it but to walk about under my umbrella, indulging in angry reflections against the haughty king for not inviting me into his hut.

When the rain had ceased, and we were again called in, he was found sitting in state as before, but this time with the head of a black bull placed before him, one horn of which, knocked off, was placed alongside, whilst four living cows walked about the court.

I was now requested to shoot the four cows as quickly as possible; but having no bullets for my gun, I borrowed the revolving pistol I had given him, and shot all four in a second of time; but as the last one, only wounded, turned sharply upon me, I gave him the fifth and settled him. Great applause followed this *wonderful* feat, and the cows were given to my men. The king now loaded one of the carbines I had given him with his own hands, and giving it full-cock to a page, told him to go out and shoot a man in the outer court; which was no sooner accomplished than the little urchin returned to announce his success, with a look of glee such as one would see in the face of a boy who had robbed a bird's nest, caught a trout, or done any other boyish trick. The king said to him, 'And did you do it well?' 'Oh yes, capitally.' He spoke the truth, no doubt, for he dared not have trifled with the king; but the affair created hardly any interest. I never heard, and there appeared no curiosity to know, what individual human being the urchin had deprived of life.

3. CONFIRMATION OF THE NILE SOURCE

18 July. Here at last I stood on the brink of the Nile; most beautiful was the scene, nothing could surpass it! It was the very perfection of the kind of effect aimed at in a highly kept park; with a magnificent stream from 600 to 700 yards wide, dotted with islets and rocks, the former occupied with fishermen's huts, the latter by sterns and crocodiles basking in the sun—flowing between fine high grassy banks, with rich trees and plantains in the background, where herds of the nsunnu [Uganda Kob] and hartebeest could be seen grazing, while the hippopotami were snorting in the water, and florikan and guinea-fowl rising at our feet. . . .

I told my men they ought to shave their heads and bathe in the holy river, the cradle of Moses—the waters of which, sweetened with sugar, men carry all the way from Egypt to Mecca, and sell to the pilgrims. But Bombay, who is a philosopher of the Epicurean school, said, 'We don't look on these things in the same fanciful manner that you do; we are contented with all the common-places of life, and look for nothing beyond the present. If things don't go well, it is God's will; and if they do go well, that is His will also.' . . .

I marched up the left bank of the Nile at a considerable distance from the water, to the Ismaba Rapids, passing through rich jungle and plantain-gardens. Nango, an old friend, first refreshed us with a dish of plantain-squash and dried fish, with *pombe*.

24 July. He then took us to see the nearest falls of the Nile—extremely beautiful, but very confined. The water ran deep between its banks, which were covered with fine grass, soft cloudy acacias, and festoons of lilac convolvuli; whilst here and there, where the land had slipped above the rapids, bared places of red earth could be seen, like that of Devonshire; there, too, the waters, impeded by a natural dam, looked like a huge mill-pond, sullen and dark, in which two crocodiles, laving about, were looking for prey. From the high banks we looked down upon a line of sloping islets lying across the stream, which divide its waters, and, by interrupting them, cause at once both dam and rapids. The whole was more fairy-like, wild, and romantic than—I must confess that my thoughts took that shape—anything I ever saw outside a theatre. . . .

Start again and . . . after a long struggling march, plodding through huge grasses and jungle, we reached a district which I cannot otherwise describe than by calling it a 'Church Estate'. It is dedicated in some mysterious manner to Lubari (Almighty) and although the king appeared to have authority over some of the inhabitants of it, yet others had apparently a sacred character, exempting them from the civil power, and he had no right to dispose of the land itself.

At last, with a good push for it, crossing hills and threading huge grasses, as well as extensive village plantations lately devastated by elephants—they had eaten all that was eatable, and what would not serve for food they had destroyed with their trunks, not one plantain or one hut being left entire —we arrived at the extreme end of the journey, the farthest point ever visited by the expedition on the same parallel of latitude as King Mtesa's palace, and just forty miles east of it. We were well rewarded; for the 'stones' as the Waganda call the falls, was by far the most interesting sight I had seen in Africa. Everybody ran to see them at once, though the march had been long and fatiguing, and even my sketch-block was called into play. Though beautiful, the scene was not exactly what I had expected; for the broad surface of the lake was shut out from view by a spur of a hill, and the falls, about 12 feet deep, and 400 to 500 feet broad, were broken by rocks. Still it was a sight that attracted one to it for hours: the roar of the waters, the thousands of passenger-fish, leaping at the falls with all their might, the Wasoga and Waganda fishermen coming out in boats and taking post on all the rocks with rod and hook, hippopotami and crocodiles lying sleepily on the water, the ferry at work above the falls, and cattle driven down to drink at the margin of the lake, made, in all, with the pretty nature of the country—small hills, grassy-topped, with trees in the folds, and gardens on the lower slopes—as interesting a picture as one could wish to see.

The expedition had now performed its functions. I saw that old father Nile without any doubt rises in the Victoria Nyanza and, as I had foretold, that lake is the great source of the holy river which cradled the first expounder of our religious belief.

✿

DR DAVID LIVINGSTONE

(1813–1873)

Scottish missionary, doctor, and explorer. Devoted his life to fighting the slave trade. His body was brought back by his faithful servants and buried in Westminster Abbey.

1, 3: *Missionary Travels and Researches* (London, 1857); 2: Livingstone's African Journal, 1853–1856, vol. i, ed. I. Schapera (London, 1963); 4, 5: *The Last Journals of David Livingstone in Central Africa; continued by a narrative of his last moments and sufferings, obtained from his faithful servants, Chuma and Susi*, ed. H. Waller (London, 1874).

1. A LION ENCOUNTER (1843)

It is well known that if one in a troop of lions is killed the others take the hint and leave that part of the country. So the next time the herds were attacked, I went with the people, in order to encourage them to rid themselves of the annoyance by destroying one of the marauders. We found the lions on a small hill about a quarter of a mile in length, and covered with trees. A circle of men was formed round it, and they gradually closed up, ascending pretty near to each other. Being down below on the plain with a native schoolmaster, named Mebalwe, a most excellent man, I saw one of the lions sitting on a piece of rock within the now closed circle of men. Mebalwe fired at him before I could, and the ball struck the rock on which the animal was sitting. He bit at the spot struck, as a dog does at a stick or stone thrown at him; then leaping away, broke through the opening circle and escaped unhurt. The men were afraid to attack him, perhaps on account of their belief in witchcraft. When the circle was re-formed, we saw two other lions in it; but we were afraid to fire lest we should strike the men, and they allowed the beasts to burst through also. If the Bakatla had acted according to the custom of the country, they would have speared the lions in their attempt to get out. Seeing we could not get them to kill one of the lions, we bent our footsteps towards the village; in going round the end of the hill, however, I saw one of the beasts sitting on a piece of rock as before, but this time he had a little bush in front. Being about thirty yards off, I took a good aim at his body through the bush, and fired both barrels into it. The men then called out, 'He is shot, he is shot!' Others cried, 'He has been shot by another man too; let us go to him!' I did not see any one else shoot at him, but I saw the lion's tail erected in anger behind the bush, and, turning to the people, said, 'Stop a little till I load again.' When in the act of ramming down the bullets I heard a shout. Starting, and looking half round, I saw the lion just in the act of springing upon me. I was upon a little height; he caught my shoulder as he sprang, and we both came to the ground below together. Growling horribly close to my ear, he shook me as a terrier dog does a rat. The shock produced a stupor similar to that which seems to be felt by a mouse after the first shake of the cat. It caused a sort of dreaminess, in which there was no sense of pain nor feeling of terror, though quite conscious of all that was happening. It was like what patients partially under the influence of chloroform describe, who see all the operation, but feel not the knife. This singular condition was not the result of any mental process. The shake annihilated fear, and allowed no sense of horror in looking round at the beast. This peculiar state is probably produced in all animals killed by the carnivora; and if so, is a merciful provision by our benevolent Creator for lessening the pain of death. Turning round to relieve myself of the weight, as he had one paw on the back of my head, I saw his eyes directed to Mebalwe, who was trying to shoot him at a distance of ten or fifteen yards. His gun, a flint one, missed fire in both barrels; the lion immediately left me, and, attacking Mebalwe, bit his thigh. Another man, whose life I had saved before, after he had been tossed by a buffalo, attempted to spear the lion while he was biting Mebalwe. He left Mebalwe and caught this man by the shoulder, but at that moment the bullets he had received took effect, and he fell down dead. The whole was the work of a few moments, and must have been his paroxysm of dying rage. In order to take out the charm from him, the Bakatla on the following day made a huge bonfire over the carcase, which was declared to be that of the largest lion they had ever seen. Besides crunching the bone into splinters, he left eleven teeth wounds on the upper part of my arm.

A wound from this animal's tooth resembles a gun-shot wound; it is generally followed by a great deal of sloughing and discharge, and pains are felt in the part periodically ever afterwards. I had on a tartan jacket on the occasion, and I believe that it wiped off all the virus from the teeth that pierced the flesh, for my two companions in this affray have both suffered from the peculiar pains, while I have escaped with only the inconvenience of a false joint in my limb. The man whose shoulder was wounded showed me his wound actually burst forth afresh on the same month of the following year. This curious point deserves the attention of inquirers.

2. ILL IN THE INTERIOR (1853)

As the result of experience my boatman Mashauana remarked, 'This is a bad town to become ill in.' The cause seems to be an abominable ditch or moat made when the people of Santuru were forming the site. This is the receptacle of all manner of filth and is covered with rank vegetation. Indeed, the whole country is covered with rank vegetable matter, either dead or spread as manure through the coarse grasses' spring. When dried during the winter it is held up by strong stalks, so that in walking one has to lift the feet about a foot high before one can proceed. The lechwee [waterbuck] sometimes hide under this mat in order to bring forth their young.

The intermittent [fever] attacked four of us at the same hour. The urine contains much brick-dust-like sediment. The action of the heart is increased in quickness and is irregular, giving three or four loud beats, then returning to its general quick action. In the cold stage I vomit all the matters contained in the stomach. This produces perspiration, but it soon dries up and the teeth chatter again. If the sweating stage is interrupted by throwing off the clothes the fever continues, and the ugly phantoms which are often seen in continued fever appear and prevent sleep. If, however, the sweating stage is not interrupted too soon, or if I fall asleep, I awake in the morning exhausted and wet with perspiration. No appetite, and a feeling of great lassitude and disinclination to speak. There seems in every attack to be either an obstruction in the small intestines or a stoppage of the secretions there. Unless this is removed by a purgative combined with quinine there is a succession of attacks, with discharge of blood.

The people have applied in great numbers for medicine, but having but a small stock with me I am compelled to refuse all except the more urgent cases. Many sore eyes are seen among them, and some ugly skin diseases.

3. Discovery and Naming of Victoria Falls (1856)

I resolved on the following day to visit the falls of Victoria, called by the natives Mosioatunya, or more anciently Shongwe. Of these we had often heard since we came into the country: indeed one of the questions asked by Sebituane was, 'Have you smoke that sounds in your country?' They did not go near enough to examine them, but, viewing them with awe at a distance, said, in reference to the vapour and noise, 'Mosi oa tunya' (smoke does sound there). It was previously called Shongwe, the meaning of which I could not ascertain. The word for a 'pot' resembles this, and it may mean a seething cauldron; but I am not certain of it. Being persuaded that Mr Oswell and myself were the very first Europeans who ever visited the Zambesi in the centre of the country, and that this is the connecting link between the known and unknown portions of that river, I decided to use the same liberty as the Makololo did, and gave the only English name I have affixed to any part of the country. . . .

Sekeletu intended to accompany me, but, one canoe only having come instead of the two he had ordered, he resigned it to me. After twenty minutes' sail from Kalai, we came in sight, for the first time, of the columns of vapour, appropriately called 'smoke', rising at a distance of five or six miles, exactly as when large tracts of grass are burned in Africa. Five columns now arose, and bending in the direction of the wind, they seemed placed against a low ridge covered with trees; the tops of the columns at this distance appeared to mingle with the clouds. They were white below, and higher up became dark, so as to simulate smoke very closely. The whole scene was extremely beautiful; the banks and islands dotted over the river are adorned with sylvan vegetation of great variety of colour and form. At the period of our visit several trees were spangled over with blossoms. Trees have each their own physiognomy. There, towering over all, stands the great burly baobab, each of whose enormous arms would form the trunk of a large tree, beside groups of graceful palms, which, with their feathery-shaped leaves depicted on the sky, lend their beauty to the scene. As a hieroglyphic they always mean 'far from home', for one can never get over their foreign air in a picture or landscape. The silvery mohonono, which in the tropics is in form like the cedar of Lebanon, stands in pleasing contrast with the dark colour of the motsouri, whose cypress-form is dotted over at present with its pleasant scarlet fruit. Some trees resemble the great spreading oak, others assume the character of our own elms and chestnuts; but no one can imagine the beauty of the view from anything witnessed in England. It had never been seen before by European eyes; but scenes so lovely must have been gazed upon by angels in their flight. The only want felt is that of mountains in the background. The falls are bounded on three sides by ridges 300 or 400 feet in height, which are covered with forest, with the red soil appearing among the trees. When about half a mile from the falls, I left the canoe by which we had come thus far, and embarked in a lighter one, with men well acquainted with the rapids, who, by passing down the centre of the stream in the eddies and still places caused by many jutting rocks, brought me to an island situated in the middle of the river, and on the edge of the lip over which the water rolls. In coming hither, there was danger of being swept down by the streams which rushed along on each side of the island; but the river was now low, and we sailed where it is totally impossible to go when the water is high. But though we had reached the island, and were within a few yards of the spot, a view from which would solve the whole problem, I believe that no one could perceive where the vast body of water went; it seemed to lose itself in the earth, the opposite lip of the fissure into which it disappeared being only 80 feet distant. At least I did not comprehend it until, creeping with awe to the verge, I peered down into a large rent which had been made from bank to bank of the broad Zambesi, and saw that a stream of a thousand yards broad leaped down a hundred feet, and then became suddenly compressed into a space of fifteen or twenty yards. The entire falls are simply a crack made in a hard basaltic rock from the right to the left bank of the Zambesi, and then prolonged from the left bank away through thirty or forty miles of hills. If one imagines the Thames filled with low, tree-covered hills immediately beyond the tunnel, extending as far as Gravesend; the bed of black basaltic rock instead of London mud; and a fissure made therein from one end of the tunnel to the other, down through the keystones of the arch, and prolonged from the left end of the tunnel through thirty miles of hills; the pathway being 100 feet down from the bed of the river instead of what it is, with the lips of the fissure from 80 to 100 feet apart; then fancy the Thames leaping bodily into the gulf; and forced there to change its direction, and flow from the right to the left bank; and then rush boiling and roaring through the hills—one may have some idea of what takes place at this, the most wonderful sight I had witnessed in Africa. In looking down into the fissure on the right of the island, one sees nothing but a dense white cloud, which, at the time we visited the spot, had two bright rainbows on it. (The sun was on the meridian, and the declination about equal to the latitude of the place.) From this cloud rushed up a great jet of vapour exactly like steam, and it mounted 200 or 300 feet high; there condensing, it changed its hue to that of dark smoke, and came back in a constant shower, which soon wetted us to the skin. This shower falls chiefly on the opposite side of the fissure, and a few yards back from the lip, there stands a straight hedge of evergreen trees, whose leaves are always wet. From their roots a number of little rills run back into the gulf; but as they flow down the steep wall there, the column of vapour, in its ascent, licks them up clean off the rock, and away they mount again. They are constantly running down, but never reach the bottom.

4. THE ANIMAL PLEASURE OF TRAVELLING (1866)

The mere animal pleasure of travelling in a wild unexplored country is very great. When on lands of a couple of thousand feet elevation, brisk exercise imparts elasticity to the muscles, fresh and healthy blood circulates through the brain, the mind works well, the eye is clear, the step is firm, and a day's exertion always makes the evening's repose thoroughly enjoyable.

We have usually the stimulus of remote chances of danger either from beasts or men. Our sympathies are drawn out towards our humble, hardy companions by a community of interests, and, it may be, of perils, which make us all friends. Nothing but the most pitiable puerility would lead any manly heart to make their inferiority a theme for self-exaltation; however, that is often done, as if with the vague idea that we can, by magnifying their deficiencies, demonstrate our immaculate perfections.

The effect of travel on a man whose heart is in the right place is that the mind is made more self-reliant: it becomes more confident of its own resources—there is greater presence of mind. The body is soon well-knit; the muscles of the limbs grow as hard as a board, and seem to have no fat; the countenance is bronzed, and there is no dyspepsia. Africa is a most wonderful country for appetite, and it is only when one gloats over marrow bones or elephant's feet that indigestion is possible. No doubt much toil is involved, and fatigue of which travellers in the more temperate climes can form but a faint conception; but the sweat of one's brow is no longer a curse when one works for God: it proves a tonic to the system, and is actually a blessing. No one can truly appreciate the charm of repose unless he has undergone severe exertion.

5. MEETING WITH STANLEY (1871)

When my spirits were at their lowest ebb, the good Samaritan was close at hand, for one morning Susi came running at the top of his speed and gasped out, 'An Englishman! I see him!' and off he darted to meet him. The American flag at the head of a caravan told of the nationality of the stranger. Bales of goods, baths of tin, huge kettles, cooking pots, tents, etc. made me think, 'This must be a luxurious traveller, and not one at his wits' end like me.'

It was Henry Moreland [sic] Stanley, the travelling correspondent of the New York Herald, sent by James Gordon Bennett, junior, at an expense of more than £4,000, to obtain accurate information about Dr Livingstone if living, and if dead to bring home my bones. The news he had to tell to one who had been two full years without any tidings from Europe made my whole frame thrill. The terrible fate that had befallen France, the telegraphic cables successfully laid in the Atlantic, the election of General Grant, the death of good Lord Clarendon—my constant friend, the proof that Her Majesty's Government had not forgotten me in voting £1,000 for supplies, and many other points of interest, revived emotions that had lain dormant in Manyuema. Appetite returned, and instead of the spare, tasteless, two meals a day, I ate four times daily, and in a week began to feel strong. I am not of a demonstrative turn; as cold, indeed, as we islanders are usually reputed to be, but this disinterested kindness of Mr Bennett, so nobly carried into effect by Mr Stanley, was simply overwhelming. I really do feel extremely grateful, and at the same time I am a little ashamed at not being more worthy of the generosity. Mr Stanley has done his part with untiring energy; good judgement in the teeth of very serious obstacles. His helpmates turned out depraved blackguards, who, by their excesses at Zanzibar and elsewhere, had ruined their constitutions, and prepared their systems to be fit provender for the grave. They had used up their strength by wickedness, and were of next to no service, but rather downdrafts and unbearable drags to progress.

❊

SIR HENRY MORTON STANLEY

(1841–1904)

British-American journalist and explorer. Born in Wales, he ran away to sea and the USA, where he fought in the Civil War on both sides. Sent to Africa by the New York Herald *to find Livingstone. Ruthless but effective on later journeys.*

1: *How I Found Livingstone* (London, 1872); 2: *The Diary of A. J. Mounteney Jephson: Emin Pasha Relief Expedition 1887–1889* (Cambridge, 1969).

1. MEETING WITH LIVINGSTONE (1871)

We push on rapidly, lest the news of our coming might reach the people of Bunder Ujiji before we come in sight, and are ready for them. We halt at a little brook, then ascend the long slope of a naked ridge, the very last of the myriads we have crossed. This alone prevents us from seeing the lake in all its vastness. We arrive at the summit, travel across and arrive at its western rim, and—pause, reader—the port of Ujiji is below us, embowered in the palms, only five hundred yards from us! At this grand moment we do not think of the hundreds of miles we have marched, of the hundreds of hills that we have ascended and descended, of the many forests we have traversed, of the jungles and thickets that annoyed us, of the fervid salt plains that blistered our feet, of the hot suns that scorched us, nor the dangers and difficulties, now happily surmounted. At last the sublime hour has arrived!—our dreams, our hopes, and anticipations are now about to be realized! Our hearts and our feelings are with our eyes, as we peer into the palms and try to make out in which hut or house lives the white man with the grey beard we heard about on the Malagarazi.

We were now about three hundred yards from the village of Ujiji, and the crowds are dense about me. Suddenly I hear a voice on my right say,

'Good morning, sir!'

Startled at hearing this greeting in the midst of such a crowd of black people, I turn sharply around in search of the man, and see him at my side, with the blackest of faces, but animated and joyous—a man dressed in a long white shirt, with a turban of American sheeting around his woolly head, and I ask:

'Who the mischief are you?'

'I am Susi, the servant of Dr Livingstone,' said he, smiling, and showing a gleaming row of teeth.

'What! Is Dr Livingstone here?'

'Yes, sir.'

'In this village?'

'Yes, sir.'

'Are you sure?'

'Sure, sure, sir. Why, I leave him just now.' . . .

'Now, you Susi, run, and tell the Doctor I am coming.'

'Yes, sir,' and off he darted like a madman. . . .

Soon Susi came running back, and asked me my name; he had told the Doctor that I was coming, but the Doctor was too surprised to believe him, and, when the Doctor asked him my name, Susi was rather staggered.

But, during Susi's absence, the news had been conveyed to the Doctor that it was surely a white man that was coming, whose guns were firing and whose flag could be seen; and the great Arab magnates of Ujiji—Mohammed bin Sali, Sayd bin Majid, Abid bin Suleiman, Mohammed bin Gharib, and others—had gathered together before the Doctor's house, and the Doctor had come out from his veranda to discuss the matter and await my arrival.

In the meantime, the head of the Expedition had halted, and the *kirangozi* was out of the ranks, holding his flag aloft, and Selim said to me, 'I see the Doctor, sir. Oh, what an old man! He has got a white beard.' And I—what would I not have given for a bit of friendly wilderness, where, unseen, I might vent my joy in some mad freak, such as idiotically biting my hand, turning a somersault, or slashing at trees, in order to allay those exciting feelings that were well-nigh uncontrollable. My heart beats fast, but I must not let my face betray my emotions, lest it shall detract from the dignity of a white man appearing under such extraordinary circumstances.

So I did that which I thought was most dignified. I pushed back the crowds, and, passing from the rear, walked down a living avenue of people, until I came in front of the semicircle of Arabs, in the front of which stood the white man with the grey beard. As I advanced slowly towards him I noticed he was pale, looked wearied, had a grey beard, wore a bluish cap with a faded gold band round it, had on a red-sleeved waistcoat, and a pair of grey tweed trousers. I would have run to him, only I was a coward in the presence of such a mob—would have embraced him, only, he being an Englishman, I did not know how he would receive me; so I did what cowardice and false pride suggested was the best thing—walked deliberately to him, took off my hat, and said:

'Dr Livingstone, I presume?'

'YES,' said he, with a kind smile, lifting his cap slightly.

I replace my hat on my head, and he puts on his cap, and we both grasp hands, and I then say aloud:

'I thank God, Doctor, I have been permitted to see you.'

He answered, 'I feel thankful that I am here to welcome you.'

I turn to the Arabs, take off my hat to them in response to the saluting chorus of 'Yambos' I receive, and the Doctor introduces them to me by name. Then, oblivious of the crowds, oblivious of the men who shared with me my dangers, we—Livingstone and I—turn our faces towards his *tembe*. He points to the veranda, or, rather, mud platform, under the broad overhanging eaves; he points to his own particular seat, which I see his age and experience in Africa has suggested, namely, a straw mat, with a goatskin over it, and another skin nailed against the wall to protect his back from contact with the cold mud. I protest against taking this seat, which so much more befits him than me, but the Doctor will not yield: I must take it.

We are seated—the Doctor and I—with our backs to the wall. The Arabs take seats on our left. More than a thousand natives are in our front, filling the whole square densely, indulging their curiosity, and discussing the fact of two white men meeting at Ujiji—one just come from Manyuema, in the west, the other from Unyanyembe, in the east.

2. FROM THE DIARY OF JEPHSON (WHO ACCOMPANIED
STANLEY ON THE EMIN PASHA RELIEF EXPEDITION)
(1887)

3 April. At half past five I mustered the men and sent back 85 under two chiefs to join Stanley and carry loads whilst I with 8 Zanzibaris and 6 Somalis hurried up the river to Manyanga—distant four days. Having put the boat together and got the 42 loads into her we started off at about half past ten. It was peculiar what a feeling of hatred the river inspires one with. One hates it as if it were a living thing—it is so treacherous and crafty, so overpowering and relentless in its force and overwhelming strength. No two yards of its face are alike—here are whirlpools rushing round with horrid gurgles and there the water eddies up—whilst the river seethes and boils all round you—it is a bad river to navigate. The banks too have a dreary ghostly appearance, black jagged rocks stand out from the banks as if ready to devour anything that came near them and the very kites and cranes seem to add to the inexpressible dreariness of the scene— it is all like a bad nightmare. We heaved the boat over several rapids and worked our way slowly up—one has to cross the river from bank to bank to get out of the way on dangerous water, it is a constant fight, a constant strain of watching the treacherous water. The Congo river god is an evil one, I am persuaded. At about 5 we camped on the south bank after having done a hard day's work.

4 April. We started off as usual at half past five. I had slept in the boat that night to see that nothing was taken out of it. We worked our way on over rapids with here and there a stretch of tolerably clear water, though there was a strong current against us all the way. The appearance of the river improved slightly today but it is still bleak and dreary to a degree. Walker was loud in his complaints that I would not stop to give him time to cook food in the middle of the day. We had tinned food and biscuits with us and yet it was not enough for him. This constant grumbling and sulking before natives, some of whom speak English, is very bad form and is most demoralizing to them, for if they see a white man grumbling why should they not grumble, a thing they are always ready to do even without any encouragement. The result has been that I have had to deal with a discontented boat's crew who were made so by the grumbling of this man who was sent to help me.

5 April. We have had a bad day of it today. The rapids have been numerous and the progress necessarily slow. We came to one place where the river narrows terribly and flows round at right angles with overwhelming force and rapidity. On each bank are high, dreary-looking hills coming close down in cliffs to the water's edge—and standing right out into the river is the Castle Rock—a large rock with its face perfectly perpendicular to the water, which is of great depth. Round this rock the water whirls with a rush and a roar and it was over this water that the boat had to be hauled. The whole face of the river was churned into foam and one's ears were confused by 'the voice of many waters'. It was a dangerous place to get the boat over, but we managed it without any mishap; but it took a very long time, for the force of the water took the boat from side to side. In the afternoon a thunder-storm came on and drenched us and everything in the boat—I was obliged to stop against the bank till it was ended for we could make no headway against the current together with the storm of wind dead ahead. All the afternoon we pushed on in the soaking rain and encamped at about half past four, on the bank where a bend of the river formed an immense pool—we were all in a wretchedly dripping condition and all depressed and low. There were a great number of hippopotami disporting themselves in the pool and several of them came up quite close to the boat.

6 April. We started off at half past five and had many weary rapids to haul over. Walker as usual keeping up a strain of grumbling and sulking. I cannot imagine anyone caring two straws for food, so that they had enough to get on with, when there is an object in view and that object is success in what one has undertaken. Walker was actually asleep when we were navigating the boat over some rapids this morning. It is hard to get natives to work and be sharp when there is a white man lying idly snoring in the stern sheets. The consequence was we were so slow that I had to keep the men on working till half past six—the last half hour we did was by bright moonlight. The river certainly looks less dreary now and there are people about. At every little causeway of rocks standing out into the river there are men fishing—they chiefly catch a sort of white bait in large quantities in large spoon-shaped nets. . . .

8 April. My Zanzibaris have not yet come, it is very annoying that I should have toiled to do my part of the agreement and that Stanley should fail to do his—however I can only wait and curb my impatience at being kept waiting as best I can. This afternoon I went out with Durnfeldt the Chief of the Congo State Station to shoot a large crocodile we saw sleeping on a rock in the river, he shot it but it rolled into the river. What a dreadful farce this Congo Free State is—one thing it cannot last much longer, it must come to an end soon.

9 April. Still no news of my men—it is as well perhaps for I cannot move today. Last night I had a fearful night with cramps and dysentery, and today I cannot leave my bed. It is dreadful, this pain and nausea, one feels that the sight even of food would make one sick and yet I am fainting from having nothing. The lonely feeling of being left alone with nothing but native noises and native smells about one makes ones thoughts turn to home with the feeling of 'shall I ever see it again'. It is miserable, everything looks black and hopeless and useless—what is the good of doing anything, all is vain, all useless—why all this worry of oneself, why all this pushing forward, and the everlasting 'cui bono' repeats itself again and again in one's mind as one tosses backwards and forwards on one's bed trying to find an easy position and finding it nowhere.

10 April. Today thank heaven I am better and all the gloomy thoughts of yesterday are departing. I got a letter from Stanley who is at Lukungu, he says he will be in Lutete in three days and is sending me my men for the boat, but for some unaccountable reason they have only just arrived (6 p.m.). I shall not be able to start till tomorrow. Stanley will be ahead of me, how I shall catch him up I don't know—it is a great shame to have left me in the lurch like this. I am still as weak as a cat and cannot eat anything, the very thought of food makes me sick.

11 April. Got up this morning after a real good night's rest and everything seems bright again. I started on the march and had a delightful meal of fresh eggs, lovely mellow bananas, and tea before I started—this morning I felt fit for anything. Oh the relief it was to turn away from the treacherous river and from that fever-stricken place Manyanga—five out of six of my Somalis are down with fever and one of my Zanzibaris—I intend to swear at Stanley for having kept me in that fever-stricken place for such an unnecessarily long time. The delight I felt in hurrying along, at again being on the move and pushing forward. My little terrier 'Spot', a very handsome little dog given me by Tippu Tib, seemed to share in my good spirits and danced round me barking and jumping up at me—his absurdities amused me and chimed in with my mood, I felt inclined to run races with him over the grassy hills, but my prestige with my men, where would it be if I gave way to such boyishness before them! And yet I had not really any reason to be in such overflowing spirits, except that I was on the move and well again. . . .

[*12 April*] After I had been in camp about a couple of hours up came Tippu Tib, in clean white cloths and turban, with his smart gilt sword and light sandals and his servants following him. He nearly embraced me in the effusion of his greeting. I was surprised to learn from him that Stanley and all of them were on the road behind—I imagined he was in front of me and was well pleased to hear to the contrary. After a couple of hours Stanley and the rest of the Expedition came up. I was so glad to see them all again after being away nearly a fortnight—they all seemed pleased to see me too. They had not much news to tell; one man had been shot whilst robbing a village and Stairs had to shoot his donkey which had fallen into a ravine and broken its leg—the Soudanese were nearly all sick and had given a great deal of trouble and the Somalis were all sick and so were a good many Zanzibaris. Stanley seemed pleased to find me there with the boat all safe and no serious mishaps to tell him of. In the evening he told me he wanted me to go on again ahead of him with the boat to the Inkisi river, three days' march off. I am to do it in three rapid marches, whilst he follows more slowly, and get the boat put together on the Inkisi river and have it in readiness to transport the Expedition across. I like being sent on like this, for one feels one is really giving some little help to the Expedition. . . .

[*14 April*] After I had been in camp about a couple of hours Casement of the Sanford Expedition[1] came up and camped by me. We bathed and he gave me a very good dinner—he is travelling most comfortably and has a large tent and plenty of servants. It was delightful sitting down to a *real* dinner at a *real* table with a table cloth and dinner napkins and plenty to eat with Burgundy to drink and cocoa and cigarettes after dinner—and this in the middle of the wilds—it will be a long time before I pass such a pleasant evening again. Hearing Stanley was camped within an hour's march of me, I determined to make an early start next morning to reach the Inkisi river and get the boat put together so as not to keep the Expedition waiting should he decide to cross it tomorrow. . . .

18 April. Left camp this morning at daylight—it was funny being with the whole expedition, it is the first time I have marched with them for 18 days, it is not half so nice as marching with one's own 50 men. The Zanzibaris are going very well now and we got into camp by ten. There were a good many deserted villages on the road; some of them must have been very pretty, as there were some fine trees. Just before getting into camp we came upon the Congo again, and one was struck afresh with its cheerless aspect—our camp is within half a mile of the river. This afternoon I went down to where the Inkalamo river falls into the Congo. It is a beautiful fall: one longed to be able to sketch it, for it would have made such a pretty sketch—the river leaping in white, foaming masses in a series of falls of ten to twelve feet each, from rock to rock, to the Congo which flowed a hundred feet below—a dark, evil-looking river all broken water and whirl-pools, with its shores of black, grim-looking rocks, with heavy jungle cover-ing the hills beyond. I climbed to a rock jutting out almost into the falls and sat there for over an hour, for I love to hear the roaring sound of water all round me—one seems so alone and away from all the little paltry bothers of the camp, and one thinks one's own thoughts and enjoys looking at the water, whilst gorgeous butterflies circle about one and sometimes even settle upon one's clothes. Stairs, who came with me, was poking about for specimens of gold-bearing quartz, but I loved to sit alone and dream—rushing water always has the effect of raising my spirits. I like this life, I like the hard work and the constant moving and pushing forward, and I would not change its hardships and unpleasantnesses for the ease of civilization. . . .

[*19 April*] It was three o'clock before the boat was ready and the ropes fixed for dragging her backwards and forwards—it was just dark when the last of the expedition with the donkeys and goats got across. I and my men were therefore obliged to camp for the night in the swamp—I noticed that

---

[1] Roger Casement, executed in 1916 for treason.

the ground was covered with a sort of four-leafed house leek growing perfectly flat on the ground and in the shape of a cross. Casement came up in the afternoon and being unable to cross with his caravan and heavy loads camped beside me. We sat outside the tents smoking and talking till eleven o'clock and could see Stanley's camp fires about half a mile off on the hillside above us.

✢

SIR SAMUEL WHITE BAKER

(1821–1893)

British hunter and explorer. A flamboyant character whose expeditions were more entertaining than productive. Travelled with his Hungarian second wife Florence, whom he had bought in a Bulgarian slave market.

1–7: *The Albert Nyanza* (London, 1866); 8: *Ismaïlia* (London, 1872).

1. MEETING WITH SPEKE AND GRANT (1863)

I had been waiting at Gondokoro twelve days, expecting the arrival of Debono's party from the south, with whom I wished to return. Suddenly on 15 February, I heard a rattle of musketry at a great distance, and a dropping fire from the south. To give an idea of the moment I must extract verbatim from my journal as written at the time.

'Guns firing in the distance; Debono's ivory porters arriving, for whom I have waited. My men rushed madly to my boat, with the report that two white men were with them who had come from the *sea*! Could they be Speke and Grant? Off I ran, and soon met them in reality; hurrah for old England!! They had come from the Victoria Nyanza, from which the Nile springs. . . . The mystery of ages solved. With my pleasure of meeting them is the one disappointment that I had not met them further on the road in my search for them; however, the satisfaction is that my previous arrangements had been such as would have ensured my finding them had they been in a fix. . . . My projected route would have brought me *vis-à-vis* with them, as they had come from the lake by the course I had proposed to take. . . . All my men perfectly mad with excitement, firing salutes as usual with ball cartridge, they shot one of my donkeys; a melancholy sacrifice as an offering at the completion of this geographical discovery.'

At the first blush on meeting them I had considered my expedition as terminated by having met them, and by their having accomplished the discovery of the Nile source; but upon my congratulating them with all my heart, upon the honour they had so nobly earned, Speke and Grant with characteristic candour and generosity gave me a map of their route, showing that they had been unable to complete the actual exploration of the Nile, and that a most important portion still remained to be determined. . . . To me this was most gratifying. I had been much disheartened at the idea that the great work was accomplished, and that nothing remained for exploration; I even said to Speke, 'Does not one leaf of the laurel remain for me?'

2. A Suit Like Speke's (1864)

After a most enjoyable march through the exciting scene of the glorious river crashing over innumerable falls—and in many places ornamented with rocky islands, upon which were villages and plantain groves—we at length approached the Karuma Falls close to the village of Atada above the ferry. The heights were crowded with natives, and a canoe was sent across to within parleying distance of our side, as the roar of the rapids prevented our voices from being heard except at a short distance. Bacheeta now explained that '*Speke's brother* had arrived from his country to pay Kamrasi a visit, and had brought him valuable presents'.

'Why has he brought so many men with him?' enquired the people from the canoe.

'There are so many presents for the M'Kamma (king) that he has many men to carry them,' shouted Bacheeta.

'Let us look at him,' cried the headman in the boat; having prepared for the introduction by changing my clothes in a grove of plantains for my dressing-room, and altering my costume to a tweed suit, something similar to that worn by Speke, I climbed up a high and almost perpendicular rock that formed a natural pinnacle on the face of the cliff, and, waving my cap to the crowd on the opposite side, I looked almost as imposing as Nelson in Trafalgar Square.

I instructed Bacheeta, who climbed up the giddy height after me, to shout to the people that an English lady, my wife, had also arrived, and that we wished immediately to be presented to the king and his family, as we had come to thank him for his kind treatment of Speke and Grant, who had arrived safe in their own country. Upon this being explained and repeated several times, the canoe approached the shore.

I ordered all our people to retire, and to conceal themselves among the plantains, that the natives might not be startled by so imposing a force, while Mrs Baker and I advanced alone to meet Kamrasi's people, who were men of some importance. Upon landing through the high reeds, they immediately recognized the similarity of my beard and general complexion to that of Speke; and their welcome was at once displayed by the most extravagant dancing and gesticulating with lances and shields, as though intending to attack, rushing at me with the points of their lances thrust close to my face, and shouting and singing in great excitement.

3. Wife Causes a Stir by Brushing Her Hair

Hardly had the few boatmen departed than some one shouted suddenly, and the entire crowd sprang to their feet and rushed towards the hut where I had left Mrs Baker. For the moment I thought that the hut was on fire, and I joined the crowd and arrived at the doorway, where I found a tremendous press to see some extraordinary sight. Everyone was squeezing for the best place; and, driving them on one side, I found the wonder that had excited their curiosity. The hut being very dark, my wife had employed her solitude during my conference with the natives in dressing her hair at the doorway, which, being very long and blonde, was suddenly noticed by some natives—a shout was given, the rush described had taken place, and the hut was literally mobbed by the crowd of savages eager to see the extraordinary novelty. The Gorilla would not make a greater stir in London streets than we appeared to create at Atada.

4. The King Suggests Wife is Left with Him

In our present weak state another year of Central Africa without quinine appeared to warrant death; it was a race against time, all was untrodden ground before us, and the distance quite uncertain. I trembled for my wife, and weighed the risk of another year in this horrible country should we lose the boats. With the self-sacrificing devotion that she had shown in every trial, she implored me not to think of any risks on her account, but to push forward and discover the lake—that she had determined not to return until she had herself reached the 'M'wootan N'zige'.

I now requested Kamrasi to allow us to take leave, as we had not an hour to lose. In the coolest manner he replied, 'I will send you to the lake and to Shooa, as I have promised; but, *you must leave your wife with me!*'

At that moment we were surrounded by a great number of natives, and my suspicions of treachery at having been led across the Kafoor river appeared confirmed by this insolent demand. If this were to be the end of the expedition I resolved that it should also be the end of Kamrasi, and, drawing my revolver quietly, I held it within two feet of his chest, and looking at him with undisguised contempt, I told him, that if I touched the trigger, not all his men could save him: and that if he dared to repeat the insult I would shoot him on the spot. At the same time I explained to him that in my country such insolence would entail bloodshed, and that I looked upon him as an ignorant ox who knew no better, and that this excuse alone could save him. My wife, naturally indignant, had risen from her seat, and maddened with the excitement of the moment, she made him a little speech in Arabic (not a word of which he understood), with a countenance almost as amiable as the head of Medusa. Altogether the *mise-en-scène* utterly astonished him; the woman Bacheeta, although savage, had appropriated the insult to her mistress, and she also fearlessly let fly at Kamrasi, translating as nearly as she could the complimentary address that 'Medusa' had just delivered.

Whether this little *coup de théâtre* had so impressed Kamrasi with British female independence that he wished to be off his bargain, I cannot say, but with an air of complete astonishment, he said, 'Don't be angry! I had no intention of offending you by asking for your wife; I will give you a wife, if you want one, and I thought you might have no objection to give me yours; it is my custom to give my visitors pretty wives, and I thought you might exchange. Don't make a fuss about it; if you don't like it, there's an end of it; I will never mention it again.' This very practical apology I received very sternly, and merely insisted upon starting. He seemed rather confused at having committed himself, and to make amends he called his people and ordered them to carry our loads. His men ordered a number of women who had assembled out of curiosity, to shoulder the luggage and to carry it to the next village where they would be relieved. I assisted my wife upon her ox, and with a very cold adieu to Kamrasi, I turned my back most gladly on M'rooli.

5. BAKER CLAIMS THE SOURCE OF THE NILE

The sun had not risen when I was spurring my ox after the guide, who, having been promised a double handful of beads on arrival at the lake, had caught the enthusiasm of the moment. The day broke beautifully clear, and having crossed a deep valley between the hills, we toiled up the opposite slope. I hurried to the summit. The glory of our prize burst suddenly upon me! There, like a sea of quicksilver, lay far beneath the grand expanse of water—a boundless sea horizon on the south and south-west, glittering in the noonday sun; and on the west, at fifty or sixty miles' distance, blue mountains rose from the bosom of the lake to a height of about 7,000 feet above its level.

It is impossible to describe the triumph of that moment; here was the reward for all our labour—for the years of tenacity with which we had toiled through Africa. England had won the sources of the Nile! Long before I reached this spot, I had arranged to give three cheers with all our men in English style in honour of the discovery, but now that I looked down upon the great inland sea lying nestled in the very heart of Africa, and thought how vainly mankind had sought these sources throughout so many ages, and reflected that I had been the humble instrument permitted to unravel this portion of the great mystery when so many greater than I had failed, I felt too serious to vent my feelings in vain cheers for victory, and I sincerely thanked God for having guided and supported us through all dangers to the good end. I was about 1,500 feet above the lake, and I looked down from the steep granite cliff upon those welcome waters—upon that vast reservoir which nourished Egypt and brought fertility where all was wilderness—upon that great source so long hidden from mankind; that source of bounty and of blessings to millions of human beings; and as one of the greatest objects in nature, I determined to honour it with a great name. As an imperishable memorial of one loved and mourned by our gracious Queen and deplored by every Englishman, I called this great lake 'the Albert Nyanza'. The Victoria and the Albert lakes are the two sources of the Nile.

The zigzag path to descend to the lake was so steep and dangerous that we were forced to leave our oxen with a guide, who was to take them to Magungo and wait for our arrival. We commenced the descent of the steep pass on foot. I led the way, grasping a stout bamboo. My wife in extreme weakness tottered down the pass, supporting herself upon my shoulder, and stopping to rest every twenty paces. After a toilsome descent of about two hours, weak with years of fever, but for the moment strengthened by success, we gained the level plain below the cliff. A walk of about a mile, through flat sandy meadows of fine turf interspersed with trees and bush, brought us to the water's edge. The waves were rolling upon a white, pebbly beach: I rushed into the lake, and thirsty with heat and fatigue, with a heart full of gratitude, I drank deeply from the Sources of the Nile.

6. 'I HAPPENED TO POSSESS A FULL-DRESS HIGHLAND SUIT'

At the hour appointed M'Gambi appeared, with a great crowd of natives. My clothes were in rags—and as personal appearance has a certain effect, even in Central Africa, I determined to present myself to the king in as favourable a light as possible. I happened to possess a full-dress Highland suit that I had worn when I lived in Perthshire many years ago; this I had treasured as serviceable upon an occasion like the present; accordingly I was quickly attired in kilt, sporran, and Glengarry bonnet, and to the utter amazement of the crowd, the ragged-looking object that had arrived in Kisoona now issued from the obscure hut, with plaid and kilt of Athol tartan. A general shout of exclamation arose from the assembled crowd; and taking my seat upon an angarep, I was immediately shouldered by a number of men, and attended by ten of my people as escort, I was carried towards the camp of the great Kamrasi.

7. THOUGHTS ON SAFE RETURN TO GONDOKORO

As I sat beneath a tree and looked down upon the glorious Nile that flowed a few yards beneath my feet, I pondered upon the value of my toil. I had traced the river to its great Albert source, and as the mighty stream glided before me, the mystery that had ever shrouded its origin was dissolved. I no longer looked upon its waters with a feeling approaching to awe for I knew its home, and had visited its cradle. Had I overrated the importance of the discovery? and had I wasted some of the best years of my life to obtain a shadow? I recalled the practical question of Commoro, the chief of Latooka: 'Suppose you get to the great lake, what will you do with it? What will be the good of it all? If you find that the large river does flow from it, what then?'

8. ENTHUSIASM OF THE WOMEN (1872)

On 8th March, I reviewed the troops, and having given the natives warning of my intention, I had a sham-fight and attack of the Fatiko mountain. Having fired several rockets at a supposed enemy, the troops advanced in two companies to the north and south extremities of the mountain, which they scaled with great activity, and joined their forces on the clean plateau of granite on the summit of the ridge. The effect was very good, and appeared to delight the natives, who had assembled in considerable numbers. After firing several volleys, the troops descended the hill, and marched back, with the band playing.

The music of our band being produced simply by a considerable number of bugles, drums, and cymbals, aided by a large military bass-drum, might not have been thought first-rate in Europe, but in Africa it was irresistible. The natives are passionately fond of music; and I believe the safest way to travel in those wild countries would be to play the cornet, if possible without ceasing, which would ensure a safe passage. A London organ-grinder would march through Central Africa followed by an admiring and enthusiastic crowd, who, if his tunes were lively, would form a dancing escort of the most untiring material.

As my troops returned to their quarters, with the band playing rather cheerful airs, we observed the women racing down from their villages, and gathering from all directions towards the common centre. As they approached nearer, the charms of music were overpowering, and, halting for an instant, they assumed what they considered the most graceful attitudes, and then danced up to the band.

In a short time my buglers could hardly blow their instruments for laughing, at the extraordinary effect of their performance. A fantastic crowd surrounded them as they halted in our position among the rocks; and every minute added to their number.

The women throughout the Shooli are entirely naked, thus the effect of a female crowd, bounding madly about as musical enthusiasts, was very extraordinary. Even the babies were brought out to dance, and these infants, strapped to their mothers' backs, and covered with pumpkin shells, like young tortoises, were jolted about without the slightest consideration for the weakness of their necks, by their infatuated mothers.

As usual, among all tribes in Central Africa, the old women were even more determined dancers than the young girls. Several old Venuses were making themselves extremely ridiculous, as they sometimes do in civilized countries when attempting the allurements of younger days.

❋

FLORENCE VON SASS BAKER
(LADY BAKER)

(c.1841–1918)

The Hungarian second wife of Samuel Baker. She travelled through Africa with him on several expeditions. When they finally settled down in England, she became a grand old lady.

A. Baker, *Morning Star* (London, 1972).

LETTER TO HER ELDEST STEPDAUGHTER (1871)

Africa
White Nile
Gondokoro
May 19, 1871

My own darling Edith,

At last we are arrived here—after a fearful struggle and weary journey in dragging a flotilla of 59 vessels including a steamer of 32 horsepower over high grass and marshes. We started from Tewfikia on the 1 December and arrived here on the 14 April, thinking this spot a perfect Paradise.

It would be quite impossible by any description to give you an idea of the obstacles to navigation through which we have toiled with the fleet, but you can imagine the trouble when you hear that we were 32 days with 1,500 men in accomplishing a distance of only 2½ miles.

Formerly the voyage from Khartoum to Gondokoro was a weary and tedious journey, but nevertheless it was only an affair of from 40 to 45 days. Now the great river has become blocked up by many miles of dense floating vegetation which, compressed by the force of the stream, has formed a compact mass which thoroughly obstructs navigation.

The Bahr Giraffe, now the only route to the Upper Nile, was more or less unnavigable for about 48 miles, alternately blocked up by floating marsh of high grass and mud through which we had to cut canals. Having overcome these obstacles the stream divided into numerous channels, all of which were so shallow as to be utterly impassable.

Our vessels drew four feet of water but in many places the depth of the river was only two feet. These terrible shallows extended over about twenty miles with intervals of deep water.

The whole force wearied with the hard work of cutting canals through the floating marshes. We were broken-hearted on arrival at the shallows, and the men made up their minds that we must turn back. The river was falling rapidly, thus it was a race against time, as it might be perfectly dry by the time we should have overcome a present obstruction. It appeared that the expedition must be utterly ruined.

Thank goodness dear Papa had foreseen and provided for the difficulties by having a large supply of good tools—such as spades, hoes, billhook, etc., and he always went many many miles ahead in a small rowing boat to sound the depth of water and to explore the miserable and fearful country generally. There was no dry land—neither was there depth, nothing but horrible marsh and mosquitoes. Many of our men died.

At length, after deepening the channel in many places with spades, we,

196

by degrees, after some months' heavy labour dragged our fleet with ropes to the limit where the water ceased altogether and the fleet was hard and fast aground in a long but narrow lake from which the water had escaped before we could cut a canal in advance.

To arrive at this narrow lake, Papa had dammed up certain streams so as to keep the entire water in one channel, but we were now apparently hopelessly ruined as there was no possibility of advance or retreat until the next rainy season should raise the river level, by which time half of our men would have been dead.

Thank God dear Papa with all the responsibility and hard work and anxiety of the expedition never lost his health—this was most fortunate or we should have been entirely ruined. On the day when all appeared hopeless he spent five hours in dragging a small boat over high grass and marsh with about fifteen men, and he happily discovered a large lake of deep water the overflow of which formed the difficult channel through which we have been ploughing our way during three months.

On the following day he explored the whole lake in the little boat and after rowing and sailing for sixteen miles, to the delight of all he returned at night with the good news that he had discovered the true White Nile junction—he had even drunk water out of the great river.

The difficulty was how to *reach* the lake? The fleet was fast aground and [with] no navigable channel before us we now determined to cut a channel to the lake and then to make a large dam across the river *behind* the fleet, so that not a drop of water should escape and the rise in the level would then float the vessels and enable them to pass up the shallow channel.

For two days *1,500* men were preparing large bundles of grass and mud together with 500 sacks of sand. During this time a strong framework of piles was erected across the river.

All being ready, the bugles and drums called every available man to work, and the scene was most exciting as they used every energy to dam up the river by throwing the sacks and hurdles against the wooden frame and heaping mud and grass until they had formed a solid bank about a hundred yards wide which completely closed the river. The effect was magical. The water rose nearly three feet in a few hours and the fleet of 59 vessels lately so helplessly aground floated about joyfully, and the steamer actually led the way, being towed by two sailing vessels into the lake (the paddles had been dismounted months ago).

Once in the lake the great difficulties passed away, and we shortly entered the great White Nile. The dam saved the expedition from utter failure.

My deal Edith, you can imagine what anxiety and trouble it must have given to dear Papa to lead an expedition through an unnavigable river.

We arrived at Gondokoro on 14 April, and it appeared really quite like heaven to us after the horrible country through which we had been struggling for four months and ten days. Nevertheless we found great changes since we last saw this spot. The whole of the villages are destroyed—not a dwelling is left and the country is strewn with the skulls and bones of the inhabitants. Those who are left are forced to take refuge from the attacks of their enemies upon low unhealthy islands in the river. The whole country is in a state of the wildest anarchy owing to the acts of the ivory and slave traders. We shall have to support some tribes and subdue others before any hope [of] order can be entertained.

The difficulties of this country were always great, but they have terribly increased what with the obstructions to navigation and the delays thus caused in a voyage that formerly was an affair of only 40 days from Khartoum, together with the hostile state of the tribes and the large force of troops necessary to support the new Government. We have great anxiety respecting the supply of provisions. We are cut off from all communication with Khartoum for twelve months until reinforcements shall arrive with the North Wind next season. With many mouths, about 2,000 including sailors and camp-followers, this is a serious matter; and Papa is driving all hands forward in the work of cultivation, as the rainy season has commenced and we shall be entirely dependent upon our crops of corn.

We have also to build the new settlement, to be named 'Ismailia', and then to convey the sections of steamers to be reconstructed ninety miles from this above the cataracts for the Albert Nyanza.

It is a very hard task to command such people in a difficult enterprise— they have no 'élan' in their disposition and they work without the energy natural to Europeans. On the other hand, Europeans are not adapted for African climate and hardships.

Already our English party is diminished by four: the unfortunate Doctor Gedge died at Khartoum last year; Mr Wood (private Secretary) returned in ill health—and you know that Lewis and Margaret returned together long ago!!!!!

We have now Mr Higginbotham (the chief engineer) and six mechanics to erect the steamers. Thank God throughout the trying journey dear Papa and I have had excellent health; also Julian had always good health, except once or twice he had a touch of fever with biliousness, but now is quite strong and well.

While I am writing your letter, my darling, our vessels are arriving very fast now after their long and weary journey—some of the boats have been six months from Khartoum.

What a change has taken place in this spot! Formerly there were numerous neat little villages scattered over the country, each surrounded by a tall hedge of euphorbia. Now there is not a dwelling. All have been destroyed—the slave traders have set every tribe against its neighbour, and the result is desolation.

We found the great nogara or war drum of the beaten tribe lying among the ruins of a village near to where we camped; two of our little kids have taken possession of the empty drum which serves them for a house. Not one brick remains upon another of the old Austrian Mission station.

The long avenue of lemon trees planted by the hands of the departed Missionaries still flourishes, although uncared for; the trees have grown to a great size and the ground beneath is literally covered with many thousands of lemons which have fallen from the trees. The natives will not eat the fruit, and they have entirely neglected and destroyed all that the industry of civilization had introduced. A few pomegranate trees can be discovered among the thorns, but utter ruin is the only result of the years of labour that the unfortunate Mission bestowed upon this ungrateful land.

Papa has arranged an excellent plan for the new settlement to be named 'Ismailia'. The port will be upon the cliff above the river commanding all approaches, and the old Mission station with the avenue of lemon trees will be enclosed and kept as the Government gardens. Once more civilization will make an effort in this God-forsaken country, and the slave trade being abolished by the presence of a thousand bayonets, there may be some hope of future improvement.

We are now cut off from all communication with the outer world, as no vessels can arrive from Khartoum for the next twelve months, when we trust to receive reinforcements. None but a large force would possibly work the vessels through the obstructions of the river. We are necessarily dependent upon the locality for supplies; thus all hands are now engaged in cultivation. . . .

How often we think and talk of you all at home, what would I give to have a long chat with you, and see you surrounded with your darling children, but with so much hard work before us we can hardly dare to think of our return home; but I cannot tell you, my own dear Edith, the happiness and the pleasure I shall have when we meet again. It is really too happy and exciting to think about home and all the dear faces—My darling I hope and trust that you quite got over your dreadful accident and that you feel as strong and as well as ever. I am very anxious to hear all about yourself and how many children there are? . . .

My dear Edith, I will trouble you now with a mission. Will you be good enough to send me out by the first opportunity addressed to dear Papa. His Excellency, Sir Samuel Baker Pasha, to the care of the British Consulate, Cairo, to be forwarded immediately:—

6 pairs of the best brown gauntlet gloves
6 pair of different colour gloves
1 pair of best rather short French stays with 6 pair of silk long stay laces.
2 pair of yellow gloves for Papa, I think they are number $7\frac{1}{2}$ but they must be the best you can get.
2 dozen lead pencils. . . .
6 pair of best steels for stays.

Give my very warmest and affectionate love to dear Robert and darling Agnes, and give plenty of kisses to my dear own grandchildren.

Ever my own Edith
Your very loving
Florence Baker

The stays to be $23\frac{1}{2}$ inches.
My darling Edith, I forget to beg you also to send me out

12 good fine handkerchiefs
6 for dear Papa.

We are getting very short of handkerchiefs—in fact we are getting short of everything.

✲

REVD CHARLES NEW

(1840–1875)

British missionary. He was the first European actually to touch the snow of Kilimanjaro, in 1871.

Life, Wanderings and Labours in Eastern Africa; with an Account of the First Successful Ascent of the Equatorial Snow Mountain, Kilm-Njaro, and Remarks upon East African Slavery (London, 1873).

REACHING THE SNOW (1866)

I had not gone far . . . before I came to a tremendous gulf, dropping almost sheer down between myself and the patch of snow to which I hoped

I was making my way. This gulf was all that now remained between myself and it, but what an *all*! The snow was on a level with my eye, but my arm was too short to reach it. My heart sank, but before I had time fairly to scan the position my eyes rested upon snow at my very feet! There it lay upon the rocks below me in shining masses, looking like newly washed and sleeping sheep! Hurrah! I cannot describe the sensations that thrilled my heart at that moment. Hurrah! I thought of Tofiki. Returning a short distance, I called to him at the top of my voice, and in a little while he made his appearance, looking horrified. What had I seen? Strengthless as he was, my cries went through him like an arrow, and gave him new vigour. He expected to find me in the hands of some monster, about to be tossed into some abysmal depth! Reaching the spot where I had seen the snow, he exclaimed, 'There is snow! What more do you want, Buana?' 'Nothing,' I observed; 'but we must carry some of it away.' It was frozen as hard as the rock itself, but with the spiked end of the spear I carried, I broke off several large masses. Tofiki put them into his blanket, slung them over his shoulders, and away we went downhill in triumph! I made the more haste as my head was so giddy that I was afraid of swooning; Tofiki, too, looked wild and strange; and besides this, as noon was approaching, the mists would soon come sweeping up the mountain and make it difficult for us to find our party. As it was, we followed down our footprints in the sand, and coming to the rocky region, steered our course by the smoke which rose from the fires of our people. Reaching our party, they looked at us enquiringly, as much as to say, 'Well, what success?' Tofiki threw down the burden of snow, saying, 'There's the white stuff; look at it; Kibo is beaten at last!' When I took the snow and began crunching it, as if it were the greatest delicacy, the men looked at each other as much as to say, 'What *uganga* is the *Mzungu* up to now?' while some said, 'Who ever saw a man eating stones before?' Mtema stared and gaped, looked first at the snow and then at me, but remained dumb with astonishment. '*Luma* [eat] yourself,' I said. He looked afraid, but after a while, putting it to his mouth, he instantly shouted, '*Mringa! mringa!* [Water! water!] Let us take it to the *mange*!' 'Yes,' said my guide, 'and I shall take some to the coast, where I shall sell it for medicine! Everybody will want a piece of the white stuff that came from Kilima Njaro!' I told them it would melt before we could reach Moche, but they smiled incredulously, saying, 'Who ever heard of stones melting?' It was broken up and put into one of the calabashes. Tofiki and I were feeling all right again now; no sooner had we entered the lower stratum of the atmosphere than our strength returned to us, and we felt quite new men. . . .

Next day, reaching the border, the natives performed a ceremony to disenchant us, and our whole party was christened with a professionally prepared liquor, supposed to possess the potency of neutralizing evil influences, and removing the spell of wicked spirits.

At camp we were very heartily received—the people crowding about us in large numbers to hear the news. None were more curious than the *mange*. He was very disappointed to hear that the 'white matter' was not silver. 'But', said Mtema, emphatically, 'it is water, *mange*! nothing but water, *mange*! Here it is in the calabash; look at it, *mange*.'

The stones and plants which we had brought down with us were closely examined; they were quite unknown to the people and greatly astonished them. They left the camp, saying, 'The white man is *Erua* [a god]!'

✻

GEORG AUGUST SCHWEINFURTH
(1836–1925)

German botanist and energetic explorer. He was the first European to meet pygmies in the Congo forests, and he also ranged widely in the Sahara. His primary interest was collecting plants.

The Heart of Africa (London, 1873).

'THE UNHAPPIEST DAY OF MY LIFE' (1870)

The unhappiest day of my life had begun with the routine to which I had grown accustomed of late. I had spent the morning writing letters and had just started my unpretentious midday meal when I was suddenly startled by a Negro's cry of *Poddu, poddu!* (fire!). Always on the alert for that cry, I realized in that same moment the whole import of the tragedy. At that time of day the perpetual north-east wind was at its strongest and, coming from that quarter, drove the flames straight onto my dwelling. I had a bare two minutes in which to salvage my possessions. My servants managed to extricate five of the trunks and two cases. Hundred-foot flames issued from the sunblinds while showers of burning thatch filled the air.

Then I noticed with horror that the packing-cases were beginning to smoulder! They contained all my manuscripts, daily records of my travels, memorandum books. The dogs followed me, howling, on burnt paws and we pulled up at last, panting, under a big tree.

The bone-dry grassy steppe had purposely been left uncut since the corn had not all been harvested. Now it caught fire; the entire countryside was like a sea of flame. And the whole disaster lasted barely half an hour.

My lovely equipment for the (second) projected Niam-Niam expedition, the very latest collections (the most deplorable loss being the whole of my entomological acquisitions and many valuable examples of African art and skill); the manuscripts with all the meteorological observations which I had entered every day since I set out from Suakin, and which in themselves alone contained some 7,000 barometric readings; the travel journals with their experiences and comments covering 825 days; finally the sterometric entries and vocabularies so laboriously obtained—within a few moments they had all fallen a prey to the flames. From the first I had retained possession of the diaries and the collection of insects for fear of any contingency that might arise in course of transmission: now, it was equally certain, they lay at the bottom of the Nile.

So there I now sat, in silent resignation, on the salvaged bedding among my tobacco plants. Evening came; the cow paid me her usual visit with her calf, and yielded me two glasses of milk. Around me the dogs howled with the pain of their burned feet. The servants and slaves were as cheerful as ever—they had had nothing to lose!

The *seriba*, however, was rebuilt—not only on the same spot but actually in the same compact style as before. I had more than six months ahead of me before I could board the trading-vessels for the return journey down the Nile. Gloomily, doggedly, I took up my work again, right from the very beginning, struggling more grimly than before with shortages and privation, no better off than a beggar. Now, however, patience took the place of enthusiasm—and patience can overcome every misfortune.

✿

JOSEPH THOMSON

(1858–1895)

Scottish explorer and cartographer. Second in command to Keith Johnston on an expedition sent by the Royal Geographical Society in 1878. Johnston died soon after they left Zanzibar and Thomson took over, to become one of the most attractive and prolific of African travellers. Thomson's Gazelle was named in his honour.

1: *To the Central African Lakes and Back* (London, 1881); 2–4: *Through Masai Land* (London, 1887).

1. DETERMINATION TO CONTINUE WHEN JOHNSTON DIES
(1878)

Full of enthusiasm, and in every respect a scientific traveller, he would have led the Expedition in a clear, well-defined pathway. Without him the way seemed dark and uncertain indeed.

The position into which I was thus thrown was one of peculiar difficulty, and the question arose within me whether I should go forward or not. I was myself ill with fever. I was almost totally destitute of the special scientific knowledge of a geographical traveller; in fact, I knew little of anything that was most needful to know; and my age was but twenty-two. But though the question arose, it was soon disposed of. With my foot on the threshold of the unknown, I felt I must go forward, whatever might be my destiny. Was I not the countryman of Bruce, Park, Clapperton, Grant, Livingstone, and Cameron? Though the mantle of Mr Johnston's knowledge could not descend upon me, yet Elijah-like he left behind him his enthusiasm for geographical research, and I resolved to carry out his designs as far as lay in my power.

2. FIRST DESCRIPTIONS OF THE GREAT GAME PLAINS
OF EAST AFRICA (1883)

There, towards the base of Kilimanjaro, are three great herds of buffalo slowly and leisurely moving up from the lower grazing-grounds to the shelter of the forest for their daily snooze and rumination in its gloomy depths. Further out on the plains, enormous numbers of the harmless but fierce-looking wildebeest continue their grazing, some erratic members of the herd gambolling and galloping about with waving tail and strange, uncouth movements. Mixed with these are to be seen companies of that loveliest of all large game, the zebra, conspicuous in their beautiful striped skin, here marching with stately step, with heads down bent, there enjoying themselves by kicking their heels in mid-air or running open-mouthed in mimic fight, anon standing as if transfixed, with heads erect and projecting ears, watching the caravan pass. But these are not all. Look! Down in that grassy bottom there are several specimens of the great, unwieldy rhinoceros, with horns stuck on their noses in a most offensive and pugnacious manner. Over that ridge a troop of ostriches are scudding away out of reach of danger, defying pursuit, and too wary for the stalker. See how numerous are the herds of hartebeest, and notice the graceful pallah springing into mid-air with great bounds, as if in pure enjoyment of existence. There also, among the tall reeds near the marsh, you perceive the dignified waterbuck, in twos and threes, leisurely cropping the dewy grass. The wart-hog, disturbed at his morning's feast, clears off in a bee-line with tail erect, and with a steady military trot truly comical. These do not exhaust the list, for there are many other species of game. Turn in whatever direction you please, they are to be seen in astonishing numbers, and so rarely hunted that unconcernedly they stand and stare at us, within gunshot.

Look, now, further ahead. Near a dark line of trees which conspicuously mark out the course of the Ngare N'Erobi (cold stream) in the treeless expanse around, you observe in the clear morning air columns of curling smoke, and from the vicinity strange, long, dark lines are seen to emerge like the dark columns of an advancing army. The smoke marks the kraals of the Masai, and the advancing lines are their cattle moving towards the pasture-ground. If you will now imagine a long line of men moving in single file across this prairie region, carrying boxes, bales, packages of iron wire, etc., headed by myself, and brought up in the rear by Martin, while a cold, piercing wind blows with the freezing effect suggestive of an early spring in Scotland, you will be able to form a picture of the scene which presented itself on that memorable morning in April. In order to find a frame for the picture, just glance round at the circle of mountains. There to the right rises Mount Meru, now seen in all its simple but grand proportions, forming a fitting pillar to the 'door' of the Masai. On your left stands the second great pillar, Kibo. From these circles an apparently almost unbroken range of mountains, rising into the picturesque masses of Donyo Erok and Ndapduk in the north, and finally sweeping round in the less conspicuous ranges of the Guaso N'Ebor (white water) in the direction of Ngurumani and the cold heights of Gelei, behind which lies unseen the still active volcano of Donyo Engai.

Let us now hurry forward, for the day is big with fate! As we stride on, continually tempted to try our 'shooting-irons', the Masai begin to appear. First a woman, well-dressed in bullock's hide and loaded with wire, beads, and chains, appears driving a donkey before her as she wends her way fearlessly towards Kibonoto to buy the vegetable food eaten by the married people and children. It is war to the death between the male Masai and Wa-chaga, but a treaty allows the women to go unhurt and without protection. Next, two or three poor men are descried, engaged in the menial task of herding and tending the cattle. As we near the kraals, the El-Moran (warriors or unmarried men) begin to turn out in parties to see the 'latest thing' in men. They do not hurry themselves, however. They survey you leisurely, and by neither word nor sign betray any feelings of astonishment. As we pass them in succession we pluck some grass and gravely shake hands. Addressing them as El-Moran, we wait till an inarticulate sound intimates they have ears. Then we say 'Subai', to which they reply 'Ebai', and our introduction is over. Greatly struck by the unusual manners of these savages, so different from the notion we have formed of them, we move on, not a bit inconvenienced by crowding or annoyed by rude remarks.

Before noon we had all reached the ice-cold waters of the snow-fed Ngare N'Erobi, which rises in its full volume at the base of the mountain. We camped in a sharp bend of the stream where it almost surrounds a bit of level sward. Our first care, of course, was to make the *boma* [enclosure], and thoroughly fortify ourselves. So far everything had gone on swimmingly, though I was quite bewildered by my unexpected reception, and felt as if there was something portentous in the whole affair.

The news of our arrival soon spread. The Masai men and women began to crowd into camp, and we mutually surveyed each other with equal interest. The women had all the style of the men. With slender, well-shaped figures, they had brilliant dark eyes, Mongolian in type, narrow, and with an upward slant. Their expression was distinctly lady-like (for natives), and betrayed their ideas in more ways than one. Obviously they felt that they were a superior race, and that all others were but as slaves before them. . . .

Conceive yourself standing in the centre of the plain. In your immediate vicinity there is not a blade of grass to relieve the barren aspect of the damp, muddy sand, which, impregnated with various salts, is unfavourable to the growth of any vegetation. Here and there, however, in the horizon are to be detected a few sheets of water, surrounded by rings of green grass, and a few straggling trees or scrubby bushes. Other green patches of tall waving sedges and papyrus mark the position of various marshes. These ponds and marshes indicate springs of fresh water which here well forth, loaded with salts in solution, to deposit their burden on the evaporation of the water. Beside these, there extend considerable tracts covered with a pure white crust of natron and saltpetre, formed by the efflorescence of the salts left by the dried-up marshes of the wet season. These areas appear to the eye as sheets of pure white snow or lakes of charmingly clear water. At other times, struck by the rays of the sun, they shine with the dazzling splendour of burnished silver. A weird haze envelopes the land with an influence shadowy and ghostly, while the mirage adds to the strange effects, until indeed everything seems unreal and deceptive. The exceptional nature of the sight is emphasized by the stupendous mass of Kilimanjaro, the pyramidal form of Meru, the double peak of Ndapduk, and the dark height of Donyo Erok, which are all faintly traceable through the dull grey sheen. In spite of the desolate and barren aspect of the country, game is to be seen in marvellous abundance. The giraffe, fit denizen of such a region, appears against the horizon like some unearthly monster, or browses among the trees and bushes. The wildebeest, imp-like and fierce in appearance, frisks with uncouth movements, or speeds with stiff ungainly gallops across the natron plain. Zebras in long lines pace leisurely along from some distant pasture-ground. Hyenas slink home from their meal of carrion. Lions satisfied with the night's venture express their sense of repletion with reverberating roars. The enquiry that naturally rises to one's mind is, How can such enormous numbers of large game live in this extraordinary desert? A curious illusion is produced by the damp, heated air rising from the sands. This gives a marvellously beautiful waving motion to the black-and-white stripes of the zebra, which seem to quiver up and down with an effect not unlike the well-known electric advertisements. As we stand in this phantom plain, awestruck with the impressive spectacle, the haze gradually thickens in the distance, and eclipses the smaller mountains. Then a morning breeze laden with moisture from the sea touches the peak of Kimawenzi, and, cooled by its influence, leaves a cloud. Passing across to Kibo, it enshrouds it in a winding-sheet of stratus. In a little while the mountain wholly disappears from view like the 'baseless fabric of a vision'.

3. Naming the Thomson Falls

Next day, as we dared not advance till we had prospected the country ahead, I dispatched a small party for that purpose, and then set off myself down the Ururu to visit its falls. On reaching them, I was impressed mightily by the stupendous thundering of the waters which in magnificent mass plunged down several hundred feet without a break into a fearful gloomy gorge. The rock is a very compact lava with a tendency to a columnar arrangement, forming near the falls precipices of a very imposing character. The crevices give support to a splendid drapery of creepers and bushes, the spray from the waters yielding the necessary sustenance. Among other plants wild bananas are to be seen. A short way down the gorge the walls become less precipitous, and recede at a high angle. The gorge and falls have been formed by a gradual cutting back through the lavas of Settima, which run some distance north and then turn west. The aspect of the great Angata (plain) Bus suggests in a very striking manner the theory that at one time it was a lake which has been thus drained by the surplus waters gradually cutting the transverse ridge away. The marshes of Kope-Kope are doubtless the remnant of this lake. After photographing the falls, and naming them the 'Thomson Falls', I proceeded through the forest in the hope of shooting something.

4. FACING DOWN THE NATIVES

I saw it was necessary to be firm, and show them we were not to be easily frightened. At last, however, as I was getting hustled nastily, my bile was raised, and before the principal young agitator knew what he was about I had dexterously laid him on his back. It was a sight to see the picture of demoniacal and ungovernable rage which he presented as he sprang to his feet. He poised his spear, and pranced about like a madman, trying to get clear of his father, who kept in front of him, and prevented him from launching it at me. The moment was very critical. All my men held their guns ready. Brahim covered the young warrior with my Express rifle, while on the other hand hundreds of warriors grasped their spears as if only waiting a signal to precipitate themselves upon our small party. As for myself, I simply folded my arms and laughed derisively, a piece of acting I have always found to have a remarkable effect upon the natives, who at once conclude that I have supernatural powers of offence and defence. The old man succeeded at last in carrying off his son, very much to my relief—for in spite of my heroic attitude I was anything but comfortable inwardly, and in reality I had made a very narrow escape. We were now masters of the field, and were allowed to leave peaceably.

✻

COUNT SAMUEL TELEKI

(1845–1916)

Hungarian explorer. The first European to see, and name, Lakes Rudolf and Stefanie.

The Discovery of Lakes Rudolf and Stefanie: A Narrative of Count Samuel Teleki's Exploring & Hunting Expedition in Eastern Equatorial Africa in 1887 & 1888 by His Companion Lieut. Ludwig von Hoehnel, trans. N. Bell (London, 1894).

ARRIVAL AT LAKE RUDOLF (1885)

Steep rocky slopes alternated with ravines strewn with debris, which gave one the impression of being still glowing hot and of having but recently been flung forth from some huge forge. And this glaring monotony continued until about two o'clock. The good spirits with which the thought that we were nearing the end of our long tramp had filled us in the morning had long since been dissipated, and our hopes had become restricted to finding some little pool with slimy green water at which to quench our thirst, when all of a sudden, as we were climbing a gentle slope, such a grand, beautiful, and far-stretching scene was spread out before us, that at first we felt we must be under some delusion and were disposed to think the whole thing a mere phantasmagoria. As we got higher up, a single peak gradually rose before us, the gentle contours rising symmetrically from every side, resolving themselves into one broad pyramidal mountain, which we knew at once to be a volcano. A moment before we had been gazing into empty space, and now here was a mighty mountain mass looming up before us, on the summit of which we almost involuntarily looked for snow. This was, however, only the result of an optical delusion caused by the suddenness with which the mountain had come in sight, and [by] the fact that the land sank rapidly on either side of it whilst we were gazing up at it from a considerable height. On the east of the mountain the land was uniformly flat, a golden plain lit up by sunshine, whilst on the [west] the base of the volcano seemed to rise up out of a bottomless depth, a void which was altogether a mystery to us. We hurried as fast as we could to the top of our ridge, the scene gradually developing itself as we advanced, until an entirely new world was spread out before our astonished eyes. The void down in the depths beneath became filled as if by magic with picturesque mountains and rugged slopes, with a medley of ravines and valleys, which appeared to be closing up from every side to form a fitting frame for the dark-blue gleaming surface of the lake stretching away beyond as far as the eye could reach.

For a long time we gazed in speechless delight, spell-bound by the beauty of the scene before us, whilst our men, equally silent, stared into the distance for a few minutes, to break presently into shouts of astonishment at the sight of the glittering expanse of the great lake which melted on the horizon into the blue of the sky. At that moment all our dangers, all our fatigues were forgotten in the joy of finding our exploring expedition crowned with success at last. Full of enthusiasm and gratefully remembering the gracious interest taken in our plans from the first by his Royal and Imperial Highness, Prince Rudolf of Austria, Count Teleki named the sheet of water, set like a pearl of great price in the wonderful land-scape beneath us, Lake Rudolf.

Our guide, Lembasso, proved himself very well acquainted with the neighbourhood.

❄

MARY KINGSLEY

(1862–1900)

English traveller in West Africa, in whose memory the African (now the Royal African) Society was founded in 1901. Niece of Charles Kingsley.

Travels in West Africa (London, 1897).

IN THE FOREST (1893)

A certain sort of friendship soon arose between the Fans and me. We each recognized that we belonged to that same section of the human race with whom it is better to drink than to fight. We knew we would each have killed the other, if sufficient inducement were offered, and so we took a certain amount of care that the inducement should not arise. Grey Shirt and Pagan also, their trade friends, the Fans treated with an independent sort of courtesy; but Silence, Singlet, the Passenger, and above all Ngouta, they openly did not care a row of pins for, and I have small doubt that had it not been for us other three they would have killed and eaten these very amiable gentlemen with as much compunction as an English sportsman would kill as many rabbits. They on their part hated the Fan, and never lost an opportunity of telling me 'these Fan be bad man too much'.

I must not forget to mention the other member of our party, a Fan gentleman with the manners of a duke and the habits of a dustbin. He came with us, quite uninvited by me, and never asked for any pay; I think he only wanted to see the fun, and drop in for a fight if there was one going on, and to pick up the pieces generally. He was evidently a man of some importance, from the way the others treated him; and moreover he had a splendid gun, with a gorilla-skin sheath for its lock, and ornamented all over its stock with brass nails. His costume consisted of a small piece of dirty rag round his loins; and whenever we were going through dense undergrowth, or wading a swamp, he wore that filament tucked up scandalously short. Whenever we were sitting down in the forest having one of our nondescript meals, he always sat next to me and appropriated the tin. Then he would fill his pipe and, turning to me with the easy grace of aristocracy, would say what may be translated as 'My dear Princess, could you favour me with a lucifer?'

I used to say, 'My dear Duke, charmed, I'm sure', and give him one ready-lit.

I dared not trust him with the box whole, having a personal conviction that he would have kept it. I asked him what he would do suppose I was not there with a box of lucifers; and he produced a bush-cow's horn with a neat wood lid tied on with tie tie, and from out of it he produced a flint and steel and demonstrated. Unfortunately, all his Grace's minor possessions, owing to the scantiness of his attire, were in one and the same pineapple-fibre bag which he wore slung across his shoulder; and these possessions, though not great, were as dangerous to the body as a million sterling is said to be to the soul, for they consisted largely of gunpowder and snuff, and their separate receptacles leaked and their contents commingled, so that demonstration on fire-making methods among the Fan ended in an awful bang and blow-up in a small way, and the Professor and his pupil sneezed like fury for ten minutes, and a cruel world laughed till it nearly died, for twenty. Still, that bag with all its failings was a wonder for its containing power.

The first day in the forest we came across a snake[1]—a beauty with a new red-brown and yellow-patterned velvety skin, about three feet six inches long and as thick as a man's thigh. Ngouta met it, hanging from a bough, and shot backwards like a lobster, Ngouta having among his many weaknesses a rooted horror of snakes. This snake the Ogowe natives all hold in great aversion. For the bite of other sorts of snakes they profess to have remedies, but for this they have none. If, however, a native is stung by one he usually conceals the fact that it was this particular kind, and tries to get any chance the native doctor's medicine may give. The Duke stepped forward and with one blow flattened its head against the tree with his gun butt, and then folded the snake up and got as much of it as possible into the bag, while the rest hung dangling out. Ngouta, not being able to keep ahead of the Duke, his Grace's pace being stiff, went to the extreme rear of the party, so that other people might be killed first if the snake returned to life, as he surmised it would. He fell into other dangers from this caution, but I cannot chronicle Ngouta's afflictions in full without running

---

[1] *Vipera nasicornis*; M'pongwe, *Ompenle*.

this book into an old-fashioned folio size. We had the snake for supper, that is to say the Fan and I; the others would not touch it, although a good snake, properly cooked, is one of the best meats one gets out here, far and away better than the African fowl.

The Fans also did their best to educate me in every way: they told me their names for things, while I told them mine ...

They also showed me many things: how to light a fire from the pith of a certain tree, which was useful to me in afterlife, but they rather overdid this branch of instruction one way and another; for example, Wiki had, as above indicated, a mania for bush-ropes and a marvellous eye and knowledge of them; he would pick out from among the thousands surrounding us now one of such peculiar suppleness that you could wind it round anything, like a strip of cloth, and as strong withal as a hawser; or again another which has a certain stiffness, combined with a slight elastic spring, excellent for hauling, with the ease and accuracy of a lady who picks out the particular twisted strand of embroidery silk from a multi-coloured tangled ball. He would go into the bush after them while other people were resting, and particularly after the sort which, when split, is bright yellow, and very supple and excellent to tie round loads.

On one occasion, between Egaja and Esoon, he came back from one of these quests and wanted me to come and see something, very quietly; I went, and we crept down into a rocky ravine, on the other side of which lay one of the outermost Egaja plantations. When we got to the edge of the cleared ground, we lay down, and wormed our way, with elaborate caution, among a patch of Koko; Wiki first, I following in his trail.

After about fifty yards of this, Wiki sank flat, and I saw before me some thirty yards off, busily employed in pulling down plantains, and other depredations, five gorillas: one old male, one young male, and three females. One of these had clinging to her a young fellow, with beautiful wavy black hair with just a kink in it. The big male was crouching on his haunches, with his long arms hanging down on either side, with the backs of his hands on the ground, the palms upwards. The elder lady was tearing to pieces and eating a pineapple, while the others were at the plantains destroying more than they ate.

They kept up a sort of a whinnying, chattering noise, quite different from the sound I have heard gorillas give when enraged, or from the one you can hear them giving when they are what the natives call 'dancing' at night. I noticed that their reach of arm was immense, and that when they went from one tree to another, they squattered across the open ground in a most inelegant style, dragging their long arms with the knuckles downwards. I should think the big male and female were over six feet each. The others would be from four to five. I put out my hand and laid it on Wiki's gun to prevent him from firing, and he, thinking I was going to fire, gripped my wrist.

I watched the gorillas with great interest for a few seconds, until I heard Wiki make a peculiar small sound, and looking at him saw his face was working in an awful way as he clutched his throat with his hand violently.

Heavens! think I, this gentleman's going to have a fit; it's lost we are entirely this time. He rolled his head to and fro, and then buried his face into a heap of dried rubbish at the foot of a plantain stem, clasped his hands over it, and gave an explosive sneeze. The gorillas let go all, raised themselves up for a second, gave a quaint sound between a bark and a howl, and then the ladies and the young gentleman started home. The old male rose to his full height (it struck me at the time this was a matter of ten feet at least, but for scientific purposes allowances must be made for a lady's emotions) and looked straight towards us, or rather towards where that sound came from. Wiki went off into a paroxysm of falsetto sneezes the like of which I have never heard; nor evidently had the gorilla, who . . . went off after his family with a celerity that was amazing the moment he touched the forest, and disappeared as they had, swinging himself along through it from bough to bough, in a way that convinced me that, given the necessity of getting about in tropical forests, man has made a mistake in getting his arms shortened. I have seen many wild animals in their native wilds, but never have I seen anything to equal gorillas going through bush; it is a graceful, powerful, superbly perfect hand-trapeze performance.[2]

After this sporting adventure we returned, as I usually return from a sporting adventure, without measurements or the body. . . .

We had to hurry because Kiva, who was the only one among us who had been to Efoua, said that unless we did we should not reach Efoua that night. I said, 'Why not stay for bush?', not having contracted any love for a night in a Fan town by the experience of M'fetta; moreover, the Fans were not sure that after all the whole party of us might not spend the evening at Efoua, when we did get there, simmering in its cooking-pots. . . .

About five o'clock I was off ahead and noticed a path which I had been told I should meet with, and, when met with, I must follow. The path was slightly indistinct, but by keeping my eye on it I could see it. Presently I

[2] I have no hesitation in saying that the gorilla is the most horrible wild animal I have seen. I have seen at close quarters specimens of the most important big game of Central Africa, and, with the exception of snakes, I have run away from all of them; but although elephants, leopards, and pythons give you a feeling of alarm, they do not give that feeling of horrible disgust that an old gorilla gives on account of its hideousness of appearance.

came to a place where it went out, but appeared again on the other side of a clump of underbush fairly distinctly. I made a short cut for it and the next news was I was in a heap, on a lot of spikes, some fifteen feet or so below ground level, at the bottom of a bag-shaped game pit.

It is at these times you realize the blessing of a good thick skirt. Had I paid heed to the advice of many people in England, who ought to have known better, and did not do it themselves, and adopted masculine garments, I should have been spiked to the bone, and done for. Whereas, save for a good many bruises, here I was with the fulness of my skirt tucked under me, sitting on nine ebony spikes some twelve inches long, in comparative comfort, howling lustily to be hauled out. The Duke came along first, and looked down at me. I said, 'Get a bush-rope, and haul me out.' He grunted and sat down on a log. The Passenger came next, and he looked down. 'You kill?' says he. 'Not much,' say I; 'get a bush-rope and haul me out.' 'No fit,' says he, and sat down on the log. Presently, however, Kiva and Wiki came up, and Wiki went and selected the one and only bush-rope suitable to haul an English lady, of my exact complexion, age, and size, out of that one particular pit. They seemed rare round there from the time he took; and I was just casting about in my mind as to what method would be best to employ in getting up the smooth, yellow, sandy-clay, in-curved walls, when he arrived with it, and I was out in a twinkling, and very much ashamed of myself, until Silence, who was then leading, disappeared through the path before us with a despairing yell. Each man then pulled the skin cover off his gun lock, carefully looked to see if things there were all right and ready loosened his knife in its snake-skin sheath; and then we set about hauling poor Silence out, binding him up where necessary with cool green leaves; for he, not having a skirt, had got a good deal frayed at the edges on those spikes.

Then we closed up, for the Fans said these pits were symptomatic of the immediate neighbourhood of Efoua. We sounded our ground, as we went into a thick plantain patch, through which we could see a great clearing in the forest, and the low huts of a big town. We charged into it, going right through the guard-house gateway, at one end, in single file, as its narrowness obliged us, and into the street-shaped town, and formed ourselves into as imposing a looking party as possible in the centre of the street. The Efouerians regarded us with much amazement, and the women and children cleared off into the huts, and took stock of us through the door-holes. There were but few men in the town, the majority, we subsequently learnt, being away after elephants. But there were quite sufficient left to make a crowd in a ring round us. Fortunately Wiki and Kiva's friends were present, and we were soon in another world—fog, but not so bad a one as that at

M'fetta; indeed, Efoua struck me from the first favourably; it was, for one thing, much cleaner than most Fan towns I have been in.

As a result of the confabulation, one of the chiefs had his house cleared out for me. It consisted of two apartments almost bare of everything save a pile of boxes, and a small fire on the floor, some little bags hanging from the roof poles, and a general supply of insects. The inner room contained nothing save a hard plank, raised on four short pegs from the earth floor.

I shook hands with and thanked the chief, and directed that all the loads should be placed inside the huts. I must admit my good friend was a villainous-looking savage, but he behaved most hospitably and kindly. From what I had heard of the Fan, I deemed it advisable not to make any present to him at once, but to base my claim on him on the right of an amicable stranger to hospitality. When I had seen all the baggage stowed, I went outside and sat at the doorway on a rather rickety, mushroom-shaped stool in the cool evening air, waiting for my tea which I wanted bitterly. Pagan came up as usual for tobacco to buy chop with; and after giving it to him, I and the two chiefs, with Grey Shirt acting as interpreter, had a long chat. Of course the first question was, Why was I there?

I told them I was on my way to the factory of H. and C. on the Rembwe. They said they had heard of 'Ugumu', i.e. Messrs Hatton and Cookson, but they did not trade direct with them, passing their trade into towns nearer to the Rembwe, which were swindling bad towns, they said; and they got the idea stuck in their heads that I was a trader, a sort of bagman for the firm, and Grey Shirt could not get this idea out, so off one of their majesties went and returned with twenty-five balls of rubber, which I bought to promote good feeling, subsequently dashing them to Wiki, who passed them in at Ndorko when we got there. I also bought some elephant-hair necklaces from one of the chiefs' wives, by exchanging my red silk tie with her for them, and one or two other things. I saw fish-hooks would not be of much value because Efoua was not near a big water of any sort; so I held fish-hooks and traded handkerchiefs and knives. . . .

The chiefs made furious raids on the mob of spectators who pressed round the door, and stood with their eyes glued to every crack in the bark of which the hut was made. The next-door neighbours on either side might have amassed a comfortable competence for their old age, by letting out seats for the circus. Every hole in the side walls had a human eye in it, and I heard new holes being bored in all directions; so I deeply fear the chief, my host, must have found his palace sadly draughty. I felt perfectly safe and content, however, although Ngouta suggested the charming idea that 'P'r'aps them M'fetta Fan done sell we'. The only grave question I had to face was whether I should take off my boots or not; they were wet through, from wading swamps, etc., and my feet were very sore; but, on the other hand, if I took those boots off, I felt confident that I should not be able to get them on again next morning, so I decided to lef 'em.

As soon as all my men had come in, and established themselves in the inner room for the night, I curled up among the boxes, with my head on the tobacco sack, and dozed.

After about half an hour I heard a row in the street, and looking out— for I recognized his Grace's voice taking a solo part followed by choruses— I found him in legal difficulties about a murder case. An alibi was proved for the time being; that is to say, the prosecution could not bring up witnesses because of the elephant hunt; and I went in for another doze, and the town at last grew quiet. Waking up again I noticed the smell in the hut was violent, from being shut up I suppose, and it had an unmistakably organic origin. Knocking the ash-end off the smouldering bush-light that lay burning on the floor, I investigated, and tracked it to those bags, so I took down the biggest one, and carefully noted exactly how the tie had been put round its mouth; for these things are important and often mean a lot. I then shook its contents out in my hat, for fear of losing anything of value. They were a human hand, three big toes, four eyes, two ears, and other portions of the human frame. The hand was fresh, the others only so so, and shrivelled.

Replacing them I tied the bag up, and hung it up again. I subsequently learnt that although the Fans will eat their fellow friendly tribesfolk, yet they like to keep a little something belonging to them as a memento. This touching trait in their character I learnt from Wiki; and, though it's to their credit, under the circumstances, still it's an unpleasant practice when they hang the remains in the bedroom you occupy, particularly if the bereavement in your host's family has been recent. I did not venture to prowl round Efoua; but slid the bark door aside and looked out to get a breath of fresh air.

It was a perfect night, and no mosquitoes. The town, walled in on every side by the great cliff of high black forest, looked very wild as it showed in the starlight, its low, savage-built bark huts, in two hard rows, closed at either end by a guard-house. In both guard-houses there was a fire burning, and in their flickering glow showed the forms of sleeping men. Nothing was moving save the goats, which are always brought into the special house for them in the middle of the town, to keep them from the leopards, which roam from dusk to dawn.

Dawn found us stirring, I getting my tea, and the rest of the party their chop, and binding up anew the loads with Wiki's fresh supple bush-ropes. Kiva amused me much; during our march his costume was exceeding scant, but when we reached the towns he took from his bag garments, and attired himself so resplendently that I feared the charm of his appearance would lead me into one of those dreadful wife palavers which experience had taught me of old to dread: and in the morning-time he always devoted some time to repacking. I gave a big dash to both chiefs, and they came out with us, most civilly, to the end of their first plantations; and then we took farewell of each other, with many expressions of hope on both sides that we should meet again, and many warnings from them about the dissolute and depraved character of the other towns we should pass through before we reached the Rembwe.

III

NORTH AMERICA

Leif Ericsson (*c.*970–*c.*1020)   221

John Cabot (*c.*1450–*c.*1499)   223

Gaspar Corte Real (*c.*1450–1501)   225

Miguel Corte Real (*c.*1450–1502)   225

Juan Ponce de León (1460–1521)   227

Giovanni da Verrazzano (1485–1528)   228

Alvar Núñez Cabeza de Vaca (*c.*1490–*c.*1564)   232

Jacques Cartier (1491–1557)   233

Francisco Vásquez de Coronado (*c.*1510–1554)   236

Hernando de Soto (*c.*1496–1542)   239

Sir Martin Frobisher (*c.*1535–1594)   242

Sir Francis Drake (*c.*1540–1596)   247

Sir Humphrey Gilbert (*c.*1539–1583)   252

John Davis (*c.*1550–1605)   255

Samuel de Champlain (1567–1635)   257

Henry Hudson (*c.*1550–*c.*1611)   260

Luke Foxe (1586–1635)   261

Thomas James (1593–1635)   262

Samuel Hearne (1745–1792)   263

James Cook (1728–1779)   268

Sir Alexander Mackenzie (1764–1820)   270

Meriwether Lewis (1774–1809)   276

William Clark (1770–1838)   276

David Thompson (1770–1857)   280

Otto von Kotzebue (1787–1846)   281

Sir John Ross (1777–1856)   284

Sir William Parry (1790–1855)   290

Sir John Franklin (1786–1847)   292

Sir James Clark Ross (1800–1862)   298

John Charles Fremont (1813–1890)   300

John Rae (1813–1893)   307

Sir Francis Leopold McClintock (1819–1907)   309

David Hanbury (1864–1910)   311

Roald Amundsen (1872–1928)   313

Leonidas (d. 1903) and Mina (1870–1956) Hubbard   316

LEIF ERICSSON

(*c*.970–*c*.1020)

Norse explorer. Son of Eric the Red, founder of the first Scandinavian settlement in Greenland, he was probably the first European to set foot on America in about the year 1000.

The North Atlantic Saga, ed. and trans. Gwyn Jones (Oxford, 1964).

DISCOVERY OF VINLAND [?NORTH AMERICA] (*c*.1000)

There was now much talk about voyages of discovery. Leif, son of Eric the Red of Brattahlid, went to see Bjarni Herjolfsson, bought his ship from him, and found her a crew, so that they were thirty-five all told. . . .

They now prepared their ship and sailed out to sea once they were ready, and they lighted on that land first which Bjarni and his people had lighted on last. They sailed to land there, cast anchor and put off a boat, then went ashore, and could see no grass there. The background was all great glaciers, and right up to the glaciers from the sea it were a single slab of rock. The land impressed them as barren and useless. 'At least', said Leif, 'it has not happened to us as to Bjarni over this land, that we failed to get ourselves ashore. I shall now give the land a name, and call it Helluland, Flatstone Land.' After which they returned to the ship.

After that they sailed out to sea and lighted on another land. This time too they sailed to land, cast anchor, then put off a boat and went ashore. The country was flat and covered with forest, with extensive white sands wherever they went, and shelving gently to the sea. 'This land', said Leif, 'shall be given a name in accordance with its nature, and be called Markland, Wood Land.' After which they got back down to the ship as fast as they could.

From there they now sailed out to sea with a north-east wind, and were at sea two days before catching sight of land. They sailed to land, reaching an island which lay north of it, where they went ashore and looked about them in fine weather, and found that there was dew on the grass, where-upon it happened to them that they set their hands to the dew, then carried it to their mouths, and thought they had never known anything so sweet as that was. After which they returned to their ship and sailed into the sound which lay between the island and the cape projecting north from the land itself. They made headway west round the cape. There were big shallows there at low water; their ship went aground, and it was a long way to look to get sight of the sea from the ship. But they were so curious to get ashore they had no mind to wait for the tide to rise under their ship, but went hurrying off to land where a river flowed out of a lake. Then, as soon as the tide rose under their ship, they took their boat, rowed back to her, and brought her up into the river, and so to the lake, where they cast anchor, carried their skin sleeping-bags off board, and built themselves booths. Later they decided to winter there and built a big house.

There was no lack of salmon there in river or lake, and salmon bigger than they had ever seen before. The nature of the land was so choice, it seemed to them that none of the cattle would require fodder for the winter. No frost came during the winter, and the grass was hardly withered. Day and night were of a more equal length there than in Greenland or Iceland. On the shortest day of winter the sun was visible in the middle of the afternoon as well as at breakfast time.

Once they had finished their house-building Leif made an announcement to his comrades. 'I intend to have our company divided now in two, and get the land explored. Half our band shall remain here at the hall, and the other half reconnoitre the countryside—yet go no further than they can get back home in the evening, and not get separated.' So for a while that is what they did, Leif going off with them or remaining in camp by turns. Leif was big and strong, of striking appearance, shrewd, and in every respect a temperate, fair-dealing man.

One evening it turned out that a man of their company was missing. This was Tyrkir the German. Leif was greatly put out by this, for Tyrkir had lived a long while with him and his father, and had shown great affection for Leif as a child. He gave his shipmates the rough edge of his tongue, then turned out to go and look for him, taking a dozen men with him. But when they had got only a short way from the hall there was Tyrkir coming to meet them. His welcome was a joyous one. Leif could see at once that his foster-father was in fine fettle. He was a man with a bulging forehead, rolling eyes, and an insignificant little face, short and not much to look at, but handy at all sorts of crafts.

'Why are you so late, foster-father,' Leif asked him, 'and parted this way from your companions?'

By way of a start Tyrkir held forth a long while in German, rolling his eyes all ways, and pulling faces. They had no notion what he was talking about. Then after a while he spoke in Norse. 'I went no great way further than you, yet I have a real novelty to report. I have found vines and grapes.'

'Is that the truth, foster-father?' Leif asked.

'Of course it's the truth,' he replied. 'I was born where wine and grapes are no rarity.'

They slept overnight, then in the morning Leif made this announcement to his crew. 'We now have two jobs to get on with, and on alternate days must gather grapes or cut vines and fell timber, so as to provide a cargo of such things for my ship.' They acted upon these orders, and report has it that their towboat was filled with grapes. A full ship's cargo was cut, and in the spring they made ready and sailed away. Leif gave the land a name in accordance with the good things they found in it, calling it Vinland, Wineland; after which they sailed out to sea and had a good wind till they sighted Greenland and the mountains under the glaciers.

✿

JOHN CABOT
(GIOVANNI CABOTO)
(*c.*1450–*c.*1499)

Genoese-born navigator with Venetian nationality who sailed to New-foundland from Bristol in command of a British ship in 1497. A year later he set out again with five ships, but failed to return. His son Sebastian explored much of the North American coast, and was the first to seek a North-West Passage.

1: C. R. Beazley, *John and Sebastian Cabot* (London, 1898); 2: J. A. Williamson, *The Cabot Voyages and Bristol: Discovery under Henry VII* (Cambridge, 1962).

1. THE DISCOVERY OF NEWFOUNDLAND (1497)

This land was discovered by John Cabot the Venetian, and Sebastian Cabot his son, in the year of the birth of our Saviour Jesus Christ [1497], on the 24th of June in the morning, to which they gave the name Land First Seen [*Prima Terra Vista*], and to a large island which is near the said land they gave the name Saint John, because it had been discovered the same day. The people of it are dressed in the skins of animals; they use in their wars bows and arrows, lances and darts, and certain clubs of wood, and slings. It is a very sterile land. There are in it many white bears, and very large stags like horses, and many other animals; and likewise there is infinite fish, sturgeons, salmon, very large soles a yard in length, and many other kinds of fish, and the greatest of them are called Baccallaos [codfish]; and likewise there are in the same land hawks black as crows, eagles, partridges, linnets, and many other kinds of birds of different species.

2. LETTER FROM LORENZO PASQUALIGO TO HIS BROTHERS IN VENICE

That Venetian of ours who went with a small ship from Bristol to find new islands has come back and says he has discovered mainland 700 leagues away, which is the country of the Grand Khan, and that he coasted it for 300 leagues and landed and did not see any person; but he has brought here to the king certain snares which were spread to take game and a needle for making nets, and he found certain notched [or felled] trees so that by this he judges that there are inhabitants. Being in doubt he returned to his ship; and he has been three months on the voyage; and this is certain. And on the way back he saw two islands, but was unwilling to land, in order not to lose time, as he was in want of provisions. The king here is much pleased at this; and he [Cabot] says that the tides are slack and do not run as they do here. The king has promised him for the spring ten armed ships as he [Cabot] desires and has given him all the prisoners to be sent away, that they may go with him, as he has requested; and has given him money that he may have a good time until then. And he is with his Venetian wife and his sons at Bristol. His name is Zuam Talbot and he is called the Great Admiral; vast honour is paid to him, and he goes dressed in silk, and these English run after him like mad, and indeed he can enlist as many of them as he pleases, and a number of rogues as well. The discoverer of these things planted on the land which he has found a large cross with a banner of England and one of St Mark, as he is a Venetian, so that our flag has been hoisted very far afield. [London, 23 August 1497; received Venice, 23 September 1497.]

GASPAR CORTE REAL

(*c*.1450–1501)

MIGUEL CORTE REAL

(*c*.1450–1502)

Portuguese explorer brothers. Gaspar sailed in 1500 to Labrador. Next year he sailed again with two ships and was lost with his ship; the other returned safely. In 1502 Miguel set out to look for him and also perished.

Alberto Cantino to Hercules d'Este, Duke of Ferrara, 17 October 1501, on Corte Real's Voyage (Modena State Archives), trans. H. P. Biggar.

LETTER TO THE DUKE OF FERRARA CONCERNING GASPAR'S SECOND VOYAGE (1501)

Most illustrious and most excellent Prince, my very singular good Lord:

Nine months have now passed since this most serene monarch [Manoel I] sent to the northern parts two well-equipped ships, for the sole purpose of finding out if it were possible to discover in that region any lands or islands. Now on the eleventh of the present month one of them has arrived safe and with some booty; and has brought people and news, which it appeared to me ought not to pass without your Excellency's hearing thereof; and thus I have set down here below clearly and exactly all that in my presence was told the king by the captain.

First of all, they relate that, after setting sail as they did from the port of Lisbon, they made their way for four months continuously, always in the same direction and towards the same pole, and never in all that time did they see anything at all. Nevertheless, in the fifth month, still wishing to push on, they say that they met huge masses of solid snow floating upon the sea and moving under the influence of the waves, from the summit of which by the force of the sun's rays a clear stream of sweet water was melted and once dissolved ran down in little channels made by itself, eating its way splashingly to the base. Since the ships now lacked fresh water, the boats approached and took as much as was then needed. Fearing to remain in that region by reason of this present danger, they wished to turn back, but yet, spurred by hope, decided to go forward as best they could for a few days more, and having got under way, on the second day they again discovered the sea to be frozen, and were forced to give up the undertaking.

They then began to turn towards the north-west and the west, in which direction they made their way for three more months, always with favourable weather. And on the first day of the fourth month they caught sight between these two courses of a very large country [probably Newfoundland] which they approached with very great delight. And since throughout this region numerous large rivers flowed into the sea, by one of these they made their way about a league inland, where on landing they found abundance of most luscious and varied fruits, and trees and pines of such measureless height and girth, that they would be too big as a mast for the largest ship that sails the sea. No corn of any sort grows there, but the men of that country say they live altogether by fishing and hunting animals, in which the land abounds, such as very large deer, covered with extremely long hair, the skins of which they use for garments and also make houses and boats thereof, and again wolves, foxes, tigers, and sables. They [the explorers] affirm that there are, what appears to me wonderful, as many falcons as there are sparrows in our country, and I have seen some of them and they are extremely pretty.

They forcibly kidnapped about fifty men and women of this country and have brought them to the king. I have seen, touched, and examined these people, and beginning with their stature, declare that they are somewhat taller than our average, with members corresponding and well-formed. The hair of the men is long, just as we wear ours, and they wear it in curls, and have their faces marked with great signs, and these signs are like those of the [East] Indians. Their eyes are greenish and when they look at one, this gives an air of great boldness to their whole countenance. Their speech is unintelligible, but nevertheless is not harsh but rather human. Their manners and gestures are most gentle; they laugh considerably and manifest the greatest pleasure. So much for the men. The women have small breasts and most beautiful bodies, and rather pleasant faces. The colour of these women may be said to be more white than otherwise, but the men are considerably darker. In fine, except for the terribly harsh look of the men, they appear to me to be in all else of the same form and images as ourselves. They go quite naked except for their privy parts, which they cover with a skin of the above-mentioned deer. They have no arms nor iron, but whatever they work or fashion, they cut with very hard sharp stones, with which they split in two the very hardest substances. This vessel came home thence in one month and they say the distance is 2,800 miles.

JUAN PONCE DE LEÓN
(1460–1521)

Spanish conquistador who discovered and named Florida.

'History of Juan Ponce de León's Voyages to Florida', trans. T. F. Davis, *Florida Historical Quarterly*, 14 (1935).

LANDING IN FLORIDA AND DESCRIBING THE GULF STREAM
(1513)

Juan Ponce de León, finding himself without office . . . and seeing himself rich, determined to do something by which to gain honour and increase his estate; and as he had news that there were lands to the northward, he resolved to go to explore toward that part; for which he armed three vessels, well provided with food, men, and mariners, which for the purpose of discovery are most necessary. He sailed from the island Thursday, in the afternoon, the 3rd of March, setting out from the harbour of San German. He went to Aguada, in order to set from there his course. The night following he went out to sea, north-west a quarter by north, and the vessels went eight leagues of a day's run, before the sun rose. They sailed on until on Tuesday, the 8th of the said month, they came to anchor at the banks of Babueca, at an island that they call El Viejo, which is in 22.5° [latitude]. Next day they anchored in an islet of the Lucayos called Caycos. Soon they anchored in another called La Yaguna, in 24°. On the 11th of the same month they reached another island called Amaguayo, and there they remained for repairs. They passed on to the island called Manegua, which is in 24.5°. On the 14th they reached Guanahani, which is in 25°40′, where they made ready one ship to cross the Windward gulf of the islands of the Lucayos. This island, Guanahani, was the first that the admiral Don Christoval Colon discovered, and where, in his first voyage, he went ashore and named it San Salvador. They set out from here, running north-west, and on Sunday, the 27th, which was the day of the Feast of the Resurrection, which commonly they call [the feast] 'of Flowers', they saw an island but did not examine it.

And Monday, the 28th, they ran fifteen leagues in the same direction, and Wednesday went on in the same manner, and afterward, with bad weather, until the 2nd of April, running west-north-west, the water diminishing to nine fathoms, at one league from land, which was in 30° 8′, they ran along beside the coast seeking harbour, and at night anchored near the land in eight fathoms of water. And believing that this land was an island, they named it La Florida, because it had a very beautiful view of many and cool woodlands, and it was level and uniform; and because, moreover, they discovered it in the time of the Feast of Flowers [Pascua Florida], Juan Ponce wished to conform in the name to these two reasons. He went ashore to get information, and take possession.

On Friday, the 8th, they set sail, running in the same direction: and Saturday they sailed to the south a quarter by south-east; and keeping the same course until the 20th of April, they discovered some huts of Indians, where they anchored: the day following, all three vessels following the sea-coast, they saw such a current that, although they had a strong wind, they could not go forward, but rather backward, and it seemed that they were going on well; and finally it was seen that the current was so great it was more powerful than the wind. The two vessels that found themselves nearest the land anchored, but the current was so strong that the cables twisted; and the third vessel, which was a brigantine, which was farther out to sea, could find no bottom, or did not know of the current, and it was drawn away from land, and lost to their sight, though the day was clear with fair weather.

✱

GIOVANNI DA VERRAZZANO

(1485–1528)

Italian navigator who explored the North American coast for the French King Francis I.

West and by North: North America seen through the eyes of its seafaring dis-coverers, ed L. B. Wright & E. B. Fowler (New York, 1971)

DESCRIPTION OF INDIANS AND DISCOVERY OF HUDSON RIVER AND NEW YORK HARBOUR (1524)

In seeking some convenient harbour whereby to come aland and have knowledge of the place, we sailed 50 leagues in vain; and, seeing the land to run still to the southward, we resolved to return back again toward the north, where we found ourselves troubled with the like difficulty. At length, being in despair to find any port, we cast anchor upon the coast and sent our boat to shore, where we saw great store of people which came to the seaside; and seeing us to approach, they fled away, and sometimes would stand still and look back, beholding us with great admiration. But afterward, being animated and assured with signs that we made them, some of them came hard to the seaside, seeming to rejoice very much at the sight of us and, marvelling greatly at our apparel, shape, and whiteness, showed us by sundry signs where we might most commodiously come aland with our boat, offering us also of their victuals to eat.

Now I will briefly declare to Your Majesty their life and manners, as far as we could have notice thereof. These people go altogether naked, except only that they cover their privy parts with certain skins of beasts like unto martens, which they fasten unto a narrow girdle made of grass, very artificially [skilfully] wrought, hanged about with tails of divers other beasts, which round about their bodies hang dangling down to their knees. Some of them wear garlands of birds' feathers. The people are of colour russet, and not much unlike the Saracens, their hair black, thick, and not very long, which they tie together in a knot behind and wear it like a tail. They are well featured in their limbs, of mean [medium] stature, and commonly somewhat bigger than we; broad-breasted, strong arms, their legs and other parts of their bodies well-fashioned, and they are disfigured in nothing saving that they have somewhat broad visages, and yet not all of them; for we saw many of them well-favoured, having black and great eyes with a cheerful and steady look, not strong of body yet sharp-witted, nimble, and great runners, as far as we could learn by experience. And in those two last qualities they are like to the people of the East parts of the world, and especially to them of the uttermost parts of China. We could not learn of this people their manner of living nor their particular customs by reason of the short abode we made on the shore—our company being but small and our ship riding far off in the sea. . . .

The shore is all covered with small sand, and so ascendeth upward for the space of 15 feet, rising in form of little hills about 50 paces broad. And sailing forward, we found certain small rivers and arms of the sea that enter at certain creeks, washing the shore on both sides as the coast lieth. And beyond this we saw the open country rising in height above the sandy shore, with many fair fields and plains, full of mighty great woods, some very thick and some thin, replenished with divers sorts of trees, as pleasant and delectable to behold as is possible to imagine. And Your Majesty may not think that these are like the woods of Hercynia [a forest in ancient Germany of which the Black Forest was a part], or the wild deserts of Tartary, and the northern coasts full of fruitless trees; but full of palm trees, bay trees, and high cypress trees, and many other sorts of trees unknown in Europe which yield most sweet savours far from the shore; the property whereof we could not learn for the cause aforesaid and not for any difficulty to pass through the woods, seeing they are not so thick but that a man may pass through them. Neither do we think that they, partaking of the East world round about them, are altogether void of drugs or spicery and other riches of gold, seeing the colour of the land doth so much argue it. And the land is full of many beasts, as stags, deer, and hares. . . .

This land is in latitude 34 d[egrees], with good and wholesome air, temperate between hot and cold; no vehement winds do blow in those regions, and those that do commonly reign in those coasts are the northwest and west winds in the summer season (in the beginning whereof we were there), the sky clear and fair with very little rain. And if at any time the air be cloudy and misty with the southern wind, immediately it is dissolved, and waxeth clear and fair again. The sea is calm, not boisterous, the waves gentle, and, although all the shore be somewhat low and without harbour, yet it is not dangerous to the sailers [sailing ships], being free from rocks and deep, so that within four or five feet of the shore there is 20-foot deep of water without ebb or flood, the depth still increasing in such uniform proportion. There is very good riding at sea; for any ship being shaken in a tempest can never perish there by breaking of her cables, which we have proved by experience. For in the beginning of March (as is usual in all regions), being in the sea oppressed with northern winds, and riding there, we found our anchor broken before the earth failed or moved at all.

We departed from this place, still running along the coast which we found to trend toward the east, and we saw everywhere very great fires by reason of the multitude of the inhabitants. . . . We saw there many people, which came unto the shore making divers signs of friendship and showing that they were content we should come aland, and by trial we found them to be very courteous and gentle, as Your Majesty shall understand by the success.

To the intent we might send them of our things which the Indians commonly desire and esteem, as sheets of paper, glasses, bells, and suchlike trifles, we sent a young man, one of our mariners, ashore; who, swimming toward them and being within three or four yards off the shore, not trusting them, cast the things upon the shore. Seeking afterward to return, he was with such violence of the waves beaten upon the shore that he was so bruised that he lay there almost dead; which the Indians perceiving, [they] ran to catch him and, drawing him out, they carried him a little way off from the sea. The young man, perceiving they carried him [and] being at the first dismayed, began then greatly to fear and cried out piteously. Likewise did the Indians which did accompany him, going about to cheer him and give him courage; and then, setting him on the ground at the foot of a little hill, against the sun, began to behold him with great admiration, marvelling at the whiteness of his flesh. And, putting off his clothes, they made him warm at a great fire, not without our great fear which remained in the boat that they would have roasted him at that fire and have eaten him. The young man, having recovered his strength and having stayed awhile with them, showed them by signs that he was desirous to return to the ship. And they, with great love clapping him fast about with many embracings, accompanying him unto the sea and, to put him in more assurance, leaving him alone, they went unto a high ground and stood there beholding him until he was entered into the boat. This young man observed, as we did also, that these are of colour inclining to black, as the others were, with their flesh very shining; of mean stature, handsome visage, and delicate limbs, and of very little strength, but of prompt wit; further we observed not. . . .

We saw many of their boats, made of one tree, 20 feet long and four feet broad, which are not made with iron, or stone, or any other kind of metal (because that in all this country, for the space of 200 leagues which we ran, we never saw one stone of any sort). They help themselves with fire, burning so much of the tree as is sufficient for the hollowness of the boat; the like they do in making the stern and the forepart, until it be fit to sail upon the sea. . . .

We saw in this country many vines growing naturally, which growing up take hold of the trees as they do in Lombardy; which, if by husbandmen they were dressed in good order, without all doubt they would yield excellent wines; for we having oftentimes seen the fruit thereof dried, which was sweet and pleasant and not differing from ours. We do think that they do esteem the same, because that in every place where they grow they take away the under branches growing round about, that the fruit thereof may ripen the better. . . .

Having our abode three days in this country, riding on the coast for want of harbours, we concluded to depart from thence, trending along the shore between the north and the east, sailing only in the daytime and riding at anchor by night. In the space of 100 leagues' sailing we found a very pleasant place situated amongst certain little steep hills, from amidst the which hills there ran down into the sea a great stream of water, which within the mouth was very deep; and from the sea to the mouth of same [probably the mouth of the Hudson River], with the tide, which we found to rise eight feet, any great vessel laden may pass up.

But because we rode at anchor in a place well fenced from the wind, we would not venture ourselves without knowledge of the place; and we passed up with our boat only into the said river, and saw the country very well peopled. The people are almost like unto the others, and clad with the feathers of fowls of divers colours. They came toward us very cheerfully, making great shouts of admiration, showing us where we might come to land most safely with our boat. We entered up the said river into the land about half a league, where it made a most pleasant lake about three leagues in compass; on the which they rowed from the one side to the other to the number of thirty of their small boats, wherein were many people, which passed from one shore to the other to come and see us. And behold, upon the sudden (as it is wont to fall out in sailing), a contrary flaw [sudden gust] of wind coming from the sea, we were enforced to return to our ship, leaving this land to our great discontentment, for the great commodity and pleasantness thereof, which we suppose is not without some riches, all the hills showing mineral matters in them.

�֎

ALVAR NÚÑEZ CABEZA DE VACA

(*c*.1490–*c*.1564)

Spanish explorer. He survived shipwreck on the coast of Texas in 1528, and with three companions walked across to the Pacific coast and eventually Mexico City, taking eight years.

'The Relation of A. N. Cabeza de Vaca' (1542), in F. W. Hodge and T. H. Lewis, *Spanish Explorers in the Southern United States 1528 to 1543* (New York, 1906).

A HARD LIFE (1528–1536)

In this time I passed a hard life, caused as much by hunger as ill usage. Three times I was obliged to run from my masters, and each time they went in pursuit and endeavoured to slay me; but God our Lord in his mercy chose to protect and preserve me; and when the season of prickly pears returned, we again came together in the same place. After we had arranged our escape, and appointed a time, that very day the Indians separated and all went back. I told my comrades I would wait for them among the prickly-pear plants until the moon should be full. . . .

I have already stated that throughout all this country we went naked, and as we were unaccustomed to being so, twice a year we cast our skins like serpents. The sun and air produced great sores on our breasts and shoulders, giving us sharp pain; and the large loads we had, being very heavy, caused the cords to cut into our arms. The country is so broken and thick-set that often, after getting our wood in the forests, the blood flowed from us in many places, caused by the obstruction of thorns and shrubs that tore our flesh wherever we went. At times, when my turn came to get wood, after it had cost me much blood, I could not bring it out either on my back or by dragging.

✳

JACQUES CARTIER

(1491–1557)

French explorer. He named the Gulf of St Lawrence and claimed much Canadian land for France.

The Voyages of Jacques Cartier, trans. H. P. Biggar (Ottawa, 1924).

1. THE ISLE OF BIRDS (1534)

And on [Thursday] the 21st of . . . May we set forth from this [Catalina] harbour with a west wind, and sailed north, one quarter north-east of cape Bonavista as far as the Isle of Birds, which island was completely surrounded and encompassed by a cordon of loose ice, split up into cakes. In spite of this belt [of ice] our two longboats were sent off to the island to procure some of the birds, whose numbers are so great as to be incredible, unless one has seen them; for although the island is about a league in circumference, it is so exceeding full of birds that one would think they had been stowed there. In the air and round about are a hundred times as many more as on the island itself. Some of these birds are as large as geese, being black and white with a beak like a crow's. They are always in the water, not being able to fly in the air, inasmuch as they have only small wings about the size of half one's hand, with which however they move as quickly along the water as the other birds fly through the air. And these birds are so fat that it is marvellous. We call them apponats and our two longboats were laden with them as with stones, in less than half an hour. Of these, each of our ships salted four or five casks, not counting those we were able to eat fresh.

2. FIRST ASCENT OF THE ST LAWRENCE RIVER TO PRESENT-DAY QUEBEC AND ARRIVAL AT MONTREAL (1535)

From [Sunday] the 19th until [Tuesday] the 28th of the month, we continued to make our way up the river without losing a day nor an hour. During this time we saw and discovered as fine a country and as level a region as one could wish, covered, as before mentioned, with the finest trees in the world, such as oaks, elms, walnuts, pines, cedars, spruce, ash, box-wood, willows, osiers, and, better than all, a great quantity of grape-vines, which were so loaded with grapes that the sailors came on board with their arms full of them. There are likewise many cranes, swans, bustards, geese, ducks, larks, pheasants, partridges, blackbirds, thrushes, turtle-doves, goldfinches, canaries, linnets, nightingales, sparrows, and other birds, the same as in France and in great numbers. . . .

At daybreak the next day, the Captain, having put on his armour, had his men marshalled for the purpose of paying a visit to the village and home of these people, and to a mountain which lies near the town. The Captain was accompanied by the gentlemen and by twenty sailors, the remainder having been left behind to guard the longboats. And he took three Indians of the village as guides to conduct them thither. When we had got under way, we discovered that the path was as well-trodden as it is possible to see, and that the country was the finest and most excellent one could find anywhere, being everywhere full of oaks, as beautiful as in any forest in France, underneath which the ground lay covered with acorns. And after marching about a league and a half, we met on the trail one of the headmen of the village of Hochelaga, accompanied by several Indians, who made signs to us that we should rest at that spot near a fire they had lighted on the path; which we did. Thereupon this headman began to make a speech and to harangue us, which, as before mentioned, is their way of showing joy and friendliness, welcoming in this way the Captain and his company. The Captain presented him with a couple of hatchets and a couple of knives, as well as with a cross and a crucifix, which he made him kiss and then hung it about his neck. For these the headman thanked the Captain. When this was done we marched on, and about half a league thence found that the land began to be cultivated. It was fine land with large fields covered with the corn of the country, which resembles Brazil millet, and is about as large or larger than a pea. They live on this as we do on wheat. And in the middle of these fields is situated and stands the village of Hochelaga, near and adjacent to a mountain, the slopes of which are fertile and are cultivated, and from the top of which one can see for a long distance. We named this mountain 'Mont Royal'.

3. SEX AND TOBACCO

These people live with almost everything in common, much like the Brazilians. They go clothed in beasts' skins, and rather miserably. In winter they wear leggings and moccasins made of skins, and in summer they go barefoot. They maintain the order of marriage except that the men take two or three wives. On the death of their husband, the wives never marry again, but wear mourning all their lives by dyeing their faces black with brayed [pulverized] charcoal and grease as thick as the back of a knife-blade; and by this one knows they are widows.

They have another very bad custom connected with their daughters, who as soon as they reach the age of puberty are all placed in a brothel open to everyone, until the girls have made a match. We saw this with our own eyes; for we discovered wigwams as full of these girls as is a boys' school with boys in France. And furthermore betting, after their fashion, takes place in these wigwams, in which they stake all they own, even to the covering of their privy parts.

They are by no means a laborious people, and work the soil with short bits of wood about half a sword in length. With these they hoe their corn which they call ozisy, in size as large as a pea. Corn of a similar kind grows in considerable quantities in Brazil. They have also a considerable quantity of melons, cucumbers, pumpkins, peas, and beans of various colours and unlike our own. Furthermore they have a plant, of which a large supply is collected in summer for the winter's consumption. They hold it in high esteem, though the men alone make use of it in the following manner. After drying it in the sun, they carry it about their necks in a small skin pouch in lieu of a bag, together with a hollow bit of stone or wood. Then at frequent intervals they crumble this plant into powder, which they place in one of the openings of the hollow instrument, and laying a live coal on top, suck at the other end to such an extent that they fill their bodies so full of smoke that it streams out of their mouths and nostrils as from a chimney. They say it keeps them warm and in good health, and never go about without these things. We made a trial of this smoke. When it is in one's mouth, one would think one had taken powdered pepper, it is so hot.

✻

FRANCISCO VÁSQUEZ DE CORONADO

(c.1510–1554)

Spanish explorer. He was made governor of the Mexican province of New Galicia at the age of twenty-eight. In 1540 he led a large party of Spanish cavalry and Indian allies to explore the interior of North America.

Pedro de Castaneda's account of the expedition of F. V. de Coronado, 1540–2, trans. in Hammond and Rey, *Narratives of the Coronado Expedition.* (Albuquerque, N. Mex., 1940).

1. THE DEATH OF ESTEBAN* (1539)

Francisco Vázquez de Coronado at once sent the friars and the negro, named Esteban, in search of that land. Fray Marcos de Niza was chosen to go to examine this land because he had been in Peru at the time when Don Pedro de Alvarado went there overland. After the friars and the negro Esteban set out, it seems that the negro fell from the good graces of the friars because he took along the women that were given to him, and collected turquoises, and accumulated everything. Besides, the Indians of the settlements they crossed got along better with the negro, since they had seen him before. For this reason he was sent ahead to discover and pacify the land so that when the others arrived all they would have to do would be to listen and make a report of what they were searching for.

When Esteban got away from the said friars, he craved to gain honour and fame in everything and to be credited with the boldness and daring of discovering, all by himself, those terraced pueblos, so famed throughout the land. . . .

When [he] reached Cibola, he arrived there laden with a large number of turquoises and with some pretty women, which the natives had given

* A negro slave who had been one of Cabeza de Vaca's three companions.

him. The gifts were carried by Indians who accompanied and followed him through every settlement he crossed, believing that, by going under his protection, they could traverse the whole country without any danger. But as the people of that land were more intelligent than those who followed Esteban, they lodged him at a lodging-house which they had outside of the pueblo, and the oldest and those in authority listened to his words and tried to learn the reason for his coming to that land.

When they were well informed, they held councils for three days. As the negro had told them that further back two white men, sent by a great lord, were coming, that they were learned in the things of heaven, and that they were coming to instruct them in divine matters, the Indians thought he must have been a spy or guide of some nations that wanted to come and conquer them. They thought it was nonsense for him to say that the people in the land whence he came were white, when he was black, and that he had been sent by them. So they went to him, and because, after some talk, he asked them for turquoises and women, they considered this an affront and determined to kill him. So they did, without killing any one of those who came with him. They took a few boys, and the others, who must have been some sixty people, they allowed to return to their lands unmolested. As these who were now returning were fleeing in fright, they chanced to see and meet the friars in the despoblado, sixty leagues from Cibola, and gave them the sad news. The friars were seized with such fear that, not trusting these people who had accompanied the negro, they opened their bags and distributed everything they had among them, keeping only the vestments for saying mass. From there they turned back without seeing more land than what the Indians had told them of. On the contrary, they were travelling by forced marches, with their habits up to their waists.

2. BISON (1540)

I want to tell, also, about the appearance of the bulls, which is likewise remarkable. At first there was not a horse that did not run away on seeing them, for their faces are short and narrow between the eyes, the forehead two spans wide. Their eyes bulge on the sides, so that, when they run, they can see those who follow them. They are bearded like very large he-goats. When they run they carry their heads low, their beards touching the ground. From the middle of the body back they are covered with very woolly hair like that of fine sheep. From the belly to the front they have very heavy hair like the mane of a wild lion. They have a hump larger than that of a camel. Their horns, which show a little through the hair, are short and heavy. During May they shed the hair on the rear half of their body and look exactly like lions. To remove this hair they lean against some small trees found in some small barrancas and rub against them until they shed their wool as a snake sheds its skin. They have short tails with a small bunch of hair at the end. When they run they carry their tails erect like the scorpion. One peculiar thing about them is that when they are calves they are reddish like ours, and with time, as they become older, they change in colour and appearance. . . .

[The Indians] go together in companies, and move from one place to another . . . following the seasons and the pasture after their oxen.

These oxen are of the bigness and colour of our bulls, but their horns are not so great. They have a great bunch upon their fore-shoulders, and more hair on their fore part then on their hinder part: and it is like wool. They have as it were a horse-mane upon their backbone, and much hair and very long from the knees downward. They have great tufts of hair hanging down their foreheads, and it seems that they have beards, because of the great store of hair hanging down at their chins and throats. The males have very long tails, and a great knob or flock at the end: so that in some respect they resemble the lion, and in some other the camel. They push with their horns, they run, they overtake and kill a horse when they are in their rage and anger. Finally, it is a foul and fierce beast of countenance and form of body. The horses fled from them, either because of their deformed shape or else because they had never seen them. Their masters have no other riches nor substance: of them they eat, they drink, they apparel, they shoe themselves; and of their hides they make many things, as houses, shoes, apparel, and ropes; of their bones they make bodkins: of their sinews and hair, thread; of their horns, maws, and bladders, vessels; of their dung, fire; and of their calves' skins, budgets [pouches], wherein they draw and keep water. To be short, they make so many things of them as they have need of, or as many as suffice them in the use of this life.

3. CÁRDENAS* DISCOVERS THE GRAND CANYON

When Don García López de Cárdenas . . . with about twelve men . . . reached Tusayan he was well received and lodged by the natives. They provided him with guides to proceed on his journey. They set out from there laden with provisions, because they had to travel over some uninhabited land before coming to settlements, which the Indians said were more than twenty days away. Accordingly, when they had marched for twenty

* A member of Coronado's expedition.

days they came to the gorges of the river, from the edge of which it looked as if the opposite side must have been more than three or four leagues away by air. This region was high and covered with low and twisted pine trees; it was extremely cold, being open to the north, so that, although this was the warm season, no one could live in this canyon because of the cold.

The men spent three days looking for a way down to the river; from the top it looked as if the water were a fathom across. But, according to the information supplied by the Indians, it must have been half a league wide. The descent was almost impossible, but, after these three days, at a place which seemed less difficult, Captain Melgosa, a certain Juan Galeras, and another companion, being the most agile, began to go down. They continued descending within view of those on top until they lost sight of them, as they could not be seen from the top. They returned about four o'clock in the afternoon, as they could not reach the bottom because of the many obstacles they met, for what from the top seemed easy was not so; on the contrary, it was rough and difficult. They said that they had gone down one-third of the distance and that, from the point they had reached, the river seemed very large, and that, from what they saw, the width given by the Indians was correct. From the top they could make out, apart from the canyon, some small boulders which seemed to be as high as a man. Those who went down and who reached them swore that they were taller than the great tower of Seville.

❖

HERNANDO DE SOTO

(*c.*1496–1542)

Spanish conquistador. After fighting with Francisco Pizarro in Peru, he led an expedition into the interior of North America, discovering the Mississippi River.

True relation of the hardship suffered by Governor Don Fernando de Soto and certain Portuguese Gentlemen in the Discovery of the Province of Florida. Now newly set forth by a Gentleman of Elvas, trans. J. A. Robertson (Deland, Fla., 1933).

FIRST SIGHTING OF THE MISSISSIPPI (1541)

Three days having passed since they had looked for some maize (and it was little that was found in proportion to what was needed), and for this reason, even though rest was needed because of the wounded, on account of the great need of finding a place where there was maize, the governor was obliged to set out immediately for Quizquiz. He marched seven days through an unpopulated region of many swamps and thick woods, but all passable on horseback except several marshes or swamps which were crossed by swimming. He reached the town of Quizquiz without being perceived. He seized all the people of the town before they got out of their houses. The cacique's mother was captured there, and then he sent to him one of the Indians who had been seized there, bidding him come to see him and that he would give him his mother and all the other people who had been taken there. For reply, he said that his lordship should order them released and sent and that he would come to visit and serve him. Inasmuch as his men were ill and weary for lack of maize and the horses were also weak, he determined to pleasure him, in order to see whether he could have peace with him. So he ordered the mother and all the others released and dispatched them and sent them with words of kindness.

Next day when the governor was awaiting the cacique, many Indians came with their bows and arrows with the intention of attacking the Christians. The governor ordered all the horsemen to be armed and mounted and all in readiness. When the Indians saw that they were on guard, they stopped a crossbow-flight from the spot where the governor was, near a stream, and after they had stayed there for a half-hour, six of the principal Indians came to the camp and said that they were come to see what people they were and that they had learned from their ancestors that a white race would inevitably subdue them; and that they were about to return to the cacique to tell him to come immediately to render obedience and service to the governor. And after offering him six or seven skins and blankets which they brought they took leave of him and together with the others, who were waiting on the shore, returned. The cacique did not again come nor did he send another message.

Inasmuch as there was little maize in the town where the governor was, he moved to another town located a half-league from the large river, where maize was found in abundance. He went to see the river, and found there was an abundance of timber near it from which piraguas could be constructed and an excellently situated land for establishing the camp. He immediately moved thither, houses were built, and the camp was established on a level place, a crossbow-flight from the river. All the maize of

all the towns behind was collected there and the men set to work immediately to cut timber and square the planks for canoes. Immediately the
Indians came down the river, landed, and told the governor that they were
vassals of a great lord called Aquiro, who was lord of many towns and
people on the other side of the river. On his behalf they informed him that
he would come the next day with all his men to see what his lordship
would command him.

Then next day, the cacique came with 200 canoes full of Indians with
their bows and arrows, painted with red ochre and having great plumes of
white and many-coloured feathers on either side and holding shields in
their hands with which they covered the paddlers, while the warriors were
standing from prow to stern with their bows and arrows in their hands.
The canoe in which the cacique came had an awning spread in the stern
and he was seated under the canopy. Also other canoes came bearing
other Indian notables. The chief, from his position under the canopy,
controlled and gave orders to the other men. All the canoes were together
and came to within a stone's throw from the bluff. From there, the cacique
told the governor, who was walking along the river with others whom he
had brought with him, that he had come to visit him and to serve and obey
him, for he had heard that he was the greatest and most powerful lord of
all the earth and that he should bethink him in what to command him.

The governor thanked him and asked him to land so that they might
better be able to talk, but without answering this, he ordered three canoes
to come up in which he brought a quantity of fish and loaves made of the
pulp of plums in the shape of bricks. All having been received, he thanked
him and again asked him to land. But since his intent was to see whether
he might do some damage by means of that pretence, upon seeing that the
governor and his men were on their guard, they began to withdraw from
land. With loud cries, the crossbowmen, who were ready, shot at them and
struck five or six. They withdrew in splendid order; no one abandoned his
paddle even though the one near him fell. Flaunting themselves, they
retired.

Afterward they came frequently and landed, and when they went toward them, they would return to their canoes. Those canoes were very
pleasing to see, for they were very large and well built; and together with
the awnings, the plumes of feathers, the shields and banners, and the
many men in them, they had the appearance of a beautiful fleet of galleys.
During the thirty days the governor was there, they made four piraguas,
in three of which, one early morning three hours before it became light,
he ordered a dozen horse to enter four to each one—men who he was
confident would succeed in gaining the land in spite of the Indians and

241

assure the crossing or die in doing it—and with them some of foot—crossbowmen and rowers—to place them on the other side. In the other piragua, he ordered Juan de Guzman to cross with men of foot, he having become captain in place of Francisco Maldonado.

And because the current was strong, they went upstream along the shore for a quarter of a league, and in crossing they were carried down with the current of the river and went to land opposite the place where the camp was. At a distance of two stones' throw before reaching shore, the men of horse went from the piraguas on horseback to a sandy place of hard sand and clear ground, where all the men landed without any accident. As soon as those who crossed first were on the other side, the piraguas returned immediately to where the governor was and, in two hours after the sun was up, all the men finished crossing. It was nearly a half league wide, and if a man stood still on the other side, one could not tell whether he were a man or something else. It was of great depth and of very strong current. Its water was always turgid and continually many trees and wood came down it, borne along by the force of the water and current. It had abundance of fish of various kinds, and most of them different from those of the fresh waters of Spain.

✵

SIR MARTIN FROBISHER

(c.1535–1594)

English navigator and explorer. He was one of the first to search for the North-West Passage, in 1576.

> 1: *The Three Voyages of Martin Frobisher in search of a passage to Cathay and India by the North-West, A.D. 1576–8.* From the original 1578 text of George Best. Edited by Vilhjalmur Stefansson (London, 1938). 2: *A true reporte of the last voyage . . . by Capteine Frobisher, written by Dionyse Settle, one of the gentlemen who made the voyage* (London, 1577).

1. THE FIRST VOYAGE (1576)

The worthy Captain, notwithstanding these discomforts, although his mast was sprung and his top mast blown overboard with extreme foul weather, continued his course towards the north-west, knowing that the sea at length must needs have an ending, and that some land should have a beginning that way; and determined, therefore, at the least to bring true proof what land and sea the same might be, so far to the north-westwards, beyond any man that hath heretofore discovered.

The 20th of July he had sight of a high land, which he called Queen Elizabeth's Foreland [Resolution Island, off Meta Incognita Peninsula, Baffin I.] after Her Majesty's name. And sailing more northerly alongst that coast, he descried another foreland with a great gut, bay, or passage divided as it were two main lands or continents asunder. There he met with store of exceeding great ice all this coast along, and, coveting still to continue his course to the northwards, was always by contrary wind detained overthwart these straits and could not get beyond. Within few days after, he perceived the ice to be well consumed and gone . . . wherefore he determined to make proof of this place to see how far that gut had continuance and whether he might carry himself through the same into some open sea on the back side, whereof he conceived no small hope; and so entered the same the one-and-twentieth of July and passed above 50 leagues therein, as he reported, having upon either hand a great main or continent. And that land upon his right hand as he sailed westward he judged to be the continent of Asia, and there to be divided from the firm of America, which lieth upon the left hand over against the same. This place he named after his name, Frobisher's Straits, like as Magellanus at the south-west end of the world, having discovered the passage to the South Sea (where America is divided from the continent of that land which lieth under the South Pole) and called the same straits Magellan's Straits.

After he had passed 60 leagues into this foresaid strait, he went ashore and found signs where fire had been made. He saw mighty deer that seemed to be mankind [human?] which ran at him, and hardly he escaped with his life in a narrow way, where he was fain to use defence and policy to save his life.

In this place he saw and perceived sundry tokens of the peoples resorting thither. And being ashore upon the top of a hill, he perceived a number of small things fleeting in the sea afar off which he supposed to be por-poises or seals or some kind of strange fish; but, coming nearer, he dis-covered them to be men in small boats made of leather. And before he could descend down from the hill certain of those people had almost cut off his boat from him, having stolen secretly behind rocks for that purpose; where he speedily hasted to his boat, and bent himself to his halberd and narrowly escaped the danger, and saved his boat. Afterward he had sundry conferences with them, and they came aboard his ship and brought him salmon and raw flesh and fish, and greedily devoured the same before our men's faces. And to show their agility, they tried many masteries upon the ropes of the ship after our mariners' fashion, and appeared to be very strong of their arms and nimble of their bodies. They exchanged coats of seals' and bears' skins, and suchlike with our men; and received bells, looking-glasses, and other toys in recompense thereof again.

After great courtesy and many meetings, our mariners, contrary to their captain's direction, began more easily to trust them; and five of our men going ashore were by them intercepted with their boat and were never since heard of to this day again; so that the captain, being destitute of boat, bark, and all company, had scarcely sufficient number to conduct back his bark again. He could now neither convey himself ashore to rescue his men (if he had been able) for want of a boat; and again the subtle traitors were so wary as they would after that never come within our men's danger.

The captain, notwithstanding, desirous to bring some token from thence of his being there, was greatly discontented that he had not before apprehended some of them. And therefore, to deceive the deceivers he wrought a pretty policy: for knowing well how they greatly delighted in our toys, and specially in bells, he rang a pretty lowbell, making signs that he would give him the same that would come and fetch it. And because they would not come within his danger for fear, he flung one bell unto them, which of purpose he threw short that it might fall into the sea and be lost. And to make them more greedy of the matter he rang a louder bell, so that in the end one of them came near the ship side to receive the bell; which when he thought to take at the captain's hand, he was thereby taken himself. For the captain, being readily provided, let the bell fall and caught the man fast and plucked him, with main force, boat and all, into his bark out of the sea. Whereupon, when he found himself in captivity, for very choler and disdain he bit his tongue in twain within his mouth. Notwithstanding, he died not thereof, but lived until he came in England, and then he died of cold which he had taken at sea.

Now with this new prey (which was a sufficient witness of the captain's far and tedious travel toward the unknown parts of the world, as did well appear by this strange infidel whose like was never seen, read, nor heard of before and whose language was neither known nor understood of any) the said Captain Frobisher returned homeward and arrived in England in Harwich the 2 of October following, and thence came to London, 1576, where he was highly commended of all men for his great and notable attempt, but specially famous for the great hope he brought of the passage to Cataya [Cathay].

And it is especially to be remembered that at their first arrival in those parts there lay so great store of ice all the coast along, so thick together, that hardly his boat could pass unto the shore. At length, after divers attempts, he commanded his company, if by any possible means they could get ashore, to bring him whatsoever thing they could first find, whether it were living or dead, stock or stone, in token of Christian possession, which thereby he took in behalf of the Queen's most excellent Majesty, thinking that thereby he might justify the having and enjoying of the same things that grew in these unknown parts. Some of his company brought flowers, some green grass, and one brought a piece of black stone much like to a sea-coal in colour, which by the weight seemed to be some kind of metal or mineral. This was a thing of no account in the judgement of the captain at the first sight; and yet for novelty it was kept in respect of the place from whence it came.

After his arrival in London, being demanded of sundry his friends what thing he had brought them home out of that country, he had nothing left to present them withal but a piece of this black stone. And it fortuned a gentlewoman, one of the adventurer's wives, to have a piece thereof, which by chance she threw and burned in the fire, so long that, at the length being taken forth and quenched in a little vinegar, it glistered with a bright marcasite of gold. Whereupon, the matter being called in some question, it was brought to certain goldfiners [refiners] in London to make assay thereof, who gave out that it held gold [*wrongly, as it transpired*], and that very richly for the quantity. Afterward the same goldfiners promised great matters thereof if there were any store to be found, and offered themselves to adventure for the searching of those parts from whence the same was brought. Some that had great hope of the matter sought secretly to have a lease at Her Majesty's hands of those places, whereby to enjoy the mass of so great a public profit unto their own private gains.

In conclusion, the hope of more of the same gold ore to be found kindled a greater opinion in the hearts of many to advance the voyage again. Whereupon preparation was made for a new voyage against the year following, and the captain more specially directed by commission for the searching more of this gold ore than for the searching any further discovery of the passage.

2. DESCRIPTION OF INDIANS ON THE SECOND VOYAGE (1577)

They are men of a large corporature, and good proportion: their colour is not much unlike the sunburnt country man, who laboureth daily in the sun for his living. They wear their hair something long, and cut before, either with stone or knife, very disorderly. Their women wear their hair long, and knit up with two loops, showing forth on either side of their faces, and the rest foltred up on a knot. . . . They eat their meat all raw, both flesh, fish, and foul, or something parboiled with blood and a little water, which they drink. For lack of water, they will eat ice, that is hard frozen, as pleasantly as we will do sugar candy or other sugar. . . .

They . . . keep certain dogs, not much unlike wolves, which they yoke together, as we do oxen and horses, to a sled or trail: and so carry their necessaries over the ice and snow, from place to place: as the captive, whom we have, made perfect signs. And when those dogs are not apt for the same use, or when with hunger they are constrained, for lack of other victuals, they eat them: so that they are as needful for them, in respect of their bigness, as our oxen are for us. They apparel themselves in the skins of such beasts as they kill, sewed together with the sinews of them. All the fowl which they kill, they skin, and make thereof one kind of garment or other, to defend them from the cold. . . .

The men and women wear their hose close to their legs, from the waist to the knee, without any open before, as well the one kind as the other. Upon their legs they wear hose of leather, with the fur side inward, two or three pair on at once, and especially the women. In those hose, they put their knives, needles, and other things needful to bear about. They put a bone within their hose, which reacheth from the foot to the knee, whereupon they draw their said hose, and so in place of garters, they are holden from falling down about their feet. They dress their skins very soft and supple, with the hair on. In cold weather or winter, they wear the fur side inward: and in summer outward. Other apparel they have none, but the said skins. . . .

Their houses are tents, made of seal-skins, pitched with four fir quarters, four square, meeting at the top, and the skins sewed together with sinews, and laid thereupon: so pitched they are, that the entrance into them is always south, or against the sun.

They have other sorts of houses, which we found not to be inhabited, which are raised with stones and whale bones, and a skin laid over them, to withstand the rain, or other weather: the entrance of them being not much unlike an oven's mouth, whereto, I think, they resort for a time, to fish, hunt, and fowl, and so leave them for the next time they come thither again.

Their weapons are bows, arrows, darts, and slings. Their bows are of a yard long of wood, sinewed on the back with strong veins, not glued to, but fast girded and tied on. Their bow strings are likewise sinews. Their arrows are three pieces, nocked with bone, and ended with bone; with those two ends, and the wood in the midst, they pass not in length half a yard or little more. . . . They have likewise three sorts of heads to those arrows. . . . They are not made very fast, but lightly tied to, or else set in a nock, that upon small occasion, the arrow leaveth these heads behind them: and they are of small force, except they be very near, when they shoot. . . .

They have two sorts of boats, made of leather, set out on the inner side with quarters of wood, artificially [skilfully] tied together with thongs of the same: the greater sort are not much unlike our wherries, wherein sixteen or twenty men may sit; they have for a sail dressed the guts of such beasts as they kill, very fine and thin, which they sew together; the other boat is but for one man to sit and row in, with one oar.

✳

SIR FRANCIS DRAKE

(*c*.1540–1596)

English privateer and navigator. He made the second circumnavigation of the globe. Terror of the Spanish and victor of the Armada.

The World Encompassed by Sir Francis Drake . . . Carefully Collected out of the Notes of Master Francis Fletcher . . . and Divers Others His Followers in the Same (London, 1854).

DRAKE CLAIMS CALIFORNIA FOR QUEEN ELIZABETH (1579)

From Guatulco we departed the day following [16 April 1579], setting our course directly into the sea, whereon we sailed 500 leagues in longitude to get a wind, and between that and June 3, 1,400 leagues in all, till we came into 42° of north latitude, where in the night following we found such alteration of heat into extreme and nipping cold that our men in general did grievously complain thereof. . . .

In 38° 30′ we fell with a convenient and fit harbour and June 17 came to anchor therein, where we continued till the 23rd day of July following. During all which time, notwithstanding it was in the height of summer and so near the sun, yet were we continually visited with like nipping colds as we had felt before; insomuch that if violent exercises of our bodies and busy employment about our necessary labours had not sometimes compelled us to the contrary, we could very well have been contented to have kept about us still our winter clothes; yea (had our necessities suffered us), to have kept our beds; neither could we at any time, in whole 14 days together, find the air so clear as to be able to take the height of sun or star. . . .

The next day after our coming to anchor in the aforesaid harbour the people of the country showed themselves, sending off a man with great expedition [very speedily] to us in a canoe who, being yet but a little from the shore and a great way from our ship, spoke to us continually as he came rowing on. And at last, at a reasonable distance staying himself, he began more solemnly a long and tedious [slow] oration after his manner, using in the delivery thereof many gestures and signs, moving his hands, turning his head and body many ways, and after his oration ended, with great show of reverence and submission, returned back to shore again. He shortly came again the second time in like manner, and so the third time, when he brought with him (as a present from the rest) a bunch of feathers, much like the feathers of a black crow, very neatly and artificially gathered upon a string and drawn together into a round bundle, being very clean and finely cut and bearing in length an equal proportion one with another, a special cognizance (as we afterwards observed) which they that guard their king's person wear on their heads. With this also he brought a little basket made of rushes and filled with an herb which they called *tabah*, both which, being tied to a short rod, he cast into our boat. Our general intended to have recompensed him immediately with many good things he would have bestowed on him, but, entering into the boat to deliver the same, he could not be drawn to receive them by any means, save one hat which, being cast into the water out of the ship, he took up (refusing utterly to meddle with any other thing, though it were upon a board put off unto him), and so presently made his return. After which time our boat could row no way but, wondering at us as at gods, they would follow the same with admiration.

The third day following, the 21st, our ship, having received a leak at sea, was brought to anchor nearer the shore that, her goods being landed, she might be repaired; but for that we were to prevent any danger that might chance against our safety, our general first of all landed his men with all necessary provision to build tents and make a fort for the defence of ourselves and goods, and that we might under the shelter of it with more safety (whatever should befall) end our business. Which when the people of the country perceived us doing, as men set on fire to war in defence of their country, in great haste and companies, with such weapons as they had, they came down into us, and yet with no hostile meaning or intent to hurt us, standing, when they drew near, as men ravished in their minds

248

with the sight of such things as they never had seen or heard of before that time, their errand being rather with submission and fear to worship us as gods than to have any war with us as with mortal men. Which thing, as it did partly show itself at that instant, so did it more and more manifest itself afterward during the whole time of our abode amongst them. At this time, being willed by signs to lay from them their bows and arrows, they did as they were directed, and so did all the rest, as they came more and more by companies unto them, growing in a little while to a great number, both of men and women.

To the intent, therefore, that this peace which they themselves so willingly sought might, without any cause of the breach thereof on our part given, be continued, and that we might with more safety and expedition end our business in quiet, our general with all his company used all means possible gently to entreat them, bestowing upon each of them liberally good and necessary things to cover their nakedness, withal signifying unto them we were no gods but men and had need of such things to cover our own shame; teaching them to use them to the same ends, for which cause also we did eat and drink in their presence, giving them to understand that without that we could not live and therefore were but men as well as they.

Notwithstanding, nothing could persuade them nor remove that opinion which they had conceived of us that we should be gods.

In recompense of those things which they had received of us, as shirts, linen cloth, etc., they bestowed upon our general and divers of our company divers things, as feathers, cauls of network, the quivers of their arrows made of fawn-skins, and the very skins of beasts that their women wore upon their bodies. Having thus had their fill of this time's visiting and beholding of us, they departed with joy to their houses, which houses are digged round within the earth and have from the uppermost brims of the circle clefts of wood set up and joined close together at the top like our spires on the steeple of a church, which, being covered with earth, suffer no water to enter and are very warm. The door in the most part of them performs the office also of a chimney to let out the smoke; it is made in bigness and fashion like to an ordinary scuttle in a ship, and standing slopewise. Their beds are the hard ground, only with rushes strewed upon it, and lying round about the house have their fire in the midst, which, by reason that the house is but low vaulted, round, and close, gives a marvellous reflection to their bodies to heat the same.

Their men for the most part go naked; the women take a kind of bulrushes and, combing it after the manner of hemp, make themselves thereof a loose garment which, being knit about their middles, hangs down about their hips and so affords to them a covering of that which Nature teaches should be hidden; about their shoulders they wear also the skin of a deer with the hair upon it. They are very obedient to their husbands and exceedingly ready in all service, yet of themselves offering to do nothing without the consents or being called of the men. . . .

Against the end of three days more (the news having the while spread itself further and, as it seemed, a great way up into the country) were assembled the greatest number of people which we could reasonably imagine to dwell within any convenient distance round about. Amongst the rest, the king himself, a man of a goodly stature and comely personage, attended with his guard of about 100 tall and warlike men, this day, June 26, came down to see us. . . .

They made signs to our general to have him sit down, unto whom both the king and divers others made several orations, or rather, indeed, if we had understood them, supplications, that he would take the province and kingdom into his hand and become their king and patron, making signs that they would resign unto him their right and title to the whole land and become his vassals in themselves and their posterities; which that they might make us indeed believe that it was their true meaning and intent, the king himself, with all the rest, with one consent and with great reverence, joyfully singing a song, set the crown upon his head, enriched his neck with all their chains, and offering unto him many other things, honoured him by the name of *hioh*. Adding thereunto (as it might seem) a song and dance of triumph, because they were not only visited of the gods (for so they still judged us to be), but the great and chief God was now become their God, their king and patron, and themselves were become the only happy and blessed people in the world.

These things being so freely offered, our general thought not meet to reject or refuse the same, both for that he would not give them any cause of mistrust or disliking of him (that being the only place wherein at this present we were of necessity enforced to seek relief of many things), and chiefly for that he knew not to what good end God had brought this to pass or what honour and profit it might bring to our country in time to come.

Wherefore, in the name and to the use of Her Most Excellent Majesty, he took the sceptre, crown, and dignity of the said country into his hand, wishing nothing more than that it had lain so fitly for Her Majesty to enjoy as it was now her proper own, and that the riches and treasures thereof (wherewith in the upland countries it abounds) might with as great convenience be transported, to the enriching of her kingdom here at home, as it is in plenty to be attained there; and especially that so tractable and loving a people as they showed themselves to be might have means to have manifested their most willing obedience the more unto her, and by her means, as a mother and nurse of the Church of Christ, might by the preaching of the Gospel be brought to the right knowledge and obedience of the true and ever-living God.

The ceremonies of this resigning and receiving of the kingdom being thus performed, the common sort, both of men and women, leaving the king and his guard about him with our general, dispersed themselves among our people, taking a diligent view or survey of every man; and finding such as pleased their fancies (which commonly were the youngest of us), they, presently enclosing them about, offered their sacrifices unto them, crying out with lamentable shrieks and moans, weeping and scratching and tearing their very flesh off their faces with their nails; neither were it the women alone which did this, but even old men, roaring and crying out, were as violent as the women were. . . .

After that our necessary businesses were well dispatched, our general, with his gentlemen and many of his company, made a journey up into the land to see the manner of their dwelling and to be the better acquainted with the nature and commodities of the country. Their houses were all such as we have formerly described and, being many of them in one place, made several villages here and there. The inland we found to be far different from the shore, a goodly country and fruitful soil, stored with many blessings fit for the use of man. Infinite was the company of very large and fat deer which there we saw by thousands, as we supposed, in a herd; besides a multitude of a strange kind of conies by far exceeding them in number. Their heads and bodies, in which they resemble other conies, are but small, his tail, like the tail of a rat, exceeding long, and his feet like the paws of a want or mole. Under his chin, on either side, he hath a bag into which he gathereth his meat when he hath filled his belly abroad, that he may with it either feed his young or feed himself when he lists not to travel from his burrow. The people eat their bodies and make great account of their skins, for their king's holiday's coat was made of them.

This country our general named Albion, and that for two causes: the one in respect of the white banks and cliffs which lie toward the sea; the other that it might have some affinity, even in name also, with our own country, which was sometime so called.

Before we went from thence, our general caused to be set up a monument of our being there, as also of Her Majesty's and successors' right and title to that kingdom; namely, a plate of brass, fast nailed to a great and firm post, whereon is engraven Her Grace's name and the day and year of our arrival there and of the free giving up of the province and kingdom, both by the king and people, into Her Majesty's hands, together with Her Highness's picture and arms in a piece of sixpence current English money, showing itself by a hole made of purpose through the plate. Underneath was likewise engraved the name of our general, etc.

The Spaniards never had any dealing or so much as set a foot in this country, the utmost of their discoveries reaching only to many degrees southward of this place. . . .

�֍

SIR HUMPHREY GILBERT

(c.1539–1583)

English navigator. Ralegh's half-brother, he sailed to North America twice.

Voyage of Sir Humfrey Gilbert discovering of Countries to the northwards of the Cape of Florida, 1583. Written by Edward Hayes, captain of the Golden Hind. In A Complete Collection of Voyages and Travels by John Harris (London, 1705).

TAKING POSSESSION OF NEWFOUNDLAND FOR THE QUEEN
(1583)

Orders thus determined, and promises mutually given to be observed, every man withdrew himself unto his charge; the anchors being already weighed and our ships under sail, having a soft gale of wind, we began our voyage upon Tuesday, the 11th day of June, in the year of Our Lord 1583. . . .

We were in number in all about 260 men, among whom we had of every faculty good choice, as shipwrights, masons, carpenters, smiths, and such-like, requisite to such an action; also mineral men and refiners. Besides, for solace of our people and allurement of the savages, we were provided of music in good variety, not omitting the least toys, as morris dancers, hobby-horse, and May-like conceits to delight the savage people, whom we intended to win by all fair means possible. And to that end we were indifferently furnished of all petty haberdashery wares to barter with those simple people. . . .

Saturday the 27th of July we might descry not far from us as it were mountains of ice driven upon the sea, being then in 50°, which were carried southward to the weather of us, whereby may be conjectured that some current does set that way from the north.

Before we come to Newfoundland, about 50 leagues on this side, we pass the Bank, which are high grounds rising within the sea and under water, yet deep enough and without danger, being commonly not less than 25 and 30 fathom water upon them: the same (as it were some vein of mountains within the sea) do run along and from the Newfoundland, beginning northward about 52° or 53° of latitude, and do extend into the south infinitely. The breadth of this Bank is somewhere more and some-where less, but we found the same about ten leagues over, having sounded both on this side thereof and the other toward Newfoundland, but found no ground with almost 200 fathom of line, both before and after we had passed the Bank. The Portugals and French chiefly have a notable trade of fishing upon this bank, where are sometimes an hundred or more sails of ships, who commonly begin the fishing in April and have ended by July. . . . During the time of fishing, a man shall know without sounding when he is upon the Bank by the incredible multitude of seafowl hovering over the same, to prey upon the offals and garbage of fish thrown out by fishermen and floating upon the sea.

Upon Tuesday the 11th of June we forsook the coast of England. So again Tuesday the 30th of July (seven weeks after) we got sight of land, being immediately embayed in the Grand Bay, or some other great bay, the certainty whereof we could not judge: so great haze and fog did hang upon the coast as neither we might discern the land well nor take the sun's height. But by our best computation we were then in the 51° of latitude.

Forsaking this bay and uncomfortable coast (nothing appearing unto us but hideous rocks and mountains, bare of trees and void of any green herb), we followed the coast to the south, with weather fair and clear. . . .

After we had met with the *Swallow*, we held on our course southward until we came against the harbour called Saint John's, about five leagues from the former Cape of Saint Francis, where before the entrance into the harbour we found also the frigate or *Squirrel* lying at anchor, whom the English merchants . . . would not permit to enter into the harbour. Glad of so happy meeting both of the *Swallow* and frigate in one day (being Sat-urday the 3rd of August), we made ready our fights and prepared to enter the harbour, any resistance to the contrary notwithstanding, there being within of all nations to the number of 36 sails. But first the general dis-patched a boat to give them knowledge of his coming for no ill intent, having commission from Her Majesty for his voyage he had in hand. And immediately we followed with a slack gale, and in the very entrance (which is but narrow, not above two butts' length) the admiral fell upon a rock on the larboard side by great oversight, in that the weather was fair, the rock much above water fast by the shore, where neither went any sea-gate. But we found such readiness in the English merchants to help us in that danger that without delay there were brought a number of boats which towed off the ship and cleared her of danger.

Having taken place convenient in the road, we let fall anchors, the captains and masters repairing aboard our admiral, whither also came immediately the masters and owners of the fishing fleet of Englishmen, to understand the general's intent and cause of our arrival there. They were all satisfied when the general had shown his commission and purpose to take possession of those lands to the behalf of the Crown of England and the advancement of Christian religion in those paganish regions, requiring but their lawful aid for repairing of his fleet and supply of some necessaries, so far as conveniently might be afforded him, both out of that and other harbours adjoining. . . .

It was further determined that every ship of our fleet should deliver unto the merchants and masters of that harbour a note of all their wants; which done, the ships as well English as strangers were taxed at an easy rate to make supply. And besides, commissioners were appointed, part of our own company and part of theirs, to go into other harbours adjoining (for our English merchant [ships] command all there) to levy our provision; whereunto the Portugals (above other nations) did most willingly and liberally contribute, insomuch as we were presented (above our allowance) with wines, marmalades, most fine rusk or biscuit, sweet oils, and sundry delicacies. Also we wanted not of fresh salmons, trouts, lobsters, and other fresh fish brought daily unto us. . . .

Monday following the general had his tent set up, who, being accompanied with his own followers, summoned the merchants and masters, both English and strangers, to be present at his taking possession of those countries. Before whom openly was read and interpreted unto the strangers his commission, by virtue whereof he took possession in the same harbour of Saint John's and 200 leagues every way, invested the Queen's Majesty with the title and dignity thereof, had delivered unto him (after the custom of England) a rod and a turf of the same soil, entering possession also for him, his heirs and assigns for ever; and signified unto all men that from that time forward they should take the same land as a territory appertaining to the Queen of England and himself authorized under Her Majesty to possess and enjoy it and to ordain laws for the government thereof, agreeable (so near as conveniently might be) unto the laws of England, under which all people coming thither hereafter, either to inhabit or by way of traffic, should be subjected and governed. And especially at the same time for a beginning he proposed and delivered three laws to be in force immediately, that is to say: the first for religion, which in public exercise should be according to the Church of England; the second for maintenance of Her Majesty's right and possession of those territories, against which if anything were attempted prejudicial, the party or parties offending should be adjudged and executed as in case of high treason according to the laws of England; the third, if any person should utter words sounding to the dishonour of Her Majesty he should lose his ears and have his ship and goods confiscated.

These contents published, obedience was promised by general voice and consent of the multitude, as well of Englishmen as strangers, praying for continuance of this possession and government begun. After this the assembly was dismissed. And afterward were erected not far from that place the arms of England engraven in lead and infixed upon a pillar of wood.

✺

JOHN DAVIS

(c.1550–1605)

English navigator. He was another early searcher for the North-West Passage.

The Voyages and Works of John Davis The Navigator, ed. A. H. Markham (London, 1878).

MEETINGS WITH ESKIMOS (1586)

The ships being within the sounds, we sent our boats to search for shoal water, where we might anchor, which in this place is very hard to find; and as the boat[s] went sounding and searching, the people of the country, having espied them, came in their canoes towards them with many shouts and cries. But after they had espied in the boat some of our company that were the year before here with us, they presently rowed to the boat, and took hold in the oar, and hung about the boat with such comfortable joy as would require a long discourse to be uttered. They came with the boats to our ships, making signs that they knew all those that the year before had been with them. After I perceived their joy, and small fear of us, myself with the merchants and others of the company went ashore, bearing with me twenty knives. I had no sooner landed but they leapt out of their canoes, and came running to me and the rest, and embraced us with many signs of hearty welcome. At this present there were eighteen of them, and to each of them I gave a knife. They offered skins to me for reward, but I made signs that it was not sold, but given them of courtesy, and so dismissed them for that time, with signs that they should return again after certain hours.

The next day, with all possible speed, the pinnace was landed upon an isle there to be finished, to serve our purpose for the discovery, which isle was so convenient for that purpose, as that we were very well able to defend ourselves against many enemies. During the time that the pinnace was there setting up, the people came continually unto us, sometimes a hundred canoes at a time, sometimes forty, fifty, more and less, as occasion served. They brought with them seal-skins, stag-skins, white hares, seal fish, salmon . . . small cod, dry caplin, with other fish, and birds, such as the country did yield.

Myself, still desirous to have a further search of this place, sent one of the ship-boats to one part of the land, and myself went to another part, to search for the habitation of this people, with straight commandment that there should be no injury offered to any of the people, neither any gunshot. The boats that went from me found the tents of the people made with seal-skins, set up upon timber, wherein they found great store of dried caplin, being a little fish no bigger than a pilchard. They found bags of train oil [i.e. oil obtained from blubber], many little images cut in wood, seal-skins in tan tubs, with many other such trifles, whereof they diminished nothing. They also found, ten miles within the snowy mountains, a plain champion country, with earth and grass, such as our moory and waste grounds of England are. They went up into a river (which in the narrowest place is two leagues broad) about ten leagues, finding it still to continue they knew not how far . . .

I returned again to my boat, the people still following me and my company, very diligent to attend us, and to help us up the rocks, and likewise down. At length I was desirous to have our men leap with them, which was done, but our men did overleap them. From leaping they went to wrestling; we found them strong and nimble, and to have skill in wrestling, for they cast some of our men that were good wrestlers. The fourth of July we launched our pinnace, and had forty of the people to help us, which they did very willingly. At this time our men again wrestled with them, and found them as before, strong and skilful. This fourth of July the master of the *Mermaid* went to certain islands to store himself with wood, where he found a grave with divers buried in it, only covered with seal-skins, having a cross laid over them. . . .

Being among them at shore the fourth of July, one of them making a long oration, began to kindle a fire in this manner. He took a piece of a board, wherein was a hole half through; into that hole he puts the end of a . . . stick like unto a bedstaff, wetting the end thereof in train, and in fashion of a turner, with a piece of leather, by his violent motion doth very speedily produce fire, which done, with turves he made a fire, into which, with many words and strange gestures, he put divers things which we supposed to be a sacrifice. Myself and divers of my company standing by, they were desirous to have me go into the smoke. I willed them likewise to stand in the smoke, in which they by no means would do. I then took one of them, and thrust him into the smoke, and willed one of my company to tread out the fire, and to spurn it into the sea, which was done to show them that we did contemn [despise] their sorcery.

✽

SAMUEL DE CHAMPLAIN

(1567–1635)

French explorer. An ardent champion of New France, he led and sponsored many expeditions and founded many French colonies, including Quebec.

Voyages of Samuel de Champlain, ed. W. L. Grant (New York, 1907).

1. SCURVY (1609)

The snows began on the 6th of October. On the 3rd of December, we saw ice pass which came from some frozen river. The cold was sharp, more severe than in France, and of much longer duration; and it scarcely rained at all the entire winter. I suppose that is owing to the north and north-west winds passing over high mountains always covered with snow. The latter was from three to four feet deep up to the end of the month of April; lasting much longer, I suppose, than it would if the country were cultivated.

During the winter many of our company were attacked by a certain malady called the *mal de la terre*, otherwise scurvy, as I have since heard from learned men. There were produced, in the mouth of those who had it, great pieces of superfluous and drivelling flesh (causing extensive putre-faction), which got the upper hand to such an extent that scarcely any thing but liquid could be taken. Their teeth became very loose, and could be pulled out with the fingers without its causing them pain. The super-fluous flesh was often cut out, which caused them to eject much blood through the mouth. Afterward, a violent pain seized their arms and legs, which remained swollen and very hard, all spotted as if with flea-bites; and they could not walk on account of the contraction of the muscles, so that they were almost without strength, and suffered intolerable pains. They experienced pain also in the loins, stomach, and bowels, had a very bad cough, and short breath. In a word, they were in such a condition that the majority of them could not rise nor move, and could not even be raised up on their feet without falling down in a swoon. So that out of 79, who composed our party, 35 died, and more than 20 were on the point of death. The majority of those who remained well also complained of slight pains and short breath. We were unable to find any remedy for these maladies. A post mortem examination of several was made to investigate the cause of their disease.

2. KILLING IROQUOIS INDIANS

When it was evening, we embarked in our canoes to continue our course; and, as we advanced very quietly and without making any noise, we met on the 29th of the month the Iroquois, about ten o'clock at evening, at the extremity of a cape which extends into the lake on the western bank. They had come to fight. We both began to utter loud cries, all getting their arms in readiness. We withdrew out on the water, and the Iroquois went on shore, where they drew up all their canoes close to each other and began to fell trees with poor axes, which they acquire in war sometimes, using also others of stone. Thus they barricaded themselves very well.

Our forces also passed the entire night, their canoes being drawn up close to each other and fastened to poles, so that they might not get separated and that they might be all in readiness to fight, if occasion required. We were out upon the water, within arrow range of their bar-ricades. When they were armed and in array, they dispatched two canoes by themselves to the enemy to enquire if they wished to fight, to which the latter replied that they wanted nothing else; but they said that, at present, there was not much light and that it would be necessary to wait for daylight, so as to be able to recognize each other; and that, as soon as the sun rose, they would offer us battle. This was agreed to by our side. Meanwhile, the entire night was spent in dancing and singing, on both sides, with endless

insults and other talk; as, how little courage we had, how feeble a resistance we should make against their arms, and that, when day came, we
should realize it to our ruin. Ours also were not slow in retorting, telling
them they would see such execution of arms as never before, together with
an abundance of such talk as is not unusual in the siege of a town. After
this singing, dancing, and bandying words on both sides to the fill, when
day came, my companions and myself continued under cover, for fear that
the enemy would see us. We arranged our arms in the best manner possible,
being, however, separated, each in one of the canoes of the savage
Montagnais. After arming ourselves with light armour, we each took an
arquebus and went on shore. I saw the enemy go out of their barricade,
nearly 200 in number, stout and rugged in appearance. They came at a
slow pace toward us, with a dignity and assurance which greatly amused
me, having three chiefs at their head. Our men also advanced in the same
order, telling me that those who had three large plumes were the chiefs,
and that they had only these three, and that they could be distinguished
by these plumes, which were much larger than those of their companions,
and that I should do that I could to kill them. I promised to do all in my
power . . .

Our men began to call me with loud cries; and, in order to give me a
passageway, they opened in two parts, and put me at their head, where I
marched some 20 paces in advance of the rest until I was within about 30
paces of the enemy, who at once noticed me, and, halting, gazed at me,
as I did also at them. When I saw them making a move to fire at us, I
rested my musket against my cheek, and aimed directly at one of the three
chiefs. With the same shot, two fell to the ground; and one of their men
was so wounded that he died some time after. I had loaded my musket
with four balls. When our side saw this shot so favourable for them, they
began to raise such loud cries that one could not have heard it thunder.
Meanwhile, the arrows flew on both sides. The Iroquois were greatly astonished that two men had been so quickly killed, although they were
equipped with armour woven from cotton thread and with wood which
was proof against their arrows. This caused great alarm among them. As
I was loading again, one of my companions fired a shot from the woods,
which astonished them anew to such a degree that, seeing their chiefs
dead, they lost courage and took to flight, abandoning their camp and fort,
and fleeing into the woods, whither I pursued them, killing still more of
them. Our savages also killed several of them, and took ten or twelve
prisoners. The remainder escaped with the wounded. Fifteen or sixteen
were wounded on our side with arrow shots; but they were soon healed.

After gaining the victory, our men amused themselves by taking a great quantity of Indian corn and some meal from their enemies, also their armour, which they had left behind that they might run better. After feasting sumptuously, dancing and singing, we returned three hours after with the prisoners. The spot where this attack took place is . . . Lake Champlain.

❉

HENRY HUDSON
(*c*.1550–*c*.1611)

English navigator and explorer. He discovered the Hudson River in 1609 and Hudson Bay in 1610. On this, his last voyage, his men mutinied and cast him adrift in a small boat in Hudson Bay before sailing home.

Abacuck Prickett, *A Journal of Mr Hudson's Last Voyage for the Discovery of a North-West Passage*, in John Harris, *A Complete Collection of Voyages and Travels* (London 1705), I. iv.

1. HARDSHIPS (1610)

It would be tedious to relate the hardships we endured while we wintered in this place; the cold was so extreme that it lamed most of our company. But I must not forget God's great mercy to us in sending us such store of white partridges during the first three months, that we killed above a hundred dozen, besides others of sundry sorts. The spring approaching, the partridges left us, and were succeeded by other fowl, as swans, geese, ducks, and teal, but hard to come by. They came from the south and flew to the north; but if they be taken short by a northerly wind, then they fall and stay till the wind serve them, and then fly to the northward. As the summer came on, these fowls were gone, and few or none to be seen. Then we searched the woods, hills, and valleys for anything that might serve for food, though never so vile; the frogs (in the time of their engendering as loathsome as toads) were not spared, nor the moss that grew on the ground. But amongst divers sorts of vegetables, Thomas Woodhouse brought home a bud of a tree, full of a turpentine substance; of this our surgeon made a decoction to drink, and applied the buds hot to such as were troubled with aches in any part of their bodies; and I must confess I received great and present ease of my pain.

2. AFTER THE MUTINY (1611)

Now were all the poor men in the shallop . . . the carpenter got of them
a piece, and powder and shot, some pikes, an iron pot, with some meal and
other things. They then stood out of the ice, the shallop being fast to the
stern of the ship, and as soon as they were out, they cut her headfast from
the stern, and out with their topsails, and stood towards the sea in a clear
sea. Then, taking in their topsails, they righted their helm and lay under
their foresail till they had ransacked and searched all places in the ship. In
the hold they found one of the vessels of meal whole, and the other half
spent, for we had but two; we found also two firkins of butter, 27 pieces
of pork, and half a bushel of peas; in the master's cabin we found 200
biscuit cakes, a peck of meal, and about the quantity of a butt of beer. Now
the shallop was come in sight again, whereupon they let fall the mainsail,
and out with the topsails, as if they had fled from an enemy.

Then I prayed them yet to remember themselves; but William Wilson
(more than the rest) would hear of no such matter. Coming nigh the east
shore, they cast about and stood to the west, and anchoring near an island
set the boat and net ashore to see if they could have a draught, but could
not for rocks and great stones. Here they gathered good store of that weed
which we called cockle-grass in our wintering place, and we lay there that
night and best part of next day, in all which time we saw not the shallop,
nor ever saw her after.

✿

LUKE FOXE

(1586–1635)

*English explorer. In 1631 he surveyed Hudson Bay and concluded that no
North-West Passage existed.*

The Voyages of Captain Luke Foxe and Captain Thomas James in Search of a
North West Passage (London, 1894).

DINNER WITH THOMAS JAMES (1631)

I was well entertained and feasted by Captain James, with variety of such
cheer as his sea provisions could afford, with some partridges; we dined

betwixt decks, for the great cabin was not big enough to receive ourselves and followers; during which time the ship . . . threw in so much water as we could not have wanted sauce if we had had roast mutton.

Whereat I began to ponder whether it were better for his company to be impounded amongst ice, where they might be kept from putrefaction by the piercing air, or in open sea, to be kept sweet by being thus daily pickled. However, they were to be pitied; the ship taking her liquor as kindly as ourselves, for her nose was no sooner out of the pitcher but her nebe [beak], like the ducks', was in it again. The gentleman could discourse of art (as observations, calculations, and the like), and [he] showed me many instruments, so that I did perceive him to be a practitioner in the mathematics; but when I found that he was no seaman, I did blame those very much who had counselled him to make choice of that ship for a voyage of such importance, for to endure two winters in (as he must have done, if he had any such intent) before he could come about by Bonn Sperance [the Cape of Good Hope] home. Our discourse had been to small purpose if we had not pried into the errors of our predecessors. And (being demanded), I did not think much for his keeping out his flag; for my ambition was [not so] ethereal, and my thoughts not so airy, so to set my sight towards the sky, but when I either called to God or made celestial observation. To this was replied that he was going to the Emperor of Japan, with letters from his Majesty, and that, if it were a ship of his Majesty's of 40 pieces of ordnance, he could not strike his flag. 'Keep it up then,' quoth I, 'but you are out of the way to Japan, for this is not it.'

✳

THOMAS JAMES

(1593–1635)

English explorer. Financed by Bristol merchants, he sought the North-West Passage in 1631 and 1632. His subsequent book inspired Coleridge's 'Ancient Mariner'.

The Strange and Dangerous Voyage of Captain Thomas James in his Intended Discovery of the North-West Passage into the South Sea. Wherein the miseries induced both going, wintering and returning, and the rarities observed both philosophical and mathematical, are related in this journal of it (London, 1633).

THREE SORTS OF COLD (1632)

We made three differences of the cold, all according to the places: in our house; in the woods; and in the open air, upon the ice, in our going to the ship.

For the last, it would be sometimes so extreme that it was not endurable; no clothes were proof against it; no motion could resist it. It would, moreover, so freeze the hair on our eyelids that we could not see; and I verily believe that it would have stifled a man in a very few hours. We did daily find by experience that the cold in the woods would freeze our faces, or any part of our flesh that was bare, but it was yet not so mortifying as the other. Our house, on the outside, was covered two third-parts with snow, and, on the inside, frozen and hung with icesickles. The clothes on our beds would be covered with hoar frost, which, in this little habitacle, was not far from the fire. But let us come a little nearer to it. The cook's tubs, wherein he did water his meat, standing about a yard from the fire, and which he did all day ply with melted snow-water, yet, in the night season, whilst he slept but one watch, would they be firm frozen to the very bottom. And, therefore, was he fain to water his meat in a brass kettle, close adjoining to the fire; and I have many times both seen and felt, by putting my hand into it, that side which was next the fire was very warm, and the other side an inch frozen.... The surgeon, who had hung his bottles of syrups and other liquid things as conveniently as he could to preserve them, had them all frozen.

✤

SAMUEL HEARNE

(1745–1792)

British explorer. He covered huge distances in the unknown interior of Canada, often travelling alone with Indians.

A Journey from Prince of Wales Fort on Hudson's Bay to the Northern Ocean (London, 1795).

MASSACRE OF ESKIMOS BY INDIANS (1771)

[*July 1771*]   At this time (it being about noon) the three men who had been sent as spies met us on their return, and informed my companions that five tents of Esquimaux were on the west side of the river. The situation, they said, was very convenient for surprising them; and, according to their account, I judged it to be about twelve miles from the place we met the spies. When the Indians received this intelligence, no further attendance or attention was paid to my survey, but their whole thoughts were immediately engaged in planning the best method of attack, and how they might steal on the poor Esquimaux the ensuing night, and kill them all while asleep. To accomplish this bloody design more effectually, the Indians thought it necessary to cross the river as soon as possible; and by the account of the spies, it appeared that no part was more convenient for the purpose than that where we had met them, it being there very smooth, and at a considerable distance from any fall. Accordingly, after the Indians had put all their guns, spears, targets, etc. in good order, we crossed the river, which took up some time.

When we arrived on the west side of the river, each painted the front of his target or shield; some with the figure of the Sun, others with that of the Moon, several with different kinds of birds and beasts of prey, and many with the images of imaginary beings, which, according to their silly notions, are the inhabitants of the different elements, Earth, Sea, Air, etc. On enquiring the reason of their doing so, I learned that each man painted his shield with the image of that being on which he relied most for success in the intended engagement. . . .

When this piece of superstition was completed, we began to advance toward the Esquimaux tents; but were very careful to avoid crossing any hills, or talking loud, for fear of being seen or overheard by the inhabitants; by which means the distance was not only much greater than it otherwise would have been, but, for the sake of keeping in the lowest grounds, we were obliged to walk through entire swamps of stiff, marly clay, sometimes up to the knees. . . . It is perhaps worth remarking, that my crew, though an undisciplined rabble, and by no means accustomed to war or command, seemingly acted on this horrid occasion with the utmost uniformity of sentiment. There was not among them the least altercation or separate opinion; all were united in the general cause, and as ready to follow where Matonabbee led, as he appeared to be ready to lead, according to the advice of an old Copper Indian, who had joined us on our first arrival at the river where this bloody business was first proposed.

Never was reciprocity of interest more generally regarded among a number of people, than it was on the present occasion by my crew, for not one was a moment in want of any thing that another could spare . . . The number of my crew was so much greater than that which five tents could contain, and the warlike manner in which they were equipped so greatly superior to what could be expected of the poor Esquimaux, that no less than a total massacre of every one of them was likely to be the case, unless Providence should work a miracle for their deliverance.

The land was so situated that we walked under cover of the rocks and hills till we were within two hundred yards of the tents. There we lay in ambush for some time, watching the motions of the Esquimaux; and here the Indians would have advised me to stay till the fight was over, but to this I could by no means consent; for I considered that when the Esquimaux came to be surprised, they would try every way to escape, and if they found me alone, not knowing me from an enemy, they would probably proceed to violence against me when no person was near to assist. For this reason I determined to accompany them, telling them at the same time that I would not have any hand in the murder they were about to commit, unless I found it necessary for my own safety. The Indians were not displeased at this proposal; one of them immediately fixed me a spear, and another lent me a broad bayonet for my protection, but at that time I could not be provided with a target [shield]; nor did I want to be encumbered with such an unnecessary piece of lumber.

While we lay in ambush, the Indians performed the last ceremonies which were thought necessary before the engagement. These chiefly consisted in painting their faces; some all black, some all red, and others with a mixture of the two; and to prevent their hair from blowing into their eyes, it was either tied before and behind, and on both sides, or else cut short all round. The next thing they considered was to make themselves as light as possible for running; which they did, by pulling off their stockings, and either cutting off the sleeves of their jackets, or rolling them up close to their armpits; and though the muskettoes at that time were so numerous as to surpass all credibility, yet some of the Indians actually pulled off their jackets and entered the lists quite naked, except their breech-cloths and shoes. Fearing I might have occasion to run with the rest, I thought it also advisable to pull off my stockings and cap, and to tie my hair as close up as possible.

By the time the Indians had made themselves thus completely frightful, it was near one o'clock in the morning of the seventeenth; when finding all the Esquimaux quiet in their tents, they rushed forth from their ambuscade, and fell on the poor unsuspecting creatures, unperceived till close at the very eves of their tents, when they soon began the bloody massacre, while I stood neuter in the rear.

In a few seconds the horrible scene commenced; it was shocking beyond description. The poor unhappy victims were surprised in the midst of their sleep, and had neither time nor power to make any resistance; men, women, and children, in all upward of twenty, ran out of their tents stark naked, and endeavoured to make their escape; but the Indians having possession of all the land-side, to no place could they fly for shelter. One alternative only remained, that of jumping into the river; but, as none of them attempted it, they all fell a sacrifice to Indian barbarity! The shrieks and groans of the poor expiring wretches were truly dreadful; and my horror was much increased at seeing a young girl, seemingly about eighteen years of age, killed so near me that when the first spear was stuck into her side she fell down at my feet, and twisted round my legs, so that it was with difficulty that I could disengage myself from her dying grasps. . . .

The brutish manner in which these savages used the bodies they had so cruelly bereaved of life was so shocking, that it would be indecent to describe it; particularly their curiosity in examining, and the remarks they made, on the formation of the women; which, they pretended to say, differed materially from that of their own. . . . When the Indians had completed the murder of the poor Esquimaux, seven other tents on the east side the river immediately engaged their attention: very luckily, however, our canoes and baggage had been left at a little distance up the river, so that they had no way of crossing to get at them. The river at this part being little more than eighty yards wide, they began firing at them from the west side. The poor Esquimaux on the opposite shore, though all up in arms, did not attempt to abandon their tents; and they were so unacquainted with the nature of firearms that when the bullets struck the ground, they ran in crowds to see what was sent them, and seemed anxious to examine all the pieces of lead which they found flattened against the rocks. At length one of the Esquimaux men was shot in the calf of his leg, which put them in great confusion. They all immediately embarked in their little canoes, and paddled to a shoal in the middle of the river, which being somewhat more than a gun-shot from any part of the shore, put them out of the reach of our barbarians.

When the savages discovered that the surviving Esquimaux had gained the shore above mentioned, the Northern Indians began to plunder the tents of the deceased of all the copper utensils they could find; such as hatchets, bayonets, knives etc., after which they assembled on the top of an adjacent high hill, and standing all in a cluster, so as to form a solid circle, with their spears erect in the air, gave many shouts of victory, constantly clashing their spears against each other, and frequently calling out *tima! tima!* by way of derision to the poor surviving Esquimaux, who were standing on the shoal almost knee-deep in water.

After parading the hill for some time, it was agreed to return up the river to the place where we had left our canoes and baggage, which was about half a mile distant, and then to cross the river again and plunder the seven tents on the east side. This resolution was immediately put in force; and as ferrying across with only three or four canoes took a considerable time, and as we were, from the crookedness of the river and the form of the land, entirely under cover, several of the poor surviving Esquimaux, thinking probably that we were gone about our business, and meant to trouble them no more, had returned from the shoal to their habitations. When we approached their tents, which we did under cover of the rocks, we found them busily employed tying up bundles. These the Indians seized with their usual ferocity; on which, the Esquimaux having their canoes lying ready in the water, immediately embarked, and all of them got safe to the former shoal, except an old man, who was so intent on collecting his things that the Indians coming upon him before he could reach his canoe, he fell a sacrifice to their fury: I verily believe not less than twenty had a hand in his death, as his whole body was like a cullender. . . .

In making our retreat up the river, after killing the Esquimaux on the west side, we saw an old woman sitting by the side of the water, killing salmon, which lay at the foot of the fall as thick as a shoal of herrings. Whether from the noise of the fall, or a natural defect in the old woman's hearing, it is hard to determine, but certain it is, she had no knowledge of the tragical scene which had been so lately transacted at the tents, though she was not more than two hundred yards from the place. When we first perceived her, she seemed perfectly at ease, and was entirely surrounded with the produce of her labour. From her manner of behaviour, and the appearance of her eyes, which were as red as blood, it is more than probable that her sight was not very good; for she scarcely discerned that the Indians were enemies, till they were within twice the length of their spears of her. It was in vain that she attempted to fly, for the wretches of my crew transfixed her to the ground in a few seconds, and butchered her in the most savage manner.

James Cook

(1728–1779)

English naval officer. Perhaps the greatest explorer of all. On his third and last voyage, in 1778–9, he sailed through the Bering Strait and reached 70°44′, the furthest north on that side of America.

The Life and Voyages of Captain James Cook, selections with introduction and notes by C. G. Cash (London, 1901).

'Sea-Horses' and Ice (1778)

On the ice lay a prodigious number of sea-horses [walrus], and, as we were in want of fresh provisions, the boats of each ship were sent to get some. By seven o'clock in the evening we had received on board the *Resolution* nine of these animals. We lived upon them as long as they lasted, and there were few on board that did not prefer them to our salt meat.

The fat at first is as sweet as marrow, but in a few days it grows rancid, unless it be salted. The lean flesh is coarse and black, and has a rather strong taste, but the heart is nearly as well tasted as that of a bullock. The fat when melted yields a good deal of oil, which burns very well in lamps; and their hides, which are very thick, were very useful about our rigging. The teeth or tusks of most of them were at this time very small; even some of the largest and oldest of these animals had them not exceeding six inches in length.

They lie, in herds of many hundreds, upon the ice, huddling one over the other like swine, and roar or bray very loud, so that in the night or in foggy weather they gave us notice of the vicinity of the ice before we could see it. We never found the whole herd asleep, some being always upon the watch. On the approach of the boat these would wake those next to them, and, the alarm being thus gradually communicated, the whole herd would be awake presently. But they were seldom in a hurry to get away till after they had been once fired at. Then they would tumble one over the other into the sea in the utmost confusion. And if we did not, at the first discharge, kill those we fired at, we generally lost them, though mortally wounded. They did not appear to us to be that dangerous animal some authors have described, not even when attacked. They are rather more so to appearance than in reality. Vast numbers of them would follow and come close up to the boats. But the flash of a musket in the pan, or even the bare pointing of one at them, would send them down in an instant. The female will defend the young one to the very last, and at the expense of her own life, whether in the water or upon the ice. Nor will the young one quit the dam though she be dead; so that, if you kill the one, you are sure of the other. The dam, when in the water, holds the young one between her fore-fins.

It must not be understood that I supposed any part of this ice which we had seen to be fixed; on the contrary, I am well assured that the whole was a movable mass. Having but little wind, I went with the boats to examine the state of the ice. I found it consisting of loose pieces of various extent, and so close together that I could hardly enter the outer edge with a boat, and it was as impossible for the ships to enter it as if it had been so many rocks. I took particular notice that it was all pure transparent ice, except the upper surface, which was a little porous. It appeared to be entirely composed of frozen snow, and to have been all formed at sea. The pieces of ice that formed the outer edge of the field were from forty or fifty yards in extent to four or five, and I judged that the larger pieces reached thirty feet or more under the surface of the water. It appeared to me very improbable that this ice could have been the production of the preceding winter alone. I should suppose it rather to have been the production of a great many winters. Nor was it less improbable, according to my judgement, that the little that remained of the summer could destroy the tenth part of what now subsisted of this mass; for the sun had now exerted upon it the full influence of his rays. Indeed, I am of opinion that the sun contributes very little toward reducing these great masses. For although that luminary is a great while above the horizon, it seldom shines out for more than a few hours at a time, and often is not seen for several days in succession. It is the wind, or rather the waves raised by the wind, that brings down the bulk of these enormous masses, by grinding one piece against another, and by undermining and washing away those parts that lie exposed to the surge of the sea. . . .

The season was now so far advanced, and the time when the frost is expected to set in so near at hand, that I did not consider it consistent with prudence to make any further attempts to find a passage into the Atlantic this year, in any direction, so little was the prospect of succeeding. My attention was now directed toward finding out some place where we might supply ourselves with wood and water, and so spend the winter as to be in a condition to return to the north in further search of a passage the ensuing summer.

SIR ALEXANDER MACKENZIE

(1764–1820)

Scottish explorer. He followed the Mackenzie River to the Arctic Ocean thinking that it might be the Pacific. Then, later, he did reach the Pacific, and became the first European to cross the continent north of Mexico.

Voyages from Montreal, on the River St Laurence, through the continent of North America, to the frozen and Pacific Oceans in 1789 and 1793; with a preliminary account of the rise, progress, and present state of the fur trade of that country (London, 1801).

1. THE TIDE REVEALS THE ARCTIC OCEAN (1789)

At eight we encamped on the eastern end of the island, which I had named the Whale Island. It is about seven leagues in length, east and west by compass; but not more than half a mile in breadth. We saw several red foxes, one of which was killed. There were also five or six very old huts on the point where we had taken our station. The nets were now set, and one of them in five fathom water, the current setting north-east by compass. This morning I ordered a post to be erected close to our tents, on which I engraved the latitude of the place, my own name, the number of persons which I had with me, and the time we remained there.

Being awakened by some casual circumstance, at four this morning, I was surprised on perceiving that the water had flowed under our baggage. As the wind had not changed, and did not blow with greater violence than when we went to rest, we were all of opinion that this circumstance proceeded from the tide. We had, indeed, observed at the other end of the island that the water rose and fell; but we then imagined that it must have been occasioned by the wind. The water continued to rise till about six, but I could not ascertain the time with the requisite precision, as the wind then began to blow with great violence; I therefore determined, at all events, to remain here till the next morning, though, as it happened, the state of the wind was such as to render my stay here an act of necessity. Our nets were not very successful, as they presented us with only eight fish. From an observation which I obtained at noon, we were in 69°7′ north latitude. As the evening approached, the wind increased, and the weather became cold. Two swans were the only provision which the hunters procured for us.

The rain did not cease till seven this morning, the weather being at intervals very cold and unpleasant. Such was its inconstancy that I could not make an accurate observation; but the tide appeared to rise sixteen or eighteen inches.

2. INDIAN MEDICINE AND ARRIVAL AT THE PACIFIC (1793)

Friday, 19 July. Soon after I had retired to rest last night, the chief paid me a visit to insist on my going to his bed-companion, and taking my place himself; but, notwithstanding his repeated entreaties, I resisted this offering of his hospitality.

At an early hour this morning I was again visited by the chief, in company with his son. The former complained of a pain in his breast; to relieve his suffering, I gave him a few drops of Turlington's Balsam on a piece of sugar; and I was rather surprised to see him take it without the least hesitation. When he had taken my medicine, he requested me to follow him, and conducted me to a shed, where several people were assembled round a sick man, who was another of his sons. They immediately uncovered him, and showed me a violent ulcer in the small of his back, in the foulest state that can be imagined. One of his knees was also afflicted in the same manner. This unhappy man was reduced to a skeleton, and, from his appearance, was drawing near to an end of his pains. They requested that I would touch him, and his father was very urgent with me to administer medicine; but he was in such a dangerous state, that I thought it prudent to yield no further to the importunities than to give the sick person a few drops of Turlington's balsam in some water. I therefore left them, but was soon called back by the loud lamentations of the women, and was rather apprehensive that some inconvenience might result from my compliance with the chief's request.

On my return I found the native physicians busy in practising their skill and art on the patient. They blew on him, and then whistled; at times they pressed their extended fingers, with all their strength on his stomach; they also put their forefingers doubled into his mouth, and spouted water from their own with great violence into his face. To support these operations the wretched sufferer was held up in a sitting posture; and when they were concluded, he was laid down and covered with a new robe made of the skins of the lynx. I had observed that his belly and breast were covered with scars, and I understood that they were caused by a custom prevalent among them, of applying pieces of lighted touchwood to their flesh, in order to relieve pain or demonstrate their courage.

He was now placed on a broad plank, and carried by six men into the woods, where I was invited to accompany them. I could not conjecture what would be the end of this ceremony, particularly as I saw one man carry fire, another an axe, and a third dry wood. I was, indeed, disposed to suspect that, as it was their custom to burn the dead, they intended to relieve the poor man from his pain, and perform the last sad duty of surviving affection. When they had advanced a short distance into the wood, they laid him upon a clear spot, and kindled a fire against his back, when the physician began to scarify the ulcer with a very blunt instrument, the cruel pain of which operation the patient bore with incredible resolution. The scene afflicted me and I left it.

On my return to our lodge, I observed before the door of the chief's residence, four heaps of salmon, each of which consisted of between three and four hundred fish. Sixteen women were employed in cleaning and preparing them. They first separate the head from the body, the former of which they boil; they then cut the latter down the back on each side of the bone, leaving one third of the fish adhering to it, and afterwards take out the guts. The bone is roasted for immediate use, and the other parts are dressed in the same manner, but with more attention, for future provision. While they are before the fire, troughs are placed under them to receive the oil. The roes are also carefully preserved, and form a favourite article of their food.

After I had observed these culinary preparations, I paid a visit to the chief, who presented me with a roasted salmon; he then opened one of his chests, and took out of it a garment of blue cloth, decorated with brass buttons; and another of a flowered cotton, which I supposed were Spanish; it had been trimmed with leather fringe, after the fashion of their own cloaks. Copper and brass are in great estimation among them, and of the former they have great plenty: they point their arrows and spears with it, and work it up into personal ornaments, such as collars, ear-rings, and bracelets, which they wear on their wrists, arms, and legs. I presume they find it the most advantageous article of trade with the more inland tribes. . . .

I went to take the dimensions of his large canoe, in which, it was signified to me, that about ten winters ago he went a considerable distance towards the mid-day sun, with forty of his people, when he saw two large vessels full of such men as myself, by whom he was kindly received: they were, he said, the first white people he had seen. They were probably the ships commanded by Captain Cook. [*Probably not.—Ed.*] This canoe was built of cedar, forty-five feet long, four feet wide, and three feet and a half in depth. It was painted black and decorated with white figures of fish of different kinds. The gunwale, fore and aft, was inlaid with the teeth of the sea-otter.[1]

When I returned to the river, the natives who were to accompany us, and my people, were already in the canoe. The latter, however, informed me that one of our axes was missing. I immediately applied to the chief, and requested its restoration; but he would not understand me till I sat myself down on a stone, with my arms in a state of preparation, and made it appear to him that I should not depart till the stolen article was restored. The village was immediately in a state of uproar, and some danger was apprehended from the confusion that prevailed in it. The axe, however, which had been hidden under the chief's canoe, was soon returned. Though this instrument was not, in itself, of sufficient value to justify a dispute with these people, I apprehended that the suffering them to keep it, after we had declared its loss, might have occasioned the loss of everything we carried with us, and of our lives also. My people were dissatisfied with me at the moment; but I thought myself right then; and I think now that the circumstances in which we were involved justified the measure which I adopted.

At one in the afternoon we renewed our voyage in a large canoe with four of the natives. We found the river almost one continued rapid . . .

They informed us also that we were approaching a cascade. I directed them to shoot it, and proceeded myself to the foot thereof, where I re-embarked, and we went on with great velocity, till we came to a fall, where we left our canoe, and carried our luggage along a road through a wood for some hundred yards, when we came to a village, consisting of six very large houses, erected on pallisades, rising twenty-five feet from the ground . . . These people do not seem to enjoy the abundance of their neighbours, as the men who returned from fishing had no more than five salmon; they refused to sell one of them, but gave me one roasted of a very indifferent kind. In the houses there were several chests or boxes containing different articles that belonged to the people whom we had lately passed. If I were to judge by the heaps of filth beneath these buildings, they must have been erected at a more distant period than any which we passed. From these houses I could perceive the termination of the river, and its discharge into a narrow arm of the sea.

As it was now half past six in the evening, and the weather cloudy, I determined to remain here for the night, and for that purpose we possessed

[1] As Captain Cooke has mentioned that the people of the sea-coast adorned their canoes with human teeth, I was more particular in my inquiries; the result of which was the most satisfactory proof that he was mistaken: but his mistake arose from the very great resemblance there is between human teeth and those of the sea-otter.

ourselves of one of the unoccupied houses. The remains of our last meal, which we brought with us, served for our supper, as we could not procure a single fish from the natives. The course of the river is about west, and the distance from the great village upwards of thirty-six miles. There we had lost our dog, a circumstance of no small regret to me.

3. NEARING THE COAST; TROUBLESOME INDIANS

Under the land we met with three canoes, with fifteen men in them, and laden with their movables, as if proceeding to a new situation, or returning to a former one. They manifested no kind of mistrust or fear of us, but entered into conversation with our young man, as I supposed, to obtain some information concerning us. It did not appear that they were the same people as those we had lately seen, as they spoke the language of our young chief, with a different accent. They then examined everything we had in our canoe, with an air of indifference and disdain. One of them in particular made me understand, with an air of insolence, that a large canoe had lately been in this bay, with people in her like me, and that one of them, whom he called *Macubah* [Vancouver?], had fired on him and his friends, and that *Bensins* [Menzies?] had struck him on the back, with the flat part of his sword. He also mentioned another name, the articulation of which I could not determine. At the same time he illustrated these circumstances by the assistance of my gun and sword; and I do not doubt but he well deserved the treatment which he described. He also produced several European articles, which could not have been long in his possession. From his conduct and appearance, I wished very much to be rid of him, and flattered myself that he would prosecute his voyage, which appeared to be in an opposite direction to our course. However, when I prepared to part from them, they turned their canoes about, and persuaded my young man to leave me, which I could not prevent.

We coasted along the land at about west-south-west for six miles, and met a canoe with two boys in it, who were dispatched to summon the people on that part of the coast to join them. The troublesome fellow now forced himself into my canoe, and pointed out a narrow channel on the opposite shore, that led to his village, and requested us to steer towards it, which I accordingly ordered. His importunities now became very irksome, and he wanted to see everything we had, particularly my instruments, concerning which he must have received information from my young man. He asked for my hat, my handkerchief, and, in short, everything that he saw about me. At the same time he frequently repeated the unpleasant intelligence that he had been shot at by people of my colour. At some distance from the land a channel opened to us, at south-west by west, and pointing that way, he made me understand that *Macubah* came here with his large canoe. When we were in mid-channel, I perceived some sheds, or the remains of old buildings, on the shore; and as, from that circumstance, I thought it probable that some Europeans might have been there, I directed my steersman to make for that spot. The traverse is upwards of three miles north-west.

We landed, and found the ruins of a village, in a situation calculated for defence. The place itself was overgrown with weeds, and in the centre of the houses there was a temple, of the same form and construction as that which I described at the large village. We were soon followed by ten canoes, each of which contained from three to six men. They informed us that we were expected at the village, where we should see many of them. From their general deportment I was very apprehensive that some hostile design was meditated against us, and for the first time I acknowledged my apprehensions to my people. I accordingly desired them to be very much upon their guard, and to be prepared if any violence was offered to defend themselves to the last.

We had no sooner landed than we took possession of a rock, where there was no space for more than twice our number, and which admitted of our defending ourselves with advantage, in case we should be attacked. The people in the three first canoes were the most troublesome, but, after doing their utmost to irritate us, they went away. They were, however, no sooner gone, than a hat, handkerchief, and several other articles were missing. The rest of our visitors continued their pressing invitations to accompany them to their village, but finding our resolution to decline them was not to be shaken, they about sunset relieved us from all further importunities by their departure. . . .

I now mixed up some vermilion in melted grease, and inscribed, in large characters, on the south-east face of the rock on which we had slept last night, this brief memorial: 'Alexander Mackenzie, from Canada, by land, the twenty-second of July, one thousand seven hundred and ninety-three.'

MERIWETHER LEWIS

(1774–1809)

WILLIAM CLARK

(1770–1838)

US soldiers and explorers. They travelled more than 8,000 miles across North America from coast to coast and back again between 1804 and 1806. They were accompanied and guided by a pregnant Shoshone woman, Sacagawea, whose baby was born on the journey.

History of the Expedition under the Command of Lewis and Clark (New York, 1893; 1st edn. 1814).

1. LETTER FROM THOMAS JEFFERSON (1803)

Washington, US. of America, July 4, 1803

To Capt. Meriwether Lewis

Dear Sir

In the journey which you are about to undertake for the discovery of the course and source of the Missouri, and of the most convenient water communication from hence to the Pacific ocean, your party being small, it is to be expected that you will encounter considerable dangers from the Indian inhabitants. Should you escape those dangers and reach the Pacific ocean, you may find it imprudent to hazard a return the same way, and be forced to seek a passage round by sea, in such vessels as you may find on the Western coast. But you will be without money, without clothes, and other necessaries, as a sufficient supply cannot be carried with you from hence. Your resource in that case can only be in the credit of the US., for which purpose I hereby authorize you to draw on the Secretaries of State of the Treasury, of War, and of the Navy of the US., according as you may find your draughts will be most negociable, for the purpose of obtaining money or necessaries for yourself and your men. And I solemnly pledge the faith of the United States that these draughts shall be paid punctually at the date they are made payable. I also ask of the Consuls, agents, merchants and citizens of any nation with which we have intercourse or amity to furnish you with these supplies which your necessities may call for, assuring them of honorable and prompt retribution. And our own

Consuls in foreign parts where you may happen to be are hereby instructed and required to be aiding and assisting to you in whatsoever may be necessary for procuring your return back to the United States. And to give more entire satisfaction and confidence to those who may be disposed to aid you, I Thomas Jefferson, President of the United States of America, have written this letter of general credit for you with my own hand, and signed it with my name.

2. SACAGAWEA'S BABY IS BORN (1805)

11th February Monday 1805. The party that were ordered last evening set out early this morning. The weather was fair and cold, wind NW. About five o'clock this evening one of the wives of Charbonneau was delivered of a fine boy. It is worthy of remark that this was the first child which this woman had borne, and, as is common in such cases, her labour was tedious and the pain violent. Mr Jessome informed me that he had frequently administered a small portion of the rattle of the rattle-snake, which he assured me had never failed to produce the desired effect, that of hastening the birth of the child. Having the rattle of a snake by me I gave it to him, and he administered two rings of it to the woman, broken in small pieces with the fingers and added to a small quantity of water. Whether this medicine was truly the cause or not I shall not undertake to determine, but I was informed that she had not taken it more than ten minutes before she brought forth.

3. LEWIS SEES MISSOURI GREAT FALLS, AND MEETS BISON AND BROWN BEAR

June 13th. They left camp at sunrise and, ascending the river-hills, went for six miles in a course generally south-west, over a country which, though more waving than that of yesterday, may still be considered level. At the extremity of this course they overlooked a most beautiful plain, where were infinitely more buffalo than we had ever before seen at a single view. To the south-west arose from the plain two mountains of a singular appearance, more like ramparts of high fortifications than works of nature. . . . Finding that the river here bore considerably to the south, and fearful of passing the falls before reaching the Rocky mountains, they now changed their course to the south, and leaving those insulated hills to the right, proceeded across the plain.

In this direction Captain Lewis had gone about two miles when his ears were saluted with the agreeable sound of a fall of water, and as he advanced a spray, which seemed driven by the high south-west wind, arose above the plain like a column of smoke, and vanished in an instant. Toward this point he directed his steps; the noise increased as he approached, and soon became too tremendous to be mistaken for anything but the Great Falls of the Missouri. Having travelled seven miles after first hearing the sound, he reached the falls about twelve o'clock. The hills as he approached were difficult of access and 200 feet high. Down these he hurried with impatience; and, seating himself on some rocks under the centre of the falls, enjoyed the sublime spectacle of this stupendous object, which since the creation had been lavishing its magnificence upon the desert, unknown to civilization. . . .

Captain Lewis then descended the hill, and directed his course toward the river falling in from the west. He soon met a herd of at lest 1,000 buffalo, and being desirous of providing for supper, shot one of them. The animal immediately began to bleed, and Captain Lewis, who had forgotten to reload his rifle, was intently watching to see him fall, when he beheld a large brown bear which was stealing on him unperceived, and was already within twenty steps. In the first moment of surprise he lifted his rifle, but remembering instantly that it was not charged, and that he had no time to reload, he felt that there was no safety but in flight. It was in the open level plain—not a bush nor a tree within 300 yards, the bank of the river sloping and not more than three feet high, so that there was no possible mode of concealment. Captain Lewis therefore thought of retreating in a quick walk, as fast as the bear advanced, toward the nearest tree; but as soon as he turned, the bear ran open-mouthed and at full speed upon him. Captain Lewis ran about eighty yards, but finding that the animal gained on him fast, it flashed on his mind that, by getting into the water to such a depth that the bear would be obliged to attack him swimming, there was still some chance of his life; he therefore turned short, plunged into the river about waist-deep, and facing about presented the point of his espontoon. The bear arrived at the water's edge within twenty feet of him; but as soon as he put himself in this posture of defence, the bear seemed frightened and, wheeling about, retreated with as much precipitation as he had pursued. Very glad to be released from this danger, Captain Lewis returned to the shore, and observed him run with great speed, sometimes looking back as if he expected to be pursued, till he reached the woods. He could not conceive the cause of the sudden alarm of the bear, but congratulated himself on his escape when he saw his own track torn to pieces by the furious animal, and learned from the whole adventure never to suffer his rifle to be a moment unloaded.

4. SACAGAWEA MEETS HER RELATIVES

Saturday, 17 August . . . On setting out at seven o'clock, Captain Clark, with Charbonneau and his wife, walked on shore; but they had not gone more than a mile before Captain Clark saw Sacagawea, who was with her husband 100 yards ahead, begin to dance and show every mark of the most extravagant joy, turning round to him and pointing to several Indians, whom he now saw advancing on horseback, sucking her fingers at the same time, to indicate that they were of her native tribe. . . . Captain Clark discovered among them Drewyer dressed like an Indian, from whom he learned the situation of the party. While the boats were performing the circuit, he went toward the forks with the Indians, who, as they went along, sang aloud with the greatest appearance of delight.

We soon drew near the camp, and just as we approached it a woman made her way through the crowd toward Sacagawea; recognizing each other, they embraced with the most tender affection. The meeting of these two young women had in it something peculiarly touching, not only from the ardent manner in which their feelings were expressed, but also from the real interest of their situation. They had been companions in childhood; in the war with the Minnetarees they had both been taken prisoners in the same battle; they had shared and softened the rigours of their captivity till one of them had escaped from the Minnetarees, with scarce a hope of ever seeing her friend relieved from the hands of her enemies.

While Sacagawea was renewing among the women the friendships of former days, Captain Clark went on, and was received by Captain Lewis and the chief, who, after the first embraces and salutations were over, conducted him to a sort of circular tent or shade of willows. Here he was seated on a white robe, and the chief immediately tied in his hair six small shells resembling pearls, an ornament highly valued by these people, who procure them in the course of trade from the sea-coast. The moccasins of the whole party were then taken off, and after much ceremony the smoking began. After this the conference was to be opened. Glad of an opportunity of being able to converse more intelligibly, Sacagawea was sent for; she came into the tent, sat down, and was beginning to interpret, when . . . she recognized her brother. She instantly jumped up, and ran and embraced him, throwing over him her blanket, and weeping profusely. The chief was himself moved, though not in the same degree. After some conversation between them she resumed her seat and attempted to interpret for us; but her new situation seemed to overpower her, and she was frequently interrupted by her tears. After the council was finished the unfortunate woman learned that all her family were dead except two brothers, one of whom was absent, and a son of her eldest sister, a small boy, who was immediately adopted by her.

✼

DAVID THOMPSON
(1770–1857)

Canadian explorer and geographer. He was a meticulous map-maker and surveyor of large areas of unknown territory.

David Thompson's Narrative of his Explorations in Western America, ed. J. B. Tyrrell (1916).

1. LIFE AMONG THE INDIANS (1807–1811)

Both Canadians and Indians often inquired of me why I observed the sun, and sometimes the moon, in the day-time, and passed whole nights with my instruments looking at the moon and stars. I told them it was to determine the distance and direction from the place I observed to other places; neither the Canadians nor the Indians believed me; for both argued that if what I said was truth, I ought to look to the ground, and over it; and not to the stars. . . . neither argument, nor ridicule had any effect, and I had to leave them to their own opinions and yet inadvertingly on my part, several things happened to confirm their opinions. One fine evening in February two Indians came to the house to trade; the moon rose bright and clear with the planet Jupiter a few degrees on its east side; and the Canadians as usual predicted that Indians would come to trade in the direction of this star. To show them the folly of such predictions, I told them the same bright star, the next night, would be as far from the moon on its west side; this of course took place from the moon's motion in her orbit, and is the common occurence of almost every month, and yet all parties were persuaded I had done it by some occult power to falsify the predictions of the Canadians. Mankind are fond of the marvellous; it seems to heighten their character by relating they have seen such things. I had always admired the tact [i.e. keen perception] of the Indian in being able to guide himself through the darkest pine forests to exactly the place he intended to go, his keen, constant attention on everything; the removal of the smallest stone, the bent or broken twig; a slight mark on the ground, all spoke plain language to him. I was anxious to acquire this knowledge, and often being in company with them, sometimes for several months, I paid attention to what they pointed out to me, and became almost equal to some of them; which became of great use to me.

2. FINAL ENTRY ON THE PACIFIC COAST (1811)

This place was about seven miles from the sea, and too much exposed to the undulations of the waves; the quality of their goods for trade very low, but good enough for the beggarly natives about them, of the same race I have described, and with few exceptions, [they] appeared a race of worthless, idle, impudent knaves, without anything to barter, yet begging everything they saw. They were all accustomed to trade with the ships, mostly of the United States, and had learned a great part of the worst words of their language. The next day in my canoe with my men I went to Cape Disappointment, which terminates the course of this river, and remained until the tide came in; at ebb tide we noticed the current of the river riding in waves over the surface to the sea for about four miles; on all the shores of this Ocean, the agitation of the sea is constantly breaking against the rocky shore with high surges, and my men now allowed the great volume of water forming these high surges to be far superior to those of any Lake.

Thus I have fully completed the survey of this part of North America from sea to sea, and by almost innumerable astronomical observations have determined the positions of the mountains, lakes, and rivers, and other remarkable places of the northern part of this continent; the maps of all of which have been drawn, and laid down in geographical position, being now the work of twenty-seven years.

✽

OTTO VON KOTZEBUE

(1787–1846)

Russian navigator. He circumnavigated the globe twice, from 1815 to 1818 and from 1823 to 1826. On the first expedition he charted a large part of Alaska and the sound that bears his name.

A Voyage of Discovery into the South Sea and Bering's Straits, For the Purpose of Exploring a North East Passage, undertaken in the years 1815–18 (London, 1821).

1. ENCOUNTERS WITH ESKIMOS (1816)

We observed people and tents on the shore; and the wish of becoming acquainted with the inhabitants of this island, who had never been visited by any navigator, and also to give our naturalists an opportunity of examining this unknown country, induced me to pay it a visit. Two of our four-oared boats were directly put into the water, and we set out, well armed with pistols, sabres, and guns. . . .

A filthy piece of leather was spread on the floor for me to sit on; and then they came up to me one after the other—each of them embraced me, rubbed his nose hard against mine, and ended his caresses by spitting in his hands and wiping them several times over my face. Though these signs of friendship were not very agreeable to me, I bore all patiently. To suppress their further tenderness, I distributed some tobacco-leaves, which they received with much pleasure, and were going to repeat all their caresses again. I hastily took some knives, scissors, and beads, and thus happily prevented a second attack. An almost still greater misery awaited me when, in order to refresh me, they brought forth a wooden trough of whale blubber (a great delicacy among all the northern inhabitants of the sea-coasts), and I bravely took some of it, sickening and dangerous as this food is to a European stomach. This, and some other presents which I afterwards made them, sealed the bond of our friendly acquaintance. My host, the proprietor of the tent, and probably the chief of his countrymen present, after our meals ordered a dance; one of them stepped forwards, made the most comical motions with his whole body, without stirring from his place, making the most hideous grimaces; the others sung a song, consisting of only two notes, sometimes louder, sometimes lower, and the time was beat on a small tambourine. . . .

In fact, we had now a very lively barter; in half an hour, my sailors had obtained above 200 kamlaikas (a name which is derived from Kamtschatka, denoting a garment, which is of the cut of a shirt, skilfully sewed together with the entrails of seals, sea-lions, and morse [walrus]) for buttons and similar things. This garment, which is put on over the other clothes, keeps off the rain and wet, and is very useful in this climate. I have remarked that all the people of this region put on their kamlaikas over their warm clothes, in damp weather; and I myself have often experienced the benefit of it in these northern latitudes.

2. KOTZEBUE'S DISCOVERY OF HIS SOUND

I cannot describe the strange sensation which I now experienced, at the idea that I perhaps stood at the entrance of the so long sought NE passage, and that fate had chosen me to be the discoverer. I felt my heart oppressed; and, at the same time, an impatience, which would not let me rest, and was still increased by the perfect calm. To satisfy myself, at least, by going on shore, and clearly observing, from some eminence, the direction of the coast, I had two boats got ready . . .

We entered a small tent of morse-skins, made in the form of a canoe, where the wife and two children were sitting in a corner. On one side of this habitation were two boats; one was quite a small one, like those used by the Aleutians, and the other a larger one, for ten persons, which serves to transport their tent, together with all their household, from one place to another. That they are employed in the chase, was proved by the various skins which lay about in heaps. The elder boy, with a lively and animated countenance that expressed much curiosity, was particularly attentive; when he observed that we noted down the names of different objects, he took a pleasure in telling us various things, and looked eagerly when we put his words on paper. The wife of the American [eskimo] seemed to have a mind for nothing but my bright buttons, which she strove secretly to twist off; but as she did not succeed in this, she sent her two children, who were entirely wrapped in fur, and crawled about me like two young bears, to try to bite them off. To save my buttons, I gave her a looking-glass; but this occasioned a great dispute, as all the family wanted to look at themselves at once, and for that it was clearly too small. I at length interfered, and made one after the other look at his face, and each of them tried to find the stranger behind the glass, as he did not know himself.

The host now spread a morse-skin outside of the tent, on which he invited us to sit, and made each of us a present of a marten's skin, for which he received presents in return, among which the tobacco was particularly welcome. The woman was adorned in the same manner as we have seen some before, with iron and copper rings on the arms, and glass beads in the hair. I took much trouble to make my American comprehend that I wished to know how far this branch might extend. He at last comprehended me, and made me understand his answer by the following pantomime: he seated himself on the ground, and rowed eagerly with his arms; this business he interrupted nine times, closing his eyes as many times, and resting his head on his hand. I learnt by this, that it would take nine days to get to the open sea through this branch. . . .

In compliance with the general wish of my companions, I called this newly discovered sound by my own name, Kotzebue's Sound. Inconsiderable as the discovery of this sound may be, it is an acquisition to geography, and may serve the world as a proof of my zeal; for, in truth, even Cook has treated this coast rather negligently.

❈

SIR JOHN ROSS

(1777–1856)

British naval officer and explorer. He failed to find the North-West Passage because he mistakenly identified clouds as mountains, barring further progress, which he named the Croker Mountains—thus creating considerable confusion for subsequent navigators. He was the uncle of Sir James Clark Ross (q.v.).

A *Voyage of Discovery* (London, 1819).

1. ICEBERGS AND ESKIMOS (1818)

It is hardly possible to imagine anything more exquisite than the variety of tints which these icebergs display; by night as well as by day they glitter with a vividness of colour beyond the power of art to represent. While the white portions have the brilliancy of silver, their colours are as various and splendid as those of the rainbow, their ever-changing disposition producing effects as singular as they were novel and interesting.

The ships had made very little progress when we were surprised by the appearance of several men on the ice, who were hallooing, as we imagined, to the ships; the first impression was that they were shipwrecked sailors, probably belonging to some vessel that had followed us and had been crushed in the late gale; we therefore tacked, hoisted our colours, and stood in for the shore. On approaching the ice, we discovered them to be natives, drawn on rudely fashioned sledges, by dogs, which they continued to drive backwards and forwards with wonderful rapidity.

When we arrived within hail, Sacheuse called out to them, in his own language; some words were heard in return, to which a reply was again made in the Eskimaux, but neither party appeared to be in the least degree intelligible to the other. For some time they continued to regard us in silence, but, on the ship's tacking, they set up a simultaneous shout, accompanied with many strange gesticulations, and went off in their sledges with amazing velocity towards the land. After they had attained the distance of a mile or more, they halted for about two hours: as soon as this was observed, the ship was tacked, and a boat sent to place an observation-stool, of four feet in height, on the ice, on which various presents, consisting of knives and articles of clothing were left. Either, however, they did not see it, or it did not attract their attention, and a second boat was therefore sent, with directions to leave one of the Eskimaux dogs with some strings of blue beads around his neck, near the same place.

It being necessary to examine if there was a passage in this place, we took the opportunity of their absence to stand towards the head of the pool, which was about four miles off, trusting that, in the mean time, they would return to the same spot, to which it was also our intention to come back, after examining into the chances of a passage northwards. No opening was, however, found; and we therefore returned, after an absence of ten hours. The dog was found sleeping on the spot where we left him, the presents remaining untouched. A single sledge was shortly after observed at a great distance, but it immediately drove off with great rapidity.

Being extremely anxious to communicate with the natives, I caused a pole to be prepared, on which a flag was fixed with a representation of the sun and moon painted over a hand holding a sprig of heath (the only shrub seen on the shore). This pole being carried to an iceberg, midway between the ships and the shore, was there erected, and a bag containing presents, with a device of a hand pointing to a ship, painted on it, was fastened to the pole within reach, and left there; the ships, in the mean time, being moored in a convenient situation for observing what might take place.

The gale had now entirely subsided, the weather became beautiful, and the water calm; circumstances that necessarily detained us in our present situation, which, notwithstanding the imperious nature of our orders to proceed with all possible despatch, we should have been unwilling to leave, while any chance of a communication with a people, hitherto unknown, remained. Myriads of the little awks surrounded us, and afforded some sport, while they proved no less a treat to the people.

August 10. About ten o'clock this day, we were rejoiced to see eight sledges, driven by the natives, advancing by a circuitous route towards the place where we lay; they halted about a mile from us, and the people alighting, ascended a small iceberg, as if to reconnoitre. After remaining apparently in consultation for nearly half an hour, four of them descended, and came towards the flagstaff, which, however, they did not venture to approach. In the mean time a white flag was hoisted at the main in each ship, and John Sacheuse dispatched, bearing a small white flag, with some presents, that he might endeavour, if possible, to bring them to a parley. This was a service which he had most cheerfully volunteered, requesting leave to go unattended and unarmed. . . .

In executing this service, Sacheuse displayed no less address than courage. Having placed his flag at some distance from the canal, he advanced to the edge and, taking off his hat, made friendly signs for those opposite to approach, as he did; this they partly complied with, halting at a distance of 300 yards, where they got out of their sledges, and set up a loud simultaneous halloo, which Sacheuse answered by imitating it. . . . Shouts, words, and gestures were exchanged for some time to no purpose, though each party seemed, in some degree, to recognize each other's language. Sacheuse after a time thought he could discover that they spoke the Humooke dialect, drawling out their words, however, to an unusual length. He immediately adopted that dialect and, holding up the presents, called out to them, *Kahkeite*, 'Come on!' to which they answered, *Naakrie, naakrieaiplaite*, 'No, no—go away'; and other words which he made out to mean that they hoped we were not come to destroy them. The boldest then approached to the edge of the canal and, drawing from his boot a knife, repeated, 'Go away; I can kill you.' Sacheuse, not intimidated, told them he was also a man and a friend . . . They now began to ask many questions; for by this time they found the language spoken by themselves and Sacheuse had sufficient resemblance to enable them to hold some communication.

They first pointed to the ships, eagerly asking, 'What great creatures those were?' 'Do they come from the sun or the moon?' 'Do they give us light by night or by day?' Sacheuse told them that he was a man, that he had a father and mother like themselves; and, pointing to the south, said that he came from a distant country in that direction. To this they answered, 'That cannot be, there is nothing but ice there.' They again asked, 'What creatures these were?' pointing to the ships; to which Sacheuse replied, that 'they were houses made of wood'. This they seemed still to discredit, answering, 'No, they are alive, we have seen them move their wings.' Sacheuse now enquired of them what they themselves were; to which they replied, they were men, and lived in that direction, pointing to the north; that there was much water there; and that they had come here to fish for sea unicorns. It was then agreed that Sacheuse should pass the chasm to them, and he accordingly returned to the ship to make his report, and to ask for a plank. . . .

Sacheuse was directed to entice them to the ship, and two men were now sent with a plank, which was accordingly placed across the chasm.

They appeared still much alarmed, and requested that Sacheuse only should come over; he accordingly passed to the opposite side, on which they earnestly besought him not to touch them, as if he did, they should certainly die. After he had used many arguments to persuade them that he was flesh and blood, the native who had shown most courage ventured to touch his hand, then, pulling himself by the nose, set up a shout, in which he was joined by Sacheuse and the other three. The presents were then distributed, consisting of two or three articles of clothing, and a few strings of beads; after which Sacheuse exchanged a knife for one of theirs.

The hope of getting some important information, as well as the interest naturally felt for these poor creatures, made me impatient to communicate with them myself; and I therefore desired Lieutenant Parry to accompany me to the place where the party were assembled, it appearing to me that Sacheuse had failed in persuading them to come nearer the ships. We accordingly provided ourselves with additional presents, consisting of looking-glasses and knives, together with some caps and shirts, and proceeded towards the spot where the conference was held with increased energy. By the time we reached it the whole were assembled; those, who had originally been left at a distance with their sledges, having driven up to join their comrades. The party now, therefore, consisted of eight natives, with all their sledges, and about fifty dogs, two sailors, Sacheuse, Lieutenant Parry, and myself; forming a group of no small singularity; not a little also increased by the peculiarity of the situation, on a field of ice, far from the land. The noise and clamour may easily be conceived, the whole talking and shouting together, and the dogs howling, while the natives were flogging them with their long whips, to preserve order.

Our arrival produced a visible alarm, causing them to retreat a few steps towards their sledges; on this Sacheuse called to us to pull our noses, as he had discovered this to be the mode of friendly salutation with them. This ceremony was accordingly performed by each of us, the natives, during their retreat, making use of the same gesture, the nature of which we had not before understood. In the same way we imitated their shouts as well as we could, using the same interjection, *Heigh! yaw!* which we afterwards found to be an expression of surprise and pleasure. We then advanced towards them while they halted, and presented the foremost with a looking-glass and a knife, repeating the same presents to the whole, as they came up in succession. On seeing their faces in the glasses, their astonishment appeared extreme, and they looked round in silence, for a moment, at each other and at us; immediately afterwards they set up a general shout, succeeded by a loud laugh, expressive of extreme delight as well as surprise, in which we joined, partly from inability to avoid it, and willing also to show that we were pleased with our new acquaintances. . . .

As we were anxious to get them to the ship as soon as possible, I desired [Sacheuse] to persuade them to accompany us; they accordingly consented, on which their dogs were unharnessed and fastened to the ice, and two of the sledges were drawn along the plank to the other side of the chasm; three of the natives being left in charge of the dogs, and the remaining sledges; the other five followed us, laughing heartily at seeing Lieutenant Parry and myself drawn towards the ship, on the sledges, by our seamen. One of them, by keeping close to me, got before his companions, and thus we proceeded together till we arrived within a hundred yards of the ship, where he stopped. I attempted to urge him on, but in vain; his evident terror preventing him from advancing another step till his companions came up. It was apparent that he still believed the vessel to be a living creature, as he stopped to contemplate her, looking up at the masts, and examining every part with marks of the greatest fear and astonishment; he then addressed her, crying out in words perfectly intelligible to Sacheuse, and in a loud tone—'Who are you? what are you? where do you come from? is it from the sun or the moon?', pausing between every question, and pulling his nose with the utmost solemnity.

The rest now came up in succession, each showing similar surprise, and making use of the same expressions, accompanied by the same extra-ordinary ceremony. Sacheuse now laboured to assure them that the ship was only a wooden house, and pointed out the boat, which had been hauled on the ice to repair, explaining to them that it was a smaller one of the same kind. This immediately arrested their attention; they advanced to the boat, examined her, as well as the carpenters' tools and the oars, very minutely; each object, in its turn, exciting the most ludicrous ejaculations of surprise; we then ordered the boat to be launched into the sea, with a man in it, and hauled up again, at the sight of which they set no bounds to their clamour. The ice anchor, a heavy piece of iron, shaped like the letter S, and the cable excited much interest; the former they tried in vain to remove, and they eagerly enquired of what skins the latter was made.

By this time the officers of both ships had surrounded them, while the bow of the Isabella, which was close to the ice, was crowded with the crew; and certainly a more ludicrous yet interesting scene was never beheld than that which took place whilst they were viewing the ship; nor is it possible to convey to the imagination anything like a just representation of the wild amazement, joy, and fear, which successively pervaded the countenances and governed the gestures of these creatures, who gave full vent to their feelings; and, I am sure it was a gratifying scene, which never can be forgotten by those who witnessed and enjoyed it.

Their shouts, halloos, and laughter were heartily joined in and imitated by all hands, as well as the ceremony of nose pulling, which could not fail to increase our mirth on the occasion. . . . The most frequent ejaculation of surprise was *Heigh! yaw!* and, when particularly excited by any more remarkable object than the rest, they pronounced the first syllable of the interjection many times, with peculiar rapidity and emphasis, extending wide their arms, and looking at each other at the end of the exclamation, with open mouths, as if in breathless consternation.

Their knowledge of wood seemed to be limited to some heath of a dwarfish growth, with stems no thicker than the finger, and accordingly they knew not what to think of the timber they saw on board. Not being aware of its weight, two or three of them, successively, seized on the spare topmast, evidently with the view of carrying it off; and as soon as they became familiar with the people around them, they showed that desire of possessing what they admired which is so universal among savages. The only thing they looked on with contempt was a little terrier dog, judging, no doubt, that it was too small for drawing a sledge; but they shrunk back, as if in terror, from a pig, whose pricked ears and ferocious aspect, being of the Shetland breed, presented a somewhat formidable appearance. This animal happening to grunt, one of them was so terrified that he became from that moment uneasy, and appeared impatient to get out of the ship. In carrying his purpose into effect, however, he did not lose his propensity to thieving, as he seized and endeavoured to carry off the smith's anvil; finding that he could not remove it, he laid hold of the large hammer, threw it on the ice, and, following it himself, deliberately set it on his sledge, and made off. As this was an article I could not spare, I sent a person to recover it, who followed him, hallooing, and soon got pretty near him. Seeing that he must be overtaken, he artfully sunk it in the snow, and went on with the sledge, by which we were convinced that he knew he was doing wrong. The seaman, on finding the hammer, left off the pursuit, and returned, while he went off, and was seen no more that day.

2. THE CROKER MOUNTAINS

During this day much interest was excited on board by the appearance of this strait; the general opinion, however, was that it was only an inlet. Captain Sabine, who produced Baffin's account, was of opinion that we were off Lancaster Sound, and that there were no hopes of a passage until we should arrive at Cumberland Strait; to use his own words, there was 'no indication of a passage', 'no appearance of a current', 'no driftwood', and 'no swell from the north-west'. On the contrary, the land was partially seen extending across, the yellow sky was perceptible; and, as we advanced, the temperature of the water began to decrease. The mast-head and crow's-nest were crowded with those who were most anxious, but nothing was finally decided at the setting of the sun.

Soon after midnight the wind began to shift, and the ship came gradually up, enabling us to stand directly up the bay: I, therefore, made all sail, and left the *Alexander* considerably astern. At a little before four o'clock a.m., the land was seen at the bottom of the inlet by the officers of the watch; but before I got upon deck, a space of about seven degrees of the compass was obscured by the fog. The land which I then saw was a high ridge of mountains, extending directly across the bottom of the inlet. This chain appeared extremely high in the centre, and those towards the north had, at times, the appearance of islands, being insulated by the fog at their bases. Although a passage in this direction appeared hopeless, I was deter-mined completely to explore it, as the wind was favourable; and, therefore, continued all sail. . . .

At three, the officer of the watch, who was relieved to his dinner by Mr Lewis, reported, on his coming into the cabin, that there was some appear-ance of its clearing at the bottom of the bay; I immediately, therefore, went on deck, and soon after it completely cleared for about ten minutes, and I distinctly saw the land, round the bottom of the bay, forming a connected chain of mountains with those which extended along the north and south sides. . . . The mountains, which occupied the centre, in a north and south direction, were named Croker's Mountains, after the Secretary to the Admiralty.

✳

SIR WILLIAM PARRY

(1790–1855)

British explorer. He searched for the North-West Passage on three expedi-tions, the first in 1819, when he found the entrance.

Journal of a Voyage for the Discovery of a North West Passage (London, 1821).

1. EXCITEMENT AND A BOUNTY OF £5,000 (1819)

At a quarter past nine p.m., we had the satisfaction of crossing the meridian of 110° west from Greenwich, in the latitude of 74°44′ 20″; by which His Majesty's ships, under my orders, became entitled to the sum of five thousand pounds, being the reward offered by the King's order in council, grounded on a late Act of Parliament, to such of His Majesty's subjects as might succeed in penetrating thus far to the westward within the Arctic Circle. In order to commemorate the success which had hitherto attended our exertions, the bluff headland, which we had just passed, was subsequently called by the men Bounty Cape, by which name I have, therefore, distinguished it on the chart.

As we stood to the westward, we found the extreme of the land in that direction to be a low point, which was named after Samuel Hearne, the well-known American traveller, and to the north-eastward of which is a bay of considerable extent, which was perfectly free from ice. We continued our course towards Cape Hearne till midnight, when the weather being too dark to run any longer with safety, the ships were hove to with their heads to the eastward. One black whale was seen, in the course of this day's navigation, off Bridport Inlet; and some flocks of snow-buntings were flying about the ship at night.

2. ENTERTAINMENTS WHEN FORCED TO OVERWINTER

Under circumstances of leisure and inactivity, such as we were now placed in, and with every prospect of its continuance for a very large portion of the year, I was desirous of finding some amusement for the men during this long and tedious interval. I proposed, therefore, to the officers to get up a play occasionally on board the *Hecla*, as the readiest means of preserving among our crews that cheerfulness and good humour which had hitherto subsisted. In this proposal I was readily seconded by the officers of both ships; and Lieutenant Beechey having been duly elected as stage manager, our first performance was fixed for the 5th of November, to the great delight of the ships' companies. In these amusements I gladly undertook a part myself, considering that an example of cheerfulness, by giving a direct countenance to everything that could contribute to it, was not the least essential part of my duty, under the peculiar circumstances in which we were placed.

In order still further to promote good humour among ourselves, as well as to furnish amusing occupation, during the hours of constant darkness we set on foot a weekly newspaper, which was to be called the *North Georgia*

Gazette and Winter Chronicle, and of which Captain Sabine undertook to be the editor, under the promise that it was to be supported by original contributions from the officers of the two ships: and, though some objection may, perhaps, be raised against a paper of this kind being generally resorted to in ships of war, I was too well acquainted with the discretion, as well as the excellent dispositions, of my officers to apprehend any unpleasant consequences from a measure of this kind.

SIR JOHN FRANKLIN
(1786–1847)

English explorer. He died searching for the North-West Passage, and became a hero as over forty expeditions set out to look for him. On an earlier expedition starting in 1819, he and his men made one of the most punishing survival marches recorded.

Narrative of a Journey to the Shores of the Polar Sea... (London, 1823).

1. THE MARCH TO FORT ENTERPRISE (1821)

The morning of the 7th [September] cleared up a little, but the wind was still strong, and the weather extremely cold. From the unusual continuance of the storm, we feared the winter had set in with all its rigour, and that by longer delay we should only be exposed to an accumulation of difficulties; we therefore prepared for our journey, although we were in a very unfit condition for starting, being weak from fasting, and our garments stiffened by the frost. We had no means of making a fire to thaw them, the moss, at all times difficult to kindle, being now covered with ice and snow. A considerable time was consumed in packing up the frozen tents and bedclothes, the wind blowing so strong that no one could keep his hands long out of his mittens.

Just as we were about to commence our march, I was seized with a fainting fit, in consequence of exhaustion and sudden exposure to the wind; but after eating a morsel of portable soup, I recovered, so far as to be able to move on. . . .

We supped off a single partridge and some *tripe de roche*; this unpalatable weed was now quite nauseous to the whole party, and in several it produced bowel complaints. Mr Hood was the greatest sufferer from this cause. This evening we were extremely distressed at discovering that our improvident companions, since we left Hood's River, had thrown away three of the fishing-nets, and burnt the floats; they knew we had brought them to procure subsistence for the party, when the animals should fail, and we could scarcely believe the fact of their having wilfully deprived themselves of this resource, especially when we considered that most of them had passed the greater part of their servitude in situations where the nets alone had supplied them with food. Being thus deprived of our principal resource, that of fishing, and the men evidently getting weaker every day, it became necessary to lighten their burdens of everything except ammunition, clothing, and the instruments that were required to find our way. I, therefore, issued directions to deposit at this encampment the dipping needle, azimuth compass, magnet, a large thermometer, and a few books we had carried, having torn out of these such parts as we should require to work the observations for latitude and longitude. . . .

September 14. This morning, the officers being assembled round a small fire, Perrault presented each of us with a small piece of meat which he had saved from his allowance. It was received with great thankfulness, and such an act of self-denial and kindness, being totally unexpected in a Canadian voyager, filled our eyes with tears. In directing our course to a river issuing from the lake, we met Crédit, who communicated the joyful intelligence of his having killed two deer in the morning. We instantly halted, and having shared the deer that was nearest to us, prepared breakfast. After which, the other deer was sent for, and we went down to the river, which was about three hundred yards wide, and flowed with great velocity through a broken rocky channel.

Having searched for a part where the current was most smooth, the canoe was placed in the water at the head of a rapid, and St Germain, Solomon Belanger, and I embarked in order to cross. We went from the shore very well, but in mid-channel the canoe became difficult to manage under our burden as the breeze was fresh. The current drove us to the edge of the rapid, when Belanger unluckily applied his paddle to avert the apparent danger of being forced down it, and lost his balance. The canoe was overset in consequence in the middle of the rapid. We fortunately kept hold of it until we touched a rock where the water did not reach higher than our waists; here we kept our footing, notwithstanding the strength of the current, until the water was emptied out of the canoe. Belanger then held the canoe steady whilst St Germain placed me in it, and afterwards embarked himself in a very dexterous manner. It was impossible, however, to embark Belanger, as the canoe would have been hurried down the rapid, the moment he should have raised his foot from the rock on which he stood. We were, therefore, compelled to leave him in his perilous situation. We had not gone twenty yards before the canoe, striking on a sunken rock, went down. The place being shallow, we were again enabled to empty it, and the third attempt brought us to the shore.

In the mean time Belanger was suffering extremely, immersed to his middle in the centre of a rapid, the temperature of which was very little above the freezing point, and the upper part of his body covered with wet clothes, exposed in a temperature not much above zero, to a strong breeze. He called piteously for relief, and St Germain on his return endeavoured to embark him, but in vain. The canoe was hurried down the rapid, and when he landed he was rendered by the cold incapable of further exertion, and Adam attempted to embark Belanger, but found it impossible. An attempt was next made to carry out to him a line, made of the slings of the men's loads. This also failed, the current acting so strongly upon it as to prevent the canoe from steering, and it was finally broken and carried down the stream. At length, when Belanger's strength seemed almost exhausted, the canoe reached him with a small cord belonging to one of the nets, and he was dragged perfectly senseless through the rapid. By the direction of Dr Richardson, he was instantly stripped, and being rolled up in blankets, two men undressed themselves and went to bed with him: but it was some hours before he recovered his warmth and sensations. . . .

By this accident I had the misfortune to lose my portfolio, containing my journal from Fort Enterprise, together with all the astronomical and meteorological observations made during the descent of the Copper-Mine River, and along the sea-coast (except those for the dip and variation.) I was in the habit of carrying it strapped across my shoulders, but had taken it off on entering the canoe, to reduce the upper weight. The results of most of the observations for latitude and longitude had been registered in the sketch-books, so that we preserved the requisites for the construction of the chart. The meteorological observations, not having been copied, were lost. My companions, Dr Richardson, Mr Back, and Mr Hood, had been so careful in noting every occurrence in their journals that the loss of mine could fortunately be well supplied. . . .

On the morning of the 1st of October, the wind was strong, and the weather as unfavourable as before for crossing on the raft. We were rejoiced to see Mr Back and his party in the afternoon. They had traced the lake about fifteen miles further than we did, and found it undoubtedly connected, as we had supposed, with the lake we fell in with on the 22nd of September; and dreading, as we had done, the idea of coasting its barren shores, they returned to make an attempt at crossing here. St Germain now proposed to make a canoe of the fragments of painted canvas in which we wrapped our bedding. This scheme appearing practicable, a party was sent to our encampment of the 24th and 25th last, to collect pitch amongst the small pines that grew there, to pay over the seams of the canoe.

In the afternoon we had a heavy fall of snow, which continued all night. A small quantity of *tripe de roche* was gathered; and Crédit, who had been hunting, brought in the antlers and backbone of a deer which had been killed in the summer. The wolves and birds of prey had picked them clean, but there still remained a quantity of the spinal marrow which they had not been able to extract. This, although putrid, was esteemed a valuable prize, and the spine being divided into portions, was distributed equally. After eating the marrow, which was so acrid as to excoriate the lips, we rendered the bones friable by burning, and ate them also.

On the following morning the ground was covered with snow to the depth of a foot and a half, and the weather was very stormy. These circumstances rendered the men again extremely despondent: a settled gloom hung over their countenances, and they refused to pick *tripe de roche*, choosing rather to go entirely without eating than to make any exertion. The party which went for gum returned early in the morning without having found any; but St Germain said he could still make the canoe with the willows, covered with canvas, and removed with Adam to a clump of willows for that purpose. Mr Back accompanied them to stimulate his exertion, as we feared the lowness of his spirits would cause him to be slow in his operations. Augustus went to fish at the rapid, but a large trout having carried away his bait, we had nothing to replace it. . . .

The sensation of hunger was no longer felt by any of us, yet we were scarcely able to converse upon any other subject than the pleasures of eating. We were much indebted to Hepburn at this crisis. The officers were unable from weakness to gather *tripe de roche* themselves, and Samandre, who had acted as our cook on the journey from the coast, sharing in the despair of the rest of the Canadians, refused to make the slightest exertion. Hepburn, on the contrary, animated by a firm reliance on the beneficence of the Supreme Being, tempered with resignation to his will, was indefatigable in his exertions to serve us, and daily collected all the *tripe de roche* that was used in the officers' mess. Mr Hood could not partake of this miserable fare, and a partridge which had been reserved for him was, I lament to say, this day stolen by one of the men. . . .

Descending afterwards into a more level country, we found the snow very deep, and the labour of wading through it so fatigued the whole party that we were compelled to encamp, after a march of four miles and a half. Belanger and Michel were left far behind, and when they arrived at the encampment appeared quite exhausted. The former, bursting into tears, declared his inability to proceed, and begged me to let him go back next morning to the tent, and shortly afterwards Michel made the same request. I was in hopes they might recover a little strength by the night's rest, and therefore deferred giving any permission *until* morning. The sudden failure in the strength of these men cast a gloom over the rest, which I tried in vain to remove, by repeated assurances that the distance to Fort Enterprise was short, and that we should, in all probability, reach it in four days. Not being able to find any *tripe de roche*, we drank an infusion of the Labrador tea plant (*ledum palustre*), and ate a few morsels of burnt leather for supper. We were unable to raise the tent, and found its weight too great to carry it on; we therefore cut it up, and took a part of the canvas for a cover. The night was bitterly cold, and though we lay as close to each other as possible, having no shelter, we could not keep ourselves sufficiently warm to sleep. . . .

At length we reached Fort Enterprise, and to our infinite disappointment and grief found it a perfectly desolate habitation. There was no deposit of provision, no trace of the Indians, no letter from Mr Wentzel to point out where the Indians might be found. It would be impossible to describe our sensations after entering this miserable abode, and discovering how we had been neglected: the whole party shed tears, not so much for our own fate, as for that of our friends in the rear, whose lives depended entirely on our sending immediate relief from this place. . . .

On the 13th . . . Belanger . . . came in almost speechless, and covered with ice, having fallen into a rapid, and, for the third time since we left the coast, narrowly escaped drowning. He did not recover sufficiently to answer our questions, until we had rubbed him for some time, changed his dress, and given him some warm soup. My companions nursed him with the greatest kindness, and the desire of restoring him to health seemed to absorb all regard for their own situation. I witnessed with peculiar pleasure this conduct so different from that which they had recently pursued, when every tender feeling was suspended by the desire of self-preservation. They now no longer betrayed impatience or despondency, but were composed and cheerful, and had entirely given up the practice of swearing to which the Canadian voyagers are so addicted.

2. Rescued by Indians

The doctor and Hepburn were almost exhausted. The cutting of one log of wood occupied the latter half an hour; and the other took as much time to drag it into the house, though the distance did not exceed thirty yards. I endeavoured to help the doctor, but my assistance was very trifling. Yet it was evident that, in a day or two, if their strength should continue to decline at the same rate, I should be the strongest of the party.

I may here remark that, owing to our loss of flesh, the hardness of the floor, from which we were only protected by a blanket, produced soreness over the body, and especially those parts on which the weight rested in lying, yet to turn ourselves for relief was a matter of toil and difficulty. However, during this period, and indeed all along, after the acute pains of hunger, which lasted but three or four days, had subsided, we generally enjoyed the comfort of a few hours' sleep. The dreams which for the most part, but not always, accompanied it, were usually (though not invariably) of a pleasant character, being very often about the enjoyments of feasting. In the day-time we fell into the practice of conversing on common and light subjects, although we sometimes discussed with seriousness and earnestness topics connected with religion. We generally avoided speaking directly of our present sufferings, or even of the prospect of relief. I observed, that in proportion as our strength decayed, our minds exhibited symptoms of weakness, evinced by a kind of unreasonable pettishness with each other. Each of us thought the other weaker in intellect than himself, and more in need of advice and assistance. So trifling a circumstance as a change of place, recommended by one as being warmer and more comfortable, and refused by the other from a dread of motion, frequently called forth fretful expressions which were no sooner uttered than atoned for, to be repeated perhaps in the course of a few minutes. The same thing often occurred when we endeavoured to assist each other in carrying wood to the fire; none of us were willing to receive assistance, although the task was disproportioned to our strength. On one of these occasions, Hepburn was so convinced of this waywardness that he exclaimed, 'Dear me, if we are spared to return to England, I wonder if we shall recover our understandings.'

November 7. Adam had passed a restless night, being disquieted by gloomy apprehensions of approaching death, which we tried in vain to dispel. He was so low in the morning as to be scarcely able to speak. I remained in bed by his side, to cheer him as much as possible. The doctor and Hepburn went to cut wood. They had hardly begun their labour when they were amazed at hearing the report of a musket. They could scarcely believe that there was really anyone near, until they heard a shout, and immediately espied three Indians close to the house. Adam and I heard the latter noise, and I was fearful that a part of the house had fallen upon one of my companions, a disaster which had in fact been thought not unlikely. My alarm was only momentary; Dr Richardson came in to communicate the joyful intelligence that relief had arrived.

SIR JAMES CLARK ROSS

(1800–1862)

British naval officer and explorer. The nephew of John Ross, with whom he travelled on both his expeditions, as well as with Sir William Parry in the interval. Later, from 1839 to 1843, he commanded the Royal Navy's first major Antarctic expedition.

Narrative of a Second Voyage in Search of a North West Passage . . . including the reports of Capt. J. C. Ross and the Discovery of the Northern Magnetic Pole (London, 1835).

1. A MISUNDERSTANDING WITH ESKIMOS (1831)

We departed accordingly, early in the morning of the 27th of April, and approaching the huts were exceedingly disappointed at not hearing the cheerful shouts with which we had been usually greeted. That was succeeded by a very disagreeable surprise, on finding that the women and children had been all sent out of the way, since we knew this to be a signal of war; a fact of which we were speedily convinced by seeing that all the men were armed with their knives. The fierce and sullen looks of these people also boded mischief: but what the cause of all this could be it was quite impossible to conjecture.

We could see them better than they could distinguish us, as the sun was in their faces; it was the noise of our dogs which gave them notice of our arrival and proximity; and as soon as this was heard, one of them rushed out of a hut, brandishing the large knife used in attacking bears, while the tears were streaming down his aged and furrowed face, which was turning wildly round in search of the objects of his animosity. In an instant he lifted his arm to throw his weapon at myself and the surgeon, who were then within a few yards of him, having advanced in order to ascertain the cause of all this commotion. But the sun, dazzling him, caused him to suspend his arm for an instant; when one of his sons laid hold of his uplifted hand, and gave us a moment's time for reflection.

The result of that was, of course, an immediate preparation for defence; though we could have done little against such odds as our unexpected enemies displayed. We therefore retired to the sledge, where I had left my gun; and not daring again to quit it, as Mr Abernethy had no arms, waited for the result, while losing ourselves in vain conjectures respecting the cause of offence, seeing that we had parted good friends on the preceding day.

The ferocious old man Pow-weet-yah was still held fast, and now by both his sons, who had pinioned his arms behind him, though he strove hard to disengage himself; while the rest of the party seemed to be standing in readiness to second any attempt which he might make on us. That there was some difference of opinion among them, however, and that all were not equally hostile, was plain from the conduct of these young men; so that we could still hope for some parley before matters came to extremity. . . . But as I could not induce any of them to approach, or to answer my questions, we continued for nearly half an hour in this state of suspense and perplexity, when we were relieved by the courage or confidence of one of the women, who came out of a hut just as I was again raising my gun, and called to me not to fire, advancing up to our party immediately, without showing the least mark of fear.

From her, we soon learned the cause of all this hubbub, which, absurd as it was, might have had a fatal termination, as we should probably have been the chief sufferers. One of Pow-weet-yah's adopted sons, a fine boy of seven or eight years of age, whom we knew, had been killed on the preceding night by the falling of a stone on his head. This they had ascribed to our agency, through the supernatural powers which we were believed to possess; while the father, not very unnaturally under this conviction, had meditated revenge in the manner which we had experienced.

I had much difficulty in persuading the good woman that we were totally ignorant of this catastrophe, and that we were very sorry for the misfortune; she, however, repeated all that I had said to two of the men who had not taken any share in the business of the attack, and who now approached us unarmed, in token of peace.

2. ARRIVAL AT THE NORTH MAGNETIC POLE

We were now within fourteen miles of the calculated position of the magnetic pole; and my anxiety, therefore, did not permit me to do or endure anything which might delay my arrival at the long wished-for spot. I resolved, in consequence, to leave behind the greater part of our baggage and provisions, and to take onwards nothing more than was strictly necessary, lest bad weather or other accidents should be added to delay, or lest unforeseen circumstances, still more untoward, should deprive me entirely of the high gratification which I could not but look to in accomplishing this most desired object.

We commenced, therefore, a rapid march, comparatively disencumbered as we now were; and, persevering with all our might, we reached the calculated place at eight in the morning of the first of June. I believe I must leave it to others to imagine the elation of mind with which we found ourselves now at length arrived at this great object of our ambition: it almost seemed as if we had accomplished everything that we had come so far to see and to do; as if our voyage and all its labours were at an end, and that nothing now remained for us but to return home and be happy for the rest of our days. They were after-thoughts which told us that we had much yet to endure and much to perform, and they were thoughts which did not then intrude. Could they have done so, we should have cast them aside, under our present excitement: we were happy, and desired to remain so as long as we could.

The land at this place is very low near the coast, but it rises into ridges of fifty or sixty feet high about a mile inland. We could have wished that a place so important had possessed more of mark or note. It was scarcely censurable to regret that there was not a mountain to indicate a spot to which so much of interest must ever be attached; and I could even have pardoned anyone among us who had been so romantic or absurd as to expect that the magnetic pole was an object as conspicuous and mysterious as the fabled mountain of Sinbad, that it even was a mountain of iron, or a magnet as large as Mont Blanc. But Nature had here erected no monument to denote the spot which she had chosen as the centre of one of her great and dark powers; and where we could do little ourselves towards this end, it was our business to submit, and to be content in noting by mathematical numbers and signs, as with things of far more importance in the terrestrial system, what we could but ill distinguish in any other manner.

We were, however, fortunate in here finding some huts of Esquimaux, that had not long been abandoned.

✿

JOHN CHARLES FREMONT

(1813–1890)

American explorer and politician. With Kit Carson as his guide, he made two major expeditions into the remaining unknown interior of North America, in 1842 and 1843/4. In 1856 he stood for the presidency as a Republican.

The Life of Col. John Charles Fremont and His Narrative of Explorations and Adventures, in Kansas, Nebraska, Oregon and California (New York, 1856).

PLANTING THE AMERICAN FLAG UPON THE SUMMIT OF
THE ROCKY MOUNTAINS (1842)

12th [August]. Early in the morning we left the camp, fifteen in number, well armed, of course, and mounted on our best mules. A pack-animal carried our provisions, with a coffee-pot and kettle, and three or four tin cups. Every man had a blanket strapped over his saddle, to serve for his bed, and the instruments were carried by turns on their backs. We entered directly on rough and rocky ground; and, just after crossing the ridge, had the good fortune to shoot an antelope. We heard the roar, and had a glimpse of a waterfall as we rode along, and, crossing in our way two fine streams, tributary to the Colorado, in about two hours' ride we reached the top of the first row or range of the mountains. Here, again, a view of the most romantic beauty met our eyes. It seemed as if, from the vast expanse of uninteresting prairie we had passed over, Nature had collected all her beauties together in one chosen place. We were overlooking a deep valley, which was entirely occupied by three lakes, and from the brink to the surrounding ridges rose precipitously five hundred and a thousand feet, covered with the dark green of the balsam pine, relieved on the border of the lake with the light foliage of the aspen. They all communicated with each other, and the green of the waters, common to mountain lakes of great depth, showed that it would be impossible to cross them. The surprise manifested by our guides when these impassable obstacles suddenly barred our progress proved that they were among the hidden treasures of the place, unknown even to the wandering trappers of the region. Descending the hill, we proceeded to make our way along the margin to the southern extremity. A narrow strip of angular fragments of rock sometimes afforded a rough pathway for our mules, but generally we rode along the shelving side, occasionally scrambling up, at a considerable risk of tumbling back into the lake. . . .

The hills on this southern end were low, and the lake looked like a mimic sea, as the waves broke on the sandy beach in the force of a strong breeze. There was a pretty open spot, with fine grass for our mules; and we made our noon halt on the beach, under the shade of some large hemlocks. We resumed our journey after a halt of about an hour, making our way up the ridge on the western side of the lake. In search of smoother ground, we rode a little inland; and, passing through groves of aspen, soon found ourselves again among the pines. Emerging from these, we struck the summit of the ridge above the upper end of the lake.

We had reached a very elevated point, and in the valley below, and among the hills, were a number of lakes of different levels; some two or three hundred feet above others, with which they communicated by foaming torrents. Even to our great height the roar of the cataracts came up, and we could see them leaping down in lines of snowy foam. From this scene of busy waters, we turned abruptly into the stillness of a forest . . . Towards evening we reached a defile, or rather a hole in the mountains, entirely shut in by dark, pine-covered rocks.

A small stream, with scarcely perceptible current, flowed through a level bottom of perhaps eighty yards width, where the grass was saturated with water. Into this the mules were turned, and were neither hobbled nor picketed during the night, as the fine pasturage took away all temptation to stray; and we made our bivouac in the pines. The surrounding masses were all of granite. While supper was being prepared, I set out on an excursion in the neighbourhood, accompanied by one of my men. We wandered about among the crags and ravines until dark, richly repaid for our walk by a fine collection of plants, many of them in full bloom. Ascending a peak to find the place of our camp, we saw that the little defile in which we lay, communicated with the long green valley of some stream, which, here locked up in the mountains, far away to the south, found its way in a dense forest to the plains.

Looking along its upward course, it seemed to conduct, by a smooth gradual slope, directly towards the peak, which, from long consultation as we approached the mountain, we had decided to be the highest of the range. Pleased with the discovery of so fine a road for the next day, we hastened down to the camp, where we arrived just in time for supper. Our table-service was rather scant; and we held the meat in our hands, and clean rocks made good plates, on which we spread our macaroni. Among all the strange places on which we had occasion to encamp during our long journey, none have left so vivid an impression on my mind as the camp of this evening. The disorder of the masses which surrounded us—the little hole through which we saw the stars overhead—the dark pines where we slept—and the rocks lit up with the glow of our fires, made a night-picture of very wild beauty.

13th. The morning was bright and pleasant, just cool enough to make exercise agreeable, and we soon entered the defile I had seen the preceding day. . . . This road continued for about three miles, when we suddenly reached its termination in one of the grand views which, at every turn, meet the traveller in this magnificent region. Here the defile up which we had travelled opened out into a small lawn, where, in a little lake, the stream had its source. . . . I determined to leave our animals here, and make the rest of our way on foot. The peak appeared so near that there was no doubt of our returning before night; and a few men were left in charge of the mules, with our provisions and blankets. We took with us nothing but our arms and instruments, and, as the day had become warm, the greater part left our coats.

Having made an early dinner, we started again. We were soon involved in the most ragged precipices, nearing the central chain very slowly, and rising but little. The first ridge hid a succession of others; and when, with great fatigue and difficulty, we had climbed up five hundred feet, it was but to make an equal descent on the other side; all these intervening places were filled with small deep lakes, which met the eye in every direction, descending from one level to another, sometimes under bridges formed by huge fragments of granite, beneath which was heard the roar of the water. These constantly obstructed our path, forcing us to make long detours, frequently obliged to retrace our steps, and frequently falling among the rocks. Maxwell was precipitated towards the face of a precipice, and saved himself from going over by throwing himself flat on the ground. We clambered on, always expecting, with every ridge that we crossed, to reach the foot of the peaks, and always disappointed, until about four o'clock, when, pretty well worn out, we reached the shore of a little lake, in which was a rocky island. We remained here a short time to rest, and continued on around the lake, which had in some places a beach of white sand, and in others was bound with rocks, over which the way was difficult and dangerous, as the water from innumerable springs made them very slippery.

By the time we had reached the further side of the lake, we found ourselves all exceedingly fatigued, and, much to the satisfaction of the whole party, we encamped. . . . We had nothing to eat to-night. Lajeunesse, with several others, took their guns and sallied out in search of a goat, but returned unsuccessful. At sunset, the barometer stood at 20.522; the attached thermometer 50°. Here we had the misfortune to break our thermometer, having now only that attached to the barometer. I was taken ill shortly after we had encamped, and continued so until late in the night, with violent headache and vomiting. This was probably caused by the excessive fatigue I had undergone, and want of food, and perhaps also, in some measure, by the rarity of the air. The night was cold, as a violent gale from the north had sprung up at sunset, which entirely blew away the heat of the fires. The cold, and our granite beds, had not been favorable to sleep, and we were glad to see the face of the sun in the morning. Not being delayed by any preparation for breakfast, we set out immediately.

On every side, as we advanced, was heard the roar of waters, and of a torrent, which we followed up a short distance, until it expanded into a lake about one mile in length. On the northern side of the lake was a bank of ice, or rather of snow covered with a crust of ice. Carson had been our guide into the mountains, and, agreeably to his advice, we left this little valley, and took to the ridges again, which we found extremely broken, and where we were again involved among precipices. Here were ice-fields; among which we were all dispersed, seeking each the best path to ascend the peak. Mr Preuss attempted to walk along the upper edge of one of these fields, which sloped away at an angle of about twenty degrees; but his feet slipped from under him, and he went plunging down the plain. A few hundred feet below, at the bottom, were some fragments of sharp rock, on which he landed and, though he turned a couple of somersets, fortunately received no injury beyond a few bruises. Two of the men, Clement Lambert and Descoteaux, had been taken ill, and lay down on the rocks, a short distance below; and at this point I was attacked with headache and giddiness, accompanied by vomiting, as on the day before. Finding myself unable to proceed, I sent the barometer over to Mr Preuss, who was in a gap two or three hundred yards distant, desiring him to reach the peak if possible, and take an observation there. He found himself unable to proceed further in that direction . . . Carson, who had gone over to him, succeeded in reaching one of the snowy summits of the main ridge, whence he saw the peak towards which all our efforts had been directed, towering eight or ten hundred feet into the air above him. In the mean time, finding myself grow rather worse than better, and doubtful how far my strength would carry me, I sent Basil Lajeunesse, with four men, back to the place where the mules had been left.

We were now better acquainted with the topography of the country, and I directed him to bring back with him, if it were in any way possible, four or five mules, with provisions and blankets. With me were Maxwell and Ayer; and after we had remained nearly an hour on the rock, it became so unpleasantly cold, though the day was bright, that we set out on our return to the camp, at which we all arrived safely, straggling in one after the other. I continued ill during the afternoon, but became better towards sundown, when my recovery was completed by the appearance of Basil and four men, all mounted. The men who had gone with him had been too much fatigued to return, and were relieved by those in charge of the horses; but in his powers of endurance Basil resembled more a mountain-goat than a man. They brought blankets and provisions, and we enjoyed well our dried meat and a cup of good coffee. We rolled ourselves up in our blankets, and, with our feet turned to a blazing fire, slept soundly until morning.

15th. . . . When we had secured strength for the day by a hearty breakfast, we covered what remained, which was enough for one meal, with rocks, in order that it might be safe from any marauding bird, and, saddling our mules, turned our faces once more towards the peaks. This time we determined to proceed quietly and cautiously, deliberately resolved to accomplish our object if it were within the compass of human means. We were of opinion that a long defile which lay to the left of yesterday's route would lead us to the foot of the main peak. Our mules had been refreshed by the fine grass in the little ravine at the Island camp, and we intended to ride up the defile as far as possible, in order to husband our strength for the main ascent. . . .

We managed to get our mules up to a little bench about a hundred feet above the lakes, where there was a patch of good grass, and turned them loose to graze. During our rough ride to this place, they had exhibited a wonderful surefootedness. Parts of the defile were filled with angular, sharp fragments of rock, three or four and eight or ten feet cube; and among these they had worked their way, leaping from one narrow point to another, rarely making a false step, and giving us no occasion to dismount. Having divested ourselves of every unnecessary encumbrance, we commenced the ascent. This time, like experienced travellers, we did not press ourselves, but climbed leisurely, sitting down as soon as we found breath beginning to fail. At intervals we reached places where a number of springs gushed from the rocks, and about 1,800 feet above the lakes came to the snow line. From this point our progress was uninterrupted climbing. Hitherto I had worn a pair of thick moccasins, with soles of *parflèche*, but here I put on a light, thin pair, which I had brought for the purpose, as now the use of our toes became necessary to a further advance. I availed myself of a sort of comb of the mountain, which stood against the wall like a buttress, and which the wind and the solar radiation, joined to the steepness of the smooth rock, had kept almost entirely free from snow. Up this I made my way rapidly. Our cautious method of advancing at the outset had spared my strength; and, with the exception of a slight disposition to headache, I felt no remains of yesterday's illness. In a few minutes we reached a point where the buttress was overhanging, and there was no other way of surmounting the difficulty than by passing around one side of it, which was the face of a vertical precipice of several hundred feet.

Putting hands and feet in the crevices between the blocks, I succeeded in getting over it, and, when I reached the top, found my companions in a small valley below. Descending to them, we continued climbing, and in a short time reached to the crest. I sprang upon the summit, and another step would have precipitated me into an immense snow-field five hundred feet below. To the edge of this field was a sheer icy precipice; and then, with a gradual fall, the field sloped off for about a mile, until it struck the foot of another lower ridge. I stood on a narrow crest, about three feet in width . . . As soon as I had gratified the first feelings of curiosity, I descended, and each man ascended in his turn; for I would only allow one at a time to mount the unstable and precarious slab, which it seemed a breath would hurl into the abyss below. We mounted the barometer in the snow of the summit, and fixing a ramrod in a crevice, unfurled the national flag to wave in the breeze where never flag waved before. During our morning's ascent, we had met no sign of animal life, except the small sparrow-like bird . . . A stillness the most profound and a terrible solitude forced themselves constantly on the mind as the great features of the place. Here, on the summit, where the stillness was absolute, unbroken by any sound, and solitude complete, we thought ourselves beyond the region of animated life; but while we were sitting on the rock, a solitary bee came winging his flight from the eastern valley, and lit on the knee of one of the men.

It was a strange place, the icy rock and the highest peak of the Rocky mountains, for a lover of warm sunshine and flowers; and we pleased ourselves with the idea that he was the first of his species to cross the mountain barrier—a solitary pioneer to foretell the advance of civilization. I believe that a moment's thought would have made us let him continue his way unharmed; but we carried out the law of this country, where all animated nature seems at war; and, seizing him immediately, put him in at least a fit place—in the leaves of a large book, among the flowers we had collected on our way. The barometer stood at 18.293, the attached thermometer at 44°; giving for the elevation of this summit 13,570 feet above the Gulf of Mexico, which may be called the highest flight of the bee. It is certainly the highest known flight of that insect. From the description given by Mackenzie of the mountains where he crossed them, with that of a French officer still further to the north, and Colonel Long's measurements to the south, joined to the opinion of the oldest traders of the country, it is presumed that this is the highest peak of the Rocky mountains.

JOHN RAE

(1813–1893)

Scottish surgeon, fur trader, and explorer. During a survey of the Arctic coast he stumbled on the first evidence of the fate of Franklin's expedition. This did not stop further searches.

The Discovery of a North-West Passage by HMS 'Investigator', ed. S. Osborn (London, 1865).

THE LAST SIGHT OF FRANKLIN BY ESKIMOS (1854)

On the morning of the 20th (April) we were met by a very intelligent Esquimaux, driving a dog-sledge laden with musk-ox beef. This man at once consented to accompany us two days' journey, and in a few minutes had deposited his load on the snow, and was ready to join us. Having explained to him my object, he said that the road by which he had come was the best for us; and having lightened the sledges, we travelled with more facility. We were now joined by another of the natives, who had been absent seal-hunting yesterday, but, being anxious to see us, had visited our snow-house early this morning, and then followed up our track. This man was very communicative; and on putting to him the usual questions as to his having seen 'white men' before, or any ships or boats, he replied in the negative, but said that a party of 'Kabloonans' had died of starvation a long distance to the west of where we then were, and beyond a large river. He stated that he did not know the exact place, that he never had been there, and that he could not accompany us so far. The substance of the information then and subsequently obtained from various sources was to the following effect.

In the spring, four winters since (1850), while some Esquimaux families were killing seals near the north shore of a large island, named in Arrowsmith's charts King William Land, about forty white men were seen travelling in company southward over the ice, and dragging a boat and sledges with them. They were passing along the west shore of the above-named island. None of the party could speak the Esquimaux language so well as to be understood; but by signs the natives were led to believe that the ship or ships had been crushed by ice, and that they were now going to where they expected to find deer to shoot. From the appearance of the men, all of whom, with the exception of an officer, were hauling on the drag-ropes of the sledge, and looked thin, they were then supposed to be getting short of provisions; and they purchased a small seal, or piece of seal, from the natives. The officer was described as being a tall, stout, middle-aged man. When their day's journey terminated, they pitched tents to rest in.

At a later date the same season, but previous to the disruption of the ice, the corpses of some thirty persons, and some graves, were discovered on the continent, and five dead bodies on an island near it, about a long day's journey to the NW of the mouth of a large stream, which can be no other than Back's Great Fish River (named by the Esquimaux Oot-koo-hi-ca-lik), as its description and that of the low shore in the neighbourhood of Point Ogle and Montreal Island agree exactly with that of Sir George Back. Some of the bodies were in a tent, or tents; others were under the boat, which had been turned over to form a shelter, and some lay scattered about in different directions. Of those seen on the island, it was supposed that one was that of an officer (chief), as he had a telescope strapped over his shoulders, and a double-barrelled gun lay underneath him.

From the mutilated state of many of the bodies, and the contents of the kettles, it is evident that our wretched countrymen had been driven to the dread alternative of cannibalism as a means of sustaining life. A few of the unfortunate men must have survived until the arrival of the wild fowl (say until the end of May), as shots were heard and fresh bones and feathers of geese were noticed near the scene of the sad event.

There appears to have been an abundant store of ammunition . . . There must have been a number of telescopes, guns (several of them double-barrelled), watches, compasses, etc., all of which seem to have been broken up, as I saw pieces of these different articles with the natives, and I purchased as many as possible, together with some silver spoons and forks, an Order of Merit in the form of a star, and a small silver plate engraved 'Sir John Franklin, K.C.B.'.

None of the Esquimaux with whom I had communication saw the 'white' men, either when living or after death; nor had they ever been at the place where the corpses were found, but had their information from those who had been there, and who had seen the party when travelling on the ice.

From what I could learn, there is no reason to suspect that any violence had been offered to the sufferers by the natives.

Sir Francis Leopold McClintock

(1819–1907)

British explorer. He was sent in 1857 by Lady Franklin to search for her husband's remains, and he confirmed the fate of the missing men.

The Voyage of the 'Fox' in the Arctic Seas (London, 1859).

1. They Dropped by the Way (1859)

7th May. To avoid snow-blindness, we commenced night marching. Crossing over from Matty Island towards the shore of King William's Island, we continued our march southward until midnight, when we had the good fortune to arrive at an inhabited snow village. We found ten or twelve huts and thirty or forty natives of King William's Island; I do not think any of them had ever seen white people alive before, but they evidently regarded us as friends. We halted at a little distance, and pitched our tent, the better to secure small articles from being stolen whilst we bartered with them.

I purchased from them six pieces of silver plate, bearing the crests or initials of Franklin, Crozier, Fairholme, and McDonald; they also sold us bows and arrows of English woods, uniform and other buttons, and offered us a heavy sledge made of two short stout pieces of curved wood, which no mere boat could have furnished them with, but this of course we could not take away; the silver spoons and forks were readily sold for four needles each.

They were most obliging and peaceably disposed but could not resist the temptation to steal, and were importunate to barter everything they possessed. There was not a trace of fear, every countenance was lighted up with joy; even the children were not shy, nor backward either, in crowding about us, and poking in everywhere. One man got hold of our saw, and tried to retain it, holding it behind his back, and presenting his knife in exchange; we might have had some trouble in getting it from him, had not one of my men mistaken his object in presenting the knife towards me, and run out of the tent with a gun in his hand; the saw was instantly returned, and these poor people seemed to think they never could do enough to convince us of their friendliness; they repeatedly tapped me gently on the breast, repeating the words 'Kammik toomee' (We are friends).

Having obtained all the relics they possessed, I purchased some seal's flesh, blubber, frozen venison, dried and frozen salmon, and sold some of my puppies. They told us it was five days' journey to the wreck—one day up the inlet still in sight, and four days overland; this would bring them to the western coast of King William's Island; they added that but little now remained accessible of the wreck, their countrymen having carried almost everything away. In answer to an enquiry, they said she was without masts; the question gave rise to some laughter amongst them, and they spoke to each other about *fire*, from which Petersen thought they had burnt the masts through close to the deck in order to get them down.

There had been *many books*, they said, but all have long ago been destroyed by the weather; the ship was forced on there in the fall of the year by the ice. She had not been visited during this past winter, and an old woman and a boy were shown to us who were the last to visit the wreck; they said they had been at it during the preceding winter.

Petersen questioned the woman closely, and she seemed anxious to give all the information in her power. She said many of the white men dropped by the way as they went to the Great River; that some were buried and some were not . . .

2. THE SKELETON

We were now upon the shore along which the retreating crews must have marched. My sledges, of course, travelled upon the sea-ice close along the shore; and although the depth of snow which covered the beach deprived us of almost every hope, yet we kept a very sharp look-out for traces, nor were we unsuccessful. Shortly after midnight of the 25th May, when slowly walking along a gravel ridge near the beach, which the winds kept partially bare of snow, I came upon a human skeleton, partly exposed, with here and there a few fragments of clothing appearing through the snow. The skeleton—now perfectly bleached—was lying upon its face, the limbs and smaller bones either dissevered or gnawed away by small animals.

A most careful examination of the spot was, of course, made, the snow removed and every scrap of clothing gathered up. A pocket-book afforded grounds for hope that some information might be subsequently obtained respecting the unfortunate owner and the calamitous march of the lost crews, but at the time it was frozen hard. The substance of that which we gleaned upon the spot may thus be summed up.

This victim I supposed to have been a young man, slightly built, and perhaps above the common height; the dress appeared to be that of a steward or officer's servant, the loose bow-knot in which his neck-handkerchief was tied not being used by seamen or officers. In every particular the dress confirmed our conjectures as to his rank or office in the late expedition—

the blue jacket with slashed sleeves and braided edging, and the pilot-cloth great-coat with plain covered buttons. We found, also, a small clothes-brush near, and a horn pocket-comb, in which a few light-brown hairs still remained. This poor man seems to have selected the bare ridge top, as affording the least tiresome walking, and to have fallen upon his face in the position in which we found him. It is probable that, hungry and exhausted, he suffered himself to fall asleep when in this position, and that his last moments were undisturbed by suffering; at least I felt strongly impressed with this idea, and the spectacle before me brought most forcibly to my recollection the extreme danger of being overcome by sleep under intense cold.

It was a melancholy truth that the old woman spoke when she said, 'They fell down and died as they walked along.'

Of this skeleton only a portion of the skull appeared above the snow, and it so strongly resembled a bleached rounded stone that the man I called from the sledge, mistaking it for one, rested his shovel upon it, but started back with horror when the hollow sound revealed to him its true nature. Were it not for their shroud of snow, it is more than probable that our anxious search would have brought to light many another skeleton, and have still further confirmed the old woman's brief story.

❉

DAVID HANBURY

(1864–1910)

English explorer. His travels in Canada in the 1890s have been described as being in a class by themselves.

Sport and Travel in the Northland of Canada (London, 1904).

ON THE VALUE OF NATIVE INFORMATION (1898–1899)

On the main Ark-i-linik River there is a stretch of country about eighty miles in length into which no human being enters. The Eskimo do not hunt so far west, and Yellow Knives and Dog Ribs from Slave Lake do not go so far east. To penetrate this country in the dead of winter would be simply to court starvation. Then the deer have all departed, and to depend on finding musk-oxen at the end of the journey would be risky indeed.

Thus there still remains one spot in this Great Barren Northland which is sacred to the musk-ox. Here the animals remain in their primeval state, exhibiting no fear, only curiosity. I approached several herds within thirty yards, photographed them at my leisure, moving them round as I wished, and then retired, leaving them still stupidly staring at me as if in wonder. When deer were not procurable, a musk-ox was killed. Fish were plentiful all along the Ark-i-linik; in fact I never saw such a grand river for fish.

The nets were rarely set, however, when meat was procurable, as it caused considerable delay in the morning, and the nets had to be dried. Moose are to be found on the main Ark-i-linik, also black bears. On the western branch the woods decreased in extent and in size of timber as we ascended until at the height of land there were none, and we had to fall back on moss and heaths for fuel. Deer were then very scarce, and the musk-ox we had long since left behind; but something always turned up to keep the pot boiling. One day it would be a wolverine or glutton, another time a fat wolf. All animals appear to be good on the Barren Lands; or is it that one's appetite is good? An occasional goose was shot, or duck, or ptarmigan, or an arctic hare; we always had enough, being indifferent as to the exact kind of animal which satisfied our hunger.

We had the good luck to meet the Eskimo from the Arctic coast, who resort to this river to obtain wood for their sleighs. These natives had never set eyes on a white man before, and had no articles of civilization whatever. They were all dressed in deerskins, and armed with long bows, arrows, and spears, beaten out of native copper. The use of tobacco was quite unknown to them, and firearms they had only heard about. They gave me a good deal of information about their country and the copper deposits along the Arctic coast, and I obtained from them several copper implements, such as dags, spear and arrow heads, needles, all beaten out of native copper, giving them in exchange knives, files, and needles, which last appeared to have by far the most value in their eyes. They exhibited no signs of fear at our approach. They were a jovial lot, and camped with us that night. In the evening they sang together, rather nicely I thought, and next morning we separated, with many signs of friendship on their part. . . .

A few words concerning the name of the fine river we were about to descend may not be out of place. As I was the first white man to explore this river, I considered that, in virtue of this priority, I had some right to name it. On old maps it is called the Thelewdezzeth, but this Indian name seems dropping out of use, and the Indians now call it the Thelon. The main part of the river is not visited by Indians, and only Yellow Knives from Great Slave Lake occasionally visit the upper waters of its western branch. The Eskimo, on the other hand, frequent and always have frequented the lower waters of the main river, and among them it is known as the Ark-i-linik, which in their language means the Wooded River. Considering the great advantage of using local names which are not merely known to the natives but are descriptive of natural features of the country, I have no hesitation in adhering to the existing name of Ark-i-linik. The Canadian Geographical Board, however, have thought fit to take exception to the Eskimo name, and I do not know at present what name they have decided to adopt. Mr Tyrrell, who visited the river in the summer of 1900, informs me that he has named its western branch after me—an honour for which I thank him, but for which I was not at all anxious. Wherever I have been in unexplored regions I have invariably made it a strict rule to ascertain and adhere to local and native names, whether of lakes, mountains, rivers, or other physical features of the country, and I wish to lay particular stress upon the importance of following this plan, for it is of the greatest service to the traveller who finds himself in the country for the first time. If he has a map in his possession, and on this map finds the native name for every place, he will have no difficulty in making the natives understand the route he wishes to follow.

✳

ROALD AMUNDSEN

(1872–1928)

Norwegian explorer. He proved that there was a navigable route to the Pacific by being the first man through the North-West Passage in his motorized sailing ship Gjöa *in 1906.*

The North West Passage (London, 1908).

GROUNDING IN 'VIRGIN WATER' (1903)

It was 6 a.m. when we grounded. We immediately launched a boat to take soundings and ascertain the best way to get off again. The shortest way was aft. But as the two banks on which we had already struck lay higher in the water than the reef on which we stood, the prospect of getting back over them was very slight. We were therefore obliged to try forward, to the south. The soundings gave us little hope. The reef shallowed up in

313

that direction, and had not more than a fathom of water upon it in the shallowest part. Taking the shortest way ahead, the distance across the reef was about 220 yards. With a few tons of ballast the *Gjöa* had a draft of 6 feet. Loaded as she was, she drew 10 feet 2 inches. The prospect of getting across was therefore not brilliant, but we had no choice. We were compelled to lighten the vessel as much as possible. First we threw overboard 25 of our heaviest cases. They contained dog's pemmican, and weighed nearly 4 cwt. each. Then we threw out all the other cases of the deck-cargo on one side, to get the vessel to heel over as much as possible.

At 8 a.m. the current set to the north and the water fell one foot. We had grounded at high tide. We now made all preparations for the next high tide. The kedge anchor was put out, and every manœuvre was tried to make the vessel heel over. The weather continued fine and calm, with sunshine; in other words, it was just the sort of day when we could have made good headway in these waters. Yet here we lay, and could not move an inch. However, we waited and trusted to the high tide. Our 'observer' availed himself of the favourable opportunity to take our bearings. We were near a little island to the north of Matty Island. High tide was at about 7 p.m. But in spite of all preparations and all our exertions we could not get the vessel to move an inch forward. When darkness set in about 8 o'clock at night we had to give up for the day.

When I came on deck at 2 a.m. next morning it was blowing fresh from the north. At 3 a.m. the vessel began to move, as if in convulsions. I had all hands called up so as to be ready to avail ourselves of any chance that might present itself. The north wind freshened to a gale, accompanied by sleet. We hove on the kedge, time after time, but to no purpose. The vessel pitched violently. I took counsel with my comrades, as I always did in critical situations, and we decided, as a last resource, to try and get her off with the sails. The spray was dashing over the ship, and the wind came in gusts, howling through the rigging, but we struggled and toiled and got the sails set. Then we commenced a method of sailing not one of us is ever likely to forget even should he attain the age of Methusaleh. The mighty press of sail and the high choppy sea, combined, had the effect of lifting the vessel up and pitching her forward again among the rocks, so that we expected every moment to see her planks scattered on the sea. The false keel was splintered, and floated up. All we could do was to watch the course of events and calmly await the issue.

As a matter of fact, I cannot say I did feel calm, as I stood in the rigging and followed the dance from one rock to another. I stood there with the bitterest self-reproach. If I had set a watch in the crow's-nest, this would never have happened, because he would have observed the reef a long way off and reported it. Was my carelessness to wreck our whole undertaking, which had begun so auspiciously? Should we, who had got so much further than anyone before us—we who had so fortunately cleared parts of the passage universally regarded as the most difficult—should we now be compelled to stop and turn back crestfallen? Turn back, yes! that might yet be the question. If the vessel broke up, what then? I had to hold fast with all my strength whenever the vessel, after being lifted, pitched down on to the rocks, or I should have been flung into the sea. Supposing she were broken up. There was a very good prospect of it. The water on the reef got shallower, and I noted how the sea broke on the outer edge. It looked as if the raging north wind meant to carry us just to that bitter end. The sails were as taut as drumheads, the rigging trembled, and I expected it to go overboard every minute. We were steadily nearing the shallowest part of the reef, and sharper and sharper grew the lash of the spray over the vessel.

I thought it almost impossible the ship could hold together if she could get on the outer edge of the reef, which, in fact, was almost lying dry. There was still time to let down a boat and load it with the most indispensable necessaries. I stood up there, in the most terrible agony, struggling for a decision. On me rested every responsibility, and the moment came when I had to make my choice—to abandon the *Gjöa*, take to the boats, and let her be smashed up, or to dare the worst, and perchance go to meet death with all souls on board.

I slid as quickly as I could down one of the back-stays on to the deck. 'We will clear the boats and load them with provisions, rifles, and ammunition.' Then Lund, who stood nearest, asked whether we might not make a last attempt by casting the remainder of the deck cargo overboard. This was, in fact, my own secret ardent desire, to which I had not dared to yield, for the sake of the others. Now, all with one accord agreed with Lund, and hey presto! we went for the deck cargo. We set to in pairs, and cases of 4 cwt. were flung over the rail like trusses of hay. This done, up I climbed into the rigging again. There was not more than a boat's length between us and the shallowest part. The spray and sleet were washing over the vessel, the mast trembled, and the *Gjöa* seemed to pull herself together for a last final leap. She was lifted up high and flung bodily on to the bare rocks, bump, bump—with terrific force. . . . In my distress I sent up (I honestly confess it) an ardent prayer to the Almighty. Yet another thump, worse than ever, then one more, and we slid off.

I flew up to the top; not a moment was to be lost; everything now depended on our finding a way out among all the shoals which were lying close around us. Lieutenant Hansen stood at the wheel, cool and collected, a splendid fellow. And now he called out: 'There is something wrong with the rudder, it will not steer.' Should this, after all, be the end, should we drift down on the island there on our lea? Then the boat pitched once more over a crest, and I heard the glad shout: 'The rudder is all right again.'

A most wonderful thing had happened: the first shock had lifted the rudder so that it rested with the pintles on the mountings. But the last shock had brought it back into its place. It was a rare thing to see any frantic enthusiasm on board the *Gjöa*; we were all pretty quiet and cool by nature. But this time the jubilation could not be controlled, and it burst out unrestained.

The manœuvres that followed were far from agreeable. The banks lay all round us, and the vessel would not answer the helm as well as she usually did. We were drenched to the skin, and our teeth chattered with cold. The lead-line was brought into requisition and from that hour the *Gjöa* did not make another quarter of a mile of the North-West Passage without one man aloft and another plying the lead. We had been taught one lesson, and we did not want another of the same kind.

✿

LEONIDAS AND MINA HUBBARD
L. H. (d. 1903) M. H. (1870–1956)

A remarkable Canadian couple. Leonidas died exploring Labrador, and his wife retraced his steps to find out what happened.

A Woman's Way through Unknown Labrador (London, 1908).

1. LEONIDAS'S LAST DIARY ENTRY (1903)

I saw it was probably useless for me to try to go further with the boys, so we counselled last night, and decided they should take merely half a blanket each, socks, etc., some tea, tea pail, cups, and the pistols, and go on. They will try to reach the flour tomorrow. Then Wallace will bring a little and come back to me. George will go on to the milk and lard and to Skipper Blake if he can, and send or lead help to us. I want to say here

316

that they are two of the very best, bravest, and grandest men I ever knew, and if I die it will not be because they did not put forth their best efforts. Our past two days have been trying ones. I have not written my diary because so very weak. Day before yesterday we caught sight of a caribou, but it was on our lee, and, winding us, got away before a shot could be fired.

Yesterday at an old camp, we found the end we had cut from a flour bag. It had a bit of flour sticking to it. We boiled it with our old caribou bones and it thickened the broth a little. We also found a can of mustard we had thrown away. I sat and held it in my hand a long time, thinking how it came from Congers and our home, and what a happy home it was. Then I took a bite of it and it was very good. We mixed some in our bone broth and it seemed to stimulate us. We had a bit of caribou skin in the same pot. It swelled up thick and was very good. Last night I fell asleep while the boys were reading to me. This morning I was very, very sleepy. After the boys left—they left me tea, the caribou bones, and another end of flour sack found here, a rawhide caribou moccasin, and some yeast cakes—I drank a cup of strong tea and some bone broth. I also ate some of the really delicious rawhide, boiled with the bones, and it made me stronger—strong to write this. The boys have only tea and one half-pound pea meal. Our parting was most affecting. I did not feel so bad. George said, 'The Lord help us, Hubbard. With His help I'll save you if I can get out.' Then he cried. So did Wallace. Wallace stooped and kissed my check with his poor, sunken, bearded lips—several times—and I kissed his. George did the same, and I kissed his cheek. Then they went away. God bless and help them.

I am not so greatly in doubt as to the outcome. I believe they will reach the flour and be strengthened, that Wallace will reach me, that George will find Blake's cache and camp and send help. So I believe we will all get out.

My tent is pitched in open tent style in front of a big rock. The rock reflects the fire, but now it is going out because of the rain. I think I shall let it go and close the tent, till the rain is over, thus keeping out wind and saving wood. Tonight or tomorrow perhaps the weather will improve so I can build a fire, eat the rest of my moccasins and have some bone broth. Then I can boil my belt and oil-tanned moccasins and a pair of cowhide mittens. They ought to help some. I am not suffering. The acute pangs of hunger have given way to indifference. I am sleepy. I think death from starvation is not so bad. But let no one suppose that I expect it. I am prepared, that is all. I think the boys will be able with the Lord's help to save me.

2. THE END OF MINA'S BOOK (1907)

At the foot of the hill below the house, Mrs Ford stood waiting. Her eyes shone like stars as she took my hand and said, 'You are very welcome, Mrs Hubbard. Yours is the first white woman's face I have seen for two years.' We went on up the hill to the house. I do not remember what we talked about. I only remember Mrs Ford's eyes, which were very blue and very beautiful now in her excitement. And when we reached the little piazza and I turned to look back, there were the men sitting quietly in the canoes. The Eskimo had drawn canoes, men and outfit across the mud to where a little stream slipped down over a gravelly bed, which offered firmer footing, and were now coming in single file towards the post each with a bag over his shoulder.

Why were the men sitting there? Why did they not come too?

Suddenly I realized that with our arrival at the post our positions were reversed. They were my charges now. They had completed their task and what a great thing they had done for me. They had brought me safely, triumphantly on my long journey, and not a hair of my head had been harmed. They had done it too with an innate courtesy and gentleness that was beautiful, and I had left them without a word. With a dull feeling of helplessness and limitation I thought of how differently another would have done. No matter how I tried, I could never be so generous and self-forgetful as he. In the hour of disappointment and loneliness, even in the hour of death, he had taken thought so generously for his companions. I, in the hour of my triumph, had forgotten mine. We were like Light and Darkness and with the light gone how deep was the darkness. Once I had thought I stood up beside him, but in what a school had I learned that I only reached to his feet. And now all my effort, though it might achieve that which he would be glad and proud of, could never bring him back.

I must go back to the men at once, and leaving Mr and Mrs Ford I slipped down the hill again, and out along the little stream across the cove. They came to meet me when they saw me coming and Heaven alone knows how inadequate were the words with which I tried to thank them. We came up the hill together now, and soon the tents were pitched out among the willows. As I watched them from the post window busy about their new camping ground, it was with a feeling of genuine loneliness that I realised that I should not again be one of the little party.

IV

CENTRAL AND
SOUTH AMERICA

CHRISTOPHER COLUMBUS (1451–1506)   321
AMERIGO VESPUCCI (1454–1512)   326
ALONSO DE OJEDA (c.1465–1515)   328
VASCO NÚÑEZ DE BALBOA (1475–1519)   329
BARTOLOMÉ DE LAS CASAS (1474–1566)   330
HERNAN CORTÉS (1485–1547)   331
ANTONIO PIGAFETTA (1491–1535)   334
FATHER PEDRO SIMÓN (fl. 1535)   336
ULRICH SCHMIDT (fl. 1535)   337
FRANCISCO DE ORELLANA (c.1511–1546)   340
HANS STADEN (fl. 1547–1555)   343
SIR FRANCIS DRAKE (c.1540–1596)   345
WILLIAM DAVIES (fl. 1614)   347
ALEXANDER VON HUMBOLDT (1769–1859)   349
CHARLES WATERTON (1782–1865)   351
CHARLES ROBERT DARWIN (1809–1882)   356
ALFRED RUSSELL WALLACE (1823–1913)   359
HENRY WALTER BATES (1825–1892)   361
RICHARD SPRUCE (1817–1893)   363
SIR RICHARD BURTON (1821–1890)   367
EDWARD WHYMPER (1840–1911)   368
HIRAM BINGHAM (1876–1956)   370
THEODORE ROOSEVELT (1858–1919)   372

CHRISTOPHER COLUMBUS

(1451–1506)

Genoese explorer. He revealed the existence of America to Europe, even if he may not have been the first European to get there.

The Voyage of Christopher Columbus: Columbus' Own Journal of Discovery Newly Restored and Translated, by J. Cummins (London, 1992).

FIRST IMPRESSIONS OF A NEW CONTINENT AND ITS INHABITANTS (1492)

Wednesday 10 October. Sailed WSW at about eight knots, sometimes up to nine and a half, occasionally only five and a half. Sixty-two and a half leagues in the twenty-four hours; I told the men only forty-six and a half. They could contain themselves no longer, and began to complain of the length of the voyage. I encouraged them as best I could, trying to raise their hopes of the benefits they might gain from it. I also told them that it was useless to complain; having set out for the Indies I shall continue this voyage until, with God's grace, I reach them.

Thursday 11 October. Course WSW. A heavy sea, the roughest in the whole voyage so far. We saw petrels, and a green reed close to the ship, and then a big green fish of a kind which does not stray far from the shoals. On the *Pinta* they saw a cane and a stick, and they picked up another little piece of wood which seemed to have been worked with an iron tool; also a piece of cane and another plant which grows on land, and a little board. On the *Niña* too they saw signs of land, and a thorn-branch laden with red fruits, apparently newly cut. We were all filled with joy and relief at these signs. Sailed twenty-eight and a half leagues before sunset. After sunset I resumed our original course westward, sailing at about nine knots. By two o'clock in the morning we had sailed about sixty-eight miles, or twenty-two and a half leagues.

When everyone aboard was together for the 'Salve Regina', which all seamen say or sing in their fashion, I talked to the men about the grace which God had shown us by bringing us in safety, with fair winds and no obstacles, and by comforting us with signs which were more plentiful every day. I urged them to keep a good watch and reminded them that in the first article of the sailing instructions issued to each ship in the Canaries

I gave orders not to sail at night after we had reached a point seven hundred leagues from there; I was sailing on because of everyone's great desire to sight land. I warned them to keep a good lookout in the bows and told them that I would give a silk doublet to the man who first sighted land, as well as the prize of 10,000 *maravedis* promised by Your Majesties.

I was on the poop deck at ten o'clock in the evening when I saw a light. It was so indistinct that I could not be sure it was land, but I called Pedro Gutiérrez, the Butler of the King's Table, and told him to look at what I thought was a light. He looked, and saw it. I also told Rodrigo Sánchez de Segovia, Your Majesties' observer on board, but he saw nothing because he was standing in the wrong place. After I had told them, the light appeared once or twice more, like a wax candle rising and falling. Only a few people thought it was a sign of land, but I was sure we were close to a landfall.

Then the *Pinta*, being faster and in the lead, sighted land and made the signal as I had ordered. The first man to sight land was called Rodrigo de Triana. The land appeared two hours after midnight, about two leagues away. We furled all sail except the *treo*, the mainsail with no bonnets, and jogged off and on until Friday morning, when we came to an island. We saw naked people, and I went ashore in a boat with armed men, taking Martín Alonso Pinzón and his brother Vicente Yáñez, captain of the *Niña*. I took the royal standard, and the captains each took a banner with the Green Cross which each of my ships carries as a device, with the letters F and Y, surmounted by a crown, at each end of the cross.

When we stepped ashore we saw fine green trees, streams everywhere and different kinds of fruit. I called to the two captains to jump ashore with the rest, who included Rodrigo de Escobedo, secretary of the fleet, and Rodrigo Sánchez de Segovia, asking them to bear solemn witness that in the presence of them all I was taking possession of this island for their Lord and Lady the King and Queen, and I made the necessary declarations which are set down at greater length in the written testimonies.

Soon many of the islanders gathered round us. I could see that they were people who would be more easily converted to our Holy Faith by love than by coercion, and wishing them to look on us with friendship I gave some of them red bonnets and glass beads which they hung round their necks, and many other things of small value, at which they were so delighted and so eager to please us that we could not believe it. Later they swam out to the boats to bring us parrots and balls of cotton thread and darts, and many other things, exchanging them for such objects as glass beads and hawk bells. They took anything, and gave willingly whatever they had.

322

However, they appeared to me to be a very poor people in all respects. They go about as naked as the day they were born, even the women, though I saw only one, who was quite young. All the men I saw were quite young, none older than thirty, all well built, finely bodied and handsome in the face. Their hair is coarse, almost like a horse's tail, and short; they wear it short, cut over the brow, except a few strands of hair hanging down uncut at the back.

Some paint themselves with black, some with the colour of the Canary islanders, neither black nor white, others with white, others with red, others with whatever they can find. Some have only their face painted, others their whole body, others just their eyes or nose. They carry no weapons, and are ignorant of them; when I showed them some swords they took them by the blade and cut themselves. They have no iron; their darts are just sticks without an iron head, though some of them have a fish tooth or something else at the tip.

They are all the same size, of good stature, dignified and well formed. I saw some with scars on their bodies, and made signs to ask about them, and they indicated to me that people from other islands nearby came to capture them and they defended themselves. I thought, and still think, that people from the mainland come here to take them prisoner. They must be good servants, and intelligent, for I can see that they quickly repeat everything said to them. I believe they would readily become Christians; it appeared to me that they have no religion. With God's will, I will take six of them with me for Your Majesties when I leave this place, so that they may learn Spanish.

I saw no animals on the island, only parrots.

Saturday 13 October. In the early morning many of the islanders came to the beach, all young, as I have said, tall and handsome, their hair not curly, but flowing and thick, like horsehair. They are all broader in the forehead and head than any people I have ever seen, with fine, large eyes. None of them is black; they are rather the same colour as the folk on the Canary Islands, which is what one might expect, this island being on the same latitude as Hierro in the Canaries, which lies due E. Their legs are very straight, and they are all the same height, not stout in the belly but well shaped. They came out to the ship in *almadías* made from a tree-trunk, like a long boat, all of a piece, wonderfully shaped in the way of this land, some big enough to carry forty or fifty men, others smaller, with only one man. They row them with paddles like a baker's shovel, very swiftly, and if the boat overturns they all jump into the sea to turn it over again and bale it out with gourds. . . .

I kept my eyes open and tried to find out if there was any gold, and I saw that some of them had a little piece hanging from a hole in their nose. I gathered from their signs that if one goes south, or around the south side of the island, there is a king with great jars full of it, enormous amounts. I tried to persuade them to go there, but I saw that the idea was not to their liking.

I decided to wait until tomorrow and then to set off to the south-west, for many of them seemed to be saying that there is land to the S and SW and NW, and that the people from the NW often come to attack them, and continue to the SW in search of gold and precious stones. This island is large and very flat, with green trees and plenty of water; there is a large lake in the middle, no mountains, and everything is green and a delight to the eye. The people are very gentle; they are so eager for our things that if we refuse to give them something without getting something in exchange they seize what they can and jump into the water with it. But they will give whatever they have for anything one gives them; they even bargained for pieces of broken plate and broken glasses. I saw them take three Portuguese *ceotís*, the equivalent of one Castilian *blanca*, for sixteen balls of cotton which must have contained more than an *arroba* of thread. I had forbidden anyone to take this, except that I had given orders to take it all for Your Majesties if it was in sufficient quantity. It grows on this island, though in the little time available I could not swear to this, and the gold they wear hanging from their noses is also from the island, but so as not to waste time I wish to set off to see if I can reach the island of Cipango.

It is now after nightfall and they have all gone ashore in their *almadías*. . . .

Monday 15 October . . . The people here are like those on the other two islands, with the same language and ways, except that these seem rather more civilized and subtle in their dealings; when they have brought cotton and other little things to the ship I have noticed that they are better at bargaining over the price than the others. Also I have noticed woven cotton cloths here like kerchiefs, and the people are more lively, and the women wear a little cotton thing in front which just covers their private part. . . .

The fish here show amazing differences from our own. Some are like cocks, with the handsomest colouring in the world: blue, yellow, red, all colours; others are marked in a thousand different ways. No man could look at them without amazement and delight, the colours are so beautiful. There are also whales. Ashore I have seen no animals of any kind; only parrots and lizards. A ship's boy told me he had seen a large snake. I have seen no sheep, goats, or other beasts. I have not been here long, for it is only midday, but if there were any I could not have failed to see some of them. . . .

Sunday 28 October . . . I never saw a lovelier sight: trees everywhere, lining the river, green and beautiful. They are not like our own, and each has its own flowers and fruit. Numerous birds, large and small, singing away sweetly. There are large numbers of palm trees, different from our own and those in Guinea; they are of medium height, without the skirt round the base; the leaves are very large, and are used to thatch the houses. The land is very level. . . .

Monday, 29 October . . . The houses are better looking than the ones we have seen so far, and I expect the closer I come to the mainland the better they will be. They are built in the shape of a campaign tent, very large, and arranged not in streets but haphazardly, like tents in an army encampment. They are clean and well swept inside, with all their equipment neatly arranged. The houses are all made of beautiful palm branches.

We found many statues in the shape of a woman, and finely carved heads like masks. I do not know if they are for decoration or worship. There were dogs which never barked, and wild birds living tame in the houses, and wonderfully crafted fishing nets and hooks and other fishing gear. None of this was touched. I think all these people on the coast must be fishermen who take their catch inland, for the island is very large. It is so beautiful that I could go on and on in its praise. I found trees with wonderfully flavoured fruit, and there must be cows and other domestic animals, for I saw skulls like those of cattle. The birds, large and small, and the song of the crickets in the night are a great joy to us all; the night air is sweet and fragrant, neither too hot nor too cold. We had very hot weather coming from the other islands to this one, but here it is warm and pleasant, like May. The other islands were probably hot because they are very flat, and because as we were coming here we had easterly winds, which are warm.

The water in the rivers here is brackish near the mouth. I do not know where the Indians get their water; they have fresh water in their houses. Ships could tack about to enter and leave this river, and there are very clear leading marks. There is seven or eight fathoms' depth at the mouth and five inside. I think this whole sea must always be as calm as the river at Seville, and the water seems perfect for pearls. I found some large snails, different from those in Spain, with no taste. . . .

Tuesday 6 November. The two men I sent inland to explore came back last night and told me they had gone twelve leagues when they reached a village of fifty houses. There were about a thousand inhabitants, for they live many to a house. The houses are like big campaign tents. The men said they were received with great ceremony, according to the customs of the place. Everyone, men and women, came to see them, and they were lodged in the best houses. The people kept touching them and kissing their hands and feet in amazement, thinking they had come from Heaven, and so they gave them to understand. They were given food, and they told me that when they arrived the foremost men in the village led them by the arm to the most important house and sat them on curious chairs, carved out of a single piece of wood in the shape of an animal with short arms and legs and its tail raised a little to form a backrest, though this is as broad as the seat to give comfortable support; there is a head in front with eyes and ears of gold. They call these chairs *duhos*. All the men sat around them on the ground. The Indian who was with my men told them about our way of life, saying that we were good people. Then all the men went out and the women came in and sat around them in the same way, kissing their hands and feet and touching them to see if they were flesh and blood like themselves. They gave them some cooked roots to eat which tasted like chestnuts. They invited them to stay for at least five days. . . .

My two men met many people crossing their path to reach their villages, men and women, carrying in their hand a burning brand and herbs which they use to produce fragrant smoke. They came across no village of more than five houses, and they were treated with the same attention by all the people. They saw many kinds of trees, plants, and scented flowers, and birds of many varieties, different from those of Spain, except that there were partridges, and nightingales singing, and geese; of these there are plenty. They saw no four-footed beasts except silent dogs. The land is very fertile and well worked . . .

✿

AMERIGO VESPUCCI

(1454–1512)

Florentine navigator whose name was given to America. In 1499–1500 he crossed the Atlantic with Alonso de Ojeda (q.v.), a Spanish conquistador who had sailed with Columbus on his second voyage. During this voyage Vespucci saw the mouth of the Amazon, which lies exactly on the equator.

El Nuevo Mundo, trans. R. Levillier (Buenos Aires, 1951).

1. A LETTER FROM SEVILLE TO HIS PATRON, LORENZO DE' MEDICI (1500)

We were absent thirteen months on this voyage, exposing ourselves to terrible dangers, and discovering a very large part of Asia, and a great many islands, most of them inhabited. According to the calculations I have several times made with the compass, we sailed about five thousand leagues. . . . We passed the equinoctial line six and a half degrees to the south, and afterwards turned to the north, which we penetrated so far that the north star was at an elevation of thirty-five degrees and a half above our horizon. To the west we sailed eighty-four degrees distant from the meridian of . . . Cadiz. We discovered immense regions, saw a vast number of people, all naked, and speaking various languages. On the land we saw many wild animals, various kinds of birds, and an infinite number of trees, all aromatic. We brought home pearls in their growing state, and gold in the grain. We brought two stones, one of emerald colour, the other of amethyst, which was very hard, at least half a span long and three fingers thick. The sovereigns esteem them most highly, and have preserved them among their jewels. . . . We brought many other stones which appeared beautiful to us, but of all these we did not bring a large quantity, as we were continually busy in our navigation, and did not stay long in any one place.

When we arrived in Cadiz, we sold many slaves, finding two hundred remaining to us . . . thirty-two having died at sea. After deducting the cost of transport, we made only about five hundred ducats, which, having to be divided into fifty-five parts, made the share of each very small. However, we are satisfied with having saved our lives, and thank God that during the whole voyage, out of fifty-seven Christian men, which was our number, only two had died, having been killed by the Indians. . . .

2. CANNIBALISM

Almost every day many people came to the beach, but never would they converse with us. And the seventh day we landed, and found that they had brought their women with them. And when we jumped ashore, the men of the land sent many of their women to talk with us. And seeing that they did not take courage, we decided to send them one of our men who was a very agile and energetic youth; and we, to give them greater confidence, entered the boats. And he went among the women, and when he approached them they made a great circle around him; and touching him and gazing at him, they displayed their wonder. Meanwhile we saw a woman approaching from the hill, and she carried a big club in her hand. And when she reached the place where our Christian stood, she came up behind him, and raising her club, struck him such a hard blow that she stretched him out dead on the ground. In a moment the other women seized him by the feet and dragged him toward the hill; and the men sprang toward the beach and began to shoot at us with their bows. Our people, sitting in the boats which were made fast by anchors to the shore, were so demoralized by the shower of arrows that nobody thought of laying hand on his weapons. We fired four Lombard shots, but without hitting anyone. When the reports were heard, they all fled toward the hill, where the women were already cutting up the Christian. And by a great fire which they had built they were roasting him before our eyes, displaying the pieces to us, and eating them.

✵

ALONSO DE OJEDA

(c.1465–1515)

Spanish conquistador. After several journeys to the New World, Ojeda was granted the governorship of the Uraba region, where he founded the colony of San Sebastian.

F. A. Kirkpatrick, *The Spanish Conquistadores* (London, 1934).

PAINFUL TREATMENT FOR A POISONED ARROW WOUND (1509)

Ojeda sailed in November 1509 with 300 men and twelve mares. Nicuesa sailed a few days later with six horses and above 700 men, since his charming personality, together with the golden fame of Veragua since Columbus's last voyage, attracted many recruits to the second enterprise. The horse was still unknown on the continent and a monstrous terror to the inhabitants. Of the 1,000 men and more who thus set out in two companies in quest of fortune, there survived after a few months less than 100. Some fell in fight or by shipwreck or by poisoned arrows shot by lurking savages from ambush in the forest. But the greater number simply died of starvation and hardship. This tragedy was the prologue to the discovery of the South Sea and to the conquest of half a continent.

Ojeda anchored in the wide bay where afterwards stood the city of Cartagena: he at once landed with seventy men to attack the Indians: but his careless confidence received a rude shock; he himself, flying with his men, only escaped death, with one companion, by his speed of foot and by skill in using his shield, which showed the marks of twenty-three arrows, while the rest of his company, including Juan de la Cosa, Chief Pilot of the Crown of Spain, were struck by poisoned arrows and died raving. After taking fierce vengeance on the inhabitants, Ojeda made a settlement further west on the Gulf of Uraba: but his men were dying of hunger, besides losses by poisoned arrows. He himself, with careless audacity, fell into an ambush, was pierced through the thigh by a poisoned arrow, and saved his life by binding two red-hot iron plates to the wound, threatening to hang the surgeon unless he applied this fearsome cautery.

✳

VASCO NÚÑEZ DE BALBOA

(1475–1519)

Spanish explorer and conquistador. He was the first European to see the Pacific Ocean, which he called the South Sea, a name which stuck for many years.

Gonzalo Fernández de Oviedo y Valdés, *Historia general y natural de las Indias* (Seville, 1547), in J. H. Parry, *The Discovery of South America* (London, 1979).

FIRST SIGHTING AND CLAIMING OF THE PACIFIC (1513)

On Tuesday 25 September[1] 1513, at 10 o'clock in the morning, Captain Vasco Núñez, having gone ahead of his company, climbed a hill with a bare summit, and from the top of this hill saw the South Sea. Of all the Christians in his company, he was the first to see it. He turned back toward his people, full of joy, lifting his hands and his eyes to Heaven, praising Jesus Christ and His glorious Mother the Virgin, Our Lady. Then he fell upon his knees on the ground and gave great thanks to God for the mercy He had shown him, in allowing him to discover the sea, and thereby to render so great a service to God and to the most serene Catholic Kings of Castille, our sovereigns. . . .

[1] Presumably an error for 27 September. 25 September 1513 was a Sunday.

And on the 29th, St Michael's Day, Vasco Núñez named twenty-six men, those who seemed to him best fitted, to accompany him with their arms, and left the rest of his force encamped at the village of Chape. He marched with this party down to the shore of the South Sea, to the bay which they had named Saint Michael, which was about half a league from their camp. They found a large inlet, lined with forest, and emerged on the beach about the hour of vespers. The water was low, and great areas of mud exposed; so they sat by the shore waiting for the tide to rise, which presently it did, rushing into the bay with great speed and force. Then Captain Vasco Núñez held up a banner with a picture of the Blessed Virgin, Our Lady, with her precious Son Our Lord Jesus Christ in her arms, and below, the royal arms of Castille and León; and with his drawn sword in his hand and his shield on his arm, he waded into the salt sea up to his knees, and paced back and forth, reciting 'Long live the most high and most mighty monarchs, Don Fernando and Doña Juana, sovereigns of Castille and Aragon and Navarre, etc., in whose names, and for the royal crown of Castille, I now take possession, in fact and in law, of these southern seas, lands, coasts, harbours and islands, with all territories, kingdoms and provinces which belong to them or may be acquired, in whatever manner, for whatever reason, by whatever title, ancient or modern, past, present or future, without let or hindrance.'

❋

BARTOLOMÉ DE LAS CASAS

(1474–1566)

Spanish priest. He defended the Amerindians against the abuses of the conquistadors and settlers.

F. Hernández de Córdoba, *The Discovery of Yucatan* (Berkeley, Calif., 1942).

TROUBLE WITH INDIANS OVER WATER* (1517)

The Spaniards passed on through the town which contained more than 4,000 houses. As the Indians saw that the Spaniards did not attack them or take their fortresses as they were believed to be but went on, they [the

* At Catoche in Yucatán, limestone conntry where water is precious and not to be removed.

Indians] came to them unarmed with joyful and kindly faces making signs of peace to them. All together they returned, as if they had known each other for a long time and as friends, to the beginning of the town where they had come in and all sat down outside under a large tree. A son of the lord and a woman brought to the captain of the Spaniards a cooked turkey, one of the large ones like peacocks, and some masks of fine gold. . . . When this had been done they asked the captain by signs what he wanted to which he replied 'water to drink'. The Indians showed him a round walled-up well of good water, where the Spaniards went to sleep. Then they took all the water needful for the ships. The Spaniards kept guard that night, and no less did the Indians do in their town. When day broke, all the Indians came out of their town armed with bows and arrows, shields and lances. They surrounded the town on the side where the Spaniards were and sent three to tell them to go to their ships. This they did with signs and with threats that if they did not go they would shoot arrows at them and do them harm. The Spaniards obeyed their order and went aboard their boats and thence to their ships.

✿

HERNAN CORTÉS

(1485–1547)

Spanish conquistador. The conqueror of Mexico. On 8 November 1519 he entered Montezuma's capital, on the site of present-day Mexico City.

1: Hernando Cortés, *Cartas de relación . . .* , trans. and ed. A. R. Pagden as Hernan Cortés, *Letters from Mexico* (New York, 1971); 2: *The Broken Spears: The Aztec Account of the Conquest of Mexico*, trans. Nahuatl–Spanish A. M. Garibay; trans. Spanish–English Lysander Kemp (Boston, 1962).

1. CORTÉS'S DESCRIPTION OF THE CITY (1519)

This great city of Temixtitan is built on the salt lake, and no matter by what road you travel there are two leagues from the main body of the city to the mainland. There are four artificial causeways leading to it, and each is as wide as two cavalry lances. The city itself is as big as Seville or Córdoba. The main streets are very wide and very straight; some of these are on the land, but the rest and all the smaller ones are half on land, half canals where they paddle their canoes. All the streets have openings in places so that the water may pass from one canal to another. Over all these openings, and some of them are very wide, there are bridges made of long and wide beams joined together very firmly and so well made that on some of them ten horsemen may ride abreast. . . .

This city has many squares where trading is done and markets are held continuously. There is also one square twice as big as that of Salamanca, with arcades all around, where more than 60,000 people come each day to buy and sell, and where every kind of merchandise produced in these lands is found; provisions as well as ornaments of gold and silver, lead, brass, copper, tin, stones, shells, bones, and feathers. They also sell lime, hewn and unhewn stone, adobe bricks, tiles, and cut and uncut woods of various kinds. There is a street where they sell game and birds of every species found in this land: chickens, partridges and quails, wild ducks, fly-catchers, widgeons, turtle-doves, pigeons, cane birds, parrots, eagles and eagle owls, falcons, sparrowhawks and kestrels, and they sell some of the skins of these birds of prey with their feathers, heads, and claws. They sell rabbits and hares, and stags, and small gelded dogs which they breed for eating. . . .

They sell honey, wax, and a syrup made from maize canes, which is as sweet and syrupy as that made from the sugar cane. They also make syrup from a plant which in the islands is called *maguey*, which is much better than most syrups, and from this plant they also make sugar and wine, which they likewise sell. There are many sorts of spun cotton, in hanks of every colour, and it seems like the silk market at Granada, except that there is a much greater quantity. They sell as many colours for painters as may be found in Spain and all of excellent hues. They sell deerskins, with and without the hair, and some are dyed white or in various colours. They sell much earthenware, which for the most part is very good; there are both large and small pitchers, jugs, pots, tiles, and many other sorts of vessel, all of good clay and most of them glazed and painted. They sell maize both as grain and as bread and it is better both in appearance and in taste than any found in the islands or on the mainland. . . .

There are, in all districts of this great city, many temples or houses for their idols. . . .

Amongst these temples there is one, the principal one, whose great size and magnificence no human tongue could describe, for it is so large that within the precincts, which are surrounded by a very high wall, a town of some five hundred inhabitants could easily be built. All round inside this wall there are very elegant quarters with very large rooms and corridors where their priests live. There are as many as forty towers, all of which are

332

so high that in the case of the largest there are fifty steps leading up to the main part of it; and the most important of these towers is higher than that of the cathedral of Seville. They are so well constructed in both their stone and woodwork that there can be none better in any place, for all the stonework inside the chapels where they keep their idols is in high relief with figures and little houses, and the woodwork is likewise of relief and painted with monsters, and other figures and designs. All these towers are burial places of chiefs, and the chapels therein are each dedicated to the idol which he venerated. . . . I will say only that these people live almost like those in Spain, and in as much harmony and order as there, and considering that they are barbarous and so far from the knowledge of God and cut off from all civilized nations, it is truly remarkable to see what they have achieved in all things. . . .

The most important of these idols, and the ones in whom they have most faith, I had taken from their places and thrown down the steps; and I had those chapels where they were cleaned, for they were full of the blood of sacrifices; and I had images of Our Lady and of other saints put there, which caused Mutezuma and the other natives some sorrow.

A Contemporary Indian View of the Spaniards

When the Spaniards were installed in the palace, they asked Montezuma about the city's resources and reserves and about the warriors' ensigns and shields. They questioned him closely and then demanded gold. Montezuma guided them to it. They surrounded him and crowded close with their weapons. He walked in the centre, while they formed a circle around him. When they arrived at the treasure house called Teucalco, the riches of gold and feathers were brought out to them: ornaments made of quetzal feathers, richly worked shields, disks of gold, the necklaces of the idols, gold nose plugs, gold greaves and bracelets and crowns.

The Spaniards immediately stripped the feathers from the gold shields and ensigns. They gathered all the gold into a great mound and set fire to everything else, regardless of its value. Then they melted down the gold into ingots. As for the precious green stones, they took only the best of them; the rest were snatched up by the Tlaxcaltecas. The Spaniards searched through the whole treasure house, questioning and quarrelling, and seized every object they thought was beautiful.

Next they went to Montezuma's storehouse, in the place called Totocalco [Place of the Palace of the Birds], where his personal treasures were kept. The Spaniards grinned like little beasts and patted each other with delight. When they entered the hall of treasures, it was as if they had arrived in

Paradise. They searched everywhere and coveted everything; they were slaves to their own greed. All of Montezuma's possessions were brought out: fine bracelets, necklaces with large stones, ankle rings with little gold bells, the royal crowns and all the royal finery—everything that belonged to the king and was reserved to him only. They seized these treasures as if they were their own, as if this plunder were merely a stroke of good luck. And when they had taken all the gold, they heaped up everything else in the middle of the patio.

ANTONIO PIGAFETTA

(1491–1535)

Italian chronicler of Magellan's first circumnavigation of the world.

The First Voyage round the World, by Magellan, trans. and ed. Lord Stanley of Alderley (London, 1874).

DESCRIPTION OF INDIANS (1520)

That land of Verzin is wealthier and larger than Spain, France, and Italy put together, and belongs to the king of Portugal. The people of that land are not Christians, and have no manner of worship. They live according to the dictates of nature, and reach an age of 125 and 140 years. They go naked, both men and women. They live in certain long houses, which they call *boii*, and sleep in cotton hammocks called *amache* which are fastened to those houses by each end to large beams. A fire is built on the ground under those hammocks. In each of those *boii*, there are 100 men with their wives and children, and they make a great racket. They have boats called canoes made of one single huge tree, hollowed out by the use of stone hatchets. These people employ stones as we do iron, as they have no iron. Thirty or forty men occupy one of those boats. They paddle with blades like the shovels of a furnace, and thus, black, naked, and shaven, they resemble, when paddling, the inhabitants of the Stygian marsh. Men and women are as well proportioned as we. They eat the flesh of their enemies, not because it is good, but because it is a certain established custom.

Those people paint the whole body and the face in a wonderful manner with fire in various fashions, as do the women also. The men are smooth-shaven and have no beard, for they pull it out. They clothe themselves in a dress made of parrot feathers, with large round arrangements at their buttocks made from the largest feathers, and it is a ridiculous sight. Almost all the people, except the women and children, have three holes pierced in the lower lip where they carry round stones, one finger or thereabouts in length and hanging down outside. Those people are not entirely black, but of a dark brown colour. They keep the privies uncovered, and the body is without hair, while both men and women always go naked. Their King is called *cacich*. They have an infinite number of parrots, and gave us eight or ten for one mirror; and little monkeys that look like lions, only yellow and very beautiful. They make round white bread from the marrowy substance of trees, which is not very good, and is found between the wood and the bark and resembles buttermilk curds.[1] They have swine which have their navels on their backs[2] and large birds with beaks like spoons and no tongues.[3] The men gave us one or two of their young daughters as slaves for one hatchet or one large knife, but they would not give us their wives in exchange for anything at all. . . . The women cultivate the fields, and carry all the food from the mountains in panniers or baskets on the head or fastened to the head. But they are always accompanied by their husbands, who are armed only with a bow of brazil-wood or of black palm-wood, and a bundle of cane arrows, doing this because they are jealous. The women carry their children hanging in a cotton net from their necks. . . .

One day was suddenly saw a naked man of giant stature on the shore of the port. . . . He was so tall that we reached only to his waist, and he was well proportioned.[4] His face was large and painted red all over, while about his eyes he was painted yellow; and he had two hearts painted on the middle of his cheeks. His scanty hair was painted white. He was dressed in the skins of animals skilfully sewn together. That animal has a head and ears as large as those of a mule, a neck and body like those of a camel, the legs of a deer, and the tail of a horse, like which it neighs, and that land has very many of them.[5] His feet were shod with the same kind of skins, which covered his feet in the manner of shoes. In his hand he carried a short, heavy bow, with a cord somewhat thicker than those of a lute, and made from the intestines of the same animal, and a bundle of rather short cane arrows feathered like ours, and with points of white and black flint stones in the manner of Turkish arrows, instead of iron. . . . The captain-general called those people Patagoni.[6] They all clothe themselves in the skins of the animal above mentioned; and they have no houses, except

---

[1] Cassava?   [2] Peccaries.   [3] Muscovy ducks?
[4] Many explorers remarked on the tall stature of the Amerindians, compared with wiry little European sailors; the legend of the Patagonian giants persisted for centuries.
[5] Guanacos.
[6] i.e. 'big feet', presumably from the habit of wrapping their feet in guanaco skin.

those made from the skin of the same animal, and they wander hither and thither with those houses just as the Cingani[7] do. They live on raw flesh and on a sweet root which they call *chapae*. Each of the two whom we captured ate a basketful of biscuit and drank one-half pailful of water at a gulp. They also ate rats without skinning them.

✻

FATHER PEDRO SIMÓN

(*fl.* 1535)

Spanish priest. In 1535 he was a member of an expedition led by Luis Alonso de Lugo against the Tairona Indians.

M. J. Forero (ed.), *Noticias Historiales de las Conquistas de Terre Firme en las Indias Occidentales* (1625) (Bogotá, 1953).

AN ASS WHICH DESERVES TO BE NUMBERED AMONG THE CONQUISTADORES (1535)

At dawn, as they lay hidden in the cornfields which surrounded the village, awaiting the moment to attack, they heard an ass bray. They knew that the Indians did not possess such animals, and did not believe that an ass could have climbed the high crags which barred the way from the coast. Some maintained that there was no ass there—unless it had wings—and that the noise was made by the Indians in mockery; the sentries, perhaps, had detected their presence, and were proclaiming that they would give the invaders such a drubbing as one might give an ass. One man, a foreigner named Malatesta, who had some knowledge of the classics, said that it must be the ass in the story of Silenus which, because it had helped Jupiter against the giants and served well in the war, had been taken up to Heaven; but had fallen again because it was too heavy, and had landed in these mountains . . . and was urging the Spaniards to get up from among the cornstalks and attack . . .

When the place had been pacified and looted, they enquired about the ass. . . . The Indians said that it had come in a ship, which had been wrecked on the coast. . . . They had killed those of the ship's company who

[7] Gypsies.

got ashore, but had kept the ass, and had carried it up into the mountains, trussed with ropes and slung between two poles, along with all the other loot they found in the ship, which included shirts, doublets, coloured bonnets, hatchets, picks, and shovels; of which there were indeed great quantities, adorning the persons of the Indians or lying about the village. So our soldiers, deeming it inappropriate and contrary to native custom that such articles should be in the hands of Indians, collected them all up, along with everything else that took their fancy, including the ass, and took it back to the coast. But the trails were rough, more suited to cats than men, and the descent was as hard as the ascent had been, so they made the Indians carry the donkey down just as they had brought it up; and very useful it turned out to be. Surely, as the first of its race to penetrate those mountains, it deserved to be numbered among the *conquistadores*. It served in other *entradas* later, and finally in the expedition which Hernando de Quesada, brother and deputy of Gonzalo Jiménez de Quesada the discoverer, led in search of El Dorado. It was ridden by Fray Vicente Requejada of the Order of Saint Augustine. . . . The ass served the friar well until, on the return march, they all ran out of food and, in the extremities of hunger, killed it for food. They left not a scrap of it. They collected its blood, made sausages of its guts, and even devoured its hide, well boiled. It had served them well in life, and served them better still in death, by its timely rescue from starvation; a salutary reminder of the hardships which in those days were the daily lot of discoverers.

✶

ULRICH SCHMIDT

(*fl.* 1535)

German explorer. He took part in many expeditions in what are now Argentina and Paraguay with Pedro de Mendoza, Juan de Ayolas, and Domingo Martínez de Irala.

Reise nach Sud-Amerika in den Jahren 1534 bis 1554 (1576) (London, 1891).

INDIANS, HUNGER, AND CANNIBALISM (1535)

So by the grace of God we arrived at Rio de La Plata, Anno 1535, and found there an Indian place inhabited by about two thousand people, named Zechurias, who have nothing to eat but fish and meat. These, on our arrival did leave the place, and fled away with their wives and children,

so that we could not find them. This Indian people go quite naked, the
women having only their privities covered, from the navel to the knees,
with a small piece of cotton cloth.

Now the captain, Pedro de Mendoza, commanded to bring the people
into the ships again, and to convey them to the other side of the Parana,
where it is not broader than eight miles. There we built a new town and
called it Buenos Aires, that is, in German, *Guter Wind*. We also brought
from Hispania on board the fourteen ships seventy-two horses and mares.

Here, also, we found a place inhabited by Indian folk, named Carendies,
numbering about 3,000 people, including wives and children, and they
were clothed in the same way as the Zechurias, from the navel to the
knees. They brought us fish and meat to eat. These Carendies have no
houses, but wander about, as do the gypsies with us at home, and in
summer they often travel upwards of thirty miles on dry land without
finding a single drop of water to drink. And when they meet with deer or
other wild beasts (when they have killed them) they drink their blood. Also
if they find a root, called Cardes, they eat it to slake their thirst. . . .

These Carendies brought us daily their provision of fish and meat to our
camp, and did so for a fortnight, and they did only fail once to come to us.
So our captain, Pedro de Mendoza, sent to them, the Carendies, a judge,
named Johan Pabon, with two foot-soldiers, for they were at a distance of
four miles from our camp. When they came near to them, they were all
three beaten black and blue, and were then sent back again to our camp.
Pedro de Mendoza, our captain, hearing of this from the judge's report
(who for this cause raised a tumult about it in our camp), sent Diego de
Mendoza, his own brother, against them with 300 foot-soldiers and 30
well-armed mounted men, of whom I also was one, straightway charging
us to kill or take prisoners all these Indian Carendies and to take possession of their settlement. But when we came near them there were now
some 4,000 men, for they had assembled all their friends. And when we
were about to attack them, they defended themselves in such a way that
we had that very day our hands full. They also killed our commander,
Diego de Mendoza, and six noblemen. Of our foot-soldiers and mounted
men over 20 were slain, and on their side about 1,000. Thus did they
defend themselves valiantly against us, so that indeed we felt it.

The said Carendies use for their defence hand-bows and tardes [darts]
which are made in the shape of half-pikes, and the head of them is made
out of flint-stone, like a flash; they have also bullets made out of stone with
a long piece of string attached to them, of the size of our leaden bullets
at home in Germany. They throw such bullets round the feet of a horse
or a deer, causing it to fall; it is also with these bullets that they killed our

commander and the noblemen, as I have seen it done myself, but the foot-soldiers were killed by the aforesaid tardes.

Thus God Almighty graciously gave us the victory, and allowed us to take possession of their place; but we did not take prisoner any of the Indians, and their wives and children also fled away from the place before we attacked them. At this place of theirs we found nothing but furrier-work made from marten or so-called otter; also much fish, fish meal, and fish fat. There we remained three days and then returned to our camp, leaving on the spot 100 of our men, in order that they might fish with the Indians' nets for the providing of our folk, because there was there very good fishing. Everyone received only six half-ounces of wheaten flour a day, and one fish every third day. The fishing lasted for two months, and if anyone wanted to eat a fish over and above his allowance, he had to go four miles for it.

And when we returned again to our camp, our folk were divided into those who were to be soldiers, and the others workers, so as to have all of them employed. And a town was built there, and an earthen wall, half a pike high, around it, and inside of it a strong house for our chief captain. The town wall was three foot broad, but that which was built one day fell to pieces the day after, for the people had nothing to eat, and were starved with hunger, so that they suffered great poverty, and it became so bad that the horses could not go. Yea, finally, there was such want and misery for hunger's sake, that there were neither rats, nor mice, nor snakes to still the great dreadful hunger and unspeakable poverty, and shoes and leather were resorted to for eating and everything else.

It happened that three Spaniards stole a horse, and ate it secretly, but when it was known, they were imprisoned and interrogated under the torture. Whereupon, as soon as they admitted their guilt, they were sentenced to death by the gallows, and all three were hanged.

Immediately afterwards, at night, three other Spaniards came to the gallows to the three hanging men, and hacked off their thighs and pieces of their flesh, and took them home to still their hunger.

A Spaniard also ate his brother, who died in the city of Buenos Aires.

FRANCISCO DE ORELLANA

(*c*.1511–1546)

*Spanish conquistador. He fought as second in command under Gonzalo
Pizarro, his childhood friend and the brother of Francisco Pizarro. While
searching for El Dorado east of the Andes, he and some fifty-eight companions became separated from the main party and sailed all the way down
the Amazon to its mouth, taking nine months and losing only fourteen men.*

*The Discovery of the Amazon according to the Account of Friar Gaspar de
Carvajal and other Documents*, trans. B. T. Lee (New York, 1934).

1. THE DECISION TO CONTINUE DOWNSTREAM (1540)

. . . after taking counsel as to what should be done, talking over our afflic-
tion and hardships, it was decided that we should choose of two evils the
one which to the Captain and to all should appear to be the lesser, which
was to go forward and follow the river . . . and so it was that, it being
Monday evening, which by count was the eighth day of the month of January, while eating certain forest roots they heard drums very plainly very far
from where we were, and the Captain was the one who heard them first
and announced it to the other companions, and they all listened, and they
being convinced of the fact, such was the happiness which they all felt that
they cast out of their memories all the past suffering because we were now
in an inhabited country and no longer could die of hunger. . . .

After the companions had somewhat recovered from the effects of the
hunger and suffering that they had undergone, being now in a mood to
work, the Captain, seeing that it was necessary to make plans for what was
ahead, gave orders to call all the companions together and repeated to
them that they could see that with the boat which we were using and the
canoes, if God saw fit to guide us to the sea, we could not go on out to a
place of rescue and that for this reason it was necessary to apply our wits
to building another brigantine of greater burden so that we might sail on
the sea, and this he advised in spite of the fact that among us there was
no skilled craftsman who knew that trade, for what we found most difficult
of all was how to make the nails . . . and there was found among us a
woodworker named Diego Mexía, who, though it was not his trade, gave
instructions as to how the task was to be done; and thereupon the Captain
ordered an apportionment of the work among all the companions whereby

each man in one group was to bring one frame and two futtocks, and others in another to bring the keel, and others the stem pieces, and others to saw planks, so that all had enough to occupy themselves with, not without considerable physical toil, because, as it was winter and the timber was very far away, each had to take his axe and go to the woods and cut down the amount that he was supposed to and bring it in on his back, and, while some carried, others formed a rear guard for them, in order that the Indians might not do them any harm, and in this way within seven days all the timber for the said brigantine was cut; and when this task was finished another was immediately assigned, for he ordered some of the men to make charcoal in order to manufacture nails and other things. It was a wonderful thing to see with what joy our companions worked and brought the charcoal, and in this same way everything else needed was supplied. There was not a man among all of us that was accustomed to such lines of work as these; but, notwithstanding all these difficulties, Our Lord endowed all of them with the proper skill for what had to be done, since it was in order to save their lives, for, had we gone on down from there using only the original boat and the canoes, coming, as we afterwards did, upon warlike people, we could neither have defended ourselves nor left the river in safety. . . . Such great haste was applied to the building of the brigantine that in thirty-five days it was constructed and launched, caulked with cotton and tarred with pitch, all of which the Indians brought because the Captain asked them for these things. Great was the joy of our companions over having accomplished that thing which they so much desired to do. . . .

2. CONFLICT WITH INDIANS AND AMAZONS

Before we had come within two leagues of this village, we saw the villages glimmering white, and we had not proceeded far when we saw coming up the river a great many canoes, all equipped for fighting, gaily coloured, and the men with their shields on, which are made out of the shell-like skins of lizards and the hides of manatees and of tapirs, as tall as a man, because they cover them entirely. They were coming on with a great yell, playing on many drums and wooden trumpets, threatening us as if they were going to devour us. Immediately the Captain gave orders to the effect that the two brigantines should join together so that one might aid the other, and that all should take their weapons and look to what they had before them. . . .

. . . the Indians still not ceasing to follow us and force upon us many combats . . . There went among these and the war canoes four or five sorcerers, all daubed with whitewash and with their mouths full of ashes, which they blew into the air, having in their hands a pair of aspergills, with which as they moved along they kept throwing water about the river as a form of enchantment; and, after they had made one complete turn about our brigantines in the manner which I have said, they called out to the warriors, and at once these began to blow their wooden bugles and trumpets and beat their drums and with a very loud yell they attacked us; but, as I have already said, the arquebuses and crossbows, next to God, were our salvation; and so they led us along in this manner until they got us into a narrows in an arm of the river. . . . Those on the water resolved to wipe us out, and they being now quite determined to do so, being now very close to us, there stood out before them their captain-general distinguishing himself in a very manly fashion, at whom a companion of ours, named Celis, took aim and fired with an arquebus, and he hit him in the middle of the chest, so that he killed him; and at once his men became disheartened and they all gathered around to look at their overlord, and in the mean time we seized the opportunity to get out into the wide part of the river . . .

At the hour of vespers we came to a village that was on a high bank, and as it appeared small to us the Captain ordered us to capture it, and also because it looked so pleasant that it seemed as if it might be a recreation spot of some overlord of the inland. And so we directed our course with a view to capturing it; the Indians put up a defence for more than an hour, but in the end they were beaten and we were masters of the village, where we found very great quantities of food, of which we laid in a supply. In this village there was a villa in which there was a great deal of porcelain ware of various makes, both jars and pitchers, very large, with a capacity of more than twenty-five *arrobas*, and other small pieces such as plates and bowls and candelabra of this porcelain of the best that has ever been seen in the world, for that of Malaga is not its equal, because it is all glazed and embellished with all colours, and so bright are these colours that they astonish, and, more than this, the drawings and paintings which they make on them are so accurately worked out that one wonders how with only natural skill they manufacture and decorate all these things, making them look just like Roman articles . . .

It must be explained that they are the subjects of, and tributaries to, the Amazons, and, our coming having been made known to them, they went to them to ask help, and there came as many as ten or twelve of them, for we ourselves saw these women, who were there fighting in front of all the Indian men as women captains, and these latter fought so courageously that the Indian men did not dare to turn their backs, and anyone who did turn his back they killed with clubs right there before us, and this is the reason why the Indians kept up their defence for so long. These women are very white and tall, and have hair very long and braided and wound about the head, and they are very robust and go about naked, but with their privy parts covered, with their bows and arrows in their hands, doing as much fighting as ten Indian men, and indeed there was one woman among these who shot an arrow a span deep into one of the brigantines, and others less deep, so that our brigantines looked like porcupines. . . .

✵

HANS STADEN

(*fl.* 1547–1555)

German gunner. He was employed by the Portuguese to manage the artillery in one of their forts on the Brazilian coast. Captured by Tupinamba Indians in 1552, he managed to survive five years of captivity.

The Captivity of Hans Stade of Hesse in A.D. 1547–1555, Among the Wild Tribes of Eastern Brazil, trans. A. Tootal (London, 1874).

1. CAPTURE (1552)

As I was going through the forest I heard loud yells on either side of me, such as savages are accustomed to utter, and immediately a company of savages came running towards me, surrounding me on every side and shooting at me with their bows and arrows. Then I cried out: 'Now may God preserve my soul.' Scarcely had I uttered the words when they threw me to the ground and shot and stabbed at me. God be praised they only wounded me in the leg, but they tore my clothes from my body, one the jerkin, another the hat, a third the shirt, and so forth. Then they commenced to quarrel over me. One said he was the first to overtake me, another protested that it was he that caught me, while the rest smote me with their bows. At last two of them seized me and lifted me up, naked as I was, and taking me by the arms, some running in front and some behind, they carried me along with them through the forest at a great pace towards the sea where they had their canoes. As we approached the sea I saw the canoes about a stone's-throw away, which they had dragged out of the water and hidden behind the shrubs, and with the canoes were great multitudes of savages, all decked out with feathers according to their custom. When they saw me they rushed towards me, biting their arms and threatening me, and making gestures as if they would eat me. Then a king approached me carrying the club with which they kill their captives, who spoke saying that having captured me from the Perot, that is to say the Portuguese, they would now take vengeance on me for the death of their friends, and so carrying me to the canoes they beat me with their fists. Then they made haste to launch their canoes, for they feared that an alarm might be raised at Brikioka, as indeed was the case.

Before launching the canoes they bound my hands together, but since they were not all from the same place and no one wanted to go home empty-handed, they began to dispute with my two captors, saying that they had all been just as near to me when I was taken, and each one demanding a piece of me and clamouring to have me killed on the spot.

Then I stood and prayed, expecting every moment to be struck down. But at last the king, who desired to keep me, gave orders to carry me back alive so that their women might see me and make merry with me. For they intended to kill me 'Kawewi Pepicke', that is, to prepare a drink and gather together for a feast at which they would eat me. At these words they desisted, but they bound four ropes round my neck, and I was forced to climb into a canoe, while they made fast the ends of the ropes to the boats and then pushed off and commenced the homeward journey.

2. A SLAVE IS EATEN

There was a slave among the savages belonging to the nation called Carios . . . This man had been a slave among the Portuguese, but had escaped from them. The savages do not kill those who escape in this wise unless they commit some crime, but keep them as slaves to serve them. . . .

It happened about the year 1554, in the sixth month of my captivity, that this Cario fell ill, and his master besought me to help him and make him well again, so that he might catch game for us to eat, especially since, as I knew well, the food that was brought in was shared with me. . . . And the man had been ill for nine or ten days.

Now the savages are accustomed to use for several purposes the teeth of a wild beast called Backe, which they sharpen, and when the blood is sluggish they cut the skin with one of these teeth so that the blood flows freely. This is equivalent with us to letting blood. I took one of these teeth, intending to open the median vein, but I could not cut it as the tooth was too blunt, and the savages stood round about. As I left him I saw that it was useless, but the savages continued to enquire whether he would recover, to which I replied that I could do nothing and that, as they saw, the blood would not flow. Then they said: 'He will surely die. Let us kill him before he is dead.' I answered: 'No, do not kill him, for possibly he may recover', but I could not restrain them. They dragged him in front of the hut of the king Vratinge, while two men held him, although he was so ill that he did not know what they were doing. Then the man came up to whom the Cario had been given, and beat out his brains, after which they left him lying before the huts ready to be eaten. But I warned them that he was a sick man, and that they might also fall sick if they ate him, and they knew not what to do. Nevertheless, one came from the huts where I was and called the womenfolk to make a fire beside the body. Then he cut off the head, for the man had lost an eye from his disease and his appearance was horrible, and throwing away the head, he singed the body at the fire. After this he cut him up and divided the flesh equally, as is their custom, and they devoured everything except the head and intestines, which they did not fancy, on account of the man's sickness.

As I went to and fro in the huts I saw them roasting here the feet, there the hands, and elsewhere a piece of the trunk, and I told the savages that this Cario whom they were roasting and eating had always spoken ill of me, saying that while I was among the Portuguese I had shot several of their friends, and that he lied, for he had never seen me before. 'Now see,' said I, 'he had been several years with you and had never been sick, but on account of his lying stories about me, my God was angry with him and smote him with sickness and put it into your minds to kill and eat him. So will my God do to all evil persons who seek or have sought to injure me.' And they were greatly terrified at my words, but I thanked God that he had in this wise shown his might and power through me. Note reader, and mark well my writing, for I do this not in order to tell you strange things, but only to make known the wonderful works of God.

❈

SIR FRANCIS DRAKE

(c.1540–1596)

English privateer. He sailed through the Strait of Magellan in 1577 on his way to making the second-ever circumnavigation of the world.

N. M. Penzer (ed.), *'The World Encompassed' and Analogous Contemporary Documents Concerning Sir Francis Drake's Circumnavigation of the World* (London, 1926).

PENGUINS AND INDIANS OF PATAGONIA (1577)

In these islands we found great relief and plenty of good victuals, for infinite were the numbers of the fowl, which the Welsh men name Penguin and Magellan termed them Geese. This fowl cannot fly, having but stub wings without feathers, covered over with a certain down as it were young goslings of two months old, as are also all their body besides. In their head, eyes, and feet they be like a duck but almost as a goose. They breed and lodge at land and in the day-time go down to the sea to feed, being so fat that they can but go [i.e. walk]; and their skins cannot be taken from their bodies without tearing of the flesh because of their exceeding fatness. They dig earth in the ground as conies do, wherein they lay their eggs and lodge themselves, and breed their young ones. It is not possible to find a bird of their bigness to have greater strength than they; for our men putting in cudgels into their earths to force them out, they would take hold of them with their bills and would not let go their hold fast, and yet trying all their strength [our men] could not in long time draw them out of their holes, being large and wide within. Some of them have upon their heads standing upright a little tuft of feathers like a peacock and have red circles about their eyes which become them well. The fat which came from their bodies is most piercing and of the nature and quality of the oil of the sea calves or seals whereof we have spoken.

We departing from these islands had somewhat a hard passage, and with difficulty many times did proceed in our way, and that for diverse causes. First, the mountains, being very high and some reaching into the frozen region, did every one send out their several winds, sometimes behind us to send us in our way, sometimes on the starboard side to drive us to the larboard and so the contrary, sometimes right against us to drive us further back in an hour than we would recover again in many. But of all others this was the worst, that sometimes two or three of these winds would come together and meet as it was in one body whose forces, being become one, did so violently fall into the sea, whirling or, as the Spaniard says, with a tornado, that they would pierce into the very bowels of the sea and make it swell upwards on every side. The hollowness they made in the water and the wind breaking out again did take the swelling banks so raised into the air, and being dispersed abroad it ran down again a mighty rain. Besides this, the sea is so deep in all this passage that upon life and death there is no coming to anchor. Neither may I omit the grisly sight of the cold and frozen mountains, reaching their heads, yea, the greatest part of their bodies, into the cold and frozen region, where the power of the reflection of the sun never toucheth to dissolve the ice and snow. . . .

The islands and plain grounds further off were very far sweet and fruitful, frequented by a comely and harmless people but naked men and women and children, whom we could not perceive to have either set places or dwelling or any ordinary means of living as tillage, breeding of cattle, or any other profession, but wanderers from place to place and from island to island, staying in a place so long as it would naturally yield them provision to live without labour save only to kill, gather, and eat, for the which purpose they builded little cottages of poles, and bowers like arbours in our gardens in England, wherein they themselves for the time lodge and keep their household stuff. . . . I took an inventory of all the particulars of one as it seemed of the chiefest lords' house among them as followeth:

1. One water pail
2. Two drinking cups
3. Two boxes of stuff to paint
4. Two wooden spits and one pair of racks
5. Two hatchets, one knife

These are the substance and riches of this people, all of which they leave behind them in the place when they remove till they return again, at what time there is a new increase of creatures for the supply of their nourishment.

✻

WILLIAM DAVIES
(*fl.* 1614)

English barber surgeon. He visited the Amazon in 1608.

Samuel Purchas, *Purchas His Pilgrims* (London, 1625).

DESCRIPTION AND DISCOVERY OF THE RIVER OF AMAZONS
(1608)

In this river I continued ten weeks, seeing the fashion of the people and country there. This country is altogether full of woods, with all sorts of wild beasts, as lions, bears, wolves, leopards, baboons, strange boars, apes, monkeys, martens, sanguines, marmosets, with divers other strange beasts; also these woods are full of wildfowl of all sorts, and parrots more plentiful than pigeons in England, and as good meat, for I have often eaten of them. Also this country is very full of rivers, having a king over every river. In this place is continual tempests, as lightning, thunder, and rain, and so extreme that it continues most commonly sixteen or eighteen hours in four and twenty. There are many standing waters in this country, which be full of alligators, guianes [iguanas], with many other several water serpents, and great store of fresh fish, of strange fashions. This country is full of muskitas, which is a small fly, which much offends a stranger coming newly into the country.

The manner, fashion, and nature of the people is this. They are altogether naked, both men and women, having not so much as one thread about them to cover any part of their nakedness. The man taketh a round cane as big as a penny candle, and two inches in length, through the which he pulls the foreskin of his yard, tying the skin with a piece of the rind of a tree about the bigness of a small pack-thread, then making of it fast about his middle; he continueth thus till he have occasion to use him. In each ear he weareth a reed or cane, which he bores through it, about the bigness of a swan's quill, and in length half an inch, and the like through the midst of the lower lip. Also at the bridge of the nose he hangs in a reed a small glass bead or button which, hanging directly afore his mouth, flies to and fro still as he speaks, wherein he takes great pride and pleasure. He wears his hair long, being rounded below to the nether part of his ear, and cut short, or rather, as I judged, plucked bald on the crown like a friar. But the women use no fashion at all to set forth themselves, but stark naked as they were born, with hair long of their heads; also their breasts hang very low, by reason they are never laced or braced up. They do use to anoint their bodies, both men and women, with a kind of red earth, [so that] the muskitas or flies shall not offend them.

These people are very ingenious, crafty, and treacherous, very light of foot, and good bowmen, whose like I have never seen, for they do ordinarily kill their own food, as beasts, fowl, and fish . . . then having each killed his own food, as well flesh and fowl as fish, they meet together, to the number of fifty or sixty in a company, then make a fire after this fashion. They take two sticks of wood, rubbing one hard against another, till such time as they be fired; then, making of a great fire, every man is his own cook to broil that which he hath gotten, and thus they feed without bread or salt, or any kind of drink but water, and tobacco, neither do they know what it means.

In these countries we could find neither gold nor silver ore, but great store of hens. For I have bought a couple for a jew's harp, when they would refuse ten shillings in money. This country is full of delicious fruit, as pine[apple]s, plantains, guavas, and potato roots, of which fruits and roots I would have bought a man's burden for a glass button or bead. The manner of their lodging is this. They have a kind of net made of the rind of a tree which they call haemac, being three fathom in length and two in breadth, and gathered at both ends at length, then fastening either end to a tree, to the full length about a yard and a half from the ground; when he hath desire to sleep, he creeps unto it.

The king of every river is known by this manner. He wears upon his head a crown of parrots' feathers, of several colours, having either about his middle or about his neck a chain of lions' teeth or claws, or of some other strange beast, having a wooden sword in his hand, and hereby is he known to be the king. Oftentimes one king wars against another in their canoes, which are boats cut out of a whole tree. Sometimes taking one another, the conquerors eat the captives.

✤

ALEXANDER VON HUMBOLDT

(1769–1859)

Prussian explorer. For five years, between 1799 and 1804 he travelled with Aimé Bonpland throughout South America collecting a vast amount of scientific data.

Personal Narrative of Travels to the Equinoctial Regions of America during the years 1799–1804, trans. from the French and ed. T. Ross (London, 1852).

1. STUDYING ELECTRIC EELS (1800)

To catch the *gymnoti* with nets is very difficult, on account of the extreme agility of the fish, which bury themselves in the mud. We would not employ the *barbasco*, that is to say, the roots of the *Piseidea erithyrna*, the *Jacquinia armillaris*, and some species of *phyllanthus*, which, thrown into the pool, intoxicate or benumb the eels. These methods have the effect of enfeebling the *gymnoti*. The Indians therefore told us that they would 'fish with horses' (*embarbascar con caballos*). We found it difficult to form an idea of this extraordinary manner of fishing; but we soon saw our guides return from the savannah, which they had been scouring for wild horses and mules. They brought about thirty with them, which they forced to enter the pool.

The extraordinary noise caused by the horses' hoofs makes the fish issue from the mud, and excites them to the attack. These yellowish and livid eels, resembling large aquatic serpents, swim on the surface of the water, and crowd under the bellies of the horses and mules. A contest between animals of so different an organization presents a very striking spectacle. The Indians, provided with harpoons and long slender reeds, surround the pool closely; and some climb up the trees, the branches of which extend horizontally over the surface of the water. By their wild cries, and the length of their reeds, they prevent the horses from running away and reaching the bank of the pool. The eels, stunned by the noise, defend themselves by the repeated discharge of their electric batteries. For a long interval they seem likely to prove victorious. Several horses sink beneath the violence of the invisible strokes which they receive from all sides, in organs the most essential to life; and stunned by the force and frequency of the shocks, they disappear under the water. Others, panting, with mane erect, and haggard eyes expressing anguish and dismay, raise themselves, and endeavour to flee from the storm by which they are overtaken. They are driven back by the Indians into the middle of the water; but a small number succeed in eluding the active vigilance of the fishermen. These regain the shore, stumbling at every step, and stretch themselves on the sand, exhausted with fatigue, and with limbs benumbed by the electric shocks of the *gymnoti*.

2. The Inconvenience of Insects

The frequency of gnats and mosquitoes characterizes unhealthy climates only so far as the development and multiplication of these insects depend on the same causes that give rise to miasmata. These noxious animals love a fertile soil covered with plants, stagnant waters, and a humid air never agitated by the wind; they prefer to an open country those shades, that softened day, that tempered degree of light, heat, and moisture which, while it favours the action of chemical affinities, accelerates the putrefaction of organized substances. . . . When you are exposed day and night, during whole months, to the torment of insects, the continual irritation of the skin causes febrile commotions and, from the sympathy existing between the dermoid and the gastric systems, injures the functions of the stomach. Digestion first becomes difficult, the cutaneous inflammation excites profuse perspirations, an unquenchable thirst succeeds, and, in persons of a feeble constitution, increasing impatience is succeeded by depression of mind, during which all the pathogenic causes act with increased violence. It is neither the dangers of navigating in small boats, the

savage Indians, nor the serpents, crocodiles, or jaguars, that make Spaniards dread a voyage on the Orinoco; it is, as they say with simplicity, *el
sudar y las moscas* (the perspiration and the flies). We have reason to
believe that mankind, as they change the surface of the soil, will succeed
in altering by degrees the constitution of the atmosphere. The insects will
diminish when the old trees of the forest have disappeared; when, in those
countries now desert, the rivers are seen bordered with cottages, and the
plains covered with pastures and harvests.

�֍

CHARLES WATERTON
(1782–1865)

*English naturalist. He spent twelve years between 1812 and 1824, collect-
ing and observing plants and wildlife in the interior of Guiana.*

Wanderings in South America (London, 1825).

1. LIFE IN THE FOREST (1812)

Courteous reader, here thou hast the outlines of an amazing landscape
given thee; thou wilt see that the principal parts of it are but faintly traced,
some of them scarcely visible at all, and that the shades are wholly wanting. If thy soul partakes of the ardent flame which the persevering Mungo
Park's did, these outlines will be enough for thee: they will give thee some
idea of what a noble country this is; and if thou hast but courage to set
about giving the world a finished picture of it, neither materials to work
on, nor colours to paint it in its true shades, will be wanting to thee. It may
appear a difficult task at a distance; but look close at it, and it is nothing
at all; provided thou hast but a quiet mind, little more is necessary, and the
genius which presides over these wilds will kindly help thee through the
rest. She will allow thee to slay the fawn, and cut down the mountain-
cabbage for thy support, and to select from every part of her domain
whatever may be necessary for the work thou art about; but having killed
a pair of Doves in order to enable thee to give mankind a true and proper
description of them, thou must not destroy a third through wantonness, or
to show what a good marksman thou art; that would only blot the picture
thou art finishing, not colour it. . . .

Leave behind you your high-seasoned dishes, your wines and your delicacies; carry nothing but what is necessary for your own comfort and the object in view, and depend upon the skill of an Indian, or your own, for fish and game. A sheet, about twelve feet long, ten wide, painted, and with loop-holes on each side, will be of great service; in a few minutes you can suspend it betwixt two trees in the shape of a roof. Under this, in your hammock, you may defy the pelting shower, and sleep heedless of the dews of night. A hat, a shirt, and a light pair of trousers will be all the raiment you require. Custom will soon teach you to tread lightly and barefoot on the little inequalities of the ground, and show you how to pass on, unwounded, amid the mantling briars.

Snakes in these wilds are certainly an annoyance, though perhaps more in imagination than reality; for you must recollect that the serpent is never the first to offend; his poisonous fang was not given him for conquest: he never inflicts a wound with it but to defend existence. Provided you walk cautiously, and do not absolutely touch him, you may pass in safety close by him. As he is often coiled up on the ground, and amongst the branches of the trees above you, a degree of circumspection is necessary, lest you unwarily disturb him.

Tigers are too few, and too apt to fly before the noble face of man, to require a moment of your attention.

The bite of the most noxious of the insects, at the very worst, only causes a transient fever, with a degree of pain more of less. . . .

Nothing could be more lovely than the appearance of the forest on each side of this noble river. Hills rose on hills in fine gradation, all covered with trees of gigantic height and size. Here their leaves were of a lively purple, and there of the deepest green. Sometimes the caracara extended its scarlet blossoms from branch to branch, and gave the tree the appearance as though it had been hung with garlands.

This delightful scenery of the Essequibo made the soul overflow with joy, and caused you to rove in fancy through fairyland; till, on turning an angle of the river, you were recalled to more sober reflections on seeing the once grand and towering mora, now dead and ragged in its topmost branches, while its aged trunk, undermined by the rushing torrent, hung as though in sorrow over the river, which, ere long, would receive it, and sweep it away for ever. . . .

The tigers had kept up a continued roaring every night since we had entered the Essequibo. The sound was awfully fine. Sometimes it was in the immediate neighbourhood; at other times it was far off, and echoed amongst the hills like distant thunder.

It may, perhaps, not be amiss to observe here, that when the word tiger is used, it does not mean the Bengal tiger. It means the jaguar, whose skin is beautifully spotted, and not striped like that of the tiger in the East. It is, in fact, the tiger of the new world, and receiving the name of tiger from the discoverers of South America, it has kept it ever since. It is a cruel, strong, and dangerous beast, but not so courageous as the Bengal tiger.

2. RIDING A CAYMAN (1820)

The day was now declining apace, and the Indian had made his instrument to take the cayman. It was very simple. There were four pieces of tough hard wood, a foot long, and about as thick as your little finger, and barbed at both ends; they were tied round the end of the rope, in such a manner, that if you conceive the rope to be an arrow, these four sticks would form the arrow's head; so that one end of the four united sticks answered to the point of the arrow-head, while the other ends of the sticks expanded at equal distances round the rope. Now it is evident that, if the cayman swallowed this (the other end of the rope, which was thirty yards long, being fastened to a tree), the more he pulled, the faster the barbs would stick into his stomach. This wooden hook, if you may so call it, was well baited with the flesh of the acouri, and the entrails were twisted round the rope for about a foot above it.

Nearly a mile from where we had our hammocks, the sand-bank was steep and abrupt, and the river very still and deep; there the Indian pricked a stick into the sand. It was two feet long, and on its extremity was fixed the machine; it hung suspended about a foot from the water, and the end of the rope was made fast to a stake driven well into the sand.

The Indian then took the empty shell of a land tortoise and gave it some heavy blows with an axe. I asked him why he did that. He said it was to let the cayman hear that something was going on. In fact the Indian meant it as the cayman's dinner-bell. Having done this, we went back to the hammocks, not intending to visit it again till morning. During the night, the jaguars roared and grumbled in the forest, as though the world was going wrong with them, and at intervals we could hear the distant cayman. The roaring of the jaguars was awful; but it was music to the dismal noise of these hideous and malicious reptiles.

About half-past five in the morning, the Indian stole off silently to take a look at the bait. On arriving at the place he set up a tremendous shout. We all jumped out of our hammocks, and ran to him. The Indians got there before me, for they had no clothes to put on, and I lost two minutes in looking for my trousers and in slipping into them. We found a cayman, ten feet and a half long, fast to the end of the rope. Nothing now remained to do, but to get him out of the water without injuring his scales . . .

I informed the Indians that it was my intention to draw him quietly out of the water, and then secure him. They looked and stared at each other, and said I might do it myself; but they would have no hand in it; the cayman would worry some of us. On saying this, they squatted on their hams with the most perfect indifference. The Indians of these wilds have never been subject to the least restraint; and I knew enough of them to be aware, that if I tried to force them against their will, they would take off, and leave me and my presents unheeded, and never return. . . . My Indian was now in conversation with the others, and they asked if I would allow them to shoot a dozen arrows into him, and thus disable him. This would have ruined all. I had come above three hundred miles on purpose to get a cayman uninjured, and not to carry back a mutilated specimen. I rejected their proposition with firmness, and darted a disdainful eye upon the Indians. . . .

I now walked up and down the sand, revolving a dozen projects in my head. The canoe was at a considerable distance, and I ordered the people to bring it round to the place where we were. The mast was eight feet long, and not much thicker than my wrist. I took it out of the canoe, and wrapped the sail round the end of it. Now it appeared clear to me, that if I went down upon one knee, and held the mast in the same position as the soldier holds his bayonet when rushing to the charge, I could force it down the cayman's throat, should he come open-mouthed at me. When this was told to the Indians, they brightened up, and said they would help me to pull him out of the river. . . .

I now took the mast of the canoe in my hand (the sail being tied round the end of the mast) and sank down upon one knee, about four yards from the water's edge, determining to thrust it down his throat, in case he gave me an opportunity. I certainly felt somewhat uncomfortable in this situation, and I thought of Cerberus on the other side of the Styx ferry. The people pulled the cayman to the surface; he plunged furiously as soon as he arrived in these upper regions, and immediately went below again on their slackening the rope. I saw enough not to fall in love at first sight. I now told them we would run all risks, and have him on land immediately. They pulled again, and out he came. This was an interesting moment. I kept my position firmly, with my eye fixed steadfast on him.

By this time the cayman was within two yards of me. I saw he was in a state of fear and perturbation; I instantly dropped the mast, sprang up, and jumped on his back, turning half round as I vaulted, so that I gained my seat with my face in a right position. I immediately seized his forelegs and, by main force, twisted them on his back; thus they served me for a bridle. He now seemed to have recovered from his surprise, and probably fancying himself in hostile company, he began to plunge furiously, and lashed the sand with his long and powerful tail. I was out of reach of the strokes of it, by being near his head. He continued to plunge and strike, and made my seat very uncomfortable. It must have been a fine sight for an unoccupied spectator. The people roared out in triumph, and were so vociferous that it was some time before they heard me tell them to pull me and my beast of burden further inland. I was apprehensive the rope might break, and then there would have been every chance of going down to the regions under water with the cayman.

The people now dragged us above forty yards on the sand: it was the first and last time I was ever on a cayman's back. Should it be asked how I managed to keep my seat, I would answer: I hunted some years with Lord Darlington's fox-hounds.

After repeated attempts to regain his liberty, the cayman gave in, and became tranquil through exhaustion. I now managed to tie up his jaws, and firmly secured his forefeet in the position I had held them. We had now another severe struggle for superiority, but he was soon overcome and again remained quiet. While some of the people were pressing upon his head and shoulders, I threw myself on his tail, and by keeping it down to the sand, prevented him from kicking up another dust. He was finally conveyed to the canoe, and then to the place where we had suspended our hammocks. There I cut his throat; and, after breakfast was over, commenced the dissection. . . .

The back of the cayman may be said to be almost impenetrable to a musket-ball, but his sides are not near so strong, and are easily pierced with an arrow; indeed, were they as strong as the back and the belly, there would be no part of the cayman's body soft and elastic enough to admit of expansion after taking in a supply of food. The cayman has no grinders; his teeth are entirely made for snatch and swallow; there are thirty-two in each jaw. Perhaps no animal in existence bears more decided marks in his countenance of cruelty and malice than the cayman. He is the scourge and terror of all the large rivers in South America near the line.

CHARLES ROBERT DARWIN

(1809–1882)

English naturalist. He first developed his theories of evolution while on the five-year voyage of the Beagle, *which set off in 1831.*

1–3: *Journal of Researches into the Geology and Natural History of the Various Countries Visited during the Voyage of HMS 'Beagle' Round the World* (London, 1839); 4: *Charles Darwin's Diary of the Voyage of HMS 'Beagle'*, ed. N. Barlow (Cambridge, 1933).

1. THE BRAZILIAN FOREST (1832)

Bahia, or San Salvador, Brazil, Feb. 29th. The day has passed delightfully. Delight itself, however, is a weak term to express the feelings of a naturalist who, for the first time, has wandered by himself in a Brazilian forest. The elegance of the grasses, the novelty of the parasitical plants, the beauty of the flowers, the glossy green of the foliage, but above all the general luxuriance of the vegetation, filled me with admiration. A most paradoxical mixture of sound and silence pervades the shady parts of the wood. The noise from the insects is so loud that it may be heard even in a vessel anchored several hundred yards from the shore; yet within the recesses of the forest a universal silence appears to reign. To a person fond of natural history, such a day as this brings with it a deeper pleasure than he can ever hope to experience again. After wandering about for some hours, I returned to the landing-place; but, before reaching it, I was overtaken by a tropical storm. I tried to find shelter under a tree, which was so thick that it would never have been penetrated by common English rain; but here, in a couple of minutes, a little torrent flowed down the trunk. It is to this violence of the rain that we must attribute the verdure at the bottom of the thickest woods: if the showers were like those of a colder clime, the greater part would be absorbed or evaporated before it reached the ground. . . .

The naturalist in England, in his walks, enjoys a great advantage over others in frequently meeting with something worthy of attention; here he suffers a pleasant nuisance in not being able to walk a hundred yards without being fairly tied to the spot by some new and wondrous creature. . . .

It has been said that the love of the chase is an inherent delight in man—a relic of an instinctive passion. If so, I am sure the pleasure of living in the open air, with the sky for a roof and the ground for a table, is part of the same feeling. It is the savage returning to his wild and native habits. I always look back to our boat cruises and my land journeys, when through unfrequented countries, with a kind of extreme delight which no scenes of civilization could create. I do not doubt every traveller must remember the glowing sense of happiness from the simple consciousness of breathing in a foreign clime where the civilized man has seldom or never trod.

2. MARINE LIFE (1834)

If we turn from the land to the sea, we shall find the latter as abundantly stocked with living creatures as the former is poorly so. In all parts of the world a rocky and partially protected shore perhaps supports, in a given space, a greater number of individual animals than any other station. There is one marine production which from its importance is worthy of a particular history. It is the kelp, or *Macrocystis pyrifera*. This plant grows on every rock from low-water mark to a great depth, both on the outer coast and within the channels. I believe, during the voyages of the *Adventure* and *Beagle*, not one rock near the surface was discovered which was not buoyed by this floating weed. . . .

The number of living creatures of all Orders, whose existence intimately depends on the kelp, is wonderful. A great volume might be written, describing the inhabitants of one of these beds of seaweed. Almost all the leaves, excepting those that float on the surface, are so thickly encrusted with corallines as to be of a white colour. We find exquisitely delicate structures, some inhabited by simple hydra-like polypi, others by more organized kinds, and beautiful compound Ascidiae. On the leaves, also, various patelliform shells, Trochi, uncovered molluscs, and some bivalves are attached. Innumerable crustacea frequent every part of the plant. On shaking the great entangled roots, a pile of small fish, shells, cuttlefish, crabs of all orders, sea-eggs, starfish, beautiful Holuthuriae, Planariae, and crawling nereidous animals of a multitude of forms, all fall out together. Often as I recurred to a branch of the kelp, I never failed to discover animals of new and curious structures. In Chiloe, where the kelp does not thrive very well, the numerous shells, corallines, and crustacea are absent; but there yet remain a few of the Flustraceae, and some compound Ascidiae; the latter, however, are of different species from those in Tierra del Fuego: we here see the fucus possessing a wider range than the animals which use it as an abode. I can only compare these great aquatic forests of the southern hemisphere with the terrestrial ones in the inter-tropical regions.

Yet if in any country a forest was destroyed, I do not believe nearly so many species of animals would perish as would here, from the destruction of the kelp. Amidst the leaves of this plant numerous species of fish live, which nowhere else could find food or shelter; with their destruction the many cormorants and other fishing birds, the otters, seals, and porpoises, would soon perish also; and lastly, the Fuegian savage, the miserable lord of this miserable land, would redouble his cannibal feast, decrease in numbers, and perhaps cease to exist.

3. THOUGHTS ON THE FINCHES OF THE GALAPAGOS ISLANDS (1835)

The natural history of these islands is eminently curious, and well deserves attention. Most of the organic productions are aboriginal creations, found nowhere else: there is even a difference between the inhabitants of the different islands. Yet all show a marked relationship with those of America, though separated from that continent by an open space of ocean, between 500 and 600 miles in width. . . .

Of land-birds I obtained twenty-six kinds, all peculiar to the group and found nowhere else, with the exception of one lark-like finch from North America (*Dolichonyx oryzivorus*), which ranges on that continent as far north as 54°, and generally frequents marshes. The other twenty-five birds consist, firstly, of a hawk, curiously intermediate in structure between a buzzard and the American group of carrion-feeding *polybori*; and with these latter birds it agrees most closely in every habit and even tone of voice. Secondly, there are two owls, representing the short-eared and white barn owls of Europe. Thirdly, a wren, three tyrant fly-catchers (two of them species of *pyrocephalus*, one or both of which would be ranked by some ornithologists as only varieties), and a dove—all analogous to, but distinct from, American species. Fourthly, a swallow, which though differing from the *Progne purpurea* of both Americas only in being rather duller-coloured, smaller, and slenderer, is considered by Mr [John] Gould as specifically distinct. Fifthly, there are three species of mocking-thrush—a form highly characteristic of America.

The remaining land-birds form a most singular group of finches, related to each other in the structure of their beaks, short tails, form of body, and plumage: there are thirteen species, which Mr Gould has divided into four sub-groups. All these species are peculiar to this archipelago; and so is the whole group, with the exception of one species of the sub-group *cactornis*, lately brought from Bow Island, in the Low Archipelago. Of *cactornis*, the two species may be often seen climbing about the flowers of the great cactus-trees; but all the other species of this group of finches, mingled together in flocks, feed on the dry and sterile ground of the lower districts. The males of all, or certainly of the greater number, are jet black, and the females (with perhaps one or two exceptions) are brown. The most curious fact is the perfect gradation in the size of the beaks in the different species of *geospiza*, from one as large as that of a hawfinch to that of a chaffinch, and (if Mr Gould is right in including his sub-group, *certhidea*), even to that of a warbler.

✲

ALFRED RUSSELL WALLACE
(1823–1913)

English naturalist. He spent five years collecting on the Amazon with Henry Bates before travelling to the Far East.

A *Narrative of Travels on the Amazon and Rio Negro, with an account of the Native Tribes and Observations on the Climate, Geology, and Natural History of the Amazon Valley* (London, 1853).

1. SOUNDS, SIGHTS, AND TASTES OF THE FOREST (1848)

Every night, while in the upper part of the river, we had a concert of frogs, which made most extraordinary noises. There are three kinds, which can frequently be all heard at once. One of these makes a noise something like what one would expect a frog to make, namely a dismal croak, but the sounds uttered by the others were like no animal noise that I ever heard before. A distant railway train approaching, and a blacksmith hammering on his anvil, are what they exactly resemble. They are such true imitations that, when lying half-dozing in the canoe, I have often fancied myself at home, hearing the familiar sounds of the approaching mail-train, and the hammering of the boilermakers at the iron-works. Then we often had the *guarhibas*, or howling monkeys, with their terrific noises, the shrill grating whistle of the cicadas and locusts, and the peculiar notes of the suacuras and other aquatic birds; add to these the loud, unpleasant hum of the mosquito in your immediate vicinity, and you have a pretty good idea of our nightly concert on the Tocantins.

On the morning of the 19th, at Panaja, where we had passed the night,

I took my gun and went into the forest, but found nothing. I saw, however, an immense silk-cotton tree, one of the buttresses of which ran out twenty feet from the trunk. On the beach was a pretty yellow *Enothera*, which is common all along this part of the river, as well as a small white passion-flower. Mr Leavens here bought some rubber, and we then rowed or sailed on for the rest of the day. In the afternoon I took the montaria, with Isidora, to try and shoot some of the pretty yellow orioles. I killed one, but it stuck in a thick prickly tree, and we were obliged to come away without it. We passed Patos in the afternoon; near it was a tree covered with a mass of bright yellow blossoms, more brilliant than laburnum, and a really gorgeous sight.

The next day we left the land of the blue macaw without a single specimen. From this place to the Falls we had seen them every day, morning and evening, flying high over the river. At almost every house feathers were on the ground, showing that this splendid bird is often shot for food. Alexander once had a chance at them, but his gun missed fire, and they immediately flew off. Lower down the river they are scarcely ever seen, and never below Baião, while from this place up they are very abundant. What can be the causes which so exactly limit the range of such a strong-flying bird? It appears with the rock, and with this there is no doubt a corresponding change in the fruits on which the birds feed.

Our Indians, seeing a likely place on the beach for turtles' eggs, went on shore in the montaria, and were fortunate enough to find 123 buried in the sand. They are oily and very savoury, and we had an immense omelette for dinner. The shell is leathery, and the white never coagulates, but is thrown away, and the yolk only eaten. The Indians eat them also raw, mixed with farinha. We dined on the beach, where there was abundance of a plant much resembling chamomile. The sands were very hot, so that it was almost impossible to walk over them barefooted. The Indians, in crossing extensive beaches, stop and dig holes in the sand to cool their feet in. We now got on very slowly, having to tack across and across the river, the wind blowing up it, as it always does at this season.

HENRY WALTER BATES

(1825–1892)

English naturalist. A self-taught entomologist, he made a huge collection during eleven years on the Amazon, from 1848 to 1859. On his return he became the first paid secretary of the Royal Geographical Society.

The Naturalist on the River Amazon (London, 1863).

1. ANTS (1860)

One night my servant woke me three or four hours before sunrise by calling out that the rats were robbing the farinha baskets. The article at that time was scarce and dear. I got up, listened, and found the noise was very unlike that made by rats. So I took the light and went into the store-room, which was close to my sleeping-place. I there found a broad column of Saüba ants, consisting of thousands of individuals, as busy as possible, passing to and fro between the door and my precious baskets. Most of those passing outwards were laden each with a grain of farinha, which was, in some cases, larger and many times heavier than the bodies of the carriers. Farinha consists of grains of similar size and appearance to the tapioca of our shops; both are products of the same root, tapioca being the pure starch, and farinha the starch mixed with woody fibre, the latter ingredient giving it a yellowish colour. It was amusing to see some of the dwarfs, the smallest members of their family, staggering along, completely hidden under their load. The baskets, which were on a high table, were entirely covered with ants, many hundreds of whom were employed in snipping the dry leaves which served as lining. This produced the rustling sound which had at first disturbed us. My servant told me that they would carry off the whole contents of the two baskets (about two bushels) in the course of the night, if they were not driven off; so we tried to exterminate them by killing them with our wooden clogs. It was impossible, however, to prevent fresh hosts coming in as fast as we killed their companions. They returned the next night; and I was then obliged to lay trains of gunpowder along their line, and blow them up. This, repeated many times, at last seemed to intimidate them, for we were free from their visits during the remainder of my residence at the place.

2. TROPICAL FOREST

To obtain a fair notion of the number and variety of the animal tenants of these forests, it is necessary to follow up the research month after month and explore them in different directions and at all seasons. During several months I used to visit this district two or three days every week, and never failed to obtain some species new to me, of bird, reptile, or insect. It seemed to be an epitome of all that the humid portions of the Para forests could produce. This endless diversity, the coolness of the air, the varied and strange forms of vegetation, the entire freedom from mosquitoes and other pests, and even the solemn gloom and silence, combined to make my rambles through it always pleasant as well as profitable. Such places are paradises to a naturalist, and if he be of a contemplative turn there is no situation more favourable for his indulging the tendency. There is something in a tropical forest akin to the ocean in its effects on the mind. Man feels so completely his insignificance there, and the vastness of nature. A naturalist cannot help reflecting on the vegetable forces manifested on so grand a scale around him. A German traveller, Burmeister, has said that the contemplation of a Brazilian forest produced on him a painful impression, on account of the vegetation displaying a spirit of restless selfishness, eager emulation, and craftiness. He thought the softness, earnestness, and repose of European woodland scenery were far more pleasing, and that these formed one of the causes of the superior moral character of European nations.

3. A MEETING WITH A BOA CONSTRICTOR

One day as I was entomologizing alone and unarmed, in a dry Ygapo, where the trees were rather wide apart and the ground coated to the depth of eight or ten inches with dead leaves, I was near coming into collision with a boa constrictor. I had just entered a little thicket to capture an insect, and whilst pinning it was rather startled by a rushing noise in the vicinity. I looked up to the sky, thinking a squall was coming on, but not a breath of wind stirred in the tree-tops. On stepping out of the bushes I met face to face a huge serpent coming down a slope, and making the dry twigs crack and fly with his weight as he moved over them. I had very frequently met with a smaller boa, the Cutim-boia, in a similar way, and knew from the habits of the family that there was no danger, so I stood my ground. On seeing me the reptile suddenly turned, and glided at an accelerated pace down the path. Wishing to take a note of his probable size and the colours and markings of his skin, I set off after him; but he increased his speed, and I was unable to get near enough for the purpose. There was very little of the serpentine movement in his course. The rapidly moving and shining body looked like a stream of brown liquid flowing over the thick bed of fallen leaves, rather than a serpent with skin of varied colours. He descended towards the lower and moister parts of the Ygapo. The huge trunk of an uprooted tree here lay across the road; this he glided over in his undeviating course, and soon after penetrated a dense swampy thicket, where of course I did not choose to follow him.

4. INCIDENT WITH TOUCANS

None of the Arassaris, to my knowledge, make a yelping noise like that uttered by the larger toucans (*Ramphastos*); the notes of the curl-crested species are very singular, resembling the croaking of frogs. I had an amusing adventure one day with these birds. I had shot one from a rather high tree in a dark glen in the forest, and leaving my gun leaning against a tree-trunk in the pathway, went into the thicket where the bird had fallen, to secure my booty. It was only wounded, and on my attempting to seize it, it set up a loud scream. In an instant, as if by magic, the shady nook seemed alive with these birds, although there was certainly none visible when I entered the thicket. They descended towards me, hopping from bough to bough, some of them swinging on the loops and cables of woody lianas, and all croaking and fluttering their wings like so many furies. Had I had a long stick in my hand I could have knocked several of them over. After killing the wounded one I rushed out to fetch my gun, but, the screaming of their companion having ceased, they remounted the trees, and before I could reload, every one of them had disappeared.

�֍

RICHARD SPRUCE

(1817–1893)

English botanist. He collected on the Amazon and in the Andes for nearly fifteen years between 1849 and 1864. He wrote no book, but his friend Wallace published a posthumous collection of his letters and journals.

Notes of a Botanist on the Amazon and Andes, ed. A. R. Wallace (London, 1908).

1. MUTINY OF HIS MEN (1854)

Nov. 23 (Thursday). This day about noon I left San Carlos. My crew consisted of four Indians; two of them were sons of the pilot (Pedro Deno). On the same day at 4 p.m. we reached the pilot's cunuco . . . and stayed the night. Here a plot was laid to kill me. There were several people at the cunuco, including the pilot's wife, other sons and daughters, a son-in-law, etc. They were engaged in distilling bureche, and my men on arrival began to test its quality, which, though not of the best, sufficed to turn their heads and set them vomiting, all except the son-in-law (Pedro Yurebe), who drank enough to make him noisy but not to render his movements unsteady.

The cunuco consisted of two sheds, open at the sides, in one of which the still was at work. The port where the canoe was anchored was perhaps some 80 yards distant, down a rather steep descent. I had my hammock taken up and fastened under one of the sheds, and when night fell, after eating a small quantify of the forequarter of an alligator which I bought of Yurebe, I turned in. The Indians were very noisy, but as nothing is more tiresome than the conversation of these people when intoxicated, I paid little attention to it, save that I noticed one of the pilot's sons was inviting his brother-in-law Yurebe to make the voyage with us to the Barra. After a while I heard them talk so much about 'heinali' ['the man'] that I could not help listening attentively to what they said, and it was well I did so.

Pedro Yurebe owed some forty-three pesos to the Comisario of San Carlos and others, but he had no scruple to leave this unpaid till his return from the Barra, and a brilliant idea had just struck him. 'The man', he said, was going to his own country, whence he would return to more. In the morning he (Yurebe) would offer his services for the voyage and get the pay beforehand (according to custom); they would then embark, and on reaching the mouth of the river Guasie, which they might do in three or four days, they would take the montaria while I was sleeping and make their way up that river, whence they could at any time return to their own territory, as it is but a short cut (a day overland) from the upper part of the Guasie to several tributaries of the Guainia. They would thus shirk the long, tedious voyage for which they had already received pay. This was largely discussed and approved by all. It then entered Yurebe's head to ask if 'the man' had much merchandise with him. 'Hulasikali! Wala!' ('He has plenty. He has everything') was the reply. But they deceived themselves, for most of my boxes were filled with paper and plants, and not with woven goods as they supposed. 'Then', said he, 'we must not leave him without carrying off as much as we can of his goods, and for this purpose it will be necessary to kill him.'

This also was approved of and the consequences discussed at length . . . 'Why should we not kill the man now?' said he; 'we have him here sleeping in the midst of the forest, far removed from all observers. When he left San Carlos every one knew him for a sick man, and no one will be surprised to hear of his death.' 'Hena nu camisha' ('I have no shirt'), 'and no sign will remain of violence having been used.' (In fact, his only clothing was a strip of bark between his legs.) This he repeated a great many times, and all his companions applauded the idea. Three questions remained for them to discuss: the disposal of the body, of the goods, and of themselves. . . .

It may be supposed that I listened to all this with breathless attention, and I could hardly believe that their acts would be conformable with their words, till I heard them begin to lash themselves into a fury by recapitulating all the injuries they had received from the white men, all of which they considered themselves justified in retaliating on my devoted head—though in my short intercourse with them I had shown them only kindness, and particularly to Pedro Yurebe, whose little daughter I had a short time before cured of a distressing colic, which for many consecutive days and nights had allowed her no rest.

I had on me a slight attack of diarrhoea—this is mostly the case with me on the first day I embark, when the excessive heat causes me to drink a great deal of water—and I had been obliged to leave my hammock two or three times since nightfall. It was now past midnight, and just as I lay down the last time I heard them deciding that the best way would be to strangle me as soon as I should be asleep again, which Yurebe undertook to do, and one of the others undertook to ascertain when I had fallen asleep. The fires had gone out and only the dim light of the stars illuminated the interior of the cabins. Though reclining in my hammock, I kept my feet on the ground ready to spring up should I be attacked. The darkness prevented their noticing this, and as I kept perfectly still for some time the man who had placed himself to watch me reported I was sleeping. I heard them all whispering one to the other, 'Iduali! Iduali!' ('Now it is good—now it is good'), and as Yurebe hesitated a moment, I got up and walked leisurely towards the forest as if my necessities had called me thither again; but instead I turned when I got a few paces and walked straight down to the canoe, unlocked the door of the cabin, which I entered, and having fortified the open doorway by putting a bundle of paper before it, I laid my double-barrelled loaded gun, along with a cutlass and knife, by my side, and thus awaited the attack which I still expected would be made.

At intervals I could hear angry exclamations from the Indians, wondering that I did not return to my hammock; and it may be imagined in what a state of mind I passed the rest of the night, never allowing my eye and ear to relax their watchfulness for a moment. However, they did not once stir to see what had become of me, and at length the break of day relieved me partly from my anxiety, but not entirely, for in that lonely place the dark deed contemplated might have been done almost as secretly by day as by night; and when shortly afterwards Pedro Yurebe came to offer to accompany me to the Barra, I took care while conversing with him never to move out of reach of my gun. Of course I declined his offer, excusing myself on the supposition that the commandant of the Brazilian frontier would not allow him to pass on account of his name not being entered in the passport along with the others.

Though Pedro Yurebe was left behind, I took care throughout the rest of the voyage that the Indians should never approach me unarmed, and I never spent a gloomier time.

2. NEAR CHIMBORAZO IN THE HIGH ANDES (1864)

Here the icy cope of Chimborazo seemed so near that one might have touched it by stretching out the hand—an illusion caused by the transparency of the atmosphere. The temperature was pleasant, for the bright sun tempered the cool breeze, and there was no sand. But as I returned, a few weeks afterwards, I crossed the paramo in a piercingly cold misty rain, and when I reached Mocha I scarcely knew whether I had any hands or feet. If you have been up Teesdale as far as the Weel, you have seen in that chilly treeless solitude something very like the paramos of the Andes. The Weel itself is not unlike the small lagoons scattered about in hollows on Sanancajas. They are often to be seen covered with small wild ducks that no one cares to disturb. Herds of shaggy wild cattle roam over the paramo, and pick up a scanty subsistence from the sedgy herbage.

You may have read of the paramero—the deadly cold wind, charged with frost, that sometimes blows over the paramos, and withers every living thing it meets. A person has told me that when a boy he was once crossing the highest point of Sanancajas, towards Guayaquil, along with his father, when they saw a man sitting by the wayside and apparently grinning at them with all his might. 'See', said the boy, 'how that man is laughing at us!' 'Silence, my son,' replied the father, 'or say a prayer for the repose of his soul—the man is dead!'

I have had to face a paramero, but never of this intense kind. Its approach is indicated by the wind beginning to whistle shrilly in the distance among the dead grass-stalks. When he hears that ominous sound, the horseman takes a pull at his flask, draws his wraps close around him, and his hat down over his eyes; and his horse too seems to nerve himself for the encounter of the withering blast—carries his head low, and throws forward his shaggy mane. It seems to be the first shock of the cold blast that kills. If a man can sustain it unscathed, he generally escapes with his life.

✻

SIR RICHARD BURTON

(1821–1890)

British explorer, soldier and, later, diplomat. After all his Asian and African travels he was posted to Brazil, as consul to Santos. He travelled inland and descended the São Francisco River.

Explorations of the Highlands of Brazil (London, 1869).

THE FALLS OF PAULO AFONSO* (1865)

Paulo Afonso differs essentially from Niagara, whose regular supply by the inland seas admits little alteration of weight, or size, or strength of stream, except in the rare winters when it is frozen over. About December, as the floods run high, this tiny creek will swell to an impassable boiling rapid, ending in a fine fall about the 'Vampire's Cave'. Upon this 'Goat Island', where if there are no goats the walking is fit for them only, are short tracts of loose sand alternating with sheets of granite, and of syenite, with here and there a 'courtil' of greener grass. The walk leads to a table of jutting rock on the west side, where we cling to a dry tree-trunk, and peer, fascinated, into the 'hell of waters' boiling below.

The Quebrada, or gorge, is here 260 feet deep, and in the narrowest part it is choked to a minimum breadth of 51 feet. It is filled with what seems not water, but the froth of milk, a dashing and dazzling, a whirling and churning surfaceless mass, which gives a wondrous study of fluid in motion. And the marvellous disorder is a well-directed anarchy: the course and sway, the wrestling and writhing, all tend to set free the prisoner from the prison walls. Ces eaux! mais ce sont des âmes: it is the spectacle of a host rushing down in 'liquid vastness' to victory, the triumph of motion, of

---

* These are now exploited for hydroelectricity, and almost all the flow now goes through the power plant.

momentum over the immovable. Here the luminous whiteness of the chaotic foam-crests, hurled in billows and breakers against the blackness of the rock, is burst into flakes and spray that leap half way up the immuring trough. There the surface reflections dull the dazzling crystal to a thick opaque yellow, and there the shelter of some spur causes a momentary start and recoil to the column, which, at once gathering strength, bounds and springs onwards with a new crush and another roar. The heaped-up centre shows fugitive ovals and progressive circles of a yet more sparkling, glittering, dazzling light, divided by points of comparative repose, like the nodal lines of waves. They struggle and jostle, start asunder, and interlace as they dash with steadfast purpose adown the inclined plane. Now a fierce blast hunts away the thin spray-drift, and puffs it to leeward in rounded clouds, thus enhancing the brilliancy of the gorge-sole. Then the steam boils over and canopies the tremendous scene. Then in the stilly air of dull warm grey, the mists surge up, deepening still more, by their veil of ever ascending vapour, the dizzy fall that yawns under our feet. The general effect of the picture—and the same may be said of all great cataracts—is the 'realized' idea of power, of power tremendous, inexorable, irresistible.

✵

EDWARD WHYMPER

(1840–1911)

British explorer, mountaineer, and artist. The first man to climb the Matterhorn (in 1865), he also climbed both Chimborazo and Cotopaxi in the Andes.

Travels Amongst the Great Andes of the Equator (London, 1879).

CLIMBING CHIMBORAZO (1879)

At about 11 a.m. we fancied we saw the Pacific, above the clouds which covered the whole of the intervening flat country; and shortly afterwards commenced to enter the plateau which is at the top of the mountain, having by this time made half the circuit of the western dome. We were then twenty thousand feet high, and the summits seemed within our grasp. We could see both—one towards our right, and the other a little further away on our left, with a hollow plateau about a third of a mile across between them. We reckoned that in another hour we could get to the top of either; and, not knowing which of the two was the higher, we made for the nearest. But at this point the condition of affairs completely changed. The sky became overclouded, the wind rose, and we entered upon a tract of exceedingly soft snow, which could not be traversed in the ordinary way. The leading man went in up to his neck, almost out of sight, and had to be hauled out by those behind. Imagining that we had got into a labyrinth of crevasses, we beat about right and left to try to extricate ourselves; and, after discovering that it was everywhere alike, we found the only possible way of proceeding was to flog every yard of it down, and then to crawl over it on all fours; and, even then, one or another was frequently submerged, and almost disappeared.[1]

Needless to say, time flew rapidly. When we had been at this sort of work for three hours, without having accomplished half the remaining distance, I halted the men, pointed out the gravity of our situation, and asked them which they preferred, to turn or to go on. They talked together in patois, and then Jean-Antoine said, 'When you tell us to turn we will go back; until then we will go on.' I said, 'Go on', although by no means feeling sure it would not be best to say 'Go back'. In another hour and a half we got to the foot of the western summit, and, as the slopes steepened, the snow became firmer again. We arrived on the top of it about a quarter to four in the afternoon, and then had the mortification of finding that it was the lower of the two. There was no help for it; we had to descend to the plateau, to resume the flogging, wading, and floundering, and to make for the highest point, and there again, when we got on to the dome, the snow was reasonably firm, and we arrived upon the summit of Chimborazo standing upright like men, instead of grovelling, as we had been doing for the previous five hours, like beasts of the field.

The wind blew hard from the north-east, and drove the light snow before it viciously. We were hungry, wet, numbed, and wretched, laden with instruments which could not be used. With much trouble the mercurial barometer was set up; one man grasped the tripod to keep it firm, while the other stood to windward holding up a poncho to give a little protection. . . . Planting our pole with its flag of serge on the very apex of the dome, we turned to depart, enveloped in driving clouds which entirely concealed the surrounding country.

Scarcely an hour and a quarter of daylight remained, and we fled across the plateau. There is much difference between ascending and descending

[1] Louis Carrel could not touch bottom with a twelve-foot pole that he was carrying. It would have continued to descend by its own weight if he had left hold of it.

soft snow, and in the trough or groove which had already been made we moved down with comparative facility. Still it took nearly an hour to extricate ourselves, and we then ran—ran for our lives, for our arrival at camp that night depended upon passing 'the breach' before darkness set in. We just gained it as daylight was vanishing, and night fell before it was left behind; a night so dark that we could neither see our feet nor tell, except by touch, whether we were on rock or snow. Then we caught sight of the camp fire, twelve hundred feet below, and heard the shouts of the disconsolate Perring, who was left behind as camp-keeper, and stumbled blindly down the ridge, getting to the tent soon after 9 p.m., having been out nearly sixteen hours, and on foot the whole time.

✿

HIRAM BINGHAM

(1876–1956)

American explorer and historian. On 24 July 1911 he stumbled on what was to become the most famous ruin in South America.

'The Discovery of Macchu Picchu', *Harper's Monthly Magazine*, Apr. 1913.

MACCHU PICCHU (1911)

It would make a dull story, full of repetition and superlatives, were I to try to describe the countless terraces, the towering cliffs, the constantly changing panorama, with the jungle in the foreground and glaciers in the lofty background. Even the so-called road got a bit monotonous, although it ran recklessly up and down rock stairways, sometimes cut out of the side of the precipice, at others running on frail bridges propped on brackets against the granite cliffs overhanging the swirling rapids. We made slow progress, but we lived in wonderland.

With what exquisite pains did the Incas, or their predecessors, rescue narrow strips of arable land from the river! Here the prehistoric people built a retaining wall of great stones along the very edge of the rapids. There they piled terrace on *andene* until stopped by a solid wall of rock. On this sightly bend in the river, where there is a particularly fine view up and down the valley, they placed a temple flanked by a great stone stairway. On that apparently insurmountable cliff they built unscalable walls, so that it should be actually, as well as seemingly, impregnable. They planted the lower levels with bananas and coca, and also yucca, that strange little tree whose roots make such a succulent vegetable. On the more lofty terraces they grew maize and potatoes.

In the afternoon we passed a hut called La Maquina, where travellers frequently stop for the night. There is some fodder here, but the density of the tropical forest, the steepness of the mountains, and the scarcity of anything like level land make living very precarious. We arrived at Mandorpampa, another grass-thatched hut, about five o'clock. The scenery and the road were more interesting than anything we had seen so far, or were likely to see again. Our camp was pitched in a secluded spot on the edge of the river. Carrasco, the sergeant sent with me from Cuzco, talked with a muleteer who lives near by, a fellow named Melchor Arteaga, who leases the land where we were camping. He said there were ruins in the vicinity, and some excellent ones at a place called Machu Picchu on top of the precipice near by, and that there were also ruins at Huayna Picchu, still more inaccessible, on top of a peak not far distant from our camp.

The next day, although it was drizzling, the promise of a *sol* (fifty cents gold) to be paid to him on our return from the ruins, encouraged Arteaga to guide me up to Machu Picchu. I left camp at about ten o'clock, and went from his house some distance upstream. The valley is very narrow, with almost sheer precipices of solid granite on each side. On the road we passed a snake that had recently been killed. Arteaga was unable to give any other name for it than *vivora*, which means venomous, in distinction from *culebra*, or harmless snake.

Our naturalist spent the day in the bottom of the valley, collecting insects; the surgeon busied himself in and about camp; and I was accompanied on this excursion only by Carrasco and the guide, Arteaga. At 10.45, after having left the road and plunged down through the jungle to the river-bank, we came to a primitive bridge, made of four logs bound together with vines, and stretching across the stream a few inches above the roaring rapids. On the other side we had a fearfully hard climb for an hour and twenty minutes. A good part of the distance I went on all fours. The path was in many places a primitive stairway, or crude stepladder, at first through a jungle, and later up a very steep, grass-covered slope. The heat was excessive, but the view was magnificent after we got above the jungle. Shortly after noon we reached a hut where several good-natured Indians welcomed us and gave us gourds full of cool, delicious water, and a few cooked sweet potatoes. All that we could see was a couple of small grass

371

huts and a few terraces, faced with stone walls. The pleasant Indian family had chosen this eagle's nest for a home. They told us there were better ruins a little further along.

One can never tell, in this country, whether such a report is worthy of credence. . . . Accordingly we were not unduly excited. Nor was I in a great hurry to move. The water was cool, the wooden bench, covered with a woollen poncho, seemed most comfortable, and the view was marvellous. . . .

Leaving the huts, we climbed still further up the ridge. Around a slight promontory the character of the stone-faced *andenes* began to improve, and suddenly we found ourselves in the midst of a jungle-covered maze of small and large walls, the ruins of buildings made of blocks of white granite, most carefully cut and beautifully fitted together without cement. Surprise followed surprise until there came the realization that we were in the midst of as wonderful ruins as any ever found in Peru. It seemed almost incredible that this city, only five days' journey from Cuzco, should have remained so long undescribed and comparatively unknown. Yet so far as I have been able to discover, there is no reference in the Spanish chronicles to Machu Picchu. It is possible that not even the conquistadores ever saw this wonderful place.

✿

THEODORE ROOSEVELT

(1858–1919)

American president. When he retired from politics at the age of fifty-four, he went to Brazil in search of adventure. With his son Kermit and the great Brazilian explorer Candido Rondon, he made the first descent, in 1914, of a previously unknown tributary of the Amazon, 1,525 km. long, which was subsequently named the Rio Roosevelt.

Through the Brazilian Wilderness (London, 1914).

1. THE RIVER OF DOUBT (1914)

On 27 February 1914, shortly after midday, we started down the River of Doubt into the unknown. We were quite uncertain whether after a week we should find ourselves in the Gy-Parana, or after six weeks in the Madeira, or after three months we knew not where. That was why the river was rightly christened the Duvida.

We had been camped close to the river, where the trail that follows the telegraph line crosses it by a rough bridge. As our laden dugouts swung into the stream, Amilcar and Miller and all the others of the Gy-Parana party were on the banks and the bridge to wave farewell and wish us goodbye and good luck. It was the height of the rainy season, and the swollen torrent was swift and brown. Our camp was at about 12° 1′ latitude south and 60° 15′ longitude west of Greenwich. Our general course was to be northward toward the Equator, by waterway through the vast forest.

We had seven canoes, all of them dugouts. One was small, one was cranky, and two were old, waterlogged, and leaky. The other three were good. The two old canoes were lashed together, and the cranky one was lashed to one of the others. Kermit with two paddlers went in the smallest of the good canoes; Colonel Rondon and Lyra with three other paddlers in the next largest; and the doctor, Cherrie, and I, in the largest with three paddlers. The remaining eight *camaradas*—there were sixteen in all—were equally divided between our two pairs of lashed canoes. Although our personal baggage was cut down to the limit necessary for health and efficiency, yet on such a trip as ours, where scientific work has to be done and where food for twenty-two men for an unknown period of time has to be carried, it is impossible not to take a good deal of stuff; and the seven dugouts were too heavily laden.

The paddlers were a strapping set. They were expert river-men and men of the forest, skilled veterans in wilderness work. They were lithe as panthers and brawny as bears. They swam like water-dogs. They were equally at home with pole and paddle, with axe and machete; and one was a good cook and others were good men around camp. They looked like pirates in the pictures of Howard Pyle or Maxfield Parrish; one or two of them were pirates, and one worse than a pirate; but most of them were hard-working, willing, and cheerful.

2. A Red-Letter Day

In the morning when we stared the view was lovely. There was a mist, and for a couple of miles the great river, broad and quiet, ran between the high walls of tropical forest, the tops of the giant trees showing dim through the haze. Different members of the party caught many fish, and shot a monkey and a couple of jacu-tinga—birds akin to a turkey, but the size of a fowl—

373

so we again had a camp of plenty. The dry season was approaching, but there were still heavy, drenching rains. On this day the men found some new nuts of which they liked the taste; but the nuts proved unwholesome and half of the men were very sick and unable to work the following day. In the balsa only two were left fit to do anything, and Kermit plied a paddle all day long.

Accordingly, it was a rather sorry crew that embarked the following morning, April 15. But it turned out a red-letter day. The day before, we had come across cuttings, a year old, which were probably but not certainly made by pioneer rubber-men. But on this day . . . we found on the left bank a board on a post, with the initials J. A., to show the furthest-up point which a rubber-man had reached and claimed as his own. An hour further down we came on a newly built house in a little planted clearing; and we cheered heartily. No one was at home, but the house, of palm-thatch, was clean and cool. A couple of dogs were on watch, and the belongings showed that a man, a woman, and a child lived there, and had only just left. Another hour brought us to a similar house where dwelt an old black man, who showed the innate courtesy of the Brazilian peasant. . . .

In mid-afternoon we stopped at another clean, cool, picturesque house of palm-thatch. The inhabitants all fled at our approach, fearing an Indian raid; for they were absolutely unprepared to have anyone come from the unknown regions upstream. They returned and were most hospitable and communicative; and we spent the night there. Said Antonio Correa to Kermit: 'It seems like a dream to be in a house again, and hear the voices of men and women, instead of being among those mountains and rapids.' The river was known to them as the Castanho, and was the main affluent, or rather the left or western branch, of the Aripuanan; the Castanho is a name used by the rubber-gatherers only; it is unknown to the geographers. We were, according to our informants, about fifteen days' journey from the confluence of the two rivers; but there were many rubber-men along the banks, some of whom had become permanent settlers. We had come over 300 kilometres, in 48 days, over absolutely unknown ground; we had seen no human being, although we had twice heard Indians. Six weeks had been spent in steadily slogging our way down through the interminable series of rapids. It was astonishing before, when we were on a river of about the size of the upper Rhine or Elbe, to realize that no geographer had any idea of its existence. But, after all, no civilized man of any kind had ever been on it. Here, however, was a river with people dwelling along the banks, some of whom had lived in the neighbourhood for eight or ten years; and yet on no standard map was there a hint of the river's existence.

374

3. NEARING SAFETY

For the first time this great river, the greatest affluent of the Madeira, was to be put on the map; and the understanding of its real position and real relationship, and the clearing-up of the complex problem of the sources of all these lower right-hand affluents of the Madeira, was rendered possible by the seven weeks of hard and dangerous labour we had spent in going down an absolutely unknown river, through an absolutely unknown wilderness. . . .

We had passed the period when there was a chance of peril, of disaster, to the whole expedition. There might be risk ahead to individuals, and some difficulties and annoyances for all of us; but there was no longer the least likelihood of any disaster to the expedition as a whole. We now no longer had to face continual anxiety, the need of constant economy with food, the duty of labour with no end in sight, and bitter uncertainty as to the future.

It was time to get out. The wearing work, under very unhealthy conditions, was beginning to tell on everyone. Half of the *camaradas* had been down with fever and were much weakened; only a few of them retained their original physical and moral strength. . . . I was in worse shape. The after-effects of the fever still hung on; and the leg which had been hurt while working in the rapids with the sunken canoe had taken a turn for the bad and developed an abscess. The good doctor, to whose unwearied care and kindness I owe much, had cut it open and inserted a drainage tube. . . . No man has any business to go on such a trip as ours unless he will refuse to jeopardize the welfare of his associates by any delay caused by a weakness or ailment of his. It is his duty to go forward, if necessary on all fours, until he drops. Fortunately, I was put to no such test. I remained in good shape until we had passed the last of the rapids of the chasms. When my serious trouble came we had only canoe-riding ahead of us. It is not ideal for a sick man to spend the hottest hours of the day stretched on the boxes in the bottom of a small open dugout, under the well-nigh intolerable heat of the torrid sun of the mid-tropics, varied by blinding, drenching downpours of rain; but I could not be sufficiently grateful for the chance.

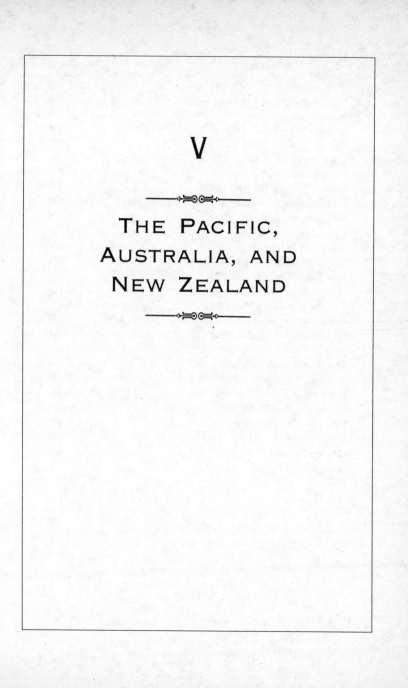

V

THE PACIFIC, AUSTRALIA, AND NEW ZEALAND

Ferdinand Magellan (c.1480–1521)   379

Alvaro de Mendaña de Neira (c.1542–1595)   382

Abel Janszoon Tasman (1603–1659)   384

William Dampier (c.1650–1715)   388

Jacob Roggeveen (1659–1729)   391

Philip Carteret (d. 1796)   395

Samuel Wallis (1728–1795)   396

Louis-Antoine Comte de Bougainville (1729–1811)   402

Sir Joseph Banks (1743–1820)   406

James Cook (1728–1779)   410

Gregory Blaxland (1778–1853)   418

George William Evans (1778–1852)   421

John Joseph Oxley (1783–1828)   422

Charles Sturt (1795–1869)   424

Edward John Eyre (1815–1901)   432

Friedrich Wilhelm Ludwig Leichhardt (1813–?1848)   438

Thomas Brunner (1821–1874)   441

John McDouall Stuart (1815–1866)   443

Robert O'Hara Burke (1820–1861)   446

William John Wills (1834–1861)   446

Peter Warburton (1813–1889)   451

Ernest Giles (1835–1897)   453

John Forrest (1847–1918)   458

Alexander Forrest (1849–1901)   461

Charles Douglas (1840–1874)   461

⬖⭃≣◖⪡⬥

FERDINAND MAGELLAN

(c.1480–1521)

Portuguese navigator. Appointed captain-general of a fleet of five ships and 241 men, he was sent by the King of Spain in 1519 to explore a new route westward to the East Indies. Finding a way through what is now called the Strait of Magellan, he continued with his three remaining ships across the Pacific Ocean, only to be killed in a skirmish with natives on the island of Cebu. One of his ships, the Victoria, *finally completed the first circum-navigation of the globe with just eighteen survivors on board. One was the navigator, Antonio Pigafetta, who wrote the subsequent account.*

Antonio Pigafetta, *First Voyage around the World*, trans. J. A. Robertson (Cleveland, 1906).

1. THROUGH THE STRAIT OF MAGELLAN AND ACROSS THE PACIFIC (1520)

A great storm struck us that night, which lasted until the middle of next day, which necessitated our lifting anchor, and letting ourselves drift hither and thither about the bay. The other two ships suffered a headwind and could not double a cape formed by the bay almost at its end, as they were trying to return to join us; so that they thought that they would have to run aground. But on approaching the end of the bay, and thinking that they were lost, they saw a small opening which did not appear to be an opening, but a sharp turn. Like desperate men they hauled into it, and thus they discovered the strait by chance. Seeing that it was not a sharp turn, but a strait with land, they proceeded further, and found a bay. And then further on they found another strait and another bay larger than the first two. Very joyful, they immediately turned back to inform the captain-general. We thought that they had been wrecked, first, by reason of the violent storm, and second, because two days had passed and they had not appeared, and also because of certain [signals with] smoke made by two of their men who had been sent ashore to advise us. And so, while in suspense, we saw the two ships with sails full and banners flying to the wind, coming toward us. When they neared us in this manner, they suddenly discharged a number of mortars, and burst into cheers. Then all together thanking God and the Virgin Mary, we went to seek the strait further on. . . .

379

Wednesday, 28 November 1520, we debouched from that strait, engulfing ourselves in the Pacific Sea. We were three months and twenty days without getting any kind of fresh food. We ate biscuit, which was no longer biscuit, but powder of biscuits swarming with worms, for they had eaten the good. It stank strongly of the urine of rats. We drank yellow water that had been putrid for many days. We also ate some ox-hides that covered the top of the mainyard to prevent the yard from chafing the shrouds, and which had become exceedingly hard because of the sun, rain, and wind. We left them in the sea for four or five days, and then placed them for a few moments on top of the embers, and so ate them; and often we ate sawdust from boards. Rats were sold for one half-ducado apiece, and even then we could not get them. But above all the other misfortunes the following was the worst. The gums of both the lower and upper teeth of some of our men swelled, so that they could not eat under any circumstances and therefore died. Nineteen men died from that sickness, and the giant together with an Indian from the country of Verzin. Twenty-five or thirty men fell sick [during that time], in the arms, legs, or in another place, so that but few remained well. However, I, by the grace of God, suffered no sickness. We sailed about 4,000 leagues during those three months and twenty days through an open stretch in that Pacific Sea. In truth it is very pacific, for during that time we did not suffer any storm. We saw no land except two desert islets, where we found nothing but birds and trees, for which we called them the Ysolle Infortunate [the Unfortunate Isles]. They are 200 hundred leagues apart. We found no anchorage, [but] near them saw many sharks. The first islet lies in 15° of south latitude, and the other in 9°. Daily we made runs of 50, 60, or 70 leagues at the catena or at the stern. Had not God and His blessed mother given us so good weather we would all have died of hunger in that exceeding vast sea. Of a verity I believe no such voyage will ever be made [again].

2. DEATH OF MAGELLAN (1521)

When morning came, forty-nine of us leaped into the water up to our thighs, and walked through water for more than two crossbow flights before we could reach the shore. The boats could not approach nearer because of certain rocks in the water. The other eleven men remained behind to guard the boats. When we reached land, those men had formed in three divisions to the number of more than 1,500 persons. When they saw us, they charged down upon us with exceeding loud cries, two divisions on our flanks and the other on our front. When the captain saw that, he formed us into two divisions, and thus did we begin to fight.

The musketeers and crossbowmen shot from a distance for about a half-hour, but uselessly; for the shots only passed through the shields which were made of thin wood and the arms [of the bearers]. The captain cried to them, 'Cease firing! cease firing!' but his order was not at all heeded. When the natives saw that we were shooting our muskets to no purpose, crying out they determined to stand firm, but they redoubled their shouts. When our muskets were discharged, the natives would never stand still, but leaped hither and thither, covering themselves with their shields. They shot so many arrows at us and hurled so many bamboo spears (some of them tipped with iron) at the captain-general, besides pointed stakes hardened with fire, stones, and mud, that we could scarcely defend ourselves. Seeing that, the captain-general sent some men to burn their houses in order to terrify them.

When they saw their houses burning, they were roused to greater fury. Two of our men were killed near the houses, while we burned twenty or thirty houses. So many of them charged down upon us that they shot the captain through the right leg with a poisoned arrow. On that account, he ordered us to retire slowly, but the men took to flight, except six or eight of us who remained with the captain. The natives shot only at our legs, for the latter were bare; and so many were the spears and stones that they hurled at us that we could offer no resistance. The mortars in the boats could not aid us as they were too far away. So we continued to retire for more than a good crossbow flight from the shore, always fighting up to our knees in the water. The natives continued to pursue us, and picking up the same spear four or six times, hurled it at us again and again. Recognizing the captain, so many turned upon him that they knocked his helmet off his head twice, but he always stood firmly like a good knight, together with some others.

Thus did we fight for more than one hour, refusing to retire further. An Indian hurled a bamboo spear into the captain's face, but the latter immediately killed him with his lance, which he left in the Indian's body. Then, trying to lay hand on sword, he could draw it out but halfway, because he had been wounded in the arm with a bamboo spear. When the natives saw that, they all hurled themselves upon him. One of them wounded him on the left leg with a large cutlass, which resembles a scimitar, only being larger. That caused the captain to fall face downward, when immediately they rushed upon him with iron and bamboo spears and with their cutlasses, until they killed our mirror, our light, our comfort, and our true guide. When they wounded him, he turned back many times to see whether we were all in the boats. Thereupon, beholding him dead, we, wounded, retreated as best we could to the boats, which were already pulling off. The Christian king would have aided us, but the captain charged him before we landed, not to leave his balanghai, but to stay to see how we fought. When the king learned that the captain was dead, he wept.

Had it not been for that unfortunate captain, not a single one of us would have been saved in the boats, for while he was fighting the others retired to the boats. I hope through the efforts of your most illustrious Lordship that the fame of so noble a captain will not become effaced in our times. Among the other virtues which he possessed, he was more constant than ever anyone else in the greatest of adversity. He endured hunger better than all the others, and more accurately than any man in the world did he understand sea charts and navigation. And that this was the truth was seen openly, for no other had had so much natural talent nor the boldness to learn how to circumnavigate the world, as he had almost done.

❀

ALVARO DE MENDAÑA DE NEIRA
(c.1542–1595)

Galician explorer. In 1568 he discovered the Solomon Islands, sailing from Peru. In 1595 he tried to return as governor with six ships, 378 colonists, 280 soldiers, and his wife. He failed to find the Solomons again, but he did discover the Marquesas and the Santa Cruz Islands, where he died. Command passed to his widow and his Portuguese pilot Pedro Fernandez de Quiros (c.1565–1615), who safely brought the remaining survivors to the Philippines.

The Voyages of Pedro Fernandez de Quiros, 1595–1606, trans. and ed. Sir C. Markham (London, 1904).

DEATH OF MENDAÑA (1595)

After putting into port in the great island of Santa Cruz, for this was the name given it, the Commander-in-Chief ordered Captain Don Lorenzo, brother of his wife, to go with the frigate to seek the Admiral's ship, which disappeared on the night in which we saw the island, respecting which I make no favourable conjecture; it was sought for this and two other times, and was not found, but only the shoals which I have mentioned. What was seen in the way of victuals in this port consisted of pigs, hens, plaintains, sweet canes, one, two, or three kinds of roots like sweet potatoes, which they eat roast and boiled, and make biscuit with it, *buyos*, two kinds of good almonds, and two kinds of pine-nuts, wood-pigeons, doves, ducks, grey and white herons, swallows, pot-herbs, pumpkins of Castille, the fruit which I mentioned in the first islands, and chestnuts and nuts. There is a very strongly scented sweet basil, and red flowers, which at this port they keep in the gardens, and two other species of another sort, also red. There is another fruit on high trees, like pippins for their good smell and savour. There is a great quantity of ginger, which grows there without its being cultivated, and much *yerba chiquilite*, with which they make indigo. There are agave trees, and a great deal of sagia, and many cocoa nuts. Marble was seen, and pearl shells, and large snail shells, like those which are brought here from China. There is a very copious spring, and five or six other rivers, though not very large.

The settlement was established close to this spring. The natives attempted to defend themselves; and as the arquebus tells at a distance, seeing the evil effects, they did not defend themselves much, but, on the contrary, gave some of what they possessed. In this matter of going for provisions there were a few things happened, which were not very good treatment of the natives, for they killed the native who was our best friend, and the lord of that island; his name was Malope; and two or three others, who were also friendly. Of the whole island no more was seen than a matter of 3 leagues around the camp. The people of this island are black: they have small canoes made of one tree, in which they go about their villages, and other very large canoes with which they go out to sea.

On Sunday 8 October, the Commander-in-Chief ordered the Master of the Camp to be killed by stabbing, and they killed Tomas de Ampuero in the same manner, and they cut off the head of the Ensign, Juan de Buitrago, and he wished to put to death two other friends of the Master of the Camp; but he left them alone, because we entreated him to do so. The cause of this was public, because they wished to go away from the country, and abandon it, and there must have been other reasons, but I am unacquainted with them. What I saw was much dissoluteness and shamelessness, and more than enough improper conduct. On 18 October the Commander-in-Chief died: on the 17th there had been a total eclipse of the moon. On 2 November his brother-in-law, Don Lorenzo, who had succeeded as Captain-General, died; and, seven or eight days before, the priest, Antonio de Serpa; and on 8 November the Vicar, Juan de Espinosa. There was great sickness amongst our people, and as there was little care for want of an apothecary and doctor, many of them died; and they begged the lady Governor, Doña Ysabel Barreto, to take them out of the country.

☆

ABEL JANSZOON TASMAN

(1603–1659)

Dutch navigator. In the course of sailing south of Australia without sighting the mainland, he discovered Tasmania and New Zealand in 1642. In spite of strict instructions from the Dutch East India Company's governor-general, van Diemen, to be careful in his dealings with 'barbarous' people, most of his encounters ended in violence.

A. Sharp, *The Voyages of Abel Janszoon Tasman* (Oxford, 1968).

1. EXTRACTS FROM TASMAN'S INSTRUCTIONS (1642)

Instructions for the skipper commander Abel Jansen Tasman, . . . assigned to the discovering of the unknown and found Southland, the South East coast of Nova Guinea, together with the islands located thereabout.

It is known that up to 150 years ago, only about a third part of the globe (divided into Europe, Asia, and Africa) had been known, and that the kings of Castile and Portugal (Ferdinand Catholicus and don Emanuel) have caused the unknown part of the earth usually named America or new world (and by the cosmographers divided into North and South America) to be discovered by the very famous sea-heroes Christopher Columbus and Amerigo Vespucci (to their undying glory), as also about the same time, the unexplored coasts and islands of Africa and East India were first sailed to by the renowned Vasco da Gama and other Portuguese captains. What inestimable riches, profitable tradings, useful exchanges, fine dominions, great might and powers, the said kings have brought to their kingdoms and crowns by this discovering and its sequel, and also untold blind heathens have come to the salutary light of the Christian religion, is also well known to the experienced, and deemed most highly laudable by all knowledgeable men, appropriately served other European princes as an example for the discovery of many Northern lands.

Nevertheless, up till now there has not been any serious attempt by any Christian kings, princes, or republics opportunely to discover the remaining unknown part of the globe (that situated in the south, and probably almost as large, as is the old or new world), although it is to be judged for good reasons, many attractive and fruitful lands are located therein . . .

You shall use great care at all places in landing with small craft, because it is apparent, the Southlands are peopled with very rough wild people, for which reason you must always be well armed and carefully on guard, since in all parts of the world, it has been found by experience, no barbarous people are to be trusted, because they usually think that the people who appear so exceedingly strange and unexpected come only to take over their lands, which (because of carelessness and easy trust) has caused many a treacherous murder in the discovery of America. For which reason the barbarous people whom you may meet and come to speech with, you shall make contact with properly and amicably; small affronts of thievery, or other things, which they might visit on our people, you shall let pass unmarked, in order not to cause any enmity towards us by punishing them, but by showing of good countenances, attract them to us, so that you may the better find out, in what circumstances they and their lands are, and whether anything useful is to be got or done there.

Of the nature of the lands, what fruits and livestock be there, what sort of structure of houses, the form and appearance of the inhabitants, their clothing, weapons, customs, manners, food, livelihood, religion, government, war, and other notable things, particularly whether they are good or ill-natured, you shall as time allows, duly try to observe, showing them various samples of the goods, given for this purpose, in order to find out what wares and materials they have, and what they want of ours in return, all which you shall keenly observe, properly draw and correctly describe, keeping for this purpose a full and suitably extensive journal, in which all your encounters are completely noted, in order therewith on your return to be able to make appropriate report to us.

If you visit any land populated with civilized people (as is not likely), you shall take more account of them than of the wild savages, trying to get in conversation and acquaintance with the leaders and subjects, informing them, you come there to trade, showing the samples of the wares, given for this purpose, as you shall be able to see in invoice, duly observing what they esteem, and to what goods they are most attracted, particularly finding out what wares are among them, likewise about gold and silver, and if it is in valued regard by them, representing yourself to be not eager for it, in order to keep them unaware of the value of the same, and if they should give you gold or silver in any bartering, you must conduct yourself as if you did not value this specie, showing copper, spelter, and lead, as if these minerals were with us of greater value.

All insolence and hostility of the crew towards the discovered peoples you will carefully prevent, and take care no harm is done to them in their houses, gardens, craft, property or women, etc. Likewise, no inhabitants brought away from their land against their will, but if any are somewhat willingly inclined thereto, you may then duly bring these hither.

2. THE DISCOVERY OF TASMANIA

In the morning early sent the pilot major Francoijs Iacobsz. with our sloop including 4 musketeers and 6 rowers, each provided with a pike and side-arms, together with the small boat of the *Zeehaen* and one of their under-mates, and 6 musketeers to an inlet, which was situated north-west a full mile from us, to find out what commodities (as of fresh water supplies, timber and otherwise) might be available there. About three hours before the evening our boats came back, bringing various samples of greens (which they had seen growing in plenty), some not unlike certain greenstuff which grows at the Cabo de Bona Esperance and is suitable to use as pot-herbs, another being long and salty, which has not a bad likeness to sea parsley. The pilot major and the under-mate of the *Zeehaen* reported as follows:

That they had rowed fully a mile round said point where [they] had found high yet level land with greenstuff (unplanted, being forthcoming from God and nature), fruit-bearing timber in abundance, and a running water place many empty valleys; which water indeed good but rather difficult to get; also was running so gradually that no more than with a bowl could be scooped.

That [they] had heard some sound of people, also playing almost like a horn or small gong, which was not far from them; but [they] had never-theless not managed to see anyone.

That [they] have seen two trees about 2–2½ fathom thick, 60–65 feet high under the boughs, in which trees gashed with flints and the bark was peeled off (thereby to climb up and gather the bird-nests) in shape of steps, each being measured fully 5 feet from one another. So that they presumed here to be very tall people or that these same by some means must know how to climb up said trees. In one tree these carved steps appeared so fresh and green as if the same was cut not four days before.

That [they] had noted the spoor or furrows of some animals in the earth not unlike the claws of a tiger, [they] also brought some excrements of (as far as [they] presumed and could observe) four-footed animals to the ships together with a little (to the eye) fine Gum which is dripping from trees, and has an Odour of Gommalacca.

3. FIRST MEETING WITH MAORIS IN WHAT TASMAN
CALLED 'MURDERERS' BAY

In the evening about one hour after sunset, saw many lights on land and four vessels near the shore, two of which betook themselves toward us, when our two boats returned to the ships; reporting that [they] had found not less than 13 fathoms water, and with the hiding of the sun (which sank behind the high land) [they] had been still about half a mile from land; after our people have been on board about one glass, those from the two canoes begin to call out to us in a gruff hollow voice, but [we] could not in the least understand any of it. However, [we] called back to them in token of answer, when they began again several times, but did not come nearer than a stonepiece's shot, blew also many times on an instrument which gave sound like the moors' trumpets. We had one of our sailors (who could play somewhat on the trumpet) blow back to them in answer. After this several times was done on both sides, and the dark evening was falling more and more, those in the vessels have finally stopped and paddled away; (for security and to be duly on guard) we made our people (as are accustomed at sea) keep watch with full quarters, and took care that [we] lay ammunition of war as muskets, pikes, and swords sufficiently ready; have blown off the guns on the upper deck, and got [them] ready again, in order that [we] might prevent all mischances and defend ourselves, if it happened that these people wished to try something evil. . . .

In the morning early, a vessel of this people having in it thirteen men approached our ships to about a cast away; they called out several times, which [we] could not understand the speech . . . these people were (as far as [we] could see) of ordinary height but rough in voice and bones, their colour between brown and yellow, had black hair right on top of the crown of the head fastened together in style and form like the Japanese at the back of the head but a bit longer and thicker of hair; upon which stood a large, thick white feather. Their craft were two long narrow canoes beside each other, over which some planks or other seating was laid, such that above water one can see through under the vessel their paddles about a large fathom long, narrow and sharp in front; [they] could proceed speedily with these vessels. Their clothing was (so it appeared) some of mats, others cottons, some and almost all the upper body naked. We waved to them many times that [they] should come to the ships, showed white cloth and some knives, from what were given to us as cargo; but however [they] did not come nearer but paddled finally back again . . .

They who lay before us, between the two ships, began to paddle so vigorously to it that about a little more than half way to our ship, [they] struck the *Zeehaen's* small boat with their stem on the side, dashed over that same violently, whereupon the foremost in this canoe of rogues, pushed the quartermaster Cornelis Ioppen in the neck several times with a long blunt pike, so fiercely that he had to fall overboard, whereupon the rest of them set to with short, thick pieces of wood (which we at first thought to be heavy blunt parangs) and their paddles, overpowering the small boat, in which violence three of the *Zeehaen's* people were killed, and the fourth through the heavy blows was mortally injured. The quartermaster and two more sailors swam towards our ship and [we] sent our sloop for them into which they got alive. After this monstrous deed and detestable thing, the murderers let the small boat drift, have pulled one of the dead into their canoe, and drowned another. We and those of the *Zeehaen*, seeing this, shot hard with muskets and cannon, but although [we] did not indeed hit them, [they] nevertheless hastened back, and paddled for land out of shooting range. We fired many shots with our forward upper and bow guns by and about their vessels, but struck none. Our Skipper, Ide Tercxsen Holman, rowed with our sloop, well manned and armed, towards the small boat of the *Zeehaen* (which these accursed men, luckily for us, still let drift) and returned with the same quickly to the ship. Finding one of the dead and the mortally wounded one therein, we raised our anchors and went under sail, because [we] could not expect to make here any friendship with this people . . .

✻

WILLIAM DAMPIER

(*c*.1650–1715)

English explorer and buccaneer. He sailed around the world three times, became a bestselling author, and was appointed leader of a naval discovery expedition in 1699 commissioned to explore the coast of New Holland (Australia).

The Voyages of Captain William Dampier, ed. J. Masefield (London, 1906).

1. NATIVE FOOD AND DRINK ON THE BATAN ISLANDS IN THE PHILIPPINES (1687)

I did never see them kill any of their goats or hogs for themselves, yet they would beg the paunches of the goats that they themselves did sell to us;

and if any of our surly seamen did heave them into the sea, they would take them up again and the skins of the goats also. They would not meddle with hogs' guts, if our men threw away any besides what they made chitterlings and sausages of. The goat-skins these people would carry ashore, and making a fire they would singe off all the hair, and afterwards let the skin lie and parch on the coals, till they thought it eatable; and then they would gnaw it, and tear it in pieces with their teeth, and at last swallow it. The paunches of the goats would make them an excellent dish; they dressed it in this manner. They would turn out all the chopped grass and crudities found in the maw into their pots, and set it over the fire, and stir it about often. This would smoke and puff, and heave up as it was boiling, wind breaking out of the ferment, and making a very savoury stink. While this was doing, if they had any fish, as commonly they had two or three small fish, these they would make very clean (as hating nastiness belike) and cut the flesh from the bone, and then mince the flesh as small as possibly they could, and when that in the pot was well boiled, they would take it up and, strewing a little salt into it, they would eat it, mixed with their raw minced flesh. The dung in the maw would look like so much boiled herbs minced very small; and they took up their mess with their fingers, as the Moors do their pilau, using no spoons.

They had another dish made of a sort of locusts, whose bodies were about an inch and a half long, and as thick as the top of one's little finger, with large thin wings and long and small legs. At this time of the year these creatures came in great swarms to devour their potato-leaves and other herbs; and the natives would go out with small nets, and take a quart at one sweep. When they had enough, they would carry them home, and parch them over the fire in an earthen pan; and then their wings and legs would fall off, and their heads and backs would turn red like boiled shrimps, being before brownish. Their bodies being full, would eat very moist, their heads would crackle in one's teeth. I did once eat of this dish, and liked it well enough; but their other dish my stomach would not take.

Their common drink is water, as it is of all other Indians. Besides which they make a sort of drink with the juice of the sugar-cane, which they boil, and put some small, black sort of berries among it. When it is well boiled, they put it into great jars, and let it stand three or four days and work. Then it settles, and becomes clear, and is presently fit to drink. This is an excellent liquor, and very much like English beer, both in colour and taste. It is very strong, and I do believe very wholesome, for our men, who drank briskly of it all day for several weeks, were frequently drunk with it, and never sick after it. The natives brought a vast deal of it every day to those aboard and ashore, for some of our men were ashore at work on Bashee

Island; which island they gave that name to from their drinking this liquor there, that being the name which the natives called this liquor by; and as they sold it to our men very cheap, so they did not spare to drink it as freely. And, indeed, from the plenty of this liquor, and their plentiful use of it, our men called all these islands the Bashee Islands.

2. ENCOUNTER WITH AUSTRALIAN ABORIGINES (1699)

When we came near the shore we saw three tall, black, naked men on the sandy Bay ahead of us; but as we rowed in, they went away. . . . While we were at work there came nine or ten of the natives to a small hill a little way from us, and stood there menacing and threatening of us, and making a great noise. At last one of them came towards us, and the rest followed at a distance. I went out to meet him, and came within 50 yards of him, making to him all the signs of peace and friendship I could; but then he ran away, neither would they any of them stay for us to come nigh them; for we tried two or three times. At last I took two men with me, and went in the afternoon along by the sea-side, purposely to catch one of them, if I could, of whom I might learn where they got their fresh water. There were ten or twelve of the natives a little way off who, seeing us three going away from the rest of our men, followed us at a distance. I thought they would follow us; but there being for a while a sandbank between us and them, that they could not then see us, we made a halt, and hid ourselves in a bending of the sandbank. They knew we must be thereabouts, and being three or four times our number, thought to seize us. So they dispersed themselves, some going to the sea-shore, and others beating about the sandhills. We knew by what rencounter we had had with them in the morning that we could easily outrun them. So a nimble young man that was with me, seeing some of them near, ran towards them; and they for some time ran away before him. But he soon overtaking them, they faced about and fought him. He had a cutlass, and they had wooden lances; with which, being many of them, they were too hard for him.

When he first ran towards them I chased two more that were by the Shore; but fearing how it might be with my young man, I turned back quickly, and went up to the top of a sandhill, whence I saw him near me, closely engaged with them. Upon their seeing me, one of them threw a lance at me, that narrowly missed me. I discharged my gun to scare them, but avoided shooting any of them; till, finding the young man in great danger from them, and myself in some, and that, though the gun had a little frighted them at first, yet they had soon learnt to despise it, tossing up their hands and crying, 'Pooh, Pooh, Pooh'; and coming on afresh with a great noise, I thought it high time to charge again, and shoot one of them, which I did. The rest, seeing him fall, made a stand again; and my young man took the opportunity to disengage himself, and come off to me; my other man also was with me, who had done nothing all this while, having come out unarmed; and I returned back with my men, designing to attempt the natives no further, being very sorry for what had happened already. They took up their wounded companion; and my young man, who had been struck through the cheek by one of their lances, was afraid it had been poisoned; but I did not think that likely. His wound was very painful to him, being made with a blunt weapon, but he soon recovered of it.

✻

JACOB ROGGEVEEN

(1659–1729)

Dutch explorer. He navigated further south than any before him. He discovered Samoa, Easter Island, and the Society Islands.

The Journal of Jacob Roggeveen, ed. A. Sharp (Oxford, 1970).

DISCOVERY OF EASTER ISLAND (1722)

Saw a turtle, greenery, and birds. About the tenth glass in the afternoon watch, de Africaansche Galey, which was sailing ahead, headed into the wind in order to wait for us, giving signal of seeing land. Coming up to her after running out of four glasses, as the breeze was light, we asked what she had seen, whereupon it was answered that they had seen very distinctly ahead to starboard a low, flat island, lying in the west by north $5\frac{1}{2}$ miles from them. Hereupon it was found fitting to run on with small sail till the end of the first watch, and then to let drift so as to wait for the coming of the day. This being thus decided, we gave to Captain Bouman, who was astern, the relevant information, and to the land the name of the Paasch Island, because it was discovered and found by us on Easter Day. There was great joy among the people, as everybody hoped that this low land was the precursor of the extended coast of the unknown Southland....

In the 9th glass of the afternoon we saw smoke rising from various places, from which it was concluded that it was inhabited by people....

The President accordingly proposes, in order not to be guilty of any default and negligence, that we shall this night stand off and on with our ships, so as at the coming of the day to go to land with two well-manned sloops, fittingly armed (so that in case of hostile encounter there would be a state of defence), and showing all friendliness to the inhabitants try to see and find out what they wear and use for ornament or other thing, and also whether any supplies of greens, fruit, or livestock are to be got there by barter. . . .

It was very unstable weather, with thunder, lightning, heavy rain, and variable winds from the north-west, also calm, so that our landing could not be put into effect. In the morning Captain Bouman (because a canoe came from the land to his ship) brought to our ship a Paaschlander with his vessel who was quite naked, without having the least covering in front of what modesty forbids being named more clearly. This poor person appeared to be very glad to see us, and marvelled greatly at the construction of our ship, and what he observed about it, as the great height of the masts, the thickness of the ropes, the sails, the cannon, which he handled accurately, and furthermore at all that he saw, but particularly when his face was shown to him in a mirror, so he looked with a quick movement of the head to the back of the mirror, evidently to find there the reason for this appearance. After we had amused ourselves enough with him, and he with us, we sent him back to shore in his canoe, having been presented with two blue strings of beads round his neck, a small mirror, a pair of scissors, and other such trifles, in which he seemed to take special pleasure and satisfaction. . . .

After the serving of breakfast sent our sloop well manned and armed as also the sloop of the ship *Thienhoven* to the shore, which, having carried out their order, reported that the inhabitants there were very finely dressed, with some materials of all sorts of colours, and that they made many signs that one should come ashore to them; but as our order was not to do this, when the numbers of the Indians present might be too large, this was not done. Furthermore, some thought they had seen that the inhabitants had silver plates in their ears, and mother-of-pearl shells round their necks for ornament. . . .

Very many canoes came to the ships. These people showed at this time their great eagerness for all that they saw, and were so bold that they took the hats and caps of the sailors from their heads and jumped with their plunder overboard, for they are extremely good swimmers, as was shown by the fact that a large number came swimming from land to the ships. Also there was one Paaschlander who climbed from his canoe through the window of the cabin of de Africaansche Galey, and seeing a cloth on the table, with which it was covered, having judged it as a good prize, took flight with it, so that particular care had to be taken to guard everything well. Further it was arranged to make a landing with 134 men for an investigation of the report of our envoys.

We set out in the morning with three boats and two sloops, manned with 134 men, and all armed with a musket, cartridge pouch, and sword. Coming to the shore, we put the boats and sloops close to one another at their grapnels, and as protection for them left in them twenty men, with arms as above, but the boat of de Africaansche Galey was also equipped with two barkers [small cannon] forward on the bow. Having arranged all this, we marched, quite close to one another, but not in order of rank, over the rocks, which lay in great quantity on the sea-shore, up to the level land or plain, indicating by hand that the inhabitants, who came towards us in great numbers, should give way and make room. Having arrived here, the *corps de bataille* of all the sailors of the three ships was formed . . . we marched forward a little, in order to give some room for some of our people who were in the rear to get themselves into line, then halting so that the hindmost should come up. To our great astonishment and without any expectation it was heard that four to five musket-shots from behind us were made, with a strong shout 'It's time, it's time, fire', whereupon, as in a glance of an eye, more than thirty muskets were let off, and the Indians being completely surprised and frightened by this fled, leaving behind ten to twelve dead, besides the wounded. The heads of this expedition, standing at the front, stopped the foremost from firing at the fugitives, asking moreover who had given the order to shoot, and for what reason he had been moved to do this. After lapse of a little time, the under-mate of the ship *Thienhoven* came to me saying that he with six men was the last, that one of the inhabitants grasped the muzzle of his musket in order to take it from him by force, whom he pushed back; then that another Indian tried to pull the coat of a sailor off his body, and that some of the inhabitants, seeing our resistance, picked up stones with a menacing gesture of throwing at us, by which by all appearance the shooting by my small troop had been caused, but that he had given no order whatever for this; then, as it was not the time for taking appropriate information about this, it was postponed till a better opportunity. After the astonishment and fear of the inhabitants had abated a little, since they saw that no continuance of hostility took place and it was made known to them by signs that the dead had threatened to make an attack on us with stones, the inhabitants who had all the time been near and about the front came back to the Chief Officers, and particularly one, who as it seemed to us had authority over the others, for giving order that all that they had, consisting of fruits, vegetables and fowls, should be fetched and brought from all sides for us. This command was accordingly received with respect and bowing of the body and at once obeyed, as the outcome testified, because after lapse of a little time they brought a large quantity of sugar-cane, fowls, yams, and bananas; but we gave them to understand by signs that we wanted nothing except only the fowls, being about sixty, in number, and thirty bunches of bananas, for which we paid them the value amply with striped linen, with which they appeared to be well pleased and satisfied. . . .

Concerning the religion of these people, of this we could get no full knowledge because of the shortness of our stay; we merely observed that they set fires before some particularly high erected stone images, and then, sitting down on their heels with bowed heads, they bring the palms of their hands together, moving them up and down. These stone images at first caused us to be struck with astonishment, because we could not comprehend how it was possible that these people, who are devoid of heavy thick timber for making any machines, as well as strong ropes, nevertheless had been able to erect such images, which were fully 30 feet high and thick in proportion; but this astonishment ceased with the discovery by the removal of a piece of stone that these images were formed from clay or greasy earth, and that small smooth stones had been stuck therein which, being arranged very closely and neatly together, made the appearance of a human being. Further, there was seen extending downward from the shoulders a faint relief or projection, which outlined the arms, since all the images appeared to show that they were hung round with a long garment from the neck to the soles of the feet, having on the head a basket, in which lay heaped white painted stones.

Moreover, it was incomprehensible to us how these people cook their food, as nobody could note or see that they had any earthen pots, pans or vessels. Solely it appeared to us from what we saw that they dug pits in the earth with their hands and laid in them large and small pieces of rock (for we saw no other sort of stone); then, having brought dried brushwood from the field and laid it on them, set it on fire, and, after lapse of a little time, they brought a cooked fowl (wrapped in a sort of rushes, very attractive, white and hot) to us to eat, but they were thanked by signs, because we had sufficient other tasks in looking after our people, to keep them in good order, so that they should not cause any mischief, and also, in case of disorder, not be taken off guard, because although these people showed us every mark of friendship, the experience of others has taught us that no Indian should be trusted too much, as the journal of the Nassau Fleet reports that they, because of the helpfulness of the inhabitants of Terra de

Feu, on one occasion lost seventeen men, having been deceived through the giving of good services.

✲

PHILIP CARTERET

(d. 1796)

English naval officer. Accompanying Samuel Wallis (q.v.) in the sloop Swallow, *he became separated after taking four months to pass the Strait of Magellan. Following a more southerly route across the Pacific, he discovered Pitcairn Island, which was to be landed on for the first time twenty-three years later by the mutineers from the* Bounty.

John Hawksworth, *An Account of the Voyages undertaken by Order of His Present Majesty for making Discoveries in the Southern Hemisphere* (London, 1773).

FIRST SIGHTING OF PITCAIRN (1767)

We continued our course westward till the evening of Thursday the 2nd of July, when we discovered land to the northward of us. Upon approaching it the next day, it appeared like a great rock rising out of the sea: it was not more than five miles in circumference, and seemed to be uninhabited; it was, however, covered with trees, and we saw a small stream of fresh water running down one side of it. I would have landed upon it, but the surf, which at this season broke upon it with great violence, rendered it impossible. I got soundings on the west side of it, at somewhat less than a mile from the shore, in twenty-five fathom, with a bottom of coral and sand; and it is probable that in fine summer weather landing here may not only be practicable but easy. We saw a great number of sea birds hovering about it, at somewhat less than a mile from the shore, and the sea here seemed to have fish. It lies in latitude 20° 2′ S, longitude 133° 21′ W, and about a thousand leagues to the westward of the continent of America. It is so high that we saw it at the distance of more than fifteen leagues, and it having been discovered by a young gentleman, son to Major Pitcairn of the marines, who was unfortunately lost in the *Aurora*, we called it Pitcairn's Island.

Samuel Wallis

(1728–1795)

English naval captain. Commanding the Dolphin, *he sailed across the Pacific slightly to the north of Carteret's* Swallow *after they were separated, and so discovered Tahiti.*

John Hawksworth, *An Account of the Voyages undertaken by Order of His Present Majesty for making Discoveries in the Southern Hemisphere* (London, 1773).

Discovery of Tahiti (1767)

At two in the morning, it being very clear, we made sail again; at day-break we saw the land, at about five leagues distance, and steered directly for it; but at eight o'clock, when we were close under it, the fog obliged us again to lie to, and when it cleared away, we were much surprised to find ourselves surrounded by some hundreds of canoes. . . . When they came within pistol shot of the ship, they lay by, gazing at us with great astonishment, and by turns conferring with each other. In the mean time we showed them trinkets of various kinds, and invited them on board. Soon after, they drew together, and held a kind of council, to determine what should be done: then they all paddled round the ship, making signs of friendship, and one of them holding up a branch of the plantain tree, made a speech that lasted near a quarter of an hour, and then threw it into the sea. Soon after, as we continued to make signs of invitation, a fine, stout, lively young man ventured on board: he came up by the mizzen chains, and jumped out of the shrouds upon the top of the awning. We made signs to him to come down upon the quarter-deck, and handed up some trinkets to him: he looked pleased, but would accept of nothing till some of the Indians came alongside, and after much talk, threw a few branches of plantain tree on board the ship. He then accepted our presents, and several others very soon came on board . . .

As we had no anchorage here, we stood along the shore, sending the boats at the same time to sound at a less distance. . . . About three o'clock in the afternoon, we brought to, abreast of a large bay, where there was an appearance of anchorage. The boats were immediately sent to sound it, and while they were thus employed, I observed a great number of canoes gather round them. I suspected that the Indians had a design to attack them, and as I was very desirous to prevent mischief, I made the signal for the boats to come aboard, and at the same time, to intimidate the Indians, I fired a nine-pounder over their heads. As soon as the cutter began to stand towards the ship, the Indians in their canoes, though they had been startled by the thunder of our nine-pounder, endeavoured to cut her off. The boat, however, sailing faster than the canoes could paddle, soon got clear of those that were about her; but some others, that were full of men, waylaid her in her course, and threw several stones into her, which wounded some of the people. Upon this, the officer on board fired a musket, loaded with buck-shot, at the man who threw the first stone, and wounded him in the shoulder. The rest of the people in the canoes, as soon as they perceived their companion wounded, leapt into the sea, and the other canoes paddled away, in great terror and confusion. . . .

While our people were on shore, several young women were permitted to cross the river, who, though they were not averse to the granting of personal favours, knew the value of them too well not to stipulate for a consideration: the price, indeed, was not great, yet it was such as our men were not always able to pay, and under this temptation they stole nails and other iron from the ship. The nails that we brought for traffic were not always in their reach, and therefore they drew several out of different parts of the vessel, particularly those that fastened the cleats to the ship's side. This was productive of a double mischief; damage to the ship, and a considerable rise at market. . . .

On Tuesday the 7th [July], I sent one of the mates, with thirty men, to a village at a little distance from the market, hoping that refreshments might there be bought at the original price; but here they were obliged to give still more than at the waterside. In the mean time, being this day able to get up for the first time, and the weather being fine, I went into a boat, and rowed about four miles down the coast. I found the country populous, and pleasant in the highest degree, and saw many canoes on the shore; but not one came off to us, nor did the people seem to take the least notice of us as we passed along. About noon I returned to the ship.

The commerce which our men had found means to establish with the women of the island rendered them much less obedient to the orders that had been given for the regulation of their conduct on shore, than they were at first. I found it necessary, therefore, to read the articles of war, and I punished James Proctor, the corporal of marines, who had not only quitted his station and insulted the officer, but struck the Master at Arms such a blow as brought him to the ground.

The next day, I sent a party up the country to cut wood, and they met with some of the natives, who treated them with great kindness and hospitality. Several of these friendly Indians came on board in our boat, and seemed, both by their dress and behaviour, to be of a superior rank. To these people I paid a particular attention, and to discover what present would most gratify them, I laid down before them a Johannes, a guinea, a crown piece, a Spanish dollar, a few shillings, some new halfpence, and two large nails, making signs that they should take what they liked best. The nails were first seized, with great eagerness, and then a few of the halfpence, but the silver and gold lay neglected. Having presented them, therefore, with some nails and halfpence, I sent them on shore superlatively happy.

From this time, our market was very ill supplied, the Indians refusing to sell provisions at the usual price, and making signs for large nails. It was now thought necessary to look more diligently about the ship, to discover what nails had been drawn; and it was soon found that all the belaying cleats had been ripped off, and that there was scarcely one of the hammock nails left. All hands were now ordered up, and I practised every artifice I could think of to discover the thieves, but without success. I then told them that till the thieves were discovered, not a single man should go on shore: this, however, produced no effect, except that Proctor, the corporal, behaved in a mutinous manner, for which he was instantly punished.

On Saturday the 11th, in the afternoon, the gunner came on board with a tall woman, who seemed to be about five and forty years of age, of a pleasing countenance and majestic deportment. He told me that she was but just come into that part of the country, and that seeing great respect paid her by the rest of the natives, he had made her some presents; in return for which she had invited him to her house, which was about two miles up the valley, and given him some large hogs; after which she returned with him to the watering-place, and expressed a desire to go on board the ship, in which he had thought it proper, on all accounts, that she should be gratified. She seemed to be under no restraint, either from diffidence or fear, when she first came into the ship; and she behaved, all the while she was on board, with an easy freedom that always distinguishes conscious superiority and habitual command. I gave her a large blue mantle, that reached from her shoulders to her feet, which I threw over her and tied on with ribands; I gave her also a looking-glass, beads of several sorts, and many other things, of which she accepted with a very good grace and much pleasure. She took notice that I had been ill, and pointed to the shore. I understood that she meant I should go thither to perfect my recovery, and I made signs that I would go thither the next morning. . . .

The next morning I went on shore for the first time, and my . . . queen . . . soon after came to me, followed by many of her attendants. As she perceived that my disorder had left me very weak, she ordered her people to take me in their arms and carry me not only over the river but all the way to her house; and observing that some of the people who were with me, particularly the First Lieutenant and Purser, had also been sick, she caused them also to be carried in the same manner, and a guard, which I had ordered out upon the occasion, followed. In our way, a vast multitude crowded about us, but upon her waving her hand, without speaking a word, they withdrew and left us a free passage. When we approached near her house, a great number of both sexes came out to meet her: there she presented to me, after having intimated by signs that they were her relations, and taking hold of my hand, she made them kiss it. We then entered the house, which covered a piece of ground 327 feet long, and 42 feet broad. . . . As soon as we entered the house, she made us sit down, and then calling four young girls, she assisted them to take off my shoes, draw down my stockings, and pull off my coat, and then directed them to smooth down the skin, and gently chafe it with their hands: the same operation was also performed upon the First Lieutenant and the Purser, but upon none of those who appeared to be in health.

While this was doing, our Surgeon, who had walked till he was very warm, took off his wig to cool and refresh himself: a sudden exclamation of one of the Indians who saw it, drew the attention of the rest, and in a moment every eye was fixed upon the prodigy, and every operation was suspended: the whole assembly stood some time motionless, in silent astonishment, which could not have been more strongly expressed if they had discovered that our friend's limbs had been screwed on to the trunk; in a short time, however, the young women who were chafing us, resumed their employment, and having continued it for about half an hour, they dressed us again, but in this they were, as may easily be imagined, very awkward; I found great benefit, however, from the chafing, and so did the Lieutenant and Purser.

After a little time, our generous benefactress ordered some bales of Indian cloth to be brought out, with which she clothed me, and all that were with me, according to the fashion of the country. At first I declined the acceptance of this favour, but being unwilling not to seem pleased with what was intended to please me, I acquiesced. When we went away, she ordered a very large sow, big with young, to be taken down to the boat, and accompanied us thither herself. She had given directions to her people to carry me, as they had done when I came, but as I chose rather to walk, she took me by the arm, and whenever we came to a plash of water or dirt, she lifted me over with as little trouble as it would have cost me to have lifted over a child if I had been well. . . .

On the 21st, the queen came again on board, and brought several large hogs as a present, for which, as usual, she would accept of no return. When she was about to leave the ship, she expressed a desire that I should go on shore with her, to which I consented, taking several of the officers with me. When we arrived at her house, she made us all sit down, and, taking off my hat, she tied to it a bunch or tuft of feathers of various colours, such as I had seen no person on shore wear but herself, which produced by no means a disagreeable effect. She also tied round my hat, and the hats of those who were with me, wreaths of braided or plaited hair, and gave us to understand that both the hair and workmanship were her own: she also presented us with some mats, that were very curiously wrought.

In the evening she accompanied us back to the beach, and when we were getting into the boat, she put on board a fine large sow, big with young, and a great quantity of fruit. As we were parting, I made signs that I should quit the island in seven days: she immediately comprehended my meaning, and made signs that I should stay twenty days; that I should go two days' journey into the country, stay there a few days, bring down plenty of hogs and poultry, and after that leave the island. I again made signs that I must go in seven days; upon which she burst into tears, and it was not without great difficulty that she was pacified.

The next morning, the gunner sent off no less than twenty hogs, with great plenty of fruit. Our decks were now quite full of hogs and poultry, of which we killed only the small ones, and kept the others for sea stores; we found, however, to our great mortification, that neither the fowls nor the hogs could, without great difficulty, be brought to eat anything but fruit, which made it necessary to kill them faster than we should otherwise have done: two, however, a boar and a sow, were brought alive to England, of which I made a present to Mr Stephens, Secretary to the Admiralty; the sow afterwards died in pigging, but the boar is still alive. . . .

At break of day, on Monday the 27th, we unmoored, and at the same time I sent the barge and cutter to fill the few water-casks that were now empty. When they came near the shore, they saw, to their great surprise, the whole beach covered with inhabitants, and having some doubt whether it would be prudent to venture themselves among such a multitude, they were about to pull back again for the ship. As soon as this was perceived from the shore, the queen came forward, and beckoned them; at the same time guessing the reason of what had happened, she made the natives retire to the other side of the river; the boats then proceeded to the shore, and filled the casks; in the mean time she put some hogs and fruit on board, and when they were putting off would fain have returned with them to the ship. The officer, however, who had received orders to bring off none of the natives, would not permit her; upon which she presently launched a double canoe, and was rowed off by her own people. Her canoe was immediately followed by fifteen or sixteen more, and all of them came up to the ship. The queen came on board, but not being able to speak, she sat down and gave vent to her passion by weeping. After she had been on board about an hour, a breeze springing up, we weighed anchor and made sail. Finding it now necessary to return into her canoe, she embraced us all in the most affectionate manner, and with many tears; all her attendants also expressed great sorrow at our departure. Soon after it fell calm, and I sent the boats ahead to tow, upon which all the canoes returned to the ship, and that which had the queen on board came up to the gun-room port, where her people made it fast. In a few minutes she came into the bow of her canoe, where she sat weeping with inconsolable sorrow. I gave her many things which I thought would be of great use to her, and some for ornament; she silently accepted of all, but took little notice of anything. About ten o'clock we were got without the reef, and a fresh breeze springing up, our Indian friends, and particularly the queen, once more bade us farewell, with such tenderness of affection and grief, as filled both my heart and my eyes. . . .

The benefit that we received while we lay off this island, with respect to the health of the ship's company, was beyond our most sanguine expectations, for we had not now an invalid on board, except the two Lieutenants and myself, and we were recovering, though still in a very feeble condition.

It is certain that none of our people contracted the venereal disease here, and therefore, as they had free commerce with great numbers of the women, there is the greatest probability that it was not then known in the country. It was, however, found here by Captain Cook, in the *Endeavour*, and as no European vessel is known to have visited this island before Captain Cook's arrival, but the *Dolphin*, and the *Boudeuse* and *Etoile*, commanded by M. Bougainville, the reproach of having contaminated with that dreadful pest a race of happy people to whom its miseries had till then been unknown must be due either to him or to me, to England or to France; and I think myself happy to be able to exculpate myself and my country beyond the possibility of doubt.

LOUIS-ANTOINE COMTE DE BOUGAINVILLE

(1729–1811)

French soldier and explorer. He completed the first French circumnavigation of the world, visiting Tahiti a year after Wallis. It is interesting to compare their accounts of Tahiti, and to note how each blames the other for introducing the venereal diseases which caused such havoc.

A *Voyage Around the World*, trans. J. R. Forster (London, 1772).

DESCRIPTION OF TAHITI (1768)

All our transactions were carried on in as friendly a manner as possible, if we except thieving. Our people were daily walking in the isle without arms, either quite alone or in little companies. They were invited to enter the houses, where the people gave them to eat; nor did the civility of their landlords stop at a slight collation, they offered them young girls; the hut was immediately filled with a curious crowd of men and women, who made a circle round the guest, and the young victim of hospitality. The ground was spread with leaves and flowers, and their musicians sung a hymeneal song to the tune of their flutes. Here Venus is the goddess of hospitality, her worship does not admit of any mysteries, and every tribute paid to her is a feast for the whole nation. They were surprised at the confusion which our people appeared to be in, as our customs do not admit of these public proceedings. However, I would not answer for it, that every one of our men had found it impossible to conquer his repugnance, and conform to the customs of the country. . . .

I presented the chief of the district in which we were with a couple of turkeys, and some ducks and drakes; they were to be considered as the mites of the widow. I likewise desired him to make a garden in our way, and to sow various sorts of seeds in them, and this proposal was received with joy. In a short time, Ereti prepared a piece of ground, which had been chosen by our gardeners, and got it enclosed. I ordered it to be dug; they admired our gardening instruments. They have likewise around their houses a kind of kitchen gardens, in which they plant an eatable hibiscus or okra, potatoes, yams, and other roots. We sowed for their use some wheat, barley, oats, rice, maize, onions, and pot herbs of all kinds. We have reason to believe that these plantations will be taken care of; for this nation appeared to love agriculture, and would I believe be easily accustomed to make advantage of their soil, which is the most fertile in the universe.

During the first days of our arrival, I had a visit from the chief of a neighbouring district, who came on board with a present of fruits, hogs, fowls, and cloth. This lord, named Toutaa, has a fine shape, and is prodigiously tall. He was accompanied by some of his relations, who were almost all of them six feet (French measure) high: I made them presents of nails, some tools, beads, and silk stuffs. We were obliged to repay this visit at his house, where we were very well received, and where the good-natured Toutaa offered me one of his wives, who was very young and pretty handsome. The assembly was very numerous, and the musicians had already began the hymenean. Such is their manner of receiving visits of ceremony.

On the 10th [March], an islander was killed, and the natives came to complain of this murder. I sent some people to the house, whither they had brought the dead body; it appeared very plain that the man had been killed by a firearm. However, none of our people had been suffered to go out of the camp, or to come from the ships with firearms. The most exact enquiries which I made to find out the author of this villainous action proved unsuccessful. The natives doubtless believed that their countryman had been in the wrong; for they continued to come to our quarters with their usual confidence. However, I received intelligence that many of the people had been seen carrying off their effects to the mountains, and that even Ereti's house was quite unfurnished. I made him some more presents, and this good chief continued to testify the sincerest friendship for us. . . .

Now that the ships are in safety, let us stop a moment to receive the farewell of the islanders. At daybreak, when they perceived us setting sail, Ereti leaped alone into the first periagua he could find on shore, and came on board. There he embraced all of us, held us some moments in his arms, shedding tears, and appearing much affected at our departure. Soon after, his great periagua came on board, laden with refreshments of all kinds; his wives were in the periagua; and with them the same islander who, on the first day of our land-fall, had lodged on board the *Etoile*. Ereti took him by the hand, and, presenting him to me, gave me to understand, that this man, whose name was Aotourou, desired to go with us, and begged that I would consent to it. He then presented him to each of the officers in particular, telling them that it was one of his friends, whom he entrusted with those who were likewise his friends, and recommending him to us with the greatest signs of concern. We made Ereti more presents of all sorts; after which he took leave of us, and returned to his wives, who did not cease to weep all the time of the periagua's being alongside of us. In it there was likewise a young and handsome girl, whom the islander that stayed along with us went to embrace. He gave her three pearls which he had in his ears, kissed her once more; and, notwithstanding the tears of this young wife or mistress, he tore himself from her, and came aboard the ship. Thus we quitted this good people; and I was no less surprised at the sorrow they testified on our departure than at their affectionate confidence on our arrival. . . .

This isle, though abounding with very high mountains, does not seem to contain any minerals, since the hills are everywhere covered with trees and other plants. At least it is certain that the islanders do not know any metals. They give the same name of *aouri*, by which they asked us for iron, to all the kinds of metals we could show them. But in what manner they became acquainted with iron is not easily understood; however, I shall soon mention what I think on this subject. I know of only a single rich article of commerce, viz. very fine pearls. The wives and children of the chief people wear them at their ears; but they hid them during our stay amongst them. They make a kind of castanets of the shells of the pearl-oyster, and this is one of the instruments employed by their dancers.

We have seen no other quadrupeds than hogs, a small but pretty sort of dogs, and rats in abundance. The inhabitants have domestic cocks and hens, exactly like ours. We have likewise seen beautiful green turtle-doves, large pigeons of a deep blue plumage and excellent taste, and a very small sort of perrokeets, very singular on account of the various mixture of blue and red in their feathers. The people feed their hogs and their fowls with nothing but plantains. . . . this isle has another inestimable advantage, which is that of not being infested by those myriads of troublesome insects that are the plague of other tropical countries: neither have we observed any venomous animals in it. The climate upon the whole is so healthy that, notwithstanding the hard work we have done in this island, though our men were continually in the water, and exposed to the meridian sun, though they slept upon the bare soil and in the open air, none of them fell sick there. Those of our men who were sent on shore because they were afflicted with the scurvy have not passed one night there quietly, yet they regained their strength, and were so far recovered in the short space of time they stayed on shore that some of them were afterwards perfectly cured on board. . . .

Vegetables and fish are [the islanders'] principal food; they seldom eat flesh, their children and young girls never eat any; and this doubtless serves to keep them free from almost all our diseases. I must say the same of their drink; they know of no other beverage than water. The very smell of wine or brandy disgusted them; they likewise showed their aversion to tobacco, spices, and in general to everything strong.

The inhabitants of Tahiti consist of two races of men, very different from each other, but speaking the same language, having the same customs, and seemingly mixing without distinction. The first, which is the most numerous one, produces men of the greatest size; it is very common to see them measure six (Paris) feet and upwards in height. I never saw men better made . . . The second race are of a middle size, have frizzled hair as hard as bristles, and both in colour and features they differ but little from mulattoes. . . .

I have met with only a single cripple amongst them; and he seemed to have been maimed by a fall. Our surgeon assured me that he had on several of them observed marks of the smallpox; and I took all possible measures to prevent our people's communicating the other sort to them; as I could not suppose that they were already infected with it.

The inhabitants of Tahiti are often seen quite naked, having no other clothes than a sash, which covers their natural parts. However, the chief people among them generally wrap themselves in a great piece of cloth, which hangs down to their knees. This is likewise the only dress of the women; and they know how to place it so artfully as to make this simple dress susceptible of coquetry. As the women of Tahiti never go out into the sun without being covered, and always have a little hat, made of canes and adorned with flowers, to defend their faces against its rays, their complexions are, of course, much fairer than those of the men. . . . Another custom at Tahiti, common to men and women, is to pierce their ears, and to wear in them pearls or flowers of all sorts. The greatest degree of cleanliness further adorns this amiable nation; they constantly bathe, and never eat nor drink without washing before and after it. . . .

I learnt from Aotourou that about eight months before our arrival at his island, an English ship had touched there. It is the same which was commanded by Mr Wallace [sic]. The same chance by which we have discovered this isle has likewise conducted the English thither, whilst we lay in Rio de la Plata. They stayed there a month; and excepting one attack of the islanders, who had conceived hopes of taking the ship, everything has passed very friendly between them. From hence, doubtless, proceeds the knowledge of iron, which we found among the natives of Tahiti, and the name of *aouri*, by which they call it, and which sounds pretty like the English word *iron*. I am yet ignorant whether the people of Tahiti, as they owe the first knowledge of iron to the English, may not likewise be indebted to them for the venereal disease, which we found had been naturalized amongst them.

SIR JOSEPH BANKS

(1743–1820)

English botanist. He sailed with Captain Cook on his circumnavigation. He was 'to be found in the first boat which visited each unknown land', and was later to become President of the Royal Society from 1778–1820.

> Journal of the Right Hon. Sir Joseph Banks, Bart., KB, PRS, during Captain Cook's first voyage in HMS 'Endeavour' in 1768–71 to Terra del Fuego, Otahite, New Zealand, Australia, the Dutch East Indies, etc., ed. Sir J. D. Hooker (London, 1896).

1. TAHITI (1769)

This morn early, Oborea and Co. came to the tents bringing a large quantity of provisions as a present, among the rest a very fat dog. We had lately learnt that these animals were eaten by the Indians and esteemed more delicate food than pork; now, therefore, was our opportunity of trying the experiment. He was immediately given over to Tupia, who, finding that it was a food that we were not accustomed to, undertook to stand butcher and cook both. He killed him by stopping his breath, holding his hands fast over his mouth and nose, an operation which took up above a quarter of an hour; he then proceeded to dress him much in the same manner as we would do a pig, singeing him over the fire which was lighted to roast him and scraping him clean with a shell. He then opened him with the same instrument and, taking out his entrails, pluck, etc., sent them to the sea where they were most carefully washed, and then put into coconut shells with what blood he had found in him. The stones were now laid and the dog, well covered with leaves, laid upon them. In about two hours he was dressed, and in another quarter of an hour completely eaten. A most excellent dish he made for us who were not much prejudiced against any species of food; I cannot, however, promise that European dog would eat as well, as these scarce in their lives touch animal food, coconut kernel, breadfruit, yams, etc. being what their masters can best afford to give them and what, indeed, from custom I suppose they prefer to any kind of food.

2. AUSTRALIAN COAST AND PEOPLE (1770)

25 April. Large fires were lighted this morn about 10 o'clock; we supposed that the gentlemen ashore had a plentiful breakfast to prepare. The country, though in general well-enough clothed, appeared in some places bare; it resembled in my imagination the back of a lean cow, covered in general with long hair, but nevertheless, where her scraggy hip-bones have stuck out further than they ought, accidental rubs and knocks have entirely bared them of their share of covering. In the even it was calm. All the fires were put out about 5 o'clock. . . .

The land this morn appeared cliffy and barren without wood. An opening appearing like a harbour was seen, and we stood directly in for it. A small smoke arising from a very barren place directed our glasses that way, and we soon saw about ten people, who on our approach left the fire and retired to a little eminence where they could conveniently see the ship. Soon after this, two canoes carrying two men each landed on the beach under them; the men hauled up their boats and went to their fellows upon the hill. Our boat which had been sent ahead to sound now aproached the place, and they all retired higher up on the hill; we saw, however, that at the beach or landing-place one man at least was hid among some rocks who never that we could see left that place. Our boat proceeded along shore and the Indians followed her at a distance. When she came back, the officer who was in her told me that in a cove a little within the harbour they came down to the beach and invited our people to land by many signs and word[s] which he did not at all understand; all, however, were armed with long pikes and a wooden weapon made something like a short scimitar.

During this time, a few of the Indians who had not followed the boat remained on the rocks opposite the ship, threatening and menacing with their pikes and swords—two in particular who were painted with white, their faces seemingly only dusted over with it, their bodies painted with broad strokes drawn over their breasts and backs resembling much a soldier's cross-belts, and their legs and thighs also with suchlike broad strokes drawn round them which imitated broad garters or bracelets. Each of these held in his hand a wooden weapon about $2^{1}/_{2}$ feet long, in shape much resembling a scimitar; the blades of these looked whitish and some thought shining, insomuch that they were almost of opinion that they were made of some kind of metal; but myself thought they were no more than wood smeared over with the same white pigment with which they paint their bodies. These two seemed to talk earnestly together, at times brandishing their crooked weapons at us as in token of defiance.

By noon we were within the mouth of the inlet, which appeared to be very good. Under the south head of it were four small canoes; in each of these was one man who held in his hand a long pole with which he struck fish, venturing with his little imbarkation almost into the surf. These people seemed to be totally engaged in what they were about: the ship passed within a quarter of a mile of them and yet they scarce lifted their eyes from their employment; I was almost inclined to think that attentive to their business and deafened by the noise of the surf they neither saw nor heard her go past them. At one we came to an anchor abreast of a small village consisting of about six or eight houses. Soon after this an old woman followed by three children came out of the wood; she carried several pieces of stick and the children also had their little burdens; when she came to the houses three more, younger children came out of one of them to meet her. She often looked at the ship but expressed neither surprise nor concern. Soon after this she lighted a fire, and the four canoes came in from fishing; the people landed, hauled up their boats, and began to dress their dinner, to all appearance totally unmoved at us, though we were within a little more than half a mile of them. Of all these people we had seen so distinctly through our glasses we had not been able to observe the least signs of clothing: myself to the best of my judgement plainly discerned that the woman did not copy our mother Eve even in the fig-leaf. . . .

29 April 1770. The fires (fishing fires as we supposed) were seen during the greatest part of the night. In the morn we went ashore at the houses, but found not the least good effect from our present yesterday: no signs of people were to be seen; in the house in which the children were yesterday was left every individual thing which we had thrown to them; Dr Solander and myself went a little way into the woods and found many plants, but saw nothing like people. At noon all hands came on board to dinner. The Indians, about twelve in number, as soon as they saw our boat put off came down to the houses. Close by these was our watering-place at which stood our cask: they looked at them but did not touch them; their business was merely to take away two of four boats which they had left at the houses; this they did, and hauled the other two above high-water mark, and then went away as they came. In the evening fifteen of them, armed, came towards our waterers; they sent two before the rest, our people did the same; they, however, did not wait for a meeting but gently retired. Our boat was about this time loaded, so everybody went off in her, and at the same time the Indians went away. Myself with the Captain, etc., were in a sandy cove on the northern side of the harbour, where we hauled the seine and caught many very fine fish, more than all hands could eat. . . .

The Captain, Dr Solander, myself, and some of the people, making in all 10 muskets, resolved to make an excursion into the country. We accordingly did so, and walked till we completely tired ourselves, which was in the evening, seeing by the way only one Indian, who ran from us as soon as he saw us. The soil wherever we saw it consisted of either swamps or light sandy soil, on which grew very few species of trees, one which was large yielding a gum much like *sanguis draconis*,[1] but every place was covered with vast quantities of grass. We saw many Indian houses and places where they had slept upon the grass without the least shelter; in these we left beads, ribbons, etc. We saw one quadruped about the size of a rabbit;[2] my greyhound just got sight of him and instantly lamed himself against a stump which lay concealed in the long grass; we saw also the dung of a large animal that had fed on grass which much resembled that of a stag;[3] also the footsteps of an animal clawed like a dog or wolf and as large as the latter;[4] and of a small animal whose feet were like those of a polecat or weasel.[5] The trees over our heads abounded very much with loryquets and cocatoos, of which we shot several; both these sorts flew in flocks of several scores together. . . .

The morn was rainy, and we who had got already so many plants were well contented to find an excuse for staying on board to examine them a little at least. In the afternoon, however, it cleared up, and we returned to our old occupation of collecting, in which we had our usual good success. Tupia, who strayed from us in pursuit of parrots, of which he shot several, told us on his return that he had seen nine Indians who ran from him as soon as they perceived him.

Our collection of plants was now grown so immensely large that it was necessary that some extraordinary care should be taken of them lest they should spoil in the books. I therefore devoted this day to that business and carried all the drying paper, near 200 quires of which the larger part was full, ashore and, spreading them upon a sail in the sun, kept them in this manner exposed the whole day, often turning them and sometimes turning the quires in which were plants inside out. By this means they came on board at night in very good condition. . . .

When the damp of the even made it necessary to send my plants and books on board, I made a small excursion in order to shoot anything I could meet with and found a large quantity of quails, much resembling our English ones, of which I might have killed as many almost as I pleased had I given my time up to it, but my business was to kill variety and not too many individuals of any one species. The Captain and Dr Solander employed the day in going in the pinnace into various parts of the harbour. They saw fires at several places and people who all ran away at their approach with

---

[1] 'Dragon's blood': in earlier English parlance 'gum-dragon', the resinous tragacanth which exuded from the tragacanth shrub or its allied species.

[2] An outdoor Australian would probably be inclined to guess here a bandicoot or a kangaroo-rat; but in the absence of much better evidence than 'a bad sight' we are not entitled to identify.

[3] No doubt a kangaroo.　　[4] Probably a dingo, the native Australian dog.

[5] Probably one of the native cats.

the greatest precipitation, leaving behind the shellfish which they were cooking; of this our gentlemen took the advantage, eating what they found and leaving beads, ribbons, etc. in return. They found also several trees which bore fruit of the Jambosa kind, much in colour and shape resembling cherries; of these they ate plentifully and brought home also abundance, which we ate with much pleasure though they had little to recommend them but a light acid. . . .

As tomorrow was fixed for our sailing, Dr Solander and myself were employed the whole day in collecting specimens of as many things as we possibly could to be examined at sea. The day was calm and the mosquitoes, of which we have always had some, more than usually troublesome.

※

JAMES COOK

(1728–1779)

English naval captain and explorer. A brilliant cartographer, he was the most respected of Pacific explorers, spending eleven years on voyages of discovery.

Capt. James Cook, the Circumnavigator, and Capt. James King, *A Voyage to the Pacific Ocean* (London, 1784).

1. DISCOVERY AND NAMING OF BOTANY BAY (1770)

Saturday 28 April. At daylight in the morning we discovered a bay which appeared to be tolerably well sheltered from all winds, into which I resolved to go with the ship, and with this view sent the master in the pinnace to sound the entrance while well kept turning up with the ship, having the wind right out. At noon the entrance bore NNW distance 1 mile.

Sunday 29 April. Saw as we came in, on both points of the bay, several of the natives and a few huts, men, women, and children on the south shore abreast of the ship, to which place I went in the boats in hopes of speaking with them, accompanied by Mr Banks, Dr Solander, and Tupia. As we approached the shore they all made off, except two men who seemd resolved to oppose our landing. As soon as I saw this I ordered the boats to lay upon their oars in order to speak to them, but this was to little purpose, for neither us nor Tupia could understand one word they said. We then threw them some nails, beads, etc., ashore, which they took up and seemed not ill-pleased, insomuch that I thought that they beckoned to us to come ashore; but in this we were mistaken, for as soon as we put the boat in they again came to oppose us, upon which I fired a musket between the two, which had no other effect than to make them retire back where bundles of their darts lay; and one of them took up a stone and threw at us, which caused my firing a second musket loaded with small shot, and although some of the shot struck the man yet it had no other effect than to make him lay hold of shield or target to defend himself. Immediately after this we landed, which we had no sooner done than they throwed two darts at us. This obliged me to fire a third shot, soon after which they both made off, but not in such haste but what we might have taken one, but Mr Banks, being of opinion that the darts were poisoned, made me cautious how I advanced into the woods. We found here a few small huts made of the bark of trees, in one of which were four or five small children, with whom we left some strings of beads, etc. A quantity of darts lay about the huts; these we took away with us. . . .

Friday 4 May. In the a.m., as the wind would not permit us to sail, I sent out some parties into the country to try to form some connections with the natives. One of the midshipmen met with a very old man and woman and two small children; they were close to the waterside, where several more were in their canoes gathering shellfish, and he being alone was afraid to make any stay with the two old people lest he should be discovered by those in the canoes. He gave them a bird he had shot, which they would not touch, neither did they speak one word but seemed to be much frightened; they were quite naked, even the woman had nothing to cover her nudity. Dr Munkhouse and another man, being in the woods not far from the watering place, discovered six more of the natives, who at first seemed to wait his coming, but as he was going up to them had a dart thrown at him out of a tree which narrowly escaped him; as soon as the fellow had thrown the dart he descended the tree and made off, and with him all the rest, and these were all that were met with in the course of this day.

Sunday 6 May. In the evening the yawl returned from fishing, having caught two sting-rays weighing near 600 pounds. The great quantity of new plants, etc. Mr Banks and Dr Solander collected in this place occasioned my giving it the name of Botany Bay. It is situated in the latitude of 34° 0′ S, Longitude 208° 37′ west; it is capacious, safe, and commodious. . . .

2. OBSERVATION OF CANNIBALISM AMONG THE MAORIS (1773)

Tuesday 23 November. Calm or light airs from the northward so that we could not get to sea as I intended. Some of the officers went on shore to amuse themselves among the natives, where they saw the head and bowels of a youth who had lately been killed. The heart was stuck upon a forked stick and fixed to the head of their largest canoe. The gentlemen brought the head on board with them; I was on shore at this time but soon after returned on board, when I was informed of the above circumstances, and found the quarterdeck crowded with the natives. I now saw the mangled head, or rather the remains of it, for the under jaw, lips, etc. were wanting. The skull was broke on the left side just above the temple; the face had all the appearance of a youth about fourteen or fifteen. A piece of the flesh had been broiled and eaten by one of the natives in the presence of most of the officers. The sight of the head and the relation of the circumstances just mentioned struck me with horror and filled my mind with indignation against these cannibals, but when I considered that any resentment I could show would avail but little, and being desirous of being an eyewitness to a fact which many people had their doubts about, I concealed my indignation and ordered a piece of the flesh to be broiled and brought on the quarterdeck, where one of these cannibals ate it with a seeming good relish before the whole ship's company, [having] such effect on some of them as to cause them to vomit. . . .

That the New Zealanders are cannibals can now no longer be doubted; the account I gave of it in my former voyage was partly founded on circumstances and was, as I afterwards found, discredited by many people. I have often been asked, after relating all the circumstances, if I had actually seen them eat human flesh myself; such a question was sufficient to convince me that they either disbelieved all I had said or formed a very different opinion from it. Few consider what a savage man is in his original state and even after he is in some degree civilized; the New Zealanders are certainly in a state of civilization, their behaviour to us has been manly and mild, showing always a readiness to oblige us; they have some arts among them which they execute with great judgement and unwearied patience; they are far less addicted to thieving than the other islanders and are, I believe, strictly honest among themselves. This custom of eating their enemies slain in battle (for I firmly believe they eat the flesh of no others) has undoubtedly been handed down to them from the earliest times, and we know that it is not an easy matter to break a nation of its ancient customs, let them be even so inhuman and savage, especially if that nation is void of all religious principles, as I believe the New Zealanders in general

412

are and like them without any settled form of government. As they become more united they will of consequence have fewer enemies and become more civilized, and then, and not till then, this custom may be forgot; at present they seem to have but little idea of treating other men as they themselves would wish to be treated, but treat them as they think they should be treated under the same circumstances. If I remember right, one of the arguments they made use of against Tupia, who frequently expostulated with them against this custom, was that there could be no harm in killing and eating the man who would do the same by you if it was in his power, for, said they, 'can there be any harm in eating our enemies whom we have killed in battle, would not those very enemies have done the same to us?'

3. DESCRIPTIONS OF HAWAII, INCLUDING SURFING (1778)

These people are scanty in their clothing; very few of the men wear anything more than the maro, but the women have a piece of cloth wrapped round the waist, so as to hang down like a petticoat as low as the knee; all the rest of the body is naked. Their ornaments are bracelets, necklaces, and amulets, which are made of shells, bone, or stone. They have also neat tippets made of red and yellow feathers, and caps and cloaks covered with the same or some other feathers; the cloaks reach to about the middle of the back, and are like the short cloaks worn by the women in England, or like the riding cloaks worn in Spain. The caps are made so as to fit very close to the head, with a semicircular protuberance on the crown exactly like the helmets of old. These and also the cloaks they set so high a value upon that I could not procure one; some were, however, got. . . .

They are an open, candid, active people and the most expert swimmers we had met with; in which they are taught from their very birth: it was very common for women with infants at the breast to come off in canoes to look at the ships, and when the surf was so high that they could not land them in the canoe they used to leap overboard with the child in their arms and make their way ashore through a surf that looked dreadful. . . .

A diversion the most common is upon the water, where there is a very great sea, and surf breaking upon the shore. The men sometimes 20 or 30 go without the swell of the surf, and lay themselves flat upon an oval piece of plank about their size and breadth; they keep their legs close on the top of it, and their arms are used to guide the plank. They wait the time for the greatest swell that sets on shore, and altogether push forward with their arms to keep on its top; it sends them in with a most astonishing velocity, and the great art is to guide the plank so as always to keep in a proper direction on the top of the swell, and as it alters its direction. If the swell drives him close to the rocks before he is overtaken by its break, he is much praised. On first seeing this very dangerous diversion I did not conceive it possible but that some of them must be dashed to mummy against the sharp rocks; but just before they reach the shore, if they are very near, they quit their plank, and dive under till the surf is broke, when the piece of plank is sent many yards by the force of the surf from the beach. The greatest number are generally overtaken by the break of the swell, the force of which they avoid, diving and swimming under the water out of its impulse. By suchlike exercises, these men may be said to be almost amphibious. The women could swim off to the ship, and continue half a day in the water, and afterwards return. The above diversion is only intended as an amusement, not as a trial of skill, and in a gentle swell that sets on must, I conceive, be very pleasant—at least they seem to feel a great pleasure in the motion which this exercise gives.

4. The Death of Cook, Recorded by Captain James King (1779)

During our absence, a difference, of a more serious and unpleasant nature, had happened. The officer, who had been sent in the small boat, and was returning on board, with the goods which had been restored, observing Captain Cook and me engaged in the pursuit of the offenders, thought it his duty to seize the canoe, which was left drawn up on the shore. Unfortunately, this canoe belonged to Pareea, who, arriving at the same moment from on board the *Discovery*, claimed his property, with many protestations of his innocence. The officer refusing to give it up, and being joined by the crew of the pinnace, which was waiting for Captain Cook, a scuffle ensued, in which Pareea was knocked down, by a violent blow on the head, with an oar. The natives, who were collected about the spot and had hitherto been peaceable spectators, immediately attacked our people with such a shower of stones as forced them to retreat, with great precipitation, and swim off to a rock at some distance from the shore. The pinnace was immediately ransacked by the islanders and, but for the timely interposition of Pareea, who seemed to have recovered from the blow, and forgot it at the same instant, would soon have been entirely demolished. Having driven away the crowd, he made signs to our people that they might come and take possession of the pinnace, and that he would endeavour to get back the things which had been taken out of it. After their departure, he followed them in his canoe, with a midshipman's cap, and some other trifling articles of the plunder, and, with much apparent concern at what had happened, asked if the *Orono* would kill him, and whether he would permit him to come on board the next day? On being assured, that he should be well received, he joined noses (as their custom is) with the officers, in token of friendship, and paddled over to the village of Kowrowa.

When Captain Cook was informed of what had passed, he expressed much uneasiness at it, and as we were returning on board, 'I am afraid', said he, 'that these people will oblige me to use some violent measures; for', he added, 'they must not be left to imagine that they have gained an advantage over us.' However, as it was too late to take any steps this evening, he contented himself with giving orders that every man and woman on board should be immediately turned out of the ship. As soon as this order was executed, I returned on shore; and our former confidence in the natives being now much abated by the events of the day, I posted a double guard on the *Morai*, with orders to call me if they saw any men lurking about the beach. At about eleven o'clock, five islanders were observed creeping round the bottom of the *Morai*; they seemed very cautious in approaching us, and, at last, finding themselves discovered retired out of sight. About midnight, one of them venturing up close to the observatory, the sentinel fired over him; on which the men fled, and we passed the remainder of the night without further disturbance. Next morning, at daylight, I went on board the *Resolution* for the time-keeper, and, in my way, was hailed by the *Discovery* and informed that their cutter had been stolen during the night from the buoy where it was moored.

When I arrived on board I found the marines arming, and Captain Cook loading his double-barrelled gun. Whilst I was relating to him what had happened to us in the night, he interrupted me, with some eagerness, and acquainted me with the loss of the *Discovery's* cutter, and with the preparations he was making for its recovery. It had been his usual practice, whenever anything of consequence was lost at any of the islands in this ocean, to get the king, or some of the principal *Erees*, on board, and to keep them as hostages till it was restored. This method, which had been always attended with success, he meant to pursue on the present occasion; and at the same time had given orders to stop all the canoes that should attempt to leave the bay, with an intention of seizing and destroying them, if he could not recover the cutter by peaceable means. Accordingly, the boats of both ships, well manned and armed, were stationed across the bay; and, before I left the ship, some great guns had been fired at two large canoes, that were attempting to make their escape.

It was between seven and eight o'clock when we quitted the ship together;

Captain Cook in the pinnace, having Mr Phillips and nine marines with him, and myself in the small boat. The last orders I received from him were to quiet the minds of the natives, on our side of the bay, by assuring them they should not be hurt; to keep my people together; and to be on my guard. We then parted; the Captain went toward Kowrowa, where the king resided; and I proceeded to the beach. My first care, on going ashore, was to give strict orders to the marines to remain within the tent, to load their pieces with ball, and not to quit their arms. Afterward I took a walk to the huts of old Kaoo and the priests, and explained to them as well as I could the object of the hostile preparations, which had exceedingly alarmed them. I found that they had already heard of the cutter's being stolen, and I assured them that, though Captain Cook was resolved to recover it and to punish the authors of the theft, yet that they and the people of the village on our side need not be under the smallest apprehension of suffering any evil from us. I desired the priests to explain this to the people, and to tell them not to be alarmed, but to continue peaceable and quiet. Kaoo asked me, with great earnestness, if Terreeoboo was to be hurt? I assured him, he was not; and both he and the rest of his brethren seemed much satisfied with this assurance.

In the mean time, Captain Cook, having called off the launch, which was stationed at the north point of the bay, and taken it along with him, proceeded to Kowrowa and landed with the Lieutenant and nine marines. He immediately marched into the village, where he was received with the usual marks of respect; the people prostrating themselves before him and bringing their accustomed offerings of small hogs. Finding that there was no suspicion of his design, his next step was, to enquire for Terreeoboo, and the two boys, his sons, who had been his constant guests on board the *Resolution*. In a short time the boys returned along with the natives who had been sent in search of them, and immediately led Captain Cook to the house where the king had slept. They found the old man just awoke from sleep; and, after a short conversation about the loss of the cutter, from which Captain Cook was convinced that he was in no wise privy to it, he invited him to return in the boat, and spend the day on board the *Resolution*. To this proposal the king readily consented, and immediately got up to accompany him.

Things were in this prosperous train, the two boys being already in the pinnace, and the rest of the party having advanced near the waterside, when an elderly woman called Kanee-kabareea, the mother of the boys and one of the king's favourite wives, came after him and, with many tears and entreaties, besought him not go on board. At the same time two chiefs, who came along with her, laid hold of him and, insisting that he should go no further, forced him to sit down. The natives, who were collecting in prodigious numbers along the shore, and had probably been alarmed by the firing of the great guns, and the appearances of hostility in the bay, began to throng round Captain Cook and their king. In this situation, the Lieutenant of marines, observing that his men were huddled close together in the crowd, and thus incapable of using their arms if any occasion should require it, proposed to the Captain to draw them up along the rocks, close to the water's edge; and the crowd readily making way for them to pass, they were drawn up in a line, at the distance of about thirty yards from the place where the king was sitting.

All this time the old king remained on the ground, with the strongest marks of terror and dejection in his countenance; Captain Cook, not willing to abandon the object for which he had come on shore, continued to urge him, in the most pressing manner, to proceed; whilst, on the other hand, whenever the king appeared inclined to follow him, the chiefs who stood round him interposed, at first with prayers and entreaties, but afterward having recourse to force and violence, and insisted on his staying where he was. Captain Cook, therefore, finding that the alarm had spread too generally, and that it was in vain to think any longer of getting him off without bloodshed, at last gave up the point; observing to Mr Phillips that it would be impossible to compel him to go on board without the risk of killing a great number of the inhabitants.

Though the enterprise which had carried Captain Cook on shore had now failed, and was abandoned, yet his person did not appear to have been in the least danger, till an accident happened, which gave a fatal turn to the affair. The boats which had been stationed across the bay, having fired at some canoes that were attempting to get out, unfortunately had killed a chief of the first rank. The news of his death arrived at the village where Captain Cook was, just as he had left the king and was walking slowly toward the shore. The ferment it occasioned was very conspicuous; the women and children were immediately sent off; and the men put on their war-mats, and armed themselves with spears and stones. One of the natives, having in his hands a stone and a long iron spike (which they call a *pahooa*) came up to the Captain, flourishing his weapon, by way of defiance, and threatening to throw the stone. The Captain desired him to desist; but the man persisting in his insolence, he was at length provoked to fire a load of small-shot. The man having his mat on, which the shot were not able to penetrate, this had no other effect than to irritate and encourage them. Several stones were thrown at the marines; and one of the *Erees* attempted to stab Mr Phillips with his *pahooa*; but failed in the attempt, and received from him a blow with the butt end of his musket.

417

Captain Cook now fired his second barrel, loaded with ball, and killed one of the foremost of the natives. A general attack with stones immediately followed, which was answered by a discharge of musquetry from the marines, and the people in the boats. The islanders, contrary to the expectations of everyone, stood the fire with great firmness; and before the marines had time to reload, they broke in upon them with dreadful shouts and yells. What followed was a scene of the utmost horror and confusion.

Our unfortunate Commander, the last time he was seen distinctly, was standing at the water's edge and calling out to the boats to cease firing and to pull in. If it be true, as some of those who were present have imagined, that the marines and boatmen had fired without his orders, and that he was desirous of preventing any further bloodshed, it is not improbable that his humanity, on this occasion, proved fatal to him. For it was remarked that, whilst he faced the natives, none of them had offered him any violence, but that, having turned about to give his orders to the boats, he was stabbed in the back, and fell with his face into the water. On seeing him fall the islanders set up a great shout, and his body was immediately dragged on shore and surrounded by the enemy who, snatching the dagger out of each other's hands, showed a savage eagerness to have a share in his destruction.

Thus fell our great and excellent Commander! After a life of so much distinguished and successful enterprise, his death, as far as regards himself, cannot be reckoned premature; since he lived to finish the great work for which he seems to have been designed; and was rather removed from the enjoyment than cut off from the acquisition of glory.

✻

GREGORY BLAXLAND

(1778–1853)

English farmer who emigrated to Australia in 1805. He, William Lawson (1774–1850), and William Charles Wentworth (1792–1872) were the first settlers, in 1813, to cross the Blue Mountains in search of grazing.

'A Journal of a Tour of Discovery across the Blue Mountains in New South Wales', *Journal and Proceedings of the Royal Australian Historical Society*, vol. xxiii. 1 (n.d.).

THE DISCOVERY OF NEW LAND (1813)

On Saturday, the 22nd [May], they proceeded in the track marked the preceding day rather more than three miles, in a south-westerly direction, when they reached the summit of the third and highest ridge of the mountains southward of Mt. Banks. From the bearing of Prospect Hill and Grose Head, they computed this spot to be 18 miles in a straight line from the River Nepean, at the point at which they crossed it. On the top of this ridge they found about 2,000 acres of land clear of trees, covered with loose stones, and short coarse grass, such as grows on some of the commons in England. Over this heath they proceeded for about a mile and a half, in a south-westerly direction, and encamped by the side of a fine stream of water with just wood enough on the banks to serve for firewood. From the summit, they had a fine view of all the settlements and country eastward, and of a great extent of country to the westward and south-west. But their progress in both the latter directions was stopped by an impassable barrier of rock, which appeared to divide the interior from the coast as with a stone wall, rising perpendicularly out of the side of the mountain.

In the afternoon, they left their little camp in the charge of three of the men, and made an attempt to descend the precipice by following some of the streams of water or by getting down at some of the projecting points where the rocks had fallen in; but they were baffled in every instance. . . . On the next day they proceeded about three miles and a half; but the trouble occasioned by the horses when they got off the open land induced them to recur to their former plan of devoting the afternoon to marking and clearing a track for the ensuing day . . . They encamped on the side of a swamp, with a beautiful stream of water running through it.

Their progress on the next day was four miles and a half, in a direction varying from north-north-west, to south-south-west; they encamped, as before, at the head of a swamp. This day, between 10 and 11 a.m., they obtained a sight of the country below, when the clouds ascended. As they were marking a road for the morrow, they heard a native chopping wood very near them, but he fled at the approach of the dogs.

On Tuesday, the 25th, they could proceed only three miles and a half in a varying direction, encamping at two o'clock at the side of a swamp. The underwood, being very prickly and full of small thorns, annoyed them very much. This day they saw the track of a wombat for the first time. On the 26th they proceeded two miles and three-quarters. The brush still continued to be very thorny. The land to the westward appeared sandy and barren. This day they saw the fires of some natives below; the number they computed at about thirty men, women, and children. They noticed also more tracks of the wombat. On the 27th they proceeded five miles and a quarter; part of the way over another piece of clear land, without trees; they saw more native fires, and about the same number as before, but more in their direct course. From the top of the rocks, they saw a large piece of land below, clear of trees, but apparently a poor reedy swamp. They met with some good timber in this day's route. . . .

On the 28th, they proceeded about five miles and three-quarters. Not being able to find water, they did not halt till five o'clock, when they took up their station on the edge of the precipice. To their great satisfaction, they discovered that what they had supposed to be sandy barren land below the mountain was forest land, covered with good grass and with timber of an inferior quality. In the evening they contrived to get their horses down the mountain by cutting a small trench with a hoe, which kept them from slipping, where they again tasted fresh grass for the first time since they left the forest land on the other side of the mountain. They were getting into miserable condition. Water was found about two miles below the foot of the mountain. The second camp of natives moved before them about three miles. In this day's route little timber was observed fit for building.

On the 29th, having got up the horses, and laden them, they began to descend the mountain at seven o'clock through a pass in the rock, about thirty feet wide, which they had discovered the day before, when the want of water put them on the alert. Part of the descent was so steep that the horses could but just keep their footing without a load, so that, for some way, the party were obliged to carry the packages themselves. A cart road might, however, easily be made by cutting a slanting trench along the side of the mountain, which is here covered with earth. This pass is, according to their computation, about twenty miles north-west in a straight line from the point at which they ascended the summit of the mountains. They reached the foot at 9 a.m., and proceeded two miles north-north-west, mostly through open meadow land, clear of trees, the grass from two to three feet high. They encamped on the bank of a fine stream of water. The natives, as observed by the smoke of their fires, moved before them as yesterday. The dogs killed a kangaroo, which was very acceptable, as the party had lived on salt meat since they caught the last. The timber seen this day appeared rotten and unfit for building.

Sunday the 30th, they rested in their encampment. One of the party shot a kangaroo with his rifle, at a great distance across a wide valley. The climate here was found very much colder than that of the mountain or of the settlements on the east side, where no signs of frost had made its appearance when the party set out. During the night the ground was covered with a thick frost, and a leg of the kangaroo was quite frozen.

From the dead and brown appearance of the grass it was evident that the weather had been severe for some time past. They were all much surprised at this degree of cold and frost in the latitude of about 34°. The track of the emu was noticed at several places near the camp.

On the Monday they proceeded about six miles, south-west and west, through forest land, remarkably well watered, and several open meadows, clear of trees, and covered with high good grass. They crossed two fine streams of water. Traces of the natives presented themselves in the fires they had left the day before, and in the flowers of the honeysuckle tree scattered around, which had supplied them with food. These flowers, which are shaped like a bottle-brush, are very full of honey. The natives on this side of the mountains appear to have no huts like those on the eastern side, nor do they strip the bark or climb the trees. From the shavings and pieces of sharp stones which they had left, it was evident that they had been busily employed in sharpening their spears.

The party encamped by the side of a fine stream of water, at a short distance from a high hill, in the shape of a sugar loaf. In the afternoon, they ascended its summit, from whence they descried all around, forest or grassland, sufficient in extent, in their opinion, to support the stock of the colony for the next thirty years.

✵

GEORGE WILLIAM EVANS

(1778–1852)

English surveyor. He was sent by the surveyor-general of lands in Sydney to explore the country beyond the Blue Mountains. He discovered the Macquarie and Lachlan Rivers between 1813 and 1815.

G. W. Evans's Journal in *Historical Records of Australia* (Sydney, 1916).

DISCOVERY OF THE LACHLAN RIVER (1815)

... the country is good indeed; these fine flats are flooded; there are rising lands clear of it, as I before stated, but no hill that will afford a prospect; tomorrow I am necessitated to return, and shall ascend a very high hill I left on my right hand early this morning. I could leave no mark here more than cutting trees; on one situated in an angle of the river and a wet creek, bearing up north, I have deeply carved 'Evans 1st June 1815'. The country continues good, and better than ever I expected to discover.

Friday 2 June. In travelling back, I left the river; at about a mile from it, the land is not so rich; the soil changed to red loam, as deep coloured as a burnt brick, wherein the grass is poor and the box trees small. I am glad to observe that the deficiency is made up by useful pine trees from one inch to three feet in diameter, as straight as arrows, some of them at least 40 feet high before the branches begin to shoot out; those, growing on what I term pine hills, are stunted; the trunks of them rise but a few feet from the ground before their branches spread, which I think may be accounted for by those hills being chiefly a mass of granite rock. I ascended the height; no country can possibly have a more interesting aspect; so much so that, if a further trace into the interior is required at a future period, I respectfully beg leave to offer myself for the service. I see no end to travelling. I am deficient in abilities to describe it properly, but shall endeavour to do so by comparing the country to an ocean, as it is nearly level, with the horizon from NW to SW; small hillocks are seen at great distances of a pale blue, showing as land appears when first discovered at sea; spaces clear of trees may be imagined islands, and the natives' smokes, rising in various points, vessels; it is a clear calm evening near sunsetting, which showed every part advantageously.

The river I can distinctly discover to continue near due west, and rest confident that, when it is full, boats may go down it in safety; my meaning of being full is its general height in moderate seasons, which the banks show, about five feet about the present level; it would then carry boats over trees and narrows that now obstruct the passage; no doubt the stream connects with Macquarie or some other river further west; the channel then sure is of great magnitude; I should think so to carry off the body of water that must in time of floods cover these very extensive flats. . . .

Monday 5th June. Left the river, which I have now called 'The River Lachlan'.

✻

JOHN JOSEPH OXLEY

(1783–1828)

English emigrant to Australia who became surveyor-general in 1812. In 1817 he set off to explore the interior, following the Lachlan River until it disappeared into marshes. He concluded that Australia had an inland sea, a hypothesis not disproved until 1860.

Journals of Two Expeditions into the Interior of New South Wales, undertaken by order of the British Government, 1817–1818 (London, 1820).

DOWN THE LACHLAN TO THE MARSHES (1817)

It is impossible to fancy a worse country than the one we were now travelling over, intersected by swamps and small lagoons in every direction; the soil a poor clay, and covered with stunted, useless timber. It was excessively fatiguing to the horses, which travelled along the banks of the river, as the rubus and bromus were so thickly intermingled that they could scarcely force a passage. After proceeding about eight miles, a bold rocky mount terminated on the river, and broke the sameness which had so long wearied us: we ascended this hill, which I named Mount Amyot, and from the summit had one of the most extensive views that can be imagined. On the opposite side of the river was another hill precisely similar to Mount Amyot, leaving a passage between them for the river, and the immense tract of level country to the eastward; this hill was named Mount Stuart. Vast plains clear of timber lay on the south side of the river, and which, from our having travelled on a level with them, it was impossible for us to distinguish before. These plains I named Hamilton's Plains, and they were bounded by hills of considerable elevation to the southward; whilst the whole level country thus bounded was honoured with the designation of Princess Charlotte's Crescent. . . .

I have reason to believe that the whole of the extensive tract named Princess Charlotte's Crescent is at times drowned by the overflowing of the river; the marks of flood were observed in every direction, and the waters in the marshes and lagoons were all traced as being derived from the river. During a course of upwards of seventy miles, not a single running stream emptied itself into the river on either side; and I am forced to conclude that in common seasons this whole tract is extremely badly watered, and that it derives its principal if not only supply from the river within the bounding ranges of Princess Charlotte's Crescent. There are doubtless many small eminences which might afford a retreat from the inundations, but those which were observed by us were too trifling and distant from each other to stand out distinct from the vast level surface which the crescent presents to the view. The soil of the country we passed over was a poor and cold clay; but there are many rich levels which, could they be drained and defended from the inundations of the river, would amply repay the cultivation. These flats are certainly not adapted for cattle; the grass is too swampy, and the bushes, swamps, and lagoons are too thickly intermingled with the better portions, to render it either a safe or desirable grazing country. The timber is universally bad and small; a few large misshapen gum trees on the immediate banks of the river may be considered as exceptions. If, however, the country itself is poor, the river is rich in the most excellent fish, procurable in the utmost abundance. One man in less than an hour caught eighteen large fish, one of which was a curiosity from its immense size and the beauty of its colours. In shape and general form it most resembled a cod, but was speckled over with brown, blue, and yellow spots, like a leopard's skin; its gills and belly a clear white, the tail and fins a dark brown. It weighed entire seventy pounds . . .

✣

CHARLES STURT

(1795–1869)

English soldier. Posted to Australia with his regiment in charge of convicts in 1826, he explored the courses of the Darling and Murray Rivers. Later he was to receive a Royal Geographical Society Gold Medal for an expedition to the Simpson Desert, near the centre of the continent, which he was the first white man to enter.

1–3: *Two Expeditions into the Interior of Southern Australia, during the years 1828, 1829, 1830, and 1831* (2 vols., London, 1833); 4: *Narrative of an Expedition into Central Australia, performed under the authority of Her Majesty's Government, during the years 1844, 5, and 6* (2 vols., London, 1849).

1. A NARROW ESCAPE (1830)

We had proceeded about nine miles when we were surprised by the appearance in view, at the termination of a reach, of a long line of magnificent trees of green and dense foliage. As we sailed down the reach, we observed a vast concourse of natives under them, and, on a nearer approach, we not only heard their war-song, if it might so be called, but remarked that they were painted and armed, as they generally are, prior to their engaging in deadly conflict. Notwithstanding these outward signs of hostility . . . I continued to steer directly in for the bank on which they were collected. I found, however, when it was almost too late to turn into the succeeding reach to our left, that an attempt to land would only be attended with loss of life. The natives seemed determined to resist it. We approached so near that they held their spears quivering in their grasp ready to hurl. They were painted in various ways. Some who had marked their ribs, and thighs, and faces with a white pigment, looked like skeletons, others were daubed over with red and yellow ochre, and their bodies shone with the grease with which they had besmeared themselves. A dead silence prevailed among the front ranks, but those in the background, as well as the women, who carried supplies of darts, and who appeared to have had a bucket of whitewash capsized over their heads, were extremely clamorous. As I did not wish a conflict with these people, I lowered my sail, and putting the helm to starboard, we passed quietly down the stream in mid-channel. Disappointed in their anticipations, the natives ran along the bank of the river, endeavouring to secure an aim at us; but, unable to throw with certainty, in consequence of the onward motion of the boat, they flung themselves into the most extravagant attitudes, and worked themselves into a state of frenzy by loud and vehement shouting.

It was with considerable apprehension that I observed the river to be shoaling fast, more especially as a huge sandbank, a little below us, and on the same side on which the natives had gathered, projected nearly a third-way across the channel. To this sandbank they ran with tumultuous uproar, and covered it over in a dense mass. Some of the chiefs advanced to the water to be nearer their victims, and turned from time to time to direct their followers. With every pacific disposition, and an extreme reluctance to take away life, I foresaw that it would be impossible any longer to avoid an engagement; yet with such fearful numbers against us I was doubtful of the result. The spectacle we had witnessed had been one of the most appalling kind, and sufficient to shake the firmness of most men; but at that trying moment my little band preserved their temper coolness, and if anything could be gleaned from their countenances, it was that they had determined on an obstinate resistance. I now explained to them that their only chance of escape depended, or would depend, on their firmness. . . . As we neared the sandbank, I stood up and made signs to the natives to desist; but without success. I took up my gun, therefore, and cocking it, had already brought it down to a level. A few seconds more would have closed the life of the nearest of the savages. The distance was too trifling for me to doubt the fatal effects of the discharge; for I was determined to take deadly aim, in hopes that the fall of one man might save the lives of many. But at the very moment when my hand was on the trigger and my eye was along the barrel, my purpose was checked by M'Leay, who called to me that another party of blacks had made their appearance upon the left bank of the river. Turning round, I observed four men at the top of their speed. The foremost of them, as soon as he got ahead of the boat, threw himself from a considerable height into the water. He struggled across the channel to the sandbank, and in an incredibly short space of time stood in front of the savage against whom my aim had been directed. Seizing him by the throat, he pushed him backwards and, forcing all who were in the water upon the bank, he trod its margin with a vehemence and an agitation that were exceedingly striking. At one moment pointing to the boat, at another shaking his clenched hand in the faces of the most forward, and stamping with passion on the sand; his voice, that was at first distinct and clear, was lost in hoarse murmurs. Two of the four natives remained on the left bank of the river, but the third followed his leader . . . to the scene of action. The reader will imagine our feelings on this occasion: it is impossible to describe them. We were so wholly lost in interest at the scene that was passing that the boat was allowed to drift at pleasure. For my own part I was overwhelmed with astonishment, and in truth stunned and confused; so singular, so unexpected, and so strikingly providential had been our escape.

We were again roused to action by the boat suddenly striking upon a shoal, which reached from one side of the river to the other. To jump out and push her into deeper water was but the work of a moment with the men, and it was just as she floated again that our attention was withdrawn to a new and beautiful stream, coming apparently from the north. The great body of the natives having posted themselves on the narrow tongue of land formed by the two rivers, the bold savage who had so unhesitatingly interfered on our account was still in hot dispute with them, and I really feared his generous warmth would have brought down upon him the vengeance of the tribes. I hesitated, therefore, whether or not to go to his assistance. It appeared, however, both to M'Leay and myself that the tone of the natives had moderated, and the old and young men having listened to the remonstrances of our friend, the middle-aged warriors were alone holding out against him. A party of about seventy blacks were upon the right bank of the newly discovered river, and I thought that by landing among them we should make a diversion in favour of our late guest; and in this I succeeded. If even they had still meditated violence, they would have to swim a good broad junction, and that, probably, would cool them, or we at least should have the advantage of position. I therefore, ran the boat ashore, and landed with M'Leay amidst the smaller party of natives, wholly unarmed, and having directed the men to keep at a little distance

426

from the bank. Fortunately, what I anticipated was brought about by the stratagem to which I had had recourse. The blacks no sooner observed that we had landed than curiosity took place of anger. All wrangling ceased, and they came swimming over to us like a parcel of seals.

Thus, in less than a quarter of an hour from the moment when it appeared that all human intervention was at an end, and we were on the point of commencing a bloody fray which, independently of its own disastrous consequences, would have blasted the success of the expedition, we were peacefully surrounded by the hundreds who had so lately threatened us with destruction; nor was it until after we had returned to the boat, and had surveyed the multitude upon the sloping bank above us, that we became fully aware of the extent of our danger, and of the almost miraculous intervention of Providence in our favour. There could not have been less than six hundred natives upon that blackened sward. . . .

It was my first care to call for our friend, and to express to him, as well as I could, how much we stood indebted to him, at the same time that I made him a suitable present; but to the chiefs of the tribes I positively refused all gifts, notwithstanding their earnest solicitations. We next prepared to examine the new river, and turning the boat's head towards it, endeavoured to pull up the stream. . . .

As soon as we got above the entrance of the new river, we found easier pulling, and proceeded up it for some miles, accompanied by the once more noisy multitude. The river preserved a breadth of one hundred yards, and a depth of rather more than twelve feet. Its banks were sloping and grassy, and were overhung by trees of magnificent size. Indeed, its appearance was so different from the waterworn banks of the sister stream that the men exclaimed, on entering it, that we had got into an English river. Its appearance certainly almost justified the expression; for the greenness of its banks was as new to us as the size of its timber. Its waters, though sweet, were turbid, and had a taste of vegetable decay, as well as a slight tinge of green. Our progress was watched by the natives with evident anxiety. They kept abreast of us, and talked incessantly. At length, however, our course was checked by a net that stretched right across the stream. I say checked because it would have been unfair to have passed over it, with the chance of disappointing the numbers who apparently depended on it for subsistence that day. The moment was one of intense interest to me. As the men rested upon their oars, awaiting my further orders, a crowd of thoughts rushed upon me. The various conjectures I had formed of the course and importance of the Darling passed across my mind. Were they indeed realized? An irresistible conviction impressed me that we were now sailing on the bosom of that very stream from whose banks I had been twice forced to retire. I directed the Union Jack to the hoisted and, giving way to our satisfaction, we all stood up in the boat and gave three distinct cheers. It was an English feeling, an ebullition, an overflow, which I am ready to admit that our circumstances and situation will alone excuse. The eye of every native had been fixed upon that noble flag, at all times a beautiful object, and to them a novel one, as it waved over us in the heart of the desert. They had until that moment been particularly loquacious, but the sight of that flag and the sound of our voices hushed the tumult, and while they were still lost in astonishment, the boat's head was speedily turned, the sail was sheeted home, both wind and current went in our favour, and we vanished from them with a rapidity that surprised even ourselves, and which precluded every hope of the most adventurous among them to keep up with us. . . .

Not having as yet given a name to our first discovery, when we re-entered its capacious channel on this occasion, I laid it down as the Murray River, in compliment to the distinguished officer, Sir George Murray, who then presided over the colonial department, not only in compliance with the known wishes of his Excellency General Darling, but also in accordance with my own feelings as a soldier. . . .

2. Description of Natives

We had found the interior more populous than we had any reason to expect; yet as we advanced into it, the population appeared to increase. It was impossible for us to judge of the disposition of the natives during the short interviews we generally had with them, and our motions were so rapid that we did not give them time to form any concerted plan of attack, had they been inclined to attack us. They did not, however, show any disposition to hostility, but, considering all things, were quiet and orderly; nor did any instances of theft occur, or, at least, none fell under my notice. The most loathsome of diseases prevailed throughout the tribes, nor were the youngest infants exempt from them. Indeed, so young were some whose condition was truly disgusting that I cannot but suppose they must have been born in a state of disease; but I am uncertain whether it is fatal or not in its results, though most probably it hurries many to a premature grave. How these diseases originated it is impossible to say. Certainly not from the colony, since the midland tribes alone were infected. Syphilis raged amongst them with fearful violence; many had lost their noses, and all the glandular parts were considerably affected. . . .

From the size and number of the huts, and from the great breadth of the foot-paths, we were still further led to conclude that we were passing through a very populous district. What the actual number of inhabitants was it is impossible to say, but we seldom communicated with fewer than 200 daily. They sent ambassadors forward regularly from one tribe to another, in order to prepare for our approach, a custom that not only saved us an infinity of time, but also great personal risk. Indeed, I doubt very much whether we should ever have pushed so far down the river had we not been assisted by the natives themselves. I was particularly careful not to do anything that would alarm them, or to permit any liberty to be taken with their women. Our reserve in this respect seemed to excite their surprise, for they asked sundry questions, by signs and expressions, as to whether we had any women, and where they were. The whole tribe generally assembled to receive us, and all, without exception, were in a complete state of nudity; and really the loathsome condition and hideous countenances of the women would, I should imagine, have been a complete antidote to the sexual passion. It is to be observed that the women are very inferior in appearance to the men. The latter are, generally speaking, a clean-limbed and powerful race, much stouter in the bust than below, but withal active and, in some respects, intelligent; but the women are poor, weak, and emaciated. This, perhaps, is owing to their poverty and paucity of food, and to the treatment they receive at the hands of the men; but the latter did not show any unkindness towards them in our presence. . . .

3. ARRIVAL AT THE COAST

From the top of the hill from which we had obtained our first view of the lake, I observed the waves breaking upon the distant headland and enveloping the cliff in spray; so that, independent of the clearness of the horizon beyond it, I was further led to conclude that there existed a great expanse of water to the SW, and, as that had been the direction taken by the river, I thought it probable that, by steering at once to the SW down the lake, I should hit the outlet. . . .

It is difficult to give a just description of our passage across the lake. The boisterous weather we had had seemed to have blown over. A cool and refreshing breeze was carrying us on at between four and five knots an hour, and the heavens above us were without a cloud. It almost appeared as if nature had resisted us in order to try our perseverance, and that she had yielded in pity to our efforts. The men, relieved for a time from the oar, stretched themselves at their length in the boat, and commented on the scenery around them, or ventured their opinions as to that which was before them. . . .

It was now near sunset, and one of the most lovely evenings I had ever seen. The sun's radiance was yet upon the mountains, but all lower objects were in shade. The banks of the channel, with the trees and the rocks, were reflected in the tranquil waters, whose surface was unruffled save by the thousands of wildfowl that rose before us, and made a noise as of a multitude clapping hands in their clumsy efforts to rise from the waters. Not one of them allowed us to get within shot.

We proceeded about a mile below the hill on which the natives were posted; some few still following us with violent threats. We landed, however, on a flat, bounded all round by the continuation of the hills. It was an admirable position, for, in the centre of it, we could not be taken by surprise, and, on the other hand, we gave the natives an opportunity of communicating with us if they would. The full moon rose as we were forming the camp, and, notwithstanding our vicinity to so noisy a host, the silence of death was around us, or the stillness of the night was only broken by the roar of the ocean, now too near to be mistaken for wind, or by the silvery and melancholy note of the black swans as they passed over us, to seek for food, no doubt, among the slimy weeds at the head of the lake. We had been quite delighted with the beauty of the channel, which was rather more than half a mile in width. Numberless mounds, that seemed to invite civilized man to erect his dwelling upon them, presented themselves to our view. The country round them was open, yet ornamentally wooded, and rocks and trees hung or drooped over the waters.

We had in one day gained a position I once feared it would have cost us infinite labour to have measured. Indeed, had we been obliged to pull across the lake, unless during a calm, I am convinced the men would have been wholly exhausted. We had to thank a kind Providence that such was not the case, since it had extended its mercy to us at so critical a moment. We had, indeed, need of all the little strength we had remaining, and could ill have thrown it away on such an effort as this would have required. I calculated that we could not have run less than forty-five miles during the day, a distance that, together with the eight miles we had advanced the evening previously, would give the length of the lake at fifty-three miles. . . .

A little before high water we again embarked. A seal had been observed playing about, and we augured well from such an omen. The blacks had been watching us from the opposite shore, and as soon as we moved, rose to keep abreast of us. With all our efforts we could not avoid the shoals. We walked up to our knees in mud and water, to find the least variation in the depth of the water so as to facilitate our exertions, but it was to no purpose. We were ultimately obliged to drag the boat over the flats (there were some of them a quarter of a mile in breadth) knee-deep in mud, but at length got her into deep water again. The turn of the channel was now before us, and we had a good run for about four or five miles. We had completed the bend, and the channel now stretched to the ESE. At about nine miles from us there was a bright sand-hill visible, near which the channel seemed to turn again to the south; and I doubted not that it terminated there. It was to no purpose, however, that we tried to gain it. Shoals again closed in upon us on every side. We dragged the boat over several, and at last got amongst quicksands. I, therefore, directed our efforts to hauling the boat over to the south side of the channel, as that on which we could most satisfactorily ascertain our position. After great labour we succeeded, and, as evening had closed in, lost no time in pitching the tents.

While the men were thus employed, I took Fraser with me, and, accompanied by M'Leay, crossed the sand-hummocks behind us, and descended to the sea-shore. I found that we had struck the south coast deep in the bight of Encounter Bay. We had no time for examination, but returned immediately to the camp, as I intended to give the men an opportunity to go to the beach. They accordingly went and bathed, and returned not only highly delighted at this little act of good nature on my part, but loaded with cockles, a bed of which they had managed to find among the sand. Clayton had tied one end of his shirt up, and brought a bag full, and amused himself with boiling cockles all night long.

4. Caught by the Drought (1845)

At the distance of seven miles we arrived at the entrance of the little rocky glen through which the creek passes, and at once found ourselves on the brink of a fine pond of water, shaded by trees and cliffs. The scenery was so different from any we had hitherto seen that I was quite delighted, but the ground, being sandy, was unfit for us; we therefore turned down the creek towards the long sheet of water Mr Poole had mentioned, and waited there until the drays arrived, when we pitched our tents close to it, little imagining that we were destined to remain at that lonely spot for six weary months. We were not then aware that our advance and our retreat were alike cut off. . . . We pitched our tents at the place to which I have led him, and which I shall henceforth call the 'Depot', on the 27th of January 1845. They were not struck again until the 17th of July following.

This ruinous detention paralysed the efforts and enervated the strength of the expedition, by constitutionally affecting both the men and animals and depriving them of the elasticity and energy with which they commenced their labours. It was not, however, until after we had run down every creek in our neighbourhood, and had traversed the country in every direction, that the truth flashed across my mind, and it became evident to me that we were locked up in the desolate and heated region into which we had penetrated as effectually as if we had wintered at the Pole. It was long indeed ere I could bring myself to believe that so great a misfortune had overtaken us, but so it was. Providence had, in its allwise purposes, guided us to the only spot, in that widespread desert, where our wants could have been permanently supplied, but had there stayed our further progress into a region that almost appears to be forbidden ground.

✷

EDWARD JOHN EYRE

(1815–1901)

Australian immigrant. He achieved the first crossing of the continent from east to west, in 1841. Later he was to serve as lieutenant-governor of New Zealand and governor of Jamaica.

Journals of Expeditions of discovery into Central Australia and Overland from Adelaide to King George's Sound, in the Years 1840–41 (2 vols., London, 1845).

1. THE MURDER OF HIS OVERSEER, JAMES BAXTER (1841)

27 April. We had now entered upon the last fearful push, which was to decide our fate. This one stretch of bad country crossed, I felt a conviction we should be safe. That we had at least 150 miles to go to the next water I was fully assured of; I was equally satisfied that our horses were by no means in a condition to encounter the hardships and privations they must meet with in such a journey; for though they had had a long rest, and in some degree recovered from their former tired-out condition, they had not picked up in flesh or regained their spirits; the sapless, withered state of the grass and the severe cold of the nights had prevented them from deriving the advantage that they ought to have done from so long a respite from labour. Still I hoped we might be successful. We had lingered day by day, until it would have been folly to have waited longer; the rubicon was, however, now passed, and we had nothing to rely upon but our own exertions and perseverance, humbly trusting that the great and merciful God who had hitherto guarded and guided us in safety would not desert us now. . . .

29 April. The horses having been all hobbled and turned out to feed, the whole party proceeded to make break-winds of boughs to form a shelter from the wind, preparatory to laying down for the night. We had taken a meal in the middle of the day, which ought to have been deferred until night, and our circumstances did not admit of our having another now, so that there remained only to arrange the watching of the horses before going to sleep. The native boys had watched them last night, and this duty of course fell to myself and the overseer this evening. The first watch was from 6 p.m. to 11, the second from 11 until 4 a.m., at which hour the whole party usually arose and made preparations for moving on with the first streak of daylight.

Tonight the overseer asked me which of the watches I would keep, and as I was not sleepy, though tired, I chose the first. At a quarter before six, I went to take charge of the horses, having previously seen the overseer and the natives lay down to sleep, at their respective break-winds, ten or twelve yards apart from one another. The arms and provisions, as was our custom, were piled up under an oilskin, between my break-wind and that of the overseer, with the exception of one gun, which I always kept at my own sleeping-place. I have been thus minute in detailing the position and arrangement of our encampment this evening because of the fearful consequences that followed, and to show the very slight circumstances upon which the destinies of life sometimes hinge. Trifling as the arrangement of the watches might seem, and unimportant as I thought it at the time whether I undertook the first or the second, yet was my choice, in this respect, the means under God's providence of my life being saved, and the cause of the loss of that of my overseer.

The night was cold, and the wind blowing hard from the south-west, whilst scud and nimbus were passing very rapidly by the moon. The horses fed tolerably well, but rambled a good deal, threading in and out among the many belts of scrub which intersected the grassy openings, until at last I hardly knew exactly where our camp was, the fires having apparently expired some time ago. It was now half past ten, and I headed the horses back in the direction in which I thought the camp lay, that I might be ready to call the overseer to relieve me at 11. Whilst thus engaged, and looking steadfastly around among the scrub to see if I could anywhere detect the embers of our fires, I was startled by a sudden flash, followed by the report of a gun, not a quarter of a mile away from me. Imagining that the overseer had mistaken the hour of the night and, not being able to find me or the horses, had taken that method to attract my attention,

I immediately called out, but as no answer was returned, I got alarmed and, leaving the horses, hurried up towards the camp as rapidly as I could. About a hundred yards from it, I met the King George's Sound native (Wylie), running towards me, and in great alarm, crying out, 'Oh Massa, oh Massa, come here', but could gain no information from him as to what had occurred. Upon reaching the encampment, which I did in about five minutes after the shot was fired, I was horror-struck to find my poor over-seer lying on the ground, weltering in his blood, and in the last agonies of death.

Glancing hastily around the camp, I found it deserted by the two younger native boys, whilst the scattered fragments of our baggage, which I left carefully piled under the oilskin, lay thrown about in wild disorder, and at once revealed the cause of the harrowing scene before me.

Upon raising the body of my faithful but ill-fated follower, I found that he was beyond all human aid; he had been shot through the left breast with a ball, the last convulsions of death were upon him, and he expired almost immediately after our arrival. The frightful, the appalling truth now burst upon me that I was alone in the desert. He who had faithfully served me for many years, who had followed my fortunes in adversity and in prosperity, who had accompanied me in all my wanderings, and whose attachment to me had been his sole inducement to remain with me in this last, and to him, alas, fatal, journey was now no more. For an instant I was almost tempted to wish that it had been my own fate instead of his. The horrors of my situation glared upon me in such startling reality as for an instant almost to paralyse the mind. At the dead hour of night, in the wildest and most inhospitable wastes of Australia, with the fierce wind raging in unison with the scene of violence before me, I was left with a single native, whose fidelity I could not rely upon, and who for aught I knew might be in league with the other two, who perhaps were even now lurking about with the view of taking away my life as they had done that of the overseer. Three days had passed away since we left the last water, and it was very doubtful when we might find any more. Six hundred miles of country had to be traversed before I could hope to obtain the slightest aid or assistance of any kind, whilst I knew not that a single drop of water or an ounce of flour had been left by these murderers, from a stock that had previously been so small. . . .

After obtaining possession of all the remaining arms, useless as they were at the moment, with some ammunition, I made no further examination then, but hurried away from the fearful scene, accompanied by the King George's Sound native, to search for the horses, knowing that if they got away now, no chance whatever would remain of saving our lives. Already the wretched animals had wandered to a considerable distance; and although the night was moonlit, yet the belts of scrub, intersecting the plains, were so numerous and dense that for a long time we could not find them. Having succeeded in doing so at last, Wylie and I remained with them, watching them during the remainder of the night; but they were very restless, and gave us a great deal of trouble. With an aching heart, and in most painful reflections, I passed this dreadful night. Every moment appeared to be protracted to an hour, and it seemed as if the daylight would never appear. About midnight the wind ceased, and the weather became bitterly cold and frosty. I had nothing on but a shirt and a pair of trousers, and suffered most acutely from the cold; to mental anguish was now added intense bodily pain. Suffering and distress had well-nigh overwhelmed me, and life seemed hardly worth the effort necessary to prolong it. Ages can never efface the horrors of this single night, nor would the wealth of the world ever tempt me to go through similar ones again.

30 April. At last, by God's blessing, daylight dawned once more, but sad and heart-rending was the scene it presented to my view, upon driving the horses to what had been our last night's camp. The corpse of my poor companion lay extended on the ground, with the eyes open, but cold and glazed in death. The same stern resolution and fearless open look which had characterized him when living stamped the expression of his countenance even now. He had fallen upon his breast four or five yards from where he had been sleeping, and was dressed only in his shirt. In all probability the noise made by the natives in plundering the camp had awoken him; and upon his jumping up, with a view of stopping them, they had fired upon and killed him. Around the camp lay scattered the harness of the horses, and the remains of the stores that had been the temptation to this fatal deed.

As soon as the horses were caught and secured, I left Wylie to make a fire, whilst I proceeded to examine into the state of our baggage, that I might decide upon our future proceedings. Among the principal things carried off by the natives were the whole of our baked bread, amounting to twenty pounds' weight, some mutton, tea, and sugar, the overseer's tobacco and pipes, a one-gallon keg full of water, some clothes, two double-barrelled guns, some ammunition, and a few other small articles. There were still left forty pounds of flour, a little tea and sugar, and four gallons of water, besides the arms and ammunition I had secured last night. . . .

At eight o'clock we were ready to proceed; there remained but to perform the last sad offices of humanity towards him, whose career had been cut short in so untimely a manner.

2. An 'Unwholesome Diet'

Our stage today was only twelve miles, yet some of our horses were nearly knocked up, and we ourselves in but little better condition. The incessant walking we were subject to, the low and unwholesome diet we had lived upon, the severe and weakening attacks of illness caused by that diet, having daily, and sometimes twice a day, to dig for water, to carry all our firewood from a distance upon our backs, to harness, unharness, water, and attend to the horses, besides other trifling occupations making up our daily routine, usually so completely exhausted us that we had neither spirit nor energy left. . . . On our march we felt generally weak and languid —it was an effort to put one foot before the other, and there was an indisposition to exertion that it was often very difficult to overcome. After sitting for a few moments to rest—and we often had to do this—it was always with the greatest unwillingness we ever moved on again. I felt, on such occasions, that I could have sat quietly and contentedly and let the glass of life glide away to its last sand. There was a dreamy kind of pleasure which made me forgetful or careless of the circumstances and difficulties by which I was surrounded, and which I was always indisposed to break in upon. Wylie was even worse than myself; I had often much difficulty in getting him to move at all, and not infrequently was compelled almost forcibly to get him up. Fortunately he was very good-tempered, and on the whole had behaved extremely well under all our troubles since we had been travelling together alone.

18 May. Having seen some large kangaroos near our camp, I sent Wylie with the rifle to try and get one. At dark he returned bringing home a young one, large enough for two good meals; upon this we feasted at night, and for once Wylie admitted that his belly was full. He commenced by eating a pound and a half of horse-flesh, and a little bread; he then ate the entrails, paunch, liver, lights, tail, and two hind legs of the young kangaroo; next followed a penguin that he had found dead upon the beach; upon this he forced down the whole of the hide of the kangaroo after singeing the hair off, and wound up this meal by swallowing the tough skin of the penguin. He then made a little fire, and laid down to sleep and dream of the pleasures of eating, nor do I think he was ever happier in his life than at that moment. . . .

Travelling for two miles further, we came to a very pretty fresh-water lake, of moderate size, and surrounded by clumps of tea-tree. It was the first permanent fresh water we had found on the surface since we commenced our journey from Fowler's Bay—a distance of nearly seven hundred miles. . . .

31 May. There were many grass-trees in the vicinity, and as several of these had been broken down and were dead they were full of white grubs of which the natives are so fond. From these Wylie enjoyed a plentiful and, to him, luxurious supper. I could not bring myself to try them, preferring the root of the broad flag-reed which, for the first time, we met with at this stream, and which is an excellent and nutritious article of food. This root, being dug up and roasted in hot ashes, yields a great quantity of a mealy, farinaceous powder interspersed among the fibres; it is of an agreeable flavour, wholesome, and satisfying to the appetite. In all parts of Australia, even where other food abounds, the root of this reed is a favourite and staple article of diet among the aborigines. . . .

3. ARRIVAL AT KING GEORGE'S SOUND

Before reaching the Sound, we met a native who at once recognized Wylie, and greeted him most cordially. From him we learnt that we had been expected at the Sound some months ago, but had long been given up for lost, whilst Wylie had been mourned for and lamented as dead by his friends and his tribe. The rain still continued falling heavily as we ascended to the brow of the hill immediately overlooking the town of Albany—not a soul was to be seen—not an animal of any kind—the place looked deserted and uninhabited, so completely had the inclemency of the weather driven both man and beast to seek shelter from the storm.

For a moment I stood gazing at the town below me—that goal I had so long looked forward to, had so laboriously toiled to attain, was at last before me. A thousand confused images and reflections crowded through my mind, and the events of the past year were recalled in rapid succession. The contrast between the circumstances under which I had commenced and terminated my labours stood in strong relief before me. The gay and gallant cavalcade that accompanied me on my way at starting—the small but enterprising band that I then commanded, the goodly array of horses and drays, with all their well-ordered appointments and equipment, were conjured up in all their circumstances of pride and pleasure; and I could not restrain a tear as I called to mind the embarrassing difficulties and sad disasters that had broken up my party, and left myself and Wylie the two sole wanderers remaining at the close of an undertaking entered upon under such hopeful auspices.

Whilst standing thus upon the brow overlooking the town, and buried in reflection, I was startled by the loud, shrill cry of the native we had met on the road and who still kept with us: clearly and powerfully that voice rang through the recesses of the settlement beneath, whilst the blended name of Wylie told me of the information it conveyed. For an instant there was a silence still almost as death—then a single repetition of that wild joyous cry, a confused hum of many voices, a hurrying to and fro of human feet, and the streets which had appeared so shortly before gloomy and untenanted were now alive with natives—men, women, and children, old and young, rushing rapidly up the hill, to welcome the wanderer on his return, and to receive their lost one almost from the grave.

It was an interesting and touching sight to witness the meeting between Wylie and his friends. Affection's strongest ties could not have produced a more affecting and melting scene—the wordless, weeping pleasure, too deep for utterance, with which he was embraced by his relatives, the cordial and hearty reception given him by his friends, and the joyous greeting bestowed upon him by all might well have put to the blush those heartless calumniators who, branding the savage as the creature only of unbridled passions, deny to him any of those better feelings and affections which are implanted in the breast of all mankind, and which nature has not denied to any colour or to any race.

Upon entering the town I proceeded direct to Mr Sherratt's, where I had lodged when in King George's Sound, in 1840. By him and his family I was most hospitably received, and every attention shown to me; and in the course of a short time, after taking a glass of hot brandy and water, performing my ablutions, and putting on a clean suit of borrowed clothes, I was enabled once more to feel comparatively comfortable, and to receive the many kind friends who called upon me. . . .

✷

FRIEDRICH WILHELM LUDWIG LEICHHARDT

(1813–?1848)

Prussian explorer. He became a national hero in Australia, leading several expeditions. On the last one, a second attempt to cross the continent from Sydney to Perth, he disappeared with six companions. No trace of them has been found. The following extracts are from an earlier expedition from Queensland to the north coast.

Journal of an Overland Expedition in Australia from Moreton Bay to Port Essington, a distance of upwards of 3,000 miles, during the years 1844–1845 (London, 1847).

1. THE DEATH OF JOHN GILBERT, AN ENGLISH
ORNITHOLOGIST (1845)

After dinner, Messrs Roper and Calvert retired to their tent, and Mr Gilbert, John, and Brown were plaiting palm leaves to make a hat, and I stood musing near their fire place, looking at their work, and occasionally joining in their conversation. Mr Gilbert was congratulating himself upon having succeeded in learning to plait; and, when he had nearly completed a yard, he retired with John to their tent. This was about 7 o'clock; and I stretched myself upon the ground as usual, at a little distance from the fire, and fell into a doze, from which I was suddenly roused by a loud noise, and a call for help from Calvert and Roper. Natives had suddenly attacked us. They had doubtless watched our movements during the afternoon, and marked the position of the different tents; and, as soon as it was dark, sneaked upon us, and threw a shower of spears at the tents of Calvert, Roper, and Gilbert, and a few at that of Phillips, and also one or two towards the fire. Charley and Brown called for caps, which I hastened to find, and, as soon as they were provided, they discharged their guns into the crowd of the natives, who instantly fled, leaving Roper and Calvert pierced with several spears, and severely beaten by their waddies. Several of these spears were barbed, and could not be extracted without difficulty. I had to force one through the arm of Roper, to break off the barb; and to cut another out of the groin of Mr Calvert. John Murphy had succeeded in getting out of the tent, and concealing himself behind a tree, whence he fired at the natives, and severely wounded one of them, before Brown had discharged his gun. Not seeing Mr Gilbert, I asked for him, when Charley told me that our unfortunate companion was no more! He had come out of his tent with his gun, shot, and powder, and handed them to him, when he instantly dropped down dead. Upon receiving this afflicting intelligence, I hastened to the spot, and found Charley's account too true. He was lying on the ground at a little distance from our fire, and, upon examining him, I soon found, to my sorrow, that every sign of life had disappeared. . . .

The spear that terminated poor Gilbert's existence, had entered the chest, between the clavicle and the neck; but made so small a wound, that, for some time, I was unable to detect it.

2. A MEETING WITH FRIENDLY NATIVES

Whilst we were waiting for our bullock, which had returned to the running brook, a fine native stepped out of the forest with the ease and grace of an Apollo, with a smiling countenance, and with the confidence of a man to whom the white face was perfectly familiar. He was unarmed, but a great number of his companions were keeping back to watch the reception he should meet with. We received him, of course, most cordially; and upon being joined by another good-looking little man, we heard him utter distinctly the words, 'Commandant', 'come here', 'very good', 'what's your name?' If my readers have at all identified themselves with my feelings throughout this trying journey; if they have only imagined a tithe of the difficulties we have encountered, they will readily imagine the startling effect which these, as it were, magic words produced: we were electrified —our joy knew no limits, and I was ready to embrace the fellows, who, seeing the happiness with which they inspired us, joined, with a most merry grin, in the loud expression of our feelings. We gave them various presents, particularly leather belts, and received in return a great number of bunches of goose feathers, which the natives use to brush away the flies. They knew the white people of Victoria, and called them Balanda, which is nothing more than 'Hollanders', a name used by the Malays, from whom they received it. We had most fortunately a small collection of words, made by Mr Gilbert when at Port Essington, so that we were enabled to ask for water (obert); for the road (allun); for Limbo cardja, which was the name of the Harbour. I wished very much to induce them to become our guides; and the two principal men, Eooanberry and Minorelli, promised to accompany us, but they afterwards changed their minds. . . .

The native were remarkably kind and attentive, and offered us the rind of the rose-coloured Eugenia apple, the cabbage of the Seaforthia palm, a fruit which I did not know, and the nut-like swelling of the rhizome of either a grass or a sedge. The last had a sweet taste, was very mealy and nourishing, and the best article of the food of the natives we had yet tasted. They called it 'Allamurr' (the natives of Port Essington, 'Murnatt'), and were extremely fond of it. The plant grew in depressions of the plains, where the boys and young men were occupied the whole day in digging for it. The women went in search of other food; either to the sea-coast to collect shellfish—and many were the broad paths which led across the plains from the forest land to the salt water—or to the brushes to gather the fruits of the season, and the cabbage of the palms. The men, armed with a wommala, and with a bundle of goose spears made of a strong reed or bamboo, gave up their time to hunting. It seemed that they speared the geese only when flying; and would crouch down whenever they saw a flight of them approaching: the geese, however, knew their enemies so well that they immediately turned upon seeing a native rise to put his spear into the throwing stick. Some of my companions asserted that they had seen them hit their object at the almost incredible distance of 200 yards: but, making all due allowance for the guess, I could not help thinking how formidable they would have been had they been enemies instead of friends. . . .

✼

THOMAS BRUNNER

(1821–1874)

New Zealand explorer. Unusually, he travelled with Maori guides and their wives. His objective was to find the legendary tableland in the Southern Alps. The greatest danger in New Zealand travel is crossing rivers.

  The Great Journey: An Expedition to Explore the Interior of the Middle Island, New Zealand, 1846–8 (Christchurch, 1952).

THE GREAT JOURNEY (1847)

[*5 January*] At this place my two female travelling companions quarrelled and fought. Their husbands taking part in the combat, I had much difficulty in reconciling them, and persuading them to continue their journey.

  6th. This morning found the weather changed into a regular soaking wet day. *7th*. Raining incessantly the whole day.

  8th. The sun has again made his appearance, dispersed the clouds, and, with the assistance of a south-wester, given us a fine day. Great fresh in the river. Collecting fern-root. *9th*. A dull dirty day, with rain in showers.

  10th. Very fine and warm. I again ascended a hill to the southward, but could see nothing but hills, or rather mountains, all round.

  11th. Started this morning to wade the river Tiraumea. We passed the Mai, or waterfall, once celebrated as a kakapo station. Two or more persons crossing a river will find it much easier and safer to hold altogether by one long stick, using both hands, and holding it on the palm, the elbow downwards, the strongest of the party up the stream. The quicker you walk the better, taking care to keep the step of the leader. It is a curious feeling, particularly to your feet, which, from the force of the stream and the slipperiness of the stones, seem scarcely to touch the bottom. . . .

  10th [*March*]. The illness, I fear, is catching, for this morning my female companions declared their inability to proceed. I believe it is a species of influenza; however, be it what it may, they tried a novel kind of cure, cutting themselves all about the painful parts with a sharp stone, and then

441

bathing in the river. We caught enough eels for a meal, and hope for better luck on the morrow.

11th. Natives worse instead of better, but we managed to accomplish about a quarter of a mile to a fresh eel-station.

12th. The illness of one of the women has settled in her leg, and she can only bring her toe to the ground. A dirty, showery day, and we lay under the nominal shelter of a large birch tree.

13th. Contrary to my experience on all previous days, the natives packed up for a start during a shower of rain, and we came on about half a mile, when it began to pour down, and the sick woman was not within hail, so Ekehu had to return and seek her, while Epike and self erected a shelter of the fern tree. Ekehu and wife arrived just at dark, and the wind, changing its quarter, blew a gale, driving the rain and smoke of our fire under our shelter. We all passed a most miserable night, not having room either to lie down or sit up, and the woman moaning with pain.

14th. Increased our shelter, which, but for the wind and rain, would be comparatively comfortable. Our fern-root almost exhausted, and no food to be found.

15th. Proposed starting, but the natives refused, stating that the woman could not accomplish above half a mile a day; that the weather showed for rain, and that it was too much work building houses at such short distances. Showery.

16th. I suppose the same arguments serve for today, as we are here still, and I am tired of urging our onward progress, for I only breed discontent, and do not carry my point; so I am determined, come what may, to become passive in urging them forward, although I do not relish gradual starvation on one meal of fern-root in twenty-four hours. I am afraid to quarrel with the natives, for I am told to look out for myself if I choose, and they will do the same.

17th. No alteration in the appearance of the weather, or any apparent abatement of the illness of the native woman, yet they prepared for a start; so we all packed up, and, I think, managed to pass over rather a long mile of ground, and camped. Caught a meal of eels. The woman did not arrive until about midnight. I begin to fear her illness will cause us many days' hunger, if not real starvation, and I will not hear of the natives' suggestion of leaving her to her fate.

18th. Rain drives us on about a quarter of a mile. *19th*. Under shelter all day. Heavy rain. *20th*. Continual rain.

21st. Rain continuing, dietary shorter, strength decreasing, spirits failing, prospects fearful. . . .

22nd [*May*]. A bitterly cold day. We, however, managed to accomplish a short day's walk, at last surmounting the precipice which had so long detained us, and slept without shelter: the rain, however, gave us a wetting during the night.

23rd. Hunger again compelled us to shift our quarters in search of food, but finding none, I was compelled, though very reluctantly, to give my consent to killing my dog Rover. The flesh of a dog is very palatable, tasting something between mutton and pork. It is too richly flavoured to eat by itself. . . .

[*October*] I believe I have now acquired the two greatest requisites for bushmen in New Zealand, the capability of walking barefoot, and the proper method of cooking and eating fern-root. I had often looked forward with dread to the time when my shoes would be worn out, often fearing I should be left a bare-footed cripple in some desolate black birch forest, or on this deserted coast; but now I can trudge along merrily barefoot, or with a pair of native sandals, called by the natives *pairairai*, made of the leaves of the flax, or, what is more durable, the leaves of the *ti* or flax tree. I can make a sure footing in crossing rivers and ascending or descending precipices; in fact I feel I am just beginning to make exploring easy work. A good pair of sandals will last about two days' hard work, and they take only about twenty minutes to make.

✿

JOHN MCDOUALL STUART

(1815–1866)

Scottish emigrant. He accompanied Sturt on his attempt to reach the centre of Australia, before succeeding himself in 1860. Later, he made the second south–north crossing of the continent and, unlike Burke and Wills, survived.

The Journals of John McDouall Stuart during the years 1858, 1859, 1860, 1861 and 1862, edited from Mr Stuart's manuscript by William Hardman (London, 1864).

1. REACHING THE CENTRE (1860)

Sunday, 22 April, Small Gum Creek, under Mount Stuart, Centre of Australia. Today I find from my observations of the sun, 111° 00′ 30″, that I am now camped in the centre of Australia. I have marked a tree and planted the British flag there. There is a high mount about two miles and a half to the north-north-east. I wish it had been in the centre; but on it tomorrow I will raise a cone of stones, and plant the flag there, and name it 'Central Mount Stuart'. We have been in search of permanent water today, but cannot find any. I hope from the top of Central Mount Stuart to find something good to the north-west. Wind south. Examined a large creek; can find no surface water, but got some by scratching in the sand. It is a large creek divided into many channels, but they are all filled with sand; splendid grass all round this camp.

Monday, 23 April, Centre. Took Kekwick and the flag, and went to the top of the mount, but found it to be much higher and more difficult of ascent than I anticipated. After a deal of labour, slips, and knocks, we at last arrived on the top. It is quite as high as Mount Serle, if not higher. The view to the north is over a large plain of gums, mulga, and spinifex, with watercourses running through it. The large gum creek that we crossed winds round this hill in a north-east direction; at about ten miles it is joined by another. After joining they take a course more north, and I lost sight of them in the far-distant plain. To the north-north-east is the termination of the hills; to the north-east, east and south-east are broken ranges, and to the north-north-west the ranges on the west side of the plain terminate. To the north-west are broken ranges; and to the west is a very high peak, between which and this place to the south-west are a number of isolated hills. Built a large cone of stones, in the centre of which I placed a pole with the British flag nailed to it. Near the top of the cone I placed a small bottle, in which there is a slip of paper, with our signatures to it, stating by whom it was raised. We then gave three hearty cheers for the flag, the emblem of civil and religious liberty, and may it be a sign to the natives that the dawn of liberty, civilization, and Christianity is about to break upon them. . . .

2. ARRIVAL AT THE GULF OF CARPENTARIA (1862)

Thursday, 24 July, Thring Creek, Entering the Marsh. Started at 7.40, course north. I have taken this course in order to make the sea-coast, which I suppose to be distant about eight miles and a half, as soon as possible; by this I hope to avoid the marsh. I shall travel along the beach to the north of the Adelaide. I did not inform any of the party, except Thring and Auld, that I was so near to the sea, as I wished to give them a surprise on reaching it. Proceeded through a light soil, slightly elevated, with a little ironstone on the surface, the volcanic rock cropping out occasionally; also

444

some flats of black alluvial soil. The timber much smaller and more like scrub, showing that we are nearing the sea. At eight miles and a half came upon a broad valley of black alluvial soil, covered with long grass; from this I can hear the wash of the sea. On the other side of the valley, which is rather more than a quarter of a mile wide, is growing a line of thick heavy bushes, very dense, showing that to be the boundary of the beach. Crossed the valley and entered the scrub, which was a complete network of vines. Stopped the horses to clear a way, whilst I advanced a few yards on to the beach, and was gratified and delighted to behold the water of the Indian Ocean in Van Diemen Gulf, before the party with the horses knew anything of its proximity. Thring, who rode in advance of me, called out 'The Sea!' which so took them all by surprise, and they were so astonished, that he had to repeat the call before they fully understood what was meant. Then they immediately gave three long and hearty cheers.

The beach is covered with a soft blue mud. It being ebb tide, I could see some distance; found it would be impossible for me to take the horses along it; I therefore kept them where I had halted them, and allowed half the party to come on to the beach and gratify themselves by a sight of the sea, while the other half remained to watch the horses until their return. I dipped my feet, and washed my face and hands in the sea, as I promised the late Governor Sir Richard McDonnell I would do if I reached it. The mud has nearly covered all the shells; we got a few, however. I could see no seaweed. There is a point of land some distance off, bearing 70°. After all the party had had some time on the beach, at which they were much pleased and gratified, they collected a few shells; I returned to the valley, where I had my initials cut on a large tree, as I did not intend to put up my flag until I arrived at the mouth of the Adelaide. Proceeded, on a course of 302°, along the valley; at one mile and a half, coming upon a small creek, with running water, and the valley being covered with beautiful green grass, I have camped to give the horses the benefit of it. Thus have I, through the instrumentality of Divine Providence, been led to accomplish the great object of the expedition, and take the whole party safely as witnesses to the fact, and through one of the finest countries man could wish to behold—good to the coast, and with a stream of running water within half a mile of the sea. From Newcastle Water to the sea-beach, the main body of the horses have been only one night without water, and then got it within the next day. If this country is settled, it will be one of the finest Colonies under the Crown, suitable for the growth of any and everything—what a splendid country for producing cotton!

ROBERT O'HARA BURKE

(1820–1861)

WILLIAM JOHN WILLS

(1834–1861)

*Burke was an Irish police officer, who had served in the Austrian army.
On emigrating to Australia in 1853 he became a district inspector of police,
and was appointed leader of the Great Northern Exploration Expedition in
1860. Wills, a surveyor from Devon, was made second in command.*

*The expedition travelled fast from New South Wales to the Gulf of
Carpentaria. A depot was left at Cooper's Creek with most of the men and
supplies, only four members (Burke, Wills, Gray, and King) continuing.
On their return, the three survivors found that it had been abandoned only
that day. Burke and Wills died of starvation. King was kept alive by the
aborigines and eventually rescued. Wills wrote the only surviving journal.*

The Burke and Wills Exploring Expedition (a pamphlet from the field-book of
Wills) (Melbourne, 1861).

1. GRAY'S THRASHING AND DEATH (1861)

Monday, 25 March, Native Dog Camp, 27 R. Started at half-past five, looking
for a good place to halt for the day. This we found at a short distance down
the creek, and immediately discovered that it was close to Camp 89 of our
up journey. Had not expected that we were so much to the westward.
After breakfast took some time altitudes, and was about to go back to last
camp for some things left, when I found Gray behind a tree, eating
skilligolee. He explained that he was suffering from dysentery, and had
taken the flour without leave. Sent him to report himself to Mr Burke, and
went on. He, having got King to tell Mr Burke for him, was called up and
received a good thrashing. There is no knowing to what extent he has been
robbing us. Many things have been found to run unaccountably short. . . .

Monday, 8 April, Camp 50, R. Camped a short distance above Camp 75.
The creek here contains more water, and there is a considerable quantity
of green grass in its bed, but it is much dried up since we passed before.
Halted fifteen minutes to send back for Gray, who gammoned he could
not walk. . . .

Wednesday, 10 April, Camp 52, R. Remained at Camp 52, R. all day to cut up and jerk the meat of the horse Billy, who was so reduced and knocked up for want of food that there appeared little chance of his reaching the other side of the desert; and as we were running short of food of every description ourselves, we thought it best to secure his flesh at once. We found it healthy and tender, but without the slightest trace of fat in any portion of the body. . . .

Wednesday, 17 April. This morning, about sunrise, Gray died. He had not spoken a word distinctly since his first attack, which was just as we were about to start. . . .

Sunday, 21 April. Arrived at the depot this evening, just in time to find it deserted. A note left in the plant by Brahe communicates the pleasing information that they have started today for the Darling; their camels and horses all well and in good condition. We and our camels being just done up, and scarcely able to reach the depot, have very little chance of overtaking them. Brahe has fortunately left us ample provisions to take us to the bounds of civilization, namely: flour, 50 lb.; rice, 20 lb.; oatmeal, 60 lb.; sugar, 60 lb.; and dried meat, 15 lb. These provisions, together with a few horseshoes and nails and some odds and ends, constitute all the articles left, and place us in a very awkward position in respect to clothing. Our disappointment at finding the depot deserted may easily be imagined—returning in an exhausted state, after four months of the severest travelling and privation, our legs almost paralysed, so that each of us found it a most trying task only to walk a few yards. Such a leg-bound feeling I never before experienced, and hope I never shall again. The exertion required to get up a slight piece of rising ground, even without any load, induces an indescribable sensation of pain and helplessness, and the general lassitude makes one unfit for anything. Poor Gray must have suffered very much many times when we thought him shamming. It is most fortunate for us that these symptoms, which so early affected him, did not come on us until we were reduced to an exclusively animal diet of such an inferior description as that offered by the flesh of a worn-out and exhausted horse. . . .

2. Last Diary Entries

Wednesday, 1 May, from Camp No. 6. Started at twenty minutes to nine, having loaded our only camel, Rajah, with the most necessary and useful articles, and packed up a small swag each of bedding and clothing for our own shoulders. . . .

Thursday, 2 May, Camp No. 7. Breakfasted by moonlight, and started at half-past six. Following down the left bank of the creek in a westerly direction, we came, at a distance of six miles, on a lot of natives, who were camped on the bed of a creek. They seemed to have just breakfasted, and were most liberal in the presentations of fish and cake. We could only return the compliment by some fish-hooks and sugar. . . . Rajah showed signs of being done up. He had been trembling greatly all the morning. On this account his load was further lightened to the amount of a few pounds, by the doing away with the sugar, ginger, tea, cocoa, and two or three tin plates. . . .

Monday, 6 May . . . The present state of things is not calculated to raise our spirits much. The rations are rapidly diminishing; our clothing, especially the boots, are all going to pieces, and we have not the materials for repairing them properly; the camel is completely done up, and can scarcely get along, although he has the best of feed, and is resting half his time. I suppose this will end in our having to live like the blacks for a few months.

Tuesday, 7 May, Camp No. 9. Breakfasted at daylight, but when about to start, found that the camel would not rise, even without any load on his back. After making every attempt to get him up, we were obliged to leave him to himself. Mr Burke and I started down the creek to reconnoitre. At about eleven miles we came to some blacks fishing. They gave us some half-a-dozen fish each for luncheon, and intimated that if we would go to their camp, we should have some more, and some bread. . . . On our arrival at the camp, they led us to a spot to camp on, and soon afterwards brought a lot of fish and bread, which they call nardoo. The lighting of a fire with matches delights them, but they do not care about having them. In the evening, various members of the tribe came down with lumps of nardoo and handfuls of fish, until we were positively unable to eat any more. They also gave us some stuff they call bedgery, or pedgery. It has a highly intoxicating effect, when chewed even in small quantities. It appears to be the dried stems and leaves of some shrub.

Friday, 10 May, Camp No. 9. Mr Burke and King employed in jerking the camel's flesh, whilst I went out to look for the nardoo seed, for making bread. In this I was unsuccessful, not being able to find a single tree of it in the neighbourhood of the camp. I, however, tried boiling the large kind of bean which the blacks call padlu; they boil easily, and when shelled are very sweet, much resembling in taste the French chestnut. They are to be found in large quantities nearly everywhere. . . .

Friday, 17 May. Nardoo. Started this morning on a black's path, leaving the creek on our left, our intention being to keep a south-easterly direction until we should cut some likely-looking creek, and then to follow it down. On approaching the foot of the first sand-hill King caught sight in the flat of some nardoo seeds, and we soon found that the flat was covered with them. This discovery caused somewhat of a revolution in our feelings, for we considered that with the knowledge of this plant we were in a position to support ourselves, even if we were destined to remain on the creek and wait for assistance from town. . . .

Friday, 24 May. Started with King to celebrate the Queen's birthday by fetching from Nardoo Creek what is now to us the staff of life. Returned at a little after 2 p.m., with a fair supply, but find the collecting of the seed a slower and more troublesome process than could be desired. . . .

Monday, 27 May. Started up the creek this morning for the depot, in order to deposit journals and a record of the state of affairs here. . . .

Tuesday, 28 May . . . Obtained some mussels near where Landa died and halted for breakfast. Still feel very unwell from the effects of the constipation of the bowels. . . .

Thursday, 30 May. Reached the depot this morning, at 11 o'clock. No traces of any one except blacks having been here since we left. Deposited some journals, and a notice of our present condition. . . .

Tuesday, 4 June. Started for the blacks' camp, intending to test the practicability of living with them, and to see what I could learn as to their ways and manners. . . .

Thursday, 6 June. Returned to our own camp, found that Mr Burke and King had been well supplied with fish by the blacks. Made preparation for shifting our camp nearer to theirs on the morrow.

Friday, 7 June. Started in the afternoon for the blacks' camp with such things as we could take, found ourselves all very weak, in spite of the abundant supply of fish that we have lately had. I myself could scarcely get along, although carrying the lightest swag—only about thirty pounds. Found that the blacks had decamped, so determined on proceeding tomorrow up to the next camp, near the nardoo field.

Saturday, 8 June. With the greatest fatigue and difficulty we reached the nardoo camp, no blacks, greatly to our disappointment. Took possession of their best mia-mia, and rested for the reminder of the day. . . .

Thursday, 20 June. Night and morning very cold, sky clear. I am completely reduced by the effects of the cold and starvation. King gone out for nardoo. Mr Burke at home pounding seed; he finds himself getting very weak in the legs. King holds out by far the best; the food seems to agree with him pretty well. . . . I cannot understand this nardoo at all; it certainly will not agree with me in any form. We are now reduced to it alone, and we manage to get from four to five pounds per day between us. . . .

Friday, 21 June. . . . I feel much weaker than ever, and can scarcely crawl out of the mia-mia. Unless relief comes in some form or other, I cannot possibly last more than a fortnight. It is a great consolation, at least, in this position of ours, to know that we have done all we could, and that our deaths will rather be the result of the mismanagement of others than of any rash acts of our own. Had we come to grief elsewhere, we could only have blamed ourselves; but here we are, returned to Cooper's Creek, where we had every reason to look for provisions and clothing; and yet we have to die of starvation, in spite of the explicit instructions given by Mr Burke, that the depot party should await our return, and the strong recommendation to the committee that we should be followed up by a party from Menindie. . . .

Saturday, 22 June . . . Mr Burke and King out for nardoo. The former returned much fatigued. I am so weak today as to be unable to get on my feet.

Sunday, 23 June. All hands at home. I am so weak as to be incapable of crawling out of the mia-mia. King holds out well, but Mr Burke finds himself weaker every day.

Monday, 24 June. A fearful night. At about an hour before sunset, a southerly gale sprang up and continued throughout the greater portion of the night; the cold was intense, and it seemed as if one would be shrivelled up. . . .

Tuesday, 23 June [sic] . . . Mr Burke and King remain at home cleaning and pounding seed. They are both getting weaker every day. The cold plays the deuce with us, from the small amount of clothing we have. . . .

Friday 26 June [sic] . . . I am weaker than ever although I have a good appetite, and relish the nardoo much, but it seems to give us no nutriment, and the birds here are so shy as not to be got at. Even if we got a good supply of fish, I doubt whether we could do much work on them and the nardoo alone. Nothing now but the greatest good luck can now save any of us; and as for myself, I may live four or five days if the weather continues warm. My pulse [sic] are at forty-eight, and very weak, and my legs and arms are nearly skin and bone. I can only look out, like Mr Micawber, 'for something to turn up'; but starvation on nardoo is by no means very unpleasant, but for the weakness one feels, and the utter inability to move oneself, for as far as appetite is concerned, it gives me the greatest satisfaction. Certainly, fat and sugar would be more to one's taste, in fact, those seem to me to be the great standby for one in this extraordinary continent; not that I mean to depreciate the farinaceous food, but the want of sugar and fat in all substances obtainable here is so great that they become almost valueless to us as articles of food, without the addition of something else.

PETER WARBURTON

(1813–1889)

English emigrant. He made several expeditions into the interior. His last, in 1873, was from Alice Springs through the Great Sandy Desert to the west coast.

Journey across the Western Interior of Australia, ed. H. W. Bates (London, 1875).

1. Capture of Native Women (1873)

On the 30th [September], just before reaching the lake, we had captured a young native woman; this was considered a great triumph of art, as the blacks all avoided us as though we had been plague-stricken. We kept her a close prisoner, intending that she should point out native wells to us; but whilst we were camped today the creature escaped from us by gnawing through a thick hair-rope, with which she was fastened to a tree. We were quickly on her tracks directly we discovered our loss, but she was too much for us, and got clear away. We had not allowed her to starve during her captivity, but she supplied herself from the head of a juvenile relation with an article of diet which our stores did not furnish.

2nd. West again today, eighteen miles over bad sand-hills and rough spinifex. Ran up a smoke, and found a native well. There are hills in sight; those towards the north look high and hopeful, but they are quite out of our course. Other detached, broken hills lie to the west, so our intention is to go towards them.

3rd. North-west by west, to a sandstone hill, but, arrived at the top, nothing was to be seen from it except several 'hunting smokes' in different directions. Found a deep well in a gully some distance up the hill, but we could not use it, for, when cleared out, the sides fell, and it was dangerous for any one to descend.

4th. Marched six miles west, and found a native camp and a well. Could not catch a native there, they being too quick for us; not far, however, from the camp a howling, hideous old hag was captured, and, warned by the former escape, we secured this old witch by tying her thumbs behind her back, and haltering her by the neck to a tree. She kept up a frightful howling all night, during which time we had to watch her by turns, or she would have got away also. I doubt whether there is any way of securing these creatures if you take your eyes off them for ten minutes. . . .

6th. . . . We let the old witch go. She was the most alarming specimen

451

of a woman I ever saw; she had been of no use to us, and her sex alone saved her from punishment, for under pretence of leading us to some native wells, she took us backwards and forwards over heavy sand-hills, exhausting the camels as well as my small stock of patience. The well we found was in the opposite direction to the one she was taking us to.

2. CURING CAMEL MEAT

It may be as well here to insert the method in which the camel meat was cured, and the animal generally disposed of, for many more than this one were doomed to fall under the knife, and the treatment in every case was precisely similar. The inner portions of the beast were first eaten, not the liver and other dainty parts only, but *all*, every single scrap was greedily devoured, and whenever eating is mentioned, it must be taken *au pied de la lettre*, and not with the loose signification we attach to it in England; to eat a bird meant with the explorer to pluck him and then to eat him *right through*, and to eat a camel meant exactly the same thing. No shred was passed over; head, feet, hide, tail, all went into the boiling pot; even the very bones were stewed down for soup first, and then broken for the sake of the marrow they contained. The flesh was cut into thin, flat strips and hung upon the bushes to dry in the sun, three days being requisite to effect the process properly. The tough thick hide was cut up and par-boiled, the coarse hair was then scraped off with a knife, and the leather-like substance replaced in the pot and stewed until it became like the inside of a carpenter's glue-pot, both to the taste and to the smell. Nour-ishment there was little or none; but it served to fill up space, and as such was valuable to starving men, who could afford to discard nothing. The head was steadily attacked and soon reduced to a polished skull, tongue, brains, and cheeks all having disappeared; the foot was much esteemed as a delicacy, though a great deal of time was requisite to cook it to perfec-tion. The method of preparing one is as follows.

Light a good fire some time beforehand, and let the wood burn down to bright glowing embers; cut the foot off at the hock, and scrape and singe as much hair off it as time and appetite will permit of. Having done this, stick the end into the glowing coals, burn it for some considerable time, and then, withdrawing it, place it on its side on the ground, and strike the other side smartly with the back of a tomahawk, when, if charred enough, the sole will come off, a large flat slab composed of tough spongy horn; if it refuses to part from the flesh, stuff it into the fire again until it becomes more reasonable. This would seem rather a long process for a hungry man to perform, and the reader doubtless thinks he is now about to reap the reward of his patience, having no further task but to devour the dainty morsel. Not so. Having got the sole off, place the foot in a bucket, and keep it steadily boiling for thirty-six hours; if your fire goes out, or you drop asleep, of course it will require longer; then at last you may venture to hope that your teeth—if good—will enable you to masticate your long-deferred dinner.

✿

ERNEST GILES

(1835–1897)

English-born explorer of Australia. On his second expedition he reached the edge of the Gibson desert and made a quick trip into it with one companion—a young man called Gibson.

Australia Twice Traversed: The Romance of Exploration (2 vols., London, 1889).

THIRST, AND THE DISAPPEARANCE OF GIBSON (1874)

The afternoon had been very oppressive, and the horses were greatly disinclined to exert themselves, though my mare went very well. It was late by the time we encamped, and the horses were much in want of water, especially the big cob, who kept coming up to the camp all night, and tried to get at our water-bags, pannikins, etc. The instinct of a horse when in the first stage of thirst in getting hold of any utensil that ever had water in it is surprising and most annoying, but teaching us by most persuasive reasons how akin they are to human things. We had one small water-bag hung in a tree. I did not think of this just at the moment, when my mare came straight up to it and took it in her teeth, forcing out the cork and sending the water up, which we were both dying to drink, in a beautiful jet, which, descending to earth, was irrevocably lost. We now had only a pint or two left. Gibson was now very sorry he had exchanged Badger for the cob, as he found the cob very dull and heavy to get on; this was not usual, for he was generally a most willing animal, but he would only go at a jog, while my mare was a fine walker. There had been a hot wind from the north all day. The following morning there was a most strange dampness in the air, and I had a vague feeling, such as must have been felt by augurs and seers of old, who trembled as they told events to come; for this was the last day on which I ever saw Gibson. . . .

We were now 90 miles from the Circus water, and 110 from Fort McKellar. The horizon to the west was still obstructed by another rise three or four miles away; but to the west-north-west I could see a line of low stony ridges, ten miles off. To the south was an isolated little hill, six or seven miles away. I determined to go to the ridges, when Gibson complained that his horse could never reach them, and suggested that the next rise to the west might reveal something better in front. The ridges were five miles away, and there were others still further preventing a view. When we reached them we had come 98 miles from the Circus. Here Gibson, who was always behind, called out and said his horse was going to die, or knock up, which are synonymous terms in this region. . . . The hills to the west were 25–30 miles away, and it was with extreme regret I was compelled to relinquish a further attempt to reach them. Oh, how ardently I longed for a camel! how ardently I gazed upon this scene! At this moment I would even my jewel eternal have sold for power to span the gulf that lay between! But it could not be, situated as I was; compelled to retreat—of course with the intention of coming again with a larger supply of water—now the sooner I retreated the better. These far-off hills were named the Alfred and Marie Range, in honour of their Royal Highnesses the Duke and Duchess of Edinburgh. Gibson's horse having got so bad had placed us both in a great dilemma; indeed, ours was a most critical position. We turned back upon our tracks, when the cob refused to carry his rider any further and tried to lie down. We drove him another mile on foot, and down he fell to die. My mare, the Fair Maid of Perth, was only too willing to return; she had now to carry Gibson's saddle and things, and we went away walking and riding by turns of half an hour. The cob, no doubt, died where he fell; not a second thought could be bestowed on him.

When we got back to about thirty miles from the Kegs I was walking, and having concluded in my mind what course to pursue, I called to Gibson to halt till I walked up to him. We were both excessively thirsty, for walking had made us so, and we had scarcely a pint of water left between us. However, of what we had we each took a mouthful, which finished the supply, and I then said—for I couldn't speak before—'Look here, Gibson, you see we are in a most terrible fix with only one horse, therefore only one can ride, and one must remain behind. I shall remain; and now listen to me. If the mare does not get water soon she will die; therefore ride right on; get to the Kegs, if possible, tonight, and give her water. Now the cob is dead there'll be all the more for her; let her rest for an hour or two, and then get over a few more miles by morning, so that early tomorrow you will sight the Rawlinson, at twenty-five miles from the Kegs. Stick to the tracks, and never leave them. Leave as much water in one keg for me as you can afford after watering the mare and filling up your own bags, and, remember, I depend upon you to bring me relief. Rouse Mr Tietkens, get fresh horses and more water-bags, and return as soon as you possibly can. I shall of course endeavour to get down the tracks also.'

He then said if he had a compass he thought he could go better at night. I knew he didn't understand anything about compasses, as I had often tried to explain them to him. The one I had was a Gregory's Patent, of a totally different construction from ordinary instruments of the kind, and I was very loath to part with it, as it was the only one I had. However, he was so anxious for it that I gave it him, and he departed. I sent one final shout after him to stick to the tracks, to which he replied, 'All right', and the mare carried him out of sight almost immediately. That was the last ever seen of Gibson.

I walked slowly on, and the further I walked the more thirsty I became. I had thirty miles to go to reach the Kegs, which I could not reach until late tomorrow at the rate I was travelling, and I did not feel sure that I could keep on at that. . . .

24 April to 1 May. So soon as it was light I was again upon the horse tracks, and reached the Kegs about the middle of the day. Gibson had been here, and watered the mare, and gone on. He had left me a little over two gallons of water in one keg, and it may be imagined how glad I was to get a drink. I could have drunk my whole supply in half an hour, but was compelled to economy, for I could not tell how many days would elapse before assistance could come: it could not be less than five, it might be many more. After quenching my thirst a little I felt ravenously hungry, and on searching among the bags, all the food I could find was eleven sticks of dirty, sandy, smoked horse, averaging about an ounce and a half each, at the bottom of a pack-bag. I was rather staggered to find that I had little more than a pound weight of meat to last me until assistance came. However, I was compelled to eat some at once, and devoured two sticks raw, as I had no water to spare to boil them in.

After this I sat in what shade the trees afforded, and reflected on the precariousness of my position. I was 60 miles from water, and 80 from food, my messenger could hardly return before six days, and I began to think it highly probable that I should be dead of hunger and thirst long before anybody could possibly arrive. I looked at the keg; it was an awkward thing to carry empty. There was nothing else to carry water in, as Gibson had taken all the smaller water-bags, and the large ones would require several gallons of water to soak the canvas before they began to tighten enough to hold water. The keg when empty, with its rings and straps, weighed fifteen pounds, and now it had twenty pounds of water in it. I could not carry it without a blanket for a pad for my shoulder, so that with my revolver and cartridge-pouch, knife, and one or two other small things on my belt, I staggered under a weight of about fifty pounds when I put the keg on my back. I only had fourteen matches.

After I had thoroughly digested all points of my situation, I concluded that if I did not help myself Providence wouldn't help me. I started, bent double by the keg, and could only travel so slowly that I thought it scarcely worthwhile to travel at all. I became so thirsty at each step I took, that I longed to drink up every drop of water I had in the keg, but it was the elixir of death I was burdened with, and to drink it was to die, so I restrained myself. By next morning I had only got about three miles away from the Kegs, and to do that I travelled mostly in the moonlight. The next few days I can only pass over as they seemed to pass with me, for I was quite unconscious half the time, and I only got over about five miles a day.

To people who cannot comprehend such a region it may seem absurd that a man could not travel faster than that. All I can say is, there may be men who could do so, but most men in the position I was in would simply have died of hunger and thirst, for by the third or fourth day—I couldn't tell which—my horsemeat was all gone. I had to remain in what scanty shade I could find during the day, and I could only travel by night.

When I lay down in the shade in the morning I lost all consciousness, and when I recovered my senses I could not tell whether one day or two or three had passed. At one place I am sure I must have remained over 48 hours. At a certain place on the road—that is to say, on the horse tracks—at about 15 miles from the Kegs—at 25 miles the Rawlinson could again be sighted—I saw that the tracks of the two loose horses we had turned back from there had left the main line of tracks, which ran east and west, and had turned about east-south-east, and the tracks of the Fair Maid of Perth, I was grieved to see, had gone on them also. I felt sure Gibson would soon find his error, and return to the main line. I was unable to investigate this any further in my present position. I followed them about a mile, and then returned to the proper line, anxiously looking at every step to see if Gibson's horse tracks returned into them.

They never did, nor did the loose horse tracks either. Generally speaking, whenever I saw a shady desert oak-tree there was an enormous bull-dog ants' nest under it, and I was prevented from sitting in its shade. On what I thought was the 27th I almost gave up the thought of walking any further, for the exertion in this dreadful region, where the triodia was almost as high as myself, and as thick as it could grow, was quite overpowering, and being starved, I felt quite light-headed. After sitting down, on every occasion when I tried to get up again, my head would swim round, and I would fall down oblivious for some time. Being in a chronic state of burning thirst, my general plight was dreadful in the extreme. A bare and level sandy waste would have been Paradise to walk over compared to this. My arms, legs, thighs, both before and behind, were so punctured with spines, it was agony only to exist; the slightest movement and in went more spines, where they broke off in the clothes and flesh, causing the whole of the body that was punctured to gather into minute pustules, which were continually growing and bursting. My clothes, especially inside my trousers, were a perfect mass of prickly points.

My great hope and consolation now was that I might soon meet the relief party. But where was the relief party? Echo could only answer— where? About the 29th I had emptied the keg, and was still over 20 miles from the Circus. Ah! who can imagine what 20 miles means in such a case? But in this April's ivory moonlight I plodded on, desolate indeed, but all undaunted, on this lone, unhallowed shore. At last I reached the Circus, just at the dawn of day. Oh, how I drank! how I reeled! how hungry I was! how thankful I was that I had so far at least escaped from the jaws of that howling wilderness, for I was once more upon the range, though still 20 miles from home. There was no sign of the tracks, of anyone having been here since I left it. The water was all but gone. The solitary eagle still was there. I wondered what could have become of Gibson; he certainly had never come here, and how could he reach the fort without doing so?

I was in such a miserable state of mind and body that I refrained from more vexatious speculations as to what had delayed him: I stayed here, drinking and drinking, until about 10 a.m., when I crawled away over the stones down from the water. I was very footsore, and could only go at a snail's pace. Just as I got clear of the bank of the creek, I heard a faint squeak, and looking about I saw, and immediately caught, a small dying wallaby, whose marsupial mother had evidently thrown it from her pouch. It only weighed about two ounces, and was scarcely furnished yet with fur. The instant I saw it, like an eagle I pounced upon it and ate it, living, raw, dying—fur, skin, bones, skull, and all. The delicious taste of that creature I shall never forget. I only wished I had its mother and father to serve in the same way. I had become so weak that by late at night, I had only accomplished 11 miles, and I lay down about 5 miles from the Gorge of Tarns, again choking for water. While lying down here, I thought I heard the sound of the foot-falls of a galloping horse going campwards, and vague ideas of Gibson on the Fair Maid—or she without him—entered my head. I stood up and listened, but the sound had died away upon the midnight air. On the 1st of May, as I afterwards found, at one o'clock in the morning, I was walking again, and reached the Gorge of Tarns long before daylight, and could again indulge in as much water as I desired; but it was exhaustion I suffered from, and I could hardly move.

My reader may imagine with what intense feelings of relief I stepped over the little bridge across the water, staggered into the camp at day-light, and woke Mr Tietkens, who stared at me as though I had been one new risen from the dead. I asked him had he seen Gibson, and to give me some food. I was of course prepared to hear that Gibson had never reached the camp; indeed, I could see but two people in their blankets the moment I entered the fort, and by that I knew he could not be there. None of the horses had come back, and it appeared that I was the only one of six living creatures—two men and four horses—that had returned, or were now ever likely to return, from that desert, for it was now, as I found, nine days since I last saw Gibson.

✻

John Forrest
(1st Baron of Bunbury)
(1847–1918)

Australian surveyor and first premier of Western Australia. On his third expedition, in 1874, he made the first and only traverse of Australia from west to east by an interior route with horses.

Explorations in Australia (London, 1875).

1. Horses versus Camels (1874)

By half-past nine on the morning of the 18th [April] we had made a fair start. The day was intensely hot, and as we had only three riding-horses, half of the party were compelled to walk. We travelled in a north-easterly direction for eleven miles, and reached a spring called Wallala, which we dug out, and so obtained sufficient water for our horses. I may mention here that Colonel Warburton and other explorers who endeavoured to cross the great inland desert from the east had the advantage of being

provided with camels—a very great advantage indeed in a country where
the water supply is so scanty and uncertain as in central Australia. As we
ascertained by painful experience, a horse requires water at least once in
twelve hours, and suffers greatly if that period of abstinence is exceeded.
A camel, however, will go for ten or twelve days without drink without
being much distressed. This fact should be remembered, because the
necessity of obtaining water for the horses entailed upon us many weary-
ing deviations from the main route and frequent disappointments, besides
great privation and inconvenience to man and beast.

The 19th was Sunday, and, according to practice, we rested. Every Sunday
throughout the journey I read Divine Service, and, except making the daily
observations, only work absolutely necessary was done. Whenever possible,
we rested on Sunday, taking, if we could, a pigeon, a parrot, or such other
game as might come in our way as special fare. Sunday's dinner was an
institution for which, even in those inhospitable wilds, we had a great
respect. . . .

2. An Orgy of Naming

25th [*May*]. Travelled onwards about N. 40° E. for eight miles, passing a
low granite range at six miles. Came to a fine brook trending a little south
of east, which we followed downwards seven miles, running nearly east.
This brook was full of water, some of the pools being eight or ten feet
deep, ten yards wide, and sixty yards long. It flowed out into a large flat,
and finally runs into a salt lake. I named this brook Sweeney Creek, after
my companion and farrier, James Sweeney. Leaving the flat, we struck
NNE for four miles, and came to a salt marsh about half a mile wide,
which we crossed. Following along, came into some high ranges, which I
named the Frere Ranges, after Sir Bartle Frere, the distinguished President of the Royal Geographical Society. . . .

26th. Ascended the Frere Ranges and got a fine view to the north and
east. Fine high hills and ranges to the north; a salt marsh and low ranges
to the east and SE. Continued on NE for four miles then NNW for three
miles, passing plenty of water in clay-holes and clay-pans in bed of marsh;
we camped at a fine pool in a large brook that runs into the marsh, which
I called Kennedy Creek, after my companion James Kennedy. The prospect ahead is very cheering, and I hope to find plenty of water and feed
for the next 100 miles. . . .

27th. Followed up the Kennedy Creek, bearing NNE and N. for about
seven miles, passing a number of shallow pools, when we came to some
splendid springs, which I named the Windich Springs, after my old and

well-tried companion Tommy Windich, who has now been on three exploring expeditions with me. They are the best springs I have ever seen—flags in the bed of the river, and pools twelve feet deep and twenty chains long—a splendid place for water. We therefore camped, and found another spot equally good a quarter of a mile west of camp in another branch. There is a most magnificent supply of water and feed—almost unlimited and permanent. A fine range of hills bore north-west from the springs, which I named Carnarvon Range, after the Right Honourable the present Secretary of State for the Colonies. The hills looked very remarkable, being covered with spinifex almost to their very summit. We shot five ducks and got three opossums this afternoon, besides doing some shoeing. . . .

29th. . . . Spinifex in every direction, and the country very miserable and unpromising. I went ahead with Windich. Steering about N. 15° E. for about eight miles over spinifex sand-hills, we found a spring in a small flat, which I named Pierre Spring, after my companion Tommy Pierre. It was surrounded by the most miserable spinifex country, and is quite a diamond in the desert. We cleared it out and got sufficient water for our horses. . . .

2nd [*June*]. Early this morning went with Pierre to look for water, while my brother and Windich went on the same errand. We followed up the brook about south for seven miles, when we left it and followed another branch about SSE, ascending which, Pierre drew my attention to swarms of birds, parakeets, etc., about half a mile ahead. We hastened on, and to our delight found one of the best springs in the colony. It ran down the gully for twenty chains, and is as clear and fresh as possible, while the supply is unlimited. Overjoyed at our good fortune, we hastened back, and, finding that my brother and Windich had not returned, packed up and shifted over to the springs, leaving a note telling them the good news. After reaching the springs we were soon joined by them. They had only found sufficient water to give their own horses a drink; they also rejoiced to find so fine a spot. Named the springs the Weld Springs, after his Excellency Governor Weld, who has always taken such great interest in exploration, and without whose influence and assistance this expedition would not have been organized. There is splendid feed all around. I intend giving the horses a week's rest here, as they are much in want of it, and are getting very poor and tired.

ALEXANDER FORREST

(1849–1901)

Younger brother of John Forrest. A distinguished explorer in his own right, he was his brother's second in command on his two main expeditions. In 1879 he crossed the Kimberleys, to discover excellent grazing.

North-West Exploration: Journal of an Expedition from De Grey River to Port Darwin (Perth, 1880).

FIRST SIGHT OF THE PLAINS (1879)

20 July. We made an early start this morning, steering ENE through a magnificent and well-watered country, little brooks crossing our track at intervals of nearly every mile, till, after travelling fourteen miles, we came to a larger stream, upon which we camped for the rest of the day. The whole of the country consisted of granite rises and clear open flats. From the summit of a low range to which Hicks and I walked this afternoon, we found spread out before us the most splendid grassy plain it has ever been my lot to see. As far as the eye could reach to the SSE and SW was one vast level expanse of magnificent feeding-ground, and at our feet a running stream, which we could trace far out into the distance. These plains, which are granitic in formation, comprise, according to my calculation, not less than 1,000,000 acres, and, judging from the richness of their herbage, would carry, I imagine, no less a number of sheep. This is, in my estimation, the finest part of Western Australia that I have seen, and I hope that before long it will be covered with flocks and herds.

✿

CHARLES DOUGLAS

(1840–1874)

Known as Mr Explorer Douglas. He travelled over much unexplored country in the South Island.

Mr Explorer Douglas, ed. J. Pascoe (Wellington, 1957).

MOSQUITOES, RABBITS, RIVERS, AND SNOW (1891)

Wednesday 4 Feby. . . . I am perfectly aware that the mosquito and sandfly have a purpose in this world, but why don't they attend to it? Their destiny is to keep down microscopic insects, who I believe would otherwise taint the air, and give us fevers instead of the present bad temper, so science says, but their sphere of use is when they are in the grub state. Why don't they stick at that and not trouble innocent unoffending prospectors who can't carry a curtain? The mosquitoes are worse this season than ever I saw them, and make a fellow think irreverently of Old Noah, if he gave them a passage in the ark, in early days. But hold on, a brilliant idea has just entered my head. Perhaps the butterfly, locust, mosquito, and others are enjoying their heaven, their reward for strictly doing their duty when in the grub state. A percentage who don't loaf, but do their best, as a reward blossom into winged insects and enjoy a higher existence for a brief period, so don't let us growl at them and call their existence useless. . . .

Friday 27 Feby. Made an early start up the creek, found a place point G. about 500 feet up, where I got a good view of Mt. Aspiring, and sketched it in as quick as possible, as clouds were fast collecting. Just got it and a few bearings finished in time. The three waterfalls show[n] on the sketch are intermittent every hour or so. Great masses of snow comes pouring down instead of water. Some of the falls lasted as long as twenty minutes, and the noise sounded like low thunder. I don't think the glacier is of great extent, but from the size of the snowfield above and the sunless den in which it is jammed it must be of immense thickness.

Although the weather didn't look very tempting, I made up my mind to make a run for it, and scale Mt. Ragan, a hill that must be nearly 7,000 feet. I got up the bed of the creek for a good way, then took the bush out to the open country. So far the travelling wasn't out of the common, but the last 2,000 feet look apalling. It wasn't a cliff, but a smooth slope of rock dipping towards me, as I thought, at an angle of 60°; but on getting closer, the angle got less, and on arriving at the foot of the slope I found it was smooth as if chiselled by the hand of man, hardly a break or a crack the whole way up, but the slope was only about 25°.

I had never tackled such a distance of sloping rock before. The puzzle was this: a fellow might get tired and want a rest, and perhaps not get one and so come down by the run again, or he might slip on a steeper part. My boots weren't very good; 25° don't look much but I found it quite plenty. I went up a few yards and slipped once, so I off boots, put them in my bag, and started as the Scotch would say in my stocking feet, and it was the grandest piece of climbing I ever did. I don't think I was more than half an hour getting to the top. . . .

As nothing was to be seen and the weather was getting thicker, I started down the way I came, got to the foot of the slope, put on my boots over what remained of the socks and reached the camp. Boiled the billy and then had time to traverse the flat to the head; it is about two miles long and say 25 chain broad. The rabbits are swarming at the head of the flat. They are barking and killing all the trees, and it is evident they have been up here for years. Perhaps they will gradually exterminate the Westland bush as they did in St Helena and Ascension. The trees off the ranges, all the little soil the country possess[es] will be washed away down the river and deposited at the mouth—a bright look-out for the cockatoos. Breed ferrets in galore, spread poison as you like, this island will never get rid of the rabbits. What is the use of destroying them down-country, when they can retire to the wilds and breed in safety? People don't seem to know the geography of this island, or to enable them to borrow more money from home, they don't want to know. Why, at least a fourth of the country will never even be inhabited, and consequently will remain a breeding-ground for armies of vermin, who have been introduced in the country by the dense ignorance of the people. . . .

Wednesday 4 March. Heavy storm of wind and rain. . . . Betsey Jane generally lies at my feet and the weather was so bad that poor Poker determined to try and get under the tent also. He couldn't lie before the fire, there was no room, so he commenced a piece of generalship, to try and get Betty out and himself in, but she knew too much for him and wouldn't budge. Then he made an appeal to my feelings: he shivered and looked at me, then he craned his neck over, and evidently thought there was room for him between me and the back of the tent; he looked with eyes that plainly told me so. He takes up as much room as a two-year-old donkey, but the weather outside was certainly miserable, and his cute hints were too much for me and I let him in, and there he now is jammed behind and giving vent to his happiness in occasional groans of satisfaction. . . .

Saturday 7 March. . . . This is about the first time I ever was on a journey like this, and showed such bad generalship as to have my tucker on one side of a river and myself on the other; but the weather looked so tempting when I went up and I made so sure of being able to cross and recross on the upper flats that I chanced it.

The river was very high, coming down, which gave me a great deal more bush travelling, and although I got it in four branches all nearly about a size, it was touch and go getting across. I thought at one time I would have had to give it up and make down the east side, or chance being washed up on the right bank.

On the subject of fording, how few people really know what precautions to take. I am not speaking of those dunderheads who take the foot of a straight rapid, or cross at a certain place simply because that happened to be the ford when they were there a few years ago. Such people are past speaking to. But take the men who do know a little, just watch them going into a river; they never look to see where the current they are going to cross runs to—where they would land if a tumble took place, and every man jack of them partly unhitches his swag with the full intention of chucking it away if a tumble does take place. Why, the fools, unless they are carrying stones or ironmongery, an ordinary swag will float for two or three minutes, and is as good to hold onto as a small raft, and if a man will only throw it off but keep the straps in his hand, it gives a splendid purchase to enable you to gain your feet if, as is more than probable, footing is there to be gained.

Today my swag would certainly have sunk, as I had a rifle, axe, and a lot of rocks and very little else. But I had two good billies, and I rolled them empty in the centre of the swag, with their lids tightened on with a strip of greased calico, and I am sure that swag would have kept me above water for half an hour. A bundle of flax sticks broken into small pieces and jammed into a bag will float a man easily, but the art in safe fording is to always select a place with the current running into a back. You are out and clawing up on the shore almost before you are aware that you have got washed off your feet. . . .

While waiting in the shelter of a rock I got a glimpse of Spectre [mountain] but I was so cold that I couldn't get my compass out, and couldn't have held it if I had. The wind was getting worse, and the snow was already ankle-deep, and I saw if I remained any longer I would become a spectre myself. So I made a bee-line down the Saddle Creek at a run, and I am doubtful if any human being will ever go down that creek at the rate I did. How splendid it was to get down out of the wind. The climate appeared to suddenly become tropical by the contrast. When well down the creek with a safe run ahead of me, I stopped and had a smoke, and began to see the narrow escape I had of dropping from exposure.

Inside my shirt, held by the belt, was a beautiful all-round bustle of snow that drifted in, and fast as I had come down, there had not been heat enough in my carcase to melt it; and there was another small patch unmelted in my only pocket, and the compass satchel was full of fine snow. Had I remained much longer I no doubt would have become sleepy and lain down to waken—Where—I believe the reason I escaped, both this time and on other occasions, was the idea of perishing never entered my head. Nothing is so bad as terror for lowering a man's stamina.

VI

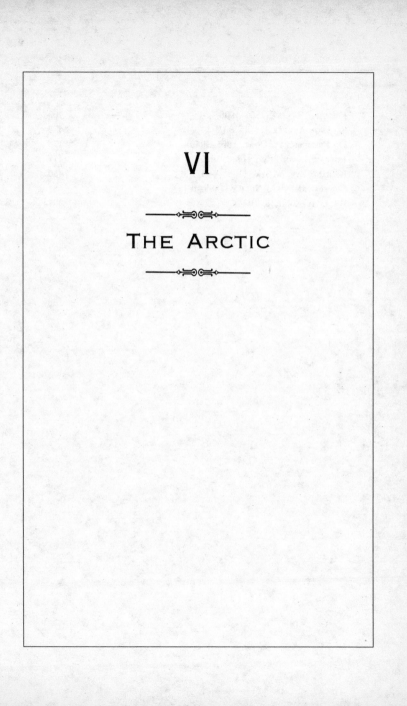

THE ARCTIC

FRIDTJOF NANSEN (1861–1930)   469
SALOMON ANDRÉE (1854–1897)   474
DR FREDERICK A. COOK (1865–1940)   476
ROBERT EDWIN PEARY (1856–1920)   477
RICHARD EVELYN BYRD (1888–1957)   480
GENERAL UMBERTO NOBILE (1885–1978)   481
WALLY HERBERT (b. 1934)   484

FRIDTJOF NANSEN

(1861–1930)

Norwegian polar explorer. In 1888 he made the first crossing of the Green-
land ice-cap. Between 1893 and 1896 he deliberately drifted in his ship,
the Fram, *in pack ice to prove the existence of Arctic currents. Meanwhile*
he and one other, Hjalmar Johansen, made an attempt on the North Pole
on foot, reaching the then furthest north. Later he lent the Fram *to Amund-*
sen for his successful attempt on the South Pole. Nansen was awarded the
Nobel Peace Prize in 1922 for his relief work after the Russian Revolution.

1: *The First Crossing of Greenland* (London, 1890); 2–4. *Farthest North,*
(London, 1897).

1. GREENLAND CROSSING (1888)

Everything seemed to point to the conclusion that we had reached the
high plateau of the interior. The announcement of this to the party produced general rejoicing, for we were all heartily tired of the long slopes we
had to climb, and which just lately had been especially trying. Sanguine as
we were, we hoped soon to reach the westward slope, when it would all
be downward travelling and pure delight, and it was in the most triumphant mood that we saw the sun sink that evening in all his glory behind
the banks of clouds and transform the western sky into one scheme of
glowing colour. All that we knew of beauty in this desert was contained in
the evening and setting of the sun; our hopes lay in the same direction, but
it was destined to be long before we saw the goal which it all seemed to
hide from us.

The snow was incredibly heavy going today, heavier than it has ever
been before, though the surface was hard and firm. The wind-packed snow
is no better than sand. We had the wind to pull against, too. . . .

It began to snow in the middle of the day and our work was heavier than
ever. It was worse even than yesterday, and to say that it was like hauling
in blue clay will scarcely give an idea of it. At every step we had to use all
our force to get the heavy sledges along, and in the evening Sverdrup and
I, who had had to go first and plough a way for ourselves, were pretty well
done up. The others who followed us were a little better off, and besides

their steel runners moved easier. The evening in the tent, however, with a savoury stew, helped us to forget the toils of the day.

Meantime the wind was steadily increasing, and the sails had to be taken in more and more to prevent the sledges overrunning me. As we were all getting hungry biscuits were served out, but no halt was made to eat them.

It was rapidly getting dark, but the full moon was now rising, and she gave us light enough to see and avoid the worst crevasses. It was a curious sight for me to see the two vessels coming rushing along behind me, with their square viking-like sails showing dark against the white snowfield and the big round disc of the moon behind.

Faster and faster I go flying on, while the ice gets more and more difficult. There is worse still ahead, I can see, and in another moment I am into it. The ground is here seamed with crevasses, but they are full of snow and not dangerous. Every now and then I feel my staff go through into space, but the cracks are narrow and the sledges glide easily over. Presently I cross a broader one and see just in front of me a huge black abyss. I creep cautiously to its edge on the slippery ice, which here is covered by scarcely any snow, and look down into the deep, dark chasm. Beyond it I can see crevasse after crevasse, running parallel with one another and showing dark blue in the moonlight.

2. PRESSURE (1894)

Severe pressure has been going on this evening. It began at 7.30 astern in the opening, and went on steadily for two hours. It sounded as if a roaring waterfall were rushing down upon us with a force that nothing could resist. One heard the big floes crashing and breaking against each other. They were flung and pressed up into high walls, which must now stretch along the whole opening east and west, for one hears the roar the whole way. It is coming nearer just now; the ship is getting violent shocks; it is like waves in the ice. They come on us from behind, and move forward. We stare out into the night, but can see nothing, for it is pitch-dark. Now I hear cracking and shifting in the hummock on the starboard quarter; it gets louder and stronger, and extends steadily. At last the waterfall roar abates a little. It becomes more unequal; there is a longer interval between each shock. I am so cold that I creep below.

But no sooner have I seated myself to write than the ship begins to heave and tremble again, and I hear through her sides the roar of the packing. As the bear-trap may be in danger, three men go off to see to it, but they find that there is a distance of 50 paces between the new pressure-ridge and the wire by which the trap is secured, so they leave it as it is. The pressure-ridge was an ugly sight, they say, but they could distinguish nothing well in the dark.

Most violent pressure is beginning again. I must go on deck and look at it. The loud roar meets one as one opens the door. It is coming from the bow now, as well as from the stern. It is clear that pressure-ridges are being thrown up in both openings, so if they reach us we shall be taken by both ends and lifted lightly and gently out of the water. There is pressure near us on all sides. Creaking has begun in the old hummock on the port quarter; it is getting louder, and, so far as I can see, the hummock is slowly rising. A lane has opened right across the large floe on the port side; you can see the water, dark as it is. Now both pressure and noise get worse and worse; the ship shakes, and I feel as if I myself were being gently lifted with the stern-rail, where I stand gazing out at the welter of ice-masses, that resemble giant snakes writhing and twisting their great bodies out there under the quiet, starry sky, whose peace is only broken by one aurora serpent waving and flickering restlessly in the north-east. I once more think what a comfort it is to be safe on board the *Fram*, and look out with a certain contempt at the horrible hurly-burly nature is raising to no purpose whatever; it will not crush us in a hurry, nor even frighten us.

3. LAND (1895)

Wednesday, 24 July. At last the marvel has come to pass—land, land, and after we had almost given up our belief in it! After nearly two years, we again see something rising above that never-ending white line on the horizon yonder—a white line which for countless ages has stretched over this lonely sea, and which for millenniums to come shall stretch in the same way. We are leaving it, and leaving no trace behind us; for the track of our little caravan across the endless plains has long ago disappeared. A new life is beginning for us; for the ice it is ever the same.

It has long haunted our dreams, this land, and now it comes like a vision, like fairyland. Drift-white, it arches above the horizon like distant clouds, which one is afraid will disappear every minute.... While I was on ahead at one time yesterday morning, Johansen went up on to a hummock to look at the ice, and remarked a curious black stripe over the horizon; but he supposed it to be only a cloud, he said, and I thought no more about the matter. When, some while later, I also ascended a hummock to look at the ice, I became aware of the same black stripe; it ran obliquely from the horizon up into what I supposed to be a white bank of clouds. The longer I looked at this bank and stripe the more unusual I thought them, until I was constrained to fetch the glass. No sooner had I fixed it

on the black part than it struck me at once that this must be land, and that
not far off. There was a large snow-field out of which black rocks projected. It was not long before Johansen had the glass to his eye, and convinced himself that we really had land before us. We both of us naturally
became highly elated. I then saw a similar white arching outline, a little
further east; but it was for the most part covered with white mist from
which it could hardly be distinguished, and moreover was continually
changing form. It soon, however, came out entirely, and was considerably
larger and higher than the former, but there was not a black speck to be
seen on it. So this was what land looked like now that we had come to it!
I had imagined it in many forms, with high peaks and glittering glaciers,
but never like this. There was nothing kindly about this, but it was indeed
no less welcome, and on the whole we could not expect it to be otherwise
than snow-covered, with all the snow which falls here.

Sunday, 1 December. Wonderfully beautiful weather for the last few
days; one can never weary of going up and down outside, while the moon
transforms the whole of this ice world into a fairyland. The hut is still in
shadow under the mountain which hangs above it, dark and lowering; but
the moonlight floats over ice and fjord, and is cast back glittering from
every snowy ridge and hill. A weird beauty, without feeling, as though of
a dead planet, built of shining white marble. . . .

Above us the sky, clear and brilliant with stars, sheds its peace over the
earth; far in the west falls shower after shower of stars, some faint, scarcely
visible, others bright like Roman candles, all with a message from distant
worlds. Low in the south lies a bank of clouds, now and again outlined by
the gleam of the northern lights; but out over the sea the sky is dark; there
is open water there. It is quite pleasant to look at it; one does not feel so
shut in; it is like a connecting link with life that dark sea, the mighty artery
of the world, which carries tidings from land to land, from people to
people, on which civilization is borne victorious through the earth; next
summer it will carry us home.

4. A HUMAN VOICE—CAPE FLORA, FRANZ JOSEF LAND (1896)

17 June. Suddenly I thought I heard a shout from a human voice, a strange
voice, the first for three years. How my heart beat, and the blood rushed
to my brain, as I ran up on to a hummock, and hallooed with all the
strength of my lungs. Behind that one human voice in the midst of the icy
desert, this one message from life, stood home and she who was waiting
there; and I saw nothing else as I made my way between bergs and ice-
ridges. Soon I heard another shout, and saw, too, from an ice-ridge, a dark

form moving among the hummocks further in. It was a dog; but further off came another figure, and that was a man. Who was it? Was it Jackson or one of his companions, or was it perhaps a fellow countryman? We approached one another quickly; I waved my hat: he did the same. I heard him speak to the dog, and I listened. It was English, and as I drew nearer I thought I recognized Mr Jackson, whom I remembered once to have seen.

I raised my hat; we extended a hand to one another, with a hearty 'How do you do?' Above us a roof of mist, shutting out the world around, beneath our feet the rugged, packed drift-ice, and in the background a glimpse of the land, all ice, glacier, and mist. On one side the civilized European in an English check suit and high rubber waterboots, well-shaved, well-groomed, bringing with him a perfume of scented soap, perceptible to the wild man's sharpened senses; on the other side the wild man, clad in dirty rags, black with oil and soot, with long, uncombed hair and shaggy beard, black with smoke, with a face in which the natural fair complexion could not possibly be discerned through the thick layer of fat and soot which a winter's endeavours with warm water, moss, rags, and at last a knife had sought in vain to remove. . . .

Jackson: 'I'm immensely glad to see you.'

'Thank you, I also.'

'Have you a ship here?'

'No; my ship is not here.'

'How many are there of you?'

'I have one companion at the ice-edge.'

As we talked, we had begun to go in towards land. I took it for granted that he had recognized me, or at any rate understood who it was that was hidden behind this savage exterior, not thinking that a total stranger would be received so heartily. Suddenly he stopped, looked me full in the face, and said quickly:

'Aren't you Nansen?'

'Yes, I am.'

'By Jove! I am glad to see you!'

And he seized my hand and shook it again, while his whole face became one smile of welcome, and delight at the unexpected meeting beamed from his dark eyes.

SALOMON ANDRÉE

(1854–1897)

Swedish aeronaut. He attempted to float over the North Pole in a balloon in 1897. Landing after three days, he and his two companions perished some months later. Andrée's diary was not found for thirty years.

The Andrée Diaries (London, 1931).

1. IN THE BALLOON (1897)

12 July. Although we could have thrown out ballast, and although the wind might, perhaps, carry us to Greenland, we determined to be content standing still. We have been obliged to throw out very much ballast today and have not had any sleep nor been allowed any rest from the repeated bumpings, and we probably could not have stood it much longer. All three of us must have a rest, and I sent Strindberg and Fraenkel to bed at 11.20 o'clock, and I mean to let them sleep until 6 or 7 o'clock, if I can manage to keep watch until then. Then I shall try to get some rest myself. If either of them should succumb it might be because I had tired them out.

It is not a little strange to be floating here above the Polar Sea. To be the first that have floated here in a balloon. How soon, I wonder, shall we have successors? Shall we be thought mad or will our example be followed? I cannot deny but that all three of us are dominated by a feeling of pride. We think we can well face death, having done what we have done. Is not the whole, perhaps, the expression of an extremely strong sense of individuality which cannot bear the thought of living and dying like a man in the ranks, forgotten by coming generations? Is this ambition?

2. ON THE ICE, WITH BEARS

13 August. Just when we had passed the fissure Strindberg cried 'three bears'. We were at once in motion and full of excited expectation. Warned by our preceding disappointments, we now went to work carefully. We concealed ourselves behind a hummock and waited, but no bears came. Then I chose myself as a bait and crept forward along the plain whistling softly. The she-bear became attentive, came forward winding me, but turned round again and lay down. At last it was too cold for me to lie immovably in the snow, and then I called out to the others that we should rush up to the bears. We did so. Then the she-bear came towards me but was met by a shot which missed. I sprang up however and shot again while the bears that were fleeing stopped for a moment; then the she-bear was wounded at a distance of 80 paces but ran a little way, whereupon I dropped her on the spot at 94 paces. . . . Today the weather has been extremely beautiful, and that is a good thing for otherwise the work would have been ticklish. When a bear is hit he brings out a roar and tries to flee as quick as he can. We have been butchers the whole day. I have been trying the business of tanning in order to get skin to mend the sleeping-sack with. The skin of the forelegs seems to be the most suitable, being the lightest. With fairly clear air today we have not seen land in any direction.

22 August. The country today has been terrible and I repeat what I wrote yesterday that we have not previously had such a large district with ice so pressed. There can scarcely be found a couple of metres of ice which does not present evident traces of pressure and the entire country consisting of a boundless field of large and small hummocks. One cannot speak of any regularity among them. The leads today have been broken to pieces and the floes small, but in general it has been easy to get across. Now they are so frozen that neither ferrying nor rafting can be employed. Today a lead changed just when we had come across it (five minutes later and it would have been impossible) and we had an opportunity of seeing a very powerful pressing. The floes came at a great speed and there was a creaking round about us. It made a strange and magnificent impression. The day has been extremely beautiful. Perhaps the most beautiful we have had. With a specially clear horizon we have again tried to catch sight of Gillis Land but it is impossible to get a glimpse of any part of it. . . . The clear air was utilized by Strindberg to take lunar distances. He saw haloes on the snow; an inner more sharply defined with the inner boundary red. . . . Observed from the ground these haloes seemed to be the extremities of parabolas or of ellipses. Magnificent Venetian landscape with canals between lofty hummock edges on both sides, water-square with ice-fountain and stairs down to the canals.

DR FREDERICK ALBERT COOK

(1865–1940)

American medical doctor and explorer. He claimed to have been the first to the North Pole, but was later discredited and accused of fraud.

My Attainment of the Pole: being the record of the expedition that first reached the Boreal Center, 1907–1909, with the final summary of the Polar controversy (London, 1911).

ARRIVAL AT THE POLE (1908)

Cracking our whips, we bounded ahead. The boys sang. The dogs howled. Midnight of April 21 had just passed. Over the sparkling snows the post-midnight sun glowed like at noon. I seemed to be walking in some splendid golden realms of dreamland. As we bounded onward the ice swam about me in circling rivers of gold. E-tuk-i-shook and Ah-we-lah, though thin and ragged, had the dignity of the heroes of a battle which had been fought through to success.

We all were lifted to the paradise of winners as we stepped over the snows of a destiny for which we had risked life and willingly suffered the tortures of an icy hell. The ice under us, the goal for centuries of brave, heroic men, to reach which many had suffered terribly and terribly died, seemed almost sacred. Constantly and carefully I watched my instruments in recording this final reach. Nearer and nearer they recorded our approach. Step by step, my heart filled with a strange rapture of conquest.

At last we step over coloured fields of sparkle, climbing walls of purple and gold—finally, under skies of crystal blue, with flaming clouds of glory, we touch the mark! The soul awakens to a definite triumph; there is sunrise within us, and all the world of night-darkened trouble fades. We are at the top of the world! The flag is flung to the frigid breezes of the North Pole! . . .

By a long and consecutive series of observations and mental tabulations of various sorts on our journey northward, continuing here, I knew, beyond peradventure of doubt, that I was at a spot which was as near as possible, by usual methods of determination, 520 miles from Svartevoeg, a spot toward which men had striven for more than three centuries—a spot known as the North Pole, and where I stood first of white men. In my own achievement I felt, that dizzy moment, that all the heroic souls who had braved the rigours of the Arctic region found their own hopes' fulfilment.

I had realized their dream. I had culminated with success the efforts of all the brave men who had failed before me. I had finally justified their sacrifices, their very death; I had proven to humanity humanity's supreme triumph over a hostile, death-dealing Nature. It seemed that the souls of these dead exulted with me, and that in some substrata of the air, in notes more subtle than the softest notes of music, they sang a paean in the spirit with me.

We had reached our destination. My relief was indescribable. The prize of an international marathon was ours. Pinning the Stars and Stripes to a tent-pole, I asserted the achievement in the name of the ninety millions of countrymen who swear fealty to that flag. And I felt a pride as I gazed at the white-and-crimson barred pinion, a pride which the claim of no second victor has ever taken from me.

✿

ROBERT EDWIN PEARY

(1856–1920)

American naval officer and explorer. He certainly arrived close to the North Pole, but his calculations have been seriously questioned since.

The North Pole (London, 1910).

'MY LIFE WORK IS ACCOMPLISHED' (1909)

This was the time for which I had reserved all my energies, the time for which I had worked for twenty-two years, for which I had lived the simple life and trained myself as for a race. In spite of my years, I felt fit for the demands of the coming days and was eager to be on the trail. As for my party, my equipment, and my supplies, they were perfect, beyond my most sanguine dreams of earlier years. My party might be regarded as an ideal which had now come to realization—as loyal and responsive to my will as the fingers of my right hand.

My four Eskimos carried the technique of dogs, sledges, ice, and cold as their racial heritage. Henson and Ootah had been my companions at the furthest point on the expedition three years before. Egingwah and Seegloo had been in Clark's division, which had such a narrow escape at that time, having been obliged for several days to subsist upon their sealskin boots, all their other food being gone.

And the fifth was young Ooqueah, who had never before served in any expedition; but who was, if possible, even more willing and eager than the others to go with me wherever I should elect. For he was always thinking of the great treasures which I had promised each of the men who should go to the furthest point with me—whale-boat, rifle, shotgun, ammunition, knives, etc.—wealth beyond the wildest dreams of Eskimos, which should win for him the daughter of old Ikwah of Cape York, on whom he had set his heart.

All these men had a blind confidence that I would somehow get them back to land. But I recognized fully that all the impetus of the party centred in me. Whatever pace I set, the others would make good; but if I played out, they would stop like a car with a punctured tyre. I had no fault to find with the conditions, and I faced them with confidence. . . .

With every passing day even the Eskimos were becoming more eager and interested, notwithstanding the fatigue of the long marches. As we stopped to make camp, they would climb to some pinnacle of ice and strain their eyes to the north, wondering if the Pole was in sight, for they were now certain that we should get there this time. . . .

The bitter wind burned our faces so that they cracked, and long after we got into camp each day they pained us so that we could hardly go to sleep. The Eskimos complained much, and at every camp fixed their fur clothing about their faces, waists, knees, and wrists. They also complained of their noses, which I had never known them to do before. The air was as keen and bitter as frozen steel. . . .

The last march northward ended at ten o'clock of the forenoon of April 6. I had now made the five marches planned from the point at which Bartlett turned back, and my reckoning showed that we were in the immediate neighbourhood of the goal of all our striving. After the usual arrangements for going into camp, at approximate local noon, on the Columbia meridian, I made the first observation at our polar camp. It indicated our position as 89° 57'.

We were now at the end of the last long march of the upward journey. Yet with the Pole actually in sight I was too weary to take the last few steps. The accumulated weariness of all those days and nights of forced marches and insufficient sleep, constant peril and anxiety, seemed to roll across me all at once. I was actually too exhausted to realize at the moment that my life's purpose had been achieved. As soon as our igloos had been completed, and we had eaten our dinner and double-rationed the dogs, I turned in for a few hours of absolutely necessary sleep, Henson and the

Eskimos having unloaded the sledges and got them in readiness for such repairs as were necessary. But, weary though I was, I could not sleep long. It was, therefore, only a few hours later when I woke. The first thing I did after awaking was to write these words in my diary: 'The Pole at last. The prize of three centuries. My dream and goal for twenty years. Mine at last! I cannot bring myself to realize it. It seems all so simple and commonplace.' . . .

After I had planted the American flag in the ice, I told Henson to time the Eskimos for three rousing cheers, which they gave with the greatest enthusiasm. Thereupon, I shook hands with each member of the party— surely a sufficiently unceremonious affair to meet with the approval of the most democratic. The Eskimos were childishly delighted with our success. While, of course, they did not realize its importance fully, or its worldwide significance, they did understand that it meant the final achievement of a task upon which they had seen me engaged for many years. . . .

We had now left the ice of the polar sea and were practically on terra firma. When the last sledge came to the almost vertical edge of the glacier's fringe, I thought my Eskimos had gone crazy. They yelled and called and danced until they fell from utter exhaustion. As Ootah sank down on his sledge he remarked in Eskimo: 'The devil is asleep or having trouble with his wife, or we should never have come back so easily.' . . .

It was almost exactly six o'clock on the morning of April 23 when we reached the igloo of 'Crane City' at Cape Columbia and the work was done. That day I wrote these words in my diary: 'My life work is accomplished. The thing which it was intended from the beginning that I should do, the thing which I believed could be done, and that I could do, I have done. I have got the North Pole out of my system after twenty-three years of effort, hard work, disappointments, hardships, privations, more or less suffering, and some risks. I have won the last great geographical prize, the North Pole, for the credit of the United States. This work is the finish, the cap and climax of nearly four hundred years of effort, loss of life, and expenditure of fortunes by the civilized nations of the world, and it has been accomplished in a way that is thoroughly American. I am content.'

RICHARD EVELYN BYRD

(1888–1957)

American aviator and Polar explorer. On 9 May 1926, with Floyd Bennett,
he flew over the North Pole.

Exploring with Byrd (New York, 1937).

THE FLIGHT (1926)

We were now getting into areas never before viewed by mortal eye. The
feelings of an explorer superseded the aviator's. I became conscious of that
extraordinary exhilaration which comes from looking into virgin territory.
At that moment I felt repaid for all our toil.

At the end of this unknown area lay our goal, somewhere beyond the
shimmering horizon. We were opening unexplored regions at the rate of
nearly 10,000 square miles an hour, and were experiencing the incomparable
satisfaction of searching for new land. Once, for a moment, I mistook a
distant, vague, low-lying cloud formation for the white peaks of a faraway
land. To the right, somewhere, the rays of the midnight sun shone down
on the scenes of Nansen's heroic struggles to reach the goal that we were
approaching at the rate of nearly 100 miles an hour. To our left lay Peary's
trail.

When our calculations showed us to be about an hour from the Pole, I
noticed through the cabin window a bad leak in the oil tank of the starboard motor. Bennett wrote on a note: 'That motor will stop.' Bennett
then suggested that we try a landing to fix the leak. But I thought that
more dangerous still. We decided to keep on for the Pole. We would be
in no worse fix should we come down near the Pole than we would be if
we had a forced landing where we were. When I took to the wheel again,
I kept my eyes glued on that oil leak and the oil-pressure indicator. Should
the pressure drop, we would lose the motor immediately. It fascinated me.
There was no doubt in my mind that the oil pressure would drop any
moment. But the prize was actually in sight. We could not turn back.

At 9.02 a.m., 9 May 1926, Greenwich civil time, our calculations showed
us to be at the Pole! The dream of a lifetime had at last been realized.

We headed to the right to take two confirming sights of the sun, then
turned and took two more. After that we made some moving and still
pictures, then went on for several miles in the direction we had come, and
made another larger circle to be sure to take in the Pole. Thus we made

a non-stop flight around the world in a very few minutes. In doing that we lost a whole day in time; and, of course, when we completed the circle, we gained that day back again. . . .

The elements were surely smiling that day on us, two insignificant specks of mortality flying over that great, vast white area in a small plane with only one companion, speechless and deaf from the motors, just a dot in the centre of 10,000 square miles of visible desolation. We felt no larger than a pinpoint and as lonely as the tomb; as remote and detached as a star. Here, in another world, far from the herds of people, the smallnesses of life fell from our shoulders. What wonder that we felt no great emotion of achievement or fear of death that lay stretched beneath us, but instead, impersonal, disembodied. On, on we went. It seemed forever onward.

Our great speed had the effect of quickening our mental processes, so that a minute appeared as many minutes, and I realized fully then that time is only a relative thing. An instant can be an age, an age an instant.

✻

GENERAL UMBERTO NOBILE

(1885–1978)

Italian aeronautical engineer and explorer. On 12 May 1926, with Roald Amundsen and Lincoln Ellsworth on board, he flew his airship, the Norge, *over the North Pole. Later, in 1928, he crashed a similar airship, the* Italia, *which resulted in the loss of seventeen lives, though he survived.*

My Polar Flights, trans. F. Fleetwood (London, 1961).

1. THE FLIGHT TO THE NORTH POLE (1926)

We were passing over Dane Island, whence Andrée had started out 29 years before, on the flight from which he did not return. Here the sky cleared again to blue. . . .

Before us the sunlit icy plain stretched as far as eye could see, under a pure blue sky. Measuring with a stop-watch the speed of our shadow upon the ice, I obtained a result of 6½ seconds, corresponding to a ground-speed of 33½ m.p.h. That meant a fairly strong head-wind, characteristic of the margin of the pack. I decided to come lower, in the hope of making more headway, and as the airship was still heavy, it sufficed to bring it onto a level keel, for us to lose height at the rate of nearly 4 ft. to the second. At 600 ft., a new speed-measurement showed that we had gained $9\frac{1}{2}$ m.p.h. We continued for about an hour at this height.

At this low altitude we could see many details of the frozen sea. We caught sight of a white fox. A little further on there were the first traces of bears: two lines drawn close together—the imprints of their paws. We saw the first channel, then occasional irregularly shaped pools, in which glimmered some 'white fish'—the last living creature we met on our journey. Beyond this the pools disappeared and the ice once more became compact. . . .

The flight went on monotonously, calmly, without anything particular happening. The ship was still from 800 to 1,000 lb. heavy, but everything in it was working smoothly. Our morale on board was excellent. Everyone was excited at the thought that in a few hours we would reach the Pole. The sunlight on the vast ice-field gave it a semblance of life, so that no one on board felt that we were flying over a desert, no one was oppressed by that enormous desolation. Why, then—was it as simple and easy as this to go to the Pole?

Cecioni, when he come to the cabin to tell me that his engines were running well, remarked jubilantly: 'So this is the terrible Pole!' 'Just wait!' I replied, 'Perhaps you are crowing too early!' . . . At 6.45 p.m. the port engine suddenly stopped. When we investigated, we found that the fuel lead of the carburettor had been blocked by a piece of ice about 8 in. long, which had formed in a bend. This curious phenomenon, probably due to water-vapour in the jackets, happened once again shortly before we reached the Pole. . . .

Towards 10.30 the snow, which had been very thick for an hour and ten minutes, grew somewhat thinner, so that we caught glimpses of the pack. Soon afterwards it ceased altogether. The sky had again clouded over, and the landscape all of a sudden looked sad and solemn. There is nothing better than sunshine to give life and sparkle even to inanimate things, but its absence made us realize the mortal stillness that brooded over all. Upon the immense frozen plain, scattered patches of fog showed up as drab spots. The whole atmosphere had acquired a pearly grey shade. . . . I definitely started to descend. By one o'clock we were at 1,000 ft., and a few minutes later at 750. Now we were very near the Pole. Riiser-Larsen at a porthole, bent over the sextant in his hands, was ready to snatch any instant when the sun peeped out from the clouds.

As we approached, the excitement on board went on growing. Nobody spoke, but one could read the happy impatience in their faces. I called

Alessandrini: 'Get the flag ready!' The little Norwegian and American flags, fixed like pennants to their staves, had been kept ready in the control cabin since the beginning of the flight; but ours was too big for that. We had to take it out of its casket, unfold it, and fasten it to the staff which my officers had prepared at King's Bay. Alessandrini went, and as he took a long time fixing it with loving care, I urged him impatiently: 'Hurry up!' . . .

At 1.30 a.m. [12 May] the height of the sun, shining from time to time among the clouds, told us that we were at the Pole. We came down lower still, to something like 600 ft.: wishing to get as close as possible to the surface of the limitless frozen sea, I had the engines slowed down. Their rhythm died away, so that the silence of the desert became more apparent. In that silence we solemnly dropped the flags. . . .

My comrades watched the stirring scene. One of them, Alessandrini, came to me a few minutes later in the cabin, radiant, saying: 'Ours was the most beautiful!'

2. THE CRASH (1928)

We were flying between 600 and 900 ft. up. The dirigible was still light, so to keep it at the proper height we had to hold the nose down. At 10.30 I again ordered a speed measurement. When this had been taken I walked to the front of the cabin and looked out of the right-hand porthole, between the steering-wheel and the elevator. To test the height, I dropped a glass ball full of red liquid, and stood there, timing its fall with a stop-watch. While I was attending to this, I heard Cecioni say excitedly: 'We are heavy!'

I turned with a start to look at the instruments. The ship was right down by the stern, at an angle of 8° to the horizon; nevertheless, we were rapidly falling.

The peril was grave and imminent. A short distance below us stretched the pack. I at once gave the orders which had to be given, the only ones that could save the ship in this emergency—if that was possible: to accelerate the two engines, start the third, and at the same time lift the nose of the dirigible still higher. I hoped by these means to overcome the unexpected heaviness. . . .

But unfortunately we went on falling. The variometer—on which my eyes were fixed—confirmed it; in fact, we seemed to be dropping even faster. I realized that there was nothing more to be done. The attempt to combat the increased weight by propulsion had failed. . . . A crash was now inevitable; the most we could do was to mitigate its consequences.

I gave the necessary orders: to stop the engines at once, so as to avoid fire breaking out as we crashed; and to drop the ballast-chain. . . . It was all that could have been ordered; it was ordered promptly and with absolute calm. The perfect discipline on board was unbroken, so that each man carried out my orders as best he could, in the vertiginous rapidity of the event.

In the meantime the pack was approaching at a fearful speed. I saw that Cecioni was finding it difficult to untie the rope which held the chain. 'Hurry up! Hurry up!' I shouted to him. Then, noticing that the engine on the left, run by Caratti, was still working, I leaned out of a porthole on that side, and at the top of my voice—echoed, I think, by one of the officers—repeated the order: 'Stop the engine!' At that moment I saw the stern-boat was only a few tens of yards from the pack. I drew back into the cabin.

The recollection of those last terrible instants is very vivid in my memory. I had scarcely had time to reach the spot near the two rudders, between Malmgren and Zappi, when I saw Malmgren fling up the wheel, turning his startled eyes on me. Instinctively I grasped the helm, wondering if it were possible to guide the ship on to a snow-field and so lessen the shock. . . . Too late! . . . There was the pack, a few yards below, terribly uneven. The masses of ice grew larger, came nearer and nearer. . . . A moment later we crashed.

There was a fearful impact. Something hit me on the head, then I was caught and crushed. Clearly, without any pain, I felt some of my limbs snap. Some object falling from a height knocked me down head foremost. Instinctively I shut my eyes, and with perfect lucidity and coolness formulated the thought: 'It's all over!' I almost pronounced the words in my mind.

It was 10.33 on May 25th. The fearful event had lasted only two or three minutes!

✷

WALLY HERBERT

(b. 1934)

British Polar explorer. He has travelled over 23,000 miles by dog-sled in both the Arctic and the Antarctic. He and three companions made the first surface crossing of the Arctic Ocean in 1968–9. If Peary's navigation was indeed at fault, they may have been the first to reach the Pole over the ice.

Across the Top of the World: The British Trans-Arctic Expedition (London, 1969).

FINDING THE POLE (1969)

Navigation in the vicinity of the Pole is a problem. If your calculation of the longitude is slightly out, then the time at which the sun crosses your meridian—in other words, that time at which the sun is due north—is wrong, and so you head in the wrong direction. And, of course, if you head in the wrong direction, you increase your errors in your dead-reckoning longitude. Your azimuth then is thrown even further into error, and you increase your errors progressively until you spiral into almost a complete circle. This is what happened to us on this particular day.

We set off and travelled for what we estimated was seven miles and stopped. We set up the theodolite, did a rough calculation, and found that we were still seven miles from the Pole. It was unbelievable. We had used up a lot of our time in getting there—the GMT date was going to change within the next seven hours and we were still seven miles short of our goal. We couldn't understand where we had gone wrong. How could one travel seven miles in the direction of the North Pole and still be seven miles from it? The only possible answer was that we must have been travelling parallel to the dateline and were thus passing the Pole. We concluded there must have been something very wrong with our azimuth taken from the position we had computed that morning; so we went into the computations again, and found an error in the longitude. We did another series of observations, all of which took time, and set off again. We travelled hard for three hours, set up a theodolite yet again, and found that we were three miles south of the Pole and on longitude zero. With Spitzbergen as our goal and being still three weeks behind schedule, we should really have carried straight on and not gone back.

But one cannot with a clear conscience say one is at the Pole when one is three miles short of it—more especially since we had told Her Majesty that by dead reckoning we had reached it. So we set off yet again, travelling on a very precise azimuth. We chopped through every single pressure ridge that came our way, cutting ourselves a dead straight line due north. But it was slow progress and the drift was going against us. We were, in fact, hardly making any progress at all. After about four hours we'd come less than a mile.

In desperation, we offloaded the sledges, laid a depot, and took on with us only the barest essentials, just enough for one night's camp. It was a risk, the only time during the whole journey that we took such a risk. But it paid off. With the lighter sledges we made faster progress, and after about three hours estimated that we must surely be at the Pole, possibly even beyond it. So we stopped, set up our tents, and did a final fix which put us at 89° 59' N., one mile south of the North Pole on longitude 180. In other words, we'd crossed the Pole about a mile back along our tracks. But the drift was now with us, so we must surely cross the Pole a second time as we drifted overnight. We got into our sleeping-bags and fell asleep.

The pad marks of thirty-five Eskimo huskies, the broad tracks of four heavy Eskimo-type sledges, and the four sets of human footprints which had approached the North Pole and halted one mile beyond it on the morning of Easter Sunday, 1969, no longer mark the spot where we took our final sun shots and snatched a few hours' rest. For even while we were sleeping, our camp was slowly drifting; and the Pole, by the time we had reloaded our sledges a few hours later and set course for the island of Spitzbergen, lay north in a different direction.

It had been an elusive spot to find and fix. At the North Pole, two separate sets of meridians meet and all directions are south. The temperature was minus 35° Fahrenheit. The wind was from the south-west, or was it from the north-east? It was Sunday, or was it Saturday? Maybe it was Monday. It was a confusing place to be—a place which lay on our course from Barrow to Spitzbergen and which had taken us 408 days to reach.

Trying to set foot upon it had been like trying to step on the shadow of a bird that was circling overhead. The surface across which we were moving was itself a moving surface on a planet the was spinning about an axis. We were standing approximately on that axis, asleep on our feet, dog-tired and hungry. Too tired to celebrate our arrival on the summit of this super-mountain around which the sun circles almost as though stuck in a groove.

We set up our camera and posed for some pictures—thirty-six shots at different exposures. We tried not to look weary, tried not to look cold. We tried only to huddle, four fur-clad figures, in a pose that was vaguely familiar—for what other proof of the attainment could we bring back than a picture posed in this way?

VII

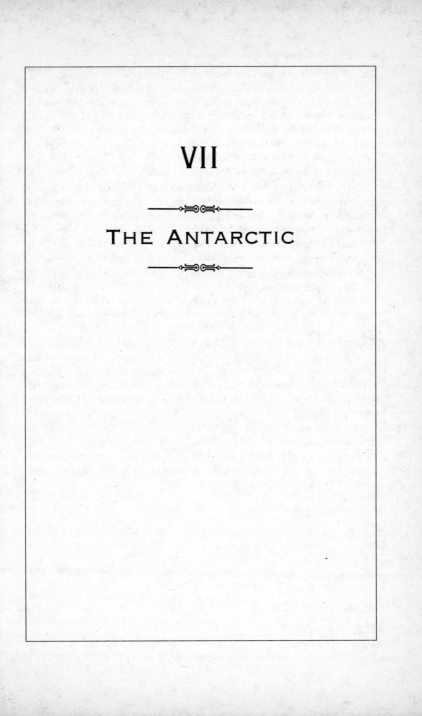

THE ANTARCTIC

Jean-Baptiste Bouvet de Lozier (1705–1788)   489
James Cook (1728–1779)   490
Edward Bransfield (c.1795–1852)   493
Nathaniel Brown Palmer (1799–1877)   495
Charles Wilkes (1798–1877)   497
Jules-Sébastien-César Dumont d'Urville (1790–1842)   499
Sir James Clark Ross (1800–1862)   501
Roald Amundsen (1872–1928)   503
Robert Falcon Scott (1868–1912)   505
Apsley Cherry-Garrard (1886–1959)   510
Sir Douglas Mawson (1882–1958)   511
Sir Ernest Shackleton (1874–1922)   516
Richard Byrd (1888–1957)   519

Jean-Baptiste Bouvet de Lozier

(1705–1788)

French (Norman) sailor. He claimed to have discovered the tip of Terra Australis (Antarctica) but it was, in fact, the small island now named after him.

John Callander, *Terra Australis Cognita* (Edinburgh, 1768).

Fog, Ice, and Celebrations (1738–9)

We left Port L'Orient July 19, 1738, and shaped our course for the island St Catharine. Hence we sailed again in search of unknown lands, which, by our instructions, we were to look for about 44° south latitude, longitude 355°. November 26, in latitude 35°, longitude 344°, we began to meet with fogs, which continued close with us, and wet our clothes like rain, and was often so thick that even when the two ships were so near that we would cheer our consort's crew working, yet we could not see them. We always fired guns during the day, and had our lanthorns lighted at night, notwithstanding all which we had much difficulty to keep together. . . .

December 10, we found ourselves at the intersection of the 44th parallel with the first meridian, where the charts commonly place the Terra del Visto, or the Cape of the Southern Continent. Still, however, we saw no land; whether it was that the fogs hindered us from seeing it, or that in reality there is no land thereabouts, except some small island, or perhaps islands of ice, which had been taken, at a distance, for a coast. On the 15th of December we first saw ice in a latitude corresponding to that of Paris. I was much pleased on seeing this ice, as I took it for a certain sign of land being near us. I had observed that the height of these icy isles generally corresponded with that of the lands near which they were formed, and these high lands are generally safe to approach. We saw some of these islands of ice so high that we could observe them eight leagues off, and when the fogs cleared up, they presented us with several amusing figures, resembling fortresses, houses, ships, etc.

In these unknown seas, the risks we ran were very great, for the ice is much more dangerous than the shore, as each piece of it is a floating rock against which, were we driven, there could be no hope of saving our lives. The smaller pieces of ice are even more dangerous than the larger, because they swim just level with the surface of the water, and when the sea runs high, it becomes very difficult to distinguish them. These dangers began to discourage the crews, so that, in order to animate them, I read those articles of our instructions in which rewards were promised in case the discovery was perfected.

We now made sail to the southward, but were quickly so hemmed in with ice that we were forced to stand fast in order to find some passage. The sea here was very deep, and we saw great numbers of divers, penguins, and sea wolves. The needle gave different variations on different compasses, declining 24' east on one, while on another it would vary 50' west, with the same irregularity of motion that has been observed on approaching the ice in Hudson's bay and Davis's straits.

January 1, 1739, I discovered land. It was exceedingly high, covered with snow, and almost hid in fogs. From the festival celebrated on this day, I called it Cape Circumcision; and the pilot of the *Eagle*, who first saw this land, had a reward of twenty piastres. . . . Its coasts are very high and rugged, and so pestered with ice as to be quite inaccessible. . . . On the 6th of January we were suddenly surrounded by a prodigious flight of fowls, of the size of a pigeon, and quite white. We kept standing along this course during twelve days, without daring to go near the shore, or even to send our boats ashore, on account of the fogs, the ice, and the contrary winds. Hence we stood eastward, under 57° latitude, till January 25, in which time we ran 425 leagues, always along the ice, and seeing great numbers of whales, sea wolves, and other large fishes. Despairing at length to find an inlet hereabouts, we quitted the Austral land, which seemed inaccessible, and stood to the northeast . . .

✽

JAMES COOK

(1728–1779)

English naval officer and explorer. Appointed in 1768 to command the Endeavour, *he had special orders to seek Terra Australis. He sailed around New Zealand and claimed Australia for the crown, but failed to find Antarctica. When a further expedition was mounted in 1772, he managed to circumnavigate the southern Continent without setting eyes on it.*

A *Voyage Towards the South Pole*, 2 vols. (London, 1777).

1. PART OF COOK'S INSTRUCTIONS FROM THE ADMIRALTY (1768)

Whereas the making discoveries of countries hitherto unknown, and the attaining a knowledge of distant parts which, though formerly discovered, have yet been but imperfectly explored, will redound greatly to the honour of this nation as a maritime power, as well as to the dignity of the Crown of Great Britain, and may trend greatly to the advancement of the trade and navigation thereof; and whereas there is reason to imagine that a continent or land of great extent may be found to the southward of the tract lately made by Capt. Wallis in His Majesty's ship the *Dolphin* (of which you will herewith receive a copy) or of the tract of any former navigators in pursuits of the like kind; you are therefore in pursuance of His Majesty's pleasure hereby required and directed to put to sea with the bark you command so soon as the observation of the transit of the planet Venus shall be finished, and observe the following instructions.

You are to proceed to the southward in order to make discovery of the continent above-mentioned until you arrive in the latitude of 40°, unless you sooner fall in with it. But not having discovered it or any evident signs of it in that run, you are to proceed in search of it to the westward between the latitude before mentioned and the latitude of 35° until you discover it, or fall in with the eastern side of the land discovered by Tasman and now called New Zealand.

If you discover the continent above-mentioned either in your run to the southward or to the westward as above directed, you are to employ youself diligently in exploring as great an extent of the coast as you can; carefully observing the true situation thereof both in latitude and longitude, the variation of the needle, bearings of headlands, height, direction and course of the tides and currents, depths and soundings of the sea, shoals, rocks, etc., and also surveying and making charts, and taking views of such bays, harbours and parts of the coast as may be useful to navigation.

You are also carefully to observe the nature of the soil, and the products thereof; the beasts and fowls that inhabit or frequent it, the fishes that are to be found in the rivers or upon the coast and in what plenty; and in case you find any mines, minerals, or valuable stones you are to bring home specimens of each, as also such specimens of the seeds of the trees, fruits and grains as you may be able to collect, and transmit them to our secretary that we may cause proper examination and experiments to be made of them.

You are likewise to observe the genius, temper, disposition, and number of the natives, if there be any, and endeavour by all proper means to cultivate a friendship and alliance with them, making them presents of such trifles as they may value, inviting them to traffic, and showing them every kind of civility and regard; taking care, however, not to suffer yourself to be surprised by them, but to be always upon your guard against any accident.

You are also with the consent of the natives to take possession of convenient situations in the country in the name of the King of Great Britain; or, if you find the country uninhabited, take possession for His Majesty by setting up proper marks and inscriptions, as first discoverers and possessors.

2. 'No Man Will Ever Venture Further Than I Have Done' (1775)

The risk one runs in exploring a coast, in these unknown and icy seas, is so very great, that I can be bold though to say that no man will ever venture further than I have done; and that the lands which may lie to the south will never be explored. Thick fogs, snow storms, intense cold, and every other thing that can render navigation dangerous must be encountered; and these difficulties are greatly heightened by the inexpressibly horrid aspect of the country; a country doomed by Nature never once to feel the warmth of the sun's rays, but to lie buried in everlasting snow and ice. The ports which may be on the coast are, in a manner, wholly filled up with frozen snow of vast thickness; but if any should be so far open as to invite a ship into it, she would run a risk of being fixed there for ever, or of coming out in an ice island. The islands and floats on the coast, the great falls from the ice cliffs in the port, or a heavy snow storm attended with a sharp frost would be equally fatal. . . .

We had now run down 13° of longitude, in the very latitude assigned for Bouvet's Land. I was therefore well assured that what he had seen could be nothing but an island of ice; for, if it had been land, it is hardly possible we could have missed it, though it were ever so small. Besides, from the time of leaving the southern lands, we had not met with the least signs of any other. But even suppose we had, it would have been no proof of the existence of Cape Circumcision; for I am well assured that neither seals nor penguins nor any of the oceanic birds are indubitable signs of the vicinity of land. I will allow that they are found on the coasts of all these southern lands; but are they not also to be found in all parts of the southern ocean? There are, however, some oceanic or aquatic birds which point out the vicinity of land; especially shags, which seldom go out of sight of it; land gannets, boobies, and men-of-war birds, I believe, seldom go very far out to sea.

As we were now no more than 2° of longitude from our route to the south, when we left the Cape of Good Hope, it was to no purpose to proceed any further to the east under this parallel, knowing that no land could be there. But an opportunity now offering of clearing up some doubts of our having seen land further to the south, I steered SE to get into the situation in which it was supposed to lie. . . .

Having now run over the place where the land was supposed to lie, without seeing the least signs of any, it was no longer to be doubted but that the ice-islands had deceived us as well as Mr Bouvet. The wind by this time having veered to the north, and increased to a perfect storm, attended as usual with snow and sleet, we handed the top-sails and hauled up ENE under the courses. During the night the wind abated, and veered to NW, which enabled us to steer more to the north, having no business further south.

EDWARD BRANSFIELD

(*c*.1795–1852)

English naval officer. He is usually credited with having discovered the Antarctic continent on 30 January 1820, although the Russian explorer Fabian Bellingshausen (1770–1825) may have made the first sighting two days earlier.

Unsigned articles based on information supplied by Midshipman Thomas Maine Bone, RN, draughtsman on the brig *Williams*, captained by Edward Bransfield. In the *Literary Gazette and Journal of Belles Lettres*, 5 (London, 1821).

1. PENGUINS AND PLANTING THE JACK (1820)

At noon we threw a bottle overboard, containing a paper bearing the following inscription: 'This bottle was hove overboard from the *Williams*, an English brig, on a voyage of discovery, to the southward, on the 12th of January, 1820, in latitude 57° 48′ and longitude 69° 55′ W. Should any vessel pick this up at sea, it is requested the master will note the latitude and longitude, putting it overboard again; or should it be found on any coast or harbour, the person so finding it will, I hope, inclose this paper to the Board of Longitude, in London, stating when, where, and how he came by it; signed Edward Bransfield, master of HMS *Andromache*. . . .

Several shoals of seals and a few penguins being seen, we tried for soundings about eight o'clock, but obtained no bottom with 120 fathoms. During the night we kept the lead going two hours, but unsuccessfully, still passing through and by large shoals of seals and penguins. So great a sign of land being in the neighbourhood made it necessary to keep a very vigilant look-out, when about eight o'clock in the morning, land was discovered making in a moderate height, and partly covered with snow. At nine we hove too, and sounded with 55 fathoms brown sand and ooze, the extremes of the land bearing from east to SSE; filled and bore up E.b.S. for a supposed entrance to a spacious bay, or at least where we thought we might bring up and water. In standing in, an unconnected chain of rocks, detached from the main, presented themselves, forming in very remarkable shapes. When within a mile or a mile and a half of the land, we hove to and hoisted the whale-boat out, put leads and lines, and armed her, when Mr Smith took her to go in search of an anchorage where we might lie in security. . . .

The breakers in smooth water are scarcely perceptible, except at intervals when the sea breaks. A short distance to the eastward of the cape is a small island pierced through, resembling the arch of a bridge. After determining the latitude of Cape Shireff, we ran to the eastward until abreast of an island, which, from its barren, uncomfortable appearance, was named the Island of Desolation. Its latitude is 62° 27′ S and longitude 60° 35′ and 10 miles due east of the last cape. Previous to the going down of the sun, we determined the variation, by an excellent azimuth, to be 23° 52′ east, and an amplitude soon after 22° 30′ east. During the time we were prosecuting our pursuits, we were surrounded by shoals of seals and penguins. From Desolation Island we ran in a NE direction for a cluster we perceived, which, when abreast of, were supposed to be the same seen by Mr Smith in the month of February 1819. The whole of these islands, along the part of the coast which we had already seen, were composed of black rock, and above the reach of the water patches of snow made but a dismal aspect. The main entirely capped which gave us but very faint hopes of ever being able to speak well of its fertility. . . .

At 1.30, an island was observed nearly clear of snow, bearing WSW; at four, the bluff bow [sic] NE. At five, observing the land to the SW of the island appear like a bay, we made sail, steering WSW with a moderate breeze. The necessary precautions were taken by keeping the lead going and a hand forward to look out for foul ground, and ice being taken, we rounded the island, and at 7.30 brought up with the chain cable in sixteen fathoms, coarse sand, with black gravel, the eastern point of the island bearing NE.b.E.; a small island near the bottom of the bay W.b.N. and the southern point of the bay SW. While rounding the island we observed its shore covered with penguins, whose awkward movement had the most strange appearance, and at the same time the most intolerable stench assailed our noses that I ever smelt, arising from these gentry. As soon as everything was secure, we hoisted the boats out, manned and armed the whale-boat, and after breakfast Mr Bransfield proceeded in her to effect a landing, where he might plant the Jack, and take possession of it by the name of New South Britain, in the name and behalf of HM George IV, his heirs and successors. At eight o'clock, observed the boat land on a shingle beach, which bore from the brig NNW; observed soon after, with the aid of our glasses, the Jack planted; we hoisted on board the brig, our ensign and pendant, and fired a gun; he likewise buried a bottle, containing several coins of the realm, given by different people for that purpose.

2. A Search for Water

We sent in the afternoon the boats in search of water. It would be impossible to describe the manner in which the penguins disputed our landing, both on the main and island; it was not until great slaughter was made, and a lane cut through them, that we could proceed. It is well known that every animal, however timid at other times, will defend its young with the most determined courage, and this being the breeding season with these birds will account for the decided opposition we met with. Before we had been long on shore we discovered several streams of water, but as they passed through the filth of these animals, they were unfit for use. To remedy this, a well was constructed and surrounded by stones to prevent its pollution.

✻

NATHANIEL BROWN PALMER

(1799–1877)

American sealer. His vessel, Hero, *may have been the first to make an Antarctic landfall, though Bransfield's claim seems stronger.*

J. R. Spears, *Captain Nathaniel Brown Palmer: An Old Time Sailor of the Sea* (London, 1922).

MEETING WITH CAPTAIN BELLINGSHAUSEN OF THE RUSSIAN
IMPERIAL NAVY ON BOARD THE FRIGATE *ROSTOCK* (1820)

The scene as that young Yankee captain entered the cabin of the frigate
might well be reproduced by an artist of talent. For the captain of the
frigate was seated at a table with a group of his officers, all in brilliant
uniform, around him, while the young sealer, smooth-faced, tall and slender, was dressed in a sealskin coat and boots of his own make, and he had
a sou'wester on his head. To the naval officers the boy certainly was a
bizarre figure. But when they looked into his far-seeing eyes they perceived that he was unabashed and fully able to meet them as man to man.

The captain of the frigate (he was made an admiral on his return home
and is so called in the various narratives of this incident) arose to greet
Captain Palmer, shook his hand, ordered a chair placed for him and then
said:

'You are welcome, young man. Be seated.'

The conversation which followed was as follows, so far as remembered:

'What is your name?'

'Nathaniel Palmer.'

'Where you are from?'

'Stonington, Connecticut, USA.'

'The name of your boat?'

'*Hero*.'

'What are you doing here?'

'On a sealing expedition. A fleet from Stonington is at work among the
islands, here.'

'What islands are those in sight?'

'The South Shetlands; and if you wish to visit any of them in particular
it will afford me pleasure to be your pilot; for I am well acquainted with
them.'

He also mentioned the harbour where the sealing vessels were at anchor
and added that water with an abundant supply of wildfowl might be obtained anywhere among the islands.

'I thank you,' continued the captain, 'but previous to our being enveloped in the fog we had a glimpse of those islands, and concluded we had
made a discovery; but behold, when the fog lifts, to my great surprise, here
is an American vessel, apparently in as fine order as if it were but yesterday
she had left the United States; not only this but her master is ready to pilot
my ships into port, where several of his own nation lie at anchor. We must
surrender the palm of enterprise to you Americans, and content ourselves
with following in your train.'

'You flatter me,' replied the captain, 'but there is an immense extent of land still further south; and when the fog there is entirely dissipated you may have a full view of it from your masthead.'

'How far south have you been?' asked the captain.

Captain Palmer told him the latitude and longitude of the point at which the *Hero* turned back and described the coast along which she had sailed.

'Indeed!' exclaimed the Russian. 'Then I am entirely anticipated in my object.'

He now arose much agitated and begged Captain Palmer to produce the *Hero*'s log book and chart. Palmer at once sent to the sloop for them. While waiting for the messenger to return, breakfast was served, with Palmer seated at the side of the Russian captain. While they were at the table many questions were asked about the seal fishery, the ports of the South Shetlands, the hailing port of the sealing fleet, and about the character of the vessels themselves.

The *Hero*'s log and chart arrived while the two were yet at the table, and were placed before the Russian captain. For a time he examined them without saying anything. Then he arose from the table and exclaimed.

'What do I see and what do I hear from a boy in his teens? That he is commander of a tiny boat of the size of the launch of my frigate, in which he had pushed his way to the pole through storm and ice; has sought and found the point I, in command of one of the best appointed fleets at the disposal of my august master, have for three long weary years searched day and night for.'

Then, placing his hand on Palmer's head he continued:

'What shall I say to my master? What will he think of me? But be that as it may, my grief is your joy. Wear your laurels with my sincere prayers for your welfare. I name the land you have discovered in honour of yourself, noble boy, Palmer Land.'

※

CHARLES WILKES

(1798–1877)

American naval officer. He commanded the US Exploring Expedition, a squadron of five poorly equipped ships which, during 1838–42, collected

*a mass of sometimes questionable data in the southern oceans. They did
discover and chart Wilkes Land, part of mainland Antarctica.*

G. Murray (ed.), *The Arctic Manual* (London, 1901).

LAND AND ICE (1840)

We had a beautiful and unusual sight presented to us this night: the sun
and moon both appeared above the horizon at the same time and each
throwing its light abroad. The latter was nearly full. The former illuminated
the icebergs and distant continent with his deep golden rays; while the
latter, in the opposite horizon, tinged with silvery light the clouds in its
immediate neighbourhood. There now being no doubt in any mind of the
discovery of land, it gave an exciting interest to the cruise, that appeared
to set aside all thought of fatigue, and to make every one willing to encounter any difficulty to effect a landing. . . .

The last two days we had very many beautiful snow-white petrels about.
The character of the ice had now become entirely changed. The tabular-
formed icebergs prevailed, and there was comparatively little field-ice.
Some of the bergs were of magnificent dimensions, one-third of a mile in
length, and from 150 to 200 feet in height, with sides perfectly smooth, as
though they had been chiselled. Others, again, exhibited lofty arches of
many-coloured tints, leading into deep caverns, open to the swell of the
sea, which, rushing in, produced loud and distant thunderings. The flight
of birds passing in and out of these caverns recalled the recollection of
ruined abbeys, castles, and caves, while here and there a bold projecting
bluff, crowned with pinnacles and turrets, resembled some Gothic keep.
A little further onwards would be seen a vast fissure, as if some powerful
force had rent in twain these mighty masses. Every noise on board, even
our own voices, reverberated from the massive and pure white walls. These
tabular bergs are like masses of beautiful alabaster; a verbal description of
them can do little to convey the reality to the imagination of one who has
not been among them. If an immense city of ruined alabaster palaces can
be imagined, of every variety of shape and tint, and composed of huge
piles of buildings grouped together, with long lanes or streets winding
irregularly through them, some faint idea may be formed of the grandeur
and beauty of the spectacle. The time and circumstances under which we
were viewing them, threading our way through these vast bergs, we knew
not to what end, left an impression upon me of these icy and desolate
regions that can never be forgotten.

JULES-SÉBASTIEN-CÉSAR DUMONT D'URVILLE

(1790–1842)

French naval officer and explorer. In 1838 he discovered, and named after his wife, Terre Adélie.

Voyage au Pole Sud, etc. sur les Corvettes 'L'Astrolabe' et 'La Zélée, sous le Commandement de M. J. Dumont-D'Urville, Capitaine de Vaisseau, 1845, in G. Murray (ed.), *The Antarctic Manual* (London, 1901).

CLAIMING LAND THE FRENCH WAY (1840)

It was nearly 9 o'clock when, to our great joy, we landed on the western part of the most westerly and the loftiest islet. The *Astrolabe*'s boat had arrived a moment before, and already the men had climbed up the steep sides of this rock. They hurled down the penguins, who were much astonished to find themselves so brutally dispossessed of the island, of which they were the sole inhabitants. We also jumped on shore armed with pick-axes and hammers. The surf rendered this operation very difficult. I was forced to leave several men in the boat to look after her. I then immediately sent one of our men to unfurl the tricolour flag on this land, which no human creature had either seen or stepped on before. Following the ancient custom, faithfully kept up by the English, we took possession of it in the name of France, as well as of the adjacent coast, which the ice prevented us from approaching. Our enthusiasm and joy were such that it seemed to us we had just added a province to French territory, by this wholly pacific conquest. If the abuse which has been born of such acts of possession has caused them to be often regarded as ridiculous and worthless, in this case at any rate we believed ourselves sufficiently in the right to maintain the ancient custom in favour of our country. For we dispossessed none and our titles were incontestable. We regarded ourselves, therefore, at once as being on French soil; and there is at least this advantage that it will never raise up war against our country.

The ceremony ended, as it should, with a libation. To the glory of France, which concerned us deeply just then, we emptied a bottle of the most generous of her wines, which one of our companions had had the presence of mind to bring with him. Never was Bordeaux wine called on to play a more worthy part; never was bottle emptied more fitly. Surrounded on all sides by eternal ice and snow, the cold was extreme. This generous liquor reacted with advantage against the rigours of the temperature.

All this happened in less time than it takes to write it. We then all set to work immediately to collect everything of interest in natural history that this barren land could offer. The animal kingdom was only represented by the penguins. Notwithstanding all my search we did not find a single shell. The rock was entirely bare, and did not even offer the least trace of lichens. We found only one single seaweed, and that was dry; so it had been brought there by currents or birds. We were obliged to fall back on the mineral kingdom. Each of us took a hammer and began to hew at the rock. But it was so hard, being of a granite nature, that we could only detach very small pieces. Happily, while wandering on the summit of the island, the sailors discovered large fragments of rock detached by frost, and these they took into our boats. In a short time we had enough to supply specimens to all our museums and to others besides. In examining them closely, I recognized a perfect resemblance between these rocks and some small fragments that we had found in the stomach of a penguin killed the evening before. These fragments could, if necessary, have given an exact idea of the geological formation of this land, if it had been impossible to go on shore there. However extraordinary may be this way of doing geology, it proves how much interest the smallest observations may have for the naturalist, often even helping him in his researches, by leading him sometimes on to the track of discoveries to which they seem to be the most foreign. The islet on which we landed is one of a group of eight or ten small islands rounded above, and all presenting pretty much the same form. These islands are separated from the nearest coast by a distance of 500–600 metres. We noticed along the shore several more tops quite bare, and one cape of which the base was also free from snow; but we noticed also a great quantity of ice which made the approach to it very difficult. All these islets, very close to each other, seemed to form a continuous chain parallel to the coast from east to west. . . .

We did not leave these islets till 9.30; we were entranced by the treasures we carried away. Before hoisting sail we saluted our discovery with a general hurrah, to bid it a last good-bye. The echoes of these silent regions, for the first time disturbed by human voices, repeated our cries and then returned to their habitual silence, so gloomy and so imposing . . .

SIR JAMES CLARK ROSS

(1800–1862)

*British naval officer and explorer. He commanded the Royal Navy's first
Antarctic expedition. Between 1839 and 1843 he discovered the Ross Sea,
Ross Ice Shelf, Ross Island, and Victoria Land.*

A *Voyage of Discovery and Research in the Southern and Antarctic Regions
During the Years 1839–43* (London, 1847).

1. NEW YEAR'S DAY (1841)

Being New Year's Day, an additional allowance of provisions was served to
the ships' crews, as was the practice on all the arctic voyages; and a complete
suit of warm clothing was issued gratis to each individual; this had been
provided by the liberality of the government, and on our entering the icy
regions, could not but prove to be as useful and acceptable a new-year's
gift as they could have received. Mutual congratulations passed between
the officers and crews of the ships, and the day was kept, as in old England,
in conviviality and rejoicing. Being amongst numerous icebergs and having
a great deal of loose ice about us added greatly to the interest of the day
to those who had never been amongst it before; and those who had could
not but share in some degree the excitement and delight of their companions. We had, indeed, met with the pack in a much lower latitude than we
had anticipated; but from the little we had seen of it we were by no means
dispirited by the early appearance of so serious an obstruction to our
progress, for it presented none of those evidences of impenetrability we
had been led to expect.

2. POSSESSION ISLAND

We found the shores of the mainland completely covered with ice projecting into the sea, and the heavy surf along its edge forbade any attempt to
land upon it; a strong tide carried us rapidly along between this ice-bound
coast and the islands amongst heavy masses of ice, so that our situation was
for some time most critical; for all the exertions our people could use were
insufficient to stem the tide. But taking advantage of a narrow opening that
appeared in the ice, the boats were pushed through it, and we got into an
eddy under the lee of the largest of the islands, and landed on a beach of
large loose stones and stranded masses of ice. The weather by this time

had put on a most threatening appearance, the breeze was freshening fast, and the anxious circumstances under which we were placed, together with the recall flag flying at the ship's mast-head, which I had ordered Lieutenant Bird to hoist if necessary, compelled us to hasten our operations.

The ceremony of taking possession of these newly discovered lands, in the name of our Most Gracious Sovereign, Queen Victoria, was immediately proceeded with; and on planting the flag of our country amidst the hearty cheers of our party, we drank to the health, long life, and happiness of Her Majesty and HRH Prince Albert. The island was named Possession Island. It is situated in lat. 71° 56′ and long. 171° 7′ E, composed entirely of igneous rocks and only accessible on its western side. We saw not the smallest appearance of vegetation, but inconceivable myriads of penguins completely and densely covered the whole surface of the island, along the ledges of the precipices, and even to the summits of the hills, attacking us vigorously as we waded through their ranks, and pecking at us with their sharp beaks, disputing possession; which, together with their loud coarse notes, and the insupportable stench from the deep bed of guano, which had been forming for ages, and which may at some period be valuable to the agriculturists of our Australasian colonies, made us glad to get away again, after having loaded our boats with geological specimens and penguins.

3. Volcanoes and Icy Cliffs

With a favourable breeze, and very clear weather, we stood to the southward, close to some land which had been in sight since the preceding noon, and which we then called the 'High Island'; it proved to be a mountain 12,400 ft. above the level of the sea, emitting flame and smoke in great profusion; at first the smoke appeared like snow drift, but as we drew nearer, its true character became manifest.

The discovery of an active volcano in so high a southern latitude cannot but be esteemed a circumstance of high geological importance and interest, and contribute to throw some further light on the physical construction of our globe. I named it Mount Erebus, and an extinct volcano to the eastward, little inferior in height, being 10,900 ft. high, was called Mount Terror. . . .

As we approached the land under all studding-sails, we perceived a low white line extending from its eastern extreme point as far as the eye could discern to the eastward. It presented an extraordinary appearance, gradually increasing in height as we got nearer to it, and proving at length to be a perpendicular cliff of ice, between 150 and 200 ft. above the level of the sea, perfectly flat and level at the top, and without any fissures or promontories on its even seaward face. What was beyond it we could not

502

imagine; for being much higher than our mast-head, we could not see anything except the summit of a lofty range of mountains extending to the
southward as far as the 79th degree of latitude. . . .

Meeting with such an obstruction was a great disappointment to us all,
for we had already, in expectation, passed far beyond the 80th degree, and
had even appointed a rendezvous there, in case of the ships accidentally
separating. It was, however, an obstruction of such a character as to leave
no doubt upon my mind as to our future proceedings, for we might with
equal chance of success try to sail through the Cliffs of Dover, as penetrate
such a mass.

✳

ROALD AMUNDSEN

(1872–1928)

*Norwegian explorer. He reached the South Pole thirty-five days before
Scott.*

The South Pole, trans. A. G. Chater (London, 1912).

ARRIVAL AT THE POLE (1911)

It was like the eve of some great festival that night in the tent. One could
feel that a great event was at hand. Our flag was taken out again and lashed
to the same two ski-sticks as before. Then it was rolled up and laid aside,
to be ready when the time came. I was awake several times during the
night, and had the same feeling that I can remember as a little boy on the
night before Christmas Eve—an intense expectation of what was going to
happen. Otherwise I think we slept just as well that night as any other.

On the morning of 14 December the weather was of the finest, just as
if it had been made for arriving at the Pole. I am not quite sure, but I
believe we dispatched our breakfast rather more quickly than usual and
were out of the tent sooner, though I must admit that we always accomplished this with all reasonable haste. We went in the usual order—the
forerunner, Hanssen, Wisting, Bjaaland, and the reserve forerunner. By
noon we had reached 89° 53′ by dead reckoning, and made ready to take
the rest in one stage. . . . We advanced that day in the same mechanical

way as before; not much was said, but eyes were used all the more. Hanssen's neck grew twice as long as before in his endeavour to see a few inches further. I had asked him before we started to spy out ahead for all he was worth, and he did so with a vengeance. But, however keenly he stared, he could not descry anything but the endless flat plain ahead of us. The dogs had dropped their scenting, and appeared to have lost their interest in the regions about the earth's axis.

At three in the afternoon a simultaneous 'Halt!' rang out from the drivers. They had carefully examined their sledge-meters, and they all showed the full distance—our Pole by reckoning. The goal was reached, the journey ended. I cannot say—though I know it would sound much more effective—that the object of my life was attained. That would be romancing rather too bare-facedly. I had better be honest and admit straight out that I have never known any man to be placed in such a diametrically opposite position to the goal of his desires as I was at that moment. The regions around the North Pole—well, yes, the North Pole itself—had attracted me from childhood, and here I was at the South Pole. Can anything more topsy-turvy be imagined?

We reckoned now that we were at the Pole. Of course, every one of us knew that we were not standing on the absolute spot; it would be an impossibility with the time and the instruments at our disposal to ascertain that exact spot. But we were so near it that the few miles which possibly separated us from it could not be of the slightest importance. It was our intention to make a circle round this camp, with a radius of twelve and a half miles, and to be satisfied with that. After we had halted we collected and congratulated each other. We had good grounds for mutual respect in what had been achieved, and I think that was just the feeling that was expressed in the firm and powerful grasps of the fist that were exchanged. After this we proceeded to the greatest and most solemn act of the whole journey—the planting of our flag. Pride and affection shone in the five pairs of eyes that gazed upon the flag, as it unfurled itself with a sharp crack, and waved over the Pole. I had determined that the act of planting it—the historic event—should be equally divided among us all. It was not for one man to do this; it was for *all* who had staked their lives in the struggle, and held together through thick and thin. This was the only way in which I could show my gratitude to my comrades in this desolate spot. I could see that they understood and accepted it in the spirit in which it was offered. Five weather-beaten, frost-bitten fists they were that grasped the pole, raised the waving flag in the air, and planted it as the first at the geographical South Pole. 'Thus we plant thee, beloved flag, at the South Pole, and give to the plain on which it lies the name of King Haakon VII's

Plateau.' That moment will certainly be remembered by all of us who stood there.

One gets out of the way of protracted ceremonies in those regions—the shorter they are the better. Everyday life began again at once. When we had got the tent up, Hanssen set about slaughtering Helge, and it was hard for him to have to part from his best friend. Helge had been an uncommonly useful and good-natured dog; without making any fuss he had pulled from morning to night, and had been a shining example to the team. But during the last week he had quite fallen away, and on our arrival at the Pole there was only a shadow of the old Helge left. He was only a drag on the others, and did absolutely no work. One blow on the skull, and Helge had ceased to live. 'What is death to one is food to another' is a saying that can scarcely find a better application than these dog meals. Helge was portioned out on the spot, and within a couple of hours there was nothing left of him but his teeth and the tuft at the end of his tail. This was the second of our eighteen dogs that we had lost. The Major, one of Wisting's fine dogs, left us in 88° 25′ S, and never returned. He was fearfully worn out, and must have gone away to die. We now had sixteen dogs left, and these we intended to divide into two equal teams, leaving Bjaaland's sledge behind.

Of course, there was a festivity in the tent that evening—not that champagne corks were popping and wine flowing—no, we contented ourselves with a little piece of seal meat each, and it tasted well and did us good. There was no other sign of festival indoors. Outside we heard the flag flapping in the breeze. Conversation was lively in the tent that evening, and we talked of many things. Perhaps, too, our thoughts sent messages home of what we had done.

✿

ROBERT FALCON SCOTT

(1868–1912)

British naval officer and explorer. Between 1901 and 1904 he led the British National Antarctic Expedition. With Edward Wilson and Ernest Shackleton, he made the first extensive land journeys on the continent. In January 1912 he and his companions all perished after becoming the second team to reach the South Pole.

Scott's Last Expedition (London, 1913).

1. FINAL DIARIES AND LETTERS (1912)

It is wonderful to think that two long marches would land us at the Pole. We left our depot today with nine days' provisions, so that it ought to be a certain thing now, and the only appalling possibility the sight of the Norwegian flag forestalling ours. Little Bowers continues his indefatigable efforts to get good sights, and it is wonderful how he works them up in his sleeping-bag in our congested tent. (Minimum for night –27.5°.) Only 27 miles from the Pole. We *ought* to do it now.

Tuesday, 16 January. . . . The worst has happened, or nearly the worst. . . . About the second hour of the march Bower's sharp eyes detected what he thought was a cairn; he was uneasy about it, but argued that it must be a sastrugus. Half an hour later he detected a black speck ahead. Soon we knew that this could not be a natural snow feature. We marched on, found that it was a black flag tied to a sledge bearer; near by the remains of a camp; sledge tracks and ski tracks going and coming and the clear trace of dogs' paws—many dogs. This told us the whole story. The Norwegians have forestalled us and are first at the Pole. It is a terrible disappointment, and I am very sorry for my loyal companions. Many thoughts come and much discussion have we had. Tomorrow we must march on to the Pole and then hasten home with all the speed we can compass. All the day-dreams must go; it will be a wearisome return. We are descending in altitude—certainly also the Norwegians found an easy way up.

Wednesday, 17 January. . . . The Pole. Yes, but under very different circumstances from those expected. We have had a horrible day—add to our disappointment a head wind 4 to 5, with a temperature –22°, and companions labouring on with cold feet and hands.

We started at 7.30, none of us having slept much after the shock of our discovery. We followed the Norwegian sledge tracks for some way; as far as we make out there are only two men. In about three miles we passed two small cairns. Then the weather overcast, and the tracks being increasingly drifted up and obviously going too far to the west, we decided to make straight for the Pole according to our calculations. . . . Great God! this is an awful place and terrible enough for us to have laboured to it without the reward of priority. Well, it is something to have got here, and the wind may be our friend tomorrow. We have had a fat Polar hoosh in spite of our chagrin, and feel comfortable inside—added a small stick of chocolate and the queer taste of a cigarette brought by Wilson. Now for the run home and a desperate struggle. I wonder if we can do it.

Thursday morning, 18 January. . . . We have just arrived at this tent, 2 miles from our camp, therefore about 1½ miles from the Pole. In the tent we find a record of five Norwegians having been here, as follows: 'Roald Amundsen, Olav Olavson Bjaaland, Hilmer Hanssen, Sverre H. Hassel, Oscar Wisting; 16 Dec. 1911'. The tent is fine—a small, compact affair supported by a single bamboo. A note from Amundsen, which I keep, asks me to forward a letter to King Haakon!

The following articles have been left in the tent: three half-bags of reindeer containing a miscellaneous assortment of mitts and sleeping socks, very various in description, a sextant, a Norwegian artificial horizon and a hypsometer without boiling-point thermometers, a sextant and hypsometer of English make. Left a note to say I had visited the tent with companions. . . .

This morning started with southerly breeze, set sail and passed another cairn at good speed; half-way, however, the wind shifted to W by S or WSW, blew through our wind clothes and into our mitts. Poor Wilson horribly cold, could not get off ski for some time. Bowers and I practically made camp, and when we got into the tent at last we were all deadly cold. Then temp. now midday down −43° and the wind strong. We *must* go on, but now the making of every camp must be more difficult and dangerous. It must be near the end, but a pretty merciful end. Poor Oates got it again in the foot. I shudder to think what it will be like tomorrow. It is only with greatest pains rest of us keep off frostbites. No idea there could be temperatures like this at this time of year with such winds. Truly awful outside the tent. Must fight it out to the last biscuit, but can't reduce rations.

Friday, 16 March or Saturday 17. Lost track of dates, but think the last correct. Tragedy all along the line. At lunch, the day before yesterday, poor Titus Oates said he couldn't go on; he proposed we should leave him in his sleeping-bag. That we could not do, and induced him to come on, on the afternoon march. In spite of its awful nature for him he struggled on and we made a few miles. At night he was worse and we knew the end had come.

Should this be found I want these facts recorded. Oates' last thoughts were of his mother, but immediately before he took pride in thinking that his regiment would be pleased with the bold way in which he met his death. We can testify to his bravery. He has borne intense suffering for weeks without complaint, and to the very last was able and willing to discuss outside subjects. He did not—would not—give up hope to the very end. He was a brave soul. This was the end. He slept through the night before last, hoping not to wake; but he woke in the morning—yesterday. It was blowing a blizzard. He said, 'I am just going outside and may be some time.' He went out into the blizzard and we have not seen him since.

I take this opportunity of saying that we have stuck to our sick companions to the last. In case of Edgar Evans, when absolutely out of food and he lay insensible, the safety of the remainder seemed to demand his abandonment, but Providence mercifully removed him at this critical moment. He died a natural death, and we did not leave him till two hours after his death. We knew that poor Oates was walking to his death, but though we tried to dissuade him, we knew it was the act of a brave man and an English gentleman. We all hope to meet the end with a similar spirit, and assuredly the end is not far.

I can only write at lunch and then only occasionally. The cold is intense, −40° at midday. My companions are unendingly cheerful, but we are all on the verge of serious frostbites, and though we constantly talk of fetching through I don't think any one of us believes it in his heart.

We are cold on the march now, and at all times except meals. Yesterday we had to lay up for a blizzard and today we move dreadfully slowly. We are at No. 14 pony camp, only two pony marches from One Ton Depot. We leave here our theodolite, a camera, and Oates' sleeping-bags. Diaries, etc., and geological specimens carried at Wilson's special request, will be found with us or on our sledge.

Sunday, 18 March. Today, lunch, we are 21 miles from the depot. Ill fortune presses, but better may come. We have had more wind and drift from ahead yesterday; had to stop marching; wind NW, force 4, temp. −35°. No human being could face it, and we are worn out *nearly*.

My right foot has gone, nearly all the toes—two days ago I was proud possessor of best feet. These are the steps of my downfall. Like an ass I mixed a small spoonful of curry powder with my melted pemmican—it gave me violent indigestion. I lay awake and in pain all night; woke and felt done on the march; foot went and I didn't know it. A very small measure of neglect and have a foot which is not pleasant to contemplate. Bowers takes first place in condition, but there is not much to choose after all. The others are still confident of getting through—or pretend to be—I don't know! We have the last *half* fill of oil in our primus and a very small quantity of spirit—this alone between us and thirst. The wind is fair for the moment, and that is perhaps a fact to help. The mileage would have seemed ridiculously small on our outward journey.

Monday, 19 March. Lunch. We camped with difficulty last night and were dreadfully cold till after our supper of cold pemmican and biscuit and a half a pannikin of cocoa cooked over the spirit. Then, contrary to expectation, we got warm and all slept well. Today we started in the usual dragging manner. Sledge dreadfully heavy. We are 15½ miles from the depot and ought to get there in three days. What progress! We have two day's food but barely a day's fuel. All our feet are getting bad—Wilson's best, my right foot worst, left all right. There is no chance to nurse one's feet till we can get hot food into us. Amputation is the least I can hope for now, but will the trouble spread? That is the serious question. The weather doesn't give us a chance—the wind from N to NW and −40° temp. today.

Wednesday, 21 March. Got within 11 miles of depot Monday night; had to lay up all yesterday in severe blizzard. Today forlorn hope, Wilson and Bowers going to depot for fuel.

Thursday, 22 and 23 March. Blizzard bad as ever—Wilson and Bowers unable to start—tomorrow last chance—no fuel and only one or two of food left—must be near the end. Have decided it shall be natural—we shall march for the depot with or without our effects and die in our tracks.

Thursday, 29 March. Since the 21st we have had a continuous gale from WSW and SW. We had fuel to make two cups of tea apiece and bare food for two days on the 20th. Every day we have been ready to start for our depot *11 miles* away, but outside the door of the tent it remains a scene of whirling drift. I do not think we can hope for any better things now. We shall stick it out to the end, but we are getting weaker, of course, and the end cannot be far.

It seems a pity, but I do not think I can write more.

R. SCOTT

For God's sake look after our people.

2. LETTERS TO J. M. BARRIE AND HIS WIFE

My dear Barrie,

We are pegging out in a very comfortless spot. Hoping this letter may be found and sent to you, I write a word of farewell. . . . More practically I want you to help my widow and my boy—your godson. We are showing that Englishmen can still die with a bold spirit, fighting it out to the end. It will be known that we have accomplished our object in reaching the Pole, and that we have done everything possible, even to sacrificing ourselves in order to save sick companions. I think this makes an example for Englishmen of the future, and that the country ought to help those who are left behind to mourn us. I leave my poor girl and your godson, Wilson leaves a widow, and Edgar Evans also a widow in humble circumstances. Do what you can to get their claims recognized. Goodbye. I am not at all afraid of the end, but sad to miss many a humble pleasure which I had planned for the future on our long marches. I may not have proved a great explorer, but we have done the greatest march ever made and come very near to great success. Goodbye, my dear friend.

Yours ever,
R. SCOTT

Later . . . As a dying man, my dear friend, be good to my wife and child. Give the boy a chance in life if the State won't do it. He ought to have good stuff in him. . . . I never met a man in my life whom I admired and loved more than you, but I never could show you how much your friendship meant to me, for you had much to give and I nothing.

[and to Kathleen, his wife . . .]
Make the boy [his son Peter] interested in natural history if you can; it is better than games; they encourage it at some schools. I know you will keep him in the open air.

Above all, he must guard and you must guard him against indolence. Make him a strenuous man. I had to force myself into being strenuous as you know—had always an inclination to be idle.

✿

APSLEY CHERRY-GARRARD

(1886–1959)

Brave but very short-sighted member of Scott's last expedition. Before the team, of which he was not a member, set off for the Pole, he made an extremely hazardous and nearly disastrous 'winter journey' to investigate the eggs of the Emperor penguin, in company with Bowers and Wilson.

The Worst Journey in the World (London, 1922).

FINDING THE BODIES OF SCOTT AND HIS COMPANIONS (1912)

[*12 November*] *Nearly midday.* 11–12 *miles south of One Ton.* We have found them—to say it has been a ghastly day cannot express it—it is too bad for words. The tent was there, about half-a-mile to the west of our course, and close to a drifted-up cairn of last year. It was covered with snow and looked just like a cairn, only an extra gathering of snow showing where the ventilator was, and so we found the door.

It was drifted up some 2–3 feet to windward. Just by the side two pairs of ski sticks, or the topmost half of them, appeared over the snow, and a bamboo which proved to be the mast of the sledge.

Their story I am not going to try and put down. They got to this point on 21 March, and on the 29th all was over.

Nor will I try and put down what there was in that tent. Scott lay in the centre, Bill on his left, with his head towards the door, and Birdie on his right, lying with his feet towards the door.

Bill especially had died very quietly with his hands folded over his chest. Birdie also quietly.

Oates' death was a very fine one. We go on tomorrow to try and find his body. He was glad that his regiment would be proud of him.

They reached the Pole a month after Amundsen.

We have everything—records, diaries, etc. They have among other things several rolls of photographs, a meteorological log kept up to 13 March, and, considering all things, a great many geological specimens. *And they have stuck to everything.* It is magnificent that men in such case should go on pulling everything that they have died to gain. I think they realized their coming end a long time before. By Scott's head was tobacco: there is also a bag of tea.

Atkinson gathered everyone together and read to them the account of Oates' death given in Scott's Diary: Scott expressly states that he wished it known. His (Scott's) last words are: 'For God's sake take care of our people.'

Then Atkinson read the lesson from the Burial Service from Corinthians. Perhaps it has never been read in a more magnificent cathedral and under more impressive circumstances—for it is a grave which kings must envy. Then some prayers from the Burial Service: and there with the floor-cloth under them and the tent above we buried them in their sleeping-bags— and surely their work has not been in vain.

✿

SIR DOUGLAS MAWSON

(1882–1958)

Australian geologist and explorer. He was the leader of the Australian Antarctic Expedition which discovered and explored George V Land and

511

*Queen Mary Land between 1911 and 1914. Setting out in November 1912
with 2 companions, Xavier Mertz and Lieutenant B. E. S. Ninnis, to explore the interior, he was the sole survivor of a march lasting 3 months.*

The Home of the Blizzard (London, 1915).

A TERRIBLE JOURNEY (1912–1913)

[*14 December 1912*]. On reaching the spot where Mertz had signalled and
seeing no sign of any irregularity, I jumped onto the sledge, got out the
book of tables and commenced to figure out the latitude observation taken
on that day. Glancing at the ground a moment after, I noticed the faint
indication of a crevasse. It was but one of many hundred similar ones we
had crossed and had no specially dangerous appearance, but still I turned
quickly round, called out a warning word to Ninnis and then dismissed it
from my thoughts.

   Ninnis, who was walking along by the side of his sledge, close behind my
own, heard the warning, for in my backward glance I noticed that he
immediately swung the leading dogs so as to cross the crevasse squarely
instead of diagonally as I had done. I then went on with my work. There
was no sound from behind except a faint, plaintive whine from one of
the dogs which I imagined was in reply to a touch from Ninnis's whip. I
remember addressing myself to George, the laziest dog in my own team,
saying, 'You will be getting a little of that, too, George, if you are not careful.'

   When I next looked back, it was in response to the anxious gaze of
Mertz who had turned round and halted in his tracks. Behind me, nothing
met the eye but my own sledge tracks running back in the distance. Where
were Ninnis and his sledge? I hastened back along the trail thinking that
a rise in the ground obscured the view. There was no such good fortune,
however, for I came to a gaping hole in the surface about eleven feet wide.
The lid of a crevasse had broken in; two sledge tracks led up to it on the
far side but only one continued on the other side.

   Frantically waving to Mertz to bring up my sledge, upon which there
was some alpine rope, I leaned over and shouted into the dark depths
below. No sound came back but the moaning of a dog, caught on a shelf
just visible 150 feet below. The poor creature appeared to have broken its
back, for it was attempting to sit up with the front part of its body while
the hinder portion lay limp. Another dog lay motionless by its side. Close
by was what appeared in the gloom to be the remains of the tent and a
canvas tank containing food for three men for a fortnight. We broke back
the edge of the névé lid and took turns leaning over secured by a rope,

calling into the darkness in the hope that our companion might be still alive. For three hours we called unceasingly, but no answering sound came back. The dog had ceased to moan and lay without a movement. A chill draught was blowing out of the abyss. We felt that there was little hope.

Why had the first sledge escaped the crevasse? It seemed that I had been fortunate, because my sledge had crossed diagonally, with a greater chance of breaking the snow-lid. The sledges were within thirty pounds of the same weight. The explanation appeared to be that Ninnis had walked by the side of his sledge, whereas I had crossed it sitting on the sledge. The whole weight of a man's body bearing on his foot is a formidable load and no doubt was sufficient to smash the arch of the roof.

By means of a fishing line we ascertained that it was 150 feet sheer to the ledge on which the remains were seen; on either side the crevasse descended into blackness. It seemed so very far down there and the dogs looked so small that we got out the field-glasses, but could make out nothing more by their aid. All our available rope was tied together but the total length was insufficient to reach the ledge and any idea of going below to investigate and to secure some of the food had to be abandoned.

Stunned by the unexpectedness of it all and having exhausted the few appliances we carried for such a contingency, we felt helpless. In such moments action is the only tolerable thing, and if there had been any expedient, however hazardous, which might have been tried, we should have taken all and more than the risk. Stricken dumb with the pity of it and heavy at heart, we turned our minds mechanically to what lay nearest at hand.

There were rations on the other sledge, and we found that there was a bare one and a half weeks' food for ourselves and nothing at all for the dogs. Part of the provisions consisted of raisins and almonds which had been taken as extras or 'perks,' as they were usually called. Among other losses there were both spade and ice-axe, but fortunately a spare tent-cover was saved. Mertz's burberry trousers had gone down with the sledge and the best substitute he could get was a pair of thick Jaeger woollen under-trousers from the spare clothing we possessed. Later in the afternoon Mertz and I went ahead to a higher point in order to obtain a better view of our surroundings. . . .

We returned to the crevasse and packed the remaining sledge, discarding everything unnecessary so as to reduce the weight of the load. A thin soup was made by boiling up all the old food-bags which could be found. The dogs were given some worn-out fur mitts, finnesko, and several spare raw-hide straps, all of which they devoured.

We still continued to call down into the crevasse at regular intervals in case our companion might not have been killed outright and, in the meantime, have become conscious. There was no reply. A weight was lowered on the fishing-line as far as the dog which had earlier shown some signs of life, but there was no response. All were dead, swallowed up in an instant. . . . At 9 p.m. we stood by the side of the crevasse and I read the burial service. Then Mertz shook me by the hand with a short 'Thank you!' and we turned away to harness up the dogs. . . .

7 *January* [*1913*]. Up at 8 a.m., it having been arranged last night that we would go on today at all costs, sledge-sailing, with Xavier in his bag on the sledge.' It was a sad blow to me to find that Mertz was in a weak state and required helping in and out of his bag. He needed rest for a few hours at least before he could think of travelling.

I have to turn in again to kill time and also to keep warm, for I feel the cold very much now.

At 10 a.m. I get up to dress Xavier and prepare food, but find him in a kind of fit. Coming round a few minutes later, he exchanged a few words and did not seem to realize that anything had happened. Obviously we can't go on today. It is a good day though the light is bad, the sun just gleaming through the clouds. This is terrible; I don't mind for myself but for others. . . . I pray to God to help us. I cook some thick cocoa for Xavier and give him beef-tea; he is better after noon, but very low—I have to lift him up to drink.

During the afternoon he had several more fits, then became delirious and talked incoherently until midnight, when he appeared to fall off into a peaceful slumber. So I toggled up the sleeping-bag and retired worn out into my own. After a couple of hours, having felt no movement from my companion, I stretched out an arm and found that he was stiff. My comrade had been accepted into 'the peace that passeth all understanding'. It was my fervent hope that he had been received where sterling qualities and a high mind reap their due reward. In his life we loved him; he was a man of character, generous and of noble parts.

For hours I lay in the bag, rolling over in my mind all that lay behind and the chance of the future. I seemed to stand alone on the wide shores of the world—and what a short step to enter the unknown future! My physical condition was such that I felt I might collapse in a moment. The gnawing in the stomach had developed there a permanent weakness, so that it was not possible to hold myself up in certain positions. Several of my toes commenced to blacken and fester near the tips and the nails worked loose.

Outside, the bowl of chaos was brimming with drift-snow and I wondered how I would manage to break and pitch camp single-handed. There appeared to be little hope of reaching the hut. It was easy to sleep on in the bag, and the weather was cruel outside. But inaction is hard to brook, and I thought of Service's lines:

> Buck up, do your damndest and fight,
> It's the plugging away that will win you the day.

If I failed to reach the hut it would be something done to reach some prominent point likely to catch the eye of a search party, where a cairn might be erected and our diaries cached. And so I commenced to modify the sledge and camping gear to meet fresh requirements. . . .

It was on 11 January—a beautiful, calm day of sunshine—that I set out over a good surface with a slight down grade. From the start my feet felt lumpy and sore. They had become so painful after a mile of walking that I decided to make an examination of them on the spot, sitting in the sun on the sledge. The sight of my feet gave me quite a shock, for the thickened skin of the soles had separated in each case as a complete layer, and abundant watery fluid had escaped into the socks. The new skin underneath was very much abraded and raw.

I did what appeared to be the best thing under the circumstances: smeared the new skin with lanoline, of which there was a good store, and with bandages bound the skin soles back in place, as they were comfortable and soft in contact with the raw surfaces. Outside the bandages I wore six pairs of thick woollen socks, fur boots and a crampon overshoe of soft leather. Then I removed most of my clothing and bathed in the glorious heat of the sun. A tingling sensation seemed to spread throughout my whole body, and I felt stronger and better. . . .

[*For fifteen terrible days Mawson struggled on alone.*]

On 1 February the wind and drift subsided late in the afternoon, and I clearly saw to the west the beacon which marked Aladdin's Cave. At 7 p.m. I reached this haven within the ice, and never again was I to have the ordeal of pitching the tent. Inside the cave were three oranges and a pineapple which had been brought from the ship. It was wonderful once more to be in the land of such things! I waited to mend one of the crampons and then started off for the hut; but a blizzard had commenced. To descend the five miles of steep icy slopes with my miserable crampons, in the weak state in which I found myself, would only have been as a last resort. So I camped in the comfortable cave and hoped for better weather next day.

The high wind, rising to a hurricane at times, continued for a whole week with dense drift until the 8th. I spent the long hours making crampons of a new pattern, eating, and sleeping. Eventually I became so anxious that I used to sit outside the cave for long spells, watching for a lull in the wind. At length I resolved to go down in the blizzard, sitting on the sledge as long as possible, blown along by the wind. I was making preparations for a start when the wind suddenly decreased and my opportunity had come.

In a couple of hours I was within one mile and a half of the hut. There was no sign of the ship lying in the offing, but I comforted myself with the thought that she might be still at the anchorage and have swung inshore so as to be hidden by the ice-cliffs, or on the other hand that Captain Davis might have been along the coast to the east searching there. But even as I gazed about seeking for a clue, a speck on the north-west horizon caught my eye and my hopes went down. It looked like a distant ship; it might well have been the *Aurora*. Well, what matter! the long journey was at an end—a terrible chapter of my life was finished!

Then the rocks around winter quarters began to come into view, part of the basin of the boat harbour appeared, and lo! there were human figures! They almost seemed unreal—I was in a dream—but after a brief moment one of them saw me and waved an arm, I replied, there was a commotion and they all ran towards the hut. Then they were lost, for the crest of the first steep slope hid them. It almost seemed to me that they had run away to hide.

Minutes passed, and I slowly went along with the sledge. Then a head rose over the brow of the hill and there was Bickerton, breathless after a long run. I expect he considered for a while which one of us it was. Soon we had shaken hands and he knew all in a few brief words, and I learned that the ship had left earlier in the day.

✿

SIR ERNEST SHACKLETON

(1874–1922)

British merchant naval officer and explorer. On his expedition to the Ant- arctic in 1907–9, he sledged to within 97 miles of the South Pole. When, on his second expedition, his ship Endurance *was crushed by ice in the Weddell Sea, he made an 800-mile voyage in an open boat to South Geor- gia, then made the first crossing of that island, with two others, to save the rest of his men.*

South (London, 1919).

THE END OF THE CROSSING (1916)

At 1.30 p.m. we climbed round a final ridge and saw a little steamer, a whaling-boat, entering the bay 2,500 ft. below. A few moments later . . . the masts of a sailingship lying at a wharf came in sight. Minute figures moving to and fro about the boats caught our gaze, and then we saw the sheds and factory of Stromness whaling-station. We paused and shook hands . . .

Cautiously we started down the slope that led to warmth and comfort. The last lap of the journey proved extraordinarily difficult. Vainly we searched for a safe, or a reasonably safe, way down the steep ice-clad mountainside. The sole possible pathway seemed to be a channel cut by water running from the upland. Down through icy water we followed the course of this stream. We were wet to the waist, shivering, cold, and tired. Presently our ears detected an unwelcome sound that might have been musical under other conditions. It was the splashing of a waterfall, and we were at the wrong end. When we reached the top of this fall we peered over cautiously and discovered that there was a drop of 25 or 30 ft., with impassable ice-cliffs on both sides. To go up again was scarcely thinkable in our utterly wearied condition. The way down was through the waterfall itself. We made fast one end of our rope to a boulder with some difficulty, due to the fact that the rocks had been worn smooth by the running water. Then Worsley and I lowered Crean, who was the heaviest man. He disappeared altogether in the falling water and came out gasping at the bottom. I went next, sliding down the rope, and Worsley, who was the lightest and most nimble member of the party, came last. At the bottom of the fall we were able to stand again on dry land. The rope could not be recovered. We had flung down the adze from the top of the fall and also the log-book and the cooker wrapped in one of our blouses. That was all, except our wet clothes, that we brought out of the Antarctic, which we had entered a year and a half before with well-found ship, full equipment, and high hopes. That was all of tangible things; but in memories we were rich. We had pierced the veneer of outside things. We had 'suffered, starved, and triumphed, grovelled down yet grasped at glory, grown bigger in the bigness of the whole'. We had seen God in his splendours, heard the text that Nature renders. We had reached the naked soul of man.

Shivering with cold, yet with hearts light and happy, we set off towards the whaling-station, now not more than a mile and a half distant. The difficulties of the journey lay behind us. We tried to straighten ourselves up a bit, for the thought that there might be women at the station made us painfully conscious of our uncivilized appearance. Our beards were long and our hair was matted. We were unwashed and the garments that we had worn for nearly a year without a change were tattered and stained. Three more unpleasant-looking ruffians could hardly have been imagined. Worsley produced several safety-pins from some corner of his garments and effected some temporary repairs that really emphasized his general disrepair. Down we hurried, and when quite close to the station we met two small boys ten or twelve years of age. I asked these lads where the manager's house was situated. They did not answer. They gave us one look—a comprehensive look that did not need to be repeated. Then they ran from us as fast as their legs would carry them. We reached the outskirts of the station and passed through the 'digesting-house', which was dark inside. Emerging at the other end, we met an old man, who started as if he had seen the Devil himself and gave us no time to ask any question. He hurried away. This greeting was not friendly. Then we came to the wharf, where the man in charge stuck to his station. I asked him if Mr Sorlle (the manager) was in the house.

'Yes,' he said as he stared at us.

'We would like to see him,' said I.

'Who are you?' he asked.

'We have lost our ship and come over the island,' I replied.

'You have come over the island?' he said in a tone of entire disbelief.

The man went towards the manager's house and we followed him. I learned afterwards that he said to Mr Sorlle: 'There are three funny-looking men outside, who say they have come over the island and they know you. I have left them outside.' A very necessary precaution from his point of view.

Mr Sorlle came out to the door and said, 'Well?'

'Don't you know me?' I said.

'I know your voice,' he replied doubtfully. 'You're the mate of the *Daisy*.'

'My name is Shackleton,' I said.

Immediately he put out his hand and said, 'Come in. Come in.'

'Tell me, when was the war over?' I asked.

'The war is not over,' he answered. 'Millions are being killed. Europe is mad. The world is mad.'

RICHARD BYRD

(1888–1957)

American aviator and polar explorer. After flying over the North Pole in
1926, he overflew the South Pole in 1929.

Exploring with Byrd (1937).

THE FLIGHT OVER THE SOUTH POLE (1929)

[*28 November*]. It was an awesome thing, creeping (so it seemed) through
the narrow pass, with the black walls of Nansen and Fisher on either side,
higher than the level of the wings, and watching the nose of the ship [i.e.
the aeroplane] bob up and down across the face of that chunk of rock. It
would move up, then slide down. Then move up, and fall off again. For
perhaps a minute or two we deferred the decision; but there was no
escaping it. If we were to risk a passage through the pass, we needed
greater manœuvrability than we had at that moment. Once we entered the
pass, there would be no retreat. It offered no room for turn. If power was
lost momentarily or if the air became excessively rough, we could only go
ahead, or down. We had to climb, and there was only one way in which
we could climb.

June, anticipating the command, already had his hand on the dump
valve of the main tank. A pressure of the fingers—that was all that was
necessary—and in two minutes 600 gallons of gasoline would gush out. I
signalled to wait. Balchen held to the climb almost to the edge of a stall.
But it was clear to both of us that he could not hold it long enough.
Balchen began to yell and gesticulate, and it was hard to catch the words
in the roar of the engines echoing from the cliffs on either side. But the
meaning was manifest. 'Overboard—overboard—200 pounds!'

Which would it be—gasoline or food? If gasoline, I thought, we might
as well stop there and turn back. We could never get back to the base from
the Pole. If food, the lives of all of us would be jeopardized in the event
of a forced landing. Was that fair to McKinley, Balchen, and June? It really
took only a moment to reach the decision. The Pole, after all, was our
objective. I knew the character of the three men. McKinley, in fact, had
already hauled one of the food bags to the trapdoor. It weighed 125 pounds.
The brown bag was pushed out and fell, spinning, to the glacier. The
improvement in the flying qualities of the plane was noticeable. It took
another breath and resumed the climb.

Now the down-currents over Nansen became stronger. The plane trembled and rose and fell, as if struck bodily. We veered a trifle to the right, searching for helpful rising eddies. Balchen was flying shrewdly. He maintained flight at a sufficient distance below the absolute ceiling of the plane to retain at all times enough manœuvrability to make him master of the ship. But he was hard-pressed by circumstances; and I realized that, unless the plane was further lightened, the final thrust might bring us perilously close to the end of our reserve.

'More,' Bernt shouted. 'Another bag.'

McKinley shoved a second bag through the trapdoor, and this time we saw it hit the glacier, and scatter in a soundless explosion. Two hundred and fifty pounds of food—enough to feed four men for a month—lay strewn on the barren ice. The sacrifice swung the scales. The plane literally rose with a jump; the engines dug in, and we soon showed a gain in altitude of from 300 to 400 ft. It was what we wanted. We should clear the pass with about 500 ft. to spare. Balchen gave a shout of joy. It was just as well. We could dump no more food. There was nothing left to dump except McKinley's camera. I am sure that, had he been asked to put it overboard, he would have done so instantly; and I am equally sure he would have followed the precious instrument with his own body. . . .

At six minutes after one o'clock, a sight of the sun put us a few miles ahead of our dead-reckoning position. We were quite close now. At 1.14 o'clock, Greenwich civil time, our calculations showed that we were at the Pole. I opened the trapdoor and dropped over the calculated position of the Pole the small flag which was weighted with the stone from Bennett's grave. Stone and flag plunged down together. The flag had been advanced 1,500 miles further south than it had ever been advanced by any American expedition.

For a few seconds we stood over the spot where Amundsen had stood, 14 December 1911; and where Scott had also stood, thirty-four days later, reading the note which Amundsen had left for him. In their honour, the flags of their countries were again carried over the Pole. There was nothing now to mark that scene: only a white desolation and solitude disturbed by the sound of our engines. The Pole lay in the centre of a limitless plain. To the right, which is to say to the eastward, the horizon was covered with clouds. If mountains lay there, as some geologists believe, they were concealed and we had no hint of them.

And that, in brief, is all there is to tell about the South Pole. One gets there, and that is about all there is for the telling. It is the effort to get there that counts.

We put the Pole behind us and raced for home.

BIBLIOGRAPHY

ANDERSON, J. R. L., *The Ulysses Factor: the Exploring Instinct in Man* (London, 1970).

BADGER, G., *The Explorers of the Pacific* (Kenthurst, 1988).

BEAGLEHOLE, J. C., *The Exploration of the Pacific* (London, 1966).

BIGGAR, H. P., *The Precursors of Jacques Cartier, 1494–1534* (Ottawa, 1911).

BONINGTON, C., *Quest for Adventure* (London, 1981).

CAMERON, I., *To the Farthest Ends of the Earth: the History of the Royal Geographical Society* (London, 1970).

—— *Explorers and Exploration* (London, 1991).

CRANFIELD, L., *The Challengers: British and Commonwealth Adventure since 1945* (London, 1976).

DAY, A. E., *Discovery and Exploration: A Reference Handbook. The Old World* (London, 1980).

DELPAR, H. (ed.), *The Discoverers: An Encyclopedia of Explorers and Exploration* (New York, 1980).

FERNÁNDEZ-ARMESTO, F., *The Times Atlas of World Exploration* (London, 1991).

GAVET-IMBERT, M. (ed.), *The Guinness Book of Explorers and Exploration* (Enfield, 1991).

GOODMAN, E., *The Explorers of South America* (New York, 1972).

HEMMING, J., *The Conquest of the Incas* (London, 1970).

—— *Red Gold* (London, 1978).

—— *Amazon Frontier* (London, 1987).

HERBERT, W., *The Noose of Laurels: The Discovery of the North Pole* (London, 1989).

HOPKIRK, P., *Trespassers on the Roof of the World* (London, 1982).

—— *The Great Game* (London, 1990).

KEAY, J., *When Men and Mountains Meet* (London, 1975).

—— (ed.), *The Royal Geographical Society History of World Exploration* (London, 1991).

KIRWAN, A. L. P., *The White Road: A Survey of Polar Exploration* (London, 1959).

MIDDLETON, D., *Victorian Lady Travellers* (London, 1965).

MOORHEAD, A., *The White Nile* (London, 1962).

—— *The Blue Nile* (London, 1962).

NEWBY, E., *The World Atlas of Exploration* (London, 1975).

—— *A Book of Travellers' Tales* (London, 1985).

NOYCE, W. *Springs of Adventure* (London, 1958).

PARRY, J. H., *The Discovery of the Sea* (London, 1964).

—— *The Discovery of South America* (London, 1979).

PENNINGTON, P., *The Great Explorers* (London, 1979).

PENROSE, B., *Travel and Discovery in the Renaissance* (Harvard, 1952).

QUINN, D. B., *New American World: A Documentary History of North America to 1612* (New York, 1979).

REID, A., *Discovery and Exploration: A Concise History* (London, 1980).

RIVERAIN, J., *Concise Encyclopedia of Explorations* (Glasgow and Chicago, 1966).

ROBINSON, J., *Wayward Women: A Guide to Women Travellers* (Oxford, 1990).

SEVERIN, T., *The African Adventure* (London, 1973).

—— *The Oriental Adventure: Explorers of the East* (New York and Boston, 1976).

TOURTELLOT, J. B. (ed.), *Into The Unknown* (Washington DC, 1987).

URE, J., *Trespassers on the Amazon* (London, 1986).

WALDMAN, C., and WEXLER, A., *Who Was Who in World Exploration* (New York, 1992).

WALLER, D., *The Pundits* (Lexington, 1990).

YAPP, P. (ed.), *The Travellers' Dictionary of Quotations* (London, 1983).

SOURCE ACKNOWLEDGEMENTS

Full source information is given before each extract. The editor and publisher are very grateful for permission to reproduce the following copyright material.

Roald Admundsen, from *The South Pole*, trans. A. G. Chater (London: John Murray, 1912).

Florence Baker, from *Morning Star* by Anne Baker (1972). Reprinted by permission of William Kimber, an imprint of HarperCollins Publishers Ltd.

Ibn Battúta, from *Travels of Ibn Battúta* (1983). Reprinted by permission of Routledge & Kegan Paul.

Hiram Bingham, 'The Discovery of Macchu Picchu', *Harper's Monthly Magazine*, April 1913.

Richard Byrd, from *Exploring with Byrd* (1937), copyright Richard Byrd 1937, © Richard E. Byrd III 1981.

John Cabot, from J. A. Williamson, *The Cabot Voyages and Bristol Discovery Under Henry VII* (1962), © The Hakluyt Society and reprinted by permission of Cambridge University Press on their behalf.

Jacques Cartier, from *The Voyages of Jacques Cartier*, publications of the Public Archives of Canada No. 11, published from the originals with translations, notes, and appendices by H. P. Biggar. Published by authority of the Secretary of State under the direction of the Archivist, 1924.

Apsley Cherry-Garrard, from *The Worst Journey in the World* (London, 1922).

Christopher Columbus, from *The Voyage of Christopher Columbus: Columbus' Own Journal of Discovery Newly Restored and Translated*, by John Cummins (Weidenfeld & Nicolson, 1992).

Dr Frederick Albert Cook, from *My Attainment of the Pole* (The Polar Publishing Co., 1911).

Hernan Cortés, from *Letters from Mexico*, trans. & ed. A. R. Pagden (New York: 1971); from *The Broken Spears: The Aztec Account of the Conquest of Mexico*, trans. Nahuatl–Spanish, A. M. Garibay, trans. Spanish–English, Lysander Kemp (Boston, 1962).

Alexandra David-Neel, from *My Journey to Lhasa* (London, 1927).

Charles Douglas, from *Mr Explorer Douglas*, ed. John Pascoe (A. H. & A. W. Reed, Wellington, 1957).

Leif Ericsson, from *The North Atlantic Saga*, ed. & trans. Gwyn Jones (OUP, 1964). Reprinted by permission of Oxford University Press.

Sven Hedin, from *My Life as an Explorer* (London: Cassell, 1926).

Wally Herbert, from *Across the Top of the World: The British Trans-Arctic Expedition*, © Wally Herbert 1969 (Penguin Books Ltd).

Sir Edmund Hillary, from *High Adventure* (London: Hodder & Stoughton, 1955).

Cheng Ho, from *The Overall Survey of the Ocean's Shores*, trans. J. V. G. Mills (1970), © Hakluyt Society and reprinted by permission of Cambridge University Press on their behalf.

Mina Hubbard, from *A Woman's Way Through Unknown Labrador* (London: John Murray, 1908).

F. Kingdon-Ward, from *Explorers All*, ed. Sir Percy Sykes (London: George Newnes Ltd, 1939).

Sir Douglas Mawson, from *The Home of the Blizzard*, Vol. I (London: Heinemann, 1915).

General Umberto Nobile, from *My Polar Flights*, trans. Frances Fleetwood (London: Muller, 1961).

Nathaniel Brown Palmer, from *Captain Nathaniel Brown Palmer: An Old-Time Sailor of the Sea* (Macmillan, 1922).

Jacob Roggeveen, from *The Journal of Jacob Roggeveen*, ed. Andrew Sharp, © OUP 1970. Reprinted by permission of Oxford University Press.

Eric Shipton, from *Nanda Devi* (Hodder & Stoughton, 1936). Reprinted by permission of Nick Shipton, on behalf of the Estate of Eric Shipton.

Sir Mark Aurel Stein, from *Ruins of Desert Cathay* (London: Macmillan, 1912).

Abel Janszoon Tasman, from *the Voyages of Abel Janszoon Tasman*, ed. Andrew Sharp, © OUP 1968. Reprinted by permission of Oxford University Press.

Wilfred Thesiger, from *Arabian Sands*, © Wilfred Thesiger 1959 (Penguin Books Ltd).

Bertram Thomas, from *Arabia Felix: Across the Empty Quarter of Arabia* (London: Cape, 1938).

Amerigo Vespucci, from *El Nuevo Mundo*, trans. Roberto Levillier (Buenos Aires: 1951).

Admiral Boris Andreyevich Vilkitskiy, from *Charting the Russian Northern Sea Route*, trans. & ed. William Barr (Montreal: McGill Queen's University Press, 1976). Reprinted by permission of the Arctic Institute of North America.

Timofeyevick Yermak, from *Yermak's Campaign in Siberia*, ed. T. Armstrong (London: The Hakluyt Society, 1975).

In many instances it has proved difficult to establish copyright prior to printing. Full source acknowledgement is made where material is thought to be still in copyright and if notified the publisher will be pleased to rectify any errors or omissions at the earliest opportunity.

INDEX

Aden 165
Afghanistan 77
Alaska 34, 281
Albert, Lake 193, 198
Alcock, Sir Rutherford 59
Aleutian Islands 34
Algiers 146
Alice Springs 451
Alvarado, Don Pedro de 236
Amazon River 326, 340, 349, 359, 361, 363,
    372
Amazonia 60
Ampuero, Thomas de 383
Amundsen, Roald 2, 100–2, 220, 313–16, 469,
    481, 488, 503–5, 507, 511, 520
Anadyr River 99
Andes Mountains 363, 366, 368
Andrée, Salomon 468, 474–5
Angola 132
Arabia 21, 55, 56, 66, 68, 111, 119
Arctic Ocean 99, 270
Argentina 337
Ark-i-linik River 311–13
Arkangel 99
Ascension Island 463
Aspiring, Mount 462
Assam 110
Ayolas, Juan de 337

Back, Sir George 308
Bactria 27
Badagry 151, 153
Badakhshan 12
Baffin Island 243
Baikie, Dr William 126, 161–3
Baker, Florence von Sass 126, 189–200
Baker, Sir Samuel White 126, 189–200
Balboa, Vasco Núñez de 320, 329–30
Banks, Mount 419
Banks, Sir Joseph 378, 406–11
Barents, Willem 2, 29–31
Barreto, Dona Ysabel 384
Barrie, Sir James Matthew 509

Barth, Heinrich 126, 156–60
Batan Islands 388
Bates, Henry Walter 320, 359, 361–3
Bath 170
Baxter, James 432
Bellingshausen, Fabian 493, 496
Bennett, Floyd 480
Bennett, James Gordon 181
Benue River 161
Bering, Vitus 2, 34–8
Bering Island 37
Bering Strait 34, 70, 74, 99, 268
Bingham, Hiram 320, 370–2
Bjaaland, Olav Olavson 503–5, 507
Blaxland, Gregory 378, 418–21
Blue Mountains, The 418, 421
Bonpland, Aimé 349
Borneo xi, 52
Botany Bay 410
Bougainville, Louis-Antoine de 378, 401, 405
Bouvet de Lozier, Jean-Baptiste 488–90
Bowers, Henry 506–7, 510–11
Brahmaputra River 59
Bransfield, Edward 488, 493–5
Brazil 235
Bristol 223, 263
British Museum 98
Bruce, James 126, 134–8, 204
Brunner, Thomas 378, 441–3
Buenos Aires 338
Buganda 170
Buitrago, Juan de 383
Bukhara 26, 41–3
Burke, Robert O'Hara 378, 443, 446–50
Burma 75–6
Burton, Isabel 165
Burton, Sir Richard 126, 164–70, 320, 367–8
Byrd, Richard Evelyn 468, 480–1, 488,
    519–20

Cabeza de Vaca, Alvar Núñez 220, 232–3
Cabot, John 220, 223–4
Cabot, Sebastian 25, 223

Cadiz 327
Caillié, René 126, 143–9, 157
Calcutta 110
Calicut 22–4
California 248
Campbell, Dr Archibald 46–52
Canada 264
Canary Islands 323
Canton 17
Cardenas, Don Garcia Lopez de 238
Carpentaria, Gulf of 444, 446
Carpini, Giovanni de Piano 2, 7–9
Carson, Kit 300
Cartagena 329
Carteret, Philip 378, 395
Cartier, Jacques 220, 233–6
Casement, Sir Roger David 187–8
Caspian Sea 26
Catoche 320
Cawdor, Lord 106–7
Cebu 379
Celebes 60
Ch'eng Tsu, Emperor 21
Chad, Lake 131, 157
Champlain, Samuel de 220, 257–60
Chancellor, Richard 25–6
Charbonneau, Toussaint 277, 279
Chelyuskin Cape 70
Cheng Ho 2, 21–3
Cherry Garrard, Apsley 488, 510–11
Chiang-ssu-yeh 93–8
Chiloe 357
Chimborazo 366, 368
China 12–24, 31, 32, 75, 229
Chitral 75–6
Circumcision Cape 490, 492
Clapperton, Hugh 126, 140–2, 150, 204
Clark, William 220, 276–80
Coelho, Nicolas 24
Colorado 301
Columbus, Christopher 27, 227, 320–6, 328, 384
Cook, Dr Frederick Albert 468, 476–7
Cook, James 220, 268–70, 273, 378, 401, 406–18, 488, 490–3
Cooper's Creek 446
Cordoba 331
Coronado, Francisco Vasquez de 220, 236–9
Corte-Real, Gaspar 220, 225–6
Corte-Real, Miguel 220, 225–6
Cortes, Hernan 320, 331
Cotopaxi 368
Crean, Thomas 517

Croker Mountains 284, 289–90
Cuyne 8

d'Orville, Albert 31
Damascus 17, 131
Dampier, William 378, 388–91
Darjeeling 51
Darling, Sir Ralph 428
Darling River 424, 427
Darwin, Charles 44, 60, 320, 356–9
David-Neel, Alexandra 2, 103–5
Davies, William 320, 347–9
Davis, John 220, 255–7
de la Cosa, Juan 329
Denham, Dixon 140
Desideri, Ippolito 2, 33–4
Desolation Island 494
Dogs:
  'Betsey Jane' 463
  'Faust' 64–6
  'George' 512
  'Helge' 505
  'Jacob' 101–2
  'Poker' 463
  'Rover' 443
  'The Major' 505
Doughty, Charles Montagu 2, 66–70
Douglas, Charles 378, 461–5
Drake, Sir Francis 220, 247–52, 320, 345–7
Dumont d'Urville, Jules-Sébastien-César 488, 499–500
Dunhuang 3

Easter Island 391
Egypt 17, 56, 174
El Dorado 337, 340
Elias, Ney 2, 75–7
Ellsworth, Lincoln 481
Encounter Bay 431
Erebus, Mount 502
Eric the Red 221
Ericsson, Leif 220–3
Escobedo, Rodrigo de 322
Espinosa, Juan de 283
Essequibo River 352
Esteban 236
Ethiopia 132
Evans, George William 378, 421–2
Evans, Edgar 508–9
Everest Mountain 120–4
Eyre, Edward John 378, 432–8

Fa Hsien 2–5
Ferrara, Duke of 225

Florida 227–8
Forrest, Alexander 378, 461
Forrest, John 378, 458–60
Fort Enterprise 292, 296
Fowler's Bay 436
Foxe, Luke 220, 262
Francis, Saint 7
Franklin, Sir John 220, 292–7, 307–9
Fremont, John Charles 220, 300–6
Frere, Sir Bartle 459
Frobisher, Sir Martin 220, 242–7

Galapagos Islands 358
Galton, Sir Francis 126, 155–6
Gama, Paulo da 23
Gama, Vasco da 2, 23–4, 384
Gangtok 106
Gao 129
Geographical Magazine x
George V Land 511
Ghenkis Khan 18
Gibson, Alfred 453–8
Gilbert, John 439–40
Gilbert, Sir Humphrey 220, 252–5
Giles, Ernest 378, 453–8
Gilgit 76
Gobi, the 3, 5, 66, 76, 78, 82
Gondokoro 189, 194, 196, 198
Good Hope, Cape of 23, 262
Grand Canyon 238
Grant, James Augustus 170, 189–90, 204
Gray, Charlie 446–7
Great Sandy Desert 451
Great Slave Lake 311–12
Great Wall, The 31–2
Greenland 469, 474
Grueber, Johann 2, 31–3
Guayaquil 366
Guiana 351
Guinea 133–4
Gulf Stream 227
Gutiérrez, Pedro 322
Guzman, Juan de 242

Hanbury, David 220, 311–13
Hanssen, Helmer 503–5
Harar 164–5
Hassel, Sverre 507
Haussa 141
Hawaii 413
Hearne, Samuel 220, 264–8, 291
Hedin, Sven 2, 82–93
Henson, Matthew 477–9

Herat 76
Herbert, Wally xi, 468, 484–6
Herjolfsson, Bjarni 221
Herne, Lt. 165–7
Hierro 323
Hillary, Edmund xi, 2, 120–4
Himalayas, The 59, 113
Holman, Ide Tercxsen 388
Hooker, Sir Joseph 2, 44–52
Hsuan Tsang 2, 5–7, 93, 94
Huang-ho, the Yellow River 32
Hubbard, Leonidas 220, 316–17
Hubbard, Mina 220, 316–18
Hudson, Henry 220, 260–1
Hudson Bay 260, 262
Hudson River 228, 232, 260
Humboldt, Alexander von 320, 349–50

Iacobsz, Françoijs 386
Ibn Battúta 2, 17–20, 126–31
India 3–5, 15, 23–4, 31–2, 44–5, 77–8, 93, 108,
    110, 119
Indus 4
Ioppen, Cornelis 388
Irala, Domingo Martínez de 337
Irrawaddy River 105
Irtysh River 28
Irvine, Andrew 123
Isfahan 17

Jackson, Frederick 473
Jamaica 432
James, Thomas 220, 262–3
Japan 262
Jefferson, Thomas 276–7
Jenkinson, Anthony 2, 26–7, 41
Jidda 22
Johansen, Hjalmar 469, 471–2

Kamchatka 34, 122, 282
Kanchenjunga 46–7
Karakorum 11
Kashgar 78
Kashmir 33
Kenya 120
Khartoum 196, 198–9
Kilimanjaro 155, 200–2, 204, 207
Kimberley Mountains 461
Kinabalu Mountain 52–4
King, James 414
King, John 446–50
King George IV 495
King George's Sound 434, 437–8

King Haakon VII's Plateau 504–5
King William Island 307, 309–10
Kingsley, Mary 126, 210–17
Kotzebue, Otto von 220, 281–4
Krapf, Johan Ludwig 126, 154–5
Kublai Khan 12
Kuchum 27–9
Kun-lun Mountains 92

La Plata River 337, 405
Labrador 225, 316
Labuan 52
Lachlan River 421–3
Ladak 33, 76
Laing, Alexander Gordon 159
Lander, John 150
Lander, Richard 126, 140, 150–4
Lapland 25
Las Casas, Bartolomé de 320, 330–1
Lawrence, T. E. 67
Lawson, William 418
Leh 33
Leichhardt, Ludwig 378, 438–41
Lena River 71
Leo Africanus 126, 131–4
Lewis, Meriwether 220, 276–80
Lhasa xi, 31–3, 38–9, 59, 76, 78, 103–5
Lisbon 225
Livingstone, Dr David 126, 175–84, 204
Louis IX of France 9
Low, Sir Hugh 52–4
Lugo, Luis Alonso de 336

Ma Huan 21–22
Macao 31
Macchu Picchu 370–2
McClintock, Sir Francis 220, 309–11
McDonnell, Sir Richard 445
Mackenzie, Sir Alexander 220, 270–5, 306
Mackenzie River 270
Macquarie River 421–2
Madeira River 373, 375
Magellan, Strait of 345, 379, 395
Magellan, Ferdinand 334, 378–82
Makalu 122, 123
Mali 127–8, 133
Mallory, George 123
Mangu, Khan 9–11
Manning, Thomas 2, 38–40
Markham, Sir Clements 77
Marquesas Islands 382
Matterhorn 368

Matty Island 309, 314
Mawson, Sir Douglas 488, 511–16
Mecca 22, 158, 164, 174
Medici, Lorenzo de 327
Medina 164
Mendaña de Neira, Alvaro de 378, 382–4
Mendoza, Pedro de 337–8
Mertz, Xavier 512–14
Meshed 75–6
Mexico 270, 331
Mexico City 232, 331
Mississippi River 239–42
Missouri River 278
Montezuma 331, 333–4
Montgomerie, Col. T. G. 59
Montreal 234
Moorcroft, William 2, 41–4
Morocco 145, 147
Moscow 25–6
Mozambique 23
Murray, Sir George 428
Murray River 424, 428–30
Mutesa, Kabaka of Uganda 172–5

Nain Singh 2, 59–60
Nanda Devi 113–18
Nansen, Fridtjof 468–73
Napoleon III 55
Nepal 32
Nepean River 419
New, Revd Charles 126, 200–2
New Galicia 236
New Holland 388
New South Britain 495
New South Wales 446
New York 228
New Zealand 120, 384, 432, 441
Newfoundland 223, 226, 252
Niagara Falls 367
Niger River 131, 134, 138–9, 150, 161
Nijni Novgorod 75
Nile, The xi, 17, 127–31, 134–8, 170, 175,
   192–4, 196–8, 203
Ninnis, B. E. S. 512–14
Niza, Fray Marcos de 236
Nobile, General Umberto 468, 481–4
Nordenskjold, Adolf 2, 70–4
North Pole, The xi, 25, 469, 474–86
North-East Passage 25, 70, 98, 100
North-West Passage 242, 255, 262–3, 284,
   290, 292
Norway 70
Novaya Zemlya 29

Oates, Lawrence (Titus) 507–8, 511
Ob River 71
Ojeda, Alonso de 320, 328–9
Orellana, Francisco de 320, 328–9
Ormuz (Hormuz) 31
Oudney, Walter 140
Overweg, Alfred 157
Oxley, John Joseph 378, 422–4
Oxus river 41, 43

Palgrave, William Gifford 2, 55–8
Palmer, Nathaniel Brown 488, 495–7
Pamirs, The 3, 75, 77
Paraguay 337
Parana River 338
Park, Mungo 126, 138–40, 204
Parry, Sir William 220, 290–2, 298
Patagonia 345
Paulo Afonso Falls 367
Peary, Robert Edwin 468, 477–9, 484
Peking 17, 31, 39, 75, 78
Persia 75–76
Perth, W. Australia 438
Peru 382
Peter the Great 34
Philby, Harry St John 111
Philippines 382, 388
Pigafetta, Antonio 320, 334–6, 379
Pinzón, Martín Alonso 322
Pitcairn Island 395
Pizarro, Francisco 239, 339
Pizarro, Gonzalo 339
Polar Sea 71
Polo, Marco 2, 12–16
Ponce de Leon, Juan 220, 227–8
Pope Innocent IV 7
Pope Leo X 131
Port Essington 440
Port L'Orient 489
Possession Island 501–2
Prince Albert 502
Przhevalsky, Nikolai Mikhailovich 2, 62–6, 77

Quebec 234, 257
Queen Elizabeth I 248
Queen Elizabeth II 120, 485
Queen Mary Land 512
Queen Victoria 193, 502
Queensland 438
Quesada, Gonzalo Jiménez de 337
Quesada, Hernando de 337
Quiros, Pedro Fernandez de 382

Rae, John 220, 307–8
Ralegh, Sir Walter 252
Rawlinson, Sir Henry 76
Rebmann, Johann 154
Resolution Island 243
Riyadh 56
Rocky Mountains 277, 301–6
Roggeveen, Jacob 378, 391–5
Rome 31, 39, 104
Rondon, Candido 372
Roosevelt, Kermit 372–3
Roosevelt, Theodore 320, 372–5
Roosevelt River 372
Ross, Sir James Clark 220, 284, 298–300, 488, 501–3
Ross, Sir John 220, 284–90, 298
Ross Ice Shelf 501
Ross Island 501
Ross Sea 501
Royal Geographical Society xi, 59–60, 75–7, 155, 361, 459
Rub'al-Khali, the Empty Quarter 111–13, 118–20
Rubruck, William of 2, 9–12
Russia 34–5, 76
Rustichello 12

Sacagawea 276–80
Sahara 140, 143, 202
St Helena 463
St John, Sir Spencer 2, 52–4
St Lawrence, Gulf of 233
St Lawrence River 234
St Petersburg 75
Salween River 108
Samoa 391
San Carlos 364–5
San Salvador (Bahia) 356
San Salvador (Island) 227
San Sebastian 328
Santa Cruz Islands 382
Santos 367
Saõ Francisco River 367
Schmidt, Ulrich 320, 337–9
Schweinfurth, Georg August 126, 202–3
Scott, Robert Falcon 120, 488, 505–10, 520
Seattle 102
Segovia, Rodrigo Sánchez de 322
Serpa, Antonio de 383
Seville 327, 331
Shackleton, Sir Ernest 488, 505, 516–18
Shan States 76
Shipton, Eric 2, 113–18

Siam 75
Siberia 27–9, 34, 71–2, 76, 98, 102
Sikkim 50, 106
Simla 77
Simón, Father Pedro 320, 336–7
Simpson Desert 424
Sining 32
Smyrna 31
Society Islands 391
Sokoto 140, 150
Solander, Carl 408–11
Solomon Islands 382
Soto, Hernando de 239
South Georgia 516
South Pole 100, 120, 469, 503–20
Speke, John Hanning 126, 164, 170–5, 189–91
Spruce, Richard 320, 363–7
Staden, Hans 320, 343
Stanley, Sir Henry Morton 126, 181–9
Stein, Sir (Mark) Aurel 2, 91–8
Steller, Georg Wilhelm 34
Stonington, Connecticut 496
Stromness whaling station 517
Stroyan, William 164–6
Stuart, John McDouall 378, 443–5
Stuart, Mount 443
Sturt, Charles 378, 424–32, 443
Suchow 32
Swedish Geographical Society 92
Sydney 438
Syria 56, 69

Tahiti 396, 402–6
Takla-Makan Desert 92–3
Tasman, Abel Janszoon 378, 384–8, 491
Tasmania 384, 386
Teleki, Count Samuel 126, 208–10
Tenzing Norgay, Sherpa xi, 120–4
Terre Adélie 499
Texas 232
Thesiger, Wilfred xi, 2, 118–20
Thomas, Bertram 2, 110–13
Thompson, David 220, 280–1
Thomson, Joseph 126, 203–8
Tibet 9, 32–3, 38, 46, 59, 103–10, 120
Tilman, Bill 113–18
Timbuktu 129–33, 143–9, 157–60
Tippu Tib 187
Tocantins River 359
Tromso 70

Tsangpo gorge 105–6
Tsung Ling Mountains 3, 6
Tunis 146
Turkestan 75–7, 91

Uganda 172–5
Unfortunate Isles 380
Uraba, Gulf of 328–9
Urga (Ulan Bator) 66

Van Dieman Gulf 445
Vancouver, George 274
Venice 12, 15, 31, 224
Verrazzano, Giovanni da 220, 228–32
Vespucci, Amerigo 320, 326–8, 384
Victoria, Lake 170, 175, 193
Victoria Falls 178–80
Victoria Land 501
Vilkiyskiy, Admiral Boris Andreyevich 2, 62, 98–100

Wallace, Alfred Russell 2, 60–2, 320, 359–60, 363
Wallis, Samuel 378, 395–402, 405, 491
Warburton, Peter 378, 451–3, 458
Ward, Frank Kingdon 2, 105–10
Waterton, Charles 320, 351–5
Weddell Sea 516
Wentworth, William Charles 418
Whymper, Edward 320, 368–70
Wilkes, Charles 488, 497–8
Wilkes Land 498
Willoughby, Sir Hugh 2, 25–6
Wills, William John 378, 443, 446–50
Wilson, Edward Adrian 505, 507–8, 510–11
Wisting, Oscar 503–5
Worsley, Frank 517–18
Wrangel's Land 71

Yáñez, Vicente 322
Yenissey River 71
Yermak, Timofeyevich 2, 27–9
Younghusband, Sir Francis 2, 75, 78–81
Yucatan 330
Yule, Sir Henry 59, 76
Yunan 76

Zaïre (Congo) 131–2, 184–9, 202
Zambesi River 178–80
Zanzibar 168, 203

OXFORD

MORE OXFORD PAPERBACKS

This book is just one of nearly 1000 Oxford Paperbacks currently in print. If you would like details of other Oxford Paperbacks, including titles in the World's Classics, Oxford Reference, Oxford Books, OPUS, Past Masters, Oxford Authors, and Oxford Shakespeare series, please write to:

UK and Europe: Oxford Paperbacks Publicity Manager, Arts and Reference Publicity Department, Oxford University Press, Walton Street, Oxford OX2 6DP.

Customers in UK and Europe will find Oxford Paperbacks available in all good bookshops. But in case of difficulty please send orders to the Cash-with-Order Department, Oxford University Press Distribution Services, Saxon Way West, Corby, Northants NN18 9ES. Tel: 0536 741519; Fax: 0536 746337. Please send a cheque for the total cost of the books, plus £1.75 postage and packing for orders under £20; £2.75 for orders over £20. Customers outside the UK should add 10% of the cost of the books for postage and packing.

USA: Oxford Paperbacks Marketing Manager, Oxford University Press, Inc., 200 Madison Avenue, New York, N.Y. 10016.

Canada: Trade Department, Oxford University Press, 70 Wynford Drive, Don Mills, Ontario M3C 1J9.

Australia: Trade Marketing Manager, Oxford University Press, G.P.O. Box 2784Y, Melbourne 3001, Victoria.

South Africa: Oxford University Press, P.O. Box 1141, Cape Town 8000.

Oxford Reference

The Oxford Reference series offers authoritative and up-to-date reference books in paperback across a wide range of topics.

Abbreviations
Art and Artists
Ballet
Biology
Botany
Business
Card Games
Chemistry
Christian Church
Classical Literature
Computing
Dates
Earth Sciences
Ecology
English Christian
   Names
English Etymology
English Language
English Literature
English Place-Names
Eponyms
Finance
Fly-Fishing
Fowler's Modern
   English Usage
Geography
Irish Mythology
King's English
Law
Literary Guide to Great
   Britain and Ireland
Literary Terms

Mathematics
Medical Dictionary
Modern Quotations
Modern Slang
Music
Nursing
Opera
Oxford English
Physics
Popes
Popular Music
Proverbs
Quotations
Sailing Terms
Saints
Science
Ships and the Sea
Sociology
Spelling
Superstitions
Theatre
Twentieth-Century Art
Twentieth-Century
   History
Twentieth-Century
   World Biography
Weather Facts
Word Games
World Mythology
Writer's Dictionary
Zoology